青年汉学家研修计划论文集

中外文化交流中心 编

A Collection of Research Papers of the Visiting Program for Young Sinologists

中国社会科学出版社

图书在版编目(CIP)数据

青年汉学家研修计划论文集 / 中外文化交流中心编 . — 北京：中国社会科学出版社，2022.11
ISBN 978-7-5227-1069-3

Ⅰ.①青… Ⅱ.①中… Ⅲ.①汉学—文集 Ⅳ.① K207.8-53

中国版本图书馆 CIP 数据核字 (2022) 第 224609 号

出 版 人	赵剑英
责任编辑	张冰洁
责任校对	李 妲
责任印制	王 超

出　　版	中国社会科学出版社
社　　址	北京鼓楼西大街甲 158 号
邮　　编	100720
网　　址	http：// www.csspw.cn
发 行 部	010-84083685
门 市 部	010-84029450
经　　销	新华书店及其他书店

印刷装订	北京君升印刷有限公司
版　　次	2022 年 11 月第 1 版
印　　次	2022 年 11 月第 1 次印刷

开　　本	710×1000　1/16
印　　张	43.5
字　　数	756 千字
定　　价	258.00 元

凡购买中国社会科学出版社图书，如有质量问题请与本社营销中心联系调换
电话：010-84083683
版权所有　侵权必究

青年汉学家研修计划上海班学员参观长沙简牍博物馆

Young sinologists(Shanghai) on visit to Changsha Jiandu Museum

青年汉学家研修计划上海班学员赴湖南省博物馆座谈

Young sinologists(Shanghai) on visit to Hunan Museum for discussion

青年汉学家研修计划上海班学员赴中共一大会址参观

Young sinologists(Shanghai) on visit to Site of the First CPC Congress

青年汉学家研修计划上海班学员赴中国商飞上海飞机制造有限公司参观交流

Young sinologists(Shanghai) on visit to COMAC Shanghai Aircraft Manufacturing Co.Ltd

青年汉学家研修计划西安班集中授课现场

Young sinologists(Xi'an) listen to the lecture

青年汉学家研修计划西安班学员交流讨论

Young sinologists(Xi'an) make exchange and discussion

青年汉学家研修计划西安班学员体验中国民俗文化

Young sinologists(Xi'an) experience Chinese folk culture

青年汉学家研修计划西安班学员在延安"打起腰鼓"

Young sinologists(Xi'an) play the "waist drum" in Yan'an

青年汉学家研修计划杭州班学员参观义乌市佛堂老街

Young sinologists(Hangzhou) on visit to the "Fo Tang Lao Jie" in Yi'wu

青年汉学家研修计划杭州班学员赴阿里巴巴集团总部参观调研

Young sinologists(Hangzhou) on visit to the headquarter of Alibaba Group

青年汉学家研修计划杭州班学员体验中国茶文化

Young sinologists(Hangzhou) experience Chinese tea culture

青年汉学家研修计划杭州班学员体验中国剪纸技艺

Young sinologists(Hangzhou) experience Chinese paper-cut skills

目 录

1 **城市结对：对可持续发展城市范式的展望**
  杭州—马德普拉塔跨文化合作
  小云 【阿根廷】
  普埃雷登市常务审议委员会 副主任

26 **杭州梦想小镇（互联网村）带给哥伦比亚的启示**
  安吉莉卡 【哥伦比亚】
  亚洲伊比利亚美洲文化基金会 项目经理

56 **杭州自行车服务案例研究**
  索非亚 【智利】
  智利国会图书馆 亚太区项目负责人/庞蒂菲娅大学 教授

93 **在西安，追寻古波斯的印记**
  好麦特 【伊朗】
  德黑兰大学外语学院中文系 教授

107 **解读旅游与文化的经济协同效应——以上海为例**
  马利克 【巴基斯坦】
  巴基斯坦坦萨戈达大学 讲师/澳大利亚西溪大学 博士生

135 **"一带一路"倡议下中国与阿拉伯和非洲地区的合作模式研究**
  ——以中埃苏伊士经贸合作开发区为例
  伊曼 【埃及】
  苏伊士运河大学语言学院中文系 助教

153 **日本报纸关于"一带一路"报道的考察**
  川村明美 【日本】
  自由职业者、翻译

166 **"一带一路"旅游对瑞士商务休闲旅游者的启示**
  何珊 【瑞士】
  苏黎世大学 国际关系专员

181 "一带一路"倡议对意中两国关系的影响
安馨彤 【意大利】
自由职业者

202 绿色"一带一路"与中国国有企业的社会责任
毕洛兰 【法国】
亚洲中心联合会 创始人

223 从"一带一路"倡议看老挝旅游业的发展
哈克妮兰 【老挝】
老挝外交研究所 研究员

243 "一带一路"电影节联盟：中国电影产业的国际化
何伊纱 【德国】
人民网 德语外籍专家

265 阿富汗孔子学院的发展现状调查与分析
阿布 【阿富汗】
喀布尔大学中文系（孔子学院） 讲师

289 地理标志驱动旅游业发展：以中国为例
哈韦拉 【智利】
智利大学国际问题研究所 讲师

325 格鲁吉亚国家博物馆的中国陶瓷
纳蒂亚 【格鲁吉亚】
格鲁吉亚国家博物馆东方艺术系 策展人

349 吉利公司在阿根廷的业务发展
何塞 【阿根廷】
阿根廷文化与社会研究中心 博士 / 国立科尔多瓦大学 教授

402 中国在巴西投资的机会
马睿婷 【巴西】
圣保罗大学 法学博士 / 联邦参议院监管、经济、商业和商业法 立法顾问
罗杰里奥 【巴西】
圣保罗大学 研究生 / 新卡尔达斯学院 教授

422 中国-阿根廷旅游合作发展战略
贡萨洛 【阿根廷】
弗雷罗大学拉丁美洲中国政治经济研究中心　教育主任/
亚洲—拉美关系研究员

451 通过旅游发展尼中关系
戴韦 【尼泊尔】
尼泊尔教育与科技部　秘书

478 科特迪瓦的中资企业案例研究
阿里妈咪 【科特迪瓦】
费利克斯·胡弗埃·博伊尼大学　研究员

498 阿根廷和中国的"全面战略伙伴关系"研究
艾丽卡 【阿根廷】
阿根廷外交部中国事务处　处长/拉努斯国立大学　教授

507 乌拉圭和中国：共建之路
帕马拉 【乌拉圭】
乌拉圭中国门户网站　创始人、翻译

520 通过旅游促进中肯民间外交和跨文化交流
茹丝 【肯尼亚】
内罗毕大学孔子学院　讲师

539 中欧关系—"17+1"机制下的中国与西巴尔干关系比较分析
桑亚 【塞尔维亚】
塞尔维亚共和国政府　顾问

569 "梦"在阿中两国文学中相似性之比较
穆成功 【埃及】
开罗爱资哈尔大学语言与翻译学院汉语言文学系　助理教授

588 东汉中期皇帝行幸长安初探
彭暮雷 【德国】
明斯特大学汉学系暨东亚研究所　博士研究生、助理教授

602　**试论《周易》"贞"字的含义和用法**
　　鲍葛薇·安吉塔　【拉脱维亚】
　　拉脱维亚大学亚洲研究系　副教授

626　**儒家政治思想与新丝绸之路**
　　罗杰里奥　【墨西哥】
　　墨西哥蒙特雷科学大学　国际关系项目主任

651　**丝绸之路上的罗马：关于中古汉语中"拂菻"名称起源的几点思考**
　　冯海城　【马其顿】
　　翻译

667　**中国在法律全球化中的作用：为共同繁荣立规**
　　伊丽莎维塔　【乌克兰】
　　乌克兰敖德萨州立大学　教授

CONTENTS

10 **Town Twinning: Projection Towards the Paradigm of Sustainable Cities Intercultural Cooperation: Hangzhou – Mar del Plata**
Manzo Romina Soledad/Argentina
Presidency Deliberative Council of General Pueyrredón Municipal Deliberative Council/Auxiliary Advisor

37 **Dream Town Internet Village in Hangzhou: Lessons for Colombia**
Angelica Maria Lopez Triana / Colombia
Asia Iberoamerica Cultural Foundation/Project Manager

70 **A Case Study: Hangzhou Bicycle Service**
María Sofía Calvo Foxley/Chile
Asia Pacific Program at Chilean Congress Library/Head;
Pontificia Universidad Católica de Valparaíso/Professor

98 **Quest for the Trace of Ancient Persia in Xi'an: A Negelected Persian Emperor Pattern on the Shi Jun Tomb of the Northern Zhou Dynasty**
Hamed Vafaei/Iran
Department of Chinese Language and Literature of University of Tehran, School of Foreign Languages/Professor

118 **Deciphering the Economic Synergy between Tourism and Culture: A Case study of Shanghai**
Muhammad Nauman Malik/Pakistan
Economics Department of University of Sargodha, Pakistan/Lecturer;
University of Western Australia/ PhD. student

142   Research on the Cooperation Mode between China and Arab and African Regions under the Belt and Road Initiative
—— China-Egypt Suez Economic and Trade Cooperation Development Zone as an example
Eman Magdy Mohamed Mahmoud / Egypt
Department of Chinese Language and Literature, School of Languages, Suez Canal University / Teaching Assistant

158   An Investigation into Japanese Newspapers' Reports on the Belt and Road Initiative
Kawamura Akemi / Japan
Freelancer; Freelance Translator

172   Understanding through Personal Experience: Introducing Belt and Road Tourism to Swiss Business and Leisure Travelers
Sandra Bachmann / Switzerland
University of Zurich / International Relations Officer

188   Effects of Belt and Road Initiative on Italy-China Relations
Rossi Arianna / Italy
Freelancer; Teacher

209   Greening Belt and Road Initiative and Chinese State-owned Enterprises Corporate Social Responsibility
Florence Biot / France
Asia Center / Co-founder

230   Lao Tourism Development Through the Belt and Road Initiative
Haknilan Inthalath / Laos
Institute of Foreign Affairs of Laos / Research fellow

251   The Belt and Road Film Festival Alliance: Internationalization of Chinese Film Industry
Isabelle Cosima Philomena Aphrodite Angelika Roske / Germany
People's Daily Online / German Foreign Expert

274	**Survey and Analysis on the Status of the Development of Confucius Institutes in Afghanistan** Ahmadi Abdul Razaq / Afghanistan Confucius Institute at Kabul University / Lecturer
302	**Geographical Indications as A Driver for Tourism Development: the Chinese Case** Javiera Paz Caceres Bustamante / Chile Institute of International Studies, University of Chile / Lecturer
334	**Chinese Ceramic in the Georgian National** Natia Demurishvili / Georgia Oriental Art Department of Georgian National Museum / Curator
368	**The Development of Geely and the Expansion of its Business in Argentina** Jose Maria Resiale Viano / Argentina Argentina Center for Research and Studies on Culture and Society (CIECS)-CONICET / PhD. Scholarship holder; National University of Córdoba / Professor
410	**The Opportunities for Chinese Investment in Brazil** Clarita Costa Maia / Brazil PhD. student in International Law from the University of São Paulo LL.M Business Law and Intellectual Property Law, UC Berkeley Federal Senate Legislative / Consultant on Regulatory, Economic, Commercial and Business Law Rogério Do Nascimento Carvalho / Brazil PhD. student in Latin American Integration Program from the University of São Paulo / Lawyer and Professor at Faculdade de Caldas Novas - Goiás
433	**Strategies for the Development of China-Argentina Tourism Cooperation** Gonzalo Anibal Tordini / Argentina Center for Chinese Political and Economic Studies in Latin America of Flores University / Education Director; Asia- Latin America Relations / Chairman, Researcher

461   Development of Nepal-China Relationship Through Tourism
       Devi Prasad Upadhaya / Nepal
       Ministry of Education, Science and Technology (Nepal) / Secretary

485   Local's Perceptions of Chinese Economic Engagement in Africa: Case Study of Chinese-owned Companies Operating in Côte d'Ivoire (West Africa)
       Gbane Alymamy / Côte d'Ivoire
       University Felix Houphouet Boigny / Economic PhD. student and Junior Researcher

501   Current situation of the "Strategic Comprehensive Partnership" between Argentina and China
       Erika Imhof / Argentina
       Ministry of Foreign Affairs, Argentina / Chief of the China Desk

512   Uruguay and China: Still much more Road to Build Together
       Paula De Santiago / Uruguay
       Portal China Uruguay / Co-Founder, Translator

527   Promoting People-to-People Diplomacy and Cross Cultural Interaction between China and Kenya through Tourism
       Ruth Njeri Wangui / Kenya
       Confucius Institute at the University of Nairobi / Lecturer

550   Sino-European Relations - Comparative Analysis on Sino-Western Balkans Relations within "17+1" Mechanism
       Sanja Arežina / Serbia
       Government of the Republic of Serbia / Counselor

576   Dream in Arabic and Chinese Literature: A Comparison of the Similarities
       Nageh Mohamed Ibrahim Mohamed Taha / Egypt
       Al-Azhar University, Faculty of Languages and Translation, Department of Chinese Language and Literature / Assistant Professor

593   Emperors Travelling to Chang'an in Mid Eastern Han-Dynasty

Alexander Brosch / Germany
University of Münster, Institute of Sinology and East Asian Studies / PhD. student, Assistant Professor

612　Meaning and Usage of the Word ZHEN 貞 in the "Book of Changes"
Baltgalve Agita / Latvia
Department of Asian Studies, University of Latvia / Associate Professor

635　Confucian Political Ideology and the New Silk Road
Rogelio Leal / Mexico
The Monterrey Institute of Technology and Higher Education / Director of International Relations Program

657　Rome on the Silk Road: Some Thoughts on the Origin of the Toponym " 拂菻 "(Fúlĭn) in Middle Chinese
Igor Radev / Macedonia
Translator

673　The Role of China in Formation of Legal Globalization: Setting Rules for a Common Prosperity
Ielyzaveta Lvova / Ukraine
Constitutional and International Law Department, Odessa State University of Internal Affairs / Professor

城市结对：对可持续发展城市范式的展望

杭州—马德普拉塔跨文化合作

小云 【阿根廷】
普埃雷登市常务审议委员会　副主任

本文基于跨文化策略[1]，对在国家层面发展清洁与可持续科技矩阵的转型的中阿合作关系作出展望。跨文化合作对加强人力资本、国家发展、促进基于地方可持续发展政策的经济增长至关重要。

在这一框架内，我们需要在世界各个城市之间开展结对合作，这对于建立跨文化联系、实施相关政策，如建立协调机制以制定城市发展和培训计划有着举足轻重的作用。

在本文中，笔者将以杭州市（梦想小镇—阿里巴巴—中国）和马德普拉塔市（马德普拉塔计算机和创意产业园—阿根廷）为例，进一步阐述建立城市结对关系的必要性和可行性，并以此案例为参照，制定必要的规划，促进绿色经济产业可持续发展，实现该领域内科学知识和经验的交流以及人力资本的加强。

---

[1] 文化政策和措施，即与文化有关的政策和措施，无论是在地方、国家、区域或国际层面，其核心是文化本身，或其目的是在创作、产生和传播过程中对个人、群体或社会的文化表达产生直接影响，获得他们的活动、商品和服务。参见《保护和促进文化表现形式多样性公约》第 4.6 条。

一 可持续性和跨文化合作

首先，我们将分析"可持续性"一词及其在综合实践、历史和规划中的含义。在这些具有中国特色的实践、历史和规划中，中国为创建人类命运共同体做出了巨大的贡献。尊重和互助的观念在中国代代相传，它们是中国为建立一个基于团结统一的全球新秩序而倡导的价值观。在过去的几十年里，围绕着这个主题，中国城市不断地出台相关政治决策并且采取切实的行动来践行这一使命。它们渴望实现文化上的可持续性，为跨代和合作超越这一目标的规划、实施和平衡做出了卓越的贡献。

近几十年来，中国在全球舞台上的作用和地位日益突出，给世界不同地区带来了深远的政治、经济和文化影响。中国与各国也逐渐建立起互惠互利的国际关系，这为我们今天要讨论的问题提供了支持。

为了实现可持续发展，我们必须将环境问题提到全球议程，因此我们需要可行的计划和实施者，他们将确立发展趋势，并就全球权力分配提出不同的变革方法。通过整合论坛和各种联盟，国际气候组织为自己构建一个统一的交流空间，这推动了国家间新层次的互动交流。正是从这里开始，在"可持续发展"这一涉及整个国际社会、国际体系结构和动态发展的主题下，中国这样的实施者发挥了领导者的作用。

为减轻气候变化带来的影响，中国制定的战略目标、政策和所采取的行动，以及为提高全民环保意识而进行的社会宣传，都将促进国际合作交流，进而加强应对机制，以改变目前的全球气候模式，实现人类进步发展。

同时，为应对气候变化，中国完善了这方面的法律法规体系、管理体制和劳动机制，加强了统计计算研究和系统建设，提高了科技政治研究水平，加强了教育培训，使应对能力和行动能力得到增强。

《2030年可持续发展议程》发布4年来，中国各省、自治区、直辖市都制定了相关政策以及地方应对方案，现已进入整体组织实施阶段。随后，相关部门相继发布了针对海洋、气象和生态保护区的行动计划和项目。这些计划、行动以及实施过程凸显了中国在上述领域的主导作用。在这4年里，中国在国际气候谈判领域发挥了前所未有的领导作用，并且取得了卓越的成效，主要体现在：中国成功地实现了基于"可持续发展计划"而设定的目标，坚定地捍卫了多元化发展和以联合国为中心的国际体系。

第二，我们需要不断地强调跨文化合作的价值，这对于加强人力资本、国家发展、促进基于地方可持续发展政策的经济增长至关重要。

文化的力量不可估量，联合国也宣布了文化对人类"可持续发展"的重要性[1]。目前，它在国际议程上占据着战略地位，是解决影响当代社会的经济、社会和环境问题的支柱。在鼓励创造力、创新、人类进步和人民福祉方面，文化提供了社会基础；它是发展的推动力，其价值可见一斑。

教育是一项文化权利，对于促进可持续性和社会包容性有着必不可少的作用；它与当地政策密切相关——没有教育的发展，那么整个发展必将不完整，何谈可持续发展？政府应当加强对外合作，促进文化交流，鼓励公民积极参与文化生活，建立跨文化、跨际的合作关系。

中国于2007年首次提出要建设生态文明，将可持续发展的理念纳入人类文明的范畴。从那时起，中国在政策、行动、预测以及捍卫生态文明建设方面取得了实质性进展，并与其他国家分享了这些具有中国特色的经验。

在建设生态文明过程中，中国最杰出的成就体现在全球计划和试点项目方面，涉及监管、问责和自然资源平衡等关键领域。这些领域在经济增长、社会发展和环境保护的八个关键方面（自然资源产权、国土空间开发保护、空间规划、资源综合管理和节约利用、资源有偿使用和生态补偿、环境治理与生态保护市场、生态文明评价与评估、问责与追究）有所改善。这八个方面是中国所倡导的生态文明的基本支柱，并且在中华人民共和国成立70周年之际，我们看到了巨大的成果。

习近平主席提出"坚持可持续发展，共创美好世界"。他强调，可持续发展是破解全球性问题的"金钥匙"，我们要打造开放多元的世界经济，努力建设包容互利的幸福社会，建设人与自然和谐相处的美好家园，为世界提供"中国方案"，开启可持续发展的新道路[2]。

在合作方面，中国是最早一批同二战后开始组建的国际发展合作体系（SICD）开展合作的国家。

随后，中国的合作皆以1964年的一份文件所制定的一系列原则为基础，即对外经济技术援助八项原则。几十年来，这些政治和价值支柱并没有被改变，只

---

[1] 我们还认识到世界的多样性，所有文化和文明都有助于丰富人类。我们强调文化对发展的重要性及其对实现千年发展目标的贡献。2010年9月22日联合国大会通过的决议：《兑现承诺：团结一致实现千年发展目标》。

[2] 《可持续发展是破解全球性问题的"金钥匙"》，新华社2019年6月9日。

是得到了扩大或者完善，这说明了中国的国家政策是稳定和一致的。

中国提出的国际合作为现有的国际体制结构划定了一个明确的可行性战略，主要侧重于支持发展中国家的现代化和进步。作为一个新兴世界的领导者，中国向其他国家提供援助，履行其国际义务，表明其遵守公平、互利、争取实质性成果和顺应时代的原则，促进基于共同价值观的团结统一。中国设想从战略高度，在互惠标准的基础上，通过建立和发展平等互利、共同发展的全面合作伙伴关系来处理与其他国家的关系，以解决实现可持续发展目标过程中的结构性问题。

跨文化政策旨在促进技术、科学和文化间的交流，而对这些政策进行分析，我们会学到有关促进文化模式交流、加强文化间对话和跨际交流的经验，从而实现联合国组织设定的部分目标，包括"加强执行手段和振兴世界可持续发展联盟"。

与国际城市建立结对合作关系之后，我们需要加强人力资本。这是城市之间互动的一个基本工具，有助于我们预测和实施跨文化、跨代交流的目标，从而实现城市的可持续发展。

以此为前提，我们需要对工业发展项目的战略规划进行分析，这对于科技（在本案例中为梦想小镇）以及以创新、环保为基础的知识经济的发展有着基础性的作用。

二 梦想小镇

创建梦想小镇的目的是在市场上展示创新和创业精神。这个以互联网为基础的行业充满创业热情，旨在为中国的经济结构提供一个创新和可持续的增长模式。这是一个很好的例子，它将新技术、艺术和对历史遗产的尊重结合在一起并成为中心，使年轻人在这个范围捕捉新的想法、获得新的价值观并且充分发挥青年创业精神。毫无疑问，这是一种独特的经济发展模式，充满了微妙之处，使其在通信和技术进步的时代取得前所未有的成功。

它是一个特殊科技领域的项目，有望为拥有技术基础、资源和服务组合、地方财政、专业培训和技能发展的公司提供支持。

梦想小镇位于杭州市西北部，总面积 3.47 平方公里。它成立于 2015 年 4 月，以河流和农田为特色。那里有几座历史建筑，因此梦想小镇的设计保留了现有的农田和河流，进而在上面形成了一个河网。别出心裁的步行走廊将关键办公点都连接起来，科学配置的无车区实现了对环境的保护。

梦想小镇是浙江杭州未来科技城项目（FTSC）的一部分，属于科学技术创新领域。该项目于2010年在杭州西部启动，主要规划面积为123平方公里，是国家试点计划的一部分。FSTC的目标是促进城市的科技发展，并成为国家层面创新驱动的城市化榜样。FSTC项目正在加速发展，成为科技驱动的增长极，是全球创新和发展的一个显著例子。那里不仅坐落着阿里巴巴和中国电信等大公司，还有一些包括初创企业在内的小公司也百花齐放。这使得交流和发展成为可能，保证了初创公司和项目的成长；但只有拥有关键的、优于其他企业的网络，这些公司才能在未来的市场上立于不败之地。

因此，如果公司能够获得一些援助，那对它们的发展将是至关重要的。在这里，它们可以获得长达三年的免费空间特许权，以及办公场地租金和公共服务费用补贴。此外，企业孵化器还为这些公司提供了与商业相关的财务支持（例如，商业规划、与其他初创企业和外部实体的联系、种子融资）。因此，我们创造了一个理想的环境供这些企业交流想法、交换经验和教训，并为它们之间的合作创造新的机会。另一个基本点涉及人力资源的招聘和培训。互联网行业正在迅速变化，因此，"智能"人力资源的使用可以增加商业领域的成功机会。

梦想小镇有一个战略性的城市化方针，旨在促进地方和地区层面的可持续经济发展。自20世纪70年代末实行改革开放以来，中国的城市化进程非常迅速，社会和经济发展取得了巨大成就。预计到2030年，中国城市人口将超过10亿，中国城市在国家未来发展中将发挥越来越重要的作用（世界银行和中国国务院发展研究中心，2014年）。毫无疑问，正如《国民经济和社会发展第十三个五年规划（2016—2020）》所述，城市化进程是中央政府政策中最重要的目标之一。

梦想小镇项目旨在创造新的模式，以实现可持续的城市发展。为此，它将绿色发展作为其原则。比如，梦想小镇的总体规划预见了新的和改进的城市化标准，其中包括"无车"区域和促进综合实验、交流和环境发展的社会互动空间（阿伊里乌，2016年）。

结合知识和实践来保护城市和农村历史区域及其相关传统区域，可以减少环境足迹，促进更多更好的生态可持续生产和消费模式。

梦想小镇作为一种建筑设计解决方案，鼓励在环境保护占主导地位的城市创建该建筑，这是关注可持续城市发展政策的产物。梦想小镇能够保障社区获得维持生存所需的基本环境商品和服务，使得生物和文化多样性得到更强有力的保护和更可持续的利用，并保证传统知识和技能与其他形式的科学知识和谐共存[1]。这是国家计划的一部分，旨在确立国家可持续发展战略的目标。由此，国家提出了开办这类公司应遵循的原则和政策，主要有：

- 所有气候变化政策都将一贯纳入国家可持续发展战略。
- 这些政策将始终遵循共同但有区别的责任原则（《联合国气候变化框架公约》所载的二元世界愿景）。
- 始终努力做好适应气候和缓解气候变化之间的平衡。将积极寻求减少温室气体排放的方案，但同时也应鼓励适应新的气候现实。
- 将鼓励技术的发展以适应这种现实。为此，应通过技术革命来减少温室气体排放。
- 积极参与与该主题有关的国际论坛。

2011年，《中国应对气候变化的政策和行动白皮书》发布。该文件介绍了在"第十一个五年规划（2006—2010）"期间减缓和适应气候变化的目标。

在这方面，中国将继续完善应对气候变化的法律法规体系、管理体制和劳动机制，加强统计计算调查和制度建设，提高科技和政治研究水平，加强气候变化方面的教育和培训，从而提高这方面的能力[2]。

三 马德普拉塔和该地区信息和通信技术协会（ATICMA）

马德普拉塔和该地区信息和通信技术协会（简称：信息和通信技术协会）汇集了阿根廷布宜诺斯艾利斯省马德普拉塔市和该地区ICT（信息和通信技术）部门的专业人士、企业家、公司和大学。它有一项开放和协作的工作，主要目标是提出具有技术基础的新举措，促进当地创业生态系统的发展。

信息和通信技术协会寻求通过技术促进创造力和智能创新，从而使该行业获得增长和发展。其目标是通过企业、创业部门、教育机构、科技机构和国家之间的合作，提高竞争力、促进知识产业发展，促进可持续增长。

其根据阿根廷布宜诺斯艾利斯省的现行立法及其活动，对环境因素和影响进

---

1 《杭州宣言：将文化置于可持续发展政策的核心》，中国杭州国际大会，2013年5月17日。
2 《中国应对气候变化的政策和行动白皮书》，2011年11月22日。

行了具体研究，主要目标是促进新企业的发展，开展行动，力求在信息和通信技术领域激发新职业，创造以产业、学术界和地方组织融合为特征的工作空间。为此，信息和通信技术协会希望在这些领域开展合作[1]。

稳定的监管框架、有利于公司创建和成长的税收优势以及鼓励发展良好生态系统的国家政策，是确保社会可持续发展和繁荣的必要价值观和行动，尤其是在地方。

在马德普拉塔市，ICT（信息和通信技术）部门雇用了约3500名员工，共有76家公司和500家微型企业（包括独立的专业企业和服务），每年的发票额超过30亿比索，其中40%来自出口，约13亿比索。

今天，阿根廷以69亿美元的数额占了世界出口市场份额的0.5%。其国家目标是达到世界市场份额的1%。这将带来巨大的变化，可创造15万个优质工作岗位。

从全国范围来看，马德普拉塔在信息和通信技术领域具有重要价值。根据ATICMA提供的数据，该市拥有"76家公司、500家微型企业、独立商业和专业服务，年营业额为31.5亿比索，年出口额为13亿比索，占40%"。

在阿根廷，73%的ICT公司是微型企业（最多有9名员工），21%是小型企业（10至40名员工）；4%是中型企业（50至200名员工），2%是大型企业（超过200名员工）。此外，该国还有四家明星公司（价值超过10亿美元的私营科技公司），其中一家名为Globant（格洛班特），公司总部设在马德普拉塔市。

这些数据表明了在同个地方存在核心创业生态系统的重要性，这对这类事业的发展至关重要。这里提出一种管理模式，其对不同的领域进行分组，促进团队合作，并引发经验和价值观交流以找到不同类型的解决方案。这是一种基本的管理模式，从长远来看有利于整个社区的发展。

创业和创业职业的觉醒是城市发展和获得竞争力的另一个根本问题。

信息和通信技术协会所遵守的主要法规之一由全球契约所规定。这份倡议建议雇主承诺在其组织中实施10项原则，这些原则基于适用于四个领域的普遍宣言和公约：人权、环境、劳动标准和反腐败。

信息和通信技术协会根据布宜诺斯艾利斯省的现行立法及其活动，定期对环境因素和影响进行研究。因此，从废物产生的角度来看，ATICMA组织被认为是

---

1 《地区发展的机遇》，《开放式管理》，马德普拉塔ATICMA。

废物（废弃电气和电子设备）的产生者，但事实上，其同时也是环境监测解决方案产生和应用的推动者。

信息和通信技术协会规定组织一些活动来提高大众环保意识，以便更有效地分离可回收废物并使自然资源的利用合理化。

在劳工事务方面，信息和通信技术协会专注于提供良好的工作环境、培训并整合工作团队，从而在该行业的劳动链中提供连续性和运营可持续性[1]。

在国家层面，通过与这一问题有关的国内和国际条例，该组织致力于促进发展进程中社会、环境和经济层面的表达，促进可持续性发展并减轻气候变化带来的影响。与此同时，它还提出与贫困作斗争、评估生态系统服务和使用替代能源的提议。该组织还设想加强国家、企业和社区层面的能力，以实施部门间和国际协议，旨在转变和促进有利于自然和人类环境的活动，实现跨代团结。

四　结论

通过分析，笔者认为跨文化合作对加强人力资本、国家发展、促进基于地方可持续发展政策的经济增长至关重要。在这一框架内，我们需要在世界各个城市之间开展结对合作[2]，这对于建立跨文化联系、实施相关政策，如建立协调机制以制定城市发展和培训计划有着举足轻重的作用。

与国际城市建立结对合作关系之后，我们需要加强人力资本。这是城市之间互动的一个基本工具，有助于我们预测和实施跨文化、跨代交流的目标，从而实现城市的可持续发展。开展这一必要的项目，目的是实现中国和阿根廷在省级和地级就绿色经济产业和可持续发展问题开展经验交流、进行科学活动并加强人力资本。其关键在于建立一个整体创新体系：政府、行业、公司、融资组织和学术机构等社会行为者之间的知识网络，以提高城市的经济竞争力。

中国将要遵循的道路是显而易见的——通过之前规划的国家政策，采用一种社会模式，对其公民可以获得的最高生活质量进行忠实的评估。城市规划部门作为监测可持续发展标准的中心，对于促进知识传播和新规划技术的发展具有无与

1　《信息和通信技术协会企业社会责任可持续发展手册(MGP) - ISO 26000》。
2　城市结对是一种具有特殊价值的合作机制，因为它不仅使国家之间的联系面向地方领导人，而且也面向全体人民。如果是在工业化国家的城市和发展中国家的城市之间进行的结对，会增加双方在知识和道德层面上的丰富性，有时还会为发展中的城市做出相当大的技术和物质贡献。它可以直接采用，无需行政费用，也不会损害双方的平等精神。

伦比的价值，因此笔者建议我们的城市中也可以创建这样的部门。在国际层面上对这些问题进行整合、交流和研究是必要的，中国可以成为各国效仿的榜样。这保证了城市长久的、可持续的发展。这些政策的实施和平衡有助于跨代交流目标的实现。在这一点上，笔者认为国际合作至关重要。通过合作，我们的社会可以获得加强公民文化培训的方法，从而使我们能够更好地了解国际合作的前景并衡量其效益。

Town Twinning: Projection Towards the Paradigm of Sustainable Cities Intercultural Cooperation: Hangzhou – Mar del Plata

Manzo Romina Soledad/Argentina
Presidency Deliberative Council of General Pueyrredón Municipal Deliberative Council / Auxiliary Advisor

My research proposal is based on the projection of intercultural policies[1] for development, in this case the cooperation relationship between China and the geographical locations of Argentina for the transformation of a clean and sustainable technology industry matrix at the national level. Intercultural cooperation is essential to strengthen human capital and contribute to national development, fostering economic growth based on local policies that focus on sustainable development.

Within this framework, twinning relationships between different cities in the

---

1 Cultural policies and measures: Policies and measures related to culture, whether at the local, national, regional or international level, which are centered on culture as such, or whose purpose is to have a direct effect on the cultural expressions of individuals, groups or societies, in the creation, production, dissemination, distribution and access to their activities, goods and services.
Source: Article 4.6 of the Convention on the Protection and Promotion of the Diversity of Expressions Cultural http://www.unesco.org/new/es/culture/themes/cultural-diversity/cultural-expressions/the-convention/glossary/

world are essential for the creation of intercultural links and policies that include coordinated mechanisms for the establishment of municipal development plans and training actions for training.

To achieve this purpose, I proposed to carry out a case study based on the technology park belonging to Hangzhou (Dream Town - Alibaba - People's Republic of China) and the city of Mar del Plata ("Mar del Plata Computer and Creative Industries Park" ATICMA - Argentina) respectively. Framework with the objective of creating the necessary projections to achieve an exchange of experiences, scientific knowledge and strengthening of human capital in the field of green economic industry and sustainable development.

I. Sustainability and Intercultural Cooperation

First, we will analyze the term Sustainability and its implication in the integration of practices, stories and proposals that characterize the People's Republic of China and its progressive contributions towards the creation of a community of shared destiny for humanity. Values such as respect and mutual help are those that China projects to achieve the creation of a new global order based on a solidarity integration that allows the transmission of knowledge to new generations. The actions and political decisions that have been carried out on the subject in recent decades demonstrate the commitment of Chinese cities, who aspire to be culturally sustainable, contributing to the projection, implementation and balancing of objectives of intergenerational and collaborative transcendence.

Over the last decades, the importance and growing prominence of the People's Republic of China on the global stage, have impressed such a degree of political influence in different regions of the world, which today is reflected in what we might consider, the evidence of a new framework for interaction at the level of international relations between States.

The insertion of environmental issues in the global agenda has involved the creation of new scenarios and actors that have set trends and produced different mechanisms of transition towards the distribution of global power. International climate architecture has provided itself with common and common spaces, through the integration of forums and various alliances that gave way to new levels of interaction between States. It is from there, where actors like China have placed themselves in a position of leadership in the face of a theme that involves the international community as a whole and involves changes in the international system both in its structure and dynamics.

Its strategies and goals of response to the phenomenon of climate change, policies and actions aimed at alleviating the effects, and a paradigm aimed at raising social awareness in this regard, foreseeing the strengthening of international cooperation in the area, and the promotion of response mechanisms to the modification of global climate patterns as we know them, means actions aimed at achieving the progressive development of humanity.

China has perfected its systems of laws and legal regulations and improved management regimes and labor mechanisms in dealing with climate change. It also intensified the research of statistics and calculations and the construction of its systems, raised the level of scientific, technological and political research, strengthened education and training on the subject, thereby increasing its response and action capabilities in this regard.

In the last 4 years, after the 2030 Agenda for Sustainable Development was issued, its related policies have been developed in all provinces, autonomous regions and municipalities under central jurisdiction, through the elaboration of their own local response plans to this phenomenon, entering a stage of integral organization and application. The corresponding departments successively promulgated action plans and work projects in the marine, meteorological and ecological protection areas. These actions and the taking of measures and subsequent instances in their action plans, form the leading role of China in the area, who assumed in the aforementioned years an unprecedented leadership in the field of international climate negotiations. The achievements currently obtained are demonstrated in the success involved in meeting the goals set based on the objectives of sustainable development and in its firm defense of pluralism and the international system with the United Nations in the center.

Secondly, it is important to highlight the value of Intercultural Cooperation, which is essential to strengthen human capital and contribute to national development, fostering economic growth based on local policies that have sustainable development as the epicenter.

Culture, whose importance for sustainable human development was declared by the United Nations Organization[1], currently occupies a strategic place on the international agenda, being a pillar in solving economic, social and environmental problems affecting contemporary societies. Its value as an engine for development is evidenced when it comes to providing social foundations that encourage creativity, innovation, human progress and people's well-being.

Education is a cultural right that is indispensable for the promotion of sustainability and social inclusion, intimately linked with the locality. Without cultural development, development would not be conceived as sustainable or incomplete. To seek an active participation of citizens in cultural life, through the exchange of experiences and the generation of connections between the local and the distant, implies creating cooperation ties between different groups through intercultural and intergenerational dialogue.

In this regard, it was in 2007 that China first proposed the construction of an ecological civilization, thus incorporating the concept of sustainable development into the framework of human civilization. Since then, China has advanced extensively in its actions, proposals and projections as well as in the defense of the

---

1 We also recognize the diversity of the world and that all cultures and civilizations contribute to the enrichment of humanity. We highlight the importance of culture for development and its contribution to the achievement of the Millennium Development Goals. Source: Resolution adopted by the General Assembly on September 22, 2010. 65/1. Fulfill the promise: united to achieve the Millennium Development Goals. https://undocs.org/es/A/RES/65/1

creation of an ecological civilization. Management and governance policies in this area have characterized his work and experiences, which he has shared with the rest of the nations.

Among its most outstanding policies and achievements are its global plans and pilot projects in key fields such as supervision, accountability and the balance of natural resources. These areas produced improvements in 8 key aspects for economic growth, social development and environmental protection: property rights of natural resources, exploitation and protection of national land space, space planning, general management and frugal use of resources, paid use of resources and ecological compensation, environmental governance and ecological protection market, evaluation and valuation of ecological civilization, and accountability and accountability. These eight systems constitute a fundamental pillar of the ecological civilization projected by China and that today sees great results at the dawn of its anniversary for the 70 years of the creation of the People's Republic.

President Xi Jinping has broadly proposed to insist on sustainable development and create a prosperous world. He stressed that sustainable development is like a "golden key" to solve current global problems and their proposals include jointly creating an open and plural world economy, striving to build a happy society that is inclusive and mutually beneficial, and build a beautiful place where people and nature live in harmony, providing the "China Program" for the world to open a new path to sustainable development[1].

In terms of cooperation, China has offered cooperation from the very beginning of the International Development Cooperation System (SICD) that began to be organized in the world after the Second World War.

Subsequently, Chinese cooperation will have to be characterized by being based on a set of principles embodied in a document dating from 1964, and

---

1 "Xi emphasizes in SPIEF that sustainable development is a 'golden key' to solve global problems"; 2019-06-08; On the internet: http://spanish.xinhuanet.com/2019-06/08/c_138125143.htm

which continues in full force until today: "Eight Principles for Economic Aid and Technical Assistance to Third Countries". These political and axiological pillars have not been modified, only expanded or in any case completed, which accounts for a stability and full consonance of their State policies.

The cooperation proposed by China demarcates a clear alternative strategy to the existing international institutional architecture, focusing mainly on supporting the modernization and progress of developing countries. It is an emerging world leader who provides assistance to other States thereby fulfilling their international obligations, expressing their conformity with the principles of equity, mutual benefit, striving for substantial results and keeping up with current times promoting a solidarity integration based on common values. China envisages an approach to relations with other States, based on reciprocity standards, from a strategic height, through the establishment and development of a comprehensive cooperation partnership characterized by equality, mutual benefit and shared development, on structural issues as is the fulfillment of the objectives of sustainable development.

Analyzing the projection of intercultural policies that imply a promotion aimed at the integration and technological, scientific and cultural exchange in terms of sustainable cultural and economic development, means promoting the exchange of cultural patterns, policies and experiences aimed at strengthening and promoting intercultural dialogue and intergenerational, thus fulfilling part of the objectives set by the United Nations Organization, including "Strengthening the means of execution and revitalizing the World Alliance for Sustainable Development".

The strengthening of human capital in the framework of brotherhood relations is a fundamental tool for interaction between cities that aspire to be culturally sustainable, contributing to the projection, implementation and balance of objectives of intergenerational transcendence and mutual understanding between nations.

It is within this framework that the analysis of the strategic rolls that industrial development projects with a technological and scientific base, in this case Dream Town, and its contribution to the development of a knowledge economy based on innovation, environmental care, is fundamental, creativity and entrepreneurship.

II. Dream Town

Creation and objectives

Dream Town is a Proposal that seeks to become a trend towards demonstrating innovation and entrepreneurship in the market. Filled with an atmosphere of entrepreneurial enthusiasm, this Internet-based industry seeks to provide an innovative and sustainable mode of growth for the Chinese economic structure. This is a clear example where new technologies, art and respect for historical heritage are integrated to create a center for capturing new ideas, values and entrepreneurship within the reach of new generations. Undoubtedly a unique economic development model and full of nuances that ensure unprecedented success in the era of communication and technological advances.

It has the Projection of special scientific and technological areas that are expected to be a support for companies with a technological base, the grouping of resources and services, local finances, professional training and skills development.

Dream Town is located northwest of Hangzhou City with a total area of 3.47 square kilometers. It was founded in April 2015 and is characterized by rivers and farmland. It has several historic buildings; therefore its design preserved the existing farmland and river, creating, in turn, a river network on that. It has a pedestrian corridor to link the key nodes and configures a car-free zone, thus ensuring the care of the environment.

It is a platform created as part of the Zhejiang Hangzhou Future Sci-Tech City (FTSC) project, an area of scientific and technological innovation that began in 2010 in the western part of Hangzhou, over a main planned area of 123 km, such as part of a national pilot plan. The objective of the FTSC is to promote scientific and technological development at the regional level of the city, and serve as a role model for urbanization driven by innovation at the national level. The FSTC project is developing at an accelerated pace as a growth pole driven by science and technology, being a notable example of innovation and development worldwide[1]. It houses not only large corporations such as Alibaba and China Telecom, but also smaller companies, including startups. This allows the possibility of exchange and development guaranteeing the growth of companies and projects that are just beginning, but that will see their future in the market guaranteed by having support and containment networks when developing their ventures.

The assistance that these companies receive is essential for their development, with the possibility of obtaining the concession of free space for up to three years and subsidies for the rental of accommodation on site and costs of public services. In addition, incubators provide financial support related to business (for example, business planning; connection with other startups and external entities; seed finance). Therefore, an ideal environment is created to exchange ideas, lessons, experiences and create new opportunities for collaboration between them. Another fundamental point involves the recruitment and training of human resources. The Internet sector is changing rapidly, therefore ensuring "intelligent" human resources can increase the chances of success in the area of business.

Planned urban development model

Dream Town has a strategic urbanization approach aimed at promoting sustainable economic development at local and regional levels. Since the introduction of the reform and opening period at the end of the 1970s, the country's urbanization process has accelerated unbearably contributing in this way to achieve social and economic progress. With a level of domestic urban population projected to reach more than 1 billion people by 2030, Chinese cities are expected to play an increasingly important role towards the country's future trajectory (World Bank and Development Research Center of the State Council

---

1 Pathways of sustainable urban development across China, The cases of Hangzhou, Datong and Zhuhai; Via Cerruti Editor, 2018, P. 14.

of the CPR 2014). The urbanization process definitely implies one of the most important objectives within the central government's policy, as stated in the thirteenth five-year Economic and Social Development Plan (2016-2020)[1] that describes the strategic intentions and main objectives of the country related to their cities (Part XIII: New Urbanization) (Central Committee of the Communist Party of China 2016). This plan highlights innovation as a fundamental pillar for the development perspectives of the People's Republic of China (Part II: Innovation-driven development).

Sustainability goals

Dream Town projects the creation of new models to achieve sustainable urban development. For this it has incorporated green principles and practices. For example, the Dream Town master plan foresees new and improved urbanization standards that include "car-free" areas and social interaction spaces that foster integrated experimentation, exchange and environment (Argyriou 2016).

The safeguarding of urban and rural historical areas and their associated traditional areas together with knowledge and practices reduce environmental footprints, promoting more and better patterns of ecologically sustainable production and consumption.

It is proposed as an architectural design solution that encourages the creation of urban areas where environmental care predominates, the product of policies that focus on sustainable urban development. This guarantees access to essential environmental goods and services for the sustenance of communities, guaranteeing stronger protection and more sustainable use of biological and cultural diversity, as well as by safeguarding traditional knowledge and skills, in synergy with other

---

[1] The thirteenth five-year plan of economic and social development of China delineates the new perspective of the country, Ministry of Commerce of the People's Republic of China, 11-02-2015. On the internet: http://spanish.mofcom.gov.cn/article/reportajeexterior/201511/20151101152203.shtml

forms of scientific knowledge[1].

This is part of a national plan through which the purposes of the National Strategy for Sustainable Development were established. Through it, the principles and policies to be followed to carry out such a company were raised, the main ones being:

- All climate change policies would always be framed in the National Strategy for Sustainable Development.

- These policies would always be framed by the principle of common but differential responsibilities (Binary World Vision enshrined in the United Nations Framework Convention on Climate Change - MMNUCC-).

- There will always be a balance between adaptation and mitigation commitments. A reduction in greenhouse gases would be sought but an adaptation to the new climatic reality should also be encouraged.

- The development of technology would be encouraged to achieve an adaptation to that reality. For this, a technological revolution should be mediated that would allow the reduction of greenhouse gas emissions.

- Active participation in international forums related to the subject.

In 2011, the White Paper on China Policies and Actions to address Climate Change was published. It meant a corollary of the projection and adoption of political measures aimed at the proposed mitigation and adaptation objectives, which had been proclaimed during the period of the XI Five-Year Plan (2006-2010).

China perfected the systems of laws and legal regulations and improved

---

[1] The Hangzhou Declaration: Placing Culture at the Heart of Sustainable Development Policies, Hangzhou International Congress China, Adopted in Hangzhou, People's Republic of China, on 17 May 2013. On the internet:
http://www.unesco.org/new/fileadmin/ MULTIMEDIA / HQ / CLT / images /FinalHangzhouDeclaration20130517.pdf

administrative regimes and labor mechanisms regarding the confrontation with climate change, intensified the investigation of statistics and calculations and the construction of its systems, raised the level of scientific, technological and political research, strengthened education and training in climate change, thereby increasing capacity in this regard[1].

III. Association of Information and Communication Technologies of Mar del Plata and the area (ATICMA)

Creation and objectives

ATICMA is an Association that brings together professionals, entrepreneurs, companies and universities of the ICT sector (Information and communication technologies) of the city of Mar del Plata and the area, in the province of Buenos Aires, Argentina. It has an open and collaborative work that provides as a main goal to promote new initiatives with a technological base, promoting the local entrepreneurial ecosystem.

It seeks to promote creativity and intelligent innovation through technology, to favor the growth and development of the sector. Its objective is to improve competitiveness, promote the knowledge industries and promote sustainable growth through joint work between companies, entrepreneurial sectors, educational establishments, science and technology institutions and the State.

It also carries out specific studies on the analysis of environmental aspects and impacts in accordance with the current legislation of the Province of Buenos Aires, Argentina and its activities.

The main goals are to promote new ventures, carry out actions that arouse new vocations in the area of information and communications technologies, and provide the creation of work spaces characterized by the integration between industry, academia and local organizations. For this, it aspires to a joint work

---

1 Policies and actions of China to face climate change. People's Republic of China, 22 November 2011. Available at: http://cu.chineseembassy.org/esp/zt/qhbhxxwt/t996975.htm

between such areas[1].

A stable regulatory framework, tax advantages for the creation, growth and establishment of companies, as well as state policies that develop a favorable ecosystem, are necessary values and actions that must be carried out to guarantee the sustainable development and prosperity of societies, Emphasizing the local.

Planned urban development model

In the city of Mar del Plata, the ICT (Information and Communication Technology) sector employs about 3,500 people, grouped in 76 companies and 500 micro-enterprises (which include independent professional enterprises and services) that invoice more than 3 thousand million pesos annually, of which 40 percent is exported, some 1.3 billion pesos.

Today Argentina participates with 0.5 percent of the world export market, with 6.9 billion dollars. The national objective is to reach 1 percent of the world market, which would cause a great change generating 150 thousand good quality jobs.

Nationally, Mar del Plata has an important value in the ICT sector. According to the data provided by Aticma, the city has "76 companies, 500 microenterprises, independent business and professional services, with 3,150 million pesos of annual turnover and 1,300 million pesos of annual exports, 40 percent."

In Argentina, 73 percent of ICT companies are micro (they have up to 9 workers), 21 percent are small (10 to 40 workers); 4 percent are medium (50 to 200 workers) and 2 percent are large (more than 200 workers). In addition, the country has four star companies (private technology companies valued at more than 1 billion dollars) and one of them, Globant, is based in the city of Mar del Plata.

These data demonstrate the importance of the existence of a nucleus

---

1   An opportunity for the development of the region, Open Management, Aticma Mar del Plata, On the internet: https://www.aticma.org.ar/gestion-abierta/

entrepreneurial ecosystem in the same place, which is fundamental for the development of this type of undertakings. The proposal of a management model that groups different areas, promotes teamwork and generates exchange of experiences and values to find solutions of different types, is fundamental and favors the entire community in the long term.

The awakening of the entrepreneurial and entrepreneurial vocation is another fundamental item for the development of the city and obtaining competitiveness.

Sustainability goals

One of the main regulations to which ATICMA adheres is foreseen by the Global Compact. This proposes to employers to commit to apply 10 principles in their organizations, which are based on Universal Declarations and Conventions applied in four areas: Human Rights, Environment, Labor Standards and Anti-Corruption.

ATICMA conducts periodic studies of environmental aspects and impacts in accordance with the current legislation of the Province of Buenos Aires and its activities. As a result and from the point of view of waste generation, the Organization is recognized as a generator of waste RAEEs (Waste Electrical and Electronic Equipment) but also as a generator of solutions and applications that contribute to the monitoring of the environment.

It also provides for the organization of awareness campaigns for the segregation of recyclable waste and the rationalization of natural resources.

In labor matters, it focuses on providing an excellent working environment, training and consolidation of work teams that provide continuity and operational sustainability in the sector's labor chain[1].

---

1 CSR Sustainability Manual (MGP) - ISO 26000, Aticma Mar del Plata. On the internet: https://www.aticma.org.ar/gestion-abierta/

At the national level, and through the adoption of both internal and international regulations related to the issue, the articulation of the social, environmental and economic dimensions in the development process is promoted, promoting sustainability and mitigating the effects of Climate Change. At the same time it promotes the fight against poverty, the valuation of eco systemic services and the use of alternative energies. The creation and strengthening of capacities at the state, business and community level is envisaged for the application of intersectoral and international agreements aimed at the transformation and promotion of activities that improve and promote a natural and human environment with a view to achieving intergenerational solidarity.

IV. Conclusions

After analyzing the points addressed, we can conclude that intercultural cooperation is essential to strengthen human capital and contribute to national development, promoting economic growth based on local policies that have sustainable development as the epicenter. Within this framework, the twinning relationships[1] between different cities worldwide are essential for the creation of intercultural links and policies that include coordination mechanisms for the establishment of municipal development plans and training actions.

The strengthening of human capital in the framework of brotherhood relations is a fundamental tool for interaction between cities that aspire to be culturally sustainable, contributing to the projection, implementation and balance of objectives of intergenerational transcendence and mutual understanding between nations. This

---

1   The twinning of cities is a mechanism of cooperation of exceptional value, because it puts in contact, between countries, not only to local leaders, but to entire populations. If it is done between cities in industrialized countries and cities in developing countries, twinning adds to the intellectual and moral enrichment of the parties a technical and material contribution sometimes considerable in favor of growing cities, directly usable, without administrative costs and without suffering the spirit of equality of the parties. The international cooperation of local communities can play an important role in the union of peoples. Source: Resolution 2861 of the XXVI General Assembly of the United Nations adopted in December 1971 with the theme "The twinning of cities as a means of international cooperation" . https://undocs.org/es/A/RES/2861%28XXVI%29

with the objective of creating the necessary projections to achieve an exchange of experiences, scientific knowledge and strengthening of human capital in matters of green economic industry and sustainable development at the provincial and local level between China and Argentina. The key is in the projection towards a system of integral innovation: knowledge networks between social actors such as the Government, Industry, Companies, Financing Organizations and the Academy, with the aim of improving the economic competitiveness of cities.

The path to be followed by the People's Republic of China is clearly palpable, through state policies previously planned and adapted to a model of society that aspires to become a faithful reflection of the highest standards of quality of life that can be accessed by its citizens Urban planning, which has as its epicenter the monitoring of sustainability standards, promotes knowledge and new planning technologies, possessing unparalleled value, inviting the creation and projection of such structures in our cities. The integration, exchange and study of these issues is necessary and an example to follow for our nations. This guarantees success and sustained long-term development whose implementation and balance allows the projection of intergenerational transcendence goals. At this point, I consider that international cooperation is essential for our societies to receive these types of tools that strengthen the cultural training of their citizens and thus be able to understand the scope and measure the benefits of its implementation.

References

Argyiou Iraklis. *Planning the Smart City in China: Key Policy Issues and the case of Dream Town in the city of Hangzhou*; French National Center for Scientific Researches (CNRS); Paris, France

Luque Gallegos, V. (2016). *Culture and Sustainable Development*. International Peripheral. Magazine for the Analysis of Culture and Territory, Spain; 22 - 01-1016

UN. Sustainable Development Goals, United Nations Development Agenda; Report of the Secretary General on the work of the Organization; publication September 2, 2015, New York. https://undocs.org/es/A/70/1

Resolution 2861 of the XXVI General Assembly of the United Nations adopted in December 1971 with the theme "The twinning of cities as a means of international cooperation". https://undocs.org/es/A/RES/2861%28XXVI%29

Hangzhou Declaration: Putting culture at the center of sustainable development policies. Culture: Key to sustainable development; Hangzhou International Congress; Hangzhou, China 17- 5- 2013.

http://www.unesco.org/new/fileadmin/MULTIMEDIA/HQ/CLT/images/FinalHangzhouDeclaration20130517.pdf

CSR Sustainability Manual (MGP) - ISO 26000; ATICMA 14-08-08 http://file:///C:/Users/Eurocae/Downloads/Manual%20de%20Sustentabilidad%20y%20RSE%20-%20ATICMA%20Rev0%2014-08-18.pdf

杭州梦想小镇（互联网村）带给哥伦比亚的启示

安吉莉卡 【哥伦比亚】
亚洲伊比利亚美洲文化基金会　项目经理

虽然中国已在为 5G 互联网革命做准备，但在哥伦比亚，宽带互联网接入和促进科学创新发展的政策设计仍然是一项挑战。2019 年笔者首次到访杭州，这座城市对我产生了巨大的影响。杭州的地铁系统、公共自行车、电动汽车和清洁城市都为我展示了一个创新城市的特点。有两件事给我留下了深刻的印象：第一，人们不再使用现金，所有的交易都是通过智能手机进行的；第二，访问阿里巴巴集团和梦想小镇（互联网村）。

在哥伦比亚，科学、技术和创新变得越来越重要，实际上其重要城市都在努力创新而不被国际一线城市抛在后面，如哥伦比亚首都波哥大就开展了一些项目来促进信息和通信技术（ICT）的使用，也许这就是波哥大被公认为智慧城市的原因。但波哥大真的是一个智慧城市吗？在哥伦比亚还有大量的研究者和创新者渴望发展和创造，但国家缺乏对这一产业激励的政策，使得这些人才离开本国去寻找更好的机会，而本国则继续处于传统的服务经济中，落入中等收入陷阱。

与此同时，中国直面与城市化进程相关的挑战，并努力建立促进城市可持续性的政策保障，强调智慧城市可促进可持续发展。中国是世界上拥有更多智慧城市试点的国家。2012 年，中国开始在国家层面上开发智慧城市模型，以利用人工智能和物联网的进步，保障城市运行的高效以及电力等资源的优化利用。

笔者希望通过介绍杭州的梦想小镇（互联网村）案例，以确定智慧城市模式在中国的优势,并能够应用于哥伦比亚波哥大市。通过实际研究,笔者认为中国作为哥伦比亚盟友极为重要,哥伦比亚有很多要向这个亚洲国家学习的地方。哥伦比亚一直是拉丁美洲对开放与中国的关系最持怀疑态度的国家,因为中国的制造业实力,哥伦比亚将中国视为其工业的威胁,也因为其明显亲美。

为了推动这项研究,本文首先定义智慧城市的概念及其今天的含义,确定智慧城市的三个组成变量,即:智慧治理、人才和智慧经济。我将通过确定的三个变量,对梦想小镇(互联网村)进行案例研究。然后,本文将讨论波哥大智慧城市的进展,并通过这三个变量确定哥伦比亚应该向中国学习的地方以及与中国合作的潜在机会。最后,本文将展望中国和哥伦比亚之间的关系及其未来前景。

一 智慧城市

智慧城市的概念越来越受到政府、企业和学术界重视,以促进可持续城市发展。智慧城市的概念没有明确的定义,但根据大都市层面的信息和通信技术(ICT)智慧城市的概念有所不同。智能城市不应局限于信息和通信技术,因为城市空间由理念和提供智能理念的人组成。

智力也可以指创意设计或新组织。我们可以说,一座城市的"智慧"描述了它有效地收集所有资源以实现既定目标的能力。

我将采用 Leonidas Anthopoulus 基于其他学者提供的不同定义所作的总结定义:智慧城市是一个利用信息和通信技术和创新作为手段来维持自身经济发展的城市,从社会和环境的角度,解决来自六个方面的若干挑战:人、经济、治理、流动性、环境和生活质量。

根据信息和通信技术创新能力和当地优先事项的不同,加上每个城市的情况不同,因此有不同的智能城市备选方案。Anthopoulus 确定了智能城市生态系统的八个组成部分,这些组成部分在城市之间可能有所不同:(1)智慧治理:在城市空间建立智能政府,同时提供服务、参与和承诺的技术。(2)智能人群:提高人们创造力和开放式创新的措施。(3)智慧经济:增强业务、发展、就业和城市增长的技术和创新。(4)智慧生活:创新,以提高城市空间的生活质量和宜居性。(5)智能环境:为保护和管理自然资源(废物管理系统、排放控制、回收利用、污染控制传感器等)创新和整合通信技术。(6)智能服务:使用技术和信息和通信技术提供医疗服务、教育、旅游、安全、响应控制(监控)等。(7)智能基础设施:

具有集成智能技术（例如传感器、智能电网等）的城市设施（例如，水和能源网络、街道、建筑物等）。（8）智能交通（或智能移动）：具有改进的集成实时监控系统的交通网络。

Anthopoulus 将"开放式创新系统"纳入智能人组成部分的一个重要概念是通过政府、行业、公司、融资组织、中介机构和学术界等社会行为者之间的知识网络实施综合学习过程。开放式创新系统被认为具有促进城市经济增长的潜力。

在明确了智慧城市的概念之后，我选择了构成智慧城市的三个变量：智慧治理、人才和智慧经济。本文将通过这三个变量来分析杭州梦想小镇（互联网村）的具体情况。

二 杭州梦想小镇（互联网村）

1. 中国智慧城市的背景

自改革开放以来，中国城市化进程加快，预计到 2030 年，中国城市人口将增加到 10 亿以上，因此中国城市在国家未来将发挥越来越重要的作用。事实上，正如《中国国民经济和社会发展第十三个五年规划》（2016—2020）所述，城市化是中央政府的高度政治优先事项，该计划确立了国家的战略意图和城市的主要目标，强调了创新对中国发展前景的关键作用。此外，2016 年批准的《"十三五"国家科技创新规划》强调了创新的重要性，包括互联网行业的创新活动，以促进国家层面的增长。中国城市制定的创新政策潜力巨大。总的来说，在中国中央和地方政府层面制定的政策规划中，可以看出城市化、创新和增长之间的密切联系。

以浙江省省会杭州市为例，杭州在重要历史时期曾经历了重大的城市挑战和治理改革。与上海、北京或天津等中国特大城市相比，杭州的全球影响力略逊色，但是正在成为国内外重要的经济和技术中心。

从 2000 年中期开始，杭州强调各种技术和知识密集型产业，如金融服务、电子商务、IT、生物医学和旅游业。如今，有着 743.8 万人口的杭州，拥有大量高科技领域的专家，并以其充满活力的商业环境而闻名。在过去二十年中，杭州一直以实现知识驱动经济为目标。2016 年 9 月，杭州成功举办了 G20 峰会，还被命名为充满活力的历史文化名城。杭州处于中国科技产业发展势头的前列，为中国其他城市树立了榜样。

杭州规划的城西科技走廊由三个平台组成：未来科技城（FSTC）、西溪谷互联网金融城和梦想城。城西科技走廊总占地面积达 224 平方千米，周围有高校群，如浙江大学就在附近。这些计划的一个关键，反映了该市对未来发展的更广阔愿景，即基于技术和经济创新的发展，这也是改善该市未来前景和促进经济增长的关键。在此背景下，杭州市政府还通过发展高新技术产业，牵头推动当地经济和产业结构调整。将这一变化带到城市的一个核心方法是设立科技园区，整合资源和服务、对科技型公司、本地金融创新以及专业培训和技能发展等方面提供支持。

2. 梦想小镇（互联网村）

梦想小镇是设有多个孵化器的地区，这些孵化器有助于新的互联网公司的发展并加快其进程。它位于未来科技城（FSTC）内部，由两部分组成：第一部分是互联网创业小镇，专注于互联网相关产品的研发和生产，如电子商务、游戏创作、软件设计、信息服务、大数据和云计算；第二部分是天使小镇，主要关注金融、投资和财富管理。天使小镇在第一轮融资中帮助新企业。

因此，梦想小镇是一个促进小企业发展的公共空间，汇集了浙江省专门从事互联网和金融领域的大学毕业生。目前，梦想小镇拥有近 300 家新公司，目标是达到 10000 家，吸引 3000 多亿人民币（相当于 450 多亿美元）的投资。它还涉及促进杭州空间和经济结构调整等更广泛的政治目标。此外，梦想小镇总体规划的一个关键目标是使该地区最终成为平衡社会、经济和生态因素的城市空间模型。

对于梦想小镇案例的分析，我将再选取智慧城市的三个变量，即智慧治理、人才和智慧经济。

（1）智慧治理

中国中央政府认识到，为了实现国家的增长目标，有必要建立一种新的增长模式，其基础是提高生产率和创新，以及城市发展的重要性。因此，国务院在 2015 年指示地方政府支持创新和新兴企业，以此促进国民经济增长和就业。

2012 年，住房和城乡建设部提出了"开展国家智慧城市试点"，到 2013 年，已经批准了 193 个试点项目。这些趋势反映了中央政府将智慧城市作为加速中国工业化和创新的战略予以重视。此外，中央政府将智慧城市的发展视为改善城市规划和管理的有效手段。

城市政体理论（URT）通过实证研究检验了中国城市化动力，该理论分析了促进增长议程中的主要政治经济角色的作用，这是由土地开发的特殊性驱动的。

城市政体理论的视角与中国背景的相关性涉及中国向新治理体系过渡的两个方面。首先是开放市场经济，伴随着国有企业改革和私营经济在城市事务中的巨大贡献。第二个是经济和行政责任的"权力下放"，它使中央以下各级，特别是市和区一级的政府，成为城市规划和发展的关键角色。尤其是把经济权力下放作为一种增长手段，赋予地方政府调控当地资源的权力（Wu，2007）。

显然，梦想小镇（互联网村）是中国当代推动智慧经济的典范项目，该项目是基于公私合作框架运作的城市治理创业模式。

（2）人才

梦想小镇是中国国家人才战略的一部分。原则上，创业公司必须由浙江省的大学毕业生参与，公司的法人（出资额至少占注册商业资本总额的30%）由毕业生担任且应届毕业生至少占公司员工的70%。

梦想小镇以开放创新为基础。首先与创业公司需要与他们的托管孵化器建立联系，一家设在梦想小镇内的私营公司，作为为他们提供各种支持的"保护性主体"。一个典型的孵化器可以容纳许多新企业（不超过30家），这些创业公司通常与孵化器位于同一栋大楼内。孵化器（通常有10位工作人员）主要通过三种方式帮助新企业，即：提供日常帮助（办公室和行政设施）；将内部实体（如同行）和外部实体（如投资者）建立联系；以及提供创新过程的技术和商业支持（例如，专有技术、财务规划、市场问题建议）。在某些情况下，孵化器可以投资需要提供资本的项目，以换取股份。如果初创企业决定退出孵化器，这些股份随后将被收取费用。为了最大限度地扩大投资机会，在整个互联网小镇为风险投资公司设立了一个指定的空间，即天使小镇，以促进创业公司与原则上专门从事科技融资的风险资本之间的互动。

当地政府出台了许多优惠政策来吸引新兴互联网公司，如落户（户籍）、幼儿教育、租金折扣和税收优惠等。自2015年在杭州市数字经济领域正式启动以来，互联网公司持续在梦想小镇崛起。这也使得杭州成为人才、资本、项目和其他高层次创业元素的磁石。最新数据显示，2016年，杭州在中国20个人才净收入主要城市中排名第一。领英（LinkedIn）在其最新报告中表示，杭州是中国对外国人最具吸引力的三大城市之一。近三年来，有23万多外籍人才选择落户杭州，其中94%从事信息软件、生物医药、新能源、节能和金融服务等行业。

可以看出，杭州市做了许多努力，为青年人才提供机会，让他们开创自己的项目，为创新做出贡献。此外，对于公司的进驻，有必要采取创新激励措施，以吸引人才参与该行业的发展。

（3）智慧经济

梦想小镇项目背后的逻辑是创新和创造力驱动增长和竞争力。因此，参与梦想小镇愿景和规划的政府当局强调提供支持初创企业的最佳方式，并期望取得优异的成果。梦想小镇官方政策文件规定，符合条件的智能应用必须涉及电子商务、软件设计、信息服务、集成电路、大数据、云计算、网络安全和动画设计等领域。在收集主要数据时，大多数梦想小镇创业项目都与两个智能领域有关："经济"和"生活质量"。

许多项目涉及数字经济应用，阿里巴巴在线平台提供传统的推广渠道。梦想小镇还代表了"智慧经济"更微妙的一面：当地政府的愿望是，创新园区将催生一家新的"阿里巴巴"。这将带来一些收益，比如通过就业和公司纳税带来更高的财政收入，以消费为基础的城市化（例如，阿里巴巴的1000多名员工本身就是一个大型的城市消费群体）或未来大规模城市开发带来土地价值的增值。

梦想小镇有些成功案例，比如杭州映墨科技有限公司和蚂蚁金融服务集团。映墨科技有限公司一开始只有6名员工，之后扩大到30人并获得了500万元人民币的风险投资。该公司利用与富士康和阿里巴巴合作的机会，在2016年又成功筹集了3800万元人民币的投资。如今，映墨科技已成为中国领先的虚拟现实公司，拥有研发能力和幼儿教育专业产品。蚂蚁金融服务集团于2014年10月正式成立，该集团源于支付宝，支付宝是2004年成立的全球领先的外部支付平台。支付宝技术团队由一群有海外工作经历的创业者组成，他们此前曾在Facebook、谷歌、亚马逊、eBay和微软等知名公司工作。他们带着向中小企业和个人消费者提供普惠金融服务的愿望回到中国，希望为消费者提供轻松快捷金融服务，不管他们是富人还是穷人，也不管他们来自哪个国家。

梦想小镇不仅是青年专业化人才的创新模式，也提升了创业精神，还旨在成为一种新型的城市化模式，促进社会开放，同时结合经济和环境因素，整合历史和未来的城市元素，保护现有的环境，创造一个没有汽车的社会活动空间。

三　哥伦比亚首都是一个智慧城市吗？

哥伦比亚于2018年5月作为正式成员加入经济合作与发展组织（OECD）。

该组织指出，哥伦比亚在研发方面的投资仅占国内生产总值（GDP）的0.2%，而其28个成员国的平均投资为2.4%。

然而，哥伦比亚首都波哥大被公认为是本国最具创新精神的城市之一。在过去四年中，市政府一直在努力将信息和通信技术作为虚拟化行政流程与城市的日常事务联系起来，安装了智能交通灯，并对基础教育中的技术教育进行投资。

如前所述，根据城市的信息和通信技术能力和优先级，智慧城市有多种类型，智慧城市指的是在经济、社会和环境发展中为人民、经济、治理、流动性、环境和生活质量使用智能的城市。因此，对于一个城市化项目来说，通过制造和涉及所有这些事务的是布朗克斯创意区项目（Bronx Creative District project），其中的理念是成为"创新、技术和创意中心"，该项目旨在结束波哥大是最危险的社区之一的印象，并消除任何恢复其初始状态的可能性。在这一领域，除其他活动外，预计将培养设计、美食、平面制作和广告等行业的企业和企业家，市政府打算在波哥大建立创业和创意产业中心。他们参考了里斯本的 LX 工厂，这是一个经过翻新的旧工业区，其中约有 200 家商店与摄影、文身和设计工作室、艺术家工作室、餐厅等相关行业，并举办了商业和文化活动。尽管市长办公室保证其政策延续性，但无法保证项目会成功，因为存在一些挑战，如 2020—2024 年市长的更换、该地区的安全问题以及是否有优惠政策激励公司迁往该地区。有人说，这个项目似乎更像是一种抹黑，而不是真正的城市结构的转变（Gonzalez，2019）。

另一方面，自 2015 年以来，一直在构建科技创新区，这是一个新的技术项目，阐明并激励创新生态系统，以加强波哥大橙色经济[1]和工业 4.0。该项目源于国立大学校园内为波哥大和该地区创建科技园的倡议。然而，由于各种的原因，这个园区一直没有建成。由于电子和系统系相关的教授和年轻研究人员的坚持，该项目才得以持续，并成为种子。现在，许多公共组织和大学支持这一倡议，这是波哥大智能战略专业化进程中优先考虑的科学、技术和创新的主要项目。

该科技创新区将位于延伸 3.5 公里的走廊内，有望成为城市战略点经济和社会发展的新极。它将是一个商业和人才供应的会议场所，采用科技创新 4.0 开发和阐述新的高科技举措（衍生产品、初创企业、中小企业和大公司），因此，数字经济有助于提高波哥大的生产率在哥伦比亚软件业的开发公司中占 78%；在过去 6 年中，该行业增长了 13.4%，占哥伦比亚 GDP 的 1.2%。33% 的橙色经济和

1　"橙色经济"也称为创意经济，描述了互联网文化、艺术和媒体产业在市场中的地位。

工业4.0技术将在该地区推广，如下所示：

• 橙色经济：视频游戏、数字平台、软件创建、应用程序创建、数字动画、互动内容。

• 工业4.0：人工智能、虚拟和增强现实、机器人、区块链、物联网、大数据和分析。

信息和通信技术公园是科技创新区的第一个项目，该项目于2015年开始并于2018年完成可行性研究。项目主体按计划将于2021年完成并提供如下服务和展示等功能：网络空间；信息和通信技术展厅；原型实验室；生活实验室；协同工作；企业孵化和加速；思维实验室；实验室大数据中心；一项技术推广计划和另一项技术废物处理、宽带和清洁能源共享服务计划。

科技创新区可能是更具雄心的项目的开始，这些项目是在30年前的城市中设计的，当时的技术范式似乎更像乌托邦。但首先，最重要的初始项目是：原型实验室；生活实验室；公司的孵化和加速；思维实验室；实验室大数据中心，以及其中的一个或两个介于协同工作、展示室、技术推广、共享服务之间。波哥大还没有被认为是经济、社会和未来国家的智慧城市。波哥大的乌托邦还没有写出来，而这个科技创新区可能是新经济的试路石。在哥伦比亚，技术和创新产业很少受到关注，根据世界知识产权组织编制的2019年全球创新指数，其在129个国家中排名67位。研究发现的其最显著挑战之一是缺乏长期规划和完成项目的承诺，特别是政府的承诺。

四 从中国到哥伦比亚的学习和合作机会

现在，笔者通过在梦想小镇（互联网村）中使用的智慧城市的三个组成部分，比较中国和哥伦比亚的两个案例，以确定哥伦比亚应该向亚洲国家学习的要点以及合作的机会。

尽管哥伦比亚和中国有不同的政府制度，但这并不妨碍哥伦比亚从改革后的中国吸取经验。正如中国改革开放的总设计师邓小平所说，"不管黑猫白猫，能捉到老鼠，就是好猫。"

（1）智慧治理

正如我们在梦想小镇的案例中看到的那样，政治稳定和长期规划是关键。从长远来看，中央政府提出的一项政治倡议会受到各方面的欢迎。因此，科技创新在中国的重要性并不是什么新鲜事,而是持续四十年的巨大发展。然而,哥伦比亚的不同在于政策没有延续性,政策依靠政府,但当这一届政府结束时,政策也停止了,换句话说,在哥伦比亚有政府政策,但没有国家政策。这些政策是短期的、临时制定的。

(2) 人才

中国人自信,当这种自信伴随着决心和耐心时,它就产生了无与伦比的价值。在当今世界,这一优势转化为创新能力。因此,技术创新是社会全面发展的结果,对未来充满乐观。中国正在发展成为全球创新中心,这不仅是因为在研发方面的投资,而且基本上是因为中国人相信有一个更好、完美的未来,在那里他们可以发挥重要作用。为了实现这一目标,我们还必须考虑中国在粮食、基础教育、健康或社会和平方面所做的投资,这为创新创造了条件。

科学和技术提供了解释和改变世界的工具。作为这一转型的设计师,需要为此制定具体的公共政策,而中国就是这一政治决策的一个例子。今天的中国拥有世界上最大的科技人力资本。六百多万的研究人员超过任何其他国家的研发团队。

虽然在哥伦比亚,也有优秀的人才,但他们通常会在国外找到机会。本国缺乏吸引人才的国家政策。没有很多研究人才和更好的教育,没有资金和人才分散是研发投资低的结果,是哥伦比亚科学和技术成为最落后的领域的两个原因。

中国项目在知识、创业精神和城市规划方面的成功取决于第一批项目是否最强大,是否能吸引高素质人才在其领域工作和生活。其他项目只是对之前项目的补充或铺垫。哥伦比亚注定要从简单的道路开始,而理解和达到新的、复杂的道路既缓慢又可怕。这是一种不在最前沿的社会行为。

(3) 智慧经济

在一项调查中,公众推选了中国的新发明:高铁、共享单车、支付宝和网上购物(后两项与阿里巴巴直接相关)。因此,梦想小镇可以成为高新技术园区的典范,该项目的第一阶段是通过打造技术区,预计将有一个新的区域可以找到孵化器和衍生产品。当然,中国的经验将有助于加快哥伦比亚的科技进程,对基础设施建设和城市发展也将是一个很好的模式。梦想小镇也可以成为布朗克斯创意区的典范,因为这个空间没有确定的未来,在一个缺乏教育和创业支持关注的空间里建立一个孵化器和加速器,在哥伦比亚将是一个巨大的进步。

中国政府有一个"中国制造"计划,在该计划中,中国希望将"中国制造"

一词的内涵转变为高质量和高科技产品。这一计划基于四大支柱：开放与世界日益紧密的联系，这意味着向世界学习，在技术革命需要中开展科学合作；创新，大量投资于研发；要求国际高质量标准；基于环境可持续性的战略。在智能产业的推动下，中国在信息技术、机器人技术、数控工具、航空航天铁路设备、替代能源和电子车辆等领域取得了发展。

这是哥伦比亚应该吸取的一系列经验，因为其必须从目前的基础工业过渡到考虑到社会、技术、地缘政治和环境意识的工业发展。

五 中国，哥伦比亚的盟友

2019年，中国与哥伦比亚的双边关系得到前所未有的加强。但哥伦比亚可能也是对中国最持怀疑态度的国家。驻波哥大大使馆公使衔参赞徐伟说，由于缺乏了解和信任，到目前为止，双边没有建立很好的经济和商业关系。

与此同时，哥伦比亚总统在2019年7月访问中国并与习近平主席在北京会面，双方承诺在更高的水平上推动双边关系。哥伦比亚政府认识到中国作为有潜在价值的合作伙伴、重要消费国、第四次工业革命领导者，在当前所扮演的角色，承担起与该国在三个支柱领域的合作，即：加强外交关系、促进哥伦比亚对中国的出口并吸引其对哥伦比亚重要基础设施建设项目投资。2019年10月至11月间，四个基础设施建设项目已启动。

波哥大地铁项目。10月，波哥大选择了两家中国公司——中国港湾工程有限公司和西安地铁有限公司，从2020年开始建设第一条地铁线路。这份合同将实现波哥大持续半个多世纪起起落落的地铁建造计划。之前市民们更多地把它当作一个神话，而不是一个可以完成的项目。波哥大一直是世界上最大的、没有地铁的大都市之一。

波哥大大都会地区的列车项目。波哥大的另一个基建项目是城郊列车，它将连接该市与周边四个人口最多的城市。城郊列车西部段将于2023年开通，全程41公里，全部使用电能。中国土木工程建筑公司（CCECC），中国铁道建设总公司（CRCC）的子公司是唯一提交了项目报价的企业。

麦德林和卡利的绿色巴士项目。11月，麦德林市从中国比亚迪公司购买17辆电动公交车增加到其公共交通系统Metroplus中，并又加购了64辆公交车。卡利市首批购买了中国申沃客车公司生产的26辆电动汽车，并计划继续购入125

辆电动公共汽车。

4G 高速公路。杜克总统宣布，一家中国公司被选中在该国南部修建一条公路，当然这条公路的建设困难重重。这是一条 456 公里长的高速公路，是雄心勃勃的第四代 4G 公路计划的一部分。

2020 年是关键的一年。两国需要更多地了解对方，并在彼此之间建立信任，同时也需要大量的文化外交。中国是哥伦比亚盟友，将在很多方面为其提供帮助。因此，让中国成为科技创新区的盟友将是该项目实现的保证。

"一带一路"倡议着重在基础设施和技术方面合作，参与国可获得贷款用于建造铁路线、机场、5G 项目、水坝、水电站、港口、桥梁以及其他项目。但哥伦比亚尚未签署任何补充备忘录。无论哥伦比亚是否签署该备忘录，中国已经在哥伦比亚的电信、制造业、石油和天然气、汽车和基础设施等领域进行了大量投资。

Dream Town Internet Village in Hangzhou: Lessons for Colombia

Angelica Maria Lopez Triana / Colombia

Asia Iberoamerica Cultural Foundation / Project Manager

While China is preparing for the 5G Internet revolution, in Colombia the broadband internet access and the design of policies to foster scientific and innovative development are still a challenge. It was what I found in September 2019, my first visit to China in Hangzhou City. Far from what I imagined, the city greatly impacted me, expanded my vision to an innovated city through its subway system, publicas bicycles, electric cars, and the clean city. There were two things that impressed me the most, number one, people no longer use cash, all transactions are made through their smartphones, and number two, was the visit to Alibaba Group and the Dream Town Internet Village.

In Colombia, the science, technology and innovation is becoming more important, actually the main cities are making efforts to innovative and not be left behind by the forefront cities of innovation and technology, such as Bogota, the capital of the country, which has carried out projects to promote the use of the information and communications technology (ICT), and maybe it is why Bogota has been recognized as an smart city, but the question remains: Is Bogota a smart city for real? in addition, there is an important number of researchers and creatives, eager to develop and create, but the lack of policies and incentives for this industry, makes this human capital have to leave the country in search of better opportunities, while the country continues in a traditional service economy, caught in the middle income trap.

Otherwise, China is a country that faces challenges associated with its urbanization process and strives to establish political approaches to promote urban sustainability, emphasizing on smart cities as a mechanism to promote sustainable development. China is the country that has more smart city pilots in the world. China began to develop the smart city model at the national level in 2012, in order to take advantage of the advances made in artificial intelligence and the Internet of Things to improve the mobilization of the city, facilitate the work to the control agencies and ensure efficient use of electricity and the resources.

Therefore, for this work I want to present the Dream Town Internet Village case in Hangzhou, to identify the advantages of the smart city model in China, and to be able to be applied in Colombia, specifically in the city of Bogotá. In this way, I seek to highlight the importance for Colombia of having China as an ally, considering that Colombia has much to learn from the Asian country. However, Colombia has been the most skeptical country in Latin America to the opening of its relations with China, because the Chinese manufacturing strength Colombia has seen China as a threat to its industry and also, because of its marked proximity to the United States.

In order to the development of this research, I will first define the concept of smart cities and what it implies today, I identified three variables that are components of an intelligent city, which are: intelligent governance, intelligent people and intelligent economy. Later, I will present the case study of Dream Town Internet Village through the three variables, previously identified. Then, I will discuss the progress on smart cities in Bogotá and through the three variables identify the points in which Colombia should learn from China and the opportunities for cooperation. I will conclude talking about the relations between China and Colombia and their future prospects.[1]

1. Smart cities

The concept of smart city is increasingly important in governments, businesses and the academy to promote sustainable urban development. Although there is no a clear definition of the smart city concept, it is different depending on the information and communications technology (ICT) at the metropolitan level, however, smart cities should not be limited to ICTs, thus the urban spaces that conform a city, are made of ideas and people who provide intelligent ideas.

In this way, intelligence can also refer to creative design or new organizations. So, we would say that the 'intelligence' of a city describes its ability to gather all its resources, effectively and without problems to achieve the objectives set.

To discuss the different definitions of smart city, would need a whole investigative process which does not concern here. Therefore, I will take the summary definition that Leonidas Anthopoulus made in base of the different definitions provided by other authors: Therefore we say that the smart city is the one that uses ICT and innovation as a means to sustain itself in economic, social and environmental terms and to address several challenges in six dimensions: people, economy, governance, mobility, environment and quality of life.

Therefore, depending on the ICT capacity, innovation and local priorities, each city performs differently and in this way there are different smart city alternatives. Anthopoulus identified eight components of a smart city ecosystem, which can vary between cities:

---

1   Before going forward, it is important to say two things: first, that this is an approach from the innovation economy and the entrepreneurial state, because without an entrepreneurial state it is impossible to achieve higher stages of development. Second, from September 2019 when this work idea was conceived to December of the same year, the relations between China and Colombia were transformed enormously, however, it is the beginning of a long way to go, with this work I hope to continue encouraging closer relations between the two countries.

(1) Smart governance: establishment of an intelligent government in the urban space, accompanied by technology for the provision of services, participation and commitment.

(2) Smart people: measures that improve people's creativity and open innovation.

(3) Smart economy: technology and innovation to strengthen business. development, employment and urban growth.

(4) Smart life: innovation to improve the quality of life and habitability in the urban space.

(5) Intelligent environment: innovation and incorporation of ICTs for the protection and management of natural resources (waste management systems, emission control, recycling, pollution control sensors, etc.).

(6) Smart services: use of technology and ICT for the provision of health services, education, tourism, security, response control (surveillance), etc.

(7) Smart infrastructure: city facilities (for example, water and energy networks, streets, buildings, etc.) with integrated smart technology (for example, sensors, smart grids, etc.).

(8) Intelligent transport (or intelligent mobility): transport networks with improved integrated real-time monitoring and control systems.

An important concept that Anthopoulus incorporates into the intelligent people component, is the 'open innovation systems' that refers to the exercise of the integrated learning process through networks knowledge between social actors such as the government, industry, companies, financing organizations, intermediaries and academia. Open innovation systems is considered to have the potential to boost urban economic growth.

Already having clear the concept of smart city, I will choose three variables that make up the smart city: smart governance, smart people and smart economy. Which I consider the more basic components to achieve higher stages of development. With these three components, I will analyze the particular case of Dream Town Internet Village in Hangzhou, China.

2. Dream Town Internet Village in Hangzhou

2.1 The context of the Smart Cities in China and the policies implemented in Hangzhou

Since the time of the reform at the end of the 70s, the urbanization of the country has accelerated, contributing greatly to social and economic progress. With the projection that the urban population will increase more than one billion by 2030, Chinese cities are expected to play an increasingly important role in the country's future. In fact, urbanization is a high political priority of the central government as stated in the 13th Five-Year Plan for Economic and Social Development (2016-2020) that establishes the country's strategic intentions and the main objectives of the city. This plan emphasizes the critical role of innovation for China's development prospects. In addition, a Five-Year National Plan on technological innovation, approved in 2016, underlines the importance of innovation activities, including in the Internet sector, to promote growth at the national level. Chinese cities enact innovation policies whose future potential seems significant. In general, close connections between urbanization, innovation and growth can be discerned in the Chinese policy plans defined at central and local levels.

An example of this is Hangzhou City, the capital of Zhejiang Province and a Chinese metropolis that has experienced major urban challenges and governance reforms during the regime's restructuring period. This city that may lack the global status of the country's megacities such as Shanghai, Beijing or Tianjin, aspires to become an important economic and technological center, nationally and internationally.

In mid-2000, Hangzhou's economy has been emphasizing various technology and knowledge-intensive sectors, such as financial services, electronic commerce,

IT, biomedicine and tourism. Now, with a population of 7,438,000 people, with expert users in high technology, and known for its vibrant business environment, Hangzhou has been the subject of various policy plans in the past twenty years with the aim of enacting a knowledge-driven economy . In September 2016, Hangzhou successfully hosted the G20 summit, and was named as a historical and cultural city full of vigor innovation Today, Hangzhou is at the forefront of China's momentum to develop its technology industry and serves as a model for other cities across the country.

Hangzhou has planned a Chengxi Science and Technology Corridor, consisting of three platforms that are: Future Sci-Tech City (FSTC), Xixi Valley Internet Finance Town and Dream Town. In a total area of 224 square km, it is surrounded by a group of nine universities and institutions of higher education such as Zhejiang University. A key direction of such plans, which also reflects the city's broader vision for future development, is based on the development of technological and economic innovation that is considered essential to improve the city's future prospects and boost economic growth. In this context, the Hangzhou city government leads efforts to promote local economic and industrial restructuring also through the development of new and high-tech industries. A key approach to bringing this change to the city is the designation of special scientific and technological areas that incorporate aspects such as the grouping of resources and services, support for technology-based companies, financial innovation local, and professional training and skills development.

2.2 Dream Town Internet Village

Dream Town is an area where are located several incubators, which help with the growth and accelerate the processes of new internet-based companies. It is located within FSTC and consists of two parts: the first, is the Internet Startup Village that focuses on the research, development and production of Internet-related products, such as electronic commerce, the creation of games, software design, information service, big data and cloud computing; and the second part is Angel Village, which focuses on finance, investments and wealth management. Angel Village helps new businesses during their first rounds of financing.

Therefore, Dream Town is a public space for the promotion of small businesses, which are conducted by graduates of universities in Zhejiang Province, specialized in the areas of internet and finance. Currently, Dream Town is home of almost 300 new companies with the goal of reaching 10,000 and attracting more than 300 billion RMB (equivalent to more than 45 billion dollars) of investment. It also relates to broader political objectives that revolve around the promotion of spatial and economic restructuring in Hangzhou. In addition, a key objective of Dream Town's master plan is for the site to finally become a model of an urban space that balances social, economic and ecological considerations.

For the analysis of the Dream Town case, I will take three the variables that are components of an intelligent city, governed intelligent, intelligent people and intelligent economy.

2.1.1 Smart Governance

The Chinese central government recognize that in order to achieve the country's growth objectives, it is necessary a new growth model that is based on increasing productivity and innovation, and the importance of urban development. Therefore, the State Council in 2015 ordered to the local governments to support innovation and new businesses as a way to increase the national economy, growth and job creation.

In 2012, the Ministry of Housing and Urban Rural Development made a call to "conduct a national smart cities pilot" by 2013 there were 193 pilot projects already approved. These trends reflect the assigned importance by the central government to the smart cities as a strategy to accelerate China's industrialization and innovation. In addition, the development of the smart city is seen by the central authorities as an effective means to improve urban planning and management.

The dynamics of Chinese urbanization have been examined through empirical studies informed by the Urban Regime Theory (URT) that analyze the role of dominant political-economic actors organized around a pro-growth agenda, which is driven by specificities of land development. The relevance of URT's perspectives for the Chinese context touches two urban aspects of the country's transition to a new system of governance. The first is the opening to a market-driven economy, which is accompanied by the reform of state enterprises and a strong contribution of private sectors in urban affairs. The second is the "decentralization" of economic and administrative responsibilities, which has constituted subnational state authorities, particularly at the municipal and district levels, key actors in urban planning and development. Economic decentralization in particular serves as an instrument for growth and empowers local authorities to act as resource mobilizers (Wu, 2007).

Evidently, Dream Town Internet Village represents an exemplary project of China's contemporary efforts to promote smart economy based on an entrepreneurial mode of urban governance operationalized by public-private partnership frameworks.

2.2.2 Smart people

Dream Town is part of the National Talent Strategy of China. In principle, is necessary that startups are involve with university graduates from Zhejiang Province who must serve as corporate legal persons of the company (contributing a minimum of 30% of the total registered commercial capital) and at least 70% of the company's staff.

Dream Town is based on open innovation systems. The first point of contact for startups is their hosting incubator, a private company established on the site, which acts as an "umbrella entity" that offers various supports. A typical incubator can house many new businesses (no more than 30) that are usually in the same building with the incubator. Incubators have some people (usually 10) and help new businesses in three main ways: daily problems (office and administration facilities);

networking with internal entities (eg, peers) and external entities (eg, investors); and technical and commercial support for the innovation process (eg, know-how; financial planning; advice on market issues). In certain cases, incubators can invest in projects offering capital in exchange for shares that would later be charged if the startup decides to withdraw from the incubation. To maximize investment opportunities, a designated space for venture capital companies, Angel Village, has been positioned throughout the Internet town to facilitate interactions between startups and capitals of risk that, in principle, specialize in science and technology financing.

The local government has published many favorable policies to attract emerging Internet companies, like the ones related to the hukou system (household registration), early childhood education, rental discounts and tax benefits. Internet companies have been emerging in Dream Town since its official launch in 2015 in the area of digital economy in Hangzhou City. This has also made Hangzhou a magnet for talent, capital, projects and other high-level elements of entrepreneurship. The latest figures show that in 2016 Hangzhou ranked first in the list of the 20 main cities in China that have a net talent income. In its latest report, LinkedIn said Hangzhou is among the top 3 cities in China that are most attractive to foreigners. In the last three years, more than 230,000 foreign talents chose to settle in Hangzhou and 94% of them work in information software, biomedicine, new energy, energy conservation, financial services, etc.

With the Dream Town Village, is evident that the city of Hangzhou has done many efforts to give opportunities to the youth talent to start their own project to contribute the innovation and also, for the relocation of the companies, has been necessary to creative incentives and also to attract talent to the growth in this industry.

2.2.3 Smart Economy

The logic behind the Dream Town project is that innovation and creativity drive to the growth and competitiveness. Consequently, government authorities, involved in the vision and planning of Dream Town, put emphasis on offering the best possible means of supporting startups with expectations of outstanding results. The official Dream Town policy document defines that eligible smart applications must fall into the areas of electronic commerce, software design, information services, integrated circuit, big data, cloud computing, network security and animation design. At the time of primary data collection, most Dream Town startup projects were related to two smart areas: "economy" and "quality of life".

Many of the projects are involved around digital economy applications, with Alibaba online platforms that offers a conventional promotion channel. Dream Town also represents a more subtle aspect of 'smart economy': the government authorities' aspiration is that the innovation site will lead to a new Alibaba corporation. This would bring several benefits as to bring higher incomes through employment and corporate taxes, the urbanization based on consumption (for example, Alibaba's workforce in order of a thousand employees is in itself a large urban consumption group) or increases in land values that would be taken into account in the future large-scale urban development.

Some successful stories in Dream Town are the Startups Immersion Technology and Ant Financial Services Group, the first one is specialist in Virtual Reality (VR) technology. The company started with six people. It then expanded to about 30 people and received RMB 5 million of venture capital and later, the company took advantage of opportunities to work with Foxconn and Alibaba and, in 2016, successfully raised 38 million RMB of investments. Today, Immersion Technology has become a leading Chinese virtual reality company with research and development capabilities, and specialized products in early childhood education. The second, Ant Financial Services Group—officially founded in October 2014 and is originated from Alipay, which is the world's leading external payment platform founded in 2004—formed by a community of foreign returnees, which previously worked in big-name companies such as Facebook, Google, Amazon, eBay and

Microsoft. But they returned with the desire to offer inclusive financial services to small and medium-sized businesses and to individual consumers, helping them enjoy the same financial services in an easy and fast way, regardless of whether they are rich or poor, or from which country they come from.

Dream Town, apart from being an innovation model for young professionals and promoting entrepreneurship, aims to serve as a new urbanization model that fosters social openness while combining economic and environmental considerations, integrating historical and future urban elements, protecting existing water channels and farmland, and creating a space for social activities without cars.

3. Is the capital city of Colombia is a smart city?

The Organization for Economic Cooperation and Development (OECD), a club of good practices that Colombia entered as a full member in May 2018, indicates that the country only invests 0.2 percent of gross domestic product (GDP) in R&D while the average of 28 member countries analyzed is 2.4 percent.

However, Bogota the capital of Colombia, has been recognized as one of the most innovative city in the country. In the last four years, the city government has been doing some efforts to bring closer the ICT to the daily routine of the city as virtualized administrative processes, has installed intelligent traffic lights and has invested in technological education in basic education.

As it was said before, there are many different kinds of smart cities depending on the ICT capability and priorities of the city, but also smart city refers to the use of those in economic, social and environmental development for the people, economy, governance, mobility, environment and quality of life. Therefore, for a case of urbanization project by making and involve all this things is The Bronx Creative District project in which the idea is to be a "center of innovation, technology and creativity", this project arises to end one of the most dangerous neighborhoods in Bogotá and eliminate any possibility of returning to its initial state. In this space, it is expected that entrepreneurs and entrepreneurs from sectors such as design, gastronomy, graphic production and advertising will be established, among other activities, with the city government intends to establish the center of entrepreneurship and creative industry in Bogotá. They took the reference from LX Factory in Lisbon, an old renovated industrial area in which there are about 200 stores that are related with photography, tattoo and design studios, artist workshops, restaurants, among others that belong to the industry and host This commercial and cultural offer. Although the mayor's office guarantees its structuring, there is no guarantee that the project will be successful since there are several challenges such as, the change of mayor for the period 2020-2024, the security of the area and it would be necessary to see if there is any incentive for companies to move to that area. It was says that this project seems be more a wipe the slate clean than a real transformation of the urban fabric (Gonzalez , 2019).

On the other hand, the Science Technology Innovation District has been structuring since 2015, a new technology project that articulates and energizes the innovation ecosystem to strengthen the orange economy[1](implemented from the presidency) and industries 4.0 of Bogota (from the mayor's office). Its origin derives from the initiative to create the scientific and technological park for Bogotá and the Region in the National University campus. For different reasons, this park has not been possible, however, it served, from the persistence of professors and young researchers linked to the electronics and systems departments, that the project be sustained, and was the seed. Now, many public organizations and universities support this initiative, which is the main project of science, technology and innovation prioritized in the process of Intelligent Strategic Specialization of Bogota.

This Science Technology Innovation District will be located in the corridor with an extension of 3.5 kilometers, which will be a new pole of economic and social development in a strategic point of the city. It will be a meeting place for business

---

1 The orange economy also known as the Creative Economy, describes the internet culture, arts and media industries in a market. Visual arts: design, fashion, architecture, gastronomy, dance, theater, opera, museums / Cultural industries: print media, libraries, television and cinema, photography, radio / New media: software creation, video games, advertising.

and the supply of human talent, to develop and articulate new high-tech initiatives (spin off, start ups, SMEs and large companies) in ICT 4.0, and thus contribute to boosting Bogota's productivity from The digital economy

Bogota represents 78% of the development companies in Colombia of the software industry; In the last 6 years this industry has grown 13.4% representing 1.2% of Colombia's GDP; 33% Technologies for Orange Economy and Industry 4.0 will be promoted in this district, like this:

· Orange Economy: Video games, digital platforms, software creation, app creation, digital animation, interactive content.

· Industries 4.0: Artificial intelligence, virtual and augmented reality, robotics, blockchain, Internet of things, big data and analytics.

The CTI Park, the first project of the Science Technology Innovation District. It began to be structured in 2015, the feasibility study was completed in 2018, and its construction and first building must be ready in 2021, where there will be an offer of services, such as: networking spaces; ICT showroom; prototyping laboratories; Living labs; coworking; business incubation and acceleration; ideation laboratories; a Lab Big Data Center; a program of Technological Extensions and another of Shared Services for disposal of technological waste, broadband and clean energy.

Science Technology Innovation District could be the start of much more ambitious projects that have emerged from initiatives designed for 30 years ago in the city, with the technological paradigm of that time, which seem to be more utopias. But first, the most important initial projects to be promoted are: Prototyping Laboratories; Living labs; Incubation and acceleration of companies; Ideation Laboratories; the Lab Big Data Center, and one or two of the set, between: co-working, showroom, technological extension, shared services.

Bogotá has not been yet thought of a smart city of economy, society and the state of the future. The utopia of Bogota is yet to be written, and this Science Technology

Innovation District may be the first stone of a new economy. In Colombia, the technology and innovation industry has received very little attention, according to the global innovation index for 2019, prepared by the World Intellectual Property Organization (Ompi), the country was located in the 67 position of 129 countries. One of the most notable challenges that were identified during the research was the lack of long-term planning and the commitment to complete the projects, especially from the government.

4. Opportunities to learn and cooperate, from China to Colombia

Now, through the same three components of an smart city which I used in the Dream Town Internet Village, I will compare the two cases from China and Colombia to identify the points that Colombia should learn from the country Asian, and opportunities to cooperate.

Although Colombia and China have different government systems, it does not prevent Colombia for taking lessons off growth from China after the reform. As Deng Xiaoping, the initiator of the reform, said "it doesn't matter if the cat is black or yellow as long as it catches mice, it's a good cat."

4.1 Smart governance

As we saw in the case of Dream Town, political stability and long-term planning are the key. A political initiative proposed by the central government in the long term, is welcomed by the system to all levels. So, the importance of scientific and technological innovation in China is not something new, but which takes forty years of immense development. Unlike Colombia, the policies are stand while the government who has establish is on top, but when the period is finishes the policies also stop, in other words, in Colombia there are government polices but not state policies; the policies are short-term and improvised.

4.2 Smart people

The Chinese are recognized by the self-confidence where the greatest differentiating element, and when this self-confidence is accompanied by determination and patience, it reaches an unequaled value. This advantage in the contemporary world, translates into a capacity for innovation. Therefore, technological innovation is the result of comprehensive social developments where optimism about the future prevails.

China is developing as the center of global innovation, not only for investment in R&D, but basically because the Chinese believe there is a better and perfect future, where they have an important role to play. For this to happen we must also consider the investment that China makes in food, basic education, health or social peace, which creates the conditions for innovation to flourish.

Science and technology provide tools to explain and transform the world. Being the architect of such transformation requires specific public policies for this and China is an example of this political decision. China today has the largest human capital in science and technology in the world. More than six million researchers form an R&D team that surpasses any other country.

While, in Colombia although there is also exceptional talent human quality, they generally finds opportunities out of country. There are a lack of state policies to attract human talent in the country. This is a result of the low investment in R&D, making it the most lagging sector, without money and decentralized, this are the two reasons why there is no many researches, and better education.

The success of the projects in China in terms of knowledge, entrepreneurship and urban planning, depends on the first projects being the most robust and powerful, so that attracts highly qualified people to work and live in their territory. Before other projects that are just complement or decoration to the previous ones. Colombia is given to start with the easy path, and it is slow and scary to understand and reach the new, complex and sophisticated. It is a behavior of societies that are not at the forefront.

4.3 Smart economy

In a survey was determinate the f new our great Chinese inventions, the high-speed train, the shared bicycles, Alipay and the online shopping (the last two directly related to Alibaba). Therefore, Dream Town can be a model for the CTI Park, which is the first phase of the by making Technology District and there is projected to be and area where it could find incubators and spin-off. Surely the experience of China would help accelerate the process in Colombia, in the infrastructure and urban development also would be good model. Dream Town also can be a model for the Bronx Creative District as well, since there is no certain future in this space, an incubator and accelerator in a space that has been characterized by lack of attention in education and entrepreneurship support, would be a great advance in Colombia.

The government has an state strategy call 'Made in China' program in which China wants to change the connotation of the phrase to a quality and high technology products. This strategy is based on four pillars: The opening to a growing articulation with the world, it means, learning from the world and generating scientific cooperation in the technological revolution needs; innovation with massive investment in research and development; demand international high quality standards and a grounded strategy on environmental sustainability. With this momentum from the intelligent industry China has managed to develop in the fields of information technology, robotics, numerical control of tools, aerospace railway equipment, alternative energy and electronic vehicles.

This is a set of lessons that Colombia should learn, as it must make a transition from the current basic industry to an industrial development taking into account society, technology, geopolitics, environmental awareness.

5. China, an ally that Colombia must have

In the course of the year 2019, the bilateral relations between China and Colombia have strengthened in a way never seen before and probably nor imagined. Colombia has been perhaps the most skeptical with China. The Minister Counselor of the embassy in Bogotá, Xu Wei, said 'due the lack of knowledge and trust, so far we do not have a very good economic and commercial relationship.'

However, after the visit of the president of Colombia, Iván Duque Márquez to Beijing, in July of this year, where he met President Xi Jinping, and promised to promote bilateral relations at a higher level. The Colombian government understood the current role of China as a value-added partner, consumer country and leader of the fourth industrial revolution and has been responsible for identifying the key areas of cooperation with this country and put efforts in three pillars: strengthen the diplomatic relationship, boost Colombian exports and attract investment to key infrastructure projects for the competitive development of Colombia. Four businesses that occurred between October and November of 2019 demonstrate it:

-Bogota Metro. In October Bogotá chose two Chinese companies for the construction of the first line of its subway from 2020. It is China Harbor Engineering Company Limited and Xi'an Metro Company Limited. This contract, should end a saga that lasted more than half a century in Bogota, which saw how successive plans to build it were up and down. The citizens talked about it more as a myth than a feasible reality. Bogota has been one of the largest metropolis in the world without a subway.

-Train in the metropolitan area of Bogotá. Another fundamental project for the capital is the suburban train that will connect the city with four of its most populated surrounding municipalities. The Regiotram of the West, projected to start operating in 2023, will be a tram based on electrical energy that will cover the 41 kilometers. The only one that submitted an offer was China Civil Engineering Construction Corporation (CCECC). This subsidiary of the state giant China Railway Construction Company (CRCC)

-Green buses in Medellin and Cali. In November, Medellín added 17 electric buses manufactured by the Chinese company BYD to its public transportation system Metroplus and purchased 64 buses more. In Cali, the third city of the country bought a first group of 26 electric vehicles manufactured by the Chinese company Sunwin Bus Corporation and set the goal of introducing 125 more electric buses into the transportation system.

-The 4G Highway. President Duque announced that another Chinese company was chosen to finish a highway in the south of the country that has had all kinds of problems. This is the 456-kilometer highway, which is part of the ambitious plan of fourth generation 4G roads.

In conclusion, 2019 is the beginning of a new dynamic and intelligent era with China. Real work is just beginning and 2020 is a key year in the consolidation. Both countries still need to know more about each other and generate more trust between them. A lot of cultural diplomacy is needed. China seems to be the ally that will help to make the impossible, to make the dreams true. Therefore, having China as an ally for the Science Technology Innovation District (DCTI) would be the guaranty that this project will become true.

The Belt and Road Initiative has two components: infrastructure and technology. The participating nations access millionaire loans to make train lines, airports, 5G projects, dams, hydroelectric, ports or bridges, among many other possibilities. But Colombia has not yet signed any memorandum to added. Regardless of whether or not Colombia signs the memorandum, there is already significant Chinese investment in the country in areas such as telecommunications, manufacturing, oil and gas, automotive and infrastructure.

References

Gomez D., China y Colombia ¿En qué están? https://www.elespectador.com/noticias/el-mundo/china-ycolombia-en-que-estan-articulo-871098

Holmes C., "China es un socio muy valioso para Colombia" https://www.semana.com/contenidoseditoriales/china-se-abre-al-mundo/articulo/china-es-un-socio-muy-valioso-para-colombia/587392

Castrillón D., El mejor aliado está en Oriente https://www.semana.com/contenidos-editoriales/la-cuartaoportunidad/articulo/el-mejor-aliado-esta-en-oriente/592853

Xuren L., Presidentes de China y Colombia prometen promover lazos http://spanish.xinhuanet.com/ 2019-08/01/c_138273522.htm

Colombia Boosts Development of its Orange Economy https://www.bizlatinhub.com/colombia-boostsdevelopment-orange-economy/

Troni N., Why Bogotá, Colombia, Is Latin America's Rising Creative Hotspot http://musebycl.io/creativecities/why-bogota-colombia-latin-americas-rising-creative-hotspot

Orange is the new Bronx as Bogotá launches Creative District https://thecitypaperbogota.com/bogota/ orange-is-the-new-bronx-as-bogota-launches-creative-district/20442

SPOTLIGHT Hangzhou Report 2018 http://pdf.savills.asia/selected-international-research/2018hangzhou-report-en.pdf

La innovadora Hangzhou se ubica como la ciudad más desarrollada de China https://www.prnewswire.com/news-releases/la-innovadora-hangzhou-se-ubica-como-la-ciudad-mas-desarrollada-de-china-618651043.html

Planning the Smart City in China: Key Policy Issues and the Case of Dream Town in the City of Hangzhou https://pdfs.semanticscholar.org/ ad14 abb84193bf78890f824307c98c3ee7c67 aa9.pdf_ga=2.99407705.635922636.1575237553-187458519 3.1575237553

Acosta, J., Bogotá, Los Distritos Para La Ciencia La Tecnología La Innovación, Y La City 5.0. https:// jaimeacostapuertas.blogspot.com/2019/02/bogota-los-distritospara-la-ciencia-la.html

Gonzalez G., El Bronx: la apuesta de Peñalosa para no hacer otro Tercer Milenio. Silla Cachaca. https:// lasillavacia.com/silla-cachaca/bronx-apuesta-penalosa-no-hacer-otro-tercer-milenio-70691

Bermudes A. El año del transporte chino en Colombia. Dialogo Chino. https://dialogochino.net/32359the-year-of-chinese-transport-infrastructure-in-colombia/?lang=es

Perez D. 2019: inicia era dinámica Colombo China. Portafolio https://www.portafolio.co/opinion/davidperez/2019-inicia-era-dinamica-colombo-china-536708

Semana. Ruta de la Seda: los chinos llegan a América Latina. https://www.semana.com/mundo/articulo/ ruta-de-la-seda-los-chinos-llegan-a-america-latina/614218

杭州自行车服务案例研究

索非亚 【智利】

智利国会图书馆　亚太区项目负责人 / 庞蒂菲娅大学　教授

一　引言

地球环境日益恶化，需要找到快速有效的解决方案来减少温室气体排放。交通运输对这些排放负有很大责任。从这个意义上说，所有旨在促使交通方式更加环保的行动都必须得到执行和效仿。在西方，人们认同比如共享单车这样的举措，而在中国杭州市拥有"世界上最大的公共自行车项目"，这一项目已融入公共交通网络。本文将分析支持这一低碳试点项目、公共政策的不同背景（国际、国家和地方），以及其地方特色（杭州作为低碳城市试点项目的一部分），并将详细介绍杭州自行车服务的特点及其挑战、改进和影响，以期智利可从中获得经验。

二　研究背景

1. 国际形势

面对气候变化的紧迫形势，我们来不及做出世界所需要的改变。

根据联合国环境署的《排放差距报告 2019》[1]，"我们正处于错失将全球变暖限制在 1.5℃的机会边缘"，因为到 2030 年，排放量有可能达到超过其应有水平的两倍。

事实上，科学家们一致认为，要走上将全球气温上升限制在 1.5℃的轨道，

1　详见：http://bcn.cl/2chdy

到 2030 年排放量必须迅速下降到 250 亿吨。当前，我们需要每年减少 7.6% 的碳排放量。

在这一重要背景下，联合国 2030 年可持续发展议程可以成为变革的有用指南，因为它包含 17 项可持续发展目标（SDG），为未来 10 年所有国家的国家发展和国际发展合作指明了方向，并提供了蓝图。

其中一个目标，即可持续发展目标 11，着眼于"使城市和人类居住区具有包容性、安全性、恢复力和可持续性"，同时认识到城市的扩张速度快于人口的增长。"2000—2014 年，城市所占面积的增长速度是其人口增长速度的 1.28 倍。与这一趋势密切相关的是，城市密度一直在下降，对地方、区域和全球范围的环境可持续性产生了深远的影响。"[1]

在这种情况下，实现可持续发展目标 11[2]——"到 2030 年，为所有人提供安全、负担得起、无障碍和可持续的交通系统，改善道路安全，尤其是通过扩大公共交通，特别关注弱势群体、妇女、儿童、残疾人和老年人的需求"——有助于建立一个低碳社会，并将排放降低到世界生存所需的水平。

在发展中国家，试图解决和弥补公共交通短缺的方式是通过增加汽车数量。然而以汽车为导向的交通系统与社会进步、经济效益和环境相冲突。

根据《自行车政策发展手册》（Cycling-Inclusive policy development）报道[2]，汽车使用量的增加导致了严重的交通拥堵，特别是在市中心。"拥堵导致长时间的延误、不可预测的出行时间和严重的空气污染。事实上，在大多数城市，即使是大城市，至少一半的行程距离小于 5 公里。这意味着通过支持步行和骑自行车来减少拥堵的潜力是巨大的。自行车友好型规划不仅有益于适合骑自行车的人，而且创造了更人性化的、可持续发展的和民主的城市，尤其有利于穷人或边缘化群体。"[3]

在这方面，报告中说，以汽车为中心的交通系统影响最大的三个人口群体是：低收入者、妇女和儿童。

"除了步行，自行车往往是贫困人口唯一的交通工具。然而，在一些国家，

---

[1] 《联合国可持续发展目标》，11。
[2] GTZ 代表联邦经济合作与发展部并同 I-CE(Interface for Cycling Expertise）合作，与 MacMillan 于 2009 年 4 月联合出版的手册。荷兰自行车大使馆在 "The benefits of cycling. Contribution to sustainable city development; A report for UN Habitat Governing Council 2013" 中引用，2013 年 4 月。http://bit.ly/35MbYUN
[3] 同上，第 23 页。

相当一部分人甚至买不起自行车，而且往往没有合适的自行车设施。与此同时特别是在拉丁美洲和亚洲城市，越来越多的人确实可以使用汽车或摩托车，但过度依赖汽车来满足所有交通需求，会给包括车主在内的所有人带来问题。"[1]

问题的关键是，如何才能为穷人提供优质、负担得起的交通工具，避免或消除过度依赖私家车的负面影响。

自行车是不错的选择，因为它的优势在于：重量轻，价格便宜，易于停放和维护——自行车符合低碳逻辑的短途旅行。它也有助于建立一个与周围环境相联系的、更健康的社会。

"为了优化自行车的使用及其对城市社会、经济和环境绩效的贡献，需要在自行车、步行、私人交通和公共交通之间达到更好的平衡。"[2]

促进自行车的使用以实现这种平衡的一个好方法就是通过"共享自行车"服务。

"市一级共享自行车的概念是在20世纪60年代引入的，当时所谓的白自行车（witte fietsen）被放置在阿姆斯特丹周围供公众使用。这个创意是任何人都可以借用自行车，骑到他或她的目的地，然后把自行车留在那里供其他人使用。"[3]

但我们花了30多年的时间才使这一行为流行起来，并转变为一种新的交通模式。

"大城市自行车共享概念的第一次重大创新发生在1995年，当时哥本哈根的'城市自行车'（Bycyklen）系统启动"。[4] 目前世界上有800多个城市使用该系统。

尽管这种服务倾向于由私营部门提供，但国家通过其地方政府也已成为这种新交通方式成功的关键因素。这是因为"与其他公共交通方式相比，它的总体成本较低。此外，在某些情况下，由于自行车道的互补性，它可以使公共交通在多式联运中得到最佳利用，从而有助于在多式联运中使用公共交通。这种多式联运通过整合各种移动设备（公共交通、停车场、公共自行车、出租车和其他）的芯

---

[1] GTZ 代表联邦经济合作与发展部并同 I-CE(Interface for Cycling Expertise) 合作，与 MacMillan 于 2009 年 4 月联合出版的手册。荷兰自行车大使馆在 "The benefits of cycling. Contribution to sustainable city development; A report for UN Habitat Governing Council 2013" 中引用，2013 年 4 月。http://bit.ly/35MbYUN，第 25 页。

[2] 《联合国可持续发展目标》，11。

[3] 城市土地协会：《共享单车：法国巴黎、加拿大蒙特利尔和中国杭州》，《动态交通和房地产：下一个前沿领域》，第 55 页。http://bit.ly/2Q6MQRW

[4] 同上。

片卡，对城市服务进行优化"。[1]

尽管中国是自行车使用的先驱，但直到 21 世纪才采用了共享自行车系统。尽管如此，由于它是旨在减少碳排放、同时实现可持续发展的公共政策，已经成为这方面的一个极好的例子。在这方面，自行车等交通工具已经起到了带头作用。

2. 国情

中国在 20 世纪 80 年代被称为"自行车王国"，但在过去 30 年中，由于快速的城市化和家用小汽车的普及，交通拥堵加剧，能源消耗飙升，环境恶化，中国的状况发生了变化。

中国住房和城乡建设部宣布，"北京的自行车出行份额从 1986 年的 54% 下降到 2007 年的 23%，深圳的自行车出行份额从 1995 年的 30% 下降到 2007 年的 4%。政府政策也加速了这一下降，这些政策主要集中在机动车使用上并导致人们对骑自行车的消极态度。"[2]

事实上，这种新的生活方式——以汽车为导向的交通系统——导致了中国主要城市空气质量的恶化。

中国改革开放 40 年来，粗放型经济增长模式付出了高昂的代价，迫切需要保护环境，实施可持续发展战略。

朝着这一方向迈出的第一步是 2005 年颁布了《中华人民共和国可再生能源法》和《2007 年中国国家气候变化计划》[3]。这两项计划都为低碳社会的实施和能源安全绘制了战略蓝图。[4]

LCS 一词最初是在日本—英国"可持续低碳社会"联合研究项目中提出的，其核心内容是："符合可持续发展原则；确保满足社会中所有群体的发展需求；公平地努力稳定温室气体（GHG）浓度以避免气候变化的灾难性影响；使用低碳能源

---

1 Sapag & Sapag Ingenieros consultores; "Investigación, factibilidad y gestión de concesión de bicicletas públicas"; Santiago; Agosto 2012, p. 30. http://bit.ly/2Mna857.

2 Hua Zhang, Susan A. Shaheen & Xingpeng Chen; "Bicycle Evolution in China:From the 1900s to the Present"; International Journal of Sustainable Transportation; 2014; page 318. http://bit.ly/2SfrrIZ.

3 "根据国家发展和改革委员会（NDRC）发布的《中国国家气候变化计划》——国内第一个全球变暖政策倡议，政府将迅速采取法律、经济、行政和技术等措施，共同减少温室气体排放，并向国民倡导应对气候变化的灵活方法。该计划的重点是能源的生产和使用、农业、林业和废弃物"。资料来源：SDG UN knowledge platform。
12 Cai Bo-Feng, Wang Jin-Nan, Yang Wei-Shan, Liu Lan-Cui, Cao Dong; "Low Carbon Society in China: Research and Practice"; Advances in climate change research 3(2): 106–120, 2012; p. 112. http://bit.ly/2M9lzNw.

4 同上，第 106 页。

和技术来提高能源效率，并采用符合低温室气体排放水平的消费模式和行为。"

随后中国政府在 2009 年作出了减少二氧化碳排放的承诺，国家发改委在 2010 年制定了"低碳试点计划"[1]。该计划得到加强，并作为第十一个五年计划期间（2006—2010）[2] 和第十三个五年计划的基础。两者都将减少二氧化碳排放作为变量，但重点不同。

另一方面，2016 年 3 月，第十二届全国人民代表大会第四次会议审议并批准了"十三五"规划，将 2030 年议程与国内中长期发展战略联系起来。该计划是创新、协调、绿色、开放和共享发展新理念的基础。

关于计划中提到的"绿色"，即："在可持续发展中，我们要坚持节约资源、保护环境的基本国策，坚持走生产水平提高、生活水平提高、生态系统健全的文明发展道路，加快建设资源节约型、环境友好型社会、建设和谐社会，实现人与自然和谐发展的现代化新模式。我们将继续建设美丽中国，为确保全球生态安全做出新的贡献。"[3]

在这些政策颁布的基础上，中国实施了一系列国家和地方公共政策，旨在改善其居民的生活质量及其与环境的关系。通过这种方式，重新定位自行车作为一种交通方式有助于发展低碳生活方式。浙江省是中国在推广自行车使用方面表现突出的省份之一，它已成为低碳政策最佳实践的典范。

3. 地方情况

浙江是中国东部沿海省份，以人与自然和谐发展著称。浙江省的省会杭州市是一个集传承、创新和绿色增长于一体的城市。

2016 年在杭州举行的 G20 峰会开幕式上，习近平主席致辞："杭州是中国的一个历史文化重镇和商贸中心。千百年来，从白居易到苏东坡，从西湖到大运河，杭州的悠久历史和文化传说引人入胜。杭州是创新活力之城，电子商务蓬勃发展，在杭州点击鼠标，联通的是整个世界。杭州也是生态文明之都，山明水秀，晴好雨奇，浸透着江南韵味，凝结着世代匠心"。[4]

此外，杭州有能力实现可持续发展，因为它具有财政、人力和物质基础，因

---

1 更多信息请参见"低碳试点计划"第 8 页。
2 从国家层面到省级层面，低碳发展的主要指标是节能率（包括节能和提高效率）。
3 中共中央编译局；《中华人民共和国经济和社会发展第十三个五年计划（2016—2020 年）》；第 20-21 页。
4 中华人民共和国外交部，"中华人民共和国主席习近平在 G20 峰会开幕式上的主旨演讲"，杭州，2016-9-3。详见：http://bit.ly/2mbXThg

而已经成为生态保护的领跑者。例如,《杭州市生态文明建设促进条例》[1]和《美丽杭州》就体现了这一点。

"杭州市政府于 2011 年发布了其第一个生态文明规划（2010—2020），然后将新的生态红线框架纳入 2015 年生态文明指南，其中规定当地政府必须制定各种环境保护红线，并评估生态资源和供应能力。"[2]

另一方面，"美丽杭州"是对习近平"美丽中国"框架的回应。"该计划规定，关键政策优先事项和干预措施必须纳入该市的经济、政治、文化和社会发展计划，同时强调必须实现绿色目标"。[3]

这些特点使其被选为实施"低碳城市试点项目"的城市之一。

在此背景下，杭州市率先实施有助于实现可持续发展目标的公共政策，特别是可持续发展目标 11。

"非机动交通计划（自行车和步行）是杭州可持续交通发展框架的核心政策。它涵盖交通和城市规划、基础设施提供和法规制定，目的在于在全市建立一个全面的低速 NMT 系统，为公众提供高可达性。作为 NMT 系统的一个关键要素，杭州于 2008 年启动了全国第一个'公共自行车'项目"。[4]

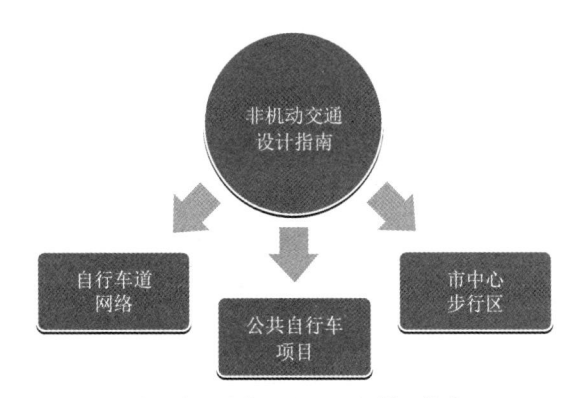

图 1 非机动交通（NMT）设计指南

资料来源：David Banister and Jian Liu。

---

[1] 详见：http://bit.ly/2QfUzxg.

[2] Jørgen Delman; "Ecological civilization Politics and Governance in Hangzhou: New pathways to green urban development?"; The Asia-Pacific Journal: Japan Focus 16(17):1-21; August 2018; pp. 5-7. http://bit.ly/394UlBt

[3] 同上，第 9 页。

[4] David Banister, Jian Liu; "Urban Transport and the Environment, Hangzhou, China"; Case study prepared for Global Report on Human Settlements 2013. P. 5.

三 低碳试点计划

国家发改委于 2010 年 7 月启动了一项低碳试点省市计划，包括八个城市，即天津、保定、杭州、重庆、南昌、贵阳、厦门和深圳，以及云南、广东、湖北、陕西、辽宁五个低碳试点省份[1]。

该计划是中央政府明确实施低碳发展的起点。

该计划的目的是鼓励城市寻找新的经济增长战略，提高人们的生活质量。该计划要求：

1. 制定低碳发展规划。该规划将调整产业结构、优化能源结构、提高节能效率和增加碳汇结合起来。

2. 制定支持低碳绿色增长的政策。鼓励市场机制实现温室气体排放控制目标。推广绿色建筑和公共交通是其中的一部分。

3. 建立低碳产业体系：这包括绿色创新和研发，将低碳技术应用于工业流程，培育能效和可再生能源领域的绿色业务。

4. 建立温室气体排放统计和管理制度。需要建立数据收集和计算系统，同时加强员工熟练管理数据的技能。

5. 倡导低碳、绿色增长的生活方式和消费模式。需要针对决策者和公众开展低碳生活方式必要性的教育和广告宣传活动。[2]

为了实现这五个目标，试点省市除制定具体的公共政策和举措外，还必须建立全面的温室气体统计数据，并建立负责任和透明的制度。

作为试点项目的城市之一的杭州，拥有近 1000 万人口，并以拥有高科技产业而闻名于世，其中包括世界领先的电子商务集团阿里巴巴。

政府选择杭州作为其试点项目并非巧合，在创新和注重绿色增长方面，它不仅在省内，而且在国家层面上都发挥了引领作用。

四 低碳城市试点：杭州

杭州分两个阶段开始规划和实施低碳城市计划。第一阶段从 2010 年到 2015

---

[1] Zheng Khanna, Nina; Fridley, David; Hong Lixuan; "Evaluating China's pilot low-carbon city initiative: national goals and local plans", page 650. http://bcn.cl/2cila.

[2] （联合国）亚洲及太平洋经济和社会委员会 (ESCAP) 文件中引用的国家发展改革委员会（NDRC）; "Low Carbon Green Growth Roadmap for Asia and the Pacific. Case Study". http://bit.ly/2s31TE5.

年，第二阶段从 2015 年到 2020 年。

"作为中国首批低碳项目城市中 GDP 最高的城市，杭州制定了比国家更雄心勃勃的碳减排目标。在此目标基础上，杭州市政府起草了更详细的计划，获得了足够的地方政府政策支持，覆盖了更多的社会服务。"[1]

需要注意的是 2013 年该市近 80% 的能源消耗来自化石燃料（56.8% 的煤炭和 22.2% 的石油）。[2]

在这种情况下实施低碳城市计划可能会限制杭州的经济增长，使得杭州不仅要遵循发改委宣布的试点城市总体目标，还要实施地方政策，以保持其领导地位。

杭州实施的低碳措施主要包括：

1）工业部门的节能；

2）建设低碳建筑和交通系统；

3）控制居住区的总废物产生量并实施废物管理；

4）分类管理；

5）宣传教育。[3]

为实现碳减排目标，杭州成立了低碳咨询小组。杭州的总体目标是，与 2005 年相比，2015 年每单位 GDP 二氧化碳排放量减少 17%，2020 年每单位 GDP 二氧化碳排放量减少 45%。此外，到 2020 年，绿色公共交通将占到 70% 的份额，从而转化为节能巴士、更多的铁线路和城市公共自行车系统等举措，这些举措将设定国家标准。

公共自行车系统符合杭州的城市特征，地势平坦，气候宜人，街道狭窄，非常适合骑自行车。在这种情况下，自行车起着基础性的作用，因为它被认为是一种低碳或"绿色"的交通方式。它在杭州的发展非常迅速，尤其是作为自行车共享系统的一部分。根据共享自行车产业报告，杭州共有 9 万辆共享自行车。截至 2017 年 4 月底，杭州市交通管理局的数字为 263000。[4]

在这种背景下，杭州自行车服务作为一项公共服务发挥了重要作用，因为它

1　IVL Swedish Environmental Research Institute, "Low-carbon Transition Road Hangzhou pilot project", p. 1. http://bit.ly/2s0hft6

2　王宇飞、宋祺佼、董文娟：《杭州、宁波低碳试点建设工程实践与启示》，《2015 年中国低碳发展年度回顾》。

3　同上。

4　段向云、陈瑞照：《杭州共享单车突围"城市丛林"的路径研究》，《经济学论坛》，2018 年 5 月，第 47 页。

是中国城市引入的第一个"公共自行车"项目，并发展了一种商业和管理模式，使其能够与私营公司竞争，并在"城市丛林"中生存。

五　杭州自行车服务

"杭州自行车服务"由政府（杭州公交集团）资助，于 2008 年 5 月启动。该项目由杭州公共自行车开发公司[1]管理，是杭州低碳城市试点项目的亮点之一，被誉为"世界上最大的公共自行车项目"。

该公司遵循以下要求："以公益为导向，市场化运作，围绕推进节能减排、建设绿色公共交通这一核心目标，坚持科学发展、不断创新的原则，努力构建方便市民和中外游客的绿色低碳公共交通体系，以改善和缓解城市公共交通的困难"。

杭州自行车服务是综合可持续交通系统的一部分，包括公共汽车、快速公交、地铁和出租车，以及良好的自行车基础设施（自行车道、自行车交通信号），智能卡可用于整个交通系统（自行车、公共汽车、地铁、快速公交、出租车和水上巴士）。

该运输系统被称为"五合一"，用于互连服务。地铁与公交、自行车和水上巴士相互补充，连接着干线。作为交通的微血管，自行车已经成为杭州交通不可或缺的一部分。[2]

事实上，"用户可以使用公共交通卡共享自行车，并获得公交优惠，因为该计划的主要目的是加强与公交的连接"。[3]

在这一交通生态系统中，"杭州自行车服务"提供"出租自行车——红色自行车——让杭州市民在每天通勤的'第一公里'和'最后一公里'以及在城市中四处走动时，可以选择方便、实惠和健康的出行方式"。[4]

杭州市政府投资 1.8 亿元（合 2635 万美元）启动该项目，并在贴现贷款方面

---

[1] 作为杭州公共交通集团的全资子公司。

[2] 张春：中国对话，"杭州：自行车上的低碳转型"；04-13-2016. http://bit.ly/2Shu5xV

[3] Susan A. Shaheen, Hua Zhang, Elliot Martin, and Stacey Guzman; "China's Hangzhou Public Bicycle. Understanding Early Adoption and Behavioral Response to Bikesharing"; transportation Research Record: Journal of the Transportation Research Board, No. 2247; Transportation Research Board of the National Academies; Washington, D.C.; 2011, P. 33.

[4] Ashden, "Hangzhou Bicycle Service and Transport Development Co Ltd / The biggest public bike share scheme in the world"，2017. http://bit.ly/2kJfZXF

投资 2.7 亿元（合 3953 万美元）。[1]

项目运营成本取决于车站规模、服务区域和车队规模，包括员工工资、新车站的建设、办公费用、自行车的购买或维护和分销。[2]

该公司通过在自行车停靠站亭上出售广告空间，筹集了大量民间资金。"杭州拥有世界上最大的自行车共享项目，除初始资本外，不需要政府资助。"[3]

根据杭州公共交通公司的数据，这种融资方式使得 80% 的出行是免费的。[4]

使用"杭州自行车服务"需要预付费电子卡。同样的卡可以在所有公共交通系统中使用，包括出租车。支付押金后，[5] "杭州自行车服务"在第一个小时内提供免费使用，一小时以后的收费标准如下：

0—59 分钟（第一小时）	免费
60—119 分钟（第 2 小时）	1 元
120—179 分钟（第 3 小时）	2 元
180—239 分钟（第 4 小时）	3 元
240—299 分钟（第 5 小时）	6 元

"杭州自行车服务"使用触摸屏亭和智能卡进行自行车借车和还车，并使用射频识别跟踪自行车信息。这些技术为用户提供自动化自助服务。[6]

"在启动时，该计划最初依靠 31 个可重新定位的移动扩展底座进行程序优化。一旦确定了使用模式，移动底座被修改为固定底座。为了限制自行车盗窃和故意破坏造成的经济损失，该计划使用便宜的单速自行车。"[7]

1. 杭州自行车服务面临的挑战

尽管"杭州自行车服务"取得了成功，但仍面临一些挑战。其中最重要的是

---

1 Energy, Smart, Communities, Initiative (ESCI); "ST-1.2 Transit-Oriented Development. Hangzhou Public Bicycle"; December 2016. h ttp://bit.ly/2McVmNX
2 Q. 李；"公共自行车经营与国有企业经营的政府引导模式：以杭州市为例"；WIT《建筑环境交易》，2014 年第 138 卷；第 5 页。
3 Urban Sustainable Exchange (USE); "Urban Public Bicycle Sharing Program". http://bit.ly/2Q4xpJV
4 同上，第 35 页。
5 300 元。这是一笔担保金，当还回自行车时，它将返还给客户。
6 Urban Sustainable Exchange (USE); "Urban Public Bicycle Sharing Program". http://bit.ly/2Q4xpJV
7 同上，第 35 页。

共享自行车的新竞争对手——黄车、蓝车等——这给服务带来了不同类型的挑战：

第一个是需求。浙江工商大学公共管理学院城市治理与公共经济系的郑春勇教授说，"最大的问题是供大于求，导致资源浪费，需要供需匹配"。[1]

杭州自行车服务公司副总经理吴国雄对此表示赞同："在杭州，我们进行了非常仔细的市场调查，得出的结论是，85800辆自行车足以为杭州服务（平均每天使用五次）。然而，私人计划增加了更多的自行车，远远超过了所需数量。他们不考虑如何利用社会中的未充分利用的资源，这才是真正的共享经济应该做的。如果没有适当的控制，在未来，它们将造成社会努力和资源的巨大浪费。我们已经在许多城市看到了这种情况，那里的自行车被丢弃在人们不去的地方。"[2]

事实上，"杭州自行车服务"已从2008年的2800辆扩大到2017年的85000多辆，每天约有350000使用次数，其中96%是免费的。除此之外，该市大部分地区还有3600个自行车停放处，相距200—300米。[3]

第二个挑战是服务本身。郑教授解释说："杭州市政府提供的红色自行车服务比黄色的要早，但红色自行车的使用必须返回到特定的地点，第一个小时是免费的。同时，黄车是一种付费服务，使用起来很方便，因为它们是移动应用程序的一部分，不需要还回到回收点。"

上述因素决定了它的需求，使"杭州自行车服务"成为老年人的最爱，老年人使用公共自行车是因为它的支付系统更接近传统的支付方式（预付卡），也因为他们的回程点靠近使用空间，例如体育和娱乐场所。年轻人选择了民营自行车服务——黄车、蓝车和其他颜色的——他们觉得这更方便实用，因为它们只需要智能手机。年轻人这种用车行为，是因为在中国，支付宝和微信支付等允许使用二维码付款的应用程序，智能手机的电子支付变得很流行。

对于红色自行车需归还到原处，杭州自行车服务局副总经理吴国雄为此解释说，当他们开始推出自行车计划时，他们必须确保其他人的道路权利没有受到侵犯。"例如，我们只在至少3.5米宽的人行道上建立停放点。这样可以确保道路不

1　本次调查基于2019年青年汉学家研修计划。
2　Charlotte Middlehurst; China dialogue; "Reinventing the wheel: Chinese cycle scheme wins innovation race"；06-19-2017. http://bit.ly/35SuDhu
3　同上，第33页。

会堵塞。但那种新型的民营共享自行车可以在任何地方停车。"[1]

2. 杭州自行车服务改进和影响

浙江工商大学公共管理学院城市治理与公共经济系的黄宏华教授表示，新竞争者的加入帮助"杭州自行车服务"提高了服务水平，例如，"在滨江区，政府提供了一项红色自行车服务，不需要将其停在固定位置，还可以采用 app 付款"。[2]

2016 年在杭州举行的 20 国集团峰会（G20）也推动了这种支付方式的实施。杭州市公共自行车服务公司总经理陶学军当时表示，"西湖地区周围的 100 个车站已升级为移动租赁，首次使用的用户只需扫描自行车旁边的二维码，通过短信注册，支付 500 元可退款押金，然后开始骑行"[3]。

另一方面，就影响而言，"杭州自行车服务"已使杭州数十万人受益，他们能够在不到一小时的行程中免费使用其服务，而综合交通系统的基础设施是关键。[4]

它还帮助减少了城市某些部门的拥堵，减少了污染，并为城市居民带来了与健康和健康生活相关的好处。这项自行车服务的影响已得到国际认可。杭州市公共自行车被评为 2017 年国际阿什顿可持续发展奖的获奖者，因其"推动必要的变革，向需要帮助的人推出可持续能源解决方案"[5]。

"阿什顿奖是可持续能源和绿色解决方案领域最负盛名的奖项之一。成立于 2001 年的阿什顿奖已经奖励了全球 200 多家企业，据说这些企业共同改善了约 8000 万人的生活，每年节省了 1000 多万吨的二氧化碳排放量"。[6]

该模式的成功和国际认可可以用陶学军的话来解释："总共有 7.6 亿辆汽车，这几乎是中国人口的一半。到目前为止，中国有 400 多个城市采用了我们的项目。我们的梦想是在中国和全世界推广我们的模式。"[7]

事实上，这种交通方式也促进了低碳文化的发展，从而形成了低碳生活方式。

---

[1] Charlotte Middlehurst; China dialogue; "Reinventing the wheel: Chinese cycle scheme wins innovation race"；06-19-2017. http://bit.ly/35SuDhu. P.42.

[2] 同上，第 42 页。

[3] 《中国日报》："杭州自行车共享热"；2016-09-01. http://bit.ly/35LGrSJ

[4] 该系统的整合方式鼓励居民选择这项服务而不是汽车。

[5] 详见：http://bit.ly/2PKlWjV

[6] 《中国日报》："杭州自行车租赁服务获奖"，2017 年 6 月 14 日。http://bit.ly/2Zbm9PZ

[7] UN News; " 'Bicycle Kingdom' makes a comeback, as China seeks solutions to tackle air pollution crisis"；6-3-2019. http://bit.ly/2Q2nqVy

六　结论

对于智利的低碳交通环境，杭州自行车服务经验值得借鉴。

根据智利在《联合国气候变化框架公约》中的第三份两年期更新报告，能源部门是智利主要的温室气体排放源，2016年占温室气体排放总量的78.0%。在燃料燃烧活动类别中，次类别能源行业最为重要，占41.5%，其次是运输业，占31.3%。[1]

报告解释说，2016年，其温室气体排放量占26936.4千吨二氧化碳当量，比1990年增加191.8%，自2013年以来增加8.4%，由于"人口增长、更强的购买力和国家道路基础设施的改善导致了全国汽车数量的增长。证据表明，气候和当地缓解面临巨大挑战，这就是为什么制定结合法规、行动和计划的政策具有战略意义。"[2]

在这方面，智利中央政府的行动旨在提高运输领域的能源效率，并制定电动汽车战略。但他们并没有将自行车视为该系统的关键交通方式。

然而环境部在上述报告中强调"2013年，智利第一个公共自行车自动化系统投入运行，地区间倡议目前覆盖了大都市区的14个地区[3]，在其运行的头两年中，已经有200个车站、2000多辆自行车和近25000名注册用户。"[4]

沿着这些路线，在一些实施了这些公共和私人系统的地区（如中国的黄色自行车），他们制订了改善道路基础设施的计划，以支持自行车与其他机动交通方式共存。与此同时，道路共存法则也被创造出来，以实现骑车人、驾车人和行人之间更和谐的互动。尽管前景看好，但这些举措仅限于首都圣地亚哥所在的地区，尚未在其他地区推行。

事实上，自2014年以来，已经有了一个"自行车道计划"项目，目标是建设190公里高标准自行车道，分布在全国15个地区，惠及32个城市。

上述计划的重要性在于，城市，特别是大都市地区自行车使用量的增加与自行车道和停车场等基础设施的建设不成正比，这导致道路生活并非总是和谐的。

1　Ministry of Environment; "Third Biennial Update Report"; p.15; 2018. h tp://bit.ly/2PJ7qsz
2　同上，第117页。
3　就政府和国家内部行政而言，智利共和国领土目前分为16个地区，这些地区又分为56个省；为了地方行政的目的，各省被细分为346个公社。
4　同上，第140页。

根据2019年世界自行车指数[1]，智利是自行车总量增长最多的国家之一[2]。其增长势头"强劲"，年增长率超过10%。然而现实表明，这一增长在各地区还不够强劲和具有决定性，这对同样希望实现可持续发展目标11的国家来说，既是挑战也是机遇。

杭州是一个旅游城市，其自然特征使其适合自行车交通。此外，其近1000万人口的庞大规模使得公共自行车的使用频率非常高。

浙江工商大学黄教授表示，这项服务是一项创新。他强调："中国政府提倡区域间竞争。例如，在浙江省，杭州需要与其他城市竞争。与民主国家不同，中国地方政府有自上而下的压力。这是城市间竞争机制背后的驱动机制。"

同时，黄教授坚持认为，像杭州公共自行车这样的创新理念的实施需要一定的条件。就中国而言，国有企业具有实施创新的综合实力。杭州自行车服务由公共企业（杭州公共自行车公司）管理，但在西方国家，首选通过私营企业提供此类服务。

黄教授提出的另一点是关于地方之间的相互学习。创新的传播或政策的扩散使得杭州公共自行车的模式能够传播到中国的其他城市。

然而，目前实施成本相对较大。事实上，最初的投资、维护和应用程序开发可能需要三年时间，还可能导致城市管理问题。

中国政府在这类举措背后有一个与"试错"相关的"免责条款"。而对于杭州公共自行车系统，人们只为基本服务付费，其竞争力就降低了。

通过分析可知，在其他国家实施公共自行车服务可以提高区域间竞争力和区域间学习，使所有参与者受益，但首先是提高公民的生活质量。

1　http://bit.ly/2s1MmEO
2　其他国家是波兰、捷克共和国、卢森堡和瑞典。

A Case Study: Hangzhou Bicycle Service

María Sofía Calvo Foxley / Chile

Asia Pacific Program at Chilean Congress Library /Head;
Pontificia Universidad Católica de Valparaíso / Professor

I. Introduction

The environmental emergency on our planet requires finding fast and effective solutions to reduce greenhouse gas emissions. Transport is one of the sectors that is most responsible for these emissions. In this sense, all actions aimed at making modes of transport more environmentally friendly must be observed and imitated. While in the West it is possible to recognize initiatives aimed at achieving this goal, such as bike-sharing, in the case of China, there is the city of Hangzhou in particular since it is known as "the biggest public bicycle project in the world", which is integrated into the public transport network. In the following paper, the different contexts (international, national and local) that support this public policy will be analyzed, the Low - carbon Pilot Program that provides new fundamentals to the initiative, as well as its local version (Hangzhou as part of Low – carbon city pilot project); the characteristics of the Hangzhou Bicycle Service will be detailed along with its challenges, improvements and impact; and some conclusions will be drawn that will allow us to glimpse what Chile could learn from this experience.

II. Research Background

2.1 International Situation

The premise is clear that we are running out of time to make changes that the world needs in the face of the climate change emergency.

According to Emissions Gap Report 2019[1] from United Nations Environment, "We are on the brink of missing the opportunity to limit global warming to 1.5°C", because emissions are on track to reach 56 Gt CO_2e by 2030, over twice what they should be.

In fact, scientists agree that to get on track to limit global temperature rise to 1.5°C, emissions must drop rapidly to 25 gigatons by 2030. Today, we need to reduce emissions by 7.6% every year.

In this critical context the 2030 Agenda for Sustainable Development of The United Nations could be a useful guide for change, because it contains 17 Sustainable Development Goals

(SDGs) that point out the direction and provide the blueprint for national development of all countries and international development cooperation in the next 10 years.

One of these goals, the SDG 11, looks to "make cities and human settlements inclusive, safe, resilient and sustainable", with the understanding that urban areas are expanding at a faster rate than their populations. "Between 2000 and 2014, areas occupied by cities grew1.28 times faster than their populations. Closely related to this trend is that the urbandensities of cities have been declining, creating profound repercussions for environmentalsustainability at the local, regional and global scale".[2]

---

1 More information in: http://bcn.cl/2chdy
2 Sustainable Development Goals UN, "Sustainable Development Goals 11

In that scenario, fulfilling the 11.2 target of the SDG 11 "by 2030, provide access to safe, affordable, accessible and sustainable transport systems for all, improving road safety, notably by expanding public transport, with special attention to the needs of those invulnerable situations, women, children, persons with disabilities and older persons"—could help to build a low carbon society and decrease the emissions at the level that the world needs to survive.

In developing countries, the way in which attempts have been made to resolve and subsidize the shortcomings of public transport has been through the expansion of the automotive fleet.

However, a car oriented transport system conflicts with social progress, economic effectiveness and the environment.

According to Cycling-Inclusive policy development[1] the increased car use has led to severe congestion, particularly in city centers. "Congestion leads to long delays, unpredictable travel times and severe pollution. It is compounded by the fact that in most cities, even large ones, at least half of all trips are less than 5 kilometers in length. This means the potential for reducing congestion by favouring walking and cycling is enormous. Cycle-friendly planning not only benefits cyclists but also creates more humane, sustainable and democratic cities, which particularly benefit the poor or marginalized".[2]

In this context the report said that the three population groups most affected by a car-centred transportation system are: low-income people, women and children.

"Aside from walking, the bicycle is often the only means of transport available to the poor. Yet in some countries, even the purchase of a bicycle remains beyond the reach of

---

1 A Handbook, April 2009, published by GTZ in association with MacMillan on behalf of the Federal Ministry for Economic Cooperation and Development, in partnership with Interface for Cycling Expertise I-CE. Cited in "The benefits of cycling. Contribution to sustainable city development; A report for UN Habitat Governing Council 2013" by Dutch Cycling Embassy; April 2013. Available in: http://bit.ly/35MbYUN
2 Ibid. p.23.

a significant part of the population and there are often no proper cycling facilities.

However, particularly in Latin-American and Asian cities more and more people do have access to a car or motorcycle, but excessive dependency on the car for all transport needs produces problems for all, including car-owners".[1]

The key question is what will it take to provide good quality, affordable transport to the poor and to avoid or undo the negative effects of disproportionate dependency on the private car.

The bicycle seems to be the answer to this question due to its constructive characteristics—light, cheap and easy to park—and of service, since it allows short-distance trips from a lowcarbon logic.

It also contributes to a healthier society (physically and mentally) that is connected with its surroundings.

"To optimize bicycle use and its contribution to a city's social, economic and environmental performance requires a better balance between cycling, walking, private and public transport".[2]

A good way to promote the use of the bicycle to achieve this balance is through "shared bicycles" services.

"The concept of bike-sharing on a municipal level was introduced in the 1960s when so-called witte fietsen (white bikes) were placed around Amsterdam for use by the public. The idea was that anyone would be able to borrow a bicycle, ride it to his or her destination, and then leave it at that location for someone else to use".[3]

But we had to spend more than 30 years for this concept to become popular and transform into a new transport model.

---

1 Ibid. p.25.
2 Ibid. p.25.
3 Urban Land Institute; "Bicycle Sharing. Paris, France; Montreal, Canada; Hangzhou, China" ; Active transportation and real estate: the next frontier; p. 55. Available in: http://bit.ly/2Q6MQRW

"The first major innovations to the bike-sharing concept in a large city occurred in 1995, when Copenhagen's Bycyklen, or "City Bikes," system was launched".[1]

There are currently more than 800 cities in the world that use this system.

Although the tendency is for this service to be provided by private parties, the State, through its local governments, has also become a key player in the success of this new form of transport. This is due to the fact that "its overall cost is lower compared to other modes of public transport." In addition, in some cases it can contribute to the use of public transport in multimodal journeys, by allowing them to be carried out optimally thanks to the complementarity of the bicycle path.

Although China was a pioneer in the use of bicycles, it was only in the 21st century that it adopted the shared bicycle systems. Nonetheless, it has become an excellent example in this regard, thanks to its public policies aimed at reducing its carbon emissions, but also achieving sustainable development, in which means of transport such as bicycles have taken the lead.

2.2 National situation

But how could the world and especially China contribute to achieving the 11.2 target of the SDG 11? In the case of China, one answer could be found in its story.

China was known as the "Kingdom of the bicycle" in the 1980s, but over the past 30 years, the country's situation has changed because of the rapid urbanization and motorization that has increased traffic congestion, soaring energy consumption, and a deteriorating environment.

"For example, as the Chinese Ministry of Housing and Urban-Rural Development declared, bicycle modal share declined from 54% in 1986 to 23% in 2007 in Beijing and from 30% in1995 to 4% in 2007 in Shenzhen. This decline was also accelerated by governmentalpolicies, which have focused primarily on motor vehicle use and

---

[1] Urban Land Institute; "Bicycle Sharing. Paris, France; Montreal, Canada; Hangzhou, China" ; Active transportation and real estate: the next frontier; p. 55. Available in: http://bit.ly/2Q6MQRW

resulted in a neg ativeattitude toward bicycling".[1]

In fact, a consequence of this new way of living -based on a car-oriented transport system has been the deterioration of air quality in the main cities of China.

Through 40 years of China's reform and opening up, the extensive economic growth mode has paid a high price, and it is in urgent need of protecting the environment and implementing a sustainable development strategy. Today China is the main greenhouse gas(GHG) emitter and it has to take action to change this situation.

The first step in that direction was the promulgation of the "Renewable Energy Law of the People's Republic of China" in 2005 and the "China National Climate Change Programme in 2007",[2] both of which have drawn a strategic blueprint for low-carbon society (LCS) implementation and energy security.[3]

According to Cai Bo-Feng, Wang Jin-Nan, Yang Wei-Shan, Liu Lan-Cui and Cao Dong from Chinese Academy for Environmental Planning, "the term of LCS was initially proposed in the Japan-UK Joint Research Project on 'Sustainable Low Carbon Society', and its core content are: to be in accord with the principle of sustainable development; to ensure that the development needs of all groups within the society are met; to make equitable efforts to stabilize greenhouse gas (GHG) concentration; to avoid catastrophic effects of climate change; to use low carbon energy sources and technologies to increase energy efficiency and to adopt the patterns of

---

1 Hua Zhang , Susan A. Shaheen & Xingpeng Chen; "Bicycle Evolution in China: From the 1900s to the Present" ; International Journal of Sustainable Transportation; 2014; p.318. Available in: http://bit.ly/2SfrrIZ

2 "According to China's National Climate Change Programme issued by the National Development and Reform Commission (NDRC), the country's first global warming policy initiative, the government will swiftly adopt measures ranging from laws, economy, administration and technology which will combine to reduce greenhouse gas emissions and imbue the country with a flexible approach to climate change. The Program focuses on energy production and use, agriculture, forestry, and waste" . Source: SDG UN knowledge platform.

3 Cai Bo-Feng, Wang Jin-Nan, Yang Wei-Shan, Liu Lan-Cui, Cao Dong; "Low Carbon Society in China: Research and Practice" ; Advances in climate change research 3(2): 106–120, 2012; p.112. Available in: http://bit.ly/2M9lzNw

consumption and behavior that are consistent with low levels of GHG emissions".[1]

Then the Chinese Government made the commitment to reduce CO_2 emissions in 2009 and the National Development and Reform Commission (NDRC)[2] created a "Low-carbon Pilot Program" in 2010.[3]

That program was reinforced and served as the basis for the 11th Five-Year Plan period(2006– 2010)[4] and the 13th Five-Year Plan. Both included decreasing CO_2 emissions as variable but with a different emphasis.

On the other hand, the 13th Five-Year Plan was reviewed and approved by the Fourth Session of the 12th National People's Congress in March 2016 linking the 2030 Agenda with domestic mid-and-long term development strategies.

That Plan was the basis of a new philosophy of innovative, coordinated, green, open, and shared development.

With respect to "green": "We need to uphold the fundamental state policy of conserving resources and protecting the environment as we pursue sustainable development, and keep to a civilized development path that ensures increased levels of production, better living standards, and sound ecosystems. We will move faster to build a resource-conserving, environmentally friendly society and bring about a new model of modernization whereby humankind develops in harmony with nature. We will move forward with building a Beautiful China and make new contributions

---

1 Ibid. p.106.
2 The goal number 10 of NDRC is "To promote the strategy of sustainable development; to undertake comprehensive coordination of energy saving and emission reduction; to organize the formulation and coordinate the implementation of plans and policy measures for recycling economy, national energy and resource conservation and comprehensive utilization; to participate in the formulation of plans for ecological improvement and environmental protection; to coordinate the solution of major issues concerning ecological building, energy and resource conservation and comprehensive utilization; to coordinate relevant work concerning environment-friendly industries and clean production promotion" More information: http://bcn.cl/2cila
3 More information from "Low-cabon Pilot Program", p.8.
4 From the national level to the provincial level, the main indicator for low carbon development is the energy-saving rate (including energy conservation and efficiency improvement).

toward ensuring global eco- security".[1]

From these foundations, China has carried out a series of national and local public policies that seek to improve the quality of life of its inhabitants and their relationship with the environment.

In that way, repositioning the bicycle as a mode of transport has contributed to developing alow carbon lifestyle.

One of the Chinese provinces that stands out for its performance in promoting the use of the bicycle is Zhejiang and it has become an example of best practices in low carbon policies.

2.3 Local situation

Zhejiang is an eastern coastal province of the People's Republic of China that is known for its harmonious development between human beings and nature. Hangzhou has a great mixture of heritage, innovation and green growth.

In fact, in his speech at the Opening Ceremony of the B20 Summit held in Hangzhou in 2016, Xi said: "Hangzhou has a fascinating history and rich and enchanting cultural heritage". Hangzhou is also an innovative and vibrant city with booming e-commerce. Just do an internet search for Hangzhou, and you will connect to a whole world. Hangzhou is also a leader in ecological conservation. Its green hills and clear lakes and rivers delight the eye on sunny days and present a special vista on rainy days. Hangzhou is imbued with a charm unique to the south of the Yangtze River that has been fostered over many generations".[2]

Furthermore, Hangzhou has the ability to carry out sustainable development thanks to the fact that it has a financial, human and material foundation and so

---

[1] Compilation and Translation Bureau, Central Committee of the Communist Party of China; "The 13th Five-Year Plan. For economic and social development of The People's Republic of China (2016–2020)" ; pp. 20 -21.

[2] Ministry of Foreign Affairs of the People's Republic of China, "Keynote Speech by H.E. Xi Jinping, President of the People's Republic of China, at the Opening Ceremony of the B20 Summit" , Hangzhou, September 3rd 2016. More information: http://bit.ly/2mbXThg

has become a leader in ecological conservation. This is expressed, for example, in "Regulations on Promoting the Construction of Hangzhou's Ecological Civilization"[1] and "Beautiful Hangzhou".

"Hangzhou's government published its first ecocivilization plan (2010-2020) in 2011 and then incorporated the new ecological red line framework into the 2015 eco-civilization guideline which stipulated that the city authorities must elaborate the various red lines for environmental protection and assess ecological resources and supply capacity".[2]

On the other hand "Beautiful Hangzhou" was a response to "Beautiful China" framework. "The plan stipulated that the key policy priorities and interventions must be incorporated into the city's economic, political, cultural, and social development plans, while emphasizing the need to meet the green targets".[3]

These characteristics led to it being selected as one of the pilot cities to implement a"low-carbon city pilot project". In this context, Hangzhou city has been a pioneer in the implementation of public policies that contribute to SDGs fulfillment, especially the SDG 11.

"The non-motorized transport (NMT) programme (cycling and walking) is the core policy in Hangzhou's sustainable transport development framework. It covers transport and urban planning, infrastructure provision and regulation preparation and it aims to establish a comprehensive low-speed NMT system across the city with high accessibility for the general public. As a key element in the NMT system, Hangzhou launched (2008) the first 'public bicycle' programme in the country".[4]

---

1 More information in: http://bit.ly/2QfUzxg
2 Jørgen Delman; "Ecological civilization Politics and Governance in Hangzhou: New pathways to green urban development?"; The Asia-Pacific Journal: Japan Focus 16(17):1-21; August 2018; pp.5-7. Available in: http://bit.ly/394UlBt
3 Ibid. p.6.
4 David Banister, Jian Liu; "Urban Transport and the Environment, Hangzhou, China" ; Case study prepared for Global Report on Human Settlements 2013. p.5.

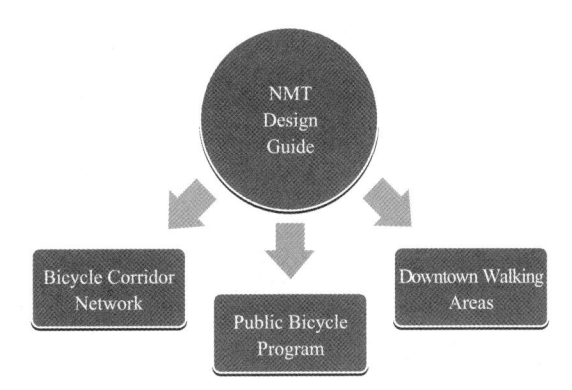

Frgure1: Non-motorized transport (NMT) design guide

Source: David Banister and Jian Liu

III. Low – carbon Pilot Program

The National Development Reform Commission (NDRC) initiated a low carbon pilot province and city program in July of 2010, including the following eight cities across the country:municipalities of Tianjin, Baoding, Hangzhou, Chongqing, Nanchang, Guiyang, Xiamen and Shenzhen and five low carbon pilot provinces of Yunnan, Guangdong, Hubei, Shaanxi, and Liaoning.[1]

This plan was the starting point of the central government to explicitly implement low carbon development.

The plan's purpose is to encourage cities to find new strategies for economic growth and improve people's quality of life. The plan requires:

- **Creating a low-carbon development plan .** The plan integrates the adjustment of the industrial structures, the optimizing of the energy structures, improving energy saving and efficiency and increasing the carbon sink.

- **Setting supportive policies for low-carbon green growth.** Market mechanisms are encouraged to achieve the greenhouse gas emission-control targets. Promoting green building and public transport are part of them.

---

[1] Zheng Khanna, Nina; Fridley, David; Hong Lixuan; "Evaluating China's pilot low-carbon city initiative: national goals and local plans" , p. 650. Available in: http://bcn.cl/2cila

- **Establishing a low-carbon industrial system:** This includes green innovation and R&D, installation of low- carbon technologies into industrial process, nurturing green business in energy efficiency and renewable energy sectors.

- **Establishing a greenhouse gas emission statistics and management system.** Data collection and accounting system need to be set up along with strengthening the skills of staff to proficiently manage it.

- **Advocating lifestyle and consuming patterns of low carbon, green growth.** Education and advertising campaigns on the imperative of low-carbon lifestyles that target both policymakers and the general public are required.[1]

To fulfil these five goals, the pilot provinces and cities have to establish comprehensive statistics with accountable and transparent systems for greenhouse gases, in addition to specific public policies and initiatives.

One of the cities that is part of the pilot program is Hangzhou, with nearly 10 million people, it is world-famous for being home to the high-tech industry, including the world's leading-commerce group, Alibaba.

The government's choice of Hangzhou for its pilot program is no coincidence and responds to the leadership it has had not only within its province, but also at the national level, from innovation and a focus on green growth.

IV. Low–carbon city pilot project: Hangzhou

Hangzhou started planning and implementing the low-carbon city program in two phases. The first was from 2010 to 2015, and the second from 2015 to 2020.

As the city with the highest GDP among the first batch of Chinese cities chosen

---

1   National Development Reform Commission (NDRC) cited in document from The Economic and Social Commission for Asia and the Pacific (ESCAP) - UN; "Low Carbon Green Growth Roadmap for Asia and the Pacific. Case Study" . Available in: http://bit.ly/2s31TE5

as low carbon project cities, Hangzhou has set a more ambitious carbon reduction target than the national one. Based on this target, Hangzhou municipal government drafted a more detailed plan, got sufficient local government policy support and covered more social sectors.[1]

One aspect to keep in mind in the analysis is that almost 80% of the city's energy consumption in 2013 came from fossil fuels (56,8% coal and 22,2% oil).[2]

The risk that this situation would limit its growth, led Hangzhou to not only follow the general objectives declared by the NDRC for the pilot cities, but also to implement local policies, which would allow it to maintain its leadership.

Low-carbon measures implemented in Hangzhou mainly focus on:

1) energy conservation in the industrial sector,

2) construction of low-carbon buildings and transportation systems,

3) controlling total waste generation in residential areas and implementing waste classification management,

4) knowledge spreading.[3]

A low-carbon advisory group was established to reach the carbon emission reduction target.

The overall target for Hangzhou was to reduce CO_2 emissions by 17% per GDP unit in 2015 and by 45% per GDP unit in 2020 compared to the level in 2005.

Moreover, there was to be a share of 70% green public transportation in 2020, that translates into initiatives like energy-efficient buses, more subway lines, and an

---

1 IVL Swedish Environmental Research Institute, "Low-carbon Transition Road Hangzhou pilot project", page 1. Available in: http://bit.ly/2s0hft6
2 Yufei Wang, Qijiao Song, Wenjuan Dong; "Hangzhou and Ningbo Low-carbon Pilot Project Practice and Enlightenment"; 2015 Annual Review of Low-Carbon Development in China; Low-carbon Development Research Group.
3 Ibid.

urban public bicycle system which sets the national standard.

The public bicycle system is consistent with the physical characteristics of Hangzhou. It has flat terrain, pleasant weather, and narrow streets, which are very suitable for cycling.

In this context, the bicycle plays a fundamental role because it is considered a low-carbon or"green" mode of transport. It's development in Hangzhou has been meteoric, especially as apart of the bicycle-sharing system.

According to the report on the shared bicycle industry, there were 90,000 shared bicycles in Hangzhou. As of the end of April 2017, the number from the Hangzhou transportationauthority was 263,000.[1]

In this context, the Hangzhou Bicycle Service has played an important role as a public service because it was the first 'public bicycle' program introduced in a Chinese City and it has developed a business and management model that has allowed it to compete with private companies and survive in the "urban jungle".

V. Hangzhou Bicycle Service

The "Hangzhou Bicycle Service" (HBS) was funded by the government (Hangzhou Public Bus Group) and started up in May 2008. It is managed by Hangzhou Public Bicycle Development Company[2] and it is one of the highlights of the low-carbon city pilot project for Hangzhou and is well known as "the biggest public bicycle project of the world".

The company follows the requirement of "public welfare orientation and market operation, focuses on the core target to promote energy saving and emission cut, and build green public transport, upholds scientific development and invariable innovation principle, endeavors to build a green and low-carbon public transport

---

1 Duan Xiangyun, Chen Ruizhao; "Research on the Path of Hangzhou Urban Bike Breaking through 'Urban Jungle'" ; Forum on Economics; Issue 574 05; May 2018. p.47.
2 As a solely-owned subsidiary of Hangzhou Public Transport Group.

system convenient for the city people and local and foreign tourists and mitigate the difficulties of urban public transport".[1]

The Hangzhou Bicycle Service is part of an integrated and sustainable transport system which includes buses, bus-rapid-transit (BRT), metro and taxis, as well as good bicycleinfrastructure (bicycle lanes, bicycle traffic signals) with smart cards that can be used across the whole transport system (cycles, buses, metro, BRT, taxis and water buses).

This transport system is called "Five in One" and works interconnecting services. The underground buses are complemented by main lines, bicycles and water buses, which connect the main lines. As traffic microvessels, bicycles have become an integral part of Hangzhou's traffic.[2]

In fact, "users can use their public transit cards for bike sharing and receive a transit discount, because the program's principal aim is to enhance and link to transit".[3]

In this transport ecosystem HBS provides "bicycles for hire -red ones- to allow the people of Hangzhou city convenient, affordable and healthy travel options for the 'first mile' and 'last mile' of daily commuting and for getting around the city".[4]

The Hangzhou government invested 180 million yuan ($26.35 million) to launch the program, and 270 million yuan ($39.53 million) in discounted loans.[5]

1　Hangzhou Public Transport Group Co, Ltd; "Bicycle Services" . Available in: http://bit.ly/35M8oKo
2　Zhang Chun; China Dialogue; "杭州：自行车上的低碳转型" ; 04-13-2016. Available in:http://bit.ly/2Shu5xV
3　Susan A. Shaheen, Hua Zhang, Elliot Martin, and Stacey Guzman; "China's Hangzhou Public Bicycle. Understanding Early Adoption and Behavioral Response to Bikesharing" ; transportation Research Record: Journal of the Transportation Research Board, No. 2247; Transportation Research Board of the National Academies; Washington, D.C.; 2011, p.33.
4　Ashden, "Hangzhou Bicycle Service and Transport Development Co Ltd / The biggest public bike share scheme in the world" , 2017. Available in: http://bit.ly/2kJfZXF
5　Energy, Smart, Communities, Initiative (ESCI); "ST-1.2 Transit-Oriented Development. Hangzhou Public Bicycle" ; December 2016. Available in: http://bit.ly/2McVmNX

The operating cost depends on the station size, service area and fleet size, including the staff salary, construction of new stations, office expense, purchase or maintenance and distribution of bicycles,.[1]

The company raises significant private funds by selling advertising space on the bike docking station kiosks. "Hangzhou has the world's largest bike-sharing program that doesn't require government funding beyond initial capital".[2]

This kind of financing results in 80% of total trips being made free of charge, according to data from Hangzhou Public Transport Corporation.[3]

A prepaid electronic card is needed to use the HBS. The same cards can be used across all public transport systems, including taxis. After paying a deposit,[4] HBS offers free use during the first hour. From the first hour until the second hour, the rental fee is one yuan per hour, increasing to 2 yuan when the third-hour starts. From the fourth hour on the fee rises to 3 yuan per hour.

0 - 59 minutes (1st hour)	Free
60 - 119 minutes (2nd hour)	1 yuan
120 - 179 minutes (3rd hour)	2 yuan
180 - 239 minutes (4th hour)	3 yuan
240 - 299 minutes (5th hour)	6 yuan

"The HBS uses touch screen kiosks and smart cards for bicycle check-in and check-out and radio frequency identification to track bicycle information. These

---

1　Q. Li; "The modes of government guidance for public bicycle operation and state-owned company operation: a case study of Hangzhou city in China" ; WIT Transactions on The Built Environment, Vol 138, 2014; p.5.
2　Urban Sustainable Exchange (USE); "Urban Public Bicycle Sharing Program" . Available in: http://bit.ly/2Q4xpJV
3　Ibid. p.35.
4　300 yuan. This amount is a guarantee and it will return to the client when coming back to the bicycle.

technologies enable automated self-service for users".[1]

"On its launch, the program initially relied on 31 mobile docking stations that could be relocated for program optimization. Once usage patterns were determined, the mobile stations were modified to fixed stations. To limit financial loss from bike theft and vandalism, the program uses inexpensive, one-speed bicycles".[2]

5.1 Hangzhou Bicycle Service's Challenges

Despite the success of HBS there are still some challenges to be faced. One of the most important is the new competitors in sharing bicycles -yellow, sky-blue ones and so on- this generates different kinds of challenges to the service:

The first one is the demand. Professor Zheng Chunyong from the Department of Urban Governance and Public Economics in the School of Public Administration of Zhejiang Gongshang University said that "the biggest problem is that supply exceeds demand, resulting in waste of resources and the need to match demand and supply".[3]

The Hangzhou Bicycle Service deputy general manager, Wu Guoxiong, is in agreement with that. "In Hangzhou we did very careful market research and concluded that 85,800 bikes were enough to service the city (with an average daily use of five times per bike). However, the private schemes have added a lot more bikes, far beyond the number needed.

They do not consider how to use the under-utilised resources in society which is what the real shared economy should do. Without proper controls, in the future, they will create a huge waste of social effort and resources. We are already seeing this in many cities where bikes are just dumped in places where people don't go to", he

---

1 Urban Sustainable Exchange (USE); "Urban Public Bicycle Sharing Program" . Available in: http://bit.ly/2Q4xpJV
2 Ibid. p.35.
3 Interview in the context of this investigation, Hangzhou, September 16, 2019.

affirms.[1]

In fact, the HBS has expanded from 2,800 bicycles in 2008 to more than 85,000 bicycles in2017, with around 350,000 hires per day, 96% of which are free of charge. Besides this, there are 3,600 bicycle stands, 200-300 metres apart, in much of the city.[2]

The second challenge is the service itself. Professor Zheng explains that "the small red bicycle service provided by the Hangzhou Municipal Government predated the yellow ones.However, the use of the red ones must be returned to a specific location and the first hour is free."

Meanwhile the yellow ones is a paid service, and it is convenient to use because "they are part of a mobile application, and don't need to be returned to a stand," he insists.

The above has determined its demand, making the HBS the favorite of older adults, who use it due to its payment system, which is closer to traditional payment practices (prepay card), also because their return points are close to the spaces of use, for example, for sports and recreation.

Younger people, who have opted for private bicycle service -yellow, sky-blue and others because they find it more convenient and practical, since they only require smartphone.

This financial behavior is explained because, in China, electronic payment from the smartphone has become popular, thanks to applications such as Alipay and WeChat Pay, which allows payments using QR codes.

But what looks like a disadvantage is defended by the Hangzhou Bicycle Service deputy general manager, Wu Guoxiong, who explains that when they started to roll

---

1　Charlotte Middlehurst; China dialogue; "Reinventing the wheel: Chinese cycle scheme wins innovation race" ; 06-19-2017. Available in: http://bit.ly/35SuDhu

2　Ibid. p.33.

out their bike scheme they had to make sure that the road rights of others were not being violated. "For example, we only build collection points on pavements that are at least 3.5 metres wide. This way we can ensure that the road is not blocked. But with this new type of private share you can park anywhere", he comments.[1]

5.2 Hangzhou Bicycle Service improvements and impact

The entry of new competitors -according to professor Huang Honghua from the Department of Urban Governance and Public Economics in the School of Public Administration of Zhejiang Gongshang University- helped HBS improve its service; for example "in Binjiang District, the government provides a red bicycle service that does not need to be parked in a fixed location, and can also collect app payments".[2]

The celebration of the G20 in Hangzhou in 2016 was also an impulse for the implementation of this form of payment. In fact, Tao Xuejun, general manager of Hangzhou Public Bicycle Service said at the time that "100 stations around the West Lake area had been upgraded to enable mobile renting and first-time users only needed to scan the QR code beside the bike, register via text message, pay a refundable deposit of 500 yuan and start riding".[3]

On the other hand, in terms of impact, HBS has benefited hundreds of thousands of people in Hangzhou, who have been able to use its services for free on tours of less than an hour, within an integrated transportation system, whose infrastructure is key.[4]

It has also helped reduce congestion in certain sectors of the city, reduce pollution, and has delivered benefits associated with health and healthy living to the inhabitants of this city.

The impact of this bicycle service has been recognized internationally. In fact, Ashden who "push for the changes needed to roll out sustainable energy solutions to

---
1　Ibid. p.42.
2　Ibid. p.42.
3　China Daily; "Hangzhou abuzz over bike sharing" ; 2016-09-01. Available in: http://bit.ly/35LGrSJ
4　The way in which the system is integrated provides incentives to the inhabitants to prefer this service to a car.

those who need them most",[1] named HBS as winner of 2017 International Ashden Award for Sustainable Travel.

"An Ashden Award is among the most prestigious honors in the field of sustainable energy and green solutions. Founded in 2001, the Ashden Awards have rewarded more than 200enterprises globally that it says have collectively improved the lives of some 80 million people, saving more than 10 million metric tons of carbon dioxide emissions every year".[2]

The success of the model and the international recognition is explained in the words of TaoXuejun: "All together there have been 760 million rides, that's almost half the population of China (…) So far, more than 400 cities in China have adopted our project. Our dream is to promote our model across China and all over the world".[3]

Indeed, this type of transport has also contributed to the development of a low-carbon culture, which has resulted in a low-carbon lifestyle.

VI. Conclusions

The Hangzhou Bicycle Service experience is interesting to analyze due to the low carbon transport landscape in Chile.

According to the Third Biennial Update Report from Chile in the United Nations Framework Convention on Climate Change, the Energy sector is the main GHG national emitter in Chile, with 78.0% of the total GHG emissions in 2016. Within the category of Fuel combustion activities, the subcategory Energy Industries is the most important with a 41.5% share, followed by Transport with 31.3%.[4]

The report explains that in 2016, its GHG emissions accounted for 26,936.4

---

1 More information in: http://bit.ly/2PKlWjV
2 China Daily; "Hangzhou bike hire service wins award", 6-14-2017. Available in: http://bit.ly/2Zbm9PZ
3 UN News: "'Bicycle Kingdom' makes a comeback, as China seeks solutions to tackle air pollution crisis"; 6-3-2019. Available in: http://bit.ly/2Q2nqVy
4 Ministry of Environment: "Third Biennial Update Report", p.15; 2018. Available in: http://bit.ly/2PJ7qsz

kt CO_2 eq, increasing by 191.8 % from 1990 and 8.4% since 2013, due to "the growth of the national automotive fleet induced by the population growth, a greater purchasing power and the improvement of the road infrastructure in the country. The evidence demonstrates a great challenge for climate and local mitigation, which is why the development of policies that combine regulations, actions and programs is strategic".[1]

In this context, the actions of Chile—from the central government- have aimed to promote energy efficiency in the transport field and develop an electromobility strategy. But they have not considered the bicycle as a key mode of transport of the system.

However, the Ministry of Environment has highlighted in the aforementioned report that "in 2013 the first automated system of public bicycles of Chile when into operation, inter-districtsinitiative which currently covers 14 districts of the Metropolitan region,53[2] and which in its first two years of operation already had 200 stations, more than 2,000 bicycles and close to 25,000 registered users".[3]

Along these lines, in some areas where these public and private systems have been implemented (like yellow bicycles in China) they have developed initiatives to improve road infrastructure to support the coexistence of bikes with other modes of motorized transportation.

Along with this, laws of road coexistence have been created to achieve a more harmonious interaction between cyclists, motorists and pedestrians.

Despite this promising panorama, these initiatives have been limited to the region where Santiago, the capital, is located and it has not caught on in other areas yet.

The fact is that since 2014 there has been a "Bike ways Plan" project with the

---

[1] "Third Biennial Update Report" p.117.
[2] For the government and the internal administration of the State, the territory of the Republic of Chile is currently divided into 16 regions, which in turn are subdivided into 56 provinces; for the purposes of local administration, the provinces are subdivided into 346 communes.
[3] "Third Biennial Update Report" p.140.

goal of constructing 190 kilometers of high standard bike ways, distributed in the 15 regions of the country and benefiting 32 cities.

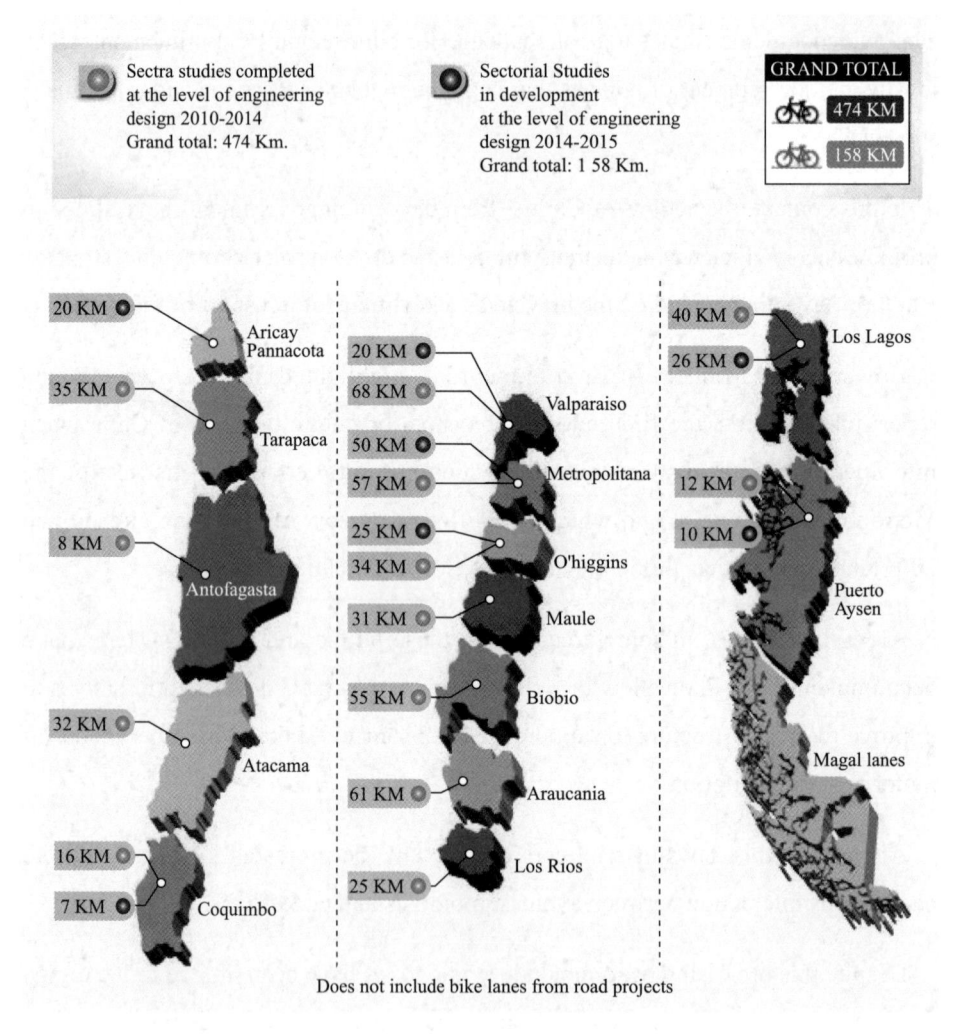

Does not include bike lanes from road projects

Frgure 2: Cycle routes   project progress status

Source: SECTRA Urban Road and Transportation Program, of the Undersecretariat of Transport of the Ministry of Transport and Telecommunications

The importance of the aforementioned plan lies in the fact that the increase in the use of bicycles in cities, especially in the Metropolitan Region, has not been proportional to the construction of infrastructure such as bicycle lanes and parking lots, which has led to the fact that road life is not always harmonious.

According to 2019 Worldwide Cycling Index,[1] Chile is one of the countries with the largest growth in number of total bicycles.[2] Its growth is "strong", with a rate that exceeds 10% per year. But, reality shows that this growth is not yet strong and conclusive enough in regions, which becomes both a challenge and an opportunity for the country that also hopes to meet SDG 11.

Hangzhou is a city recognized as touristic and has natural features that make it suitable for bicycle transport. Added to this, its large population of almost 10 million people makes the frequency of HBS use very high.

According to professor Huang from Zhejiang Gongshang University, this service is an innovation. "The Chinese government advocates inter-regional competition. For example, in Zhejiang Province, Hangzhou needs to compete with other cities. Unlike democratic countries, Chinese local governments have top-down pressure. This is the driving mechanism behind the competition mechanism between cities", he emphasizes.

And at the same time, the professor insists that the implementation of innovative ideas like HBS requires certain conditions. In the case of China, the state-owned enterprises have comprehensive strength for implementing innovation. Hangzhou Bicycle Service is managed by a public enterprise (Hangzhou Public Bicycle Company), but in the Western countries the preference is to provide this kind of service through private enterprise.

Another point made by professor Huang is about mutual learning between places. The innovation transmission or policy diffusion has allowed for the spread of word of HBS to other cities in China.

However, the implementation cost is relatively large. In fact, the initial

---

[1] Check all the index in: http://bit.ly/2s1MmEO
[2] Other ones are Poland, Czech Republic, Luxembourg and Sweden.

investment, maintenance, app development could require three years and also could cause urban management problems.

The Chinese government has a "disclaimer clause" relative to "trial and error" behind this kind of initiative. And in the case of HBS you pay just for the basic service and there is less competitiveness.

Despite that analysis, it is clear that the implementation of public bicycle service in other countries could increase interregional competitiveness and interregional learning benefiting all the key players but above all the citizens and their quality of life.

Without a doubt, Chile could be a good place to adopt this public policy, since it could benefit not only the citizens, but also the tourists who visit it, just as Hangzhou is an internationallyrecognized tourist destination and whose nature and places could be enhanced through a friendly and green mode of transport such as bicycles.

在西安，追寻古波斯的印记

好麦特 【伊朗】
德黑兰大学外语学院中文系　教授

2003 年夏，西安市文物保护考古研究所在西安北郊的井上村发掘了一座北周(580 年)的凉州萨保史君墓，[1]这是西安地区继北周安伽墓[2]之后的第二座与粟特人有关系的墓葬，出土文物及图像都很丰富，是研究北周首都长安社会文化生活以及丝绸之路的重要资料。

史君墓石墓门由门楣、门柱、门扉、门槛等组成，通高 152 厘米、宽 135 厘米，除门扉之外，均采用减地刻的技法刻绘各种图案，门扉上彩绘贴金，分别用白、黑和红色绘飞天和莲花等图案，可谓精美辉煌，极尽奢华之能事。[3]

史君墓石椁出土后引起了学界重视，学者们从自己的专业领域出发开展了对史君墓石椁的研究。2004 年至今，学者们取得了众多成果，研究内容涵盖考古学、宗教学、语言学以及古代东西方文化交流史等。笔者在前人研究的基础上结合一些最新的波斯语文献资料，发挥自己雕塑专业的优势，以史君墓石椁浮雕的雕塑手法研究为核心，深入研究其图案的详细内容。

虽然许多中国研究者认为北周史君墓上的图案是与丝路上最为活跃的民族之

1　西安市文物保护考古研究所：《西安北周凉州萨保史君墓发掘简报》，《文物》２００５年３期。
2　陕西省考古研究所：《西安发现的北周安伽墓》，《文物》2001 年 1 期；《西安北郊北周安伽墓发掘简报》，《考古与文物》2000 年 6 期；邢福来：《北朝至隋初人华粟特贵族墓围屏石榻研究》，《考古与文物》集刊 2002 年《汉唐考古》卷。
3　尹夏清：《北周史君墓石墓门及其相关问题研究》；《考古与文物》, 2018 第 2 期。

一"粟特人"有关系，但是笔者通过深入研究该坟墓上的图案并做了一些比较工作后发现，墓上的不少图是与"波斯文明"有密切的关系。大部分的中国研究者因为把史君这位商人认作为粟特人，从而把他坟墓上的图像也联系到粟特文化了。

不能否认的是作为丝路上最为活跃的民族，粟特人在汉唐之际大批涌入中国，他们在为中国带来异域商品的同时也将中国文化向四处传播。但是应该注意的是，来到中国的粟特人带来的文化遗产受到过波斯文明的影响，而且粟特该民族的不少文化因素都是起源于波斯文明。有意思的是"史君"这位粟特商人是来自中亚的"史国"；该国名称的来源也是一个"阿维斯塔语"，词意为"谷地"；阿维斯塔语是一种古老的印欧语系语言，属于伊朗语族的东伊朗语，亦是波斯古经《阿维斯塔》成书时所使用的语言。据历史记载，史君一生笃信古波斯宗教琐罗亚斯德教。[1]

2019年9月，初笔者通过参加由中国文化和旅游部主办、陕西师范大学承办的2019"青年汉学家研修计划"（西安），参观了西安博物院，考察了"北周史君墓"并对墓上面的一些图案进行了仔细的研究。

西安市文物保护考古所《西安北周凉州萨保史君墓发掘简报》对史君石椁有如下的判断："西壁第三幅画面分上下两部分（图1）。上部描绘的是一位粟特首领在树丛中狩猎的场面。画面下部的图像是一幅商队行进图。商队最前面是两个骑马的男子，其中一位可以看见腰间悬挂着箭袋。后面是两头驮载货物的骆驼，再后面是一位头戴船形帽的骑马男子，上举的右手握着望筒正在望。在两头骆驼的右上方，有两匹马和一头驴驮载着货物并行，后面一持鞭男子正驱赶它们前行。"

中国的一些研究者如北京大学的荣新江教授认同上述的判断并写道："与这些画面类似的场景，也出现在其他粟特系统石棺床的围屏上。"这位考古学家认为"日本Miho美术馆藏石棺床编号D的石板是该问题一个特别好的例子，即绘有胡人牵驼而行，骆驼背上驮有高大的包裹，骆驼右

图1　史君石椁西壁第三幅

1　申虎：《北周史君墓石椁浮雕研究》；陕西师范大学2018年硕士论文。

侧和后面各有一胡人随行，下面有三个披发的游牧民族(哒或突厥人)骑马而行"。[1]

与中国研究者不同，笔者认为史君石椁上部描绘在树丛中狩猎的场面并不是西安市文物保护考古所认为的"一位粟特首领"，而很可能是公元 5 世纪萨珊王朝著名的波斯帝国国王"巴赫拉姆·古尔"（Bahram Gur）。波斯著名史诗《列王纪》中记载说他喜爱狩猎。巴赫拉姆·古尔曾为争夺王位而进行斗争，登极后是位英明君主，制定法律保护百姓。有些神话讲到：当他的死期到来时，他在狩猎的时候大地裂开把他吞了进去。关于巴赫拉姆·古尔的传说融汇了许多古代神话。据传说，巴赫拉姆王是第一位波斯语诗人。为了证明史君石椁上部描绘在树丛中狩猎的人就是波斯历史中萨珊王朝的巴赫拉姆，除了他头上的冕冠和身上与史君墓中图像不同的皇服以外，通过与古波斯的一些相似的图案比较，我们了解到这个事实：顶面圆盘用复杂而有代表性的萨珊技艺打造，形状优美，上面描绘的故事后来收录在著于 11 世纪的伊朗史诗巨作《沙纳玛》(即《列王纪》)中。在《列王纪》中，巴赫拉姆·古尔——即巴赫拉姆五世（公元 420—438 年在位）最宠信的乐师阿扎达要和他比箭。恰如图 3 所示，巴赫拉姆·古尔用弓箭射掉了一只雄羚的双角，让它看上去像一只雌羚，接着他又向一只雌羚的头射出两支箭，让她看似长着雄羚那样的双角。

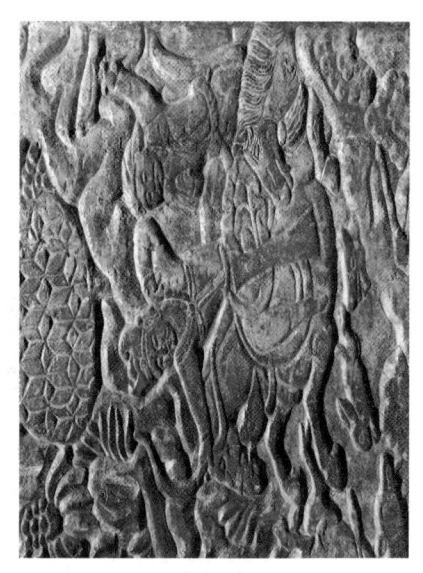

图 2　粟特首领还是波斯王子？

图 3　狩猎图盘　伊朗萨珊时期
　　　（约公元 400—500）

---

[1] 参见荣新江《Miho 美术馆粟特石棺屏风的图像 及其组合》，《艺术史研究》(第 4 辑)，中山大学出版社 2002 年收，第 213-214 页，图 8a。

图4 波斯著名诗人内扎米诗书中讲巴赫拉姆王故事的一页（公元16世纪）

图5和图6 古波斯土地上挖掘的两个盘子上都描绘了巴赫拉姆王狩猎的故事

图7 一幅讲巴赫拉姆王狩猎故事的波斯细密画

图8 萨珊王朝巴赫拉姆王时代的金币

根据图 4—8 所提供的资料，可以说史君石椁上狩猎者的身份是很有可能是萨珊王朝的国王"巴赫拉姆·古尔"（Bahram Gur）而且如果我们深入一些研究波斯语的历史资料或从古至今保留的一些细密画等艺术作品，还能确定史君石椁上的另一些图案也很有可能与这位波斯王子有关。譬如，紧挨着上述巴赫拉姆图像，转到石椁北面的第一幅，上部中心位置的帐篷内盘腿坐一男子，头戴宝冠，着翻领窄袖长袍，腰束带，右手握一长杯，脚穿长靴。帐篷前铺设一椭圆形毯子，上面跪坐一位头戴毡帽的长者，着翻领窄袖长袍，腰束带，悬挂腰刀，右手握长杯，与帐内人物对坐饮酒。帐篷两侧有三位侍者。画面的下部是一个正在休息的商队，中间有两位男子正在交谈，一人肩上还背着货囊。如果我们认可史君墓上的图像与波斯的巴赫拉姆王有关系的话，很有可能上面提出的信息也是巴赫拉姆皇宫里的一些活动。下面两幅中古的波斯细密画的内容与上述的内容很相似，并且绘画中的一些建筑、乐器、饮料等与史君墓上的图像相似。

图 9 和图 10　巴赫拉姆王宫里的两场娱乐活动

除此之外，笔者发现史君石椁上的其他图像如图 9、图 10，也与波斯文化中的神话与历史有密切的关系。

总的来说，精美的石椁入殓尸骨，为研究北朝时期以及古丝路上的历史、宗教、商贸、音乐、舞蹈等提供了丰富的研究素材。毫无疑问的是，这些珍贵的素材应该被一组不同国家的考古学家重新分析研究。

Quest for the Trace of Ancient Persia in Xi'an: A Negelected Persian Emperor Pattern on the Shi Jun Tomb of the Northern Zhou Dynasty

Hamed Vafaei / Iran

Department of Chinese Language and Literature of University of Tehran, School of Foreign Languages / Professor

In the summer of 2003, Xi'an Institute of Cultural Relics Protection and Archaeology excavated the Liangzhou Sabao Shi Jun Tomb in Jingshang Village, Xi'an City, which was built in the second year of the Daxiang Reign (A.D. 580) in the northern suburb of Xi'an City.[1] The tomb is the second tomb related to the Sogdian people in the Xi'an area after the An Jia Tomb of the Northern Zhou Dynasty[2]. The objects and images unearthed in the tomb are quite numerous, and they are important materials for studying the social and cultural life of Chang'an,

---
1 Xi'an Institute of Cultural Relics Protection and Archaeology: Brief Report on the Excavation of Liangzhou Sabao Shi Jun Tomb Discovered in Xi'an, *Cultural Relics*, No. 3, 2005.
2 Shaanxi Provincial Institute of Archaeology: An Jia Tomb in the Northern Zhou Dynasty Discovered in Xi'an, *Cultural Relics*, No. 1, 2001; Brief Report on the Excavation of An Ja Tomb in Northern Zhou Dynasty Discovered in the Northern Suburb of Xi'an, *Archaeology and Cultural Relics*, No. 6, 2000; Xing Fulai: A Research Project on the Stone Beds and Folding Screen in Sogdian Noble Tombs in China Built from the Northern Dynasties to the Early Sui Dynasty, *Volume of Han and Tang Archaeology, Archaeology and Cultural Relics*, 2002 annual collection.

the capital of the Northern Zhou Dynasty, and the Silk Road.

The door of Shi Jun's headstone consists of a doorhead, doorposts, door leaves, a threshold, etc., with a height of 152 cm and a width of 135 cm. Except for the door leaf, all kinds of patterns are carved using the bas-relief technique. The door leaf is painted in gold, and the patterns of the flying Apsaras and lotus are painted in white, black and red respectively, which are exquisite, brilliant, and extremely luxurious.[1]

After the stone outer coffin of the Shi Jun Tomb was unearthed, it attracted the great attention of academic circles. Scholars started their study of the Shi Jun Tomb in their own professional fields. Since 2004, the achievements in the past fourteen years have been fruitful, covering archaeology, religion, linguistics and the history of ancient cultural exchanges between the East and the West. On the basis of previous studies, the author combined some new Persian literature and materials, gave full play to the advantages of his studies with a major in sculpture, and focused on the research of sculpture techniques used on the stone outer coffin relief of Shi Jun Tomb, and deeply studied the detailed content of its patterns.

Although many Chinese researchers think that the patterns of the Shi Jun Tomb in the Northern Zhou Dynasty are related to the "Sogdians", one of the most active ethnic groups on the Silk Road, the author found that many pictures on the tomb are closely related to the "Persian civilization" by deeply studying and comparing the patterns of the tomb. Most Chinese researchers have linked the images of the Shi Jun Tomb to Sogdian culture because Shi Jun is a Sogdian businessman.

It cannot be denied that as the most active nation on the Silk Road, the Sogdians flooded into China in large numbers during the Han and Tang Dynasties. They not only brought foreign goods to China, but also spread Chinese culture around the world. However, it should be noted that the cultural heritage brought by the Sogdians who came to China was influenced by the Persian civilization. In

---

1 Yin Xiaqing: Research on the Stone Door of Shi Jun Tomb in the Northern Zhou Dynasty and Related Issues; *Archaeology and Cultural Relics*, No.2, 2018.

fact, many cultural factors of the Sogdians belong to the Persian civilization. Interestingly, Shi Jun, the Sogdian businessman, was from a country named Kess in Central Asia. The origin of the country's name is an "Avista" word meaning "valley"; Avista belongs to the ancient Indo-European language family, and belongs to the East Iranian language sub-family of the Iranian language family, and it was used by people when the ancient Persian book Avista was written. According to historical records, Shi Jun believed in Zoroastrianism, an ancient Persian religion, all his life.[1]

At the beginning of September 2019, the author participated in the 2019 Visiting Program for Young Sinologists (Xi'an) hosted by the Ministry of Culture and Tourism and undertaken by Shaanxi Normal University; through the program, the author visited Xi'an Museum to inspect the Shi Jun Tomb built in the Northern Zhou Dynasty and made a careful study of the patterns on the tomb.

The Xi'an Institute of Cultural Relics Protection and Archaeology issued the Brief Report on the Excavation of Liangzhou Sabao Shi Jun Tomb Discovered in Xi'an, which made the following judgment on Shi Jun's stone outer coffin: "The third picture of the west wall is divided into two parts" (see Figure a). The upper part depicts a scene of a Sogdian leader hunting in the bushes. The lower part of the picture is a caravan picture. At the front of the caravan are two men on horseback, one of whom has a quiver hanging from his waist. Behind them are two camels

Figure (a) The third picture of the west wall of Shi Jun's outer stone coffin

---

1 Shen Hu: Research on the Outer Stone Coffin Reliefs of the Shi Jun Tomb Built in the Northern Zhou Dynasty, *Journal of Shaanxi Normal University*, 2018.

carrying goods, and behind the camels is a man riding a horse and wearing a boat-shaped hat, who is watching the distant place and holding a telescope-like thing in his right hand. At the top right of the two camels, there are two horses and a donkey carrying goods in parallel, and a man with a whip behind them is riding forward.

Some researchers in China, such as Professor Rong Xinjiang of Peking University, agreed with the above judgment and wrote: "Scenes similar to those in these pictures also appear on the screens of stone funerary couches in other Sogdian relics." The archaeologist believes that "the stone slab with the number D of the stone funerary couch preserved in the Miho Art Museum in Japan is a good example. It is painted with a Hu Ren man leading a camel, a big package on the camel's back, two Hu Ren men on the right and behind the camel respectively, and three hairy nomads (Ephtals or Turks) riding below".[1]

Unlike the Chinese researchers, the author thinks that the scene of hunting in the bushes depicted in the upper part of Shi Jun's outer stone coffin is not "a Sogdian leader" as what the Xi'an Institute of Cultural Relics Protection and Archaeology said. It is very likely that he was "Bahram Gur", the famous Persian Empire king of the Sassanian Dynasty in the 5th century AD; King Bahram was written about in myths, legends and epics of Persian literature. The famous Persian epic Kings records that he loves hunting. Bahram Gur once fought for the throne. After he ascended the throne, he was a wise monarch who made laws to protect the people. Some myths say that when his

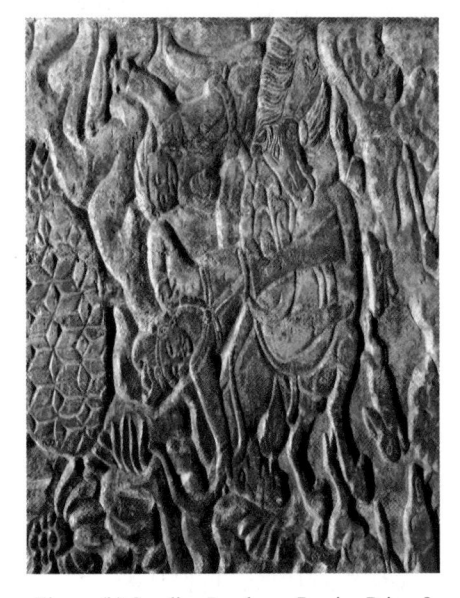

Figure (b) Sogdian Leader or Persian Prince?

---

1 Rong Xinjiang: Images and Combinations of the Screens of the Sogdian Stone Funerary Couch in Miho Art Museum, *The Study of Art History*, No.4, Sun Yat-sen University Press, 2002, pp. 213-214, Figure 8a.

death came, the earth split and swallowed him up while he was hunting. The legend about Bahram Gur is a fusion of many ancient stories; according to legends, King Bahram was the first Persian poet. The evidence to prove that the man who is hunting in the trees depicted in the upper part of Shi Jun's outer stone coffin is Bahram of the Sassanian Dynasty in Persian history include, besides the crown on his head and the imperial costume

Figure (c) Hunting plate: Iran. Sassanian period. About 400-500 AD.

unlike those in the upper images of Shi Jun's tomb, we can also learn this fact by comparing the patterns with some similar ones in ancient Persia:

The disk is made with complex and representative Sassanian skills, and its shape is beautiful. The story described in it was included in the Iranian epic masterpiece Shanama (that is, the Kings) in the 11th century. In the Kings, Azadeh, the favorite musician of Bahram Gur (i.e. Bahram V, reigned in 420-38 AD), wanted to compete with him. Just as shown in this picture, Bahram Gur shot off the horns of a male gazelle with a bow and arrow to make it look like a female gazelle, and then he shot two arrows at the head of a female gazelle to make it look like a male gazelle with horns.[1]

Figure (d) A page about the story of King Bahram in the famous Persian poet Nezami's poetry book preserved in the United States (16th AD)

---

1 [Metropolitan Museum of Art bulletin / Recent acquisitions]; Metropolitan Museum of Art bulletin. Recent acquisitions; Metropolitan Museum of Art, 1989.

Fig.(e) and Fig.(f) The two plates excavated in ancient Persian land depict the story of King Bahram hunting.

Figure (g) A Persian miniature regardomg the hunting story of King Bahram

Figure (h) Gold coins of the Sassanian Dynasty during the reign of King Bahram

According to the information provided above, it can be said that the identity of the hunter depicted on Shi Jun's outer stone coffin is probably "Bahram Gur", the king of the Sassanian Dynasty, and if we go deeper into some Persian historical data or some miniatures and other works of art that have been preserved since ancient times, it can be said that other patterns on Shi Jun's outer stone coffin are also likely to be related to this Persian prince. For example, next to the above-mentioned image, in the upper central part of the first picture on the north wall of the outer stone coffin, there is a man sitting cross-legged in a tent, wearing a treasure crown, a lapel robe with narrow sleeves, a waist belt, a long cup in his right hand and boots on his feet. An oval blanket is laid in front of the tent, on which an elderly man with a felt hat is kneeling, wearing a lapel robe with narrow sleeves, a waistband, a waist knife, a long cup in his right hand, and drinking with the people in the tent. There are three waiters on both sides of the tent. In the lower part of the picture there is a caravan that is resting. In the middle position, two men are talking, one with a cargo bag on his shoulder. If we accept the fact that the images in the Shi Jun Tomb have something to do with King Bahram of Persia, it is very likely that the information presented above is also some activities in Bahram's Palace. The contents of the following two medieval Persian miniatures are very similar to those mentioned above; some buildings, musical instruments, drinks, etc. in the miniatures are very similar to those found in the Shi Jun Tomb.

In addition, the author found that other images on Shi Jun's outer stone coffin are also closely related to the myth and history of Persian culture, but this article is limited and cannot provide all the relevant information about it. He hopes that he can go deeper into talking about the images found in the Shi Jun Tomb in another article or conference.

Generally speaking, the exquisite outer stone coffin provides abundant research materials for studying the history, religion, commerce, music and dance of the Northern Dynasties and the ancient Silk Road. There is no doubt that these precious materials should be re-analyzed and studied by a group of archaeologists from different countries.

Quest for the Trace of Ancient Persia in Xi'an:
A Negelected Persian Emperor Pattern on the Shi Jun Tomb of the Northern Zhou Dynasty

Fig.(h) and Fig.(I) Two entertainment activities in Bahram's Palace

References

[Metropolitan Museum of Art bulletin / Recent acquisitions] ; Metropolitan Museum of Art bulletin. Recent acquisitions; Metropolitan Museum of Art, 1989.

Rong Xinjiang: Images and Combinations of the Screens of the Sogdian Stone Funerary Couch in the Miho Art Museum. Sun Yat-sen University Press, 2002, 2002.12 (2003.7),199221.

Study on Art History. Sun Yat-sen University Press. 2002.

Yin Xiaqing: Research on the Stone Door of the Shi Jun Tomb in the Northern Zhou Dynasty and Related Issues; *Archaeology and Cultural Relics*, No.2, 2018.

Shen Hu: Research on the Reliefs on the Outer Stone Coffin of the Shi Jun Tomb Built in the Northern Zhou Dynasty, *Journal of Shaanxi Normal University*, 2018.

Xi'an Institute of Cultural Relics Protection and Archaeology: Brief Report on the Excavation of Liangzhou Sabao Shi Jun Tomb Discovered in Xi'an, *Cultural Relics*, No. 3, 2005.

Shaanxi Provincial Institute of Archaeology: An Jia Tomb in the Northern Zhou Dynasty

Discovered in Xi'an, Cultural Relics, No. 1, 2001; Brief Report on the Excavation of An Ja Tomb in the Northern Zhou Dynasty Discovered in the Northern Suburb of Xi'an, Archaeology and Cultural Relics, No. 6, 2000; Xing Fulai: Research on the Stone Beds and Folding Screen in Sogdian Noble Tombs in China Built from the Northern Dynasties to the Early Sui Dynasty, *Volume of Han and Tang Archaeology, Archaeology and Cultural Relics*, 2002 annual collection.

Yang Junkai. Bilingual Inscriptions on the Shi Jun Tomb Built in the Northern Zhou Dynasty and Related Issues. *Cultural Relics*. No.8, 2013.

Luo Feng. Byzantium Unearthed Gold Conis from the Shi Jun Tomb Built in the Northern Zhou Dynasty. *Cultural Relics*.

解读旅游与文化的经济协同效应——以上海为例

马利克 【巴基斯坦】

巴基斯坦坦萨戈达大学　讲师／澳大利亚西溪大学　博士生

一　背景

上海作为中国主要城市之一和中央直辖市的重要性不容忽视。它现在正在引领包括旅游市场在内的全球商业和贸易业务。文化旅游在其初始阶段受到旅游业增长的推动，后来，文化旅游本身成了一个宽泛的市场（Richards，2007）。上海似乎正在沿着这条道路前进，因为它作为全球经济活动中心的地位将有利于文化旅游的发展。

文化旅游被认为是一个基于以下类型或维度的产业：（1）有形的 [纪念馆、历史遗迹等]，（2）无形的 [文化节、美食、传统音乐、口头传统、手工艺品等]，（3）当代创意产业产品 [电影、表演艺术、时尚、设计、媒体等]，以及（4）其他 [体育、教育、购物、健康等]。这些产品的竞争力是以文化、创意和服务的渗透为前提的。在全球范围内，文化和旅游业的协同效应已经得到认可，据统计文化旅游业占全球旅游市场的近 40%。与此同时，文化旅游业在过去五年中还有所增长（这一趋势将持续下去）（UNWTO，2018）。中国于 2018 年将文化部和国家旅游局合并为"中华人民共和国文化旅游部"。这表明了中国政府的政策方向和愿景，即从这一具有潜力的领域获得最大可能的成果。最近的中美贸易紧张对世界上最大的集装箱装卸港上海来说是一个巨大的挑战。在这种反全球化行为之后，投资者可能会保持谨慎。此外，随着上海政府对环境标准的执行越来越严格，投资者可能会变得更加保守。在应对这些问题的同时,寻求其他增长和发展渠道(多样化)也很重要,如技术创新和文化旅游市场,以及与之配套的航运、贸易、金融和资本市场等。

上海的目标是提高其作为国际商业、贸易、航运、金融和技术创新中心的地位,同时遵循可持续发展的环境标准(SBF,2018)。上海如何应对和构思文化旅游非常重要,尤其是在自身的现代化上海文化(城市文化)蓬勃发展的情况下。此外,经济纽带是如何将上海的文化和旅游联系在一起的?上海正在实施或即将实施哪些新举措?这一背景成为本研究的真正动力。

本研究将围绕以下三个方面:

1. 上海是如何构思文化旅游的?上海的文化旅游在推广实践上需要什么样的支持?

2. 确定上海文化与旅游业之间的经济协同效应(文化旅游)。

3. 正在或将使上海成为国际文化旅游胜地的地标性成就/举措是什么?

二 数据收集和研究方法

框架图显示了经济协同效应,它对文化和旅游业起作用。本研究中心游客包括入境和国内(来自中国境外的游客)游客。上海的文化包括有形的、无形的、当代的和其他四种类型。

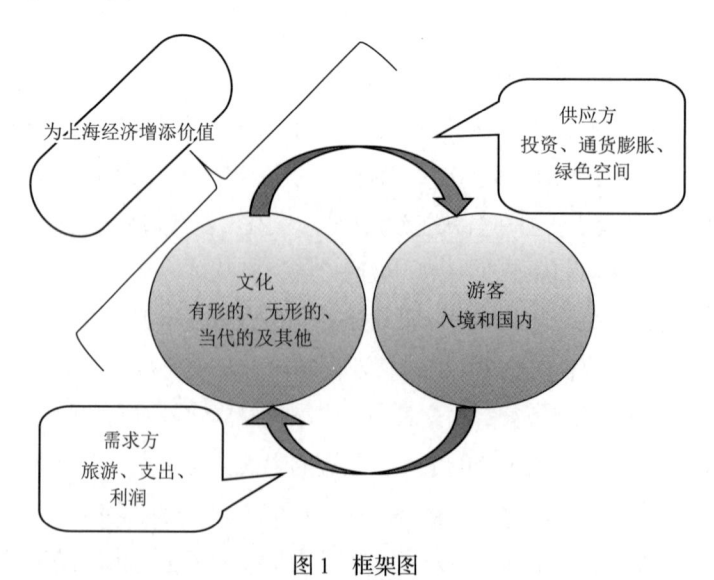

图 1 框架图

供应方将展示政府的供应是如何吸引文化游客来上海旅游的。投资将用于文化、体育和娱乐领域。

文化投资将用于有形和无形产品开发的代理。娱乐投资在这里被用来代表当代类型的文化旅游产品，体育投资将被用来代表其他类别。

此外，通货膨胀的情况也会给我们有关社区负担能力的印象。生活成本越低，社区就越欢迎游客，对游客也越有吸引力。在可持续旅游业的环境敏感性方面，绿地也是一个重要因素。

在需求方，我们会看到有多少文化游客对此感兴趣。该研究将了解有多少文化游客来到上海，他们的消费量是多少，以及旅行社如何从该行业获利并获得收入。所有这些变量都将被用来代表来上海的文化游客的需求趋势。

本研究以定性研究为基础，采用目的性抽样（非概率抽样）的方法，并利用"青年汉学家访问计划（上海）2019"（VPYS-2019）的机会。三螺旋概念被视为理解基于创新产生的现代知识经济运作的一种方式。这种螺旋关系包括政府、学术界/大学和工业界，它们之间存在相互影响的共同联系（Leydesdorff，2012）。在这种背景下，本研究力求接触学者和官员（他们曾在上海市政府的各个项目中工作）。

根据VPYS 2019的既定时间表，授课和实地考察将与关键信息人访谈（KII）一起作为信息来源。KII已用于分析本研究的目标1。二级数据可在《2018年上海统计年鉴》（SSY，2018）和《2018年上海基本事实》（2018）中获得，并用于研究目标2，而授课和实地考察则用于理解研究目标3。

三 研究发现

1. 上海文化旅游理念

上海是一座国际化城市，被认为是中国的一座奇迹城市，有着自己的传统和未来发展愿景。上海文化旅游的独特之处在于，它涵盖了UNWTO（2018）提出的文化旅游定义的所有方面。它包括"有形的"、"无形的"、"当代的"和"其他"类型（我们已经在引言中对它们进行了定义）。正是由于上海的现代化和城市化进程，才产生了自己的上海城市文化。就这些维度的重要性而言，受访者对上海所有类型的文化旅游都给予了重视。

正如其中一位受访者所说："事实上，正是所有这些类型的文化旅游的共同影响，上海的自我发展的城市文化是开放的、外向的、好客的和包容的，无论游客来自中国其他省份还是来自国外。"

然而，也有不同的回答："我认为这可能因人而异。例如，老年游客可能对有形遗产更感兴趣，年轻游客可能对当代和其他类型的文化旅游更感兴趣，包括时尚、媒体、购物、数字化等。"

它向我们表明，研究游客的行为非常重要，以便我们根据文化游客的特点了解他们的实际需求。根据这一观点，一旦我们确定入境游客和国内游客对上海的偏好，就会制定适当的政策。根据 KIIs 调查对象的观点，文化旅游约占上海旅游市场总的 30% 至 50%。

多年来，上海的入境文化游客有所增加，考虑到我们前面讨论过的文化旅游的更广泛定义，入境文化游客约占上海旅游市场总的 60% 至 70%。此外，这种增长的背后得到了政府的鼓励和支持。正如一位受访者所说，"政府的指导方向和兴趣，在这些问题上非常重要"。与此同时，上海作为游客最佳目的地的受欢迎程度，即在一个地方就能找到很多感兴趣的东西，也是其旅游业增长背后的另一个因素。

国内文化游客约占总数的 30% 至 40%，他们对无形、当代和其他类别的旅游产品非常感兴趣。但这并不意味着他们完全忽略了有形的东西，只不过国内游客相对地更容易被具有中国特色的上海大都市文化（无形、当代和其他类型的文化旅游）所吸引并为之着迷。根据受访者的观点，由于上海文化旅游的多维度性日益增强，这几年的旅游量也有所增加。因此，根据受访者的说法，近 80% 至 90% 的游客来上海要么出于文化动机，要么参与文化活动。文化在上海政府的旅游政策中占有非常重要的地位。此外，他们还注意到，营销和推广计划必须实实在在反映上海文化的方方面面，因为它现在不仅闻名亚洲而且闻名全世界。

对于上海文化旅游产业的发展，已经有不同类型的支持，这些支持或正在进行中，更多的或在未来的规划之中。它包括立法、产品开发、资金、能力建设和培训、营销、国际合作以及网络和合作。这些也是国际公认的支持文化旅游的方式（UNWTO，2018）。对于每种类型的支持，我们都得到了许多不同的回应。

其中一名受访者评论道："在立法方面，将文化部和中国国家旅游局合并或整合为'中华人民共和国文化和旅游部'是一项重大举措。此外，在上海未来的15

项工作计划中,有一项计划专门包括旅游业,其中娱乐、体育、文化和购物也被考虑在其中"。

与航运、贸易和金融等传统经济部门对比,上海此类未来规划举措表明了政府对文化旅游业的关注。旅游营销的一个显著举措是"数字化"。

其中一位受访者认为,"数字化无疑是 21 世纪旅游市场的未来。了解这一事实后,我们将推出这种虚拟现实或数字应用,甚至可以通过智能手机技术访问"。

这些应用程序将虚拟地展示博物馆及其内部产品。某些技术会提供上海的 3D 视图,其中包含游客可以找到文化景点的不同地点的信息。

在能力建设和培训方面,一种反馈是,"非常需要对旅游经营者和导游进行能力建设和培训,因为他们对上海的文化层面和遗产了解较少"。

这表明,为促进上海文化旅游业的发展,迫切需要政府重视提高人文服务质量。

在认同国际合作重要性时,有受访者认为:"毫无疑问,有必要学习国际先例。比如埃及就是这样一个例子,我们的旅游业可以从中学到很多东西。"。

另一位受访者提到,"类似中国国际进口博览会的活动表明,我们决心开展国际合作,欢迎他们不仅是为了贸易,而且是为了在包括文化旅游在内的各个方面来进行探索。"

各种项目的国际合作,无论是在有形基础设施还是在服务提供方面,都将有助于上海提升其接待入境游客的国际标准。它将增加外国入境游客的便利,并简化潜在入境游客的访问。

就网络和合作而言,一个显著的反馈是,"未来,长三角地区(城市经济带)将是一个由上海和周边三省组成的一体化区域。在这个区域,未来的发展将以上海为龙头,包括旅游业在内的所有部门都将得到整合,并相互合作和协调。"

2. 经济协同效应

上海正在迅速适应成为文化游客最受欢迎的目的地,同时保持其作为全球金融、商业和贸易活动中心的领导地位。2017 年旅游业增加值占 GDP 的比例为 6.2%。此外,自 2005 年以来,上海经济的旅游业绝对附加值持续上升(图 2)。上海的旅游业由酒店、旅行社、旅游商业、城市交通、园艺、餐饮、旅游运输和邮电等不同行业组成。这表明旅游业在上海经济中有许多前向和后向联系。

(1)需求方面

在 2010—2017 年期间,国际旅游业的外汇收入以近 6% 的速度增长。2017 年,

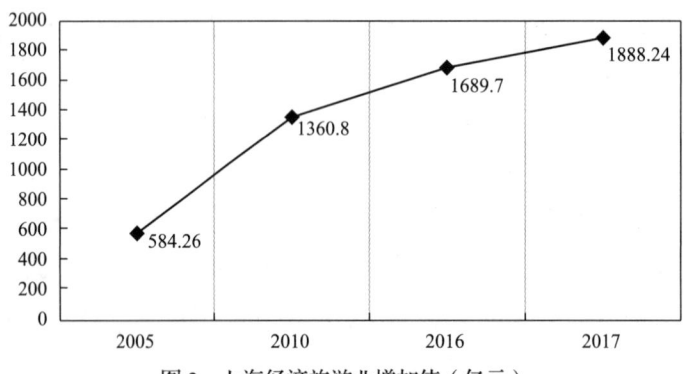

图 2 上海经济旅游业增加值（亿元）

海外收入达到 68 亿美元（图 3）。2016 年至 2017 年期间，外汇出现了 2.8% 的惊人增长，因为这远远超过了前六年的年增长率 1.95%（2010—2016）。这一指标可以用来衡量来上海的入境国际游客的消费。

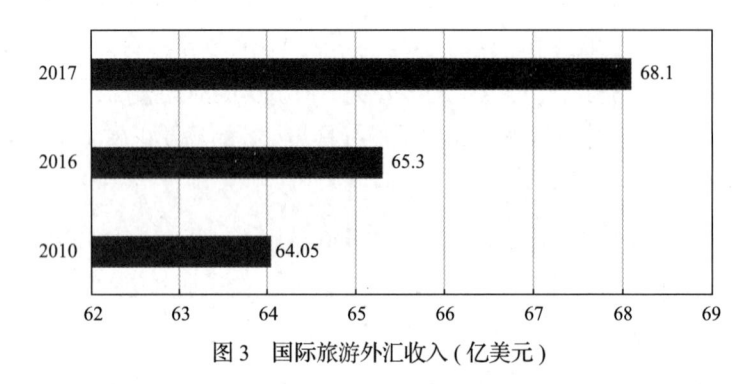

图 3 国际旅游外汇收入（亿美元）

从 2015 年到 2017 年，旅行社接待的海外游客每年增长 12%，而海关记录显示，自 2010 年以来，海外游客的年增长率为 2.6%（图 4）。

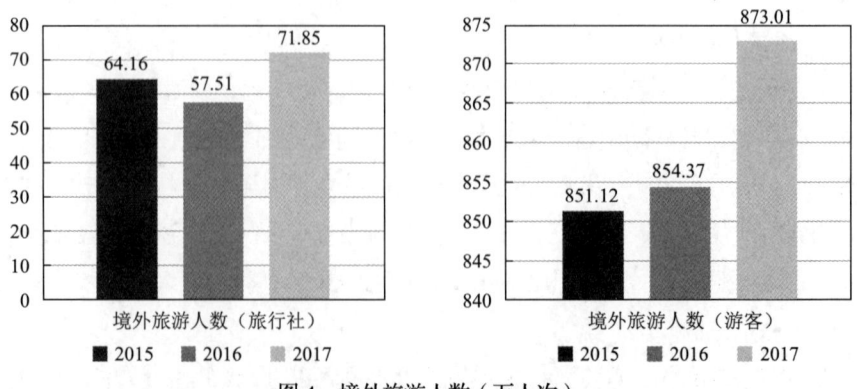

图 4 境外旅游人数（万人次）

上海酒店的平均入住率在过去几年中显著增长，2017年达到69%。此外，仅在两年内（2015—2017），旅行社的盈利能力就从3100万元人民币显著增长至8.17亿元人民币。同时，营业收入从827亿元人民币增至1396亿元人民币（SSY，2018）。

就上海入境旅游市场的国际化而言（图5），亚洲是最大的合作伙伴，占中国内地（除澳门、台湾和香港地区外）国际游客入境总人数的37%。如果加上港澳台地区的游客，亚洲的份额将进一步扩大。紧随其后的是北美游客，占上海国际游客总数的32%，其次是欧洲和大洋洲，市场份额分别为24.4%和6.6%。

国内游客市场也很繁荣（图6）。这种增长不仅体现在游客数量上，还体现在他们在上海不同活动中的人均支出上。这些国内游客既来自当地，也来自中国其他省份。游客数量和消费习惯的增加表明，他们也是上海旅游市场的重要组成部分。

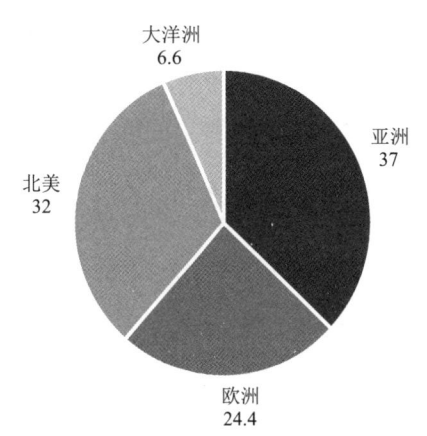

图5　2017年入境旅游市场国际化情况（%）

以上的分析可以告诉我们，文化旅游的需求面已经足够强劲，趋势也表明未来文化旅游的需求面还会继续如此强劲。它反映了上海文化对国内外游客的吸引。

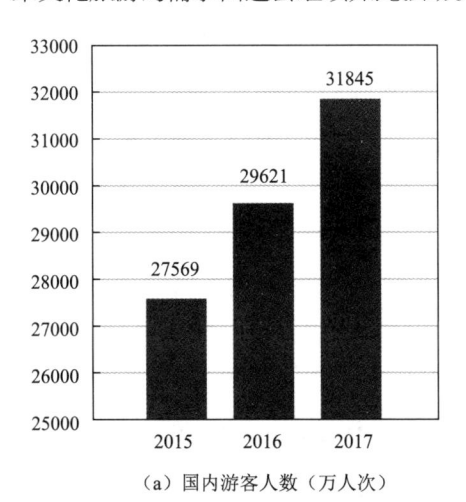

（a）国内游客人数（万人次）

年份	2015	2016	2017
人数	27569	29621	31845

（b）人均消费（元）

年份	2015	2016	2017
消费	1087	1163	1264

图6　（a）国内游客人数（万人次）与(b)人均消费（元）

（2）供应方面

为分析供应方面的情况，本研究采用了上海市政府统计的不同行业的地方固定资产投资信息。在不同部门的分类中，"文化、体育和娱乐"的类别似乎与我们已经讨论过的文化旅游维度的更广泛定义非常一致（图7）。"文化"相关投资与有形和无形的文化旅游类型有关。"娱乐"相关投资代表当代类型的文化旅游，而"体育"相关投资可以代表其他类别的文化旅游。

使用该类型投资分析的目的是分析是否进行了实际增加文化游客产品开发的特定投资。之后，每年的投资统计数据可以与来自国外（入境）和本地（国内）的游客的抵达进行比较。图7显示，我们关注的投资类别有上升趋势，这表明上海市政府对此类投资需求的兴趣。然而，2017年，投资急剧下降，这可能会对未来一年的文化旅游业造成负面的影响，但目前还没有相关数据。

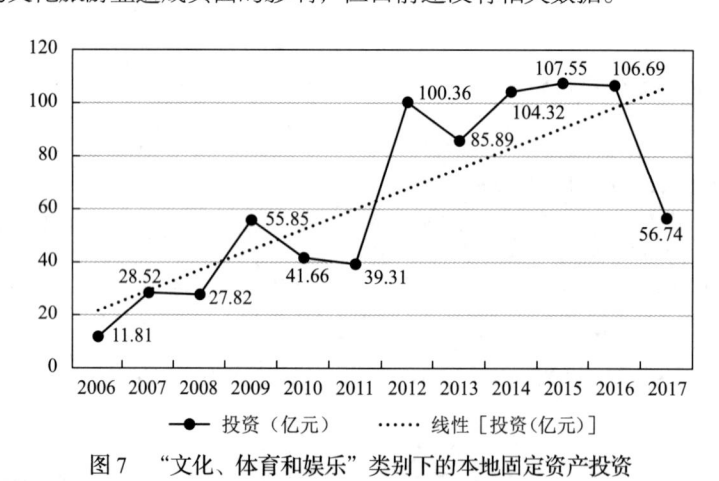

图7 "文化、体育和娱乐"类别下的本地固定资产投资

随着文化旅游产品开发投资的增加，海关入境游客数据呈上升趋势。旅行社接待入境游客的趋势线具有稳定且非负面的趋势（图8）。

自2012年至2015年，年通胀率几乎保持稳定。2016年的通货膨胀率比前一年略微上升了0.8个百分点，2017年的通货膨胀率为1.7%（图9）。即使是线性预测对未来也几乎是负线性趋势。更低的生活成本将是政府的另一项规定，使游客在上海生活更方便。与此同时，通过提高购买能力，当地社区的生活水平也会提高。

在任何地方，城市绿地都一直是提升其绿色形象的辅助工具，并具有许多附加的环境效益。上海城市绿地面积不断增加，使游客可以享受更清洁的环境（图10）。

图 8 历年游客人数（万人次）

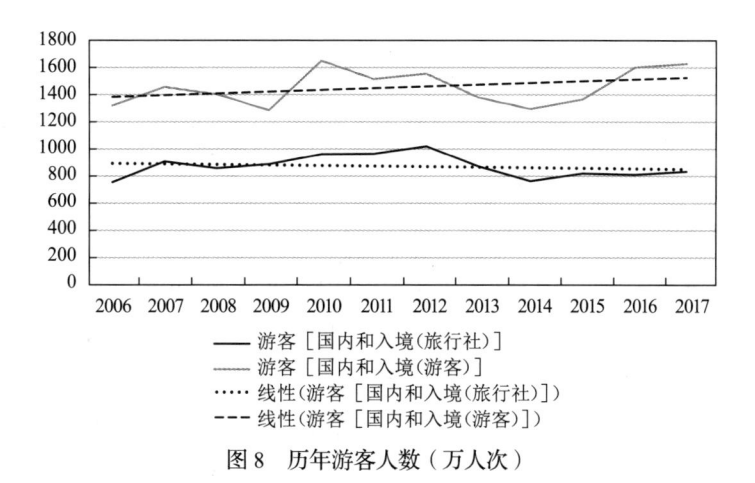

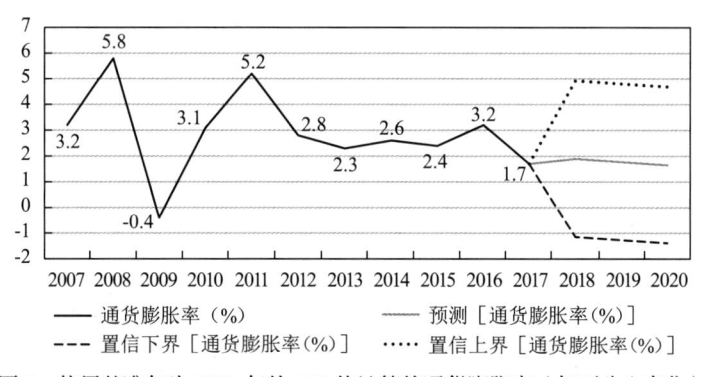

图 9 使用基准年为 1978 年的 CPI 值计算的通货膨胀率（年百分比变化）

图 10 城市绿地（公顷）

同时，政府已采取立法措施关闭不符合环保规定的工厂。最近一项将于 2019 年 7 月 1 日生效的立法是《上海生活垃圾管理条例》，该条例旨在禁止酒店内使用所有的一次性清洁用具，如牙刷、剃须刀、梳子等。

3. 措施

上海正在实施许多具有里程碑意义的举措，这些举措将使上海真正成为最理想的城市。上海已进入后工业化经济发展阶段，城市经济主要由服务业推动，2017年服务业占上海GDP总量的近69%（SSY，2018）。上海城市文化的特点是对新思想和新观念的吸收和接纳。它实际上是基于发展中的独立性、实用主义、自我完善、创新倾向、法治和爱国主义等因素（Yuezhi, 2019）。此外，未来的目标是追求基于"技术创新"的高质量增长和发展。这将是上海未来的目标，以及经济增长的金融、资本、贸易和航运领域。

上海对崇明岛的开发，为文化旅游制定了新的标准和增加了多样性。该岛属于上海市辖区，已被指定为发展农业生态农场，该农场正在推广有机农业，以确保环境保护。上海再次成为中国的先锋，在中国农村或农村地区推广绿色旅游，保护生态多样性和农村文化。崇明将建立航运和海洋产业，并为文化游客提供大量机会参观和体验的乡村农场、多样化生态保护区、风景名胜区和清洁的环境。

上海有许多博物馆，中国古代历史和中国共产党的发展史都被很好地保存下来，供游客参观游览。它们展示了中国古代和现代历史的辉煌。上海有许多传统文化和社区文化中心，展示中华文明的历史和文化遗产。这些手工艺品向游客展示了中国文化的多样性和深度。最重要的是，他们对孔子的思想进行了开发，并提供不同的文化活动，游客可以参与其中。上海是一个国际化的大都市，在世界上享有盛名。上海的社区中心为其国际居民和游客提供了许多学习中国文化和古老文明的机会，如书法、中国传统舞蹈等。

为了加强沟通和协调，计划未来几年内在上海及其三个相邻省份之间建立长三角带（长三角城市带）。该倡议旨在加强协调，并从各自的经验中共同学习，以促进不同的经济部门，如旅游业或文化旅游业、可持续发展等。

随着时间的推移，许多娱乐和创意产业品牌在上海落户并开业，比如与时尚、购物、电影节、美食、大学、媒体等相关的品牌。为了加快这些活动，上海将继续举办中国国际进口博览会和上海国际电影节等活动，从而成为国际文化旅游胜地。可以肯定的是，上海可以让每个人都可以找到其感兴趣的东西，有其独特之风格和趣味。

四 结论

上海的都市文化是最令人难以置信、最具包容性的。然而，政府继续在相关领域加大投资，如提供优质服务的人力资源管理、定期的游客出境调查等后续反馈调查、旅游营销数字化以及体育、文化和娱乐产业。同样，采取措施明确区分和管理文化游客与其他类别的游客也很重要，如商务游客、休闲游客等。通过这些持续的努力，上海将吸引比现在更多的境外游客，甚至国内游客。

Deciphering the Economic Synergy between Tourism and Culture: A Case study of Shanghai

Muhammad Nauman Malik/Pakistan

Economics Department of University of Sargodha, Pakistan/Lecturer; University of Western Australia/ PhD. student

I. Background

The significance of Shanghai, being one of the leading cities of the China and as a municipality under the direct administration of Central Government, can never be ignored. It is now steering the global businesses and trade ventures including the tourism market. Cultural tourism in its initial phase is being driven by the increased tourism and later, cultural tourism itself becomes wide spread market (Richards, 2007). It seems as Shanghai is moving on this pathway as its status as a center of global economic activities would be a boon for cultural tourism development.

Cultural tourism has been recognized as an industry based upon the following types or dimensions; (1) Tangible [monuments, historic sites etc.], (2) Intangible [cultural festivals, gastronomy, traditional music, oral traditions, Handicrafts etc.], (3) Contemporary & Creative industry [film, performing arts, fashion, design, media etc.] products, and (4) Others [sports, education, shopping, health etc].

Competitiveness of these products is premised over the permeation of culture, creativity and service in them. Globally, the synergies of culture and tourism has been endorsed and Cultural Tourism is now said to be almost 40% of the global tourism market. At the same time, there has been growth in cultural tourism for the last five (years and this trend would continue to be so (UNWTO, 2018). The Chinese Central Government under the leadership of President Xi Jinping has merged the Ministry of Culture and China National Tourism Administration into the Ministry of Culture and Tourism of the People's Republic of China' on 19th March 2018. It is an important step for China and particularly for Shanghai, being under direct control of central government. Moreover, it shows the institutional direction and vision of the Chinese government to get maximum possible outcome from this potential sector. The recent Sino-US Trade tensions is a great threat to Shanghai which is the biggest container handler in the world. Investors might be cautious in the wake of such anti-globalization acts. Moreover, they might become more parsimonious as Shanghai's government is becoming strict for the implementation of environmental standards. While coping with such issues, it is significant to pursue other venues (diversification) for growth and development like technological innovation and cultural tourism market along with shipping, trading, finance and capital market.

Shanghai is aiming to enhance its status as an international center for business, trade, shipping, finance and technological innovation while following the environmental standards of sustainable development (SBF, 2018). It is very important how cultural tourism is being addressed and conceived by the Shanghai, especially when its own modernized shanghai culture (city culture or urban culture) is thriving. Moreover, how economic linkage has knitted together culture and tourism in Shanghai along with what new initiatives are being implemented or about to be in near future. This background became the real impetus of this study.

The following research will be around 3 aspects:

1.How cultural tourism is being conceived by Shanghai and What kind of support is needed or in practice for the promotion of cultural tourism of Shanghai?

2.Identification of the economic synergy between culture and tourism in shanghai (Cultural Tourism).

3.What are the land mark achievements/initiatives which are making or would make Shanghai an international attraction for cultural tourism?

II. Data and Methodology

The Framework in figure 1 shows the economic synergy which is working for culture and tourism or collectively we can say cultural tourism. The tourists include both domestic and inbound (tourists coming from outside of China) tourists. The culture includes all of its four types for Shanghai including Tangible, Intangible, Contemporary and Others.

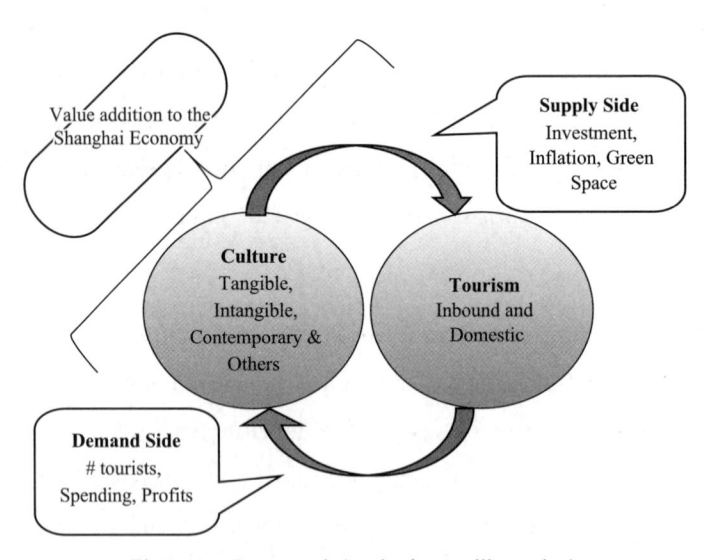

Figure 1   Framework (Author's own illustration)

The supply side would show how the government's provision is actually attracting the cultural tourists to visit Shanghai. Investment would be taken for the areas of Culture, Sports and Entertainment.

Cultural investment would be used for the proxy of tangible and intangible product development. Entertainment investment is being used here to represent the Contemporary type of cultural tourism products, and Sports investment would be used to represent Others Category.

Moreover, the situation of inflation would give us the impression of affordability power of community. As much the living cost would be less it will not only make community welcoming for tourists but also attract tourists. Green Space has been added as a factor in the context of environmental sensitivity in the context of sustainable tourism.

On the demand side, we would see how much cultural tourists are taking interest. The study would see what number of cultural tourists are coming to Shanghai, what are their spending volumes and how tour agencies are making profitability and getting revenues from this industry. All these variables would be used as proxy for the demand tendencies of cultural tourists who are coming to Shanghai.

This study has been based upon qualitative approach in its methodology having purposive sampling (non-probability sampling) using the opportunity under Visiting Program for Young Sinologists – Shanghai 2019 (VPYS-2019). Triple-Helix concept has been seen as a way to understand the working of modern knowledge economies based upon innovation generation. This helix includes Government, Academia/ University and Industry which have mutual and common linkages to interact (Leydesdorff, 2012). In this context, this study has parsimoniously endeavored to reach the Academics and the Officials (who used to work for Shanghai government in various projects).

As per given schedule in VPYS 2019, delivered lectures and field visits would be the source of information along with Key-Informant Interviews (KIIs). KIIs have been used to analyze objective 1 of this study. Secondary data, available in the Shanghai's Statistical Yearbook 2018 (SSY, 2018) and Shanghai's Basic Facts 2018 (SBF, 2018), has been used to study objective 2 whereas delivered lectures and field visits have been used to understand objective 3 of the study.

III. Research Findings

1. Concept of Cultural Tourism for Shanghai

Shanghai is an international city and known to be a miraculous city of China having its own legacy and future vision of growth and development. Shanghai cultural tourism is unique in the sense that it encompasses all dimensions of cultural tourism definition which had been put forward by UNWTO (2018). It comprises of 'Tangible', 'Intangible', 'Contemporary' and 'Other' types (*we have already defined them in Introduction*). It happens to be due to the advance modernization and urbanization of Shanghai which resulted in its own Shanghaies Urban Culture. As far as the significance of these dimensions are concerned, respondents gave importance to all types of cultural tourism for Shanghai.

> As one of the respondents said, "It is actually the joint impact of all these types of cultural tourism that Shanghai's self-evolved city culture is open, outward, welcoming and assimilating for others whether they come from other provinces of China or from abroad".

> However, one response differed as, " I think it may vary from person to person. For example, aged tourist may get more interest in tangible heritage and young tourist may get more fascinated by contemporary and other kinds of cultural tourism which includes fashion, media, shopping, digitization etc."

It shows us that it is important to study the behavior of tourist so that we get an idea about what actually the demand of cultural tourists based upon their characteristics. As per this view, appropriate policy will get shape once we determine the preferences of the inbound tourists and domestic tourists to Shanghai. It is perceived that cultural tourism is around 30% to 50% of the total tourism market of Shanghai according to the views of the respondents in KIIs.

Over the years inbound cultural tourists have increased in shanghai and it is perceived to be around 60% to 70% of the total tourism market of Shanghai, considering the broader definition of cultural tourism we discussed earlier.

Moreover, the reasons behind the increase are noted to be the government encouragement as one respondent opined, "government's direction and interests matters a lot in such matters". At the same time, popularity of Shanghai as the best place where tourists can find much at one place is another factor behind the growing tourism industry.

Domestic cultural tourists, perceived to be around 30% to 40% of total cultural tourists, take much interest in the intangible, contemporary and other categories' products of tourism. It doesn't mean they ignore tangible ones altogether, but it happens that domestic tourists relatively get more attracted and fascinated from the Shanghai's urban culture with Chinese characteristics (Intangible, contemporary and other types of cultural tourism). It has also been increased in the couple of years as per the view of respondents due to the increasing multidimensionality of Shanghai's cultural tourism. Hence, as per the opinion of respondents, nearly 80% to 90% of the tourists either motivated by culture or they participate in cultural activities. Culture has a very important place in the tourism policy of the Shanghai's government. Moreover, they also pay attention that their marketing and promotional plans must do reflect all different dimensions of Shanghai's culture for which it is now famous not only in Asia but across whole world.

There are different types of support which have been acknowledged upon which working is either going on or in future more work would be done for the promotion of cultural tourism industry of Shanghai. It includes Legislation, Product development, Funding, Capacity Building and Training, Marketing, International Collaboration, and Networking and Cooperation. They have also been internationally acknowledged ways to support the cultural tourism (UNWTO, 2018). We got numerous distinctive responses for each type of support.

> One of the respondents commented, "In terms of legislation, one big initiative has been the merger or the integration of Ministry of Culture and China National Tourism Administration into the 'Ministry of Culture

and Tourism of the People's Republic of China'. Moreover, among the 15 working-plans for the future of Shanghai one exclusively includes the tourism sector whereas Entertainment, Sports, culture and shopping would also be worked upon".

In the backdrop of traditional economic sectors of Shanghai like shipping, trade and finance, such legislative and future planning initiatives shows the interest of the government towards the cultural tourism industry. One notable initiative in the marketing of tourism is its "Digitization".

One of the respondents said, "Digitization is surely the future of travel market in 21st century." Being acquainted of this fact, we are about to launch such virtual reality or digital applications which would even be accessible on smart mobile phone technology.

These applications would virtually display museums and their inner products. Some would give a 3D view of Shanghai with information of different sites where tourists could find cultural attractions.

In the context of capacity building and training,

>One response was, "capacity building and training of tour operators and tour guides is much needed as they have lesser information about the cultural dimensions and heritage of Shanghai".

It shows that urgent attention of the government is required to improve the human service quality for the promotion of cultural tourism in Shanghai.

While endorsing the significance of International Collaboration,

>one responded, "It is no doubt necessary to learn from international precedents. One such example is of Egypt from which our tourism sector can learn a lot".

>Another respondent mentioned, "China International Import Expo like

events shows our determination for international collaboration to welcome them not only for trade but also to explore us in every aspect including cultural tourism".

International collaboration in various projects whether in physical infrastructure or in-service delivery would help Shanghai for the entrenchment of international standards for inbound tourists. It would increase the facilitation of foreign inbound tourists and streamline prospective inbound tourists' visits.

As far as networking and cooperation is concerned, one distinguished response was, "In future, Yangtze Delta Region (Economic Urban Belt) would be an integrated region comprised of Shanghai and neighboring three provinces. In this region, future development would be integrated in all sectors including tourism under the leadership of Shanghai and they would cooperate and coordinate with one another".

2. Economic Synergy

Shanghai is rapidly adapting itself to become the favorite destination for cultural tourists while sustaining its top position as a hub of global financial, business and trade activities. The ratio of value-addition of tourism to GDP was 6.2% in 2017. Moreover, there has been a consistent rise in the absolute value addition of tourism industry for Shanghai economy since 2005 (Fig 2). The tourism industry in Shanghai is comprised of different sectors like Hotels, Travel Agencies, Tourism Commerce, Urban Traffic, Gardening, Catering, Travel Transportation, and Post and Telecommunication. It shows tourism industry has many forward and backward linkages in the Shanghai economy.

2.1. Demand Side

During the period of 2010-17, foreign exchange earnings from international tourism has grown at the rate of nearly 6%. In 2017, the foreign earnings touched the level of USD 6.8 billion (Fig 3). A phenomenal growth of 2.8% in foreign exchange occur between 2016 and 2017 as it was much more than what was achieved during the preceding six years with annual growth of 1.95% (2010-16). This indicator can be taken as a proxy for the spending of inbound international tourists coming to Shanghai.

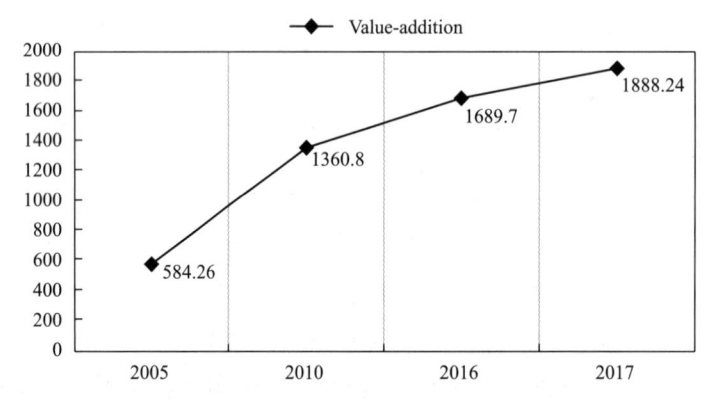

Figure 2   Value-Addition of Tourism Industry in Shanghai Economy (100 Million Yuan)

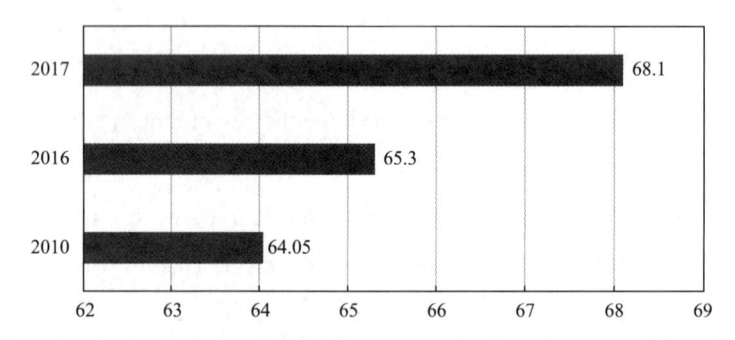

Figure 3   Foreign Exchange Earnings from International Tourism (100 million USD)

There has been an annual increase of 12 % in overseas tourists received by the tour agencies from 2015 to 2017 whereas customs records shows us that overseas tourist have been growing at an annual rate of 2.6% since 2010 (Fig 4).

The average occupancy rate of hotels in Shanghai is impressively growing for the past couple of years and it reached at 69% in 2017. Moreover, just within the time period of two years (2015-17) the profitability of tour agencies impressively grows from CNY 31 million to CNY 817 million yuan. At the same time, the operational revenues increased from CNY 82.7 billion to 139.6 billon (SSY, 2018).

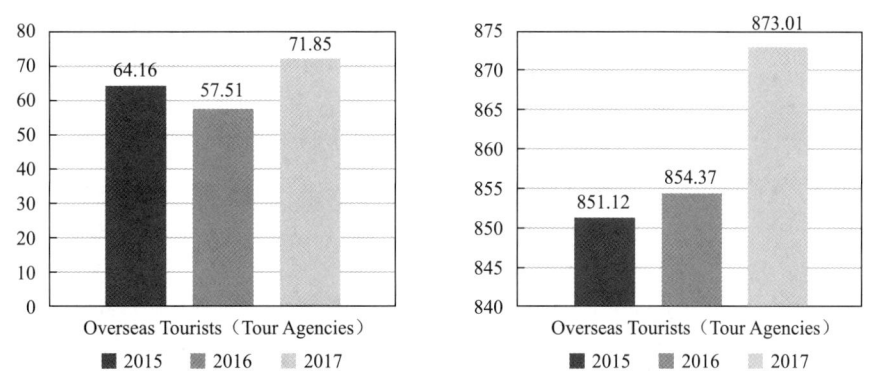

Figure 4 Overseas Tourist Arrival (10,000 persons times)

As far as the internationalization of inbound tourism market in Shanghai is concerned (Fig 5), Asia is the biggest partner with 37% of the total international tourist arrival excluding Macao, Taiwan and Hong Kong Chinese regions. The share of Asia would further get bigger with the inclusion of tourists from these Chinese regions. Subsequently, North America tourists are 32% of the total international tourists in Shanghai followed by Europe and Oceania having 24.4% and 6.6% market shares, respectively.

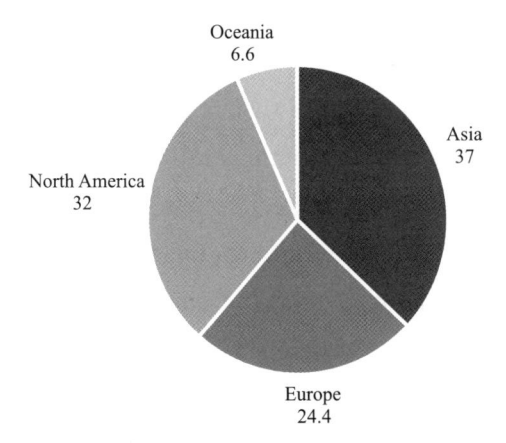

Figure 5 Internationalization of Inbound Tourism Market in 2017 (%)

The market of Domestic tourists is also flourishing (Fig 6). The increase is not only in terms of number of tourists but also in per capita expenditure which they spend on average per person in different activities in Shanghai. These domestic tourists are both local as well as come from other provinces of China. The rise in the number of tourists and there spending habits show us that they also constitute a significant part of the Shanghai tourism market.

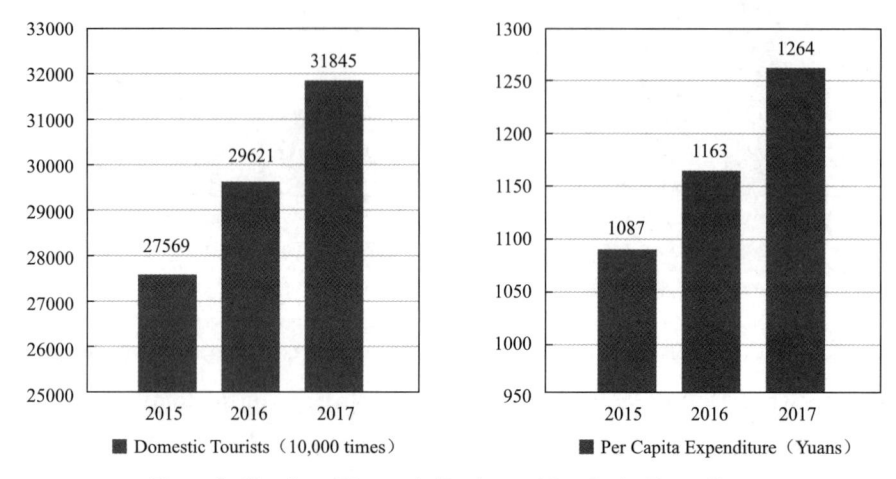

Figure 6　Number of Domestic Tourists and Per Capita Expenditure

The above analysis can show us that demand side of Cultural tourism is strong enough and trend shows us that it will continue to be so in future. It reflects the cultural impact of Shanghai upon domestic and inbound tourists.

2.2. Supply Side

In order to analyze the supply side situation, the study uses the information of Shanghai government's statistics about its local investment in fixed assets given in different sectors. Among the different sectors' categorization, the category of 'Culture, Sports and Entertainment' appears to be parsimoniously and cautiously much aligned with the broader definition of Cultural Tourism dimensions which we have already discussed (Fig 7). 'Culture' related investment is related with the types of tangible and intangible cultural tourism types. 'Entertainment' related investment represents the Contemporary type of cultural tourism whereas 'sports' related investment can be proxied for the other category of cultural tourism.

The purpose of using this type of investment is to analyze whether specific investments have been made that actually increased the product development for cultural tourists. Later, the yearly statistics of investment can be compared with the

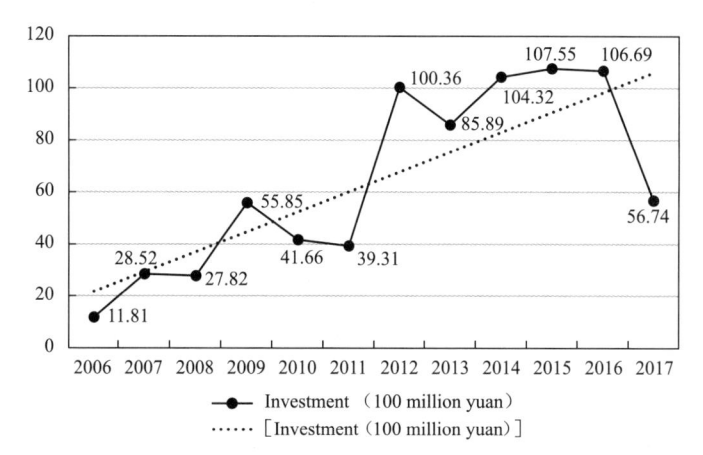

Figure 7 Investment in Local Fixed Assets under the category of "Culture, Sports and Entertainment"

arrival of visitors both from abroad (Inbound) as well as from local areas (domestic). Figure 7 shows that there has been upward trend for the investment category for which we are concerned about and it shows the interest of Shanghai government for the need of such investment. However, in 2017 there has been a sharp decline in investment which might cause an unsuitable impact on the cultural tourism in the year (s) to come whose data is not available yet.

In line with the increase in investment for the product development of cultural tourism, we have an upward trend in visitor's data having inbound visitors by Customs. The trend line having inbound visitors by tour agencies has a stable and non-negative tendency (Fig 8).

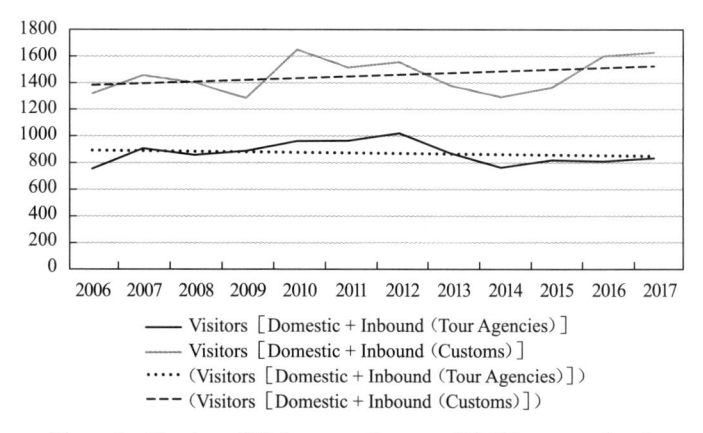

Figure 8 Number of Visitors over the years (10,000 persons times)

The annual inflation rate remains almost stable since 2012 to 2015. There has been a little increase of inflation in 2016 of 0.8% percentage point from the previous year followed by 1.7% inflation rate in 2017 (Fig 9). Even the linear forecast has almost a negative linear trend for future. A less expensive living cost would be another provision from the government so that tourists could have more convenient living in Shanghai. At the same time, the local community would have more better living standard by having more purchasing affordability.

Urban green space has always been a supportive tool to enhance the green image of any place and have many attached environmental benefits with it. There has been a consistent increase in the area of urban green space in Shanghai so that tourists could enjoy a cleaner environment (Fig 10).

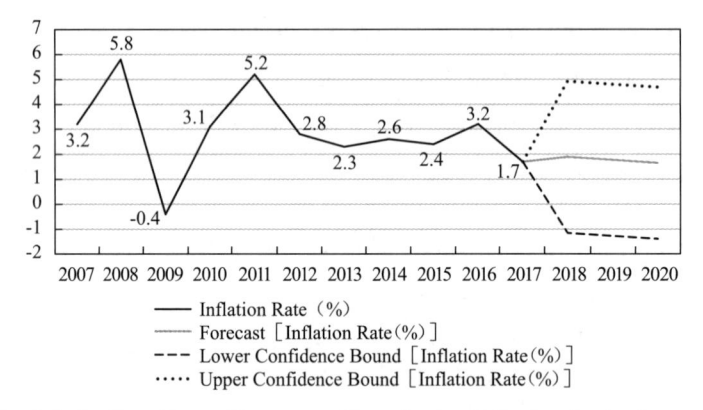

Figure 9　Inflation Rate (Annual Percentage Change) using CPI values having base year 1978

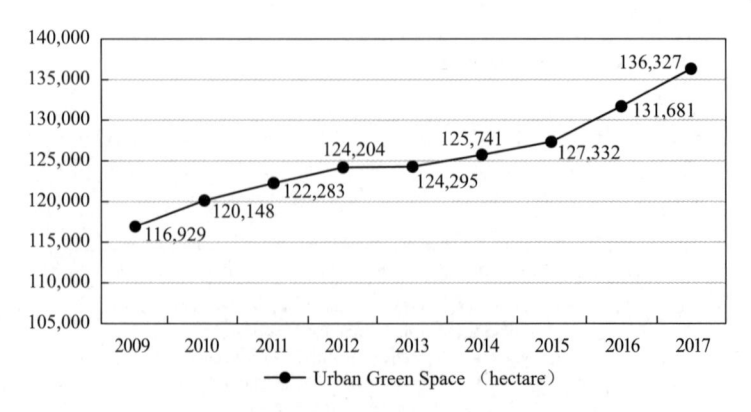

Figure 10　Urban Green Space

At the same time, legislative measures have been taken in which the factories have to shut down that failed to meet the environmental protection regulations. One recent legislation which will take effect from July 1st, 2019 is the Shanghai Life Trash Management Regulation meant to ban all disposal cleaning appliances like toothbrushes, razors, combs etc. in hotels.

3. Initiatives

There are many landmark initiatives which are on-going in Shanghai that would truly make the city the most desirable one. Shanghai has entered in the stage of post-industrialization in economic development where the city's economy is primarily being run by its services sector which is almost 69% of the total GDP of Shanghai in 2017 (SSY, 2018). The special feature of Shanghai's urban culture is its assimilation and acceptance for new ideas and initiatives. It actually based upon the factors of independence in development, Pragmaticism, Self-improvement, Inclination towards Innovation, Rule of Law and Patriotism (Yuezhi, 2019). Moreover, the future objective is to pursue high quality growth and development which requires the focus on "Technological Innovation". This would be the objective of Shanghai for future along with finance, capital, trade and shipping areas of economic growth (Z. Gang, personal communication, June 25, 2019).

Setting new standards and diversity of cultural tourism, Shanghai has developed its island with the name of "Chongming". The island has a status of a district under Shanghai municipality. Island has been designated to develop for the agro-ecological farms where organic farming is being promoted to ensure the protection of environment. Shanghai is again spearheading China in which countryside or rural areas would be promoted for green tourism where ecological biodiversity and rural culture would be preserved. Shipping and marine industry would be established in Chongming along with numerous opportunities for cultural tourists to watch and experience rural farms, preservation of ecological biodiversity, scenic spots and clean environment (W. Lu, personal communication, June 25, 2019).

There are many museums in Shanghai where both the ancient history of China and evolution of the Communist Party of China are well enshrined for tourists to observe. They demonstrate the glory of China's ancient and modern history. Many traditional cultural and community cultural centers exist in Shanghai to reveal the historical and cultural artifacts of Chinese civilization. These handicrafts and artifacts actually give a breath-taking demonstration to tourists about the diversity and depth of Chinese culture. Most importantly, they enlighten about the Confucius ideology and offer different cultural activities in which tourists can participate. Shanghai, being a cosmopolitan community, is renowned in whole world. Community centers of Shanghai offer many opportunities to its international residents and tourists to learn Chinese culture and old civilization e.g. calligraphy, traditional Chinese dance etc. (X. Ke, personal communication, June 18, 2019).

In order to increase networking and coordination, it has been planned that over the next couple of years Yantze Delta Region (Yantze Urban Belt) would be established among Shanghai and three of its neighboring provinces. This initiative has been envisaged for more coordination and to have a common learning from individual experiences for the promotion of different sectors of economy like tourism or cultural tourism, sustainable development etc. (W. Lu, personal communication, June 25, 2019).

Many brands of entertainment and creative industry exists and opening up with the passage of each day in Shanghai like brand attached with Fashion, Shopping, Film Festivals, gastronomy, universities, media etc. In order to speed up these activities, it has been decided that Shanghai would continue to conduct China International Import Expo and Shanghai International Film Festival like events to become an international cultural tourist attraction. It is for sure that Shanghai has something for each person, having different characteristics and interests.

III. Conclusion

Shanghai's urban culture is truly the most fabulous and assimilating one. However, the government has continued to make more investments in the relevant areas like human resource management for quality services, follow-up feedback surveys e.g. Tourist's Exit surveys on regular basis, digitization of tourism marketing, Sports, Culture and Entertainment industries. All these suggestions would make the necessary hard and soft infrastructure for cultural tourism promotion. It is also important to make measures to explicitly differentiate and measure cultural tourists from other categories of tourists like business tourists, leisure tourists etc. With these consistent efforts Shanghai would attract far more inbound foreign tourists and even domestic tourists than what it is receiving now.

References

Daogen Z. (2019). *How Chinese Economy Develop So Fast?*. [Lecture Notes]. Retrieved from http://sinology.chinaculture.org/html/www/news/newsdetails.html?id=254 on 21-06-2019.

Leydesdorff, L. (2012). The Triple Helix of University-Industry-Government Relations (February 2012). Encyclopedia of Creativity, Innovation, and Entrepreneurship, New York: Springer.

Mengsheng T. and Qiguang A. (2018) Steering to Prosperity – Achievements Review of China's Economic Growth in 40 Years, World Affairs Press, Beijing.

Richards, G. (2007). Cultural Tourism: Global and local perspectives. London: Routledge.

SBF (2018) Shanghai Basic Facts, Information Office of Shanghai Municipality & Shanghai Municipal Statistics Bureau, Zhongxi Book Company, Shanghai.

SSY (2018) Shanghai Statistical Yearbook 2018, Shanghai Municipal Statistics Bureau, Shanghai.

Tang, C. F., & Tan, E. C. (2018) Tourism-Led growth hypothesis: A new global evidence. Cornell Hospitality Quarterly, 59(3), 304-311.

UNWTO (2018) Tourism and Culture Synergies, World Tourism Organization (UNWTO), Madrid, DOI: https://doi.org/10.18111/9789284418978.

WEF (2017) The Travel & Tourism Competitiveness Report 2017-Paving the way for a more sustainable and inclusive future, Insight Report, World Economic Forum.

Yuezhi X. (2019) *Chinese History and Urban Culture*. [Lecture Notes]. Retrieved from http://sinology.chinaculture.org/html/www/news/newsdetails.html?id=254 on 21-06-2019.

Lectures (Personal Communications)

Xiong Yuezhi (2019) Chinese History and Urban Culture, Lecture delivered in Shanghai Academy of Social Sciences, Shanghai on 17-06-2019.

Zhang Daogen (2019) How Chinese Economy Develop So Fast? Lecture delivered in Shanghai Academy of Social Sciences, Shanghai on 18-06-2019.

Xue Ke (2019) Cultural Heritage Protection and Development of Tourism Industry, Lecture delivered in Shanghai Academy of Social Sciences, Shanghai on 18-06-2019.

Wei Lu (2019) Innovation of Service industry and Development of Cultural Tourism Industry, Lecture delivered in Shanghai Academy of Social Sciences, Shanghai on 25-06-2019.

Zeng Gang (2019) Creative Industry and Urban Tourism, Lecture delivered in Shanghai Academy of Social Sciences, Shanghai on 25-06-2019.

"一带一路"倡议下中国与阿拉伯和非洲地区的合作模式研究
——以中埃苏伊士经贸合作开发区为例

伊曼 【埃及】
苏伊士运河大学语言学院中文系　助教

"一带一路"倡议是习近平主席于 2013 年提出的。2013 年 9 月，习近平主席出访哈萨克斯坦，在纳扎尔巴耶夫大学提出共同建设"丝绸之路经济带"；2013 年 10 月，习近平在印度尼西亚提出共同建设"21 世纪海上丝绸之路"。自此，"一带一路"倡议走进世界视野，逐步引起共鸣。

一 "一带一路"倡议提出及其对阿拉伯和非洲地区的影响

"一带一路"倡议积极主动地发展与沿线国家的经济合作伙伴关系，共同打造政治互信、经济融合、文化包容的利益共同体、命运共同体和责任共同体。它体现了中国文化的智慧，通过丝绸之路沿线国家的基础设施项目，将亚洲、非洲和欧洲大陆各国的经济联系起来，创造基于宽容、和平、互相尊重以及互利互惠的世界新秩序。

自习近平主席提出"一带一路"倡议以来，国际舞台对此倡议表示热烈欢迎，通过中国举办的第一届和第二届"一带一路"国际合作高峰论坛，及其分论坛、圆桌会议、多边合作协议签署仪式，可以看到来自各个国家领导、政府首脑、国际组织主席甚至各国老百姓对该倡议的信任和期望。

截至 2019 年 3 月 3 日，同中国签署合作文件的国家和国际组织的总数已经达到 152 个。各方在互联互通的相关领域进行了密切合作，取得了积极的成果。在一些专业领域还建立了多个多边合作机制。这些都表明，"一带一路"倡议顺应了合作共赢的时代潮流。

中国是阿拉伯和非洲国家的友好伙伴，双方有着密切的联系。在"一带一路"倡议提出的 6 年间，中、阿、非三方在各个方面的合作取得巨大的发展。

二 "一带一路"倡议与中埃合作的历史形成过程

埃及是世界最古老的文明古国之一，也是阿拉伯世界和非洲地区的一个大国。埃及被誉为非洲和阿拉伯世界之"心"。中埃友谊源远流长，双方的经贸合作交流有 1000 多年的历史，两国通过"古代丝绸之路"不仅开展阿拉伯香料和中国瓷器的经贸往来，而且在文化、文明和历史等方面相互理解。在新时代，两国人民对彼此的支持越来越坚定。

埃及于 1956 年 5 月与中国建交，是第一个与中国建交的阿拉伯世界和非洲地区的国家，此后其他阿拉伯和非洲国家逐渐与中国建交。在新世纪，两国在各个层面、各个领域的合作获得快速发展。自 2013 年习近平主席提出"一带一路"倡议以来，埃及对此倡议表示完全同意和支持，与中国携手共建"一带一路"，走向发展与繁荣的合作道路。中国大力支持埃及总统塞西提出的"埃及 2030 愿景"，为帮助埃及实现经济改革而在埃及市场投入大量资金并拓展经贸合作。在两国领导的互访和支持下，双方在各个方面合作进展顺利，两国关系也提升到全面战略伙伴关系。笔者以埃及为研究对象，探讨中国跟阿拉伯和非洲国家的合作模式在体现"一带一路"倡议对沿线地区发挥的巨大作用。

整体来看，中国和埃及在政治、经贸、文化、旅游和人文领域展开了卓有成效的合作，特别是在经贸领域成果更加丰硕：

1. 据埃及投资部的统计数据显示，截至 2019 年，在埃及正式注册的中国公司和代办处及分公司共有 1345 家，资本总额为 7.92 亿美元。

2. 中国在埃及外国投资排行榜上名列第 21 名。

3. 中国公司在埃及所从事的行业是多种多样的，其中制造业 702 家、服务业 432 家、建筑建材行业 70 家、信息通讯公司 79 家、农业公司 47 家、旅游公司 6 家。

4. 中国公司和企业共为埃及人提供了 2.74 万个工作岗位。

"一带一路"倡议与"埃及2030愿景"相契合，本文以中埃苏伊士经贸合作开发区为例，体现中国在阿拉伯世界和非洲国家所做出的努力和巨大贡献。

三 "一带一路"倡议下的中埃苏伊士经贸合作开发区模式研究

中埃苏伊士经贸合作开发区是中埃在新世纪经贸合作交流中的典型代表。中国天津泰达投资控股有限公司下属中非泰达投资股份有限公司于2008年负责筹建运营中埃苏伊士经贸合作开发区，已从红海荒漠变为园区绿洲。经过10年时间，中埃经贸开发区已入驻了60多家中国企业，为埃及年轻人提供了3000多个工作机会。其中，中国巨石股份有限公司（简称：中国巨石）埃及分公司专门生产、经营玻璃纤维并将产品出口到世界各个国家。2012年，中国巨石在埃及苏伊士设立全资子公司——巨石埃及玻璃纤维股份有限公司，拉开了中埃在玻璃纤维复合材料领域产能合作的序幕。经过6年时间，中国巨石在埃及建成三条大型池窑拉丝生产线，矿粉原料、包装材料等配套项目紧跟到位，一个现代化生产基地拔地而起。

（一）中埃苏伊士经贸合作开发区基本概况

中国埃及经贸合作开发区的设立是在全球经济一体化发展浪潮中，中埃双方考量各自经济发展态势的战略选择。中埃泰达苏伊士经贸合作开发区位于亚非欧三大洲金三角地带的埃及苏伊士湾西北经济区，紧邻苏伊士运河，距离埃及第三大港口——因苏哈那港仅2公里。

中埃苏伊士经贸合作开发区的故事始于20世纪90年代中后期。1997年，两国签署政府谅解备忘录，确定中国帮助埃及在苏伊士西北地区建设特区。1998年初，中国国务院指定由天津经济技术开发区（TEDA，即泰达）参与合作，带有政府援建性质。从1998年到2008年的第一期建设期，泰达只占合营公司10%的股份，对公司的运营只提供咨询，并没有主导权，自主开发的主动性也不太强，区域没有什么实质性变化。直到2007年，泰达在埃及政府组织的苏伊士经济特区项目公开招标中中标，在新合作运营公司中持股80%，园区才真正通过商业化方式启动。

合作区初始面积为1.34平方公里，目前累计投资约1亿美元，已基本开发完成。2014年9月，中埃双方签订了合作区扩展区项目，扩展区面积6平方公里，分三期开发，开发建设总投资约 2.3 亿美元。根据扩展区建设开发规划，建成后的区域将吸引大约 150 至 180 家企业入驻。2015 年 11 月 30 日，中国天津泰达投资公司与埃方签署《苏伊士经贸合作区扩展区一期土地移交协议》，经贸合作区土地扩大 2 平方公里。2016 年 1 月，习近平主席在访问埃及期间与塞西总统共同为扩展区揭牌。

到 2017 年底，苏伊士合作区起步区共有企业 68 家，其中生产型企业 33 家（含中资成分投资企业 29 家），另有生产、生活配套型企业 35 家。合作区累计吸引协议投资额超过 9 亿美元，现已初步形成了以宏华钻机和国际钻井材料制造公司为龙头的石油装备产业园区、以西电 -EGEMAC 高压设备公司为龙头的高低压电器产业园区、以中纺机无纺布为龙头的纺织服装产业园区、以巨石玻璃纤维公司为龙头的新型建材产业园区和以牧羊仓储公司为龙头的机械制造类产业园区在内的五大产业布局，带动上下游产业入区，快速形成产业集群效应。

巨石埃及公司是最早到中埃苏伊士经贸合作开发区投资的中国企业。2012 年，巨石公司制订了 6 年工作计划，但在不到 6 年的时间内巨石埃及分公司不仅提前完成了这些工作目标，而且还有所突破。

笔者作为 2019 年青年汉学家研修班学员，在浙江工商大学学习期间，经由导师李蓉教授和《浙江日报》秦军主任的联系和组织，对中国巨石公司总部进行实地考察，了解该公司情况、埃及分公司概况及其在埃及将来的计划。

（二）中国巨石股份有限公司在埃及经营现状和未来计划

1. 调研过程。这是笔者第一次去中国经济开发区，也是第一次参观中国公司总部及其工厂。公司的行政事务部总经理陈纪明给我们介绍了巨石公司的历史、发展阶段、工业领域以及埃及分公司的概况。

20 世纪 90 年代玻璃纤维行业开始流行，那时中国玻璃纤维工业刚开始发展。巨石玻璃纤维公司成立于 1993 年，1999 年上市。巨石集团作为国家大型企业和国家火炬计划重点高新技术企业，是中国最大的玻纤生产企业，产能居亚洲第一。公司主要客户分布在能源、交通、石油和电子电力等行业，50% 以上的玻璃纤维及其制品出口美国、日本等国。

去巨石总部进行实地考察之前，笔者并不知道什么是玻璃纤维，玻璃纤维是什么样子、玻璃纤维在我们日常生活中的用途是什么。笔者在巨石总部看到玻璃纤维应用到人们生活的方方面面，如手机、汽车、家电设备、家具、餐具，甚至飞机、大卡车、大船上都有使用。在巨石工厂笔者也参观了各种各样玻璃纤维的制作过程。巨石一天生产的粗纱可绕地球 202 圈，生产的细纱可绕地球 110 圈。目前，玻纤总产能超过 180 万吨，占中国总产能的 40% 和世界总产能的 22%。

2. 巨石模式与埃及制造

（1）公司合作的精准定位和投产合理布局

巨石全球布局营销网络，销售遍布 100 多个国家和地区，埃及分公司算是巨石公司在全非洲和阿拉伯世界唯一的分公司。2011 年巨石公司副总裁曹国荣到埃及调研，在具体推进巨石国际化的几个选点中，选择了泰达苏伊士经贸合作开发区。随后公司对埃及进行多次实地考察和市场咨询，发现埃及地理位置较为核心、市场条件很好、玻璃纤维资源和埃及劳动力很丰富。2012 年最终确立了"埃及巨石要用 7 到 10 年实现 20 万吨产量"的规划，当时计划上两条生产线，尽快实现规模经济。

2012 年 1 月开始土建，2013 年底第一条池窑拉丝生产线试产，2014 年 5 月 18 日正式投产。2016 年 7 月二期投产；2017 年 9 月三期建成投产；2018 年相关配套项目陆续投产。

至此，标志着埃及巨石 20 万吨生产基地提前全部建成，项目总投资 5.8 亿美元，占地 23.4 万平方米，将实现年产值超过 2.2 亿美元。公司一共建设了三条大型池窑拉丝生产线以及矿粉原料、包装材料等配套项目，为当地直接创造 2500 个就业岗位，开启了中埃在玻璃纤维复合材料领域产能合作的序幕。埃及当地生产的玻璃纤维实现了向国外出口。尽管巨石埃及分公司在项目建设初期也遇到了一些问题如缺少电、水和天然气，但在埃及政府和中国驻埃及使馆的支持下克服了这些困难。

（2）公司经营本土化的管理策略和团队文化的建设

目前巨石在埃及分公司的员工总数为 1708 人，埃方人员 1659 人，中方 49 人，本土化率达到 97% 以上。高管有 7 人，埃方已经有 2 人，中层以上 49 人，埃方 32 人。总裁张毓强说："本土化最终是人才本土化，如果都是我们的人在管，那不等于把我们的工厂和人搬到国外吗？这不是国际化，也做不到。"

关于埃及分公司的发展计划，巨石埃及分公司总经理助理王剑飞先生指出，埃及经济情况最近两三年不断发展，公司根据埃及当地实际情况，找好的机会在新的领域进行投资，紧跟埃及的改革步伐而发展，比如公司有计划在矿产开发和经营领域投资。王剑飞也说道，公司在埃及的工作不限于产业方面，经常在埃及很多城市举办一些活动，比如每年斋月期间，公司会进行斋饭晚会、捐送斋礼包和斋饭等活动，这样有利于在埃及当地树立良好的印象，帮公司跟埃及当地社会建立和谐关系。

埃及分公司副经理艾哈迈德·苏莱曼是一位埃及青年，他的专业是机械工程学。他从2012年开始在公司工作，先来中国学习了8个月。他表示公司始终坚持尊重社会文化的观念，通过员工间文化理解加强团队建设，比如每年公司在斋月和开斋节组织集体开斋饭，向员工表示祝贺并增强他们的归属感；公司的每个工作室都有做礼拜的地方，以便埃及员工做礼拜。公司每年会在当地组织活动，不仅树立公司在当地的良好形象，还肩负起社会责任。公司通过举办各种各样的比赛并组织所有员工参加，以促进中埃员工间的了解。

艾哈迈德还说，在人才发展的框架内，巨石公司致力于给埃及员工提供旨在提高员工各个方面的工作技能的学习平台。每年公司都会组织员工到中国总部进行考察、学习和培训，让他们通过学习将先进的技术和管理思想带到埃及。除此之外，还在埃及开展多种研修班，培养本地人才。巨石公司是中国在埃及投资的最大工业企业。对艾哈迈德来说，公司在埃及会有很灿烂的未来，公司下一步会对产品结构进行调整，使其更了解市场需求，在生产组织和质量方面变得更加精准、有效、高质，从而促进公司更好地成长和发展。同时，公司将继续加强本地沟通，以及专注于发展技术和行政管理人才，将埃及生产基地建设为完全的本地管理的企业，在"一带一路"战略愿景框架内为加强两国之间的合作做出贡献。

在谈到自己的未来和梦想，艾哈迈德表示他一直追求发展，并加倍努力，以达到公司期望并满足工作要求。随着公司发展迅速，需要更加努力并提高竞争力，以便在公司的帮助下取得进步。他还表示相信公司的工作理念，即"学习、发展、创新和责任"，坚持实现这些理念是他的工作目标。

四 未来展望：中埃合作的新期待

综上所述，笔者希望通过本文将中埃在"一带一路"倡议下的发展情况作为阶段性的研究展示，让大家了解中埃合作交流的丰硕成果和中埃两国之间的密切关系与深厚友谊。笔者想提及一个令人感动的细节：在参观中国巨石公司总部历史馆时，笔者发现大部分照片和介绍大牌子都能看到"埃及"这两个字、看到埃及员工照片上的笑脸、埃及和中国员工的合影。笔者想向中国公司说"谢谢"，因为这是埃及经过苦难动荡时期后能够再次在出口产品上看到"埃及制造"。笔者相信，中埃两大文明之国一起携手，必将造福世界人民。

Research on the Cooperation Mode between China and Arab and African Regions under the Belt and Road Initiative

—— China-Egypt Suez Economic and Trade Cooperation Development Zone as an example

Eman Magdy Mohamed Mahmoud / Egypt

Department of Chinese Language and Literature, School of Languages, Suez Canal University / Teaching Assistant

The Belt and Road Initiative is an important initiative put forward by Chinese President Xi Jinping in 2013. In September 2013, President Xi Jinping visited Nazarbayev University in Kazakhstan and proposed to jointly build the Silk Road Economic Belt. In October 2013, Xi Jinping proposed to jointly build the 21st-Century Maritime Silk Road in Indonesia. Since then, the Belt and Road Initiative has entered the world vision and has gradually aroused global resonance.

I. The Belt and Road Initiative and its influence on Arab and African regions

The Belt and Road Initiative aims to actively develop economic cooperation partnerships with countries along the route named after the historical symbolic "Silk Road", and jointly build a community of common interests, common destiny and common responsibility with mutual political trust, economic integration and cultural tolerance. It is a good idea which reflects and embodies the wisdom of Chinese culture in the 21st century. Through the infrastructure projects of countries along the ancient Silk Road, it connects the economies of Asia, Africa and European countries, aiming at creating a new world order based on tolerance, peace, mutual respect and mutual benefit.

I think that the Belt and Road Initiative is a new concept of globalization that China provides to the world on the basis of co-construction, business cooperation, sharing, mutual trust and mutual benefit, which is in stark contrast with the current culture of violence and terrorism. Since President Xi Jinping put forward the Belt and Road Initiative, the international arena has warmly welcomed it. Through the first and second Belt and Road Forum for International Cooperation held by China, and their sub-forums, round-table conferences and signing ceremonies of multilateral cooperation agreements, we can see the trust and expectation of leaders, heads of government, presidents of international organizations and even the masses of most countries for the initiative.

As of March 3, 2019, the total number of countries and international organizations that have signed cooperation documents with China has reached 152. All parties have cooperated closely in the related fields of interconnection, and they have achieved positive results. A number of multilateral cooperation mechanisms have also been established in some professional fields. All these indicate that the Belt and Road Initiative conforms to the trend of win-win cooperation.

China is a friendly partner of Arab and African countries, and they have close ties. In the six years since the Belt and Road Initiative was put forward, the cooperation in various fields among China, countries in the Arab world and countries in Africa has made great progress.

II. The Belt and Road Initiative and the historical process of the formation of China-Egypt cooperation

Egypt is one of the oldest civilizations in the world, and a big country in the Arab, African and Islamic world. Egypt is known as the "heart" of Africa and the Arab world. The traditional friendship between China and Egypt has a long history, and the economic and trade cooperation and exchanges between the two sides can be traced back to 1,000 years ago. Through the Ancient Silk Road and camel caravan, the two countries not only carried out economic and trade exchanges between Arab spices and Chinese porcelain, but they also understood each other in terms of culture, civilization and history. In the new era, peoples of the two countries are strengthening the support for each other.

Egypt began to establish diplomatic relations with China in May 1956, and was the first Arab and African country to do so. Since then, other Arab and African countries have gradually established diplomatic relations with China. In the new century, the cooperation between the two countries at all levels and in all fields has been developing rapidly. Since President Xi Jinping put forward the Belt and Road Initiative in 2013, Egypt has fully agreed with and supported this initiative, and has joined hands with China in developing the Belt and Road Initiative and in moving towards the cooperative road full of development and prosperity with China. China strongly supports Egypt's 2030 Vision put forward by Egyptian President Sisi, and is investing a lot in the Egyptian market, and has expanded economic and trade cooperation to help Egypt achieve economic reform. With the exchange visits of and support from leaders of the two countries, the two sides have developed rapidly in all aspects, and the relationship between the two countries has been upgraded to a comprehensive strategic partnership. Therefore, I take Egypt as the object of my research in order to discuss how the cooperation mode between China and countries in the Arab world and in Africa, especially regarding the Belt and Road Initiative, plays a great role in the areas along the Belt and Road.

On the whole, China and Egypt have carried out fruitful cooperation in the fields of politics, economy, trade, culture, tourism and humanities, especially in the fields of economy and trade. Let's use a set of figures to illustrate the general situation of China-Egypt economic and trade relations:

1. According to the statistics of the Egyptian Ministry of Investment, as of 2019, there were 1,345 Chinese companies, representative offices and branches officially registered in Egypt, with a total capital of 792 million US dollars.

2. China ranks 21st in the list of foreign investment in Egypt.

3. Chinese companies are engaged in various industries in Egypt, including 702 manufacturing companies, 432 service companies, 70 building materials companies, 79 information and communication companies, 47 agricultural companies and 6 tourism companies.

4. Chinese companies and enterprises have provided 27,400 jobs for Egyptians.

Most of these figures are from the China-Egypt Suez Economic and Trade Cooperation Development Zone. China's Belt and Road Initiative is in line with Egypt's Vision 2030, so this paper takes the China-Egypt Suez Economic and Trade Cooperation Development Zone as a model, which reflects China's efforts and great contributions in the Arab world and in African countries.

III. Research on the mode of the China-Egypt Suez Economic and Trade Cooperation Development Zone under the Belt and Road Initiative

The China-Egypt Suez Economic and Trade Cooperation Development Zone is a typical case of China-Egypt economic and trade cooperation and exchange in the new century. China-Africa TEDA Investment Co., Ltd., a subsidiary of China TEDA Investment Holding Co., Ltd., was responsible for the establishment and operation of the China-Egypt Suez Economic and Trade Cooperation Zone in 2008, which changed the Red Sea desert into an industrial park oasis. After 10 years, more than 60 Chinese enterprises have established their businesses in the China-Egypt Suez Economic and Trade Development Zone, providing more than 3,000 job opportunities for young Egyptians. Among them, there is the China Jushi Co., Ltd. Egypt Branch which specializes in glass fiber production in Egypt and exports the glass fiber products produced to countries all over the world. In 2012, the establishment of Jushi Egypt Glass Fiber Co., Ltd., a wholly-owned subsidiary of China Jushi in Suez, Egypt, started the cooperation between China and Egypt in the field of capacity for glass fiber composites. After six years, China Jushi has built three large-scale tank-furnace fiber elongation production lines in Egypt, with supporting projects covering mineral powder raw materials and packaging materials. A modern production base sprung up here.

(I) The General situation of the China-Egypt Suez Economic and Trade Cooperation Development Zone

The establishment of the China-Egypt Suez Economic and Trade Cooperation Development Zone is a strategic choice for China and Egypt in considering their respective trends in economic development within the tide of global economic integration. The China-Egypt TEDA Suez Economic and Trade Cooperation Development Zone is located in the northwest economic zone of Egypt's Suez Bay in the golden triangle of Asia, Africa and Europe, close to the Suez Canal, and only 2km away from Sokhna, the third largest port in Egypt.

The story of the China-Egypt Suez Economic and Trade Cooperation Development Zone began in the middle and late 1990s. In 1997, the two countries signed a memorandum of understanding between their governments, which determined that China would help Egypt build a special zone in the northwestern area of Suez. At the beginning of 1998, the State Council of China appointed Tianjin Economic-Technological Development Area (TEDA) to participate in the cooperation, with government aid. From 1998 to 2008, there was the first phase of construction. TEDA only accounted for 10% of the shares of the joint venture company responsible for the Development Zone, and TEDA only provided consulting service, but did not dominate it; in addition, the joint venture had little initiative to actively develop the zone, so no substantial development could be seen in the Zone. In 2007, TEDA won the bid in the national open tender of the Suez special economic zone organized by the Egyptian government, and held 80% of the shares in the new cooperative company responsible for the development of the zone. Only then did the development of the industrial park really start in a commercial way.

The starting area of the cooperation zone covers an area of 1.34 square kilometers, with an accumulated investment of about 100 million US dollars, the development of which has been basically completed. In September 2014, China and Egypt signed the cooperation zone expansion project, which covers an area of 6 square kilometers and is to be developed in three phases, with a total investment of about 230 million US dollars. According to the construction and development plan of the expansion area, the completed area will attract about 150 to 180 enterprises to establish their business there. On November 30th, 2015, China TEDA Investment Company signed the *Agreement on the Transfer of the First Phase of the Expansion Area of the Suez Economic and Trade Cooperation Zone* with Egypt, and accepted the land of the first phase with an area of 2 square kilometers from Egypt. During President Xi Jinping's visit to Egypt in January 2016, he and President Sisi jointly attended the launching ceremony of the expansion area.

By the end of 2017, there were 68 enterprises in the starting area of the Suez Cooperation Zone, of which 33 were production-oriented enterprises (including 29 Chinese-funded enterprises) and 35 enterprises were of the supporting type for production and living. The cooperation zone has attracted more than 900 million U.S. dollars of agreed investment. At present, it has initially formed five industrial parks, including the oil equipment industrial park led by Honghua Group and the International Driller Manufacturing Company, the high-voltage and low-voltage electrical appliance industrial park led by the China XD-EGEMAC High-Voltage Equipment Company, the textile and garment industrial park led by the China Textile Machinery Nonwoven Fabric Company, the new building materials industrial park led by the Jushi Glass Fiber Company and the machinery manufacturing industrial park led by Muyang Warehousing Engineering Co., Ltd.

They have driven the businesses of upstream and downstream industries into the zone, thus rapidly forming the effect of an industrial cluster.

Jushi Egypt Company was the first Chinese enterprise to invest in the China-Egypt Suez Economic and Trade Development Zone. In 2012, the company made a work plan for the next six years. While in less than six years, the Jushi Egypt Branch overfulfilled the work goals of the plan.

I am a student of the 2019 Group of the Visiting Program for Young Sinologists, studying at Zhejiang Gongshang University. By virtue of the contact and organization of the tutor Professor Li Rong and the director Qin Jun of Zhejiang Daily, I made a field visit to the headquarters of the China Jushi Company, and personally learned about the general situation of the company, its Egypt branch and its future plan in Egypt. The following is a report on the achievements of my survey.

(II) Case study: The operating Status of the China Jushi Co., Ltd. in Egypt and its future plan of Realizing the Dream (Made in Egypt)

1. Survey process

During the one hour from Hangzhou to the Tongxiang Economic Development Zone, I was very excited. This was the first time for me to visit China's economic development zone, and it was also the first time to visit the company headquarters and its manufacturing factory in China. Upon arrival at the company headquarters, Mr. Chen Jiming, General Manager of the Administration Department of China Jushi Co., Ltd. and Mr. Zhao Jun, Senior Manager of the Development Strategy Department warmly received us. Manager Chen first introduced the history, developmental stage and the industrial field of China Jushi and the general situation of its branch in Egypt. Jushi is the model embodiment of "China's industrial power" in my view.

In the 1990s, the knowledge of the glass fiber industry became popular, when China's glass fiber industry was just beginning. In 1993, the Jushi Glass Fiber Company was established. Under the development concept of "innovation, strength and talent", the company was listed in 1999. After that, Jushi spread its wings to develop extensively. The Jushi Group is a national large-scale first-class enterprise and a key high-tech enterprise in the China Torch Program. It is the largest glass fiber manufacturer in China, and its production capacity ranks first in Asia. The company's main customers come from fields including energy, transportation, petroleum, electronic power etc., and more than 50% of glass fiber and its products are exported to the United States, Japan and other places around the world.

I had not known what fiberglass was before I visited Jushi Headquarters. What is glass fiber like? Where is glass fiber used in our everyday lives? At the headquarters, we were able to see that fiberglass has entered every aspect of people's lives, such as mobile phones, cars, household appliances, furniture, tableware, even airplanes, trucks and ships. When visiting the Jushi Factory, I saw the manufacturing process of various glass fibers. The roving produced by Jushi per day could circle the earth 202 times and its spun yarn could circle the earth 110 times. At present, the total capacity for glass fiber production exceeds 1.8 million tons, accounting for 40% of China's total production capacity and 22% of the world's total production capacity.

2. The Jushi model and Egyptian manufacturing

(1) The company has an accurate orientation towards cooperation and a reasonable production strategy

Jushi has a global marketing network, with sales business in more than 100 countries and regions. Its Egypt Branch is the only branch of Jushi Company in Africa and the Arab world. In an interview with me, Manager Zhao Jun explained that in 2011, Cao Guorong, the vice president and the capable subordinate of president Zhang Yuqiang, went to Egypt to explore the market, and chose TEDA Suez Economic and Trade Cooperation Zone from several specific sites to promote the internationalization of Jushi. Subsequently, the company conducted many field visits and market consultations in Egypt, and it found that Egypt is a geographical core in this region, and has good market conditions, abundant glass fiber resources and a sufficient labor force. In 2012, Jushi made the target plan of "fulfilling 200 thousand tons of glass fiber production in Egypt in 7 to 10 years". At that time, two production lines were planned, which could facilitate the realization of that economic scale. Civil construction began in January 2012, and the first tank-furnace fiber elongation production line was put into trial production at the end of 2013 and officially put into production on May 18th, 2014. The second phase was put into production in July 2016; the third phase was completed and put into operation in September 2017; in 2018, related supporting projects were put into operation one after another, which indicated that the 200,000-ton production base had been completed ahead of schedule. The total amount of investments in the project was 580 million US dollars, covering an area of 234,000 square meters, and the annual output value would exceed 220 million US dollars. The company has built three large-scale tank-furnace fiber elongation production lines, as well as supporting projects covering mineral powder raw materials and packaging materials, which directly created 2,500 local jobs, opening the prelude of China-Egypt capacity cooperation in the field of glass fiber production. The locally-produced glass fiber in Egypt is exported to foreign countries with the mark "Made in Egypt". Manager Zhao Jun pointed out that when starting investment in Egypt, they encountered some problems, such as revolution, power shortage, water and natural gas, but with the support of the Egyptian government and the Chinese embassy in Egypt, these difficulties were overcome.

(2) The strategy for the management of localization and the construction of team culture

At present, the Jushi Egypt Branch has a total of 1,708 employees, including 1,659 local employees and 49 employees from China, with a localization rate of employment of over 97%. There are 7 senior executives, 2 of whom are local Egyptians, and 49 middle and senior officers, 32 of whom are local Egyptians. Zhang Yuqiang said, "The ultimate localization is talent localization. If all responsible officers are employees from China, doesn't that mean moving our plants and staff from China to here? That is not internationalization, nor is it feasible and neither can it be done."

Regarding the development plan of the Egypt Branch, Mr. Wang Jianfei, assistant general manager of Jushi Egypt Branch, pointed out that Egypt's economic situation has been developing continuously in the last two or three years, and the company has found good opportunities to invest in other fields according to the actual situation in Egypt, and we will develop with the new reform of Egypt. For example, the company has plans to invest in mineral exploitation and management. Wang Jianfei also said that the company's work in Egypt is not limited to industry, and the company often holds some social activities in many Egyptian cities. For example, during Ramadan every year, the company will hold iftar parties, donate Ramadan packages and iftar, and so on, so as to foster a good image in Egypt and help the company establish a harmonious relationship with the local Egyptian community.

Ahmed Suleiman, deputy manager of the Jushi Egypt Branch, is a young Egyptian man whose major is mechanical engineering. He started working in the company in 2012 after his 8 months of study in China. He said that the company always adheres to the principle of respecting local social culture and strengthens team harmony by promoting civilization and cultural understanding among employees. For example, the company organizes a collective iftar dinner every year during Ramadan and Lasser Bairam to congratulate employees and enhance their sense of belonging; each studio of the company has a place of worship to facilitate Egyptian employees in their worshipping. The company organizes social activities every year not only to establish a good image of the company in the local area, but also to shoulder social responsibilities. The company organizes various competitions for all employees to participate in order to promote the integration of cultures.

Ahmed also said that within the framework of talent development, Jushi is committed to establishing a learning platform for Egyptian employees to improve their working skills in all aspects. Every year, the company organizes visits for employees to study and train in China headquarters to bring advanced technology and management ideas to Egypt. In addition, a variety of training programs have been held in Egypt to cultivate local talents. Jushi is the largest industrial enterprise from China investing in Egypt, and it has the most advanced technology and the fastest construction ability. In his opinion, the company will have a bright future in Egypt. In the next step, the company should adjust the product structure to make it adapt better to the market demand and become more accurate, effective and high-quality in production organization and quality, so as to promote better growth and development of the company. At the same time, the company will continue to strengthen local communication, focus on developing technical and administrative talents, build the Egyptian production base into a fully locally-managed enterprise, and contribute to strengthening cooperation between the two countries within the framework of the strategy of the Belt and Road Initiative.

Talking about his future and his dream, Ahmed said that he has been pursuing a higher level of development, for which he has spared no effort in meeting the company's expectations and job requirements. With the rapid development of the company, an employee needs to make more efforts and obtain more competitiveness to achieve the best progress with the help of the company. He also expressed his consistent belief in the company's work philosophy, namely "learning, development, innovation and responsibility", and adhering to the philosophy is his work target and challenge.

IV. Prospects: new expectations for China-Egypt cooperation

To sum up, I hope that through this paper, the development of China and Egypt under the Belt and Road Initiative can be shown to be a staged type of research, so that everyone can become familiar with the fruitful results of China-Egypt cooperation and exchange and the close relationship and profound friendship between the two countries. As a conclusion, I would like to mention two touching things: first, when visiting the History Museum of the headquarters of the China Jushi company, I found that most of the captions, introductions and photos have the word "Egypt", the smiling faces of Egyptian employees and the group photos of Egyptian and Chinese employees; second, I wish to say "thank you" to Chinese companies for having the fact that the words "Made in Egypt" can once again be seen in export products after all of Egypt's suffering and turbulence. I believe that China and Egypt, two great civilizations, together will surely bring great benefits to the people of the world.

日本报纸关于"一带一路"报道的考察

川村明美　【日本】
自由职业者、翻译

一　引言

中国国家主席习近平 2013 年提出共建"一带一路"倡议，已经过去好几年。截至 2019 年 12 月，中国同 137 个国家和 30 个国际组织签署共建"一带一路"合作文件，在众多国家展开有关"一带一路"的基础设施建设。

第一届"一带一路"国际合作高峰论坛于 2017 年 5 月在北京举行之际，日本媒体纷纷对"一带一路"倡议进行了报道，使许多日本民众知道了"一带一路"这个名称。可是，有多少日本人了解"一带一路"倡议到底是什么呢？为此，本文试图通过按时间顺序整理的日本报纸关于"一带一路"倡议的报道而对其主要内容进行分析。这次以发行量第一、第二的日本两大全国性报纸为研究对象，即《读卖新闻》和《朝日新闻》，选取的报道是从习近平主席提出"一带一路"倡议的 2013 年 9 月到第二届"一带一路"国际合作高峰论坛举行的 2019 年 4 月底，数量为 1000 多条。

二　"一带一路"倡议提出以及推进建设

习近平主席于 2013 年 9 月在哈萨克斯坦发表重要演讲，提出共同建设"丝绸之路经济带（一带）"；同年 10 月，在印度尼西亚国会演讲时提出共同建设"21世纪海上丝绸之路（一路）"。之后，将"丝绸之路经济带"与"21世纪海上丝绸之路"结合起来，称为"一带一路"。2015年3月，中国国家发展改革委员会、外交部、商务部联合发布了《推动共建丝绸之路经济带和21世纪海上丝绸之路的愿景与行动》文件。

习近平主席提出倡议的一年之后，《读卖新闻》和《朝日新闻》的报道中才出现"一带一路"这个词语，分别是2014年10月18日和12月21日。《读卖新闻》介绍称，习近平主席2013年9月访问斯里兰卡时向拉贾帕克萨总统提出共同建设"21世纪海上丝绸之路"。而《朝日新闻》在报上称，中国国务院总理李克强访问哈萨克斯坦并提出共同开发"丝绸之路经济带"计划。两家报纸都说明"一带一路"是由"丝绸之路经济带"与"21世纪海上丝绸之路"构成的经济圈构想。另外，《朝日新闻》在其报道最后提出"日本今后如何对待中国要提出的地区战略呢"？由此表现可知，这阶段日本与"一带一路"还保持一段距离。

"一带一路"第二次在两报上出现的时间是2015年3月中国全国人民代表大会期间。《朝日新闻》3月6日报道称，李克强提出要加速推进对外投资和贸易的方针，并表示其海外战略的关键就是"一带一路"建设。3月9日报道称，中国国务委员兼外交部部长王毅表示全面推进"一带一路"是今年中国外交的重点。3月28日举行的博鳌亚洲论坛，两家报纸都报道了习近平主席发表的主旨演讲内容，其中介绍"一带一路为整个地区带来利益《朝日新闻》"、"一带一路不是中国一家的独奏，而是沿线国家的合唱《读卖新闻》"等习近平的发言。但同时报道称，国际社会对"一带一路"抱有警惕。

此后，截至2017年2月的约2年时间内，关于"一带一路"的主要报道是日本以外的各国展开"一带一路"建设的消息。具体而言，两家报纸2015年4月21日报道称，习近平主席首次访问巴基斯坦，中巴双方签署了很多涉及中巴经济走廊的经济合作文件，其总投资额约为460亿美元。中巴经济走廊是"一带一路"的旗舰项目。

其他主要报道如下：由于特殊的地理位置，尼泊尔在"一带一路"构想中占有重要的位置。中国近年来在尼泊尔大力推进道路、发电站建设等大型项目（《朝日新闻》2015年5月4日）；习近平同俄罗斯总统普京会谈，两国元首一致同意"一带一路"同欧亚经济联盟对接合作（《读卖新闻》2015年7月9日）；习近平首访沙特、埃及等中东国家，同中东国家元首一致确认将推进"一带一路"合作，并表示将向中东各国提供巨额投融资（《朝日新闻》2016年1月20、23日；《读卖新闻》同年1月20、22、23日）等。从这些报道可以看出，习近平积极访问各国，同国家元首进行会谈，旨在落实推进"一带一路"构想。

另一方面，期间也有许多报道，就是向"一带一路"沿线国家提供资金支持的亚洲基础设施投资银行（AIIB）的消息，例如AIIB签约仪式、开业仪式、年会等。其中有如下报道：日本对于AIIB保持着慎重的态度，认为AIIB不设常驻理事会、融资审查标准缺乏透明性，而且若加入的话，日本将负担大额出资金（《朝日新闻》2016年1月17日）；日本和美国担心亚投行运营的透明性，因此对加入AIIB持观望的立场（《读卖新闻》1月17日）。

三 "一带一路"国际合作高峰论坛以及中日关系改善

2017年5月14日，首届"一带一路"国际合作高峰论坛在北京举行，来自130多个国家的约1500名代表参会，其中包括意大利、俄罗斯等29个国家的元首。习近平在演讲中表示，中国将在未来3年向参与"一带一路"建设的发展中国家和国际组织提供600亿元援助。此间日本主要媒体对"一带一路"倡议进行了广泛地报道。下面看其一系列的报道：

据《读卖新闻》4月25日报道，日本首相安倍晋三已决定要求"亲华派"的自民党干事长二阶俊博参加会议。接着，4月29日报道称，二阶俊博在接受香港的电视媒体采访时说"你可以认为，日本有参加亚投行的可能性"，也表示日本对"一带一路"将尽全力提供合作。

5月17日《读卖新闻》和《朝日新闻》都报道称，二阶俊博同习近平主席在钓鱼台国宾馆会谈，向习近平提交了首相安倍晋三的亲笔信。安倍在亲笔信中表示，希望今后加强双方高层对话，在合适的机会下实现互访。而对于"一带一路"倡议，安倍提出将加深两国间的对话与合作。据6月6日报道，安倍在国际会议上公开表示就"一带一路"进行有条件合作。两家报纸都在7月9日的报上做同样标题，即"首相表示就'一带一路'进行合作"，并报道称，在与习近平的会谈中，安倍评价"一带一路"构想具有潜在可能性，希望"一带一路"倡议的成果有利于实现国际社会的安定和繁荣。

据两家报纸2017年11月12日报道，安倍晋三和习近平主席在越南进行会谈，两国首脑一致同意加速改善中日关系。安倍重申了"一带一路"合作方针，并提出在"一带一路"框架下展开在第三国的中日经济合作。日本政府于12月制定并提出具体方案，根据这些方案，将在节能环保合作、产业升级、提高物流网便利性的3个领域进行中日企业的经济合作（《读卖新闻》11月28日、《朝日新闻》12月5日）。另外，两家报纸分别报道称，安倍和李克强在5月会谈时同意为了推进在第三国的中日经济合作，将设立官民联合委员会，在2018年9月召开首次会议（《读卖新闻》2018年6月7日、9月13日、《朝日新闻》同年7月20日）。

《朝日新闻》2018年7月20日报道指出，日本政府开始积极在"一带一路"框架上的合作，安倍晋三2017年6月以日本政府的立场第一次表示"一带一路"合作，此后中日关系在逐步改善。而也2018年10月27日《读卖新闻》报道称，日本政府认为以"一带一路"为"杠杆"可推进中日关系改善。

四　债务陷阱以及慎重态度

但与此同时，两家报纸也报道有些"一带一路"建设项目暂停或者被取消的消息，例如马来西亚2018年8月决定取消铁路建设等"一带一路"大型项目。《读卖新闻》2018年10月27日在报上做"亚洲国家对'一带一路'抱有警惕"的标题，并报道称，亚洲国家连续表明暂停或取消"一带一路"建设项目，发生如此情况的背景是国际社会开始怀疑会增加一些国家的"一带一路"债务以及缺乏管理透明性。"中国通过提供基础设施建设支援而造成让发展中国家负担巨额债务"（《朝日新闻》2018年11月18日）等。

根据如此情况，习近平主席2019年4月25日到27日在第二届"一带一路"国际合作高峰论坛上表示，推动企业在项目建设、运营等环节按照普遍接受的国际规则标准进行，同时确保商业和财政上的可持续性。对此，两家报纸都以"习近平强调遵守国际规则标准"为标题（4月27日）分别报道称，日本政府对"一带一路"的不透明的投资有担心（《读卖新闻》）；安倍晋三作为合作条件提出基础设施建设的开放性和透明性，对"一带一路"一直保持慎重态度（《朝日新闻》）。

五　结语

本文通过按时间顺序整理的关于"一带一路"的报纸报道，试图理解日本对"一带一路"倡议的态度。可以看到，2013年中国提出倡议后，日本政府一直持观望态度。但以2017年的国际论坛作为一个契机，日本对"一带一路"的态度发生了变化,即开始显示积极姿态。国际论坛以后,随着中日"一带一路"合作的具体化,中日关系加速改善。但与此同时,两家报纸都始终报道日本对"一带一路"抱有一定的警惕。尤其是 2018 年以后在报上频频出现"债务陷阱"这个词,因此可以看出包括日本的国际社会提高了警惕。

根据现有的报道,中日"一带一路"合作看起来停滞。为了推进两国合作,笔者认为需要更加互相了解,以消除日本对"一带一路"倡议的怀疑和警惕。

这次研究只围绕"一带一路"倡议的大趋势,阐述简单的见解。今后要从更多方面进行分析报道内容,以加深对"一带一路"的理解,也要关注"一带一路"倡议的发展。

参考文献

读卖新闻:报道数据库 Yomiuri Database service,2013—2019.

朝日新闻:报道数据库 Kikuzo Ⅱ,2013—2019.

王义桅:《"一带一路"机遇与挑战》,人民出版社 2015 年版。

后藤武秀:《亚洲文化研究所研究年报》,2017 年第 5 期。

白春骝:《常叶大学经营学部纪要》,2018 年第 2 期。

人民网. http://www.people.com.cn/

中国政府网. http://www.gov.cn/index.htm

中国一带一路网. https://www.yidaiyilu.gov.cn/

An Investigation into Japanese Newspapers' Reports on the Belt and Road Initiative

Kawamura Akemi/ Japan

Freelancer; Freelance Translator

I. Introduction

It has been more than six years since Chinese President Xi Jinping put forward the Belt and Road Initiative in 2013. By December 2019, China had signed cooperation documents with 137 countries and 30 international organizations to develop the Belt and Road Initiative, and started the construction of the infrastructure covered by the initiative in many countries.

When the Belt and Road Forum for International Cooperation was held in Beijing in May 2017, Japanese media reported on the Belt and Road Initiative, which made the name of the initiative known to many Japanese people . However, how many Japanese people know what the Belt and Road Initiative is? Therefore, this paper attempts to analyze the main contents of the reports on the Belt and Road Initiative issued by Japanese newspapers, which have been sorted into a chronological order. In this paper, the two major Japanese national newspapers with the first and second largest circulation, namely, Yomiuri Shimbun and Asahi Shimbun, were selected as research objects, and the scope of the research covers their reports on the initiative from September 2013 when the initiative was first put forward by President Xi Jinping to the end of April 2019, totally more than 1,000 articles.

II. Proposal of the Belt and Road Initiative and the Promotion of Its Development

Xi Jinping delivered an important speech in Kazakhstan in September 2013, proposing to jointly build the Silk Road Economic Belt ("the Belt"). Then, in October of the same year, in a speech to the Indonesian National Assembly, he proposed to jointly build the 21st-Century Maritime Silk Road ("the Road"). After that, the Silk Road Economic Belt was combined with the 21st-Century Maritime Silk Road, which was then called the Belt and Road Initiative for short. In March 2015, China's National Development and Reform Commission, Ministry of Foreign Affairs and Ministry of Commerce jointly released the document Vision and Actions on Jointly Building the Silk Road Economic Belt and the 21st-Century Maritime Silk Road.

It was not until one year after Xi Jinping put forward his proposal that the word "the Belt and Road Initiative" appeared in the reports of Yomiuri Shimbun and Asahi Shimbun, that is, on October 18th and December 21st, 2014 respectively. The Yomiuri Shimbun reported that Xi Jinping visited Sri Lanka in September, and he proposed to President Rajapaksa to jointly build the 21st-Century Maritime Silk Road. The Asahi Shimbun reported that Chinese Premier Li Keqiang visited Kazakhstan and put forward the plan of jointly developing the Silk Road Economic Belt. Both newspapers show that the Belt and Road Initiative is an economic circle concept made up of the Silk Road Economic Belt and the 21st-Century Maritime Silk Road. In addition, at the end of its report, Asahi Shimbun wrote, "How will Japan treat the regional strategy proposed by China in the future?" It can be seen from the performance that at this stage, Japan kept its distance from the Belt and Road Initiative.

The next time when the Belt and Road Initiative appeared in their reports was during the Chinese National People's Congress in March 2015. The Asahi Shimbun reported on March 6th that Li Keqiang put forward the policy of accelerating foreign investment and trade, and said that the key to China's overseas strategy is the development of the Belt and Road Initiative. Then, on the 9th of the same month, it reported that Chinese State Councilor and Foreign Minister Wang Yi said at the meeting that comprehensively promoting the Belt and Road Initiative was the focus of China's diplomacy this year. For the Boao Forum for Asia held on the 28th of the same month, both newspapers reported the contents of Xi Jinping's keynote speech, and introduced the contents of Xi Jinping's speech such as "the Belt and Road Initiative will bring benefits to the whole region"(Asahi Shimbun) and "the Belt and Road Initiative is not a solo by China, but a chorus of countries along the route" (Yomiuri Shimbun).

Since then, during about two years up to February, 2017, the main contents of reports about the Belt and Road Initiative were the news that countries other than Japan had started the development of the Belt and Road Initiative. Specifically, the two newspapers reported on April 21, 2015 that Xi Jinping visited Pakistan for the first time after taking office as president of the country, and China and Pakistan signed many economic cooperation documents involving the China-Pakistan Economic Corridor, with a total investment of about 46 billion US dollars. The China-Pakistan Economic Corridor is the flagship project of the Belt and Road Initiative.

Other main reports are as follows: "Because of its special geographical location, Nepal occupies an important position within the Belt and Road Initiative. In recent years, China has vigorously promoted large-scale projects such as roads and power station construction in Nepal" (Asahi Shimbun, May 4, 2015); "Xi Jinping held talks with Russian President Vladimir Putin, and the two heads of state unanimously agreed on the docking cooperation between the Belt and Road Initiative and Eurasian Economic Union" (Yomiuri Shimbun, July 9, 2015); "Xi Jinping visited

Saudi Arabia, Egypt and other Middle Eastern countries for the first time; he and the Middle Eastern heads of state unanimously confirmed that they would promote cooperation on the Belt and Road Initiative, and indicated that China would provide huge investments and financing to the Middle Eastern countries" (Asahi Shimbun, January 20th, 23rd, 2016; Yomiuri Shimbun, January 20th, 22nd, 23rd, 2016), etc. From these reports, it can be seen that Xi Jinping actively visited various countries to hold talks with heads of state, aiming at implementing the idea of promoting the Belt and Road Initiative.

On the other hand, during this period, there were many reports about the Asian Infrastructure Investment Bank (AIIB), which provided financial support to the Belt and Road Initiative, covering the signing ceremony, opening ceremony and annual meeting of AIIB. Among them, there are the following reports: "Japan maintains a cautious attitude towards AIIB, because AIIB does not have a permanent board of directors, and the financing review standard lacks transparency, and if Japan joins, it should pay a large sum of money" (Asahi Shimbun, January 17, 2016); "Japan and the United States are worried about the transparency of the operations of the AIIB, so they hold a wait-and-see position on joining the AIIB" (Yomiuri Shimbun, January 17th).

III. The Forum for International Cooperation and Improvement of China-Japan Relations

On May 14th, 2017, the first Belt and Road Forum for International Cooperation was held in Beijing. About 1,500 representatives from more than 130 countries attended the meeting, including the heads of 29 countries such as Italy and Russia. President Xi Jinping said in his speech that China will provide 60 billion yuan of assistance to developing countries and international organizations participating in the construction of the Belt and Road Initiative in the next three years. During this period, major Japanese media widely reported on the Belt and Road Initiative. Here's a series of reports:

First of all, according to the Yomiuri Shimbun's report on April 25th, Japanese Prime Minister Shinzo Abe has decided to ask Toshihiro Nikai, the Secretary-General of the Liberal Democratic Party who is "pro-China", to attend the meeting. Then, on April 29th, it was reported that in an interview with Hong Kong TV station, Toshihiro Nikai said that "You can deem that Japan has the possibility to participate in the AIIB", and he also indicated that Japan would do its best to cooperate on the development of the Belt and Road Initiative.

On May 17th, both the Yomiuri Shimbun and Asahi Shimbun reported that Toshihiro Nikai had a meeting with Xi Jinping at the Diaoyutai State Guesthouse and submitted a personal letter from Shinzo Abe to President Xi. In his personal letter, Abe expressed the hope to strengthen the high-level dialogue between the two sides in the future, and realize mutual visits under appropriate opportunities. As for the Belt and Road Initiative, Abe proposed to deepen the dialogue and cooperation between the two countries. According to the report on June 6th, Abe publicly expressed the wish of conditional cooperation on the Belt and Road Initiative at the international conference. Both newspapers made the same headline on July 9th, that is, "The Prime Minister expressed the wish of cooperation on the Belt and Road Initiative", and reported that during the talks with Xi, Abe evaluated that the Belt and Road Initiative has potential and hoped that the achievements of the Belt and Road Initiative would be conducive to the stability and prosperity of the international community.

According to the reports of the two newspapers on November 12th, 2017, Shinzo Abe and Xi Jinping held talks in Vietnam, and the heads of the two countries unanimously agreed to accelerate the improvement of China-Japan relations. Abe reiterated the Belt and Road Initiative cooperation policy, and proposed to develop China-Japan economic cooperation in a third country under framework of the Belt and Road Initiative. Then, in December, the Japanese government formulated and put forward its specific plans. According to these plans, economic cooperation between Chinese and Japanese enterprises would be carried out in three areas: cooperation on energy conservation and environmental protection, industrial upgrading, and improving the convenience of a logistics network (Yomiuri Shimbun, November 28th; Asahi Shimbun, December 5th). In addition, the two newspapers reported separately that Abe and Li Keqiang agreed during the talks in May that in order to promote China-Japan economic cooperation in a third country, a joint committee of government and civil authorities would be set up and the committee's first meeting would be held in September 2018 (Yomiuri Shimbun, June 7th, September 13th, 2018; Asahi Shimbun, July 20th, 2018).

Asahi Shimbun reported on July 20th, 2018 that the Japanese government had actively started cooperation on the framework of the Belt and Road Initiative. In June 2017, Shinzo Abe mentioned the cooperation regarding the Belt and Road Initiative for the first time on behalf of the Japanese government. Since then, China-Japan relations have been gradually improving. On October 27th, 2018, Yomiuri Shimbun reported that the Japanese government believed that the Belt and Road Initiative as a "lever" could promote the improvement of China-Japan relations.

IV. Debt Trap and Cautious Attitude

At the same time, however, the two newspapers issued reports that some construction projects under the Belt and Road Initiative had been suspended or canceled, including Malaysia's decision to cancel railway construction and other large-scale projects under the Belt and Road Initiative in August 2018. On October 27th, 2018, Yomiuri Shimbun published an article with the headline "Asian Countries Are Wary of the Belt and Road Initiative", and reported that Asian countries had continuously indicated that they would suspend or cancel the construction projects under the Belt and Road Initiative; the background of this situation was the situation in which the international community had begun to suspect that the debt of some countries increased because of the Belt and Road Initiative and they thought the management of the initiative lacked transparency. "China's support for the construction of infrastructure has caused developing countries to bear huge debts" (Asahi Shimbun, November 18, 2018), etc.

According to this situation, at the second Belt and Road Forum for International Cooperation from April 25th to 27th, 2019, Xi Jinping said that it should be promoted for enterprises to follow generally accepted international rules and standards in project construction and operation, and at the same time commercial and financial sustainability should be ensured. In this regard, both newspapers publicized the articles with the headline "Xi Jinping Emphasized Compliance with International Rules and Standards" (April 27th), and reported separately that the Japanese government was worried about the opaque investment of the Belt and Road Initiative (Yomiuri Shimbun), and Shinzo Abe put forward the openness and transparency of the project for the construction of infrastructure as a condition of cooperation, and kept a cautious attitude towards the Belt and Road Initiative (Asahi Shimbun).

V. Conclusion

This paper tries to understand how Japan treats the Belt and Road Initiative by observing the Japanese newspaper reports which have been sorted in chronological order. As a result, it can be seen that the Japanese government has been holding a wait-and-see attitude since China put forward the initiative in 2013. However, taking the forum in 2017 as an opportunity, Japan changed its attitude towards the Belt and Road Initiative, and began to show a positive attitude. After the forum, with the concretization of China-Japan cooperation under the Belt and Road Initiative, the improvement of China-Japan relations was accelerated. But at the same time, both newspapers have always reported that Japan has been wary of the Belt and Road Initiative. Especially after 2018, the word "debt trap" appears frequently in newspapers, so it can be seen that the international community, including Japan, has had a vigilant attitude.

According to the reports so far, China-Japan cooperation under the Belt and Road Initiative seems to be stagnant. In order to promote the cooperation between the two countries, I believe that it is necessary to understand each other better, so as to eliminate Japan's suspicion and vigilance against the Belt and Road Initiative.

This study only focuses on the big trend of the Belt and Road Initiative and expounds my opinions on it. In the future, we should analyze the content of reports regarding more aspects to deepen our understanding of the Belt and Road Initiative and pay attention to the evolution of the Belt and Road Initiative.

References

Yomiuri Shimbun. Report database, Yomiuri Database service, 2013-2019.

Asahi Shimbun. Report database, Kikuzo II, 2013-2019.

Wang Yiwei. Opportunities and Challenges of the Belt and Road Initiative. Beijing: People's Publishing House, 2015.

Takeshi Goto. Annual Research Report of the Asian Cultural Institute, 2017, 5:184(183)-190(177).

Bai Chunliu. Summary of the Management Department of Tokoha University. 2018.2, 5(1)(2): 121-129.

People's Network. http://www.people.com.cn/

Chinese Government Network. http://www.gov.cn/index.htm

China Belt and Road Network. https://www.yidaiyilu.gov.cn/

"一带一路"旅游对瑞士商务休闲旅游者的启示

何珊 【瑞士】

苏黎世大学 国际关系专员

一 瑞士和中国——一条旅游单向道

近几十年来，国际旅游业取得了令人瞩目的增长。1950年，全世界有2500万外国游客出入境，2018年约为13亿。根据预测，到2030年，这一数字将增至18亿。在收入增加的亚洲，国际旅游的需求增长特别快，这一发展在中国市场上表现得尤为明显。国际市场的开放、经济增长和人口金融状况的改善，促进了旅游活动的显著增加。瑞士也能感受到这种增长。2018年，中国游客在瑞士共度过136万晚——与2017年相比增长了6%（BFS，2018）。瑞士旅游中心是瑞士官方最大的旅游运营商，他们预计未来会有更大的增长。更年轻、更国际化的中国一代（40岁以下），是有着更多的旅行经验和对当地文化更感兴趣的一代，他们现在开始旅游了——参观最重要的景点和购物区仍然是大多数中国游客的主要兴趣，但户外运动（冬季和夏季）以及艺术和文化正变得越来越重要，特别是在个人旅游领域。目前户外运动还不是中国游客的主要兴趣之一，但需求正在缓慢增长。在中国，人们也受到城市生活压力、空气污染、交通堵塞或缺乏锻炼的影响，越来越多地寻求在新鲜空气中娱乐休闲，因此，中国人也可能对瑞士的徒步旅行和农业旅游越来越感兴趣。

中国作为一个旅游目的地也变得越来越重要。1997年，2370万外国人访问了中国，2007年这一数字上升到5470万，2017年达到6070万（World Bank，

2017）。然而，对于瑞士来说，中国还没有成为度假胜地。2018 年，每位瑞士居民平均进行了 3.2 次夜间旅行和 10.6 次日间旅行，67% 的夜间旅行是在国外进行的，而大部分的日间旅行是在瑞士境内进行的（88%）。瑞士人大部分时间都在邻国和欧洲其他地区旅行，只有 7% 的夜间旅行目的地在欧洲以外（BFS 2018）。在这项统计中，中国并没有被作为旅游目的地。不过，中国的旅游条件是相当有利的，有几家航空公司提供瑞士和中国之间的廉价直飞航线。例如从苏黎世到北京（10 小时）、上海和香港（12 小时）。中国还没有发展成为瑞士人的旅游目的地的原因，可能是由于文化和语言的差异，另一个可能使从瑞士到中国的旅行变得更加困难的因素，是签证费在过去一年中从 70 法郎增加到 188 法郎——事实上几乎增加了两倍。

二　瑞士游客将中国视为旅游目的地

一项针对瑞士旅行社的调查显示，瑞士大约有 24 家旅游公司专门从事组织游客到中国的旅游。他们提供各种各样的旅游项目，周期平均需要 10—19 天。旅游项目包括长江游轮、跨西伯利亚铁路旅行、香港、北京（长城和故宫）、云南（昆明和丽江）、上海、杭州、苏州、西藏、西安（兵马俑）、成都（熊猫基地）和桂林等地观光。目前只有少数瑞士旅行社提供以"新丝绸之路"为主题的旅游项目。能让瑞士游客联想到中国的关键词，包括中国长城、灯笼、人口、大排档、功夫、熊猫、茶、春节、丝绸、龙。

三　瑞士游客对"一带一路"的认识

中国和瑞士保持着非常独特的关系。瑞士是 1950 年最早与中华人民共和国建立外交关系的西方国家之一。2020 年是中国和瑞士建交 70 周年。目前两国的合作似乎也进展顺利。瑞士和中国之间的自由贸易协定于 2014 年生效（SECO，2014）。2016 年，中国国家主席习近平和约翰·N. 施耐德·安曼宣布建立两国之间的创新战略伙伴关系（SECO，2016）。2019 年 4 月底，瑞士正式加入"一带一路"倡议，两国签署了谅解备忘录。瑞士联邦理事会强调，五项核心原则应成为该项目的基础：私人资本用于私人项目、社会责任、环保标准、透明度和可持续的债务管理。

通过对过去九个月来瑞士新闻界关于这一主题的文章进行的回顾表明，最重要的事情是：尽管总体观点是积极的，但目前还不确定瑞士在"一带一路"倡议中可以发挥什么作用，以及瑞士公司可以从该倡议中受益到何种程度（见表1）。

表1 2019年4月至12月瑞士参与"一带一路"主题的瑞士新闻文章回顾

	正面观点	负面观点	瑞士可以发挥什么作用	瑞士公司如何受益
文章数量	8	5	3	4

这些关于瑞士加入"一带一路"倡议潜力的未明确问题表明，瑞士需要更多地了解该倡议。即使对于专业的和知识渊博的民众来说，也很难把握这项重大决策——更不用说对于普通公众了。目前，笔者还没有发现关于瑞士人对"一带一路"倡议总体看法的研究。如果有人想继续这方面的研究，了解瑞士公众对"一带一路"倡议的理解以及他们对"一带一路"倡议的态度是积极的还是消极的，这肯定是很有意义的。

四 旅游是相互了解的方式

让瑞士人更多地了解"一带一路"倡议的一个方式就是通过旅游业。旅游业包括不同国家人民之间的跨文化交流，将有助于增进彼此了解与和平合作（Premodh），就像你亲眼所见和所经历的比你在报纸上读到的要容易理解得多。

丝绸之路的构想已有2200年的成功历史。丝绸之路沿线有来自不同时代的各种文化资产，它们见证了不同文化之间成功的贸易或合作。这些对游客很有吸引力，同时也向游客传播贸易路线的理念。虽然沿着整个丝绸之路（例如，包括中亚国家）旅行对于理解BRI很有意义，但本文只讨论丝绸之路的中国部分。此外，本文所指旅游仅限于"一带一路"倡议陆地走廊，不涉及海上丝绸之路。

当然，世界上有许多旅游目的地可以促进不同文化之间的理解。以下是几个独特的例子。

1. 2008年北京夏季奥林匹克运动会

2008年夏季奥运会于2008年8月8日至24日在中国首都北京举行。这是中国首次举办夏季奥运会。来自204个国家的11000多名运动员参加了比赛。2008年夏季北京奥运会也吸引了来自世界各地的数百万游客。不仅在比赛期间，而且在比赛前后，游客们参观了新建的体育场馆和竞技场。通过访问中国首都，游客不仅了解了各种景点或体育景点，还了解了这个大都市的文化、语言和人民。他们买了纪念品，在当地餐馆吃饭。因此，2008年北京夏季奥运会可以被视作吸引东西方、中国和世界相互理解的非常成功的例子。

2. 梵蒂冈

梵蒂冈位于意大利首都罗马，因此被意大利完全包围。这个小国面积只有0.44平方公里，总人口约1000人。每年，数以百万计的游客在西斯廷教堂参观教皇艺术藏品，前往米开朗基罗的"最后审判"。到目前为止，梵蒂冈博物馆的年参观人数已达到600万。在梵蒂冈的一天访问中，客人可以参观天主教会最重要的场所，同时体验城邦的艺术、文化和政府形式。因此，到梵蒂冈旅游既是天主教会的一个重要收入来源，也是一个重要的公共关系工具。

3. 毕尔巴鄂古根海姆美术馆

毕尔巴鄂古根海姆博物馆（Guggenheim Museum Bilbao）是位于西班牙巴斯克自治区毕尔巴鄂的一家现代艺术博物馆，展览面积11000平方米，既有永久性展览，也有外部巡回展览。该建筑于1997年竣工，以其解构主义建筑风格而闻名。该馆花了四年时间建造，其盛大开幕式于1997年10月18日在胡安·卡洛斯国王在场的情况下举行。"毕尔巴鄂效应"一词源自博物馆建筑及其对城市的影响，是指建筑师通过壮观的建筑对场所进行有针对性的升级。算法很简单：游客越多，工作机会就越多。自从古根海姆博物馆成立以来，毕尔巴鄂一直繁荣发展。巴斯克自治区也被全世界认定为一个地区，而此前该地区之所以受到关注，是因为分离主义组织埃塔的恐怖活动。因此，毕尔巴鄂是一个独特的成功例子。弗兰克·盖里（Frank Gehry）的古根海姆博物馆为该市带来了新的经济繁荣，当时该市正与超过20%的失业率作斗争。中型城市毕尔巴鄂在博物馆开馆前曾希望有50万游客，但很快，每年就有100万游客，因为博物馆展示的艺术，也因为博物馆本身是一个令人生畏的疯狂建筑。毕尔巴鄂已经完全重新定位了自己，一个从前的工业城市变成了一个文化城市。

4. 卢塞恩文化和会议中心

卢塞恩文化和会议中心（简称KKL）是瑞士中部卢塞恩市的一座多功能建筑，其音乐厅因顶级声学效果而备受推崇，它是根据建筑师让·努维尔的计划修建的。

KKL 也在一项关于"毕尔巴鄂效应"的研究中得到了检验,它很可能也从"毕尔巴鄂效应"中获益。KKL 利用其湖边位置,强化了卢塞恩的"景观与城市的融合"(Alaily-Mattar et al., 2017)。

五 "一带一路"旅游

当然,丝绸之路沿线有无数代表新时期和古代的地方值得一游。重要的是要从众多吸引游客的景点和活动中进行选择,同时让他们更接近"一带一路"的概念。在下文各段中,笔者简要介绍了关于名胜和活动的建议。

1. 西安——秦始皇陵

西安曾经是著名的古丝绸之路起点。在一个小的空间里了解这么多的历史,在中国恐怕没有比这更合适的地方了。秦始皇兵马俑位于西安临潼区,是中国"全民旅游"的指定地点之一。它也是世界上最大的墓地之一,是中国第一位皇帝秦始皇的遗产。

2. 西安——大雁塔、大唐不夜城

大雁塔位于西安市南部,建于 652 年,位于唐高宗为纪念已故母亲而修建的"大慈悲寺"的庭院中。围绕着大雁塔(主要在南面)有一公里长的夜市,在那里你可以买到纪念品或当地小吃。两侧是古色古香的大型建筑,人们在夜市漫步,玩得很开心。那些勇于尝试的人,可以租一套传统的中国古装,体验一下穿越的感觉。

3. 甘肃——桑科草原

桑科草原位于海拔 3000 米的高原上。夏季,藏族牧民在这里扎营放牧牦牛群。敏感的生态系统可以通过出口那里生产的牦牛毛从"一带一路"倡议中受益,但也必须特别保护它,防止过度使用。

4. 甘肃——拉卜楞寺

拉卜楞喇嘛教寺院建于 1709 年,只有带上导游才能参观。目前仍有约 1200 名僧侣居住在那里。

5. 兰州——甘肃省博物馆

甘肃省博物馆收藏了大量具有丝绸之路悠久历史的文物,最著名的是 1969

年在武威发现的马踏飞燕——东汉时期张将军墓中的"铜奔马"。

6. 甘肃—嘉峪关

嘉峪关建于明朝，在当时的中国皇帝眼中，它代表着长城的西端，也是"文明世界"的终点。长城代表着与古代丝绸之路不同的防御体系，古代丝绸之路则通过与外国文化的贸易建立和平。

7. 敦煌—莫高窟

莫高窟位于古丝绸之路的战略要地。这是一个贸易和宗教的聚会场所。是联合国教科文组织认定的世界遗产。莫高窟共有491座佛教石窟，其中有2400多座雕塑，最重要的是有45000平方米的壁画。这个文化和历史遗址是中国最重要的遗址之一，记录了东西方文化在丝绸之路上的交汇和统一。在近500个色彩斑斓的佛教洞穴中，游客数量受到严格限制。建议仔细规划行程。

8. 敦煌—鸣沙山、月牙湖

敦煌城外约5公里处有一片像图画书一样的美景——鸣沙山。它高达250米，令人印象深刻的是沙漠地层由细流沙形成。在沙丘中间"躺着"一个小月牙湖，湖水来源于地下的泉水。

9. 新疆—吐鲁番市

吐鲁番绿洲是一个重要的贸易中心。他们的财富来自丝绸之路，但其存在归功于坎儿井灌溉系统，该系统如今全长2000公里。交河，一座50米高岩石高原上的废墟城市，是传说中的车师帝国的首都。13世纪被蒙古人征服后，交河被永远遗弃。昔日的城市结构至今仍清晰可见。泥泞的废墟与周围郁郁葱葱的山谷形成了鲜明的对比。

六 结论

旅游业可以为相互理解打开大门。然而，对于瑞士游客来说，中国还没有被确立为旅游目的地。参观旧丝绸之路沿线以及新丝绸之路沿线，有助于理解"一带一路"的理念和可能性。

Understanding through Personal Experience: Introducing Belt and Road Tourism to Swiss Business and Leisure Travelers

Sandra Bachmann / Switzerland

University of Zurich / International Relations Officer

I. Switzerland and China: A Tourism One-way Street

International tourism has experienced impressive growth in recent decades. While in 1950, 25 million arrivals of foreign travellers were recorded worldwide, last year it was around 1.3 billion. According to projections, this number will rise to 1.8 billion by 2030 (UNWTO, 2011). In Asia, where incomes have increased, demand for international travel rose particularly fast. This development is clearly evident in the Chinese market, where the opening of international markets, economic growth and the improved financial situation of the population have led to a significant increase in travel activity. This increase can also be felt in Switzerland. In 2018, Chinese tourists spent nights in Switzerland—that is a 6% growth compared to 2017 (BFS, 2018). The Switzerland Travel Centre, the official and largest tour operator in Switzerland, expects even greater growth in the future.A younger and more cosmopolitan Chinese generation (under 40) with more travel experience and more interest in local culture is now starting to travel—visiting the most important sights and shopping areas are still the main interests of a large majority of Chinese guests, but outdoor activities (winter and summer) as well as art and culture are gaining in importance, especially in the area of individual travel.Outdoor activities are not yet one of the main interests of Chinese guests, but demand is slowly increasing: In China, too, people are affected by stress in city life, air pollution, traffic congestion or lack of exercise and are therefore increasingly seeking recreation in the fresh air. In connection with this, the Chinese are also likely to become increasingly interested in hiking and agrotourism in Switzerland.

China is also becoming increasingly important as a tourist destination. In 1997, 23.7 million foreigners visited China, in 2007 the figure had risen to 54.7 million and by 2017 to 60.7 million (World Bank, 2017). For Switzerland, however, China has not yet become established as a holiday destination. In 2018, each Swiss resident made an average of 3.2 overnight trips and 10.6 day trips. 67% of the overnight trips were made abroad, while the majority of day trips were made within Switzerland (88%). The Swiss spend most of their time traveling in neighboring countries and the rest of Europe. Only 7% of overnight trips had a destination outside of Europe (BFS 2018). China is not visible as a travel destination in this statistic.However, the conditions would be quite favorable. Several airlines offer cheap direct flights between Switzerland and China. For example from Zurich to Beijing (10 hours), Shanghai and Hong Kong (12 hours).Why China has not yet developed as a travel destination for the Swiss may be due to cultural and language differences.Another point that could make travel from Switzerland to China more difficult is the increase in the visa fee from 70 to 188 francs in the past year—in fact it has almost tripled.

II. Perception of China as a Travel Destination for Swiss Tourists

A desk research of Swiss travel agencies showed that there are about two dozen companies in Switzerland that specialize in tours to China. They offer a variety of trips which take between 10 and 19 days on average. Organized tours include Yangtze River cruises, trips on the Trans-Siberian Railway, visits to Hong Kong, Beijing (Great Wall and Forbidden City), Yunnan (Kunming and Lijiang), Shanghai, Hangzhou, Suzhou, Tibet, Xi'an (Terracotta Army), Chengdu (Panda station) and Guilin. Only a handful of Swiss tour operators are currently offering themed tours focusing on the "New Silk Road". Keywords that Swiss tourists associate with China are following: Great Wall of China, lanterns, population, food stands, kung fu, panda bears, tea, Chinese New Year, silk, dragons.

III. Perception of Belt and Road Initiative (BRI) in Switzerland

China and Switzerland maintain a very unique relationship. Switzerland was one of the first Western countries to establish diplomatic relations with the People's Republic of China in 1950. In 2020 China and Switzerland will celebrate 70 years of diplomatic relations.And the cooperation between the two countries also seems to be going well at present. The free trade agreement between Switzerland and China came into force in 2014 (SECO, 2014).In 2016, State Presidents Xi Jinping and Johann N. Schneider-Ammann announced the establishment of an Innovative Strategic Partnership between the two countries (SECO, 2016). Most recent, at the end of April 2019, Switzerland officially joined BRI and the two countries signed a Memorandum of Understanding. The Swiss Federal Council stressed that five central principles should form the foundation of the project: Private capital for private projects, social responsibility, green criteria for environmental protection, transparency and sustainable debt management.

A literary review of the existing Swiss press articles on the subject in the past nine months shows one thing above all: despite a positive general opinion, it is still unclear what role Switzerland could play in the BRI and to what extent Swiss companies could benefit from the initiative (see table 1).

Table 1Review of Swiss press articles on the subject of the Swiss participation in the BRI April - December 2019

	positive reception	negative reception	what role can Switzerland play?	how can Swiss companies profit?
Number of articles	8	5	3	4

These unanswered questions about the potential of BRI for Switzerland indicate a need for additional knowledge about the initiative. Even for a specialized and knowledgeable audience, the large-scale project is difficult to grasp—let alone for the general public. At the present time, there is no research on the general opinion of the Swiss population on the BRI. If one wanted to continue research on the subject, it would certainly be interesting to ask the Swiss public about what they understand by the BRI and whether they have a more positive or negative attitude towards it.

IV. Tourism as a Mean for Mutual Understanding

One option that would enable the Swiss to learn more about BRI is through tourism. Tourism comprises the cross-cultural interaction between people of different nations and thus contributes to a better understanding and peaceful cooperation (Premodh). What you see and experience with your own eyes is much easier to understand than what you read in a newspaper article, for example.

The idea of the Silk Road has a 2200 year old and successful history. Along the Silk Road there are various cultural assets from different epochs, which bear witness to successful trade or cooperation between cultures. These are attractive for visitors and also teach about the idea of the trade route. Although a journey along the entire Silk Road—including, for example, the Central Asian states—would be interesting for an understanding of BRI, only the Chinese part of the Silk Road will be discussed in this paper. Furthermore, the paper will be limited to the BRI land corridor. The Maritime Silk Road is not covered in this paper.

There are certainly many tourist destinations in the world that promote understanding between cultures. Here are just a few unique examples:

1. 2008 Summer Olympics in Beijing

The 2008 Summer Olympic Games were held from August 8 to 24 2008, mainly in the Chinese capital Beijing. These were the first Summer Olympic Games ever to be held in China. Over 11000 athletes from 204 countries took part in the competitions.The summer 2008 Olympic Games in Beijing also attracted millions of tourists from all over the world. And not only during the competitions, but also before and after the games, tourists visited the newly built stadiums and arenas. With their visit to the Chinese capital, visitors not only got to know the various sights or the sports attractions. They also got to know the culture, the language and the people of the megacity.They bought souvenirs and ate in local restaurants.The 2008 Summer Olympics in Beijing can therefore be seen as an absolutely successful example for an attraction for mutual understanding between East and West, between China and the world.

2. Vatican City

The Vatican lies within the Italian capital Rome and is thus as an enclave completely surrounded by Italy. The small state has only an area of 0.44 square kilometers and a total population of about 1000 inhabitants.Each year, millions of visitors make the journey through the pontifical art collection to Michelangelo's "Last Judgement" in the Sistine Chapel. By now, the annual number of visitors to the Vatican Museums has reached the six million mark. During a one-day visit to the Vatican, a guest can see the most important sites of the Catholic Church and at the same time experience the art, culture and form of government of the city state. Tourism to the Vatican is therefore both an important source of income for the Catholic Church as well as an essential public relations tool.

3. Guggenheim Museum Bilbao

The Guggenheim Museum Bilbao is an art museum for modern art in Bilbao in the Spanish Basque Country. It has an exhibition area of 11,000 m² and shows both a permanent exhibition and external touring exhibitions. The building was completed in 1997 and is famous for its deconstructivist architectural style. The construction time took four years. The grand opening was held on 18 October 1997 in the presence of King Juan Carlos. From the museum building and its influence on the city is derived the term "Bilbao effect". The term "Bilbao effect" refers to the targeted upgrading of places through spectacular buildings by architects. The calculation is quite simple: the more visitors, the more jobs. Bilbao has flourished since the Guggenheim Museum came into existence.And the Basque Country was also positively perceived by the world as a region.Previously, the region had attracted attention rather through the terrorist activities of the separatists group ETA.Bilbao is therefore an unique example of success. Frank Gehry's Guggenheim Museum has brought a new economic boom to the city, which at the time was struggling with unemployment of more than 20 percent. Instead of half a million visitors, which had been hoped for in the medium-sized city of Bilbao before the opening, there were soon one million a year; because of the art shown in the museum, but also because of the museum itself, a formidable madness construction. Bilbao has completely repositioned itself above this, a former industrial city became a city of culture.

4. Lucerne Culture and Congress Centre

The Culture and Convention Centre Lucerne (KKL for short) is a multifunctional building in the city of Lucerne in central Switzerland with a concert hall that is highly regarded for its top-class acoustics, built according to the plans of architect Jean Nouvel.The KKL was also examined in a study regarding the "Bilbao effect". It may well also have benefited from a "Bilbao effect". The KKL plays with its lakeside location and reinforces "the fusion of landscape and city" in Lucerne (Alaily-Mattar et al 2017).

V. Belt and Road Tourism

Of course there are countless places along the Silk Road that represent the new and ancient periods and are worth visiting. It is important to choose those sights and activities from the wide range that attract tourists and at the same time bring them closer to the concept of BRI.In the paragraphs below, several suggestions for places of interest and activities are briefly presented.

1. Xi'an - Terracotta Army

Xi'an was once the renowned starting point of the ancient Silk Road. There is probably no better place in China to get to know so much history in such a small space. Located in the Lintong district of Xi'an, which is one of the designated places for China's "All for One Tourism", the terracotta army is one of the world's largest burial sites. It is the legacy of the first Chinese Emperor Qin Shi Huangdi.

2. Xi'an - Giant Wild Goose Pagoda and Night Market

The Giant Wild Goose Pagoda is located in the south of the city of Xi'an and was built in 652, in the courtyard of the "Monastery of Great Charity", which Emperor Gaozong had built in memory of his late mother. Surrounding the Giant Wild Goose Pagoda, but mainly to the south, is a kilometre-long night market where you can buy souvenirs or local snacks. Flanked by large buildings in antique style, such as the Xi'an Opera House, people stroll around the night market and are having a great time. Those who feel a bit brave, rent a traditional Chinese robe and feel like they are taken back to the old days.

3. Gansu - Sangke Grassland

The Sangke Grassland is situated on a plateau of 3000 meters above sea level. Tibetan herders camp here in summer to graze their yak herds. The sensitive ecosystem can benefit from BRI by exporting the yak wool produced there, but it must also be especially protected from overuse.

4. Gansu - Labrang Monastry

The Lamaist monastery was built in 1709 and can only be visited with a guide. Currently there are still about 1200 monks living there.

5. Lanzhou - Gansu Provincial Museum

The Gansu Provincial Museum houses an extensive collection of pieces from the long history of the Silk Road. The most famous piece is the bronze horse galloping on the back of a swallow discovered in Wuwei in 1969, the "Flying Horse" from the tomb of General Zhang of the Eastern Han Dynasty period.

6. Gansu - Western End of the Great Wall

Built in the Ming Dynasty, Jiayuguan represents the western end of the Great Wall, in the eyes of the then Chinese Emperor also the end of the "civilized world". And beyond that, only the demons and barbarians from the desert and Central Asia existed. The Great Wall represents a different defence system than the ancient Silk Road, which established peace through trade with foreign cultures.

7. Dunhuang - Mogao Caves

The Mogao Caves are located at a strategic point on the old Silk Road. This was a meeting place for trade and religions. The UNESCO World Heritage Site comprises a total of 491 Buddhist grottos, which contain over 2,400 sculptures and, above all, 45,000m2 of murals. This cultural and historical site is one of the most important in China, documenting the meeting and unification of Western and Eastern cultures on the Silk Road. Visitor numbers are strictly limited in the almost 500 colourful Buddhist caves. Careful planning of the visit is recommended.

8. Dunhuang - Singing Sand Dunes and Crescent Moon Lake

About 5km outside of Dunhuang there is a piece of picture-book desert - the Singing Sand Dunes. Up to 250m high, impressive desert formations have been formed by the fine drifting sand. In the middle of the Singing Sand Dunes lies the small Crescent Moon Lake, which is fed by an underground spring.

9. Xinjiang - Turpan

The oasis of Turfan was an important trading centre. They owed their wealth to the Silk Road, but their existence to the Karez irrigation system, which today reaches a total length of 2,000km. Jiaohe, the ruined city on a 50m high rock plateau, was the capital of the legendary Cheshi Empire. After the conquest by the Mongols in the 13th century, Jiaohe was abandoned forever. The former city structures can still be clearly seen today. The mud ruins form a beautiful contrast to the lush green of the surrounding valleys.

VI. Conclusion

Tourism can be a door opener for mutual understanding. For Swiss tourists, however, China is not yet established as a tourist destination. Visiting destinations along the old and thus also the new Silk Road creates an understanding for the idea and the possibilities of BRI. The following could be a program for a BRI tourism holiday.

References

ALAILY-MATTAR et al. (2017). "Repositioning cities through star architecture: how does it work?", Journal of Urban Design.

BFS (2018). "Beherbergungsstatistik HESTA 2018".

BFS (2018). "Reisen der Schweizer Wohnbevölkerung 2018".

PREMODH, Neepa. "Tourism as a Powerful Tool for Peace and Dialogue". ELK Asia Pacific Journals - Special Issue.

SECO (2014). "Freihandelsabkommen Schweiz-China tritt am 1. Juli 2014 in Kraft".

SECO (2016). "Gemeinsame Erklärung zwischen der Volksrepublik China und der Schweizerischen Eidgenossenschaft zur Errichtung einer Innovativen Strategischen Partnerschaft".

UNWTO (2011). "UNWTO Annual Report 2011".

World Bank (2017). "International tourism, number of arrivals - China".

"一带一路"倡议对意中两国关系的影响

安馨彤 【意大利】

自由职业者

一 前言

中意友谊扎根在深厚的历史积淀之中[1]。自罗马和秦帝国的伟大时代以来，两国的文明因古丝绸之路沿线的商人和外交官的交流而丰富，影响了彼此历史的发展。几个世纪以来，知识和商品运输的路线已经改变了它们的性质，成为通往合作和互利的新时代的道路，这体现在"一带一路"倡议中。2018年3月23日，中意建交50周年前一年，双方签署了《谅解备忘录》，重申了对实施这一宏伟项目的坚定承诺。尽管《谅解备忘录》是一份不具约束力的声明，但它对国际舆论产生了重大影响，引起了东西方的极大关注。本研究旨在通过概述"一带一路"倡议，通过对现在做法的分析，来预防风险，以实现该倡议的真正价值。鉴于这一专题的性质，笔者同时参考了最近的出版物以及经认可的新闻机构报道的和出席会议期间亲自记录的官方声明以及对著名汉学家和政治家的原始采访结果[2]。

二 中意关系：商业经济视角下的现状和最新发展

《谅解备忘录》被视为中意两国在近代历史上双边贸易和金融交流的里程

---

[1] 引自习近平主席2019年3月23日正式访问意大利前的信件"中意友谊扎根在深厚的历史积淀之中"（Renminribao, 2019）。

[2] 在本文中，采用的观点来自阿尔贝托·布拉达尼尼（Alberto Bradanini）和费迪南多·内利·费罗西·布拉达尼尼（Ferdinando Nelli Feroci Bradinini）。

碑。早在中国"走出去"政策开始之前，两国就签署了双边商业和外交条约；其中，1985年中意双边投资条约标志着互惠投资的加强。正是在21世纪初，中国在意大利的投资开始大幅增加，这也得益于欧盟的优惠政策，最重要的是2003年的中欧全面战略伙伴关系（Hirst, 2019）。该条约与2001年中国加入世贸组织和2004年中意签署全球战略伙伴关系一起，有助于创造一个旨在维护和促进可持续发展、和平与稳定的国际环境。2005年至2018年间，中国在意大利的投资达到249.9亿美元，是继英国、德国和法国之后在欧洲的第四大投资国（Casarini, 2019）[1]。特别是2014年，即"一带一路"启动后的一年，投资大幅增长，中国化工收购了倍耐力（16.89%）的多数股权，倍耐力是世界第五大轮胎制造商（Goldstein, 2016）。这使意大利成为欧洲最重要的投资目的地之一。中国国家外汇管理局（SAFE）对十家意大利最大公司的35亿欧元投资组合也证明了这一趋势（Casarini, 2015）。由于中意双方建立了一个强有力的正式框架，包括全球战略伙伴关系三年行动计划，投资流量继续以高速度增长。截至2017年年中，北京已向意大利股市上市公司投资超过50亿欧元，相当于当时中国对欧洲股票投资总额的10%（近600亿欧元）。在过去二十年中，中国公司和金融机构投资了600多家意大利企业，其中包括银行业（蒙蒂帕什迪锡耶纳银行、联合信贷银行、圣保罗联合银行、麦迪奥班卡银行）、能源业（萨皮姆、埃内尔、埃尼）、汽车制造商（菲亚特克莱斯勒汽车）、电信业（意大利电信）、电缆和系统（普赖斯曼）和保险行业（通利保险）（卡萨里尼，2019年）。

另一方面，意大利对中国的投资没有取得同样的成功。与其他西方国家一样，在20世纪，它可以从经济特区（SEZ）、特别地区和特许权内的优惠减损税收计划中获益。然而，截至2018年底，与意大利合作的中国企业只有1700家，员工约15万人，营业额220亿欧元。在中国的合资企业、外商独资企业和代表处约有2000个单位（ICE, 2019年）。意大利以及其他欧洲国家、日本和美国在中国的投资确实出现了大幅收缩，特别是因为劳动力和服务成本的增加[2]，税收优惠较低，更加关注环境保护，而其他新兴国家的吸引力日益增强（Bradanini, 2018）。

至于贸易额，2017年达到420亿欧元，比上年增长9.2%。根据2018年欧盟

---

1 这一趋势还得益于意大利于2015年加入亚洲基础设施银行（亚投行），通过2.66%的合作伙伴关系以及2018年9月签署的第三国合作谅解备忘录（Zhang, 2019）。

2 这主要是由于"中国制造2025"和"一带一路"倡议中的项目，都旨在为中国在国际舞台上赢得新的经济角色，以及改变发展模式（Ruet, 2018）。

统计局的调查，意大利是对中国的第四大欧洲出口国，出口额约为140亿美元，约占意大利总出口额的2.7%（WTO，2019）。意大利的时装、食品和家具仅占总出口量的15%，而机械和汽车行业占最大份额。迄今为止，从北京进口的商品价值超过270亿欧元，相当于中国出口市场的1.3%，使意大利成为中国的第十九大出口目的地。根据SACE SIMEST预测，在意大利的出口将经历一个积极的增长趋势，未来几年（2019—2021），汽车、制药、纺织、时装和工程行业平均增长率预计为8.8%（ICE，2019）。然而，受援国市场存在广泛的结构性缺陷，如进入壁垒高、手续冗余和法律差异，所有这些因素都显著加剧了经济不对称：尽管2017年意大利贸易赤字减少了13.7亿欧元，但意大利—中国贸易赤字仍达149亿欧元（Punzi，2019）。

三　2019年《谅解备忘录》的影响

在中意全面战略伙伴关系建立15周年之际，双方签署《谅解备忘录》，共同推动到2049年实施"一带一路"倡议，进一步深化了政治和经济关系。考虑到单边主义和贸易保护主义的浪潮日益高涨，《谅解备忘录》被许多西方国家视为一个惊人的突破，因为它表明发达国家也有可能开始接受"一带一路"倡议，将其视为一项连通性和经济发展倡议，以建立一个更加全球化、多边和自由的世界（Casarini，2019）。与古代一样，中国和意大利再次成为东西方之间的主要桥梁，肩负着创造知识、相互理解、包容性增长和创新解决方案以与全世界共享的远见卓识的使命。"一带一路"倡议涵盖的领域可概括为"连通性的五个因素"：通过文化、游客和学生交流，实现全球治理改革的政策沟通、道路连通性、未开发的贸易、货币流通和不同文明之间的相互理解（Infomercatesteri，2019）。投资项目包括贸易、金融、运输、物流、基础设施、可持续发展、流动性和合作，其中一些项目还涉及第三国。对中国来说，在意大利市场进行更大的投资意味着提升价值链和产品的适销性，并通过在意大利收购已具备全球竞争力的行业技术、专有技术和品牌，进一步建立更多的规模经济（Casarini，2019）。与此同时，对意大利企业的绿地投资将为全国企业家精神带来新的动力，并将促进意大利制造。该地区已成为全球航运贸易量19%的主要枢纽（Bressan，2019）。因此，许多有影响力的中国公司对意大利的主要港口——的里雅斯特、拉文纳和热那亚——以及国家内陆基础设施表现出兴趣，其中包括上海和宁波的港务局，中国交通建设集团公司（CCCG）和中国工商银行。他们实施了伙伴关系和新的贷款计划，以改善意大利港口，使其在国际层面上更具竞争力，并更有效地完成 BRI 下的项目 1 (Casarini, 2019)。

与此同时，备忘录的签署表明了双方恢复其国际影响力的意愿，颠覆了"华盛顿共识"体系（Bradanini，2017）。特别是，这一行动表明了他们反对单一国际社会的决心，以及勾勒出一个更加强大欧洲的新命运的意图，这个欧洲重视多方面的声音。获得七国集团[2]中一个与美国有着紧密关系的成员国的支持，中国将增强其在西方世界的政治和外交影响力，从而为"一带一路"在欧洲以及在第三国与欧盟国家的合作项目赢得合法性和信心，并支持人民币的国际使用（Casarini，2015）。

四 实施"一带一路"倡议背后价值观的可能解决方案

西方的危言耸听和批评揭示了一种根深蒂固的、以欧洲为中心的世界问题方针，这为该倡议的实施创造了一个不利的环境。例如，在关于意大利港口的《谅解备忘录》之后所签署的协议并不意味着与比雷埃夫斯港口相同特许经营权许可，因为热那亚和的里雅斯特仍将由意大利政府管辖。这些港口可能会从投资中受益，从而成为鹿特丹等欧洲主要枢纽的真正竞争对手（Negri，2019）。应当指出，在这方面，欧盟（特别是意大利）已经制定了足够的工具来防范风险和抓住机遇，以保护国家和欧洲安全，防止外国掠夺性投资（由第三方或基金进行），并于 2017 年颁布了一项法令，以加强现有的国家筛选机制，即"黄金权力"[3]。该法令对涉及基础设施等战略部门的规划、实现、维护和管理的协议或合同规定了强制性预防性通告。"黄金权力"还阻碍专业知识和技术的获

---

1 这些项目包括在意大利的"北方港口建设计划"和"投资意大利计划"中。的里雅斯特是"Trihub 项目"的一部分，该项目是欧盟和中国之间的框架协议，旨在促进相互基础设施投资。在这方面，庞大的中国交通建设公司（CCCC）致力于在威尼斯港建设码头，而 2018 年，中国招商局集团在拉文纳港投资 1000 万欧元，旨在将该市转变为欧洲海军工程中心。自 2016 年以来，北京通过持有集装箱码头 49.9% 的股份（40% 由中远海运持有，9.9% 由青岛港管理局持有）直接进入意大利西北部瓦多利古尔港（Fardella，2018）。
2 意大利是 G7 国际组织内的经济大国之一，也是欧洲经济共同体（EEC）（现为欧盟，EU）的创始国之一。
3 "黄金权力"是政府拥有的一种特殊权力，旨在保障国家安全，防止可能影响国家安全和公共秩序的投资。它来自"分享权力"的改革，这是欧盟仿效美国 CFIUS（Kirschenbaum，2019）创建的一种综合筛选机制。

取，防止低价倾销假冒产品以及预防华为和爱立信发起的 5G 项目所带来的风险（Casarini，2019）。"黄金权力"的最新内容试图具体解决围绕 5G 项目敏感信息盗用问题的担忧，尽管法国是华为投资在欧洲建立 5G 互连的主要接受者（Bai，2019）。正如意大利前驻华大使阿尔贝托·布拉迪尼尼（Alberto Bradinini）在接受采访时强调的那样，意大利体系不应该保护自己不受中国的影响，而应该保护自己不受不尊重共同体创始价值观的欧洲大国的伪善竞争的影响。意大利，以及其他欧盟成员国，仍然以一种根深蒂固的欧洲中心主义为特征：世界其他地区是由一个公开的民主公正来判断的，正如媒体对香港或 BRI 局势的态度所显示的那样。这种激进的立场实际上隐藏着无知、恐惧和被动的顺从，掩盖了"一带一路"建设的文化和理念。在利己主义的蒙蔽下，西方忽视了中国古代文明的儒家和道家哲学[1]，它正试图使用与其他经济参与者相同的工具，并遵守相同的国际法规，进入国际经济领域。意中《谅解备忘录》本身反映了标准欧洲协议的语言和结构，以及《共建丝绸之路经济带和 21 世纪海上丝绸之路的愿景与行动》(2015) 和《共建"一带一路"：理念、实践和中国贡献"(2017)》是近期中意关系的两个基础性文件。

中国承诺与国际标准接轨始于 2000 年，随着"走出去"政策的实施并于 2016 年重申，这意味着 WTO 应该更容易保护各国免受中国国内过剩产能的倾销，同样，中国企业也更容易保护自己不受指控（Casarini，2019）。在 2019 上海第二届中国国际进出口（CIE）开幕式上，习主席肯定了北京将与欧盟和国际组织，如联合国教科文组织和亚太经合组织（APEC），进行富有成效的谈判。2018 年中国政府实施的结构调整计划也证实了这一点，当时中国银行业监督管理委员会和中国保险业监督管理委员会合并，以降低金融风险和不良贷款（Bummetti，2019）。类似地，2019 年，中国立法者在《公司法》和《外国投资法》中引入了一项改革：它满足了世界贸易组织（WTO）关于统一法律体系的要求，以确保外国和本国个人以及私营和上市公司在国内领土上的公平竞争（Covington，2019）。然而，考虑到资本主义超级大国的倒退和中国日益增长的潜力，《华盛顿共识》的世界似乎无法接受资本家的达尔文主义倾向于拯救一个几十年来一直被征服和妖魔化、最近走上市场经济道路的国家。事实上，世界银行估计，"一带一路"可能为所有人带来重要利润：到 2019 年底，它将使世界贸易成本降低 1.1% 至 2.2%，

1　这包括互惠、和谐共存、双赢理论、人性、同情、繁荣、和平的概念（Asif & Ling，2018）。

并为世界发展做出 0.1% 的贡献（Farnesina，2018）。因此，有必要创造一个和谐的环境，促进各级的主动相互理解和了解[1]，以培养能力，改善这项年轻的倡议，创造"人类共同的未来"。

在这种观点下，论坛、研究项目、协会、学生和游客交流、组织和类似的国际平台对于在共存的更广泛目标下分享各种合作领域的经验和知识至关重要（Farnesina，2018）。在这一点上，2019 年上海国际展览可以作为一个例子，特别是中意关系：在"新时代，共享未来"的主题下，意大利作为 160 家企业的官方合作伙伴，在 2020 年（意大利"文化和旅游年"）签署了 3 亿欧元的意大利肉类和大米出口协议以及加强学生和游客交流的协议 (Buzzetti, 2019)。

迄今为止，意大利和中国通过坚实的制度框架丰富了友谊，包括三年合作计划、文化论坛、商业论坛，几项涉及医疗、生态、城市化、农业、航空航天的经济协议，以及大量跨领域的举措[2]。尽管这些例子代表了促进互动的适当平台，但第一个必要的步骤应该是合作，旨在找到真正履行这一承诺的工具，避免空洞的手续。从统一的国家和国际政治立场建立高效、透明的法律框架是落实"一带一路"倡议精神和促进双边对话以建立更密切关系的关键（Bai，2019）。在中意案例中，费迪南多·内利·费罗西（Ferdinando Nelli Feroci）强调了消除无用的、分散的机构和重叠角色的重要性，以创建一个灵活的合作体系，让双方重新团结起来。同样，阿尔贝托·布拉达尼尼（Alberto Bradanini）明确指出，"一带一路"的真正问题在于意大利的体系：国家政府应该用有效的工具来赋予国家权力，比如一个常设的中国部门，一个单一的、小型的、综合性的机构，完全由专家、汉学家和经济学家组成，依据专家的能力挑选合适的人员。为了有权协调国家和地方一级的公共机构，这一常设机构应并入理事会主席，并负责与研究中心、学术机构、协会、地方和国家企业合作，加深相互认知[3]。要提升中意联盟的整体潜力，两国必须超越各种政治普世主义，拥抱多元和差异（Bradanini，2018）。

---

1 这一概念可概括如下："国之交在于民相亲，民相亲在于心相通"。
2 仅提及其中一些内容：意大利外交部出版的《意大利法律框架中的中国员工双语指南》（"意大利劳动法指南"）、对凌江经济特区（重庆辖区）意大利企业的法律支持、2018 年湖南省与米兰美术学院的文化艺术交流等。
3 他的提议部分反映在现有的意大利—中国商业论坛（成立于 2014 年），该论坛定期举办会议，重点关注商业和贸易。其对中意关系产生了积极的影响，因为它建立了一个常设机构，协助政府间对话，简化信息、人才、工业项目的交流（Bradanini，2018）。

五　结论

"一带一路"为双方带来风险和机遇。一方面，意大利政府希望为国有企业和意大利制造的产品在中国获得更多的市场准入，在"一带一路"框架下获得更多的中国国内投资，并从严峻的经济和政治危机中获得救赎。另一方面，中国希望实施国家项目，以提升其软实力，促进对国际标准的调整，创建一个与《华盛顿共识》相反的结构。为了评估作为该倡议基础的项目的实际可行性，有必要揭露毫无根据的误解，通过贯穿各领域的活动和透明一致的体制框架促进相互理解，以实现双方作出的众多承诺。

Effects of Belt and Road Initiative on Italy-China Relations

Rossi Arianna / Italy

Freelancer; Teacher

I. Preface

China and Italy relations are deeply rooted in their secular and relentless exchanges[1]. Ever since the great era of the Roman and the Qin Empire, the civilizations of the two countries have been enriched by the exchanges of traders and diplomats along the Ancient Silk Road, affecting the development of the histories of one another. Over the centuries, the routes of knowledge and products have changed their nature, becoming the path towards a new era of cooperation and mutual benefit, embodied in the BRI. The strong commitment for the implementation of this ambitious project was reaffirmed on March 23rd 2018 with the signing of the MoU, one year before the 50th anniversary of the establishment of China-Italy diplomatic relations. Although the MoU is a non-binding statement, it has been exerting a major impact on the international public opinion, raising

---

1 Quoting the letter of President Xi Jinping before his official visit to Italy on 23 March 2019: "中意友谊扎根在深厚的历史积淀之中" (*People's Daily*, 2019).

considerable concerns from East to West. While China is perceived as the ruthless enemy of Western democracy and free trade, Italy is considered as the naïve 'Trojan horse' paving the way for the Dragon's entrance into Europe. This study aims to contribute to this debate by providing an overview on the actual perspectives over the BRI, unveiling biased opinions and detecting good practices to prevent existing risks and implement the real values of the initiative. Given the nature of this topic, recent publications, as well as official declarations both reported by accredited press agencies and recorded in person during attended conferences were taken into account, together with the results of original interviews to renowned sinologists and politicians[1].

The body of this paper is organized as follows: the first paragraph provides an overview on the Sino-Italian diplomatic and trade relations over recent decades. Paragraph two highlights the official intentions behind the MoU, whereas the most common misconceptions are briefly introduced in paragraph three. Paragraph four provides the rebuttal to spread alarmism, highlighting the actual risks underlying the BRI, together with possible solutions, followed by conclusions.

II. China-Italy relations: state of art and recent developments from a business-economic perspective

The MoU can be considered as the milestone of the bilateral trade and financial exchanges between China and Italy in recent history. Even before the beginning of the Chinese "Go Out policy", the two countries signed bilateral commercial and diplomatic treaties; among these, the China-Italy BIT in 1985 marked the intensification of reciprocal investments. However, it was with the beginning of the 21st century that Chinese investments in Italy began to raise significantly, also thanks to favorable EU policies, most significantly the 2003 EU-China Comprehensive Strategic Partnership (Hirst, 2019). This treaty, together with China joining the WTO in 2001 and the signing of China-Italy Global Strategic Partnership in 2004,

---

[1] In this paper, the opinions took into consideration are those of Alberto Bradanini and Ferdinando Nelli Feroci. Bradinini. The link to the interviews and the main participants biography are included in Appendix.

contributed to create an international environment, aimed to safeguard and promote sustainable development, peace and stability. Between 2005 and 2018 Chinese investments in Italy reached USD 24.99 billion – the fourth highest recipient country in Europe after the United Kingdom, Germany and France1 (Casarini, 2019). In particular, 2014, the year after the launching of the BRI, was characterized by a staggering increase in investments, with the ChemChina's acquisition of a majority stake of Pirelli (16.89%), the fifth biggest tire maker in the world (Goldstein, 2016). This put Italy among the most important European destinations of investments. This trend was also proved by the 3.5 billion euro portfolio investment by the Chinese State Administration of Foreign Exchange (SAFE) in ten of Italy's largest companies (Casarini, 2015). Thanks to a strong formal framework consisting of a Three-Year Plan of Action for global strategic Partnership, investment flows continued to grow at a positive rate. By mid-2017, Beijing had invested more than EUR 5 billion in listed companies listed on the Italian stock market, which corresponds to 10% of total Chinese investments in European stocks (almost EUR 60 billion) at that time. In the last two decades, Chinese companies and financial institutions have invested in more than 600 Italian enterprises, including banking (Monte dei Paschi di Siena, Unicredit, Intesa SanPaolo, Mediobanca), energy (Saipem, Enel, Eni), automaker (Fiat Chrysler Automobiles), telecommunication (Telecom Italia), cables and systems (Prysmian) and insurance (Assicurazioni Generali) industries (Casarini, 2019).

On the other hand, Italian investments towards the PRC did not experience the same success. As other Western countries, over the 20th Century it could benefit from favorable derogatory tax schemes inside Special Economic Zones (SEZ), special areas and concessions. Nevertheless, at the end of 2018 Chinese enterprises with an Italian partnership were only 1,700, with about 150,000 employees and a turnover of EUR 22 billion. Joint ventures, WFOEs and representative offices in

---

1   This trend also benefited from the joining of Italy in the Asian Infrastructure Bank (AIIB) in 2015, through a partnership of 2.66% and the signing of the Memorandum of Understanding for the Cooperation in Third Countries in September 2018 (Zhang, 2019).

China had around 2 thousand units (ICE, 2019). Italy, as well as other European countries, Japan, and the U.S., is indeed experiencing a sharp contraction in investments in China, particularly because of an increase in the cost of labor and services[1], a less favorable tax regime, a greater attention to environmental protection, and a growing appeal exerted by other emerging countries (Bradanini, 2018).

As for the trade volume, in 2017 it reached EUR 42 billion, 9.2 per cent more than the previous year. According to the 2018 Eurostat survey, Italy is the fourth biggest European exporter towards Beijing, with around USD 14 billion exports, which account for about 2.7% of Italy's total exports (WTO, 2019). Made in Italy fashion, food, and furniture account for just 15% of the total export volume, whereas mechanical and automotive industry holds the biggest share. To date, imports from Beijing are worth more than EUR 27 billion, which corresponds to 1.3% of the Chinese export market, making Italy the nineteenth largest export destination. According to SACE SIMEST projections, Made in Italy exports will experience a positive growth trend over the coming years: an increment at an average rate of 8.8% is predicted between 2019 and 2021 in automotive, pharmaceutical, textile, fashion and engineering industries (ICE, 2019). Yet, wide structural deficiencies exist in the recipient market, as high barriers to entry, redundant formalities, and legal discrepancies. All of these factors significantly contribute to exacerbating economic asymmetries: although the Italian trade deficit decreased by EUR 1.37 billion in 2017, the Italy-China trade deficit still amounts to EUR 14.9 billion (Punzi, 2019).

III. The implications of the 2019 Memorandum of Understanding

Over the year of the 15th anniversary of the establishment of Sino-Italian Comprehensive Strategic Partnership, the two parties further deepened their political

---

[1] This is mostly due to Made in China 2025 (中国制造 2025) and the projects embedded in the BRI, all aimed at gaining a new economic role for China on the international stage, as well as at changing the development model (Ruet, 2018).

and economic relationship by signing a MoU to jointly promote the implementation of the BRI by 2049[1]. Considering the rising wave of unilateralism and trade protectionism, the MoU was perceived as an outrageous breakthrough by many in Western countries, because it suggested the possibility that developed countries too may begin to accept the BRI as a connectivity and economic development initiative towards a more globalized, multilateral and free world (Casarini, 2019). Just like in ancient times, China and Italy are once again the main bridge between the East and the West, with a farsighted mission of creating knowledge, mutual understanding, inclusive growth, and innovative solutions to be shared with the entire world. The fields covered by the BRI may be summarized by the "five factors of connectivity": policy communication towards a global governance reform, road connectivity, untapped trade, monetary circulation and mutual understanding between civilizations through cultural, tourists and students exchanges (InfoMercatiesteri, 2019). Investment projects include trade, finance, transportation, logistics, infrastructure, sustainable development, mobility and cooperation, some of these also involving third countries. For China, larger investments in the Italian market would mean moving up the value chain and the marketability of its products, as well as further building more economies of scale, through the acquisition of technology, know-how and brands in sectors where Italy has achieved global competitiveness (Casarini, 2019). At the same time, green-field investments in Italian enterprises would give new momentum to national entrepreneurship and would enhance Made in Italy products abroad, through corporate and management restructuring[2]. In addition, business opportunities opened by the U.S.-China trade war may serve as fuel to leverage the Italy-China trade deficit, particularly thanks to the agricultural

---

1 The Belt and Road Initiative was officially announced by President Xi Jinping in late 2013, and it is expected to be fully implemented by the 100th anniversary of the foundation of the People's Republic of China in 2049.
2 Michele Geraci, the former Italian Deputy Secretary of the Ministry of Economic Development, who signed the MoU, firmly stated the necessity of green-field investments that increase employment and national GDP. The Belt and Road will open new opportunities to promote Italian immaterial assets – art, history, and culture – while developing its managerial competences and its soft power (Bressan, 2019).

commodities sector[1] (Bradanini, 2018). Despite having great potentials, the Italian economy is still struggling against the heavy effects of the 2010 European debt crisis, which affected domestic growth[2] and demand for products and services, and put its future competitiveness at risk on the third millennium global scenario (ICE, 2019). Against this backdrop, the Chinese financial and commercial intervention seems a viable option to stimulate national development by creating employment and elevating the level of internationalization of excellences. Chinese innovative projects (such as 'Made in China 2025') will probably introduce products with a higher added value on the domestic markets. In particular, importing technological assets will abide by the current focus of the Italian economic policies, centered on the creation of a smart nation – based on venture capital and on the reduction of the infrastructural and digital divide (Mise, 2019). Following the example of Huawei Technologies, which located its European headquarters in Milan, multinational companies from the PRC may benefit from local intangible assets and logistical strongholds to access European markets, while contributing to job creation and employees training (Goldstein, 2016). Sitting at the centre of the Mediterranean Sea, the end-point of the 21st Century Maritime Silk Road, Italy holds a strategic position fundamental for the success of the massive infrastructural project of Beijing. Thanks to the expansion of the Suez port, the Mediterranean region has become the principal junction for 19% of the global shipping trade volume (Bressan, 2019). Therefore, a number of influential Chinese companies are showing interest towards Italy's major ports – Trieste, Ravenna, and Genoa – and national inland infrastructure. Among them there are the port authorities of Shanghai and Ningbo; the China Communications Construction Group (CCCG) and the Industrial and Commercial Bank of China. They implemented partnerships and new loan schemes to ameliorate Italian ports, making them more competitive at an international level,

---

[1] According to Michele Geraci, due to the existing global value chain, the increase of US duties in the long run will act as a catalyst in fostering the subversion of the current world balance (Fotina, 2019).

[2] Since 2001, the average GDP growth rate has been 0.25% compared to the 1.7% EU average; while the government debt is equal to 130% of the GDP. (Zeneli, 2019)

and more efficient in fulfilling projects under the BRI[1] (Casarini, 2019).

At the same time, the singing of the Memorandum shows the will of the two parties to redeem their internationally influential role, subverting the 'Washington consensus' system (Bradanini, 2017). Particularly, this act showed their determination against a monolithic international community, and the intention of outlining a new destiny for a stronger Europe that gives importance to multisided voices. By receiving the support of one of the member states of the G7[2] with tight relations with the USA-based establishment, China will enhance its political and diplomatic influence in the Western world, hence gaining legitimacy and confidence for BRI's cooperation projects in Europe and with EU countries in third countries, and bolstering the international use of Renminbi (Casarini, 2015).

IV. Possible solutions to implement the values behind the BRI

The Western alarmism and criticism reveals a deep-rooted Eurocentric approach to world issues that is creating a confused environment for the implementation of the initiative. For example, the agreements signed right after the MoU about Italian ports do not imply the same premises of the Piraeus port concession, since Genoa and Trieste will remain under the jurisdiction of the Italian government. These ports will probably benefit from investments, so much so that they might become real competitors for European major hubs, such as Rotterdam (Negri, 2019). In this regard, it should be noted that the EU has already developed adequate tools to prevent risks and grasp opportunities: Italy, in particular, to prevent foreign predatory investments (by third parties or funds) as to safeguard national and

---

1 These projects are included in the so-called 意大利"北方港口建设计划" and "投资意大利计划". Trieste is part of the "Trihub project", a framework agreement between the EU and China to promote mutual infrastructure investments. In this regard, the giant China Communications Construction (CCCC) is committed to the construction of quays in the port of Venice, while in 2018 China Merchant Group invested EUR 10 million in the port of Ravenna, with the aim of transforming the city into a European hub of naval engineering. Since 2016, Beijing secured a direct presence in Northwest Italian port of Vado Ligure through a 49.9% stake in the container terminal (40% held by COSCO Shipping, 9.9% by the authority of Qingdao Port) (Fardella, 2018).

2 Italy is one of the economic powers sitting inside the G7 international organization and it is also one of the founding states of the European Economic Community, EEC (now European Union, EU).

European security, in 2017 put forward a Decree to strengthen the existing national screening mechanism "golden power"[1]. This decree introduced compulsory preventive notification for agreements or contracts involving projection, realization, maintenance and management in strategic sectors, such as infrastructure. The "golden power" also hinders expertise and technology acquisition, preventing the dumping of counterfeiting goods at low prices, as well as the risks entailed in the 5G projects initiated by Huawei and also by Ericsson (Casarini, 2019). The latest update of the "golden power" tries to specifically address the concern surrounding the issue about sensitive information misappropriation through 5G projects, even though France is the major receiver of Huawei investments for the creation of 5G interconnectivity in Europe (Bai, 2019), blinded by egocentrism, the West ignores the Confucian and the Daoist philosophy of the ancient Chinese civilization[2], which is attempting to enter the international economic playfield using the same tools of other economic players and respecting the same international regulation. The China-Italy MoU itself reflects the language and the structure of standard European agreements and the general principles set out in "Vision and Actions on Jointly Building Silk Road Economic Belt and 21st – Century Maritime Silk Road" (2015) and in "Building the Belt and Road: concept, practice and China's contribution" (2017), two founding documents of the recent China-Italy relations[3]. The commitment of China to align to international standards started at the wake of the 2000, with the implementation of the "Go Global Policy", and it was then reaffirmed in 2016 with the expiry of the "nonmarket economy status" of China, meaning that it is supposed to be easier for the WTO to defend countries from dumping Chinese domestic overcapacity and equally for Chinese companies to defend themselves from accusations (Casarini,

---

[1] The "golden power" is a special power owned by a government in order to guarantee the country's national security, preventing investments that could have an impact on national security and public order. It comes from the reform of the "share power", an integrated screening mechanism created by the EU following the American example of CFIUS (Kirschenbaum, 2019).

[2] This encompasses the concept of reciprocity, harmonic coexistence, win-win theory, humanity, compassion, prosperity, peace (Asif & Ling, 2018).

[3] These documents were jointly outlined by the Commission of Development and Reforms, Minister of Foreign Affairs and Ministry of Trade of the PRC.

2019). At the opening ceremony of the second edition of China International Import Export (CIIE) of Shanghai 2019, President Xi affirmed that Beijing will carry out fruitful negotiations with the EU and with international organizations, as the UNO and the Asia Pacific Economic Cooperation (APEC) to create a common ground useful to face 21st Century challenges. This was also confirmed by the Program of Structural Adjustment put in place by the Chinese government in 2018, when the China Banking Regulatory Commission and the China Insurance Commission were merged together to lower financial risks and non-performing loans (Buzzetti, 2019). Similarly, in 2019 Chinese lawmakers introduced a reform in the Company Law and in the Foreign Investment Law: it addressed the requirements of the World Trade Organization (WTO) in matter of unified body of laws that ensures fair competition on domestic territory both for foreign and national individuals, as well as private and public companies (Covington, 2019). Nevertheless, given the regression of capitalist superpowers and the growing potential of the PRC, the world of the Washington Consensus seems unable to accept that the capitalist Darwinism is favoring the redemption of a country that was subjugated and demonized for many decades and has recently took up the path of a market economy. As a matter of fact, the World Bank estimated that the BRI may lead to important profit for everyone: it would lower world trade costs between 1.1% and 2.2% and give a 0.1% contribution to the world development by the end of 2019 (Farnesina, 2018). It is therefore essential to create a harmonic environment for proactive mutual understanding and knowledge at all levels[1] to develop competencies and to ameliorate this young initiative, as to create a "shared future for humankind". Under this point of view, forums, research programs, associations, exchanges of students and tourists, organizations, and similar international platforms are fundamental to share experiences and knowledge in a variety of fields of cooperation[2] under the broader objective of growing

---

1 This concept can be summarized as follows: "国之交在于民相亲, 民相亲在于心相通" ("Friendship, which derives from close contact between the people, holds the key to sound state-to-state relations").
2 As President Xi stated during the opening ceremony of the second edition of the Belt and Road Forum (May 2017), "over the coming 5 years, China will be committed in exchanges, joint research and training programs among 5000 national and foreign experts" (Farnesina, 2018).

together. In this matter, the CIIE of Shanghai 2019 can be taken as an example, particularly for China-Italy relations: under the theme of "New Era, Shared Future", Italy, the official partner with 160 enterprises, signed a EUR 300-million agreement for the export of Italian meat and rice and an agreement for the intensification of exchanges of students and tourists in 2020 (the Italian "Year of Culture and Tourism") (Buzzetti, 2019). To date, Italy and China have enriched their friendship through a solid institutional framework, consisting of the Three-Year Plan for Cooperation, the Cultural Forum, the Business Forum, several economic agreements involving healthcare, ecology, urbanization, agriculture, aerospace and aviation, and a great number of cross-cutting initiatives[1]. Even though these examples represent adequate platforms that facilitate interaction, the first necessary step should be a joint cooperation aimed at finding tools aimed at the real implementation of this commitment, avoiding empty formalities. Establishing an efficient and transparent legal framework from a unified political national and international stance is the key to implement the spirit of the BRI and facilitating the bilateral dialogue for a more intense relation (Bai, 2019). In the China-Italy case, Ferdinando Nelli Feroci highlighted the importance of eliminating useless and scattered apparatus and overlapping roles in order to create an agile system of cooperation, in which to reunite the two parties. Equally, Alberto Bradanini specified that the real issue in the BRI matter is the Italian system: the national government should empower the country with efficient tools, such as a Permanent Department for China, a single, small, and integrated institution, entirely composed by experts, sinologists, and economists, selected on the basis of their competencies. In order to be entitled to coordinate public institutions, both at national and local level, this permanent organ should be integrated into the Presidency of the Council and should be in charge of cooperating with research centers, academies, associations, local and national

---

[1] Just to mention some of these: the bilingual guide for Chinese employees in the Italian legal framework published by the Italian Ministry of Foreign Affairs ("Guide to the Italian Labour Law"), the legal support for Italian firms in the SEZ of Lingjiang (Chongqing jurisdiction), the cultural-artistic exchange between Hunan province and the Academy of Fine Arts of Milan in 2018, and similar.

enterprises to accumulate mutual knowledge[1]. To enhance the entire potential of Sino-Italian alliance, both countries must surpass all kind of political universalism and embrace pluralism and differences (Bradanini, 2018).

V. Conclusion

The Belt and Road entails risks and opportunities for both sides. On one hand, the Italian government hopes to obtain more market access in China for national companies and Made in Italy products, more Chinese investment at home under the BRI framework and redemption from a harsh economic and political crisis. On the other hand, China wants to implement national projects to promote its soft power, to foster the adjustment to international standards, to create a counter-structure to that one of the Washington consensus. To evaluate the real feasibility of the projects underlying the initiative it is necessary to unveil unfounded misconception and promote mutual understanding through cross-cutting activities and a transparent and coherent institutional framework, aimed at implementing the many promises made by both parties.

Appendix

The synthetic version of the interviews carried out for original data collection for the present paper is available at the following link: https://forms.gle/L8LFrX161nTf7em26.

The answers considered for this study are those of:

Alberto Bradanini: current president of Study Centre for Chinese Studies (CSCC), he held important diplomatic positions: Commercial Counselor at the Italian Embassy in China (1991-1996), Italian Ambassador to China (1996-1998), Italian Ambassador to Beijing (2013-2015), Coordinator of China-Italy Governmental Committee at the Italian

---

1 His proposal partially reflects the existing Italy-China Business Forum (founded in 2014), a periodic meeting focused on business and trade. It had a real impact on China-Italy relations, since it allowed the establishment of a permanent law court that assists the intergovernmental dialogue, ease the exchange of information, knowledge, industrial projects, and strategic partnership with third countries (Bradanini, 2018).

Ministry of Foreign Affairs (2004-2007), and Italian Ambassador to Iran (2008-2012).

Ferdinando Nelli Feroci: current president of the International Affaris Institute (IAI). He was a diplomat from 1972 to 2013, he was Permanent Representative of Italy to the European Union in Brussels (2008-13), Chief of Staff (2006-08) and Director General for European Integration (2004-06) at the Italian Ministry of Foreign Affairs. Previously, he served in New York at the United Nations, in Algiers, Paris and Beijing. He also served as Diplomatic Counsellor of the Vice President of the Italian Council of Ministers (1998). In June 2014 he was appointed to the post of European Commissioner in the Commission chaired by Manuel Barroso to replace Antonio Tajani, a position he held until the end of the mandate of the Commission on 1 November 2014. Formerly a Fellow at the Center for International Affairs, Harvard University (1985-86), and Visiting Professor at the Istituto Universitario Orientale of Naples (1989), he is currently a professor at the School of Government of LUISS, Rome.

Federico Brusadelli: current Research Associate for Chinese Studies at Friedrich-Alexander-Universität Erlangen-Nürnberg and affiliate to Italian Association for Chinese Studies and to European Association for Chinese Studies and Philosophy.

References

Amighini, A. (11/09/2019). *Fact Checking: BRI, la nuova via della seta*. ISPI. https://www.ispionline.it/it/pubblicazione/fact-checking-bri-la-nuova-della-seta-23784

Asif, M. & Ling, Y. (2018). *Belt and Road Initiative: A Spirit of Chinese Cultural Thought*. Canadian Center of Science and Education: International Journal of Business and Management, Vol. 13, No. 12

Bai, J. (01/04/2019). *5G, le regole più certe sono una buona garanzia per tutti*. 中国经济信息社. http://www.classxhsilkroad.it/news/politica-economica/5g-le-regole-piu-certe-sono-una-buona-garanzia-per-tutti-201903292002271476

Bradanini, A. (2018). *Italia-Cina, come riequilibrare una relazione asimmetrica*. CSCC Policy Papers.

Bressan, M. (16/03/2019). *L'Italia nella Nuova Via della Seta: opportunità e rischi*. Inside Over. https://it.insideover.com/economia/litalia-nella-nuova-via-della-seta-opportunita-e-rischi.html

Buzzetti, E. (04/11/2019). *Il 2020 sarà un anno fondamentale per i rapporti tra Italia e Cina*. Agenzia Giornalistica Italiana. https://www.agi.it/politica/rapporti_cina_italia_via_della_seta_di_maio-6486877/news/2019-11-04/

Carcano, L. (13/03/2019). *Via della Seta, Fondazione Italia-Cina: "Usa e Ue temono nuova globalizzazione"*. LaPresse. https://www.lapresse.it/economia/via_della_seta_fondazione_italia-cina_usa_e_ue_temono_nuova_globalizzazione_-1235245/news/2019-03-13/

Casarini, N. (2015). *Is Europe to Benefit from China's Belt and Road Initiative?*. IAI Working Papers, Vol. 15, No. 40.

Casarini, N. (2019). *Rome-Beijing: Changing the Game. Italy's Embrace of China's Connectivity Project, Implications for the EU and the US*. IAI Papers. Vol. 19, No. 5.

Covington & Burling LLP. (09/04/2019). *China Adopts New Foreign Investment Law*. Convington. http://www.iberchina.org/files/2019/fie_law_covington.pdf

Dana Heide et al. (17/04/2018). *"EU Ambassadors Band Together Against Silk Road"*. Handelsblatt. https://www.handelsblatt.com/23581860.html

Fardella, E. & Prodi, G. (2018). *The Belt and Road Initiative and its Impact on Europe*. Valdai Papers, No.82

Fotina, C. (28/07/2019). *Dazi Usa, un conto salato per l'Italia: «Per noi conto da 4,5 miliardi»*. IlSole24Ore. https://www.ilsole24ore.com/art/dazi-usa-conto-salato-l-italia-per-noi-conto-45-miliardi-AC5b8Tb

Goldstein, A. (2016). *Capitalismo Rosso. Investimenti cinesi in Italia*. Milano: Università Bocconi.

Hirst, P. & Garcia, A. (2019). *China, Italy, the European Union and the "Belt and Road Initiative"*. Clyde & Co. https://www.lexology.com/library/detail.aspx?g=95486fdd-273b-4360-8895-46213f772e49

ICE. (2019). *ICE 2018-2019 Report. Italy in the world economy*. Ministry of Economic Development.

InfoMercatiesteri. (18/04/2019). *Rapporto Cina*. Italian Ministry of Foreign Affairs and International Cooperation. http://www.infomercatiesteri.it/overview.php?id_paesi=122

Kirschenbaum, J., Soula, E. & Clohessy, M. (24/09/2019). *EU Foreign Investment Screening – At Last, a Start*. GMF. https://securingdemocracy.gmfus.org/eu-foreign-investment-screening-at-last-a-start/

Kwong, D. (09/04/2008). *Italy's Ferrero wins battle against fakes in China*. Reuters. https://www.reuters.com/article/ferrero-china/italys-ferrero-wins-battle-against-fakes-in-china-idUSHKG16080620080409

Negri, A. (19/03/2019). *Vi racconto i due pesi e le due misure degli Stati Uniti su Italia, Cina e non solo*. Smartmag. https://www.startmag.it/mondo/via-seta-cina-italia/

Punzi, F. (15/03/2019). *Nuova Via della Seta: ecco perché l'Italia sottovaluta implicazioni geopolitiche e rischi economici*. Atlantico. http://www.atlanticoquotidiano.it/quotidiano/nuova-via-della-seta-ecco-perche-litalia-sottovaluta-implicazioni-geopolitiche-e-rischi-economici/

Renminribao. (21/03/2019). 东西交往传佳话 中意友谊续新篇. http://paper.people.com.cn/rmrb/html/2019-03/21/nw.D110000renmrb_20190321_3-03.htm

Ries, E. T., et al. (2018). *2018 Edelman Trust Barometer*. Edelman Institute.

Ruet, J. (03/08/2019). *Made in China 2025 and the Belt and Road Initiative*. ISPI online. https://www.ispionline.it/it/pubblicazione/made-china-2025-and-belt-and-road-initiative-21113

Studio Legale Chiomenti. (2009). *"Quadro di riferimento legislativo e fiscale per gli investimenti stranieri in Cina"*. https://www.yumpu.com/it/document/view/4509555/guida-informativa-legale-sulla-cina-studio-legale-chiomenti

The Economist Intelligence Unit (2013). *"China Going Global Investment Index"*. The Economist. https://china.ucsd.edu/_files/odi-2013/09232013_Paper_Liu_ChinaGoingGlobal.pdf

World Trade Organization. (2019). *World Trade Statistical Review 2019*. Geneva: World Trade Organization Centre William Rappard.

Zeneli, V. (03/04/2019). *Italy Signs on to Belt and Road Initiative: EU-China Relations at Crossroads?*. The Diplomat. https://thediplomat.com/2019/04/italy-signs-on-to-belt-and-road-initiative-eu-china-relations-at-crossroads/

绿色"一带一路"与中国国有企业的社会责任

毕洛兰 【法国】
亚洲中心联合会 创始人

2019年春季在北京举办的第二届"一带一路"国际合作高峰论坛上,中国提出了"绿色之路"的倡议,并在推动"生态文明"之外,展示了自己作为发展参与者的身份。中国正在回应国际社会对其的期望,肩负起作为大国的责任,同时防止因为忽视环境被人指责。海外的中企,特别是作为主要参与者的国有企业能发挥什么作用?旨在为企业提供可持续发展途径的指南和模板的企业社会责任(CSR)是否为中国实现这一目标提供了信用支持?换言之,除了中国所宣称的雄心之外,在这种背景下,企业社会责任在哪些方面提升才能够支持中国的形象,并应对可持续发展的全球挑战?

本文采用探究式的方法,试图回答上述问题,同时试图更好地理解与全球发展驱动力相关的国际期望、"一带一路"倡议(BRI)与可持续发展目标(SDG)的可能一致性,以及中国从这个角度对国有企业的动员。这意味着要根据中国的国情以及中国所制定的管理办法来考虑企业社会责任。本文重点关注行业和参与者的动态,以便更好地理解中国企业社会责任的当前趋势、局限性和潜在优势。

一 调整"一带一路"倡议(BRI)以实现可持续发展目标

1. 国际社会的期望

2016年1月1日,联合国环境规划署(UNEP)《2030年可持续发展议程》

的 17 项可持续发展目标（SDG）生效并适用于所有国家。《2030 议程》旨在确保所有国家，无论其发展水平如何，"动员力量结束一切形式的贫困，消除不平等，应对气候变化，确保没有人落后"。为了实现这些目标，在保护地球的同时促进繁荣，各国领导人认识到，在消除贫困的同时，必须制定战略，促进经济增长，满足包括教育、卫生、社会保障和就业机会在内的一系列社会需要，同时应对气候变化和保护环境[1]。中国已经采纳了这些原则，并在 2013 年启动了培育全球战略的"一带一路"倡议 (BRI)。2017 年 5 月在北京举办的首届"一带一路"国际合作高峰论坛上，65 个成员国齐聚一堂，习近平主席将"一带一路"称为"世纪工程""和谐大家庭"。因此，通过在陆地和海洋基础设施上 1 万亿美元投资，在跨大陆的规模上改善互联互通和合作的最初目标因此被超越并扩展到金融、旅游、可持续和创新方面。摩根士丹利 (Morgan Stanley) 估计，到 2027 年，中国在"丝绸之路"沿线国家的累计投资将超过 1.2 万亿美元。

在环境层面，来自世界各地的环境专家于 2018 年在《自然——可持续发展》杂志上发表专栏文章警告说，BRI 增加的贸易走廊将威胁生物的多样性，它将侵占 265 种临危物种的领地，其中 81 种濒危，39 种极危。

从气候角度来看，清华大学金融与发展中心主任马军和联合国环境规划署联合主任西蒙·扎德克在 2019 年 9 月发表的一项研究表明，"与气候相关的最大风险和机遇在于我们支持 120 多个已经加入 BRI 国家低碳发展道路的能力，这些国家目前占全球 GDP 的 23% 左右，碳排放量占全球的 28% 左右，中国除外"。

最后，由于 BRI 实施涉及的利益相关者众多，而且很难与 2030 年议程保持一致，美国战略与国际问题研究中心（CSIS）甚至明确指出，"从设计上看，BRI 更像是一个松散的品牌，而不是一个有严格标准的项目"。

2. 绿色"一带一路"："重塑形象和绿色投资"

2019 年 4 月 25 日，第二届"一带一路"国际合作高峰论坛在消除担忧和改善形象的背景下开幕。

在论坛期间，还强调了另一项倡议——由中国绿色金融委员会（GFC）与伦敦合作发起的绿色金融倡议（GFI），宣布全球 28 家公司签署了一套 BRI 绿色金融指南。基于现有的负责任融资举措，绿色投资原则旨在将可持续发展和低碳排

---

[1] 《2030 年议程》还建立了一个国际审查程序，邀请各国自愿每年报告进展情况。SDG 的实施需要各国政府以及所有参与者（公司、社区、协会、研究人员等）的积极承诺，并在每个州的层面上进行部署。

放纳入"一带一路"倡议下的项目。

2019年5月,国际可持续发展研究所(IISD)的《绿色一带一路特别政策研究》和《2030年可持续发展议程》政策报告指出,中华人民共和国生态环境部与国内外合作伙伴共同创建了"一带一路国际绿色发展联盟"。

因此,在政治话语、正在进行的多边合作和金融工具的支持下,各项公告和动员令人鼓舞。然而,"一带一路"倡议在国家和国际层面都没有一个超越参与者的单独管理机制。尽管中国民营经济蓬勃发展,但中国主要依靠占国内生产总值30%的国有企业。中国将国有企业置于"一带一路"建设的前列。在过去五年中,102家战略性央企(国务院国资委监管的央企)中有80多家实施了3116个"一带一路"沿线项目,其中50%用于基础设施建设,合同金额超过70%。

这些国有企业真的有能力在预期可持续发展的角度开展它们的项目吗?企业社会责任(Corporate Social Responsibility,简称CSR)自20世纪50年代在美国被引入以来,一直强调在企业活动中考虑社会、环境和经济问题,并与利益相关方进行互动。事实上,随着20世纪80年代末全球金融市场的建立,全球化的模式得到了加强,企业社会责任也伴随着监管途径的进步、促进跨国公司的兴起而发展起来。

3. "走出国门,讲好中国故事"中的国企公共外交

"一带一路"延伸了中国的"走出去"战略。该战略在20世纪90年代末加速实施,表现在国有企业开拓国外市场,以获得中国经济快速增长所需的资源和原材料。国有企业是中国经济外交的工具,其目的是"以经促政"和"政经结合"。

2005—2008年,中国纺织行业制定了一个标准,在电气领域主要国有企业国家电网发布了第一份报告,深圳、上海证券交易所首次制定《上市公司社会责任指引》和《上市公司环境信息披露指引》(2006—2008)。

也正是在这个时候,中国商务部发布了《关于加强出口企业环境监测的通知》和《关于加强社会责任的若干意见》。国资委于2008年发布了《中央企业履行社会责任指引》。中国的企业社会责任行动加快,2015年的报告发布量成倍增加,达到1703份(2006年为32份)。此外,越来越多的中国企业和社会组织加入了《联合全球契约》,其中许多企业采用了全球报告倡议组织(GRI)框架等国际报告标准,通过与世界领先企业进行对标,改善了企业社会责任管理和信息披露质量。截至2016年底,中国参与者为261家,包括113家大型企业、

105 家中小企业和 43 家社会组织。

对于国有企业的海外业务，中国商务部和国资委从 2013 年开始发表了支持提高企业社会责任意识的声明。为了加强实施，政府表示希望改善国家法律法规，尤其是生产质量、投资、环境保护方面的法律法规。企业优先参考这些法律法规，而不是联合国的环境、社会和公司治理（ESG）。它还打算更加重视中国在海外的专业组织（如商会），以规范最佳做法，并改进中国在海外运营公司的管理规则和指南，以及公司在实施企业社会责任方面的推动作用。

鼓励境外国有企业熟悉当地现行法律法规，尊重与当地工会、劳动、税收和环境保护有关的法律法规。与此同时，各部委将制定管理规则，将环境保护纳入外国投资和合作中，其企业社会责任的绩效和实施将在审查国外发展评估时予以考虑。国有企业在自身承担企业社会责任方面的作用得到了很好的提升，这既有利于增强其与世界上发布报告并关注环境问题的大公司相比的竞争力，也有利于在管理、资金分配和培训方面发挥内部优势。

在这种背景下，一些人认为，在国外履行社会责任已成为中央企业在世界范围内开展活动、提升品牌形象和国际竞争力的重要因素，也是塑造中国国家形象的重要因素。"一带一路"从一开始就这样宣称和鼓励，那么国家层面的企业社会责任发展是否如 2013 年期望的那样，足以通过国企来巩固其海外的部署？因此，有必要更仔细地研究中国的企业社会责任概念及其实施方式。

二 中国国有企业在社会责任方面的特殊性

1. 概念的发展与法规

1994 年，中华人民共和国第一部《公司法》生效，使公司在法律上独立，从而成为社会责任的主体，尽管没有明确提到"企业社会责任"一词。与此同时，颁布了一系列与环境和社会问题有关的法律，包括《环境保护法》（1989 年）、《工会法》（1992 年）、《消费者保护法》（1993 年）和《劳动法》。

但直到 2006 年，企业社会责任才首次得到法律和国家发展战略的承认。中国共产党第十六届中央委员会第六次全体会议在提出追求"构建社会主义和谐社会"的同时，明确要求"加强公民、企业和其他各类组织的社会责任"。

然而，2006 年，《公司法》第 5 条和《集体企业法》第 7 条（仅有的包含关于企业社会责任的声明性规定的两部国家法律）并未规定遵守企业社会责任标准和行为准则的法律义务。中央企业和合作企业的合伙人必须遵守法律、行政法规，遵守社会公德和商业道德，诚实守信，接受公众监督，承担社会责任。

因此，就像人们对企业社会责任的普遍看法一样，中国的文件主要属于规范性文件的范畴，只向私营公司提供引导，而不构成具有约束力标准的依据。

从立法角度看，2011年国外贿赂被纳入了刑法，2012年公司在工作分配方面的责任得到了强化，并且，与卖家对消费者的责任一样，2014年通过了《环境保护法》修正案，采用了污染者付费的原则。此外，在2015年，通过监测系统和澄清生产者和销售者的责任，食品安全得到了改善。如同中共中央第十八次会议所强调的，《关于全面推进法治若干重大问题的决定》明确提出了"加强企业社会责任立法"的要求。

在标准制定方面，2015年，国家质量监督检验检疫总局和国家标准局联合发布了三项社会责任国家标准，其中包括《社会责任指南》、《社会责任报告编写指南》和《社会责任履行指南》(附件6)，均于2016年1月1日生效。

与德国、瑞典和荷兰建立了国际企业社会责任合作，旨在提高企业社会责任意识和良好实践。商会和专业协会的积极参与提高了政策制定和执行的能力，为国际活动建立了企业社会责任监督和评估机制。

例如，2012年，在中国国际承包商协会在商务部的协助下，《中国国际承包商社会责任指南》得以出版。该指南详细介绍了7个主要主题，包括项目质量和安全、员工权利和职业发展、业主权利、供应链管理、公平竞争、环境保护以及社区参与和发展，提出了具体要求，并概述了企业社会责任管理的要点。它采用国际公认的标准，如"联合国全球契约组织"和ISO26000，并考虑到中国国际外包行业的发展，提供了一个适用于这些公司的框架。

2. 评估、局限性和展望

尽管所有这些努力都是为了提高认识和规范，但联合国邮政署、中国商务部国际贸易经济合作研究院和国资委研究中心发布的《中国海外企业企业社会责任研究报告》，强调中国海外企业企业社会责任发展处于初期：根据海外企业社会责任管理水平和信息披露建立的海外企业社会责任发展平均指数在2015年仅为25.67。央企是企业社会责任表现最好的企业，平均发展指数为42.77，私营企业为20.93。就行业而言，建筑公司和运输公司表现为"跟随者"(指数分别为49.92和42.00)，尤其是采矿、电力、制造业以及信息运输和技术服务业。相比之下，房地产行业和多部门行业被视为"路人"（指数约为 14）。

然而，大多数在海外成立的中国企业声称非常熟悉企业社会责任，根据 2015 年《中国海外企业可持续发展报告》，83% 的中国企业认为企业社会责任实践促进了可持续发展和竞争力的能力建设。事实上，与联合国千年发展目标和可持续发展目标、ISO26000、联合国全球契约和 GRI 等全球倡议和指导方针相比，中国跨国公司似乎对企业公民身份、利益相关者理论和三重底线（经济、环境和社会）有着更好的理解。此外，企业社会责任实践的动机有三分之二与公司自身的文化和理念等内部因素有关，有一半与总部的要求有关。尽管并非微不足道，外部因素是次要驱动力，其中含有地方政府（33%）、商业伙伴（24%）和其他包括当地社区利益相关者（23%）。

理解国际概念和与地方建立联系方面的局限性确实是中国企业在海外发展和履行社会责任的主要障碍，尤其是国有企业参与"一带一路"倡议的主要障碍，此外，国资委和中国社会科学院在 2018 年 12 月发布的关于《中央企业社会责任蓝皮书》中强调，管理体系的实施和企业社会责任报告的发布过于薄弱。

更具体地说，据被问询的公司称，他们在国外的 CSR 实践的大部分限制都是内部的。其中包括缺乏专业组织和人才，因此缺乏理论和实践支持（52%），对责任者缺乏激励和惩罚（42%），财政困难和缺乏额外资源（37%），来自东道国外部利益相关者的社会压力有限（31%），总部没有发布一致的要求或规定（26%），或缺乏企业社会责任意识和企业领导对企业社会责任的理解不够（19%）。到目前为止，只有不到 50% 的受访公司实施了专门为其海外活动设计的企业社会责任管理体系。

目前，只有 10% 的受访公司每年或定期发布针对其海外活动的企业社会责任报告，《企业社会责任蓝皮书》也指出了这一不足。中国跨国公司通常不愿意与当地媒体和机构沟通，因为它们长期以来过分重视与地方政府的关系，但在很大程度上忽视了与当地社区和非政府组织的互动。

事实上，在社区影响、经济发展和绿色信贷方面，海外的中国公司毁誉参半，他们在环境影响、劳资关系、环境评估和工作条件等领域受到了批评。这些是导致国外企业社会责任方面 62.6% 的负面评价的主要原因。然而，根据 KPMG 全球中国实践以及 CCPIT（中国国际贸易促进委员会）中国经济信息部发布的《中国企业海外绿色经营报告》，对社区和经济发展的影响、对环境的影响、就业机会、绿色信贷和劳资关系，是媒体、国家和国际研究机构在企业社会责任方面的主要关注点。其中，中国企业因提供就业机会、制定环境标准和开展慈善活动而获得好评。

因此，可以看出，在国际社会的关注和国家鼓励下，加强企业社会责任的发展，特别是在"一带一路"框架内，将是有益的。除了激励企业发布报告和与当地社区更好的沟通、考虑各种机制和手段能力之外，还可以依靠慈善事业和基金会的力量，正如《企业社会责任趋势》中所建议的那样。此外，随着大学社会责任网络等专家库的建立，教育、研究和培训似乎能够成为资金、创新和合作融合的平台，为企业社会责任的成功发展做出有益的贡献。

Greening Belt and Road Initiative and Chinese State-owned Enterprises Corporate Social Responsibility

Florence Biot / France

Asia Center / Co-founder

With the "greening" of the Belt and Road Initiative (BRI) proclaimed in spring 2019 during the second Belt and Road Forum in Beijing, China confirms the political dimension of the initiative, and displays itself as an actor of development beyond the promotion of the "ecological civilization". China then seems to meet the international expectation of a responsibility linked to its status as a major country. What role can Chinese companies play abroad, and in particular state-owned enterprises (SOE's) as main participants in the initiative? Also, does corporate social responsibility (CSR), which intends to provide companies with the guides and templates for a sustainable approach, constitute a useful lever for mobilization for China to make this intention effective? In other words, beyond the ambitions proclaimed by China, what are the CSR advances that could support the image of China in this context and respond to the global challenges of sustainable development?

Following an exploratory approach, this article attempts to answer these questions while trying to get a better understand of the international expectations linked to the global development drives, the possible alignment of the BRI in response to the Sustainable Development Goals (SDGs) and the mobilization of SOE's by China in this perspective. We will review some of China's missed appointments and the political and financial tools that could nevertheless support its approach today. That would mean considering the concept of CSR according to Chinese characteristics and the instruments specifically developed by the Party-State. Then, focus will be on the dynamics of both sector and players in order to better comprehend the current trends in Chinese CSR, its limitations and potential advantages.

I. Adjusting BRI to the Pursuit of Sustainable Development Objectives: International expectations

1.1 the Expectations from the International Community

On January 1, 2016, the 17 Sustainable Development Goals (SDGs) of the United Nations Environment Program (UNEP) 2030 Agenda for Sustainable Development entered into force. By applying to all, they aim to ensure that all countries, whatever their level of development, "mobilize energies to end all forms of poverty, combat inequalities and tackle climate change, making sure no one is left behind". With these goals, in order to promote prosperity while protecting the planet, leaders recognize that eradicating poverty must be accompanied by strategies that enhance economic growth and meet a range of social needs, including education, health, social protection and employment opportunities, while fighting climate change and protecting the environment.[1]

China, which has adopted these principles, is nurturing planetary ambitions with the launch in 2013 of the Belt and Road Initiative (BRI). During the first Belt and

---

1 The 2030 Agenda also establishes an international review process, by which States are invited, on a voluntary basis, to report annually on their progress. Deployed at the level of each State, the implementation of the SDGs calls for an active commitment from governments as well as from all actors (companies, communities, associations, researchers, etc.).

Road Forum in May 2017 in Beijing bringing together the 65 associated countries, Xi Jinping described this as the "project of the century" and the harmonious coexistence of a large family. The initial objective of improving connectivity and cooperation on a transcontinental scale through an unrivaled investment of 1,000 billion dollars in land and sea infrastructures is therefore exceeded to also include the financial, tourism, sustainable and innovation aspects to the point that Morgan Stanley estimates that the cumulative Chinese investments in the countries of the "silk roads" will exceed 1,200 billion dollars by 2027.

On the environmental level, a column published in *Nature Sustainability* in 2018 by environmental experts from around the world warns of the threat to biodiversity by the increase of trade corridors created by the BRI which would encroach on the territory of 265 threatened species 81 of which are endangered and 39 are critically endangered.

Finally, from a climate point of view, Ma Jun, director of the Center for Finance and Development at Tsinghua University and Simon Zadek, co-Director of UNEP, express in a study published in September 2019 that "the greatest risk -and opportunity -related to the climate lies in our ability to support a low carbon development path for the group of more than 120 countries that have joined the BRI Initiative while they currently represent, with the exception of China , around 23% of global GDP and around 28% of global carbon emissions ".

In the end, with both the multiplicity of stakeholders involved in the BRI implementation and the difficulty in aligning with the 2030 agenda, the CSIS even specify that "by design, the BRI is more a loose brand than a program with strict criteria".

1.2 Greening of the BRI: a rejuvenated image and green investments

The second Belt and Road Forum on April 25, 2019 then opened against a backdrop of fears to be dispelled and an image to be improved.

On the sidelines of the Forum, another initiative is also highlighted. This is the

Green Finance Initiative (GFI) led by the China Green Finance Committee (GFC) in partnership with London announcing that 28 companies around the world are subscribing to a set of green finance guidelines for the BRI. Building on existing responsible finance initiatives, the Green Investment Principles aim to integrate sustainable development and low carbon emissions into projects under the BRI.

In May 2019, the IISD's *Special Policy Study on Green Belt and Road and 2030 Agenda for Sustainable Development Policy Report* noted that the Ministry of Ecology and Environment of the People's Republic of China work together with domestic and foreign partners to create the BRI International Green Development Coalition.

The announcements and mobilizations thus seem encouraging, supported by political language, ongoing multilateral cooperation and financial instruments. However, the BRI does not have a single institution of governance beyond a network of actors, both at national and international level. Despite the dynamic of the Chinese private sector, China relies above all on its State-owned Enterprises, which represent 30% of domestic GDP, and which it places at the forefront of the BRI. Over the past five years, more than 80 of the 102 so-called strategic central companies (i.e. under the supervision of the State-owned Assets Supervision and Administration Commission of the State Council, SASAC) have thus implemented 3,116 projects along the BRI, 50% of which in the construction of infrastructure and whose contract value exceeded 70%.

However, do the SOE's actually have the capacity to carry out their projects in the expected sustainable perspective, in which the Corporate Social Responsibility (CSR) intends to contribute since it was introduced in the US the 1950s, by taking into account social, environmental and economic concerns in their activities and interactions with their stakeholders? Indeed, following the model of globalization accentuated at the end of the 1980s with the creation of financial markets at the global level, CSR developed with the rise of multinationals by advancing regulatory tools at the same time.

1.3 SOE's Public Diplomacy in "Going out and Telling Chinese story"

The BRI extends the Chinese strategy of "going out" (*zou chu qu*), which implementation accelerated at the end of the 1990s calling the SOE'S to create foreign markets and obtain access to resources and raw materials that are necessary for China's rapid economic growth. State-owned enterprises stand as the instruments of Chinese economic diplomacy, which aims to "use the economy to promote politics" (*yi jing cu zheng*) and "to combine politics and economics" (*zheng jing jie he*).

At the time multinationals embraced CSR to protect their reputation, China became a labor-intensive industry without actually achieving certification (such as SA 8000). It seems to respond pragmatically to this "technical" obstacle first, but also by the growing attention of the Chinese public to CSR: a literature on the subject emerged between 2000 and 2005 with different approaches to the concept.

Between 2005 and 2008, we observed in China the creation of a standard by the textile industry, the publication of the first report by the main SOE'S in the electrical field State Grid, and the formulation of first CSR *Guidelines for Public Companies* and the *Guidelines on the Disclosure of Environmental In-formation for Public Companies* by the Shenzhen and Shanghai stock exchanges (2006-2008).

It was also around this time that the Ministry of Commerce of the People's Republic of China (MOFCOM) issued the *Notice on Strengthening the Environmental Monitoring over Export Enterprises* and the *Several Opinions on Strengthening the Social Responsibility*. As the SASAC, it published its *Guidelines on the Fulfilment of Social Responsibility by Central Enterprises* in 2008. Since then, the CSR movement has accelerated in China and the publication of reports has multiplied to reach 1,703 in 2015 (compared to 32 in 2006). In addition, more and more Chinese companies and social organizations have joined the United Global Compact and many of them have adopted international reporting standard like the GRI framework, improving their CSR management and the quality of information disclosure by benchmarking to the world leading companies. At the end of 2016, the number of Chinese participants stood at 261, including 113 large enterprises, 105 SMEs and 43 social organizations.

For SOE's overseas, it was from 2013 that MOFCOM and SASAC published in support of greater awareness of CSR. To strengthen its implementation, the government says it wants to improve national laws and regulations -in particular for the quality of production, investments, environmental protection to which companies preferentially refer to rather than to the UN's ESGs. It also intends to give more weight to Chinese professional organizations abroad (such as chambers of commerce) to standardize best practices and improve both the rules and guidelines on the management of Chinese companies operating abroad and the driving role of companies for the implementation of CSR.

SOE's abroad are encouraged to familiarize themselves with the local laws and regulations in force and to respect those relating to the local union, labor, taxation and environmental protection. In the meantime, the ministries were to formulate the management rules that integrate environmental protection in foreign investments and cooperation whose performance and implementation of CSR would be taken into account in the review of evaluation of development abroad. The role of SOE'S in their own appropriation of CSR is well raised both for the benefit of strengthening their competitiveness compared to large companies in the world which published reports and paid attention to environmental problems, and of an internal advantage in terms of management, allocation of funds and training.

In this context, some argue that the implementation of social responsibility abroad has become an important factor for central enterprises to develop their activities in the world, improve their brand image and their international competitiveness, and become also an important element in shaping China's national image. With such declarations and encouragement from the very beginnings of the BRI, is the development of CSR at the national level suitable enough to underpin its deployment abroad through SOE's appropriation of a Chinese model as expected in

2013? It is therefore necessary to examine more closely the Chinese concept of CSR and the modalities of its implementation.

II. The Chinese Specificities of Soe's in Terms of CSR

2.1 Concept Development and Regulation

In 1994, the first company law of the PRC entered into force, making companies legally independent and thus becoming the subject of social responsibility, although the term "CSR" was not explicitly mentioned. In the meantime, a series of laws relating to environmental and social issues have been enacted, including the *Environmental Protection Act* (1989), the *Trade Union Act* (1992), the *Consumer Protection Act* (1993) and labor law.

But it was not until 2006 that CSR was recognized for the first time by law and by the national development strategy. The Sixth Plenary Assembly of the Sixteenth Central Committee of the Communist Party of China (CCCPC), in the pursuit of "building a harmonious socialist society", explicitly demands "to strengthen the social responsibilities of citizens, enterprises and other types of organizations".

However, in 2006, article 5 of the law on companies and article 7 of the law on collective enterprises, the only two national laws containing a declaratory provision on CSR, do not create a legal obligation to comply with CSR standards and codes of conduct. Central enterprise carrying out business activities and partners in cooperative enterprises must (bixu) obey laws and administrative regulations, observe social morals and business ethics, remain honest and of good faith, accept public scrutiny, and assume social responsibility

Thus, just like the common view on CSR, Chinese documentation mainly belongs to the category of normative documents (*guifanxing wenjian*) to provide only advice (*yindao*) to private companies without constituting a source of binding standards. From a legislative point of view, foreign bribery was incorporated into criminal law in 2011, the responsibility of companies in terms of work distribution was reinforced in 2012 and, like that of sellers vis-à-vis consumers, the polluter-pay principle was adopted in 2014 with the amendment of the law on environmental protection. Also, in 2015 food safety was improved by monitoring the system and clarifying the responsibility of producers and sellers. As underlined by the CCCPC during the 18th meeting, the *Decision on Several Major Issues Concerning Comprehensively Promoting the Rule of Law* explicitly put forward the requirement of "strengthening CSR legislation". Regarding the development of standards, the State Administration of Quality Control, Inspection and Quarantine and the Standards Administration of China jointly published three national standards on social responsibility in 2015 with the *Guide to Social Responsibility,* the *Guide to Writing Social Responsibility Reports* and the *Guide to Social Responsibility Performance* (Annex 6), all of which came into effect on January 1, 2016. International CSR cooperation has been established with Germany, Sweden and the Netherlands and aims to raise CSR awareness and good practice. The active involvement of chambers of commerce and professional associations enhances the capability of policy making and implementation, establishing CSR supervisory and evaluation mechanisms for international activity For example, the *Guide to Social Responsibility of Chinese International Contractors* published in 2012 was developed by the *China International Contractors Association* with the assistance of MOFCOM. The guide details 7 main topics, including project quality and safety, employee rights and career development, owner's rights, supply chain management, fair competition, environmental protection and community involvement and development, offers specific requirements and outlines the key points of CSR management. Using internationally recognized standards, such as the United Nations Global Compact and ISO26000, and taking into account the development of the international outsourcing industry in China, it provides a framework applicable to the companies.

2.2 Assessment, Limits And Perspectives

Despite all these efforts to raise awareness and to regulate, the *Research Report on Corporate Social Responsibility of Chinese Overseas Enterprises* published by the UNPD for China, the Chinese Academy of International Trade and Economic Cooperation in China at MOFCOM, and the Research Center of the Commission for SASAC, underline the near-initial stage of development of CSR by Chinese enterprises abroad: the overseas CSR development average index, established on the basis of overseas CSR management level and information disclosure, is only of 25.67 in 2015. Central enterprises are those with best CSR performances with an average development index of 42.77 versus 20.93 for private companies. In terms of industries, construction companies and transport companies perform as "followers" (with indices of 49.92 and 42.00 respectively), notably mining, electricity, manufacturing, as well as information transport and technical service. Comparatively the real estate sectors and multi-sector industries are considered as "passers-by" (with indices around 14).

However, most Chinese companies established abroad claim to be very familiar with CSR and according to the 2015 *Report on the Sustainable Development of Chinese Enterprises Overseas* 83% believe that CSR practices promote capacity building for sustainable development and competitiveness. Actually, it appears that Chinese MNEs generally have a better understanding of corporate citizenship, stakeholder theory and the triple bottom line (economic, environmental and social) than knowledge of global initiatives and guidelines -such as the UN MDGs and SDGs, ISO26000, the UN Global Compact and GRI. Also, the motivation of CSR practices is for two-thirds linked to internal factors such as the culture and philosophy of the company itself and for half linked to the requirements of the head office. External actors are a secondary, albeit not insignificant, driving force -among them local authorities (33%), business partners (24%) and other stakeholders, including local communities (23%).

These limitations in understanding international concepts and establishing links with localities are indeed pointed as the main obstacles to the development and CSR performance of Chinese companies abroad, in particular the SOE's participating in the initiative of the BRI, alongside the too weak implementation of a management system and publication of CSR reports, as highlighted in December 2018 by SASAC and the Chinese Academy of Social Sciences CASS in the first *Bluebook on Overseas Social Responsibility of Central Entreprises*.

More specifically, according to the questioned companies, most of the limitation to their CSR practices abroad are internal. They include the lack of professional organizations and talents, therefore the lack of theoretical and practical support (52%), the absence of incentives and sanctions for those responsible (42%), financial difficulties and the lack of additional resources (37%), limited social pressure from external stakeholders in the host country (31%), the absence of coherent requirements or regulations issued by the head office (26%) or of awareness and business leaders' understanding of CSR (19%). So far, less than 50% of the companies questioned have implemented a CSR management system specially designed for their activities abroad.

Similarly, up to 50% of companies do not disclose any CSR information overseas in any form whatsoever. Currently, only 10% of companies surveyed publish CSR reports specific to their overseas activities annually or regularly, a deficiency that the CSR bluebook also points out. Chinese multinationals are generally reluctant to communicate with local media and institutions as they chronically place undue importance on relationships with local governments, but more largely ignore interaction with local communities and NGOs.

Indeed, Chinese companies abroad have received a mixed reception when it comes to community impact, economic development and green credit, and they have drawn criticism in areas such as environmental impact, industrial relations, environmental assessment and working conditions. These are the main reasons for the 62.6% negative performance of CSR abroad. However, according to the *Green Operation of Chinese Enterprises Overseas* report published by KPMG Global China Practice and the Chinese Department of Economic Information of the China Council for the Promotion of International Trade (CCPIT), the impact on the community and economic development, the impact on the environment, employment opportunities, green credit and industrial relations are the main concerns of the media and national and international research institutes in terms of CSR. Among them, Chinese companies have acquired some form of credit for providing employment opportunities, setting environmental standards and carrying out philanthropic activities.

It can thus be seen with such international attention and national encouragement that strengthening development of CSR, particularly in the BRI framework, would be beneficial. Beyond the incentives for reports' publication and better communication with local communities, articulation of various mechanisms and measurement capacities, it can also rely today on the strong developments of philanthropy and foundations as suggested by Syntao in its last edition of CSR trends. Also, with the constitution of networks of experts such as the University social responsibility network, education, research and training seems to be able to be the sector where funds, innovations and cooperation could converge at the same time as useful contributions to the development of a successful CSR. But beyond a few examples of training populations in a win-win situation along the BRI as it appears in Malaysia, Laos, or Bangkok, and the strong development of Confucius institutes which, on the contrary, generate significant suspicions, the main point in the future is to see whether cooperation for an alliance development such as the university alliance of the silk road, with the UK in particular, can be established along a balanced and sustainable path.

References

"BRI Cooperation: Mainstreaming ESG Investments", Shi Yichen, Jie Bao, 2019 July, https://green-bri.org/bri-cooperation-mainstreaming-esg-investments?cookie-state-change=1569086036147

"China aims to address 'debt trap' criticism at second Belt and Road Forum", *South China Morning Post*, Catherine Wong, 25 April 2019https://www.scmp.com/news/china/diplomacy/

article/3007558/china-aims-address-debttrap-criticism-second-belt-and-road

"China expands global ambitions with a new phase of Xi's signature program", Apr 29 2019, https://www.cnbc.com/2019/04/29/belt-and-road-china-expands-global-ambitions-with-newprogram-phase.html //

"China's Belt and Road Initiative, from the inside looking out", Zhang Denghua, Yin Jianwen, 2019. 07 https://www.lowyinstitute.org/the-interpreter/china-s-belt-and-road-initiative-insidelooking-out

"China's Belt and Road Initiative: Five Years Later", Hillman, Jonathan, CSIS (2018-01-25)

"China's Flexibility on Display at the Belt and Road Forum", Institut Montaigne, Mathieu Duchatel, APRIL 2019, https://www.institutmontaigne.org/en/blog/chinas-flexibility-display-belt-and-road-forum

"China's 1st report on SOE overseas social responsibility published", Liu Yukun, 2018, http://www.chinadaily.com.cn/a/201805/25/WS5b08138ea31001b82571c624.html

"Corporate Social Responsibility on the Belt and Road", Dr Mimi Zou, jan. 2019, Australian Institute of International Affairs, http://www.internationalaffairs.org.au/australianoutlook/corporate-social-responsibility-beltroad/

"CSR of the Belt & Road Initiative", Feb. 13 2018, https://www.uscpublicdiplomacy.org/story/csr-belt-road-initiative

"Current Trends in Research on Social Responsibility in State-Owned Enterprises: A Review of the Literature from 2000 to 2017", Raquel Garde-Sanchez, María Victoria López-Pérez and Antonio M. López-Hernández, Department of Finance and Accounting, University of Granada, July 2018

"Decarbonizing the Belt and Road A GREEN FINANCE ROADMAP", Dr. Ma Jun, Dr. Simon Zadek, Sept. 2019, Tsinghua PBCSF, www.vivideconomics.com/publications/decarbonizing-the-belt-and-road-initiative-agreenfinance-roadmap

"Embracing the BRI Ecosystem in 2018 -Navigating pitfalls and seizing Opportunities", Sitao Xu, Lydia Chen, Deloitte perspective, https://www2.deloitte.com/content/dam/Deloitte/cn/Documents/ser-soe-br/deloitte-cn-briembracing-the-bri-ecosystem-in-2018-en-180403.pdf

"Further Enhancing CSR Awareness of Chinese Companies Operating Abroad", MOFCOM, http://csr2.mofcom.gov.cn/article/CEGA/pg/201303/20130300059556.shtml

"Social Responsibility' in the Governance of Chinese stateowned Enterprises", Flora Sapio,

Università degli Studi "L'Orientale", Napoli (Italy), Aug. 2019, https://papers.ssrn.com/sol3/papers.cfm?abstract_id=3431685

"SOEs leading way in CSR initiatives", 2018, China Daily

"The first social responsibility report released by the SASAC system", 2018, Shenzhen News, http://csr2.mofcom.gov.cn/article/ckts/sr/201812/20181202819469.shtml

《中国企业海外可持续发展报告 2015》, UNDP, http://www.cn.undp.org/content/china/zh/home/library/south-south-cooperation/2015-reporton-the-sustainable-development-of-chinese-enterprise/

《中央企业社会责任蓝皮书》, 中国社科院、国务院国资委, 2018 年 12 月, 1972 页

« Nouvelles Routes de la Soie : ralentissement ou second souffle ? », Jean-Raphaël Chaponnière, https://asialyst.com/fr/2019/04/30/nouvelles-routes-de-la-soie-vers-secondsouffle/

« Verdir les Nouvelles Routes de la soie : récents progrès dans l'évaluation de l'ampleur du défi, des obstacles et des leviers d'action », Sebastien Treyer, IDDRI, https://www.iddri.org/fr/publications-et-evenements/billet-de-blog/verdir-les-nouvellesroutes-de-la-soie-recents-progres

Corporate Social Responsibility In China: A Vision, An Assessment And A Blueprint, Benaoit Vermander, Wspc, 2013, p. 354

CSR Guidelines for Public Companies and the *Guidelines on the Disclosure of Environmental In-formation for Public Companies, 2006 / Notice on Strengthening the Environmental Monitoring over Export Enterprises* and the *Several Opinions on Strengthening the Social Responsibility,* 2007 / *Guidelines on the Fulfilment of Social Responsibility by Central Enterprises, 2008,* http://www.wtoguide.net/index.php?g=&m=article&a=index&id=449

CSR Report on Chinese Business Overseas Operations, Liu Baocheng / Zhang Mengsha, Globethics.net China Ethics Series No. 8

Further Enhancing CSR Awareness of Chinese Companies Operating Abroad, MOFCOM, 2013, CNTV

GoldenBee Research on CSR Reporting in China 2018, goldencsr, 2018-12-27, http://en.goldenbeechina.com/index.php/Home/News/show/id/94

Guidelines to the State-owned Enterprises Directly under the Central Government on Fulfilling Corporate Social Responsibilities, State-owned Assets Supervision and Administration Commission of the State Council, 2014, http://csr2.mofcom.gov.cn/article/policies/national/sasac/201410/20141000753366.shtml

Operation Manual for the Guide on Social Responsibility for Industries in China (GSRI-China 2.0), 2018, China Federation of Industrial Economics, http://csr2.mofcom.gov.cn/article/ckts/sr/201810/20181002801976.shtml

Research Report on the Overseas CSR Fulfillment of Central SOEs (2017): Central SOEs should improve the ability to fulfill their social responsibility overseas, http://csr2.mofcom.gov.cn/article/CEGA/pg/201303/20130300059556.shtml

Special Policy Study on GreenBelt and Roadand 2030 Agenda for Sustainable DevelopmentPolicy Report, https://www.iisd.org/sites/default/files/publications/cciced/agm/cciced-sps-green-beltroads.pdf

Sustainability reporting standards in China, April 2016, http://www.bsdconsulting.com/insights/article/sustainability-reporting-standards-in-china

The Belt and Road Initiative from a sustainability Perspective, The Swedish trade and invest council, Embassy of Sweden, Beijing, China, sept. 2018 https://www.swedenabroad.se/globalassets/ambassader/kina-peking/documents/csr-new/theimplication-of-the-bri-from-a-sustainability-perspective_20180930_final.pdf

Top 10 CSR Trends in China (2019), jan. 2019, Syntao academy, Syntao green finance, China overseas investment riskmap, ccm csr promotion center, http://en.syntao.com/syntaoEN/public/uploads/20190227/2e511a113b58ffd609e44524e16179 ad.pdf

中国企业的海外绿色运营，https://assets.kpmg.com/content/dam/kpmg/pdf/2013/10/China-enterprises-green-globalisation-201310-c.pdf

中央企业讲好中国故事的几点思考——以海外社会责任为视角 - 支纪强李青林对外传播

传播企业社会责任每日经济新闻联合商道纵横发起"首席责任官计划"，2019-01-20，www.sohu.com/a/290345489_115362

央企"一带一路"履责情况分析. 文章来源：《国资报告》杂志，发布时间：2019-03-25.

从"一带一路"倡议看老挝旅游业的发展

哈克妮兰 【老挝】

老挝外交研究所　研究员

一　引言

不可忽视的是，交通运输和旅游业与经济和科学密切相关，促进交通基础设施建设可能有助于旅游业的发展。然而，建设高铁建设成本高，同时还需要通过实地考察和规划以证明某些经济活动如旅游业是否会得到提高。本文旨在通过对各国案例的研究，阐明铁路促进老挝旅游业发展的相关因素，同时审视老挝"陆锁国向陆联国转变"发展政策的相关措施。本文最后，笔者明确老挝旅游业的机遇和挑战并提出发展建议。

二　老挝旅游形势

老挝是不发达的内陆国家，位于中南半岛中部，北面与中国接壤（416公里），西北至缅甸（236公里），西至泰国（1835公里），南至柬埔寨（492公里），东到越南（1957公里）。

老挝总面积为23.68万平方公里，约70%的地形为山区，在川圹省达到了最高海拔2820米。尤其是老挝北部和毗邻越南的地区，山峦起伏。湄公河是西部的主要地理特征，事实上，在某些地区形成了与泰国的天然边界。湄公河在老挝境内流经1900公里，塑造了众多老挝人民的生活方式。在南部，湄公河宽达20

公里，形成了一个有数千个岛屿的区域。

由于其战略地位（在中南半岛和东南亚的中心），老挝被认为是一个拥有"附加值的目的地"。因此，老挝旅游业的表现可能会受到区域层面的多个因素的影响，这些因素包括全球旅游趋势、游客流向、气候变化、政治和经济环境、自然灾害、恐怖袭击。老挝独特旅游产品的开发、老挝与邻国的旅游线路以及与区域国家旅游合作的增加将是老挝旅游业成功的关键因素（Tourismlaos，2019）。

从1990年到2015年，游客数量每年都在增加。自2016年以来，这一趋势发生了变化，2016年下降了10%（4239047人次），2017年进一步下降了8.7%（3868838人次）。然而，与2017年（4186432人）相比，2018年的游客人数略微增加了8.2%（MOICT，2018）。因此，信息、文化和旅游部制定了2016—2025年期间的国家旅游战略，该战略与政府政策相一致，政府将旅游业列为发展社会经济的八大优先项目之一。

老挝有很多旅游景点，如黄金寺庙、湄公河游轮、雄伟的瀑布、最长的河流洞穴和近24个国家公园，比如琅勃拉邦，一个与佛教相关的旅游胜地；美丽的寺庙，如香通寺；以及每天早上数十名僧侣从当地居民那里收集施舍的景象。尽管如此，老挝在2018年只接待了420万游客；与邻国相比，这是一个非常令人失望的成绩。同年，泰国有3200万游客，马来西亚有2680万游客，越南有1000多万游客（King，2017）。

根据老挝工业部的统计，2018年，旅游业以8.11亿美元的收入排名全国各行业收入第三，这意味着它是发展社会经济的重要机制之一（MOICT，2018）。

不幸的是，老挝可能拥有所有类型的旅游景点，但缺乏邻国所拥有的"3S"：阳光、海洋、沙滩（Sun，Sea，Sand）；因为没有先进的交通设施，仍有一些旅游景点尚未开发，而许多景点只有在旱季才能到达。我们也缺乏先进的基础设施，例如，一些旅游景点没有电力设施，另一个问题是熟练的技术和劳务服务仍然缺乏。

三　高铁（HSR）与旅游业的关系

高铁（HSR）和旅游业紧密相关，一旦流动性得到改善，就会促进游客的行为改变。与这一领域相关的研究论文越来越多，特别是高铁和旅游方面的研究。笔者梳理此前的研究发现，研究者从不同角度考察了高铁对旅游业发展的影响，如以国家空间结构为例,考察法国和西班牙的中型城市、马德里、巴黎和罗马等大都市地区以及高铁走廊沿线地区的中长距离高铁,证明高铁网络对旅游空间分布具有"走廊"效应,有助于中等城市发展城市旅游,有助于郊区小城市作为大都市圈的特殊次中心的发展,并对游客选择游览靠近大都市地区的其他小城市产生重大影响。研究表明,高铁系统对马德里和罗马的选择没有影响,但对巴黎作为旅游目的地的选择有影响(Yin,2019)。

交通运输业已成为全球网络系统的重要组成部分,是旅游基础设施的最重要组成部分之一。有各种各样的交通方式,人们可以方便地从一个地方到另一个地方。在古代,最早的运输方式是陆地上的动物和海上的帆船。旅游的发展源于生存的需要,源于对遥远国家的贸易扩张和发展,源于对占领新土地和领土的渴望。接着是19世纪蒸汽和电力的使用,然后是内燃机。配备喷气式发动机的飞机是在20世纪50年代推出的。随着科技的发展,旅行变得越来越快,人们可以周游世界。

鉴于旅游业与人们从居住地到旅游景点或从他们的国家到另一个国家的流动有关,每个游客都必须旅行才能到达目的地。因此,交通是旅游业的主要组成部分之一。要开发任何旅游景点,必须有适当、高效和安全的交通方式,包括航空运输(飞机)、陆路运输(汽车)、铁路运输(铁路)和水路运输(邮轮)。交通对旅游业至关重要。研究表明,游客在假日总开支中有近30%至40%用于交通,其余用于食物、住宿和其他活动,这再次凸显了交通的重要性。

从四种交通方式来看,铁路是世界上最经济、最方便、最受欢迎的交通方式,尤其是长途旅行。17世纪,德国发明了带有木制轨道的铁路。第一条铁轨是在19世纪初期在美国开发的。铁路彻底改变了19世纪和20世纪人们的交通和大规模流动。

在欧洲,有六个国家的铁路系统已经统一,使欧洲人的铁路旅行更方便。乘客可以在欧洲任何一个国家购买车票,并穿越六个国家。对于外国游客,欧铁通票提供从一周到三个月不等的特快列车旅行无限制折扣(Tourism,2019年)。

高速铁路系统旨在加强与该地区和城市的可达性和连通性,它们填补了汽车和公共汽车提供的短距离机动性与航空运输提供的中等距离机动性之间的空白。截至2016年,全球运营的高铁线路已超过3.48万公里,另有2.48万公里在建。这些线路最初被设定为联结城市之间的走廊,铁路的增长最终导致跨越扩展区域的综合系统,如日本、中国沿海和西欧(Transportgeography,2018)。一项关于日本铁路系统的研究利用统计数据,分析了日本东北和九州地区旅游需求和游客行为的变化。结果表明,在新干线网络延伸连接的城市,游客人数显著增加。此外,该文作者认为距离高铁站的距离越短,将导致对某个旅游目的地的需求增加(Kurihara,2016)。

四 老中关系和"一带一路"倡议

老挝与中国山水相连,两国人民有着深厚而悠久的关系。两国在争取独立和建设社会主义期间相互同情,相互支持。因此,可以说老中是有着共同理想、相同社会制度、相似发展道路的社会主义友好邻邦。

多年来,由于两国最高领导人相互理解和信任,老中关系不断加强和深化,两国全面战略合作伙伴关系按照四个好的方向不断扩大:邻居、好朋友、好同志、好伙伴。老中始终平等相待,相互支持,探索社会主义理论和实践创新,全面推进经济、政治、文化和社会发展,加快推进现代化建设。

2017年的前9个月,老中双边贸易额达到21亿美元,增长25.1%,中国对老挝的直接投资总额超过61亿美元,使中国成为老挝最大的投资国和第二大贸易伙伴。这种贸易合作促进了当地经济水电、采矿、服务、贸易和其他部门的发展(Vientianetime,2017)。

在地区和国际舞台上,由于人口众多,中国已成为带动区域发展的领头国家。此外,中国政府已经到了以建设社会主义和促进国际合作作为基础的新的发展时代。因此,"一带一路"倡议是2013年中国政府提出的最有意义的构想之一,是一项全球发展战略,以加强区域互联互通,并在基础设施建设上拥抱更光明的未来。

在这方面,中国"一带一路"倡议与老挝"陆锁国向陆联国"战略高度互补,老挝"八五"国家社会经济发展规划与中国"十三五"国家社会经济发展规划也具有潜在的对应关系。因此,两国政府自然而然地将这些倡议视为基于互利合作的倡议,这进一步加强了两国之间的联系,为该地区带来了和平、稳定与繁荣。

老中铁路是两国务实合作的大型项目之一。在老挝和中国政府于2010年签署铁路建设谅解备忘录(MOU)后,铁路被高度视为将老挝从"陆锁国"转变为"陆联国"并克服高运输成本的一个要素。因此,老挝将成为从中国到东南亚国家铁路线上的第一站,火车以高达每小时125英里的速度行驶,客货混装。从昆明到新加坡的火车只需 10 小时。

老中铁路的建设始于 2016 年底,预计于 2021 年 12 月完成。目前,施工进度约为 60%。这一大型项目投资 58 亿美元,从北部的卢昂南塔省的中老边境延伸到中部的首都万象,全长 420 公里。隧道全长 9595 米,分为两部分,中方 7170 米,老挝 2425 米。

铁路开工后,该地区发生了一些重大变化,例如:在建设的前六个月内,中国公司已经修建了穿过森林的道路,并在半山腰钻了隧道。

铁路部分施工段位于湄公河沿岸老挝北部琅勃拉邦地区,之前该地区没有电力供应,加上生活和生产条件差,但现在该地区已经正式通电。

老挝员工受雇于琅勃拉邦和万荣之间的铁路施工点,因此老挝员工可以从中国同事那里学习先进的技术和管理(*China Daily*,2017 年)。

除了铁路,老挝与中国的航班连接也在改善。2019 年 5 月,四川航空公司开通了昆明至万象的直达航线,海南航空公司开通了老挝通往海口的航线。

五 机遇与挑战

当然,老中铁路提供的运输服务肯定会惠及不同的利益攸关方,如政府、生产者、农民、企业家和投资者,尤其是铁路沿线的利益相关者。每一项发展都必然伴随着机遇和挑战,这是不可避免的。

1. 机遇

铁路和公路等基础设施方面将建设更好的设施,以将游客带到更广阔的大陆。显然,建成后的老中铁路将把老挝同所有东南亚国家以及中国连接起来。在这方面,许多旅游景点将修建连接道路,以便能够迎来更多的游客。正如我们在一些案例研究中所回顾的那样,交通的便利性和成本似乎是一般游客在参观某些地方之前的决定因素之一。

铁路交通可能会吸引很多中国游客在前往其他国家之前,第一站就来到老挝。据信息、文化和旅游部统计,来老挝旅游的中国游客数量逐年增加,老挝是中国人的旅游目的地之一,每年平均有 40 万中国人到访老挝。2017 年,这一数字增至 639185 人以上,增长约 12%,中国人在老挝外国游客数量中排名第三。2018 年,访问老挝的中国人增加到 80 万左右。2019 年上半年,也就是老挝—中国访问年,中国游客在老挝的记录比 2018 年同期增加到 50 万。铁路建成后,可能会吸引更多的中国游客前往沿线国家。最好的例子是泰国。2018年，泰国接待了1000万中国游客，其中大部分来自云南省（Xuxin, 2018）。此外，在第二届"一带一路"国际合作高峰论坛（BRF）期间，老挝和泰国在中国首都北京正式签署合作备忘录，在第一座泰老友谊大桥附近，将修建一座廊开和万象之间的铁路桥。这表明老挝必须为大量中国游客的访问做好准备（Hongtong, 2019）。

此外，它还可以进一步支持相关行业，如旅行社、酒店、餐饮、交通和纪念品业务。由于游客是来体验和享受的，所以对于他们可能会做什么或购买基本住宿和交通之外的其他东西没有明确的限制。可能消费的额外服务包括当地的美食、当地餐馆、电影院等娱乐场所、文化活动，甚至可能包括零售产品和服务，或电子、电信产品和服务。根据联合国世界旅游组织（UNWTO）的数据，他们列出了12个广义描述的旅游价值链行业。这些行业包括：1）旅行社和其他预订服务活动，2）铁路客运，3）公路客运，4）水上客运，5）航空客运，6）游客住宿，7）餐饮服务活动，8）运输设备租赁，9）文化活动，10）体育和娱乐活动，11）其他针对特定国家的旅游特色活动，12）针对特定国家的旅游特色商品零售业。因此，通过与旅游业相关的行业列表，我们可以看到铁路是其中之一，这意味着铁路可能是推动旅游业发展的因素之一。

因此，丰富的旅游业将创造巨大的需求，对整个经济做出更广泛的贡献。服务业的增长将产生更多和更广泛的就业机会，消费者和食品需求的增加也将支持当地的农产品。

2. 挑战

与机遇并存的，也有挑战。从旅游业来看，最难的事情是避免只成为路线而不是目的地。如上所述，老挝与泰国、缅甸和柬埔寨等东南亚国家的旅游景点大多相似，包括历史遗迹、寺庙、森林、瀑布等。在这种情况下，如果我们没有做好充分的准备，将无法吸引游客并为他们提供便利。

社会问题是我们发展后必将面临的重大挑战之一。由于该地区交通繁忙，旅游相关产业可能无法应对人口的急速增长，外来者的进入可能会扰乱当地文化，令当地民众心烦意乱。一些当地人可能会从旅游业的增长中受益，而有些人仍然没有办法从旅游业的增长中抓住机会。有些人可能会进行犯罪活动，如从游客那里赚快钱，从而导致犯罪率的上升。

此外，任何发展都会带来一些干扰。在开始修建铁路之后，有很多树木必须被清除，而为了修建隧道，有一些山必须被穿透。在未来，将建设更多的道路以方便游客，从而导致更多的交通问题，更多的噪音。更多的游客可能会浪费更多的自然资源，加上垃圾处理问题和污染增加，这将扰乱该地区的生态平衡。

3. 建议

总而言之，交通运输在促进整体社会经济发展方面发挥着重要作用，尤其是旅游业。此外，较低的运输成本将有助于投资者和当地企业家获得更合理价格的原材料来发展业务。然而，要取得交通运输领域的进一步发展，仍有一些挑战需要解决，如社会问题、环境问题和东南亚国家之间的竞争问题。

为了最大限度地利用机遇、减少挑战，在铁路完工之前，几点建议可以帮助我们提前预防挑战，以便尽可能多地收获机遇，具体如下：

老挝需要更好的基础设施，因此需要修建更多的铁路以方便游客。我们需要为旅游目的地开发交通基础设施，以便将火车站连接到另一个旅游景点。有了更舒适的旅行，我们就能更容易迎来更多的游客。此外，还需要增加签证等方面的政策便利，例如：一个签证可以在铁路沿线的每个国家旅行。据联合国世界旅游组织称，他们对签证便利化的研究表明，全球旅游业对增加游客数量，尤其是来自中国、印度、俄罗斯和巴西的游客数量产生了积极影响（UNWTO，2014）。因此，交通设施和旅游政策应被视为关键任务之一。

相关产业的发展是准备好应对和培育铁路机遇的重要力量之一。为了管理大量游客，所有利益攸关方都应该准备并讨论游客涌入对当地的影响，通过制定规则来保护当地文化。此外，需要训练有素的专业服务技能，以展示老挝人民的热情好客。

另一个扩大旅游的建议是，有关机构应研究沿线国家，并设法与其他外国机构合作，建设沿线国家的旅行团。这将是老挝旅游机构提升业务并享受更多客户的潜在机会。最重要的措施之一是要准备应对社会和环境问题。在这方面，应该严格执行与这一领域有关的规定。

Lao Tourism Development Through Belt and the Road Initiative

Haknilan Inthalath / Laos

Institute of Foreign Affairs of Laos / Research fellow

I. Introduction

It's unignorable that transportation and tourism are closely involved economic and scientific common view that promoting transportation infrastructure which may contribute to the development of tourism industry. However, in case of building a Highspeed railway, their high construction costs while also needs experiential evidence or planning stage that certain economic activities such as tourism should be reinforced. This paper aim to clarify the relevant factors of railways to foster the tourism industry in Laos focusing on case study in various countries. also, to review the relevant measures of turning lao-landlocked to land-linked policy to this regard development, and finally, identify opportunities and challenges, and provide recommendations.

II. Laos tourism situation

The Peoples' Democratic Republic of Laos is a least developing landlocked country, located in the center of Indochina, sharing borders with China to the North

(416 kilometers), Myanmar to Northwest (236 kilometers), Thailand to the West (1,835 kilometers), Cambodia to the South (492 kilometers) and Vietnam to the East (1,957 kilometers).With a total area of 236,800 square kilometers, around 70% of Laos' terrain is mountainous, reaching a maximum elevation of 2,820 meters in Xieng Khouang Province. The landscapes of northern Laos and the regions adjacent to Vietnam, in particular, are dominated by rough mountains.The Mekong River is the main geographical feature in the west and, in fact, forms a natural border with Thailand in some areas. The Mekong flows through nearly 1,900 kilometers of Laos territory and shapes much of the lifestyle of the people of Laos. In the South the Mekong reaches a breadth of 20 kilometers, creating an area with thousands of islands.

Because of its strategic location (in the center of Indochina and South-East Asia), Laos PDR is considered to be a "add on destination". Hence, Laos tourism performances are likely influenced by several factors at regional level which are global tourism trends, the flow of tourists to the region, climate change, political and economic circumstances, natural disasters, terrorist attacks, and other, Moreover, the development of unique tourism products for Laos, tourists circuits living Laos with neighboring countries and increasing in tourism cooperation with regional countries will be the essential factors to contribute to the success of Laos tourism (Tourism Laos, 2019).

In the period 1990 to 2015 the number of visitors increased every year. Since 2016 this trend has changed, with a drop of 10% in 2016 (4,239,047 visitors), and a further drop of 8.7% in 2017 (3,868,838). However, 2018 showed a slight increase in tourist arrivals by 8.2% compared to 2017 (4,186,432) (MOICT, 2018). Therefore, the Ministry of Information, Culture and Tourism has set up the National Tourism Strategy for the period 2016-2025, which is in line with the government policy to set tourism industry into one of the eight priority programmed to develop the socio-economic of the Laos government.

Even though there are so many tourist attractions such as golden temples, Mekong river cruises, mighty waterfalls, longest river caves and nearly two dozen national parks, Laos has it all. For example: Luang Prabang, a magnet for Buddhism-related tourism, beautiful temples such as Wat Xieng Thong, and the spectacle of scores of monks collecting alms every morning from local residents. Nonetheless, Laos welcomed only 4.2 million visitors in 2018; it has seen to be a very disappointed achievement compared to its neighbors. In that same year, there were 32 million tourist arrivals in Thailand, 26.8 million in Malaysia and over 10 million in Vietnam (King, 2017).

According to the statistic from Laos Ministry of industry, it shows that the tourism industry is ranked 3rd place industry that bring the income to the country with the income 811 million US dollar in 2018, meaning that it is one of the significant mechanisms to develop the socio-economic (MOICT, 2018).

Unfortunately, Laos may have all the tourist attractions, but we lack 3S: Sun Sea Sand, while all of our neighbors have, advanced transportation facilities because there are still some tourists site remain under-developed and many are accessible only in the dry season, we also lack of advanced infrastructure facilities, for instance Some tourist site, there are no electricity assessment and another problem is that skilled technical and labor services are still required.

III. Relation between Highspeed Railways (HSR) and Tourism Industry

High-speed rail (HSR) and tourism are firmly related economic activities, once the mobility improved, it is perceived to facilitate behavioral changes in tourists. There are more and more research papers related to this field, specially the topics of HSR and tourism. Previous studies have examined the impact of HSR on tourism development from different angles, such as a national spatial structure, medium-sized regional cities in France and Spain, metropolitan areas, including Madrid, Paris, and Rome, and medium- and long-distance HSR on the areas along the HSR corridor, demonstrating that HSR networks have a "corridor" effect on the tourism spatial distribution, help medium-sized cities to develop urban tourism, facilitate the development of small suburban cities as special subcenters of the metropolitan area, and have a significant effect on tourists' choice to visit other smaller cities close to a Metropolitan area. Studies have shown that an HSR system has no influence on the choice of Madrid and Rome, but has an effect on the choice of Paris, as a tourist destination(yin, 2019).

The transport industry has become crucially involved in the global network system and is one of the most important components of the tourism infrastructure. There are various mode of transportation which will allow people to travel from one place to another easily. Back then, the earliest forms of transportation, in the ancient times were animals on land and sails on the sea. Travel development from the need to survive, to expand and develop trade too far off countries, and the hunger to capture new lands and territories. This was followed by the use of steams and electricity in the nineteenth century followed by internal combustion engines. aircraft with the jet engines were introduced in the 1950s. With the development of technology, travel became faster and more and people could travel around the globe.

Seeing that tourism associated with the movement of people from their places of residence to the places of tourist attractions or from their country to another country, every tourist has to travel to reach the places of interest. Transport is, thus, one of the major components of the tourism industry. To develop any place of tourist attraction, there have to be proper, efficient, and safe modes of transportation which included Air transport(plane), land transport(car), rail transport(railway) and water transport (cruise)

Transportation is vital to tourism. Studies have shown that tourists spend almost 30 to 40 percent of their total holiday expenditure on transportation and the remaining on food, accommodation, and other activities. This aspect once again highlights the importance of transportation.

From 4 modes of transportation, the railway is the most economical, convenient, and popular mode of travel especially for long distance travel all over the world. The railroad was invented in the seventeenth century in Germany with wooden tracks. The first steel rail was developed in the USA during the early 1800s. The railways revolutionized transportation and mass movement of people seen in the nineteenth and twentieth centuries.

In Europe, the railway systems of six European countries have been clubbed to make rail travel easier for the people of Europe. A rail passenger can buy a ticket in any one country of Europe and travel through six countries. For the foreign tourists, Eurail Passes offer unlimited discounts travel in express trains for periods ranging from a week to three months (Tourism, 2019).

Highspeed rail system are represented to reinforce accessibility and connectivity with the region and cities, they fill gap between short rage mobility provided by cars and buses and medium rage mobility provided by air transport. There was as of 2016 more than 34,800 km of operational HSR lines in the world with an additional 24,800 km under construction. These lines were initially set as corridors between city-pairs and their growth eventually lead to integrated systems spanning extended regions, such as for Japan, Coastal China and Western Europe (Transportgeography, 2018). Another example is in japan, the study investigates the change of tourism demand and tourist behavior in Tohoku and Kyushu Region by using statistical data collected by MLIT and JTA. The results suggest that tourism arrivals increased significantly in cities that were connected by the extended Shinkansen network. In addition, modal share of railway showed obvious increase as well. In addition, the author suggests that the shorter distant from HSR station will result in an increase of tourism demand to a certain destination (Kurihara, 2016).

IV. Laos-China Ties and Belt and Road Initiative

Laos and China are connected by the mountain and river. The people of the two countries has a deep and long-standing relationship. The two countries had a sympathy for and provided mutual support to each other in the fight for independence in the war time and during the time for the building of socialism. therefore, we could say that Laos-china is a friendly socialist neighbor with shared ideals, the same social systems and similar paths of development.

Over the years, Laos-China tie has been continuously strengthened and deepened as a result of mutual understanding and trust between top leaders of the two countries as the comprehensive strategic cooperative partnership between the two countries has been expanding in line with four good directions- good neighbors, good friends, good comrades and good partners.Laos and China have always treated each other as equals and supported each other in exploring innovation in socialist theories and practice, in fully advancing economic, political, cultural and social development, and in accelerating modernization.

In addition, Laos-China's Bilateral trade reached US$2.1 billion in the first nine months in 2017, up by 25.1 percent and China's total direct investment in Laos exceeded US$6.1 billion which made China to become the largest investor and second largest trading partner of Laos. This trading cooperation facilitate the development of hydroelectricity, mining, services, trade and other sectors of the local economy (Vientiane time, 2017).

In the regional and international stage, China has become the leading nation in strengthening regional development given the higher number of populations. besides, The administration of the PRC has been transformed into a new development era foregrounded on building socialism as well as promoting international cooperation. thus, the belt and road initiative were introduced in 2013, One of the most significant vision proposed by Chinese government, is a global development strategy to enhance regional connectivity and embrace a brighter future involving infrastructure development.

In this connection, China's Belt and Road Initiative and the strategy of Laos to transform country from a landlocked to a land-linked are high degree of complementary while the 8th Five-Year National Socio-economic Development Plan of Laos and China's 13th Five-Year Plan is also a potential correspondent. Therefore, two government automatically viewed the initiatives as being based on mutual benefit and cooperation which even more strengthen ties between two countries bringing peace, stability and prosperity to the region.

Laos-china railways, is one of the mega projects of the practical cooperation between two countries. After the signing of the Memorandum of Understanding (MOU) for the railway construction in 2010 by the Laos and Chinese government, the railway is highly considered as a factor to transform Laos from "land-locked country" to "land-linked country" and overcome the high cost of transportation on the way around. As a result, Laos will become the first stop on one route from China to Southeast Asia countries with trains travelling at speech of up to 125 miles per hour, carrying both passengers and cargo. The route from Kunming to Singapore will take just 10 hours.

The construction of Laos-China railway started in the end of 2016 and expected to be completed in December 2021. Currently, the construction had made about 60% progress. This mega project investment costs 5.8 billion USD for the distance of 420 km stretching from the Laos-Chinese border in Luangnamtha province in the North to Vientiane Capital in the Center. The tunnel, with the total length of 9,595 meters, is divided into two parts, 7,170 meters in the Chinese side and 2,425 meters in the Laos side.

After the railway started to build, there are some great change occurs in the area, for example:

-Within the first six months of construction, Chinese companies have built roads running through forests and drill tunnels halfway up the mountains.

-Some The construction section of China Railway is located on Laos' northern Luang Prabang area along the Mekong river, there had been no power supply in the area, plus living and production conditions were poor. But now the area was officially connected to electricity.

-Laos staff were hired by the railway construction site between towns of Luang Prabang and Vangvieng, So Laos staffs could learn the advanced technology and management from their Chinese colleagues (Chinadaily, 2017).

Apart from railways, Laos' flight connections with China are improving, too. A direct link operated by Sichuan Airlines launched between Kunming and Vientiane in May, while a Hainan Airlines route to Haikou, the capital of Hainan Island.

V. Opportunities and Challenge

Of course, The transport service provided by Laos-China railway is definitely expected to benefit to different stakeholders such as government, producers, farmers, entrepreneurs and investors particularly along the railway. Moreover, it is avoidable that every development would definitely come with both opportunities and challenges.

1. Opportunities

It would build better facilities in term of infrastructure such as railway and roads to move tourist more continently. Obviously, after Laos-China railway finished, it will connect Laos to all the Southeast Asia countries as well as China. In this connection, connected roads will be built to many tourist's attraction so that we will be able to welcome more tourists to come. as we have reviewed in some case study, the convenience and cost of transportation seems to be one of determine for tourist in general before they visit some places.

Railways could attract a lot of Chinese visitors come to Laos at the first stop before moving to another countries. The number of Chinese tourists come to Laos was increase year by year, According to Ministry of information, culture and tourism, Laos is one of travel destinations of Chinese people. The average number of Chinese visiting Laos is around 400,000 people annually. In 2017, the number has increased to more than 639,185which increased around 12% and ranked Chinese people in the third for foreign visitor of Laos. The number of Chinese people visiting Laos has increased to around 800,000 in 2018. In the first half of 2019 – the Visit Laos-China Year – Chinese tourist record in Laos has increased to 500,000 compared to the same period in 2018. In this connection, after the railway finished, this could attract more Chinese visitors who would travel to countries along the route. The best example could be Thailand. In 2018, Thailand welcomes 10 million Chinese tourists in which mostly fly from Yunnan province (Xuxin, 2018). Moreover, a rail bridge between Nong Khai and Vientiane will be built close to the first Thai-Laos Friendship Bridge in which the memorandum of cooperation between Laos and Thailand was officially sign in the Chinese capital Beijing during the second Belt and Road Forum for International Cooperation (BRF). This shows the obvious opportunity that Laos will have to be prepare for massive Chinese tourist to visit (hongtong, 2019).

In addition, it could further support related industries such as travel agency, hotel, restaurants, transport, and souvenir businesses. Since tourists comes to experience and enjoy so there is not definitive limit as to what they may do or buy additional to the basic accommodations and transport. The additional services that may be consumed are local food, local restaurants, entertainment places such as cinemas, cultural activities; and may even include retail products and services or electronic and telecommunications products and services. According to UNWTO (United Nation World tourism organization), they listed 12 industries that broadly define and describe tourism industry value chain. These industries are : 1) Travel agencies and other reservation services activities, 2) Railway passenger transport, 3) Road passenger transport, 4) Water passenger transport, 5) Air passenger transport, 6) Accommodation for visitors, 7) Food and beverage serving activities, 8) Transport equipment rental, 9) Cultural activities, 10) Sports and recreational activities, 11) Other country-specific tourism characteristic activities, 12) Retail trade of country-specific tourism characteristic goods. So, by the list of industries related tourism, we could see that the railway is one of them which means that the railway could be one of the factors to boost the tourism industry.

So, the wealthy tourism industry will create a huge demand, contribute more widely to the whole economy. This will result in more and wide employment generation due to the growing of services industries. This will also support the local agriculture product due to the increasing of consumers and food demand.

2. Challenges

Along with opportunities, there are remaining challenges. The hardest things of becoming the route is to avoid becoming only a route not a destination. As having mentioned above, the tourist attractions among Laos and other South east Asia country such as Thailand, Myanmar and Cambodia, most of them are similar which are historic places, temples, forest, waterfall and So on. In this case, if we are not well prepared enough, we wouldn't be able to attract and facilitate the tourist especially the relevant industries of tourism.

The social problem is one of the significant challenges that we would definitely face after the development. Due to the heavy traffic in the region, the related industries of tourism may not be able to cope up with the rush increase leading to overcrowding, the invasion of outsider may disturb the local culture which would made the local people upset. Some local people might benefit for tourism growing while some still have no ideas to take opportunities from the tourism growing. Some people may enter to the criminal activities to fetch easy money from tourist which lead to increased criminal.

Besides, any development requires some interference After started constructing the railways, there are so many trees have to be gotten rid, there are some mountains that have to be pierced in order to build a tunnel. In the future, more road will be constructed to facilitate the tourist leading to more traffic, more noise: more tourist may waste more natural resources, waste disposal problem, pollution increase in the area which would disturbs the ecological balance of the area.

3. Recommendations

To conclude, the transportations is showing the important role to foster overall socio-economy Especially tourism that definitely require this infrastructure. Moreover, the lower transport cost will help the investor and local entrepreneur to enjoy more reasonable price of component needed to develop their business. However, to develop more to this sector, there are still some challenges that need to address such as a social problem, environmental problem and competitiveness among southeast Asia countries

In order to maximize the opportunities and minimize the challenges, there are few suggestions that might help to prevent the challenges in advance before the railway finish in order to harvest the opportunities as much as we can as follows:

Laos needs better facilities in term of infrastructure, so more roads need to be built to facilitate tourists. We need to develop traffic infrastructure for tourist destination in order to connect the railway station to another tourist attraction. With the more comfortable travelling, we would be able to welcome more tourists conveniently. Moreover, the policy facilitation such as visa also required to be added for example: one visa could travel every country along the route. According to the UNWTO, their research on visa facilitation shows a positive impact of global tourism to increase the number of travelers especially tourists from China, India, Russia and brazil (UNWTO, 2014).Therefore, the facilities both transportations and tourism policy should be considered to be one of the crucial tasks.

Related industries development is one of the significant reinforcements to be ready to handle and foster the opportunities gained by the railways. In order to manage the massive number of tourists, all the stakeholders should prepare and discuss about the impacts to local to prevent the tourist invasion by setting rule to reserve a local culture and respect the rule of law. In addition, professional Services skill need to be well trained to complement the natural hospitality of the Laos people.

Another alternative recommendation to enlarge tourism is that the agency involved should study the country in the route and find ways to cooperate with other foreign agency to set up the package tour traveling the countries along the route. This would be a potential opportunity for Laos tourism agency to level up their business as well as enjoying more costumers.

And, one of the most important measure is that to prepare for the Social and environmental problem. in this regard, regulations related to this field should be implemented precisely.

References

Chinadaily. (2017, 9 25). *business*. Retrieved from Chinadaily webste: http://www.chinadaily.com.cn/business/2017-08/07/content_30359991.htm

hongtong, T. (2019, 4 26). *thailand*. Retrieved 9 2019, from Bangkokpost: https://www.bangkokpost.com/thailand/general/1667212/govts-sign-thai-Laos-rail-deal

Hou, X. (2019, 03 09). *High-Speed Railway and City Tourism in China: A Quasi-Experimental Study on HSR Operation*. Retrieved from MDPI: https://doi.org/10.3390/su11061512

King, B. (2017, August 22). *Travel*. Retrieved from CNN: https://edition.cnn.com/travel/article/could-china-put-laos-on-the-tourist-map/index.html

Kurihara, T. (2016). The Impact of High Speed Rail on Tourism Development: A Case Study of Japan. *the open transportaion journal*, 35-40.

MOICT. (2018). *Statistical Report on Tourism in Laos*. Vientiane: Ministry of Information, culture and Tourism.

note, T. (n.d.). *tourism*. Retrieved from Tourism note: https://tourismnotes.com/tourism-transportation/

Tourism. (2019, 9-22). *Torism transportation*. Retrieved 9 2019, from Tourism notes: https://tourismnotes.com/tourism-transportation/

Tourismlaos. (2019). *Lao's in Brief*. Retrieved from Laos-simply bueatiful: https://www.tourismlaos.org/show.php?Cont_ID=41

Transportgeography. (2018, 9-22). *World High Speed Rail Systems*. Retrieved from transportgeography: https://transportgeography.org/?page_id=1921

UNWTO. (2014, 1 20). *press-release*. Retrieved 9 2019, from UN- world tourism organisation: http://media.unwto.org/press-release/2014-01-27/asean-countries-could-win-10-million-new-visitors-easing-visa-procedures

Vientianetime. (2017, 9 22). *sub-new*. Retrieved from Vientianetime: http://www.vientianetimes.org.la/sub-new/Cooperation/Cooperation_China_265.php

Xuxin. (2018, 12 10). *english*. Retrieved 9 2019, from Xinhuanet: http://www.xinhuanet.com/english/2018-12/20/c_137686283_2.htm

yin, P. (2019, 01). *How Does High-Speed Rail Affect Tourism? A Case Study of the Capital Region of China*. Retrieved from ResearchGate: https://www.researchgate.net/publication/330456363_How_Does_High-Speed_Rail_Affect_Tourism_A_Case_Study_of_the_Capital_Region_of_China#pfe

"一带一路"电影节联盟：中国电影产业的国际化

何伊纱 【德国】
人民网　德语外籍专家

　　电影节参照会议的形式，与城市结构紧密交织在一起，可以成为该城市的名片，成为国际关系中的资产，也可以通过参与者积极讨论，增强公民对这座城市的认同感，因为他们可以看到来自世界不同角落的、那些没有机会在电影院看到的、甚至不知道其存在的故事。对于影迷来说，参加电影节相当于没有离开电影院进行了两周的旅行，每天看5部电影，和其他影迷一起交流想法。在几次连续的电影节中，固定的电影节参与者组成了一个新的"家庭"，一个由对电影共同的爱好组成的社会小单位。

　　尽管中国有大量的电影节，大部分在2010年左右成立，但作为一种社会现象的西方的电影节模式还是件新鲜事。它出现在20世纪80年代末90年代初，如1993年成立的上海国际电影节（SIFF）。但这并不意味着中国在改革开放之前没有影迷或类似电影节之类的活动。自20世纪80年代以来，在家用录像机等家庭娱乐形式普及之前，电影周是一种国际电影艺术普及的重要形式。上海国际电影节为了追求电影剧目更加多样化、推动中国年轻电影业的发展以及支持民族影业的广泛性和公平性，于2018年发起成立了"一带一路"电影节联盟（BRFFA）。该组织目前由来自世界各地33个国家的38个电影节和电影机构组成。"一带一路"电影节联盟将放映"一带一路"电影周的影片。通过这一举措，上海国际电影节成功打造了具有中国特色的电影节模式，为西方电影节提供了另一种选择。为了突出电影节和电影周在发展和基本前提上的差异，笔者先简要总结两种模式的历史背景。

一 电影节和电影周

根据中国电影研究学者 Ma Ran 的说法，对电影周的组织情况描述如下：

> 一个复杂的过程，尽管其议程中存在等级层次，但涉及众多支持者，包括文化管理部门、电影行业（电影专业人士）和观众。电影周对中国的电影进口具有重要的经济意义，同时其成长也依赖中国电影业的发展。中国观众也将电影周作为接触外国电影的渠道和平台[1]。

在组织全国电影周的文化权威部门中，中国电影公司最重要。它是1951年成立的一家国有实体机构，通过其市级和省级的分支机构来协调该项活动，自1956年以来[2]，这些机构可以灵活地调整和修改电影周的计划。中国人民对外友好协会（CPAFFC）[3]和中国电影协会——这两个半官方实体都负责基层倡议和中国与伙伴国家之间的联系——都参与了组织电影周。

1950年，在北京举办了第一个人民共和国电影周展览。从20世纪50年代初到1960年，苏联电影周通过苏联和中国电影专业人员之间的交流，对中国民族电影工业的技术发展起到了重要推动作用。虽然一个重要的目标是加强共产主义国家之间的友谊，具体体现就是这些国家在中国组织电影周，然后相应地在他们国家组织中国电影周，但中国的电影周也有来自社会主义阵营以外国家的电影放映——印度（1955年）、法国（1956年）或埃及（1957年）。这些国家当时与中华人民共和国没有外交关系[4]，因此电影周被证明是文化外交的有效手段。从1953年起，在20多个城市举办了不同国家电影展映的电影周。最终，1957年亚洲电影周和1958年亚非电影节被认为是当代"一带一路"电影周的先驱。

1　R. Ma, *A genealogy of film festivals in the People's Republic of China: 'film weeks' during the 'Seventeen Years' (1949–1966)*, New Review of Film and Television Studies, Routledge, 2016, p. 43, DOI: 10.1080/17400309.2015.1107266

2　R. Ma, Ibid., p. 45.

3　R. Abel, *French Film Theory and Criticism: a history/anthology, 1907-1929*, Princeton, 1993, s. 198.

4　R. Ma, ibid., p. 47.

电影节的历史始于1932年的威尼斯电影节和1939年的戛纳电影节，尽管其形式在第二次世界大战后基本稳定下来，但奖励制度的延续取决于当时的政治气候。当电影周建立在双边关系和互利互惠的概念基础之上时，电影节不仅意味着电影之间的竞争，也意味着电影节本身乃至主办城市之间的竞争。根据戛纳电影节官方网站上公布的资料，戛纳电影节的成立归因于在意识形态和声望方面与威尼斯竞争的愿望[1]。到今天为止，电影节得到了各国政府的各种支持，该组织由非政府组织管理，电影节导演在活动内容的选择和形象塑造方面发挥着决定性作用。

电影节和电影周之间的差异也体现在电影剧目的选择和节目策划的过程。电影节的剧目由专家挑选，这些导演的视野通过他们策划的节目部分得到体现。长期稳定的节目策划人对以观众为中心的电影节（如鹿特丹国际电影节或伦敦电影节）至关重要，因为电影策展人在电影节和电影观众之间建立信任、当地信誉和熟悉感。节目策划人的名字是电影节质量的保证。另一方面，电影周由国家、省或市各级政府机构策划，策划人基本上保持匿名。

事实证明，电影节是主办城市的一个重要宣传工具，吸引了房地产、服务业的投资，不仅在影迷中促进了旅游业的发展，还让人们着迷于名人文化、电影节的声望，甚至是电影节所带来的国际化和全球性城市地位。政府和半官方机构在组织电影周时，把重点放在了国家层面上，电影在几个城市巡回放映，而电影节仍然与当地的城市文化保持着较远的距离。

电影节中心场馆进一步凸显了活动空间维度的重要性，因为这里会举办颁奖或互动问答等所有仪式，并将电影节的观众凝集在一起。电影周开幕演出在几个非固定活动场所的城市举行，观众反馈不如电影节那么有影响。这两种展示方式的主要目的也有所不同，电影节的形象还是以娱乐为导向，而电影周首先是教育。这一意图通过在电影周中展示的官方电影说明得到体现。而电影节目录介绍则以事件介绍、电影概要和专题文章为特色，其目的更多的是提供信息而不是教育。

最后一个区别是结构的局限性。17年历史的电影周是建立在双边主义和互利互惠基础上的二元封闭体系之上的，而近30年历史的世界各地电影节的快速发展却是一条不断扩张的开放之路。"一带一路"电影节联盟体现了灵活性和合作性，创建了支持网络，而伴随而来的电影周则设法将两种展览模式的结构结合起来，发挥他们的长处，避免其弊端。

1　https://www.festival-cannes.com/en/69-editions/history (20.09.2019)

二 友谊和竞争的动力

尽管电影节由导演管理，独立于政府机构而存在，但有一个组织可以对其运作进行监管。成立于 1933 年，国际电影制片人协会（FIAPF）根据行业标准将电影节分为不同类别：竞赛型非专门类电影节（A 类）、竞赛型专门类电影节（B 类）、非竞争性故事片电影节、纪录片和短片电影节[1]。迪娜·伊尔达诺娃（Dina Iordanova）总结了电影节竞赛型功能的要求，"必须至少运行九天；不应该专门化，但应该涵盖电影制作的所有方面；[必须]有至少十四部没有类型限制的电影进行专题竞争"。[2] FIAPF 的宗旨是，在不考虑主办城市之间的预算差异和经济差异的情况下，通过会员循环和认证制度，确保专业电影人的权利。尽管如此，FIAPF 在成立 86 年后，仍然是一个享有盛誉的品牌，至少在电影专业人士中是如此。它让你有机会参加最著名的电影活动，如柏林电影节、威尼斯电影节或戛纳电影节。据上海国际电影节官方网站报道，该电影节于 1994 年获得 FIAPF 的认可[3]，而这时候上海国际电影节成立才仅仅一年。

然而，如今大多数电影节都是在 FIAPF 架构之外成功举办的，通过优选的节目安排，建立稳定的观众，赢得了电影制作人的信任，获得了私人投资者的支持和声望。自 20 世纪 90 年代以来，越来越多的电影节在现有的网络之外成立，在地理上远离老的迷影中心，独立于其网络之外。FIAPF 对国际电影首映数量的高要求仍然是一个主要问题，这使得大多数备受期待的新片背后的电影人会首先选择在威尼斯、柏林和戛纳电影节上放映他们的电影，以得到更多的曝光和宣传。虽然各电影节之间的高竞争力可以起到激励作用，但只有给予会员们平等的机会，才能选出最佳影片，但 FIAPF 似乎强化了这种不公平的结构。"一带一路"电影联盟可能会成为一个可以促进电影节之间特权和声望重新分配的组织，埃琳娜·波拉奇（Elena Pollacchi）称其为"声誉节日"——结合了公共关系、文化外交和企业制度的元素，不断积累利益相关者的资本，把这个节日塑造为超级品牌的形象。上海国际电影节是一个促进中国电影产业发展的平台，但目前还缺乏足够的声望和声誉。

有趣的是，"一带一路"电影节联盟与 FIAPF 电影节体系紧密相连。在 A 类

---

[1] http://www.fiapf.org/ (20.09.2019)
[2] D. Iordanova, *Showdown of the Festivals: Clashing Entrepreneurships and Post-Communist Management of Culture*, "Film International", 4:5, 2006 Issue 23, p. 28.
[3] http://www.siff.com/a/2019-03-22/3208.html (20.09.2019)

的 15 个得到认可的电影节中[1]，其中 5 个是"一带一路"电影节联盟成员：开罗国际电影节、莫斯科国际电影节、华沙国际电影节、塔林黑夜电影节和上海国际电影节。在 24 个 B 类电影节中[2]，有 6 个是 BRFFA 的成员：明斯克国际电影节、索非亚国际电影节、伊斯坦布尔国际电影节、孟买电影节、欧亚国际电影节、特兰西瓦尼亚国际电影节[3]。此外，曾经获得认可的电影节——塞萨洛尼基国际电影节现已成为"一带一路"电影节联盟的成员。除纽约亚洲电影节继续代表美国境内的亚裔美国人社区外，加入联盟的电影节和机构具有明确的国家形象[4]。

SIFF 组织者们开始关注"一带一路"电影节联盟，而不是关注 FIAPF 成员之间的竞争，开始从电影模式中汲取灵感，这些电影周在全球各地的电影机构之间形成了跨国友谊与合作。当被问及 BRFFA 发展的未来前景时，华沙电影节导演斯特凡·劳丁[5]声称，这很大程度上取决于联盟成员本身，从时间的角度来看，最重要的是电影节之间的对话和建立友谊，而不是考虑最初的竞争前提。"一带一路"电影节联盟似乎也依赖于人际关系网（关系）。华沙电影节负责人提到他认识上海国际电影节常务主任，因为他们都是 FIAPF 电影节委员会的成员。他受邀参加了之前版本的 SIFF，并于 2018 年来到上海，亲自签署 BRFFA 联盟协议，积极参与圆桌会谈，安排联盟活动并参与电影节组织者之间的交流。

2018 年 6 月 16 日在上海签署的《关于成立促进"一带一路"电影文化交流电影节联盟的谅解备忘录》主要目标是：通过电影加强文化艺术的传播和交流；通过电影加强各国之间文化习俗和传统的沟通和理解；推动在其他国家的电影节或电影机构举办各国电影展等活动；为各国的电影节和相关活动提前推荐评委会成员和嘉宾；加强各国在电影制作、联合制作和发行方面的交流与合作；建立和促进签署方之间的信息共享机制[6]。

该联盟旗下的电影节各方参加了 SIFF 期间组织的年度论坛，进行了电影制作人、节目策划人、制作和发行公司代表以及电影评论家和研究人员之间的行

1　Retrieved from: http://www.fiapf.org/intfilmfestivals_sites.asp (20.09.2019)
2　Retrieved from: http://www.fiapf.org/intfilmfestivals_2019_sites02.asp (20.09.2019)
3　Retrieved from: http://www.siff.com/a/2019-09-23/3721.html (20.09.2019)
4　http://www.siff.com/a/2019-06-21/3509.html (20.09.2019)
5　2019 年 7 月 8 日通过电子邮件对斯特凡·劳丁（Stefan Laudyn）进行的采访。
6　http://www.siff.com/skin/default/2018%20BELT%20AND%20ROAD%20FILM%20WEEK.pdf (20.09.2019)

业小组讨论。导演斯特凡·劳丁[1]强调，SIFF 组织者愿意改变并实施联盟成员提出的建议。他提到，2018 年代表们建议将正在进行的工作纳入该计划，SIFF 主任介绍了新的内容，因为寻找已经在制作阶段的新的有趣项目对于 A 类电影节至关重要，尤其是像 SIFF 或 WFF 这样的旨在尽快挑选高质量电影首映的电影节。此前，上海国际电影节曾因电影选择平庸[2]，缺乏明确的节目方向、品牌模糊、放映好莱坞大片（在电影节之外很容易买到）以及制片人的匿名性而受到批评。然而，仅仅将西方的措施应用到中国的环境中是不够的。马然[3]解释了选择电影的两种模式——"节目策划"和"选片"之间的差异，一个由节目策划人承担，另一个由"选片人"承担。据这位学者称，2008 年之前，SIFF 电影筛选团队由专家和学者组成，并由中英文翻译协助，因为国际电影挑选中几乎总是只有英文字幕。在接下来的十年里，这个团队开始包括电影制片人和评论家。Ma 评论："评选团队大约有 100 人，其中 50 人是负责评审和评选的专家和把关人，其他人大多是当地大学的研究生，负责技术问题和初步分类。"[4] 华沙电影节还聘请研究生签订临时工作合同，从大量提交的电影作品中挑选影片[5]。这在欧洲大小电影节中非常常见。与其他顶级电影节相比，柏林电影节的电影选片委员会由 20 名选片人组成。声誉的差异可能会使 SIFF 选片人的工作更加密集和耗时，因为大多数有趣的新片已经被大多数著名的电影节推荐和挑选。Ma 还注意到，选片人扮演的角色更像是一个星探，而不是西方模式的电影策展人。她表示，推荐参赛作品并最终在 SIFF 或其他电影节获奖的选片人将获得额外的现金奖励。组织机构可能会提供其他的激励措施，但在 2019 年，电影节在网站上列出了首席选片团队及其联系信息[6]。尽管在 2019 年，节目在最后一刻发生了变化[7]，但 SIFF 支持长期担任选片人的年轻电影策展人逐渐崭露头角，他们建立了一个

---

1 2019 年 7 月 8 日通过电子邮件对斯特凡·劳丁（Stefan Laudyn）进行的采访。
2 Jean-Michel Frodon, "The Cinema Planet," in The Film Festival Reader, ed. Dina Iordanova (St. Andrews: St. Andrews Film Studies, 2013), 207.
3 R. Ma, *Programming China at the Hong Kong International Film Festival and the Shanghai International Film Festival* [in] *Chinese Film Festivals: Sites of Translation* [Eds. C. Berry, L. Robinson]. New York: Palgrave Macmillan, 2017, pp. 237-258.
4 R. Ma, *A genealogy of film festivals in the People's Republic of China: 'film weeks' during the 'Seventeen Years' (1949–1966)*, New Review of Film and Television Studies, Routledge, 2016, p. 43, DOI: 10.1080/17400309.2015.1107266
5 Ada Minge 于 2017 年在华沙电影节的电影选择团队工作。
6 R. Ma, Ibid., p. 45
7 R. Ma, Ibid., p. 44

知名且受人尊敬的品牌，比如在国际荧幕上的范丽达（Frida Fan）[1]。正如 Ma 总结的那样：

> 人们很容易认为电影节在翻译和移植中逐渐进步，电影节能够根据国际趋势更新其运作框架（如增加数字电影或短片部分，并增设电影奖和电影市场）来发展与中国社会文化和政治语境相适应的本土节目实践和话语[2]。

三 "一带一路"电影周暨巡回展

"一带一路"电影巡展始于 2015 年，当时 SIFF 举办了丝绸之路全景展[3]。随后第二年，准备与"一带一路"系列签订文化交流与合作协议。2018 年，联盟成立，2018 年 6 月至 2019 年间，由相关电影节的选片人挑选的中国电影在合作国上映。其中有：《柔情史》(2018 年，导演杨明明，纽约亚洲 FF)、《阿拉姜色》(2018 年，导演松太加，塔林黑夜 FF)或《矮婆》(2018 年，导演蒋能杰，华沙 FF)。当被问及评选过程时，斯蒂芬·劳丁（Stefan Laudyn）[4]说，WFF 团队可以从提交给"一带一路"电影周计划的 200 多个片名中进行选择。随着 2019 年巡回展览的开始，联盟成员米什科尔茨国际电影节放映了"一带一路"电影周的三部电影：《白云·苍狗》(导演臧连荣、许若谷)、《拂乡心》(导演秦海璐)、《第一次的离别》(导演王丽娜)。根据 SIFF 网站的官方新闻："《第一次的离别》入选第 36 届耶路撒冷电影节，《武林孤儿》(2018 年，导演黄璜)和《少年桑吉》(2018 年，导演张国栋)入选白俄罗斯第 26 届明斯克国际电影节"[5]。入选"一带一路"中国电影的重要要求之一是入围者在放映时用"SIFF"和"一带一路电影节联盟"为标志，这将推动 SIFF 成为"上海文化"品牌的象征，提升其在各国的综合影响力和品牌知名度[6]。这表明，"一带一路"电影周巡展的最重要目标之一是借 A 类电影

1　W. Mitchell, J. Kay, S. Wong, M. Goodfellow, Future Leaders 2019: programmers and curators - Asia, Africa and Australia. Screen International 16 May 2019. https://www.screendaily.com/features/future-leaders-2019-programmers-and-curators-asia-africa-and-australia/5139492.article (20.09.2019)

2　R. Ma, Ibid.

3　http://www.siff.com/a/2018-07-05/2901.html (20.09.2019)

4　2019 年 7 月 8 日通过电子邮件对斯特凡·劳丁（Stefan Laudyn）进行的采访。

5　http://www.siff.com/a/2019-09-23/3720.html (20.09.2019)

6　http://www.siff.com/a/2018-09-25/3039.html (20.09.2019)

节的形象东风，推动上海国际电影节成为超级品牌。

巡回展于每年六月在上海国际电影节期间随着"一带一路"电影周电影之夜以官方的演出而结束。2019 年，作为"一带一路"电影周的一部分，来自 24 个不同国家的 24 部电影上映。随后，8 个奖项获得提名：观众选择奖和媒体选择奖（这两个奖项都至少授予两次，即最佳影片和最佳导演奖）：《水晶天鹅》（*Crystal Swan*，2018 年，导演达里亚·朱克）、《第一次的离别》、《斯堪的纳维亚的沉默》（*Scandinavian Silence*，2019 年，导演马尔蒂·黑尔登）、《创世纪》（*Genesis*，2018 年，导演阿尔帕·博格丹）、印度制造（*Sui Dhaaga: Made in India*，2018 年，导演夏兰特·卡塔利亚）、比莱（*Bille*，2018 年，导演伊娜拉·科尔曼）、《早安》（*Good Morning*，2018 年，导演小津安二郎）、《头顶太阳永不落》（*The Sun Above Me Never Sets*，2019 年，导演柳博芙·鲍里索娃）。6 月 19 日，在华特·迪士尼大剧院举行的盛大典礼上，俄罗斯影片《头顶太阳永不落》获得最佳电影类别的观众选择奖和媒体选择奖，白俄罗斯的《水晶天鹅》也获得了电影的媒体选择奖，中国导演王丽娜《第一次的离别》和匈牙利导演阿尔帕·博格丹《创世纪》获得了最佳导演的媒体选择奖[1]。

时间将见证"一带一路"电影节联盟是否会长久，或者电影节巡回展是否有可能真正改变观众的观影习惯、丰富剧目和拓宽英语电影以外的电影视野。在接下来的几年里，上海国际电影节采取的举措可能会伴随着类似的国际电影交流、电影周和巡回展览计划，这在一定程度上可能类似于现有电影节的基本结构。平遥国际电影节的成立和西宁第一届国际电影节声誉的提升，也为"一带一路"沿线国家电影交流的发展创造了一个良好的视角。

1　R. Ma, ibid., p. 47.

The Belt and Road Film Festival Alliance: Internationalization of Chinese Film Industry

Isabelle Cosima Philomena Aphrodite Angelika Roske / Germany

People's Daily Online / German Foreign Expert

The origins of film festivals as a social structure can be found as far back as the 1920s French ciné-club movement lead by Riciotto Canudo and Jean Delluc. The basic premise was to promote cinema as an international art by establishing a network of events comprised of film screenings[1], lectures and discussions[2]. Modeled after the format of conferences, film festivals are closely intertwined with the city structure. They can become this city's business card, an asset in international relations, as well as they can straighten the citizen's feelings of identification with the city through active participation in discussions, seeing stories from different corners of the world which otherwise they wouldn't have the chance to see in the cinema or even wouldn't know of its existence. For cinephiles, attending the film festival is comparable to 2-week travel without leaving the cinema seat, seeing up to 5 movies a day, inventing new traditions with other cinephiles. In the course of several, continuous festival editions, the regular festival attendees become one alternative family,

---
1 Most often of the titles not distributed in mainstream cinemas.
2 R. Abel, *French Film Theory and Criticism: a history/anthology, 1907-1929*, Princeton, 1993, s. 198.

a small unit in the society joined by shared love for cinema.

Regardless of large number of film festivals in China, major part of them established in the 2010s, the Western model of film festivals as a social phenomenon is quite recent. It emerged in the late 1980s early 1990s, such as Shanghai International Film Festival established in 1993. But it definitely does not mean that in China before the reform and opening up period there were no forms of cinephilia and events comparable to film festivals. Since the 1950s in China, film weeks (*dianyingzhou*, 电影周) became an alternative to Western model and were an important form of education as well as celebration of international cinema art before the popularization of VHS and home entertainment since the 1980s. Shanghai International Film Festival in its pursuit of greater diversity in cinema repertoire, promotion of young Chinese cinema, as well as support for various national film industries and equal representation, initiated in 2018 The Belt and Road Film Festival Alliance. The organization currently consists of 38 film festivals and film institutions from 33 countries[1] from all over the world that will screen films included in The Belt and Road Film Week as part of their program. Through this initiative SIFF successfully builds a model of film festival with Chinese characteristics, offering an alternative to Western one. To highlight the differences in development and basic premises of film festivals and film weeks, I will briefly summarize the historical background of both models.

I. Two Modes of Exhibition: Film Festival and Film Week

According to Chinese film studies scholar Ma Ran, the organization of film week was:

> A complicated process that involved a range of supporters including the cultural authorities, film industries (film professionals), and audiences, although a hierarchy existed among its agendas. Film weeks were of economic significance for the PRC's film imports and also relied on the

---

1 Retrieved from: http://www.siff.com/a/2019-06-21/3509.html (20.09.2019)

Chinese film industry's development for their growth. Also, Chinese audiences relied on film weeks as contact points and platforms to access foreign films.[1]

Among the cultural authorities that organized national film weeks, the most important was China Film Corporation (*zhongguo dianying gongsi*, 中国电影公司), a state-owned entity established in 1951. It coordinated the event through the network of its municipal- and provincial-level branches that since 1956[2] had flexibility in adjusting and modifying the program of the film weeks. As Ma Ran[3] highlights, Chinese People's Association for Friendship with Foreign Countries (CPAFFC[4]) and the China Film Association - both semi-official entities responsible for grass root initiatives and personal connection between PRC and one partnership country - took part in organizing film weeks.

First such exhibition, Film Week of the People's Democratic Republic Nations in Beijing, was organized in 1950. From the beginning of 1950s until 1960, Soviet Film Weeks proved important to the technological development of national film industry through the exchange of knowledge between Soviet and Chinese film professionals. PRC film weeks reflected Cold War dynamics, that exceed the simplistic dualistic differentiation. Although one of the vital objectives was strengthening of the friendship between the communist states that took shape in organizing a film week in China and reciprocal Chinese Film Week in the featured country, but PRC's film weeks also featured cinemas from countries outside the socialist bloc - India (1955), France (1956) or Egypt (1957). These countries that did not have diplomatic ties with the PRC at that time[5], thus film weeks proved to be effective means of cultural diplomacy. From 1953 onwards there were film weeks

---

1 R. Ma, *A genealogy of film festivals in the People's Republic of China: 'film weeks' during the 'Seventeen Years' (1949–1966)*, New Review of Film and Television Studies, Routledge, 2016, p. 43, DOI: 10.1080/17400309.2015.1107266
2 R. Ma, Ibid., p. 45
3 R. Ma, Ibid., p. 44
4 Retrieved from: http://en.cpaffc.org.cn/introduction/ (20.09.2019)
5 R. Ma, ibid., p. 47

of different national cinemas organized in over 20 cities. Finally in 1957 Asian Film Week & 1958 Asia-Africa Film Festival could be perceived as a comprehensive, transnational, precursor for contemporary The Belt and Road Film Week.

The history of film festivals starts with the founding of Venice Film Festival in 1932 and Cannes Film Festival in 1939, although its form solidified after the II World War and the continuity of the awards system depended on the political condition of the times. When film weeks were based on the notion of bilateralism and reciprocity, film festivals connote competitiveness, not only among films in the programme, but also between film festivals themselves and even host cities. According to the history published on Cannes Film Festival official website, the founding of the event in Cannes is attributed to the desire to compete with Venice, in the areas of ideology as well as prestige[1]. Film festivals up until today receive varied amount of support from the national governments, the organization is managed by NGOs with film festival directors maintaining a decisive role in shaping the selection and profile of the event.

The difference between film festivals and film weeks is also visible in the process of selection and programming. Repertoire of the film festival is chosen by a group of specialists, whose auteur vision is reflected through the sections they curate. Long-term programmers are vital for audience-focused festivals such as International Film Festival Rotterdam or London Film Festival, because film curators build trust, local credibility and the feeling of familiarity between film festival and cinema-goers. The name of a programmer is a guarantee of quality of festival selection. Film weeks on the other hand were curated by governmental bodies on state, provincial or municipal levels and remained largely anonymous.

Film festivals proved to be an important promotional tool for host cities, attracting investment in real estate, service sector, boosting tourism not only among cinephiles, but the people enchanted with celebrity culture, festival's prestige or

---

1 Retrieved from https://www.festival-cannes.com/en/69-editions/history (20.09.2019)

even a notion of international global city status that film festival helps to create. While organizing film weeks governmental and semi-official bodies put emphasis on the national paradigm, films were touring around several cities, thus the event remained more detached from a local, urban culture.

The importance of spatial dimension of the event is further highlighted in the emergence of film festival centre - one building that hosts all the rituals and ceremonies such as awards or Q&As and consolidates the community of film festival goers all gathered in one place. The opening galas of film weeks were held in several cities without a specific spatial event centre, the audience feedback was not as significant as in the case of film festival. The main aim of these two modes of exhibition also differs, whereas film festivals' profile is still entertainment oriented but the film weeks were firstly supposed to educate the audience. This intention is reflected through a booklet with official film interpretation accompanying each title presented in the film week. It constituted an alternative to film festival catalogues that features event introduction, film synopsis and thematic articles, but its aim is more informational than educational.

The final difference is the limitation of structure. While film weeks during 17 Years were based on the dual, closed system of bilateralism and reciprocity, the rapid development of film festivals all over the world in the last three decades is an open circuit that only keeps expanding. The Belt and Road Film Festival Alliance indicates flexibility and cooperation, creates support network and the accompanying film week manages to combine the structures of two modes of exhibition, bringing forth their advantages and trying to avoid the drawbacks.

II. Dynamics of Friendship and Competition

Although film festivals are managed by directors and exist independently of governmental institutions, there is an organization that can regulate their operations. Established in 1933, Fédération Internationale des Associations de Producteurs de Film (FIAPF) groups associated film festivals into categories (Competitive

Features Film Festival known as "A-list", Competitive Specialized Film Festivals called "B-list", Non-Competitive Feature Film Festivals, Documentary and Short Film Festivals[1]) according to criteria. Dina Iordanova summarizes the requirements for Competitive Features Film Festival, that "[it] must run for at least nine days; it should not specialize but should cover all aspects of filmmaking; [must have] a feature competition with at least fourteen films without genre limitations[2]". Through membership circuit and accreditation system, FIAPF is supposed to secure film professionals rights when dealing with film festivals without consideration for diverse budgets and economic differences between the locations of the host cities. Nevertheless 86 years after its founding, FIAPF still remains a brand that secures a high reputation of the accredited film festival, at least among the film professionals. It gives the opportunity to enter an exclusive group of most prestigious film events such as Berlinale, Venice FF or Cannes FF. According to Shanghai International Film Festival official website, it became accredited by FIAPF already in 1994[3], just one year after the founding of the festival. The organizers continue to use the A-list status as a major promotional tool.

Nevertheless majority of film festivals nowadays are successfully organized outside of the FIAPF structure, building a steady audience, gaining trust of filmmaker, support of private investors and prestigious status through the means of exceptionally good programming. As Flora Lichaa[4] notices Marijke De Valck's analysis of the international film festival circuit brings to mind theory of rhizome proposed by Gilles Deleuze and Felix Guattari. Especially since the 1990s more and more festivals are founded outside of the already existing network, geographically far away from the old hubs of cinephilia and independent from its structures. FIAPF requirement of high amount of international film premieres in the program

---

1 Retrieved from http://www.fiapf.org/ (20.09.2019)
2 D. Iordanova, *Showdown of the Festivals: Clashing Entrepreneurships and Post-Communist Management of Culture*, "Film International" , 4:5, 2006 Issue 23, p. 28.
3 Retrieved from: http://www.siff.com/a/2019-03-22/3208.html (20.09.2019)
4 F. Lichaa, The Beijing Independent Film Festival: Translating the Non-Profit Model into China [in] Chinese Film Festivals Sites of Translation, Pelgrave Macmillian, 2017, p. 112.

continues to be a major problem, because filmmakers behind most anticipated new releases will firstly chose to present their films in Venice, Berlin, Cannes merely due to more exposure, publicity around the event. The high competitiveness among the film festivals can prove motivational, but only when the members are given equal chances to pick up best film titles, but FIAPF seems to solidifying the unfair unfair structure. The Belt and Road Film Alliance might become an organization that could facilitate the redistribution of privilege and prestige among the film festival that Elena Pollacchi[1] calls "reputational festivals" - the ones that combine elements of public relations, cultural diplomacy and corporate system to continue accumulating their stakeholders' capital and create an image of the festival as a super brand. Shanghai International Film Festival is a platform for the promotion of Chinese film industry but still lacks sufficient prestige and reputation.

Interestingly The Belt and Road Film Festival Alliance turns out to be closely connected to the FIAPF network of festivals. Among 15 accredited festivals in A-list category[2], 5 of them are members of The Belt and Road Film Festival Alliance: Cairo International Film Festival, Moscow International Film Festival, Warsaw International Film Festival, Tallinn Black Nights Film Festival and Shanghai International Film Festival. Out of 24 B-list festivals[3], 6 are members of BRFFA: Minsk International Film Festival, Sofia International Film Festival, Istanbul International Film Festival, Mumbai Film Festival, Eurasia International Film Festival, Transilvania International Film Festival[4]. Moreover, one formerly accredited festival, Thessaloniki International Film Festival, is now a member of The Belt and Road Film Festival Alliance. Film festivals and institutions joined in the alliance have explicitly national profile[5], all except for New York Asian Film

---

1 E. Pollacchi, *"Mature at Birth": The Beijing International Film Festival Between the National Film Industry and the Global Film Festival Circuit* [in] Chinese Film Festivals: Sites of Translation. (Eds. C. Berry, L. Robinson). New York: Palgrave Macmillan, 2017, p. 47.
2 Retrieved from: http://www.fiapf.org/intfilmfestivals_sites.asp (20.09.2019)
3 Retrieved from: http://www.fiapf.org/intfilmfestivals_2019_sites02.asp (20.09.2019)
4 Retrieved from: http://www.siff.com/a/2019-09-23/3721.html (20.09.2019)
5 eg. Polish Film Institute, New Zealand Film Commission, Indonesian Film Board, Georgia National Film Center, National Film Center of Latvia, Ukrainian Motion Picture Association

Festival that continues to represent Asian American community within the United States.

Instead of focusing on taking part in the competition among the FIAPF members, SIFF organizers inaugurating The Belt and Road Film Festival Alliance start to draw inspiration from the model of films weeks that connoted transnational friendship and cooperation between the film institutions around the world. When asked about the future prospects of BRFFA development, Stefan Laudyn[1], director of Warsaw Film Festival, stated that a lot depends on the members of alliance themselves and through the perspective of time the most vital are conversations and building friendship between film festivals, regardless of the original premise of competitiveness. The Belt and Road Film Festival Alliance seems also to rely on the network of interpersonal relations. The head of Warsaw Film Festival mentions he is acquainted with Fu Wenxia, Shanghai International Film Festival long-term director, since both of them are members of FIAPF Festival Committee. He was invited to previous editions of SIFF and in 2018 he managed to come to Shanghai to personally sign BRFFA alliance agreement and actively participate in the roundtable talk, scheduling the alliance activities and engaging in the exchange of knowledge between film festival organizers.

According to Memorandum of Understanding the Establishment of the Film Festival Alliance to Promote Belt and Road Film Culture Exchange signed on June 16, 2018 in Shanghai, the main objectives are to: intensify the spread and exchanges of culture and art by means of films; enhance the communication and understanding of cultural customs and traditions among countries by means of films; advance the holding of film exhibition and other activities for films of each country in film festivals or film institutions of other countries; advance the recommendation of jury members and guests for film festivals and related events among the countries; strengthen communication and cooperation in film production, co-production and distribution among the countries; set up and promote the information sharing

---

1 Interview conducted with Stefan Laudyn via email correspondence (08.07.2019)

mechanism among the signing parties[1].

The film festivals joint in the alliance participate in yearly Forum organized during SIFF to take part in industry panel discussions between filmmakers, programmers, representatives of production and distribution companies, but also film critics and researchers. Director Stefan Laudyn[2] highlights that SIFF organizers are willing to change and put into practice the advice proposed by the alliance members. He mentions that In 2018 the representatives suggested to include work-in-progress into the programme and director Fu Wenxia successfully introduced the new section. The search of new interesting projects already in the phase of production is vital for A-list festivals, especially the ones like SIFF or WFF that aim to pick high quality film premieres as soon as possible. Previously Shanghai International Film Festival had been criticized for mediocre film selection[3], lack of clear programming direction, vague branding, screening Hollywood blockbuster titles that are easily available outside of the festival circuit and anonymity of programmers. Nevertheless it is insufficient to simply apply Western measures into Chinese context. Ma Ran[4] explains the difference between the two modes of film selection - "programming" and "xuanpian" , one undertaken by a programmer and the other by "xuanpianren". According to the scholar, before 2008 SIFF film selection team was made of experts and academics assisted by Chinese-English interpreters as international film screeners almost always have only English subtitles. In the next decade the team started to include also filmmakers and critics. Ma Ran summarizes that in 2017: "The team of selectors consists of roughly 100 people, 50 of whom are experts and gatekeepers in charge of evaluation and selection, with the others being mostly postgraduate students at local universities

---

1 Retrieved from: http://www.siff.com/skin/default/2018%20BELT%20AND%20ROAD%20FILM%20WEEK.pdf (20.09.2019)
2 Interview conducted with Stefan Laudyn via email correspondence (08.07.2019)
3 Jean-Michel Frodon, "The Cinema Planet," in The Film Festival Reader, ed. Dina Iordanova (St. Andrews: St. Andrews Film Studies, 2013), 207.
4 R. Ma, *Programming China at the Hong Kong International Film Festival and the Shanghai International Film Festival* [in] *Chinese Film Festivals: Sites of Translation* [Eds. C. Berry, L. Robinson]. New York: Palgrave Macmillan, 2017, pp. 237-258.

who take care of technical issues and preliminary categorization"[1]. Warsaw Film Festival also employs postgraduate students for temporary work contracts to select titles from a large pool of film submissions[2] and it is quite common practice among bigger and smaller film festivals in Europe. To draw a comparison with other A-list film festival, Berlinale's film selection team consist of 20 programmers. It is possible that the difference in reputation makes the work of SIFF *xuanpianren* more intensive and time-consuming, because most interesting new releases have already been recommended and picked up by most renowned film festivals. Ma Ran also notices that *xuanpianren* assumes a role of a talent scout more than a Western model of programmer being a film curator. She states that the *xuanpianren*, who recommended an entry, which ended up winning awards at SIFF or other film festivals, is provided with additional cash bonus. The structure of a game might provide an additional motivation, nevertheless in 2019 the festival had listed the chief selection team on the website with their contact information[3]. Although in 2019 there had been last minute changes to the programme[4], but SIFF supports the gradual emergence of long-term *xuanpianren*, young film curators that build up a recognizable and respected brand such as Frida Fan featured in Screen International[5]. As Ma Ran brilliantly summarizes:

> It is tempting to argue that it is within the gradual progress of translations and transplantations that the festival is able to both update its operational framework according to the "international trends" (such as installing digital

---

1 M. Ran, Ibid., p. 253.
2 One of my university colleagues, Ada Minge, worked in film selection team of Warsaw Film Festival in 2017
3 Retrieved from: http://www.siff.com/a/2017-03-14/1479.html (20.09.2019)
4 P. Frater & R. Davis, *Shanghai Film Festival Abruptly Pulls Opening Film 'The Eight Hundred'*. Variety 14 June 2019. Retrieved from:
https://variety.com/2019/film/news/shanghai-film-festival-pulls-opening-film-the-eight-hundred-huayi-bros-1203243335/ (20.09.2019)
5 W. Mitchell, J. Kay, S. Wong, M. Goodfellow, Future Leaders 2019: programmers and curators - Asia, Africa and Australia. Screen International 16 May 2019. Retrieved from:
https://www.screendaily.com/features/future-leaders-2019-programmers-and-curators-asia-africa-and-australia/5139492.article (20.09.2019)

film or short film sections, and adding film award and film markets), and develop local practices and discourses of programming in sync with Chinese sociocultural and political contexts".[1]

III. Belt and Road Film Week & Touring Exhibition

The origins of Belt and Road Film Touring Exhibition reach 2015 when SIFF organized Silk Road Panorama[2]. Then in the following year the preparation had been undertaken to sign the culture exchange and cooperation agreement with The Belt and Road series. In 2018 the alliance had been established, between June 2018 and 2019 Chinese films selected by programmers of associated festivals were screened in partner countries, among them *Girls Always Happy* (柔情史, 2018, dir. Yang Mingming 杨明明) at New York Asian FF, *Ala Changso* (阿拉姜色, 2018, dir. Song Taijia 松太加) at Tallinn Black Night FF or *Yun Jie* (矮婆, 2018, dir. Jiang Nengjie 蒋能杰) at Warsaw FF. When asked about the selection process, Stefan Laudyn said that WFF team could choose from over 200 titled submitted to Belt and Road Film Week programme.[3] As 2019 Touring Exhibition starts, alliance member CineFest Miskolc had screened three films included in this year's Belt and Road Film Week: *The Road Home* (白云·苍狗, dir. Zang Lianrong 臧连荣, Xu Ruogu 许若谷), *The Return* (拂乡心, dir. Qin Hailu 秦海璐) and *A First Farewell* (第一次的离别, 2019, dir. Wang Lina 王丽娜). According to the official news at the SIFF website: "*A First Farewell* was recommended to the 36th Jerusalem Film Festival in Israel, *Wushu Orphan* [武林孤儿, 2018, dir. Huang Huang 黄璜] and *Young Sangye* [少年桑吉, 2018, dir. Zhang Guodong 张国栋] were chosen for the 26th Minsk International Film Festival in Belarus"[4]. One of the vital requirements during the screening of selected Chinese films from Belt and Road programme is that the finalists when screened will be identified by the SIFF

---

1   R. Ma, *Programming China at the Hong Kong International Film Festival and the Shanghai International Film Festival* [in] *Chinese Film Festivals: Sites of Translation* [Eds. C. Berry, L. Robinson]. New York: Palgrave Macmillan, 2017, p. 253.
2   Retrieved from: http://www.siff.com/a/2018-07-05/2901.html (20.09.2019)
3   Interview conducted with Stefan Laudyn via email correspondence (08.07.2019)
4   Retrieved from: http://www.siff.com/a/2019-09-23/3720.html (20.09.2019)

and the "Belt and Road Film Festival Alliance" logos, which will promote the SIFF as a symbol of the "Shanghai Culture" brand, enhance its comprehensive influence and brand awareness in the countries.[1] It shows that one of the most important aims of Belt and Road Film Week & Touring Exhibition is promoting SIFF as a super brand, following A-list festivals' image and Elena Pollacchi's definition of "reputational festival"[2].

The Touring Exhibition is concluded each June during SIFF with Belt and Road Film Week Film Night concluded with official gala. In 2019 there were 24 films from 24 different countries screened as part of Belt and Road Film Week. Then 8 titles were nominated for awards: Audience Choice Award and Media Choice Awards (both categories given at least twice, for best film and best director): *Crystal Swan* (2018, dir. Darya Zhuk), *A First Farewell*, *Scandinavian Silence* (2019, dir. Martti Helde), *Genesis* (2018, dir. Arpad Bogdan), *Sui Dhaaga: Made in India* (2018, dir. Sharat Katariya), *Bille* (2018, dir. Ināra Kolmane), *Good Morning* (2018, dir. Bahij Hojeij) and The Sun Above Me Never Sets (2019, dir. Lyubov Borisova). During the gala on June 19 in Walt Disney Grand Theater the Russian title in the line up, *The Sun Above Me Never Sets*, won Audience Choice Award and Media Choice Awards in Best Film category while Belarus's Crystal Swan also won the Media Choice Awards for Film while Chinese director Wang Lina (*A First Farewell*) and Hungarian director Arpad Bogdan (*Genesis*) received the Media Choice Awards for Best Director[3].

The future will verify if the Belt and Road Film Festival Alliance will be longstanding or if film festival circuit has the potential to truly change the audience's film-watching habits, diversify the repertoire and broaden the cinematic horizons beyond the English-language cinema. In the next few years the initiative undertaken by Shanghai International Film Festival might be followed by similar

---

1   Retrieved from: http://www.siff.com/a/2018-09-25/3039.html (20.09.2019)
2   E. Pollacchi, Ibid., p. 47.
3   Zhang Rui, *Russian film tops Belt and Road Film Week*, "China.org.cn" June 21, 2019. Retrieved from: http://www.china.org.cn/arts/2019-06/21/content_74907884.htm (20.09.2019)

programmes of international film exchange, film weeks and touring exhibitions, that might to some extent resemble the rhizomatic structure of existing film festivals. The founding of Pingyao International Film Festival and rising reputation of FIRST International Film Festival in Xining also creates an interesting perspectives on the development of film exchange along continental Belt and Road. The links between Chinese cinema hubs and film festivals around the world deserves a lot more research and studies, which I will continue to pursue.

References

F. Lichaa, *The Beijing Independent Film Festival: Translating the Non-Profit Model into China* [in] *Chinese Film Festivals Sites of Translation*, 2017, Pelgrave Macmillian, p. 112.

E. Pollacchi, *"Mature at Birth": The Beijing International Film Festival Between the National Film Industry and the Global Film Festival Circuit* [in] *Chinese Film Festivals: Sites of Translation* (Eds. C. Berry, L. Robinson), 2017, New York: Palgrave Macmillan, pp. 35-56.

C. Berry, *Shanghai and Hong Kong: A Tale of Two Festivals* [in] *Chinese Film Festivals: Sites of Translation* (Eds. C. Berry, L. Robinson), 2017, New York: Palgrave Macmillan, pp. 15-34.

R. Ma, *A genealogy of film festivals in the People's Republic of China: 'film weeks' during the 'Seventeen Years' (1949–1966)*, "New Review of Film and Television Studies", 2016 14:1, pp. 40-58, DOI: 10.1080/17400309.2015.1107266

R. Zhang, *Russian film tops Belt and Road Film Week*, "China.org.cn" June 21, 2019. Retrieved from: http://www.china.org.cn/arts/2019-06/21/content_74907884.htm (20.09.2019)

R. Abel, *French Film Theory and Criticism: a history/anthology, 1907-1929*, Princeton, 1993, s. 198.

J. M. Frodon, *The Cinema Planet* [in] *The Film Festival Reader*, [Ed. Dina Iordanova], St. Andrews: St. Andrews Film Studies, 2013, p. 207.

D. Iordanova, *Showdown of the Festivals: Clashing Entrepreneurships and Post-Communist Management of Culture*, "Film International", 4:5, 2006Issue 23, pp. 25-38.

R. Ma, *Programming China at the Hong Kong International Film Festival and the Shanghai International Film Festival* [in] *Chinese Film Festivals: Sites of Translation* [Eds. C. Berry, L. Robinson]. New York: Palgrave Macmillan, 2017, pp. 237-258.

P. Frater & R. Davis, *Shanghai Film Festival Abruptly Pulls Opening Film 'The Eight Hundred'*. "Variety" 14 June 2019. Retrieved from:

https://variety.com/2019/film/news/shanghai-film-festival-pulls-opening-film-the-eight-hundred-huayi-bros-1203243335/ (20.09.2019)

W. Mitchell, J. Kay, S. Wong, M. Goodfellow, *Future Leaders 2019: programmers and curators - Asia, Africa and Australia*. "Screen International" 16 May 2019. Retrieved from: https://www.screendaily.com/features/future-leaders-2019-programmers-and-curators-asia-africa-and-australia/5139492.article (20.09.2019)

阿富汗孔子学院的发展现状调查与分析

阿布 【阿富汗】
喀布尔大学中文系（孔子学院） 讲师

引 言

阿富汗地处中国—中亚—西亚经济走廊和中巴经济走廊之间，在"一带一路"建设中地位重要，区位比较优势和在地区价值链的位置重要性都非常突出。自古以来，阿富汗就是古代丝绸之路上的明珠，曾为古代丝绸之路建设和中华文化的发展做出重要的贡献。"一带一路"倡议为阿富汗人民提供的不仅是四通八达的道路，还有国际社会对内陆国家发展问题前所未有的重视和投入。2016 年 5 月，中阿签署了共建"一带一路"合作谅解备忘录。2017 年 10 月，阿富汗加入亚投行。在阿富汗安全形势不清等不利情况下，中阿货物贸易额保持了年均 10 亿美元的水平，直航和直达班列稳定运营，新的经济合作项目也在积极探讨中。这些都令中阿在"一带一路"框架下深化合作拥有坚实的基础和广阔的前景。中阿多年来的各方合作，离不开两国人民之间的日益频繁的人文交流，而孔子学院的建立，为中阿具备双边沟通与交流能力人才的需求和支撑提供了平台并发挥了纽带桥梁作用。2007 年，太原理工大学与国家汉办签署关于在阿富汗创办孔子学院协议时，合作方喀布尔大学没有一本汉语教材，没有一个汉语教师，没有一个懂阿富汗语言的老师，双方院校没有任何合作基础，一切从零开始。2009 年 11 月，喀布尔大学孔子学院和该院汉语系举行正式挂牌仪式，阿富汗自此有了第一个以汉语为专业的学术和文化交流机构，也为当地汉语教学发展奠定了坚实基础。经过近 11

年的发展，汉语及中国文化传播在阿富汗地区反响良好，已有 8 届 181 名汉语专业毕业生，这些青年学子，毕业后进入阿富汗外交部门、中资公司、中阿贸易企业和学校等各行各业工作，成为推进中阿政治、经济、文化、教育等领域交流合作的中坚力量，促进了中阿各方交流合作，加深了中阿双方友谊，促进了中阿"民心相通"。目前，虽然中文和中国文化在阿富汗很受欢迎，但是，如何才能在"一带一路"倡议的推动下，克服阿富汗安全形势不清的困难，使孔子学院的汉语传播及中国文化传播发挥更大的桥梁纽带及人才支撑作用等方面的调查研究非常薄弱，而随着中阿"一带一路"合作已逐步展开，如何充分发挥孔子学院综合文化交流平台的作用，助力"一带一路"，并实现喀布尔大学孔子学院自身可持续发展，急需全面深入调查研究。鉴于此，本文采用调查问卷、实地访谈的调查方法，以阿富汗喀布尔大学孔子学院的汉语教师、汉语学习者为调查对象，针对被访者对学习汉语和中国文化的需求，对孔子学院汉语教学和文化传播的满意度、孔子学院课程设置、汉语教师、教材、考核、文化活动等方面进行调查分析，探讨喀布尔大学孔子学院在汉语教学和文化传播方面所取得的成功经验、存在的问题及可持续发展对策建议等，以期为"一带一路"沿线其他国家孔子学院的发展提供借鉴。

一　喀布尔大学孔子学院的汉语教学现状调查分析

喀布尔大学作为阿富汗的第一所最高学府，始建于 1930 年，目前在校学生 3 万人，在校学生中女生约占 40%，教职工约 1200 人。现设有经济、社科、医学、法学、文学、艺术等专业。语言学院成立于 1944 年，该学院的学生们学习不同国家的语言。语言学院现开设了汉语、英语、法语、俄语、德语、西班牙语、土耳其语、阿拉伯语、普什图语和波斯达利语（波斯语）等 10 种语言课程。

1. 孔子学院汉语学习者的现状及分析

喀布尔大学孔子学院（中文系）中文本科从 2008 年 3 月开始招生，其中 2011 年因汉办公派汉语教师未到岗，中文系没有足够的师资，这一年没有招收新生。同年 10 月由于安全形势恶化，汉办决定暂时停止对孔院营运直到 2013 年 1 月。2012 年尽管汉办撤回了中国教师，但是仍然有 29 名新生入学开始学习中文。孔院（中文系）开设中文本科专业以来共招生 11 届 469 人，截止 2019 年，共培养本科毕业生 8 届 181 人，先后有 292 人次获得中国国家汉办孔子学院奖学金赴华深造。喀布尔大学孔子学院中文系一直以来都是春季招生,但是,从 2017 年起进行了改革,为了与世界其他国家同步,改为秋季招生。表 1 为历届毕业生情况。

表 1　　　　　　喀布尔大学孔子学院历届毕业的学生情况

类别	2008级	2009级	2010级	2011级	2012级	2013级	2014级	2015级	2016级	2017级	2018级	2019级	合计
入学	15	16	23	零	29	52	62	70	52	50	50	50	469
在读										44	42	44	130
肄业					1		2						3
退学	1		2		2	10	30		24	6			75
延期毕业						3	18						21
毕业	14	16	21		26	39	12	15	22				165

备注:2011 年没有招生。2017 级毕业的 18 名学生因在中国享受南亚师资班奖学金,于 2018 年 6 月延期毕业了。

由表 1 可以看到一个突出的问题,那就是学生的流失率比较高,达到学生总数的 20.3%。其中的原因比较复杂,有的是阿富汗高教部调剂过来的,没有报中文专业,对学习中文缺乏兴趣,有畏难情绪;有的是因为战乱或家庭困难而放弃学习。目前孔子学院采用 HSK 考核学生的汉语学习情况。表 2 为学生获得 HSK 证书情况。

表 2　　　喀布尔大学孔子学院历届本科专业学生 HSK 获得证书情况

获证情况	2008级	2009级	2010级	2011级	2012级	2013级	2014级	2015级	2016级	2017级	2018级	2019级	合计
HSK3					24	27	24	13	16	17	24	31	166
HSK4							1	5	4		38	33	81
HSK5					1	3	1				7	12	23
HSK6	1	1	6		2	2							12

备注:3 级为一年级结业时,4 级为二年级结业时,5 级为三年级结业时,6 级为四年级毕业时。

表 2 显示,学生汉语水平考试的结果不容乐观的原因是"三教"(教师、教材、教学)急缺和存在的问题以及战乱形势,同时,学校和孔子学院都没有对学生的汉语水平考试成绩提出硬性的要求,也没有与他们的毕业证挂钩,所以参加汉语

水平考试的动机主要是为了获得奖学金,因此没有打算赴中国学习的学生基本不会报名参加考试,这在某种程度上会削弱考试"考教结合、以考促学、以考促教"的作用。

2. 汉语教师的现状及分析

喀布尔大学孔子学院的成立为培养本土教师开创了平台。喀布尔大学中文系的6名汉语教师都是孔子学院培养的本土教师,他们都是通过在中国进修学习,进一步提高自己的汉语水平,提升了学历,有的还在读博或读研,虽然本土教师的学历层次不断提高,但基本都是助教职称,职称结构很不合理,原因是从中国进修返回阿富汗后,是否继续从事汉语教学有很大的不确定性。相比较而言,在岗的三名中国教师学历和职称结构都比较合理,两名老教师是中国文学专业毕业的资深汉语教师,一名助教也是国际汉语教育硕士学历。但是,从人数方面来讲,孔子学院(中文系)若要扩大教学规模,支持其他学校的汉语教学,以目前的师资人数来说,保证教学正常运行,已很紧张,但还要兼顾教学之外的财务管理、教学档案管理、学术与教学研究,工作量是比较大的。师资具体情况见表3。

表3　　　　　喀布尔大学孔子学院师资情况一览表

年龄/教师类别	21-30	31-40	41-50	51-60	合计	教授	讲师	助教	合计	博士	在读博士	硕士	在读硕士	合计
中国教师	1	1	1	1	4	1	1	1	3	1	0	3	0	4
百分比%	25	25	25	25	100	25	25	25	75	25		75		100
本土教师	6	0	0	0	6	0	0	6	6	0	1	3	2	6
百分比%	100				100			100	100		17	50	33	100

3. 汉语课程设置现状及分析

喀布尔大学孔子学院的课程设置由原来的两门课程,发展到现在的10门课程。主干课程课时也由原来的一周2课时,增加到3课时,具体课程设置情况见表4。

表4　　　　　喀布尔大学孔子学院汉语课程设置一览表

学年	综合	口语	听力	读写	阅读	写作	视听说	报刊选读	经贸汉语	翻译教程	论文指导	文化技能
2008	6	2										
2009	6	2										

续表

学年	综合	口语	听力	读写	阅读	写作	视听说	报刊选读	经贸汉语	翻译教程	论文指导	文化技能
2010	6	2										
2011												
2012	3	2	2	2	2							
2013	3	2	2	2	2							
2014	3	2	2	2	2							
2015	3	3	3	3	3	3	2	1	1	2		
2016	3	3	3	3	3	3	2	1	1	2	1	1
2017	4	3	3	3	3	3	2	1	1	2	1	1
2018	5	3	3	3	3	3	2	1	1	2	1	1
2019	5	3	3	3	3	3	2	1	1	2	1	1

表 4 所显示的课程设置是每一个学年所开课程的总体情况。2019 学年显示有 12 门课，一年级开设 5 门，即口语、综合、读写、听力、文化技能，一周 15 课时；而视听说、报刊选读、经贸汉语、翻译教程、论文指导等课程在四年级开设。

4. 课堂教学现状及分析

本文针对听力课、口语和阅读三门课程设计了不同的问卷。调查对象为一、二、三、四年级中文专业学生，共发放学生问卷 102 份，收回有效问卷 89 份。孔子学院中文系本土和中国教师共计 10 人接受了采访。调查结果显示：听力课教学效果较差，原因是教材内容陈旧，教师方法单一，能听懂的学生人数只占 16%，学生对教学内容不感兴趣；汉语口语课最大的问题是没有口语交际的语境，其次是学生自身汉语发音、语法及词汇量上存在的问题，使学生张不开口交际，第三是本土教师没有突出口语课的教学特点，教学方法缺少口语交际训练的话题设计，82% 的学生喜欢中国老师从零起点起给他们教口语，第四是口语教材内容也存在陈旧、老化的问题；孔子学院中文系学生对阅读课非常感兴趣，对阅读课教师教学方法的认可度十分高，但希望教师在阅读课上能加强汉语阅读技能的训练，还希望老师能给他们提供课外阅读资料，能快速增加汉语词汇量和提高汉语阅读能力。

5. 汉语教材的现状及分析

2017 学年，喀布尔大学孔子学院总结以往教材使用中的问题，修订了汉语本科专业培养计划，据此对课程设置做出了调整，决定统一使用北京语言大学出版社的《发展汉语》和北京大学出版社的《博雅汉语》系列教材。各课型教材存在的问题已在前节陈述。

6. 第二课堂活动

喀布尔大学孔子学院十分重视一年一度的"汉语桥"演讲比赛、孔子学院日、中国传统节日、中国书画展、文化体验活动，旨在增进中阿两国友好关系，为阿富汗民众提供展示汉语和中国文化的平台。由于受到安全问题的困扰，孔子学院在举办这些活动的时候不能大张旗鼓，只能在有限的范围内进行，其传播效果受到一定的限制。

二　喀布尔大学孔子学院的汉语教学存在的问题

调查分析显示，喀布尔大学孔子学院的汉语教学从 2008 年开设中文课程至今，面对的是阿富汗长期遭受战乱和恐怖主义破坏、种族和宗教冲突严重、国内民生状态恶劣和严峻的安全形势。孔子学院的老师们深耕战地，奉献青春，挥洒汗水，从最初的 15 名学生到 2013 年起每年招收的学生都在 50 名以上，学生的规模一直呈上升趋势；其次，从汉语本科专业课时量来看，从最初的一周 6 课时，到 2019 年的平均每周 16 课时；课程设置也由 2 门增加到 8 门。再次，孔子学院开设了教学点、孔子课堂，其他地区的汉语课程的开设也在协商当中。学院培养了一批"知华、友华、爱华"的阿富汗青年学子，保证了孔子学院工作正常运行及持续发展，为中阿两国在"一带一路"框架下深化人文交流合作，促进两国民心相通奠定了坚实基础和广阔的前景。但是，我们也看到还有很多问题亟待研究解决。

孔子学院布局单一且不均衡，不能满足当地汉语学习者的需求。目前阿富汗仅靠喀布尔大学一所孔子学院已不能满足该国各地汉语学习者的需求，如阿富汗巴米扬省，是阿富汗 34 个省中的一个省，居全国中心，也是当地占多数的哈扎拉族人的文化中心，哈扎拉族是阿富汗斯坦国内第三大民族。因历史上有名的巴米扬大佛而闻名世界，巴米扬地处丝绸之路上，是往来欧洲、波斯、中国和印度间的商队途经之地，因此巴米扬的艺术融合着希腊、波斯和印度佛教的成分，形成独特的古典的艺术风格——希腊式佛教艺术。由于自古与中国的历史渊源和独特的文化背景，巴米扬省多次申请开设孔子学院，但一直未得到足够重视和关注。

孔子学院的宣传及活动空间有限，影响了孔子学院的发展和中国文化的传播。由于自古连续不断的强邻入侵和大国角逐，铸就了今天阿富汗的社会结构、宗教文化、国土疆界和政治生态，尤其是不断恶化的安全局势，使得很多孔子学院的活动只能限制在很小的范围内举行。

生源规模有待进一步扩大到中小学，汉语有待纳入阿富汗国民教育体系。虽然阿富汗的孔子学院工作有了稳步持续发展，但生源规模始终是制约孔子学院在该地区进一步发展的瓶颈问题。目前汉语教学仅限于大学本科教学，阿富汗的中小学没有开设汉语课程，汉语教学缺乏连续性。

教学和科研水平有待提升，急需实施"质量提升+"工程。目前阿富汗孔子学院存在规模较小、课程设置不科学、本土师资水平不高、教法单一滞后、教材内容陈旧和话题针对性不强、地域特点不突出的问题。还有网络教学、远程教学等教学资源严重缺乏，科学研究水平低且滞后，尤其是针对该国孔子学院发展的相关调查研究几乎空白等问题，使得汉语及中国文化传播在阿富汗的理论支持和实践指导严重不足。

三 喀布尔大学孔子学院建设发展的相关建议

作为古丝绸之路上的重要中枢，阿富汗在中国"一带一路"建设中具有重大的意义。中国的国家安全、新疆安全稳定和"一带一路"倡议都同阿富汗局势息息相关，中国同阿富汗在经济上有极强的互补性，一直在为推进阿富汗的和平与发展发挥建设性作用。中方一直同国际社会一道，为推动阿富汗和中亚地区的和平、稳定与发展作出不懈努力，2014年10月，两国政府发表的《关于深化战略合作伙伴关系的联合声明》指出：双方将在文化、教育、青年、妇女、社会、媒体等领域加强交流与合作，未来五年中方将通过各种渠道向阿方提供500个中国政府奖学金名额，推动中阿人文交流稳步发展，民心相通是"一带一路"建设的社会根基，孔子学院平台则是实现中国与阿富汗国家民心相通最重要的桥梁纽带。如果阿富汗能够实现真正的和平和繁荣，必然对中国西部边疆的安全稳定，乃至"一带一路"建设的深入开展有保障意义。面对新形势下的新挑战、新要求，阿富汗孔子学院的发展将面临越来越多潜在的不确定因素，创新发展的任务十分紧迫，特别是如何将孔子学院搭建成"一带一路"民心相通的桥梁，这对中国及阿富汗政府来说都是一个不可轻估的挑战。

1. 注重国别特点，制定类型化孔子学院发展的中长期规划

"一带一路"倡议的持续推进，带动了孔子学院的可持续发展。但是，"一带一路"沿线各国各方情况各异，孔子学院的发展需要融入中小学、大学、社区和扎根本土，比如阿富汗孔子学院的发展特点，和欧美、非洲、南亚，甚至中亚等国家的经济、政治、文化、社会等方面水平差异巨大。目前阿富汗孔子学院要紧紧抓住"一带一路"建设为契机，将孔子学院融入"一带一路"、全球化治理，构建人类命运共同体的"大共识"下，为维护和平稳定，促进人类文明进步做贡献，以阿富汗汉语学习、研究及中国文化传播需求为出发点，制定并严格执行符合阿富汗自身孔子学院发展的中长期规划，推动孔子学院的类型化发展。

2. 注重沟通交流，多渠道、多方式开展新建孔子学院和扩大汉语教学层次范围工作

阿富汗喀布尔大学孔子学院已经历了11年发展历程，为中阿两国人文交流培养了很多懂汉语通中国文化的友好使者，为孔子学院的发展奠定了良好基础。今天，两国政府应充分考虑阿富汗国家民众对汉语学习及了解中国文化的需求，在阿富汗国情允许的情况下，可通过政府间合作、友好城市、校际合作、校企合作等牵线搭桥，逐步推进在阿富汗巴米扬开办孔子学院和将汉语纳入该国国民教育体系的论证和试点工作。

3. 注重当地需求，实施孔子学院办学"质量+"工程

阿富汗与中国在政治、经济、文化等领域的各方合作逐渐展开，学习汉语成为阿富汗青年人到中资企业就业、来华留学旅游、与中方开展业务合作的金钥匙，也是推动孔子学院融入当地需求、提升办学效益的内在动力。孔子学院应抓住这一契机在师资力量、教材适用性、教学方法和目标上进行适时调整和转型。在教师配备上，加大本土教师"汉语+应用专业"学历人才培养；在教材使用和编写上，加大教材"多语种+国别化特色"开发研究；在教学方法上，加大"传统教学+体验式教学+现代教育技术"的结合；同时，在教学中，一是围绕"一带一路"建设中当地的新需求，将汉语教学与实用培训、岗位技能有机融合，使教学更好地为学生成才服务、为当地发展服务，二是应充分挖掘丝绸之路记载的中国和阿富汗文化融汇的图景，以及中阿两国之间自古以来的千丝万缕的联系，深刻、久远且广泛的影响，并将这些内容贯穿于孔子学院汉语教学及中国文化传播中，让孔子学院成为阿富汗国民了解中国、认识中国的平台和窗口。

4. 注重科学研究，加强国别化孔子学院发展的理论指导和实践支持

在"一带一路"建设中，中国与沿线国家的交往不断拓展，联系更加密切，单一的语言教学已经不能满足当地的需求，加强文化交流与人文互动、提供商旅信息咨询服务、推进教育科技文化合作、推介东道国优秀文化成果等服务已经提上日程。阿富汗喀布尔大学孔子学院应结合中阿两国各方面的合作需求及进一步加强综合文化交流平台作用提出的新要求，推动孔子学院从单一的语言教学向多功能服务转变，从单向"走出去"向"走出去"与"引进来"双向交流和发展模式，有目的地推进阿富汗孔子学院持续发展的研究，加强交流合作，提升教学和科研水平。还应当依托中方合作方及其他院校学科、人才、科研优势，提升自身内涵建设，并积极为外方相关专家来华开展教学和研究提供帮助，为"一带一路"沿线国别化孔子学院发展提供智库支持，为促进多元文明共存共荣做出更大贡献。

参考文献

1. 赵伯乐：《阿富汗：影响南亚地缘政治格局的新因素》，《形势与政策》，2006年第1期。
2. 汪川：《"一带一路"安全评估报告之 阿富汗》，《军事文摘》，2021年第5期。

Survey and Analysis on the Status of the Development of Confucius Institutes in Afghanistan

Ahmadi Abdul Razaq / Afghanistan

Confucius Institute at Kabul University / Lecturer

Introduction

    Afghanistan, located between the China-Central Asia-West Asia Economic Corridor and the China-Pakistan Economic Corridor, plays an important role in the Belt and Road Initiative, and has outstanding advantages of comparative location and an important position in the regional value chain. Since ancient times, Afghanistan has been playing a key role in the ancient Silk Road, and has made great contributions to the ancient Silk Road and to the development of Chinese culture. The Belt and Road Initiative provides the Afghan people with not only a better road transportation system, but also unprecedented attention to and investment from the international community regarding the development of landlocked countries. In May 2016, China and Afghanistan signed a memorandum of understanding on cooperation in the Belt and Road Initiative. In October 2017, Afghanistan joined the Asian Infrastructure Investment Bank. Although under unfavorable circumstances such as the unstable security situation in Afghanistan, the volume of trade between China and Afghanistan has maintained an average annual level of US$ 1 billion, direct flights and trains are operating stably, and new economic cooperation projects are being actively explored. All these provide a solid foundation and broad prospects for deepening cooperation between China and Afghanistan within the framework of the Belt and Road Initiative. The cooperation between China and Afghanistan for many years has been carried out on the base of increasingly frequent cultural exchanges between the two countries, and the Confucius Institute provides a platform and bridge for cultivating the talents needed by bilateral communications and exchanges between China and Afghanistan. In 2007, when Taiyuan University of Technology and the Center for Language Education and Cooperation signed an agreement on the establishment of a Confucius Institute in Afghanistan, Kabul University, the partner of the project, even had no Chinese textbook, no Chinese teacher, and even no teacher who knew the national language of Afghanistan, and both sides of the project had no basis for cooperation, so everything had to start from scratch. In November 2009, the Confucius Institute of Kabul University and the Chinese Department of the Institute held an official opening ceremony. Since then, Afghanistan has had the first academic and cultural exchange institution specializing in Chinese, which has also laid a solid foundation for the development of local Chinese teaching. After nearly 11 years of development, the spread of Chinese and Chinese culture has received a good response in Afghanistan, with 181 graduates majoring in Chinese from 8 years of enrollment. After graduation, these young students have worked in many industries, such as Afghan diplomatic departments, Chinese-funded companies, Sino-Afghan trade enterprises, schools and so on. They have become the backbone of Sino-Afghan exchanges and cooperation in politics, economy, culture, education and other fields, they have promoted the exchanges and cooperation between China and Afghanistan, deepened their friendship, and promoted people-to-people bonds between the two countries. At present, although Chinese and Chinese culture are very popular in Afghanistan, surveys and research projects are still rare on how to overcome the difficulty of the unsettled security situation in Afghanistan to make communication in the Chinese language and the Chinese cultural communication of the Confucius Institute play a greater role in the Belt and Road Initiative as a bridge to cultivate the talents. With the gradual development of Sino-Afghan Belt and Road Initiative cooperation, there is still an urgent need for comprehensive deep surveys and research on how to give full play to the role of the Confucius Institute as a comprehensive cultural exchange platform to help improve the Belt and Road Initiative and realize the sustainable development of the Confucius Institute at Kabul University. In view of this, in this paper, the Chinese teachers and Chinese learners in the Confucius Institute of Kabul University, Afghanistan have been surveyed by means of questionnaires and field interviews. Aiming at the needs of the respondents for learning Chinese and Chinese culture, the author surveyed and analyzed the satisfaction of Chinese teaching and cultural communication in the Confucius Institute, the curriculum of the Confucius Institute, Chinese teachers, teaching materials, assessment and cultural activities, and discussed the successful experience, existing problems and sustainable development measures and suggestions for the Confucius Institute of Kabul University in Chinese teaching and cultural communication. The author also wishes to provide reference for the development of Confucius Institutes in other countries along the Belt and Road.

I. Survey and analysis of the current situation of Chinese teaching at the Confucius Institute of Kabul University

Kabul University, the first and the best University in Afghanistan, was founded in 1930. At present, it has 30,000 students, about 40% of whom are women, and about 1,200 faculty members. There are majors in economics, social sciences, medicine, law, literature, art, etc. Its Language School was founded in 1944, where students can learn different languages to understand the outside world. The Language School now offers 10 language courses including Chinese, English, French, Russian, German, Spanish, Turkish, Arabic, Pashto and Persian Dari (Persian).

1. The current situation and the analysis of Chinese learners in the Confucius Institute

The Confucius Institute (Chinese Department) of Kabul University began to recruit Chinese undergraduate students in March 2008. In 2011, due to the absence of Chinese teachers sent by the Center for Language Education and Cooperation, the Chinese Department did not recruit new students that year. In October of the same year, due to the deterioration of the security situation, the Center for Language Education and Cooperation decided to temporarily stop operating the Confucius Institute until January 2013. In 2012, although the Center for Language Education and Cooperation withdrew Chinese teachers, there were still 29 freshmen who had started to learn Chinese. The Confucius Institute (Chinese Department) has enrolled 469 students in 11 years since starting the Chinese undergraduate major. By the end of 2019, it had trained 181 graduates of an 8-year enrollment, and 292 people successively won the scholarship provided by the Center for Language Education and Cooperation and the Confucius Institute to support them in studying in China. The Chinese Department of the Confucius Institute at Kabul University has always enrolled students in the spring. However, since 2017, it has been reformed and enrolled students in the autumn in order to keep pace with other countries in the world. Table 1 shows the situation of previous graduates.

Table 1 The Situation of Previous Graduates of the Confucius Institute of Kabul University

Category	Grade 2008	Grade 2009	Grade 2010	Grade 2011	Grade 2012	Grade 2013	Grade 2014	Grade 2015	Grade 2016	Grade 2017	Grade 2018	Grade 2019	Total
Enrolled	15	16	23	0	29	52	62	70	52	50	50	50	469
Studying										44	42	44	130
Certified dropout					1		2						3
Dropped out	1		2		2	10	30		24	6			75
Graduation postponed						3	18						21
Graduated	14	16	21		26	39	12	15	22				165

Remarks: No enrollment in 2011. The graduation of the 18 students who should graduate in 2017 was postponed to June 2018 because they participated in the activities of the South Asia Teacher Class Scholarship in China.

From the above table, we can see a prominent problem, that is, the student turnover rate is relatively high, reaching 20.3% of the total number of students. The reasons are complicated, some of the students were transferred here by the Ministry of Higher Education of Afghanistan, they had not applied for the Chinese major, they lacked interest in learning Chinese, and they were afraid of difficulties in studying the language. Some of them gave up studying because of war or family difficulties. At present, the Confucius Institute uses HSK to assess students' Chinese learning. Table 2 shows the situation of students obtaining the HSK certificate.

Table 2 HSK Certificates Obtained by Previous Undergraduate Students of the Confucius Institute of Kabul University

Certificate situation	Grade 2008	Grade 2009	Grade 2010	Grade 2011	Grade 2012	Grade 2013	Grade 2014	Grade 2015	Grade 2016	Grade 2017	Grade 2018	Grade 2019	Total
HSK3					24	27	24	13	16	17	24	31	166
HSK4							1	5	4		38	33	81
HSK5					1	3	1				7	12	23
HSK6	1	1	6		2	2							12

Remarks: HSK 3 for finishing the first year studying, HSK 4 for finishing the second year studying, HSK 5 for finishing the third year studying and HSK 6 for finishing the fourth year studying.

The above table shows that the HSK results of students are not good because of the urgent shortage and problems of "teaching materials, teachers and teaching methods", as well as the war situation. At the same time, neither the university nor the Confucius Institute put forward rigid requirements for students' HSK results, and they do not link the results to students' graduation certificates. Therefore, the motivation to participate in the HSK is mainly to obtain scholarships, and the students who do not intend to study in China will not sign up for the examination, which weakens the principle of "combining examination with teaching, promoting learning and teaching through examination" to some extent.

2. The current situation and an analysis of Chinese teachers

The establishment of the Confucius Institute at Kabul University has created a platform for training local teachers. The 6 teachers of Chinese in the Chinese Department of Kabul University are all local teachers trained by the Confucius Institute, all of whom have further improved their level of Chinese and academic qualifications by studying in China, and some of them are still studying for PhD or postgraduate. Although the academic qualifications of local teachers are constantly improving, they are basically teaching assistants, and their professional titles are unreasonable, the reason causing this situation is the great uncertainty about whether they will continue to engage in Chinese teaching after returning to Afghanistan from China. In comparison, the academic qualifications and professional titles of the three on-the-job Chinese teachers are relatively reasonable. Two of them are old senior Chinese teachers majoring in Chinese literature, and the other one is a teaching assistant who has a master's degree in international Chinese education. However, in terms of the number of Chinese teachers, if the Confucius Institute (Chinese Department) wants to expand the scale of its teaching and support Chinese teaching in other universities and colleges, the current number of teachers is already quite insufficient to ensure the normal operation of teaching, not to mention that they also need to participate in the financial management, teaching file management, academic and teaching research, they have been overloaded. See Table 3 for details of the situations of the teaching staff.

3. The current situation and an analysis of the Chinese curriculum

The number of courses offered by the Confucius Institute of Kabul University has grown from two courses to ten courses now. The class hours of main courses have also increased from 2 class hours a week to 3 class hours. See Table 4 for the specific curriculum.

The curriculum shown in the table above is the general courses in each academic year. In the academic year of 2019, there are 12 courses, 5 of which are for the

Table 3 The Situation of the Teaching Staff at the Confucius Institute of Kabul University

Age Teacher category	21-30	31-40	41-50	51-60	Total	Professors	Lecturers	Assistants	Total	PhD	Studying for PhD	Master	Studying for master	Total
Teachers from China	1	1	1	1	4	1	1	1	3	1	0	3	0	4
Percentage%	25	25	25	25	100	25	25	25	75	25		75		100
Local teachers	6	0	0	0	6	0	0	6	6	0	1	3	2	6
Percentage%	100				100			100	100		17	50	33	100

Table 4 List of Chinese Courses at the Confucius Institute of Kabul University

Class hour Academic year;	Comprehensive Learning	Oral Chinese	Listening	Reading and writing	Reading	Writing	Viewing, listening and speaking	Newspaper reading	Business Chinese	Translation	Thesis guidance	Literacy skills
2008	6	2										
2009	6	2										
2010	6	2										
2011												
2012	3	2	2	2	2							
2013	3	2	2	2	2							
2014	3	2	2	2	2							
2015	3	3	3	3	3	3	2	1	1	2		
2016	3	3	3	3	3	3	2	1	1	2	1	1
2017	4	3	3	3	3	3	2	1	1	2	1	1
2018	5	3	3	3	3	3	2	1	1	2	1	1
2019	5	3	3	3	3	3	2	1	1	2	1	1

first-year students, including Oral Chinese, Comprehensive Learning, Reading and Writing, Listening, and Literacy Skills, with 15 class hours a week; Viewing, Listening and Speaking, Newspaper Reading, Business Chinese, Translation, Thesis Guidance and other courses are offered for the fourth-year students.

4. The current situation and an analysis of classroom teaching

This paper designs different questionnaires for listening, speaking and reading. The respondents were Chinese Majors in grades 1, 2, 3 and 4. A total of 102 student questionnaires were distributed and 89 valid questionnaires were recovered. A total of 10 local and Chinese teachers of the Chinese Department at the Confucius Institute were interviewed. The results show that the effect of the teaching of the listening class is poor because the teaching materials are outdated, and teachers' methods are not adequately up-to-date, only 16% of the students can understand the material, and students are not interested in the teaching content. The biggest problem of the class in oral Chinese is that there is no environment for oral communication, the second problem is the low level of the students' own Chinese pronunciation, grammar and vocabulary, which make them unable to communicate with each other, and the third is that local teachers fail to highlight the teaching characteristics of the class in oral Chinese, their teaching methods lack topic design for oral communication training and 82% of the students like Chinese teachers to teach them oral Chinese from scratch, and the fourth problem is that the oral teaching material is also outdated and aging. The students of the Chinese Department of the Confucius Institute are very interested in the reading class, and highly approve of the teaching methods of teachers in that class. However, they hope that teachers can strengthen the training of Chinese reading skills in the reading class, and they also hope that teachers can provide them with extracurricular reading materials, which can quickly increase their Chinese vocabulary and improve their ability at reading Chinese.

5. The current situation and an analysis of Chinese teaching materials

In the academic year of 2017, the Confucius Institute of Kabul University summarized the problems in the use of previous textbooks, revised the training plan of Chinese undergraduate majors, adjusted the curriculum accordingly, and decided to use the series of textbooks Developing Chinese published by Beijing Language and Culture University Press and Boya Chinese published by Peking University Press. The problems existing in each course textbook have been stated in the previous section.

6. The second classroom activities

The Confucius Institute of Kabul University attaches great importance to the annual "Chinese Bridge" speech contest, Confucius Institute Day, Chinese traditional festivals, Chinese painting and calligraphy exhibitions and cultural experience activities, aiming at enhancing the friendly relations between China and Afghanistan and providing a platform for Afghan people to display Chinese and Chinese culture. Due to the security problems, the Confucius Institute cannot hold these activities with great fanfare, but only in a limited range, and the effect of its circulation is limited to a certain extent.

II. The Problems of Teaching Chinese at the Confucius Institute of Kabul University

According to the above survey and analysis, Chinese language teaching at the Confucius Institute of Kabul University has been offered since 2008, against the background of Afghanistan's long-term war and terrorism, serious ethnic and religious conflicts, poor domestic livelihood of the people and severe security situation. Teachers at the Confucius Institute devote their youth and sweat to the battlefield. From the initial 15 students to more than 50 students enrolled each year since 2013, the scale of students has been on the rise. The Chinese undergraduate professional class hours rise from the initial 6 class hours a week to the average 16 class hours a week in 2019; the number of courses has also increased from 2 to 8. In addition, the Confucius Institute has opened teaching points and Confucius classrooms, and plans to offer Chinese courses in other regions. A number of young Afghan students who know China, like China and love China have finished their studies here, who have ensured the normal operation and sustainable development of the Confucius Institute, and have laid a solid foundation and provide broad prospects for deepening humanities exchanges and cooperation between China and Afghanistan under the framework of the Belt and Road Initiative, and they promote communication between the people of the two countries. However, we also see that there are still many problems to be studied and solved.

The distribution of the Confucius Institute is limited and unbalanced, which cannot meet the needs of local Chinese learners. The results of the survey show that at present, only one Confucius Institute at Kabul University in Afghanistan can no longer meet the needs of Chinese learners throughout the country. For example, Bamiyan Province in Afghanistan is one of the 34 provinces in Afghanistan, which is the national center and the cultural center of the Hazara ethnic group, which is the third-largest ethnic group in Afghanistan. Famous all over the world for the historic Bamiyan Buddhist Statue, Bamiyan is located on the Silk Road, which is a hub for caravans traveling between Europe, Persia, China and India. Therefore, art in Bamiyan combines the elements of Greek, Persian and Indian Buddhism, forming a unique classical artistic style—Greek Buddhist art. Due to historical relationships and unique cultural backgrounds between Bamiyan Province and China since ancient times, related parties have repeatedly applied for the establishment of Confucius Institutes there, while they fail to attract enough attention.

The limited publicity and space for activities at the Confucius Institute has affected the development of the Confucius Institute and the spread of Chinese culture. Since ancient times, the continuous invasion of strong neighbors and competition among big powers have created the social structure, religious culture, territorial boundaries and political ecology of Afghanistan today, especially the bad security situation, which makes many activities at the Confucius Institute limited to a small scope and cannot be publicized, so as not to cause safety incidents.

The student source needs to be further expanded to primary and secondary schools, and Chinese language education needs other support, such as being included in the Afghan national education system. Although the work of the Confucius Institute in Afghanistan has developed steadily and continuously, the scale of student source has always been the bottleneck restricting the further development of the Confucius Institute in this region. At present, Chinese teaching is limited to undergraduate teaching. There is no Chinese course in primary and secondary schools in Afghanistan, and so Chinese teaching lacks continuity.

The level of teaching and scientific research needs to be improved, and the "Quality Improvement+" project is urgently needed. The results of the survey show that the scale of the Confucius Institute in Afghanistan is small at present; the curriculum setting is unscientific; the level of local teachers is not high enough; teaching methods are not up-to-date and advanced; the content of the teaching materials is outdated, the teaching topics in the material fail to highlight topic targets and local characteristics; teaching resources such as network teaching and distance learning are seriously insufficient; the scientific level is low and lagging behind others around the world; in particular, the research on the development of Confucius Institutes in this country is almost blank, which causes serious insufficiency in theoretical support and practical guidance of Chinese and Chinese cultural communication in Afghanistan.

III. Suggestions on the Construction and Development of the Confucius Institute of Kabul University

As an important hub of the ancient Silk Road, Afghanistan is of great significance in the Belt and Road Initiative. China's national security, including Xinjiang's security and stability, and the Belt and Road Initiative are closely related to the situation in Afghanistan. China and Afghanistan are highly complementary economically and China has been playing a constructive role in promoting peace and development in Afghanistan. China, together with the international community, has made unremitting efforts to promote peace, stability and development in Afghanistan and Central Asia. In October 2014, the Joint Statement on Deepening a Strategic Partnership issued by the two governments pointed out that the two sides will strengthen exchanges and cooperation in the fields of culture, education, youth, women, civil society and media, and China will provide scholarships for 500 Afghan students through various channels in the next five years to promote the steady development of cultural exchanges between China and Afghanistan. "Connected hearts" is the social foundation to developing the Belt and Road Initiative, and the Confucius Institute platform is the most important bridge to connect people's hearts between China and Afghanistan. If Afghanistan can achieve real peace and prosperity, it will certainly be of great significance for guaranteeing the security and stability of China's western frontier and even the in-depth development of the Belt and Road Initiative. Facing the new challenges and requirements of the new situation, the development of the Confucius Institute in Afghanistan will face more and more potentially uncertain factors, and the task of innovation and development is very urgent. Especially, how to build the Confucius Institute into a bridge between the people of the countries in the Belt and Road Initiative is a challenge, to which great attention shall be paid by both Chinese and Afghan governments.

1. Formulating the medium-and long-term plan for the development of the Confucius Institute on the basis of the characteristics of each country

The continuous promotion of the Belt and Road Initiative has promoted the sustainable development of the Confucius Institute. However, countries along the Belt and Road have different situations, and the development of Confucius Institutes needs to be integrated into the education of primary and secondary schools, universities, communities and rooted in the local area. For example, the developmental characteristics of the Afghan Confucius Institute are greatly different from those of Europe, America, Africa, South Asia and even Central Asia in terms of economy, politics, culture and society. At present, the Confucius Institute in Afghanistan should seize the opportunity of the Belt and Road Initiative, integrate the Confucius Institute into the Initiative, global governance, and great consensus to build a human community with a shared future, make contributions to maintaining peace and stability and promoting the progress of human civilization, formulate and strictly implement the medium-and long-term plan in line with the development of the Confucius Institute in Afghanistan on the basis of Chinese learning, research and Chinese cultural communication in Afghanistan, and promote the typical development of the Confucius Institute.

2. Building new Confucius Institutes and expanding the scope of Chinese teaching levels through communication and exchange and by multiple channels and methods

The Confucius Institute of Kabul University in Afghanistan has experienced 11 years of development, which has cultivated many friendly messengers who understand Chinese and Chinese culture for the cultural exchanges between China and Afghanistan, and it has laid a good foundation for the development of the Confucius Institutes in general. Today, the two governments should give full consideration to the needs of Afghan people for learning Chinese and understanding Chinese culture. If Afghanistan's national conditions permit, they can gradually push forward the demonstration and pilot work of opening a Confucius Institute in Bamiyan, Afghanistan, and bringing Chinese into the national education system by cooperation between governments, sister cities, inter-school cooperation and school-enterprise cooperation.

3. Paying attention to local needs and implementing the "Quality+" project of the Confucius Institute.

Cooperation between Afghanistan and China in the political, economic, cultural and other fields has gradually begun. Learning Chinese has become the important key for young Afghans to finding jobs in Chinese-funded enterprises, studying in China and carrying out business cooperation with China, and it is also the internal driving force for the Confucius Institute to integrate into local needs and improve efficiency. The Confucius Institute should seize this opportunity to make opportune adjustments and transformations in their teaching staff, in the applicability of their teaching materials, teaching methods and objectives. In terms of teachers' allocation, it is necessary to increase the training of local teachers with Chinese+application major education; in the use and compilation of teaching materials, the research and development of multilingual+national characteristics shall be increased for teaching materials; in terms of teaching methods, the combination of traditional teaching+experiential teaching+modern educational technology should be strengthened. In the teaching process, first, Chinese teaching, practical training and job skills should be organically integrated within the new local needs for the development of the Belt and Road Initiative, so that the teaching can better cultivate students' talents and serve local development; second, the tradition of cultural integration between China and Afghanistan existing in the old Silk Road and the inextricable links between China and Afghanistan since ancient times and the related profound, long-lasting and extensive influence should be fully tapped to put these contents into the Chinese teaching process of the Confucius Institute and Chinese cultural dissemination, so as to make the Confucius Institute a platform and window for Afghan people to learn more about China.

4. Strengthening theoretical guidance and practical support for the local-characteristics development of the Confucius Institutes through special scientific research

With the development of the Belt and Road Initiative, China's exchanges with countries along the route are constantly expanding, and their links are closer. Single language teaching can no longer meet local needs. More service targets have been put on the agenda such as strengthening cultural exchanges and humanities interaction, providing information consulting services for business and tourism, promoting educational, scientific and cultural cooperation, and recommending excellent cultural achievements of the host country. The Confucius Institute of Kabul University in Afghanistan should further strengthen its role as a comprehensive cultural exchange platform in combination with the cooperation needs of all parties in China and Afghanistan, accelerate the development of the Confucius Institute from providing single language teaching to multiple function services, from the one-way "going out" pattern to the "going out"-"bringing in" two-way exchanges and pattern of development, systematically promote research on the sustainable development of Confucius Institutes in Afghanistan, strengthen exchanges and cooperation, and improve the level of teaching and research. It should also, by virtue of the advantages provided by Chinese partners and other institutions in disciplines, talents and scientific research, enhance its own establishment and actively help foreign experts to carry out teaching and research in China, provide think-tank support for the localized development of Confucius Institutes in the countries along the Belt and Road, and make greater contributions to the coexistence and common prosperity of diverse civilizations.

References

1. Zhao Bole, Afghanistan: New Factors Affecting the Geopolitical Pattern of South Asia [J]. Situation and Policy, January 2006.

2. Wang Chuan, The Belt and Road Initiative Security Assessment Report—Afghanistan [J]. Military Digest, May 09, 2021.

地理标志驱动旅游业发展：以中国为例

哈韦拉 【智利】
智利大学国际问题研究所　讲师

一　导言

中国已成为全球重要的旅游目的地。正如世界旅游组织（UNWTO）所述，中国是世界第四大旅游目的地。国际旅游业在中国发展成功的关键因素之一是其城市文化遗产方面的吸引力。对于发展中经济体，如拉丁美洲区域的经济体，旅游业可能成为其发展进程的重要经济引擎；因此，学习中国的经验可为制定合理政策的重要参考。在这方面，许多国家发现，地理标志不仅是推销产品的工具，而且是推销与这些商品相关的旅游服务的工具。

地理标志已有 100 多年的历史。法国是最早保护此类知识产权的国家之一，在法国地理标志主要用于香槟和其他酒类商品。这一保护制度被引入世界贸易组织（世贸组织），特别是与贸易有关的知识产权方面（TRIPS 协定）和其他国际公约。

学者 Suh 和 MacPherson 认为，地理标志通过基于高质量的产品差异化带来更高附加值，因为其提供有关产品属性的官方认证信息从而保护消费者，同时加强和保存了该地区的特征和文化遗产信息。

地理标志不仅被认为是知识产权，也是一种政策工具，尤其是在考虑旅游业发展的情况下。一些作者表示，如果生产者能够将旅游活动纳入其与地理标志相关的战略中，销售额可能会增加更多。例如，通过引入与受保护产品相关的美食路线（Barrera, 1999, 2006; Millán & Morales-Fernández, 2012）。

尽管有大量文献论证地理标志对旅游业发展的潜力，但在提到发展中国家时，实证支持和正面影响的证据有限，特别是针对智利等拉美国家的中国最佳实践（Marie Vivien&Biénabe, 2017; Neilson, Wright & Aklimawati, 2018; Rawat, 2017）。本文试图扩展有关中国和拉丁美洲旅游、茶文化和地理标志的文献。为了做到这一点，本文分析了中国文化遗产在浙江省旅游推广中的作用，特别是通过地理标志保护杭州龙井茶，以及它们对旅游发展的影响。为此，采用定性和描述性案例研究方法进行分析。继Yin（2011）之后，将使用主要和次要来源进行分析。文献综述基于地理标志、茶文化和旅游。为了分析茶叶地理标志对浙江省旅游业发展的影响，将调查案例研究的官方文件，以及2019年浙江省杭州市青年汉学家访问计划实地考察期间从茶农和主要参与者处收集的信息。首先，对旅游、茶文化与地理标志的关系进行了文献综述。第二，阐述中国对地理标志的保护。第三，阐述杭州龙井茶的案例研究。第四，进行了分析。最后，本文将给出一些结论和政策建议。

二　文献综述：地理标志、茶文化与旅游

地理标志（GIs）可定义为"用于具有特定地理来源且具有该来源所带来的质量或声誉的产品上的标志"（WIPO，2017）。文献将地理标志称为"资源贫乏的农民和加工者可以使用的营销工具，有可能增加或获得一些安全收入，促进社会和环境可持续的生产实践，并加强地方动态和治理"（Marie Vivien & Biénabe, 2017）。

正如Sun等（2013）所述，地理标志的保护可以发挥以下作用：

市场引导和企业组织，促进和加强名特产产业化；利用技术规范和质量监控功能，加强和提高名、特产品的质量标准化；利用市场意识和产品声誉背景，支持和推广农产品品牌战略；提高农产品的附加值，增加农民收入，从而有助于解决有关农业、农村和农民的问题。

Eguillor（2014）认为，在国家和国际层面，预计地理标志将为产品增加价值，增加需求和价格，并有助于当地发展。在欧洲，受地理标志保护的产品超过700种，其中90%来自法国、葡萄牙、意大利、希腊、西班牙和德国（Cáceres, 2019; Cambra & Villafuente, 2009）。具体而言，在西班牙，贸易保护产品的

经济价值在 18 年内增长了六倍（Millán & Morales Fernández，2012）。所有这些因素表明，将地理标志作为品牌服务，对于制定农村地区发展战略至关重要（Cambra & Villafuente，2009）。

尽管《TRIPS 协定》提出了保护地理标志的基本原则，但并未定义与原产地的联系或基于原产地的质量标准（Cáceres，2019）。该规范是通过规范或使用规则的定义在产品层面建立的（Marie Vivien & Biénabe，2017）。还必须考虑到，地理标志不仅是一项知识产权，也是一项政策工具。

Xing（2015）认为，非物质文化遗产的知识产权保护是必要和合法的，因为它有助于保持其经济价值，从而使集团享有其产权。具体而言，地理标志是最方便的保护，因为它与非物质文化遗产的结合最多。两者都具有地域性特征，既考虑自然因素，又考虑人为因素；它们决定了权利和集体主体的不可转让性。

在这种背景下，茶文化作为一种有趣的文化遗产出现，因为它发展了文化维度，形成和培育了全球茶文化。根据 Li 和 Chen（2010）的说法，"茶叶采集和饮用的历史可以追溯到公元前 1100 年的周朝"。茶文化对于促进和构建和谐社会至关重要，茶道"倡导我们选择真诚的生活态度，礼貌地社交，建立和平共处的新型人际关系……"由此，茶文化旅游结合了生态。

在考虑地理标志和旅游业时，一些研究表明，如果生产者能够将旅游活动纳入其地理标志战略，那么销售额可以增加更多。例如，通过整合与受保护产品相关的美食路线。在阿根廷和西班牙，游客数量增加，因为他们需要更多关于货物原产地的信息，更喜欢当地产品及其质量（Barrera，1999，2006；Millán & Morales Fernández，2012）。另一个重要因素是，作为改善农村地区交通和通信的一种方式，地理标志吸引了新的基础设施投资，例如，甚至酒店和火车旅游也被纳入地理标志范围，以促进地理标志相关的旅游（Cambra & Villafuente，2009）。

Suh 和 MacPherson（2007）在提到茶叶地理标志和旅游业时，对韩国的博盛（Boseong）绿茶进行了一项研究，指出当地方政府决定将该行业定位为区域发展的引擎时，它实施了一项基于收购地理标志等举措的综合创新计划，以提高产品质量。最终，地理标志提升了产品的形象，提高了公众对该地区的认识，茶园已经成为电影、电视节目等的背景。事实上，访问该地区的游客数量增加了，博城地区游客增长了 300%。地理标志提高了产量和价格，刺激了茶叶相关产业。因此，地理标志不仅可以在产品营销中发挥重要作用，还可以在场所营销中发挥重要作用。从这里开始，以及在其他国家，政府开发了各种与茶叶相关的旅游活动，如绿茶节、绿茶度假村等。

Xingdong（2017）认为，地理标志有助于维持良好的生态环境。推广地理标志产品的使用不仅有助于传播和保护优秀的传统民俗艺术，而且有助于发展生态农业、生态旅游、文化旅游等。这也将鼓励农村地区城市化的发展，以及农业产业化的发展。

正如 Huang、Tuan 和 Wongcha（2014）所言，自中国改革开放以来，农村地区的经济活动已经进行了改革。休闲农业和乡村旅游被认为是全球的朝阳产业。中国理事会表示，需要发展这一经济活动，以扩大郊区和农村地区充分就业。在这种背景下，茶文化已成为中国乡村旅游的关键。茶文化旅游的发展丰富了乡村旅游，有助于人们了解中国悠久的茶文化历史，推动了当地经济的可持续发展（Ya&Qi，2014）。

三　中国地理标志的保护

中国于 1995 年实施了地理标志保护，共有五种不同的保护类型。如今，地理标志通过双重系统得到保护，因为它们可以注册为集体商标和认证商标（Xiaobing & Kireeva，2007）。农业部还颁布了第三批农产品保护条例。中国加入世界贸易组织后，对《中华人民共和国商标法》进行了一些修改，将地理标志保护作为一种单独的商标类型。与此同时，一种独特的制度也被纳入了中国。因此，可以说中国有三种保护地理标志的方式（Sun 等，2013）：

（1）国家工商行政管理局（SAIC）地理标志商标注册。
（2）国家质量监督检验检疫总局（AQSIQ）的地理标志产品保护（特殊）。
（3）农业部农产品地理标志注册（MOA）。

根据中华人民共和国国家工商行政管理局（SAIC）的数据，截至 2014 年底，共注册了 2697 个地理标志商标，其中 85% 以上用于农产品（Yuanhua, Wei, & Nabi，2016）。

1. 商标制度

这是中国最早使用的制度，类似于美国使用的制度。中国的商标法并没有将地理标志与其他常见标志区分开来，所以只要它们不欺骗消费者，地理标志就可以成为商标。2001年，中国加入WTO后，对1993年的《商标法》进行了修订，引入了认证和集体商标作为保护地理标志的一种方式。在第16（2）条中指出（Berti，2017；Xiao Bing&Kireeva，2007；Yuanhua等，2016）：

如果商标中包含的地理标志未说明所涉商品的位置或原产地，则该术语会在公众中引起混淆，应拒绝注册。还应禁止将其作为商标使用。但善意取得登记的，继续有效。上款所述地理标志是指该地理标志是有关货物的原产地，货物的特殊品质、声誉或其他特征主要取决于所涉地理位置的自然条件或其他人文条件。

在这种情况下，申请人必须提交一套证明产品合格的文件。申请人还应采取一些监督产品质量的手段。第4条规定，申请将地理标志注册为集体商标的协会或任何其他组织应由地理标志所示区域内的成员组成(Berti, 2017; Xingdong, 2017; Yuanhua et al., 2016)。必须补充的是，在中国，地理标志不仅指在某一地理区域生产的产品，还指与产品生产有关的自然和人为因素；这在其他国家被称为原产地名称。这种保护主要被视为针对非法竞争者滥用地理商标的防御性保护。

2. 独特性

本案中最重要的条款是"地理标志产品保护规定"，该行政裁决已于2005年5月16日由国家质检总局审批。其中包括《商品地理标志（注册和保护）法》（1999（48）号）（Berti，2017；Yuanhua等，2016）。这些措施代表了一种类似于欧洲国家的保护体系。该系统主要用于向客户证明地理声明的真实性以及特定地理区域与产品质量之间的联系。

法案第10条规定，申请人必须在提交给政府的提案中说明产品原产地的限制，并提交技术文件（可能包括产品的物理、化学或感官特征及其与原产地自然和人为因素的关系）。该过程完成后，如果其他生产商有意在其产品上使用地理标志标签，则必须向当地质量技术监督局或出入境检验检疫局申请授权，出示证明相关产品源自GI地区的证书（Lin & Lian, 2018; Xingdong, 2017）。

3. 农产品

该系统始于2008年农业部颁布的《农产品地理标志管理办法》（Berti，2017）。它以商标法为基础，但类似于特殊的商标法，仅适用于农产品：如蔬菜、谷物、水果、油、茶、草药、工艺品、花卉等。它不保护葡萄酒、醋、陶瓷、玉石、针织、丝绸等。

《办法》第二条规定，农产品地理标志是指：

以地区名称命名的特殊农产品标识，旨在说明所示农产品来自特定地区，产品的质量和主要特征主要取决于该地区的自然和生态环境以及文化和历史因素（Berti，2017）。

因此，适合注册的产品只能是与生产地名称相符的产品。在这种情况下，申请人只能是农民合作经济组织和行业协会。之后，该地区的生产商必须向协会出示证书，以便合法使用地理标志，包括可以标记为地理标志的产品数量（Berti，2017；Xiao Bing & Kireeva，2007）。

四　浙江省的茶叶保护：杭州龙井茶

中国拥有悠久而丰富的茶文化。茶叶质量和产地之间的联系在中国消费者中得到了广泛认可，同时也获得了国际声誉。中国政府在茶园标准化、病虫害防治和绿色防治技术方面加大了投资。此外，还对茶叶公司实施营销门槛，以改进其生产工艺，从而提高产品质量。如图1和图2所示，从2013年到2018年，中国的茶叶生产和消费都有所增长。

浙江省是中国重要的茶叶产地，也是绿茶的主要出口基地（Sun等，2013）。2015年，浙江省在茶树栽种面积分布中排名第六，在茶叶生产中排名第四，在茶叶出口中排名第一（Liu，2015）。因此，茶叶现在是浙江省当前农村和山区农业经济的新亮点，已成为提高农业效率和农民收入的重要因素。浙江省的茶园总面

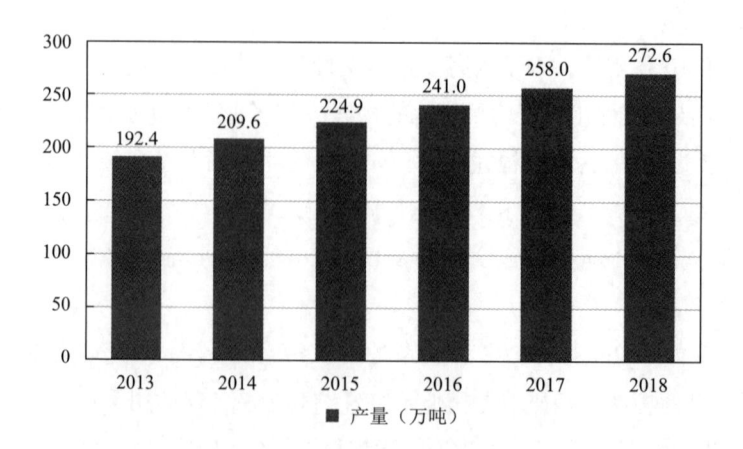

图1　2013—2018年中国茶叶产量

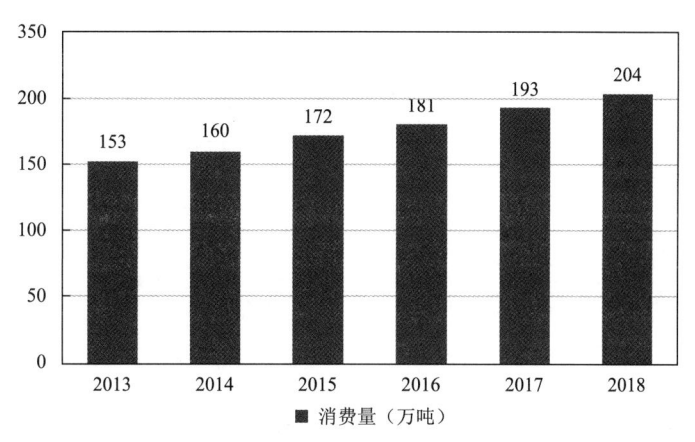

图 2 2013—2018 年中国茶叶消费量

积约为 143 万公顷，产量为 12 万吨（O-Chanet，2017），其中绿茶占 85%，红茶和乌龙茶占 15%。

浙江省的茶叶保护始于 1999 年的地理标志产品体系。龙井茶是 2001 年第一个获得原产地保护的产品，也是中国第四个国家地理标志产品（Sun 等，2013）。截至 2012 年，原国家质量监督检验检疫局已对浙江省 8 种茶叶进行了地理标志保护（表 1）。

表 1 浙江省地理标志产品（特殊保护）（Sun 等，2013）

批准的排名	批准时间	地理标志产品	地理标志产品的保护范围
4	2001.10.26	龙井茶	在浙江省，东起虎跑、茅家埠，西到杨府庙、龙门坎、何家村，南起社井、浮山，北至老东岳、金鱼井，总面积 168 平方公里
70	2004.04.06	安吉白茶	安吉县现辖行政区域
117	2004.12.13	乌牛早茶	永嘉县现辖行政区域
325	2007.03.20	开化杜仲茶	开化县现辖行政区域
422	2008.03.14	松阳茶	松阳县现辖行政区域
435	2008.05.08	建德苞茶	建德市 9 个镇、街道办事处（新安江街、洋溪街、更楼街、下崖镇、杨村桥镇、乾潭镇、梅城镇、三都镇、大洋镇）所辖的现行行政区域
665	2010.05.24	惠明茶	现为景宁畲族自治县管辖的行政区域
816	2010.12.31	三杯香茶	泰顺县现辖行政区域

1995 年，国家工商总局开始在浙江省注册茶叶的地理标志商标。

表 2　　　　浙江省作为商标的地理标志（Sun 等，2013）

商标名称	注册人
安吉白茶	安吉县农业局茶叶站
临海蟠毫茶	临海专业技术推广站
景山绿牡丹茶	江山专业技术推广站
余姚瀑布仙茗茶	余姚市瀑布仙茗茶叶协会
径山茶	杭州市余杭区径山茶业管理协会
大佛茶	新昌名茶协会
普陀佛茶	舟山市普陀区茶业协会
苍南翠龙茶	苍南县农业协会
磐安云峰茶	浙江省磐安茶业协会
嵊州珠茶	嵊州市茶业协会
龙井茶	浙江省农业厅经济作物管理局
桐庐雪水云绿茶	桐庐县雪水云绿茶业协会
建德苞茶	建德市质量计量监测中心
开化龙顶茶	开化市特产局（茶叶局）
莫干黄芽茶	德清县莫干山镇农业综合服务中心
天目青顶茶	临安市茶业协会
千岛玉叶茶	淳安茶业协会
天台山云雾茶	天台专业技术推广站
西湖龙井茶	杭州市西湖区龙井茶业协会
仙都笋峰茶	缙云茶业协会
松阳银猴茶	松阳茶业协会

农业部的地理标志农产品注册始于 2008 年。截至 2012 年，农业部已在浙江省注册了 7 种茶叶（表 3）。

表 3　　　　　　浙江省茶叶的农产品地理标志（Sun 等，2013）

产品名称	原产地的指定保护范围	申请人
长兴紫笋茶	水口乡、夹浦镇、小浦镇、煤山镇、白岘乡、龙山街道、雉城镇、林城镇、泗安镇、二界岭乡、吴山乡、和平镇、李家巷镇、洪桥镇以及长兴县的国营场站，共 15 个乡镇，92 个村（场）	长兴茶业协会
泰顺三杯香茶	罗阳镇、百丈镇、柳峰乡、松洋乡、彭溪镇、仕阳镇、万排乡、仙稔乡、筱村镇、泗溪镇、凤垟乡、横坑乡、九峰乡、月湖乡、峰文乡、雅阳镇、龟湖镇、雪溪乡、东溪乡、翁山乡、联云乡、新浦乡、包垟乡、司前镇、竹里乡、峰门乡、黄桥乡、碑排乡、南院乡、岭北乡、三魁镇、西旸镇、下洪乡、大安乡、洲岭乡、垟溪乡等 36 个乡镇 205 个村 (场)	泰顺茶业协会
千岛银珍茶	李家镇、大同镇、航头镇、寿昌镇、更楼街道、新安江街道、洋溪街道、下涯镇、莲花镇、杨村桥镇、大洋镇、梅城镇、三都镇、乾潭镇、钦堂乡等新安江沿岸广大区域，辖 16 个乡镇、街道，84 个村	建德市千岛银珍茶叶合作社
余姚瀑布仙茗茶	余姚市所有行政村	余姚市瀑布仙茗茶叶协会
天目青顶茶	太湖源镇、西天目乡、高虹镇、於潜镇、藻溪镇、太阳镇、潜川镇、乐平乡、昌化镇、河桥镇、湍口镇、龙岗镇、清凉峰镇、大峡谷镇、岛石镇共计 15 个乡镇 78 个行政村	临安市茶业协会
桐庐雪水云绿茶	桐庐县行政范围内的新合乡、钟山乡、百江镇、合村乡、分水镇、瑶琳镇、横村镇、富春江镇、凤川镇等 9 个乡镇 59 个村	桐庐县雪水云绿茶业协会
普陀佛茶	普陀区的沈家门街道、东港街道、勾山街道、展茅街道、朱家尖街道、桃花镇、六横镇、登步乡；定海区的城东街道、环南街道、解放街道、昌国街道、盐仓街道、临城街道、白泉镇、干览镇、马岙镇、小沙镇、岑港镇、双桥镇、金塘镇、北蝉乡；岱山县的高亭镇、东沙镇、岱东镇、岱西镇、衢山镇、秀山乡	舟山市农业协会

龙井茶是一种有 1200 多年历史的绿茶。它生长在浙江省杭州西湖周边地区，因为那里有肥沃的土地、多山和良好的气候。它被认为是中国十大名茶中最好的茶。

龙井茶根据不同的地理来源分为狮、龙、云、虎，代表狮峰、龙井、云栖和虎跑的种植园（China Discovery，2018）。2014 年，浙江的茶叶制造商生产了

24000 吨龙井茶（Mengxing，2015）。

　　传说清朝乾隆皇帝（公元 1711—1799 年）巡游杭州时，他去龙井狮峰学习采茶，他的随从告诉他，皇太后病了。回到北京后，皇太后闻到龙井茶的香味，喝了龙井茶后，感觉好多了（China Discovery，2018）。

　　当地还有一个关于龙井的传说：在古代有一处干净的泉水流经 12 个村庄，这似乎是中国龙赐予的水。于是，人们就在涌泉处放置了一个雕刻的龙首。有一天，一位风水师在喝完水后感觉这泉水很神奇，就建议村民们打井取水饮用。最后，他们将这口井命名为"龙井"(China Discovery，2018)。

　　一些村庄围绕茶叶相关旅游业开展了经济活动。例如，龙井村就是龙井茶的发源地。如今，这里不仅居住着 800 多人，而且还有近 800 亩的龙井茶种植园。这是一个游客可以参观茶园、狮峰胡公庙和中国国家茶叶博物馆的地方。

　　2008 年，国家工商行政管理总局商标局批准"龙井茶"被浙江省农业技术推广中心注册为地理标志认证商标，七年后，"龙井茶"被认定为地理标志原产地产品 (HKTDC，2009; Mengxing，2015)。2014 年，该中心取消了 35 家计划使用"龙井茶"商标的公司的权利，主要是因为他们在授权过期后没有申请再使用。到 2015 年，352 家公司拥有该商标的使用权。此外，该中心在 43 个国家申请商标注册，并收到马德里商标国际注册系统的注册证书，以及西班牙、意大利、德国和美国等其他国家的批准通知（Mengxing，2015）。截至 2012 年，172 家公司在使用龙井茶地理标志产品（表 1）。

五　文化遗产和地理标志是旅游业发展的驱动力

　　正如杭州中国国家茶叶博物馆（Weber，2018）所述：茶是中国对人类和世界文明的重大贡献之一。中国是茶树的发源地，也是第一个发现和使用茶叶的国家。茶产业和茶文化始于饮茶。几千年来，随着茶的习俗越来越深入地渗透到中国人的生活中，茶文化作为古老的民族文化的一部分，作为东方传统文化的瑰宝，不断得到丰富和发展。今天，作为一种世界性的饮料，茶是中国人民和世界其他地方人民之间深厚感情的纽带。

　　中国茶文化与世界其他地区之间的这种联系可以反映在旅游业的发展中。在此背景下，地理标志有助于促进民族文化的传承及其经济发展（Xingdong，2017）。地理标志可以对旅游业产生积极影响，因为公众对该地区优质茶叶的认识提高，有助于促进产品和地方营销。中国，特别是浙江省，以娱乐为基础，以家庭活动为主题，发展了浓厚的茶文化旅游；在杭州中国茶叶博物馆可以受到教育和熏陶；令人放松的风景让人身心愉悦，并提供户外空间；茶馆和传统茶道创造了和谐的室内空间。

在上述三个系统下，浙江茶叶地理标志代表了该省的自然因素，如土壤类型、天气条件、茶叶品种。此外，还有人为因素，如制茶历史、中国文化传说、种植历史等。浙江省政府机构开展了相关活动，监督龙井茶的质量以及龙井茶合法生产区域的商标使用情况，以保持其特色并吸引游客（Mengxing，2015）。浙江省工商行政管理局指出，"龙井茶"地理标志商标的成功注册有助于确立"龙井"名称使用的排他性（HKTDC，2009）。在工艺和市场准入方面，龙井茶被认定为地理标志后，西湖龙井的价格在 2000 年至 2005 年间比其他茶叶上涨了 10%，与 2005 年茶叶平均价格 23 元/公斤相比，达到了 100 元/公斤（ITC，2009）。

根据龙井村实地考察和杭州中国茶叶博物馆参观期间收集的信息，可以说龙井茶的非物质文化遗产和旅游相关活动已经培育和发展了多年。例如，2003 年联合国教科文组织通过的《非物质文化遗产保护公约》将其列入世界非物质文化遗产名录中的传统绿茶工艺。这也与 2005 年国务院发布《关于加强中国非物质文化遗产保护的意见》有关，目的是抢救和保护中国的非物质文化遗产。由此，浙江茶的传统工艺得到了开发，包括传统的制作工艺、传统的音乐等，这些都是游客在游览不同村庄时可以体验到的元素。

位于西湖西南侧的龙井村被宣传为游客可以呼吸到带有特殊茶香的清新空气的地方。游客可以去胡公庙观赏"十八御茶树"，这是乾隆皇帝为皇太后采茶的地方，还可以观赏活了 250 多年的茶树。还有占地 130 亩的龙井山地公园，有百年茶馆喝龙井茶，看炒茶的过程，参加茶道或"欣赏制作一杯茶的技巧，以表达中国纯净、优雅、真诚和和谐的茶精神"（China Discovery，2018）。还有前总理周恩来访问过的西湖西侧的梅家坞村；而位于西湖西南侧的龙坞茶村则紧靠浙江国家旅游度假区。龙坞茶村因其 666 平方米的茶园和良好的生态环境而被称为"天然氧吧"。在这些村庄里也有卖龙井茶给游客的商店，在那里他们可以买到纪念品。

龙井村已被改造成一个旅游目的地：房屋采用江南风格，以悬檐和扶壁而闻名。这种转变是由政府、生产者和村民共同出资的（Chen，2009）。此外，当地茶农经营茶园，并根据季节雇佣人员。他们平均每年的净收入超过 5 万元。事实上，各家各户都在一起卖龙井茶。即使是杭州的城市居民也希望住在龙井村，体验乡村生活中平静的风景和茶文化的传统。在营销策略上，村委会向茶叶生产商提供包装和防伪标签。

这些村庄还为那些想更深入地了解茶文化的游客开发了特别的项目。该项目被称为"龙井茶文化探索项目"，游客可以参观龙井茶园，然后与当地茶农一起提着竹篮采茶，体验完整的采茶过程。然后，游客可以看到茶叶是如何晒干的，品尝茶叶并参加茶道表演。最后，他们可以享用午餐和当地菜肴。

此外，杭州还为游客准备了茶文化博览会。这是为期三个月的茶嘉年华，重点介绍龙井茶的制作、品尝和历史。根据实地考察中收集到的信息，游客可以在博览会上品尝优质好茶，探索龙井茶背后的故事，还可以看到制作和泡茶的每一个步骤。

最后，游客可以参观中国国家茶叶博物馆，在那里可以通过视频、报告和古代材料全面了解茶的历史仪式、习俗和风格，并在整个行程中品茶。

在此，有必要强调当前地理标志保护系统的一些缺陷，这些缺陷也会影响茶叶相关旅游业的发展。首先，有时公司未经授权使用龙井茶商标。例如，浙江省农业技术促进中心起诉了位于江苏省的卡库茶叶公司，因为其未经授权使用商标对原有品牌产生了不良影响。在这起案件中，该中心要求政府机构调查和惩罚销售假冒"龙井茶"的公司，因为这些公司欺骗消费者。第二，由于不同的机构管理地理标志时采用不同的法律，使用该术语的组织之间可能会产生一些冲突，因为它受到不同立法的保护。尽管如此，它仍可能影响产品的声誉并欺骗消费者（Yuanhua等，2016）。第三，有时地理标志保护的成本会增加，因为申请者必须花费超过需要的费用，并且他们必须向两个或更多的管理组织申请。此外，国家工商总局、国家质检总局和农业部的行政职能重叠，浪费了行政资源（Yuanhua等，2016）。第四，有时茶农和生产商会将标签交给经销商，有时经销商会在非原产地生产的茶产品上贴上标签，然后以更高的价格销售产品。此外，无组织的销售渠道使得很难追溯茶叶的来源并证明其质量，使消费者受害。

六 结论和政策建议

在过去的几年里，随着消费者的偏好从数量转向质量，我们看到了"新奢侈品"的概念是如何发展的。在这种情况下，了解产品的历史和文化方面，以及与这些战略相关的营销战略和服务如何体现产品质量，变得越来越重要。因此，地理标志可以带来更高附加值的产品，保护消费者，因为它提供了有关产品质量的认证信息。这些地理标志还将有助于确定和促进特定地区的文化遗产，因为产品的质量与产地有关。

根据有限的案例以及在杭州实地考察期间收集的信息，可以得出结论，地理标志已被纳入浙江省，加强了茶文化，并鼓励了其旅游业和经济发展。地理标志被理解为政策工具，因为已经制定了更多的营销和旅游战略，表明生产者、公共机构之间的持续协作，以及那些认识到并喜欢这种产品消费者。因此，茶叶作为非物质文化遗产的代表，将继续发展。

尽管龙井茶的案例更为成功，但在促进旅游活动方面，将中国的体系与智利进行比较时，可以看出一些主要差异。在龙井茶中引入地理标志系统后，茶的形象得到了提升，得到某些商店或茶博物馆工作人员的认可。但在智利（Cáceres, 2019）。一般公众，甚至一些茶农不认识这些添加到产品中的术语或标签。在中国，由于市场强化以及种植者和政府机构为保持茶叶质量而不断开展的运动，自地理标志注册以来，价格和生产水平都有所提高，但在智利，公共机构没有同样的支持。此外，在智利，地理标志与旅游业发展之间没有明确的相关性，因为生产者认为只有注册地理标志才能获得成功的产品。他们缺乏资源和协作努力，因此很难克服这一问题。

然而，由于中国没有严格的地理标志管理，还有其他一些茶叶地理标志没有正确使用保护。这就让协会承担检查费用，以确保其他产品不会欺骗消费者。因此，尽管公众对茶文化相关旅游业的发展有很多支持，但这将取决于不同的组织以及它们如何合作来实施成功的质量活动。

关于政策建议，各机构之间需要进行更多的协调，因为似乎有必要审查所使用的系统，以便各机构之间的活动不会重叠，地理标志的注册不会最终成为组织和消费者都困惑的过程。此外，必须向公众提供更多的信息，让公众了解茶地理标志的非物质文化遗产，使他们能够识别产品，并要求特定的标签。

最后，必须强调的是，由于这类研究的政策影响，需要进行更多的研究。本文介绍了杭州龙井茶这一具体案例的研究结果。未来的比较研究可能有助于理解茶叶地理标志如何改善和影响旅游业发展，特别是在关注休闲旅游等概念时，不仅在中国其他地区，而且在其他国家也是如此。

Geographical Indications as A Driver for Tourism Development: the Chinese Case

Javiera Paz Caceres Bustamante / Chile

Institute of International Studies, University of Chile / Lecturer

I. Introduction

China has become an important tourism attraction worldwide. As stated by the World Tourism Organization (UNWTO) China is the fourth largest world destination. One of the key success factors of the growth of international tourism towards China has been the attractiveness of cultural heritage aspect within its cities. For developing economies, such as those in the Latin American region, tourism may become an important economic engine for their development processes; therefore, learning from the Chinese experience may become a critical aspect towards sound policy making. In this context, many countries have found in Geographical Indications (GIs) a tool not only to promote products, but to promote tourism services linked with these goods.

GIs have more than 100 years of history. France was one of the first countries protecting this type of intellectual property right, mainly used in champagne and other types of liquor (Sun, Xiong, Wang, & Zhong, 2013). This protection system was introduced to the World Trade Organization (WTO), specifically, to the Trade-Related Aspects of Intellectual Property Rights (TRIPS Agreement) and to other international conventions.

Suh and MacPherson (2007) argue that GIs lead to higher value-added products through product differentiation based on guaranteed quality; it protects consumers because it provides officially certified information regarding product attributes; and it enhances and preserves the identity and cultural heritage of the region.

From here, GIs are not only considered an intellectual property right, but also a policy instrument, especially if we consider tourism development. Some authors state that if producers are able to incorporate tourism activities to their GI-related strategies, sales can increase even more. For example, through the incorporation of gastronomic routes related to the protected products (Barrera, 1999, 2006; Millán & Morales-Fernández, 2012).

Even though there is extensive literature arguing GIs' potential for tourism development, limited empirical support and evidence from positive impacts have been presented when referring to developing countries, specifically Chinese best practices for Latin American countries such as Chile (Marie-Vivien & Biénabe, 2017; Neilson, Wright, & Aklimawati, 2018; Rawat, 2017). This paper attempts to expand the literature regarding tourism, tea culture and geographical indications for China and Latin America. In order to do this, this paper analyzes the incorporation of Chinese cultural heritage in the tourism promotion of Zhejiang province, specifically the protection of Hangzhou's Longjing Tea through geographical indications, and their impact on tourism development. For this objective, the analysis is carried out by means of a qualitative and descriptive case study methodology. Following Yin (2011), primary and secondary sources will be used. The literature review is based on geographical indications, tea culture and tourism. In order to analyze the impact of tea GIs on the tourism development of Zhejiang province, official documents will be reviewed for the case study, as well as the information gathered from tea growers and key actors during the field trips in the 2019 Visiting Program for Young Sinologist in Hangzhou, Zhejiang province. The paper is divided as follows: First, a literature review is presented on the relationship of tourism, tea culture and geographical indications. Second, the Chinese protection for geographical indications is offered. Third, the case study of Hangzhou's Longjing Tea is described. Fourth, the analysis is presented. Finally, some conclusions and policy recommendations will be given.

II. Literature Review: Geographical Indications, Tea Culture and Tourism

Geographical Indications (GIs) can be defined as "a sign used on products that have a specific geographical origin and possess qualities or a reputation that are due to that origin" (WIPO, 2017, p. 8). The literature has referred to GIs as "marketing tools accessible to resource-poor farmers and processors, with potential for increased or some secure incomes, for promoting socially and environmentally sustainable production practices, and for strengthening local dynamics and governance" (Marie-Vivien & Biénabe, 2017, p. 2).

As Sun et al. (2013) states the protection of GIs can give play to the effect of:

> market guidance and business organization, promote and enhance the industrialization of famous and special products; use the function of technical specifications and quality monitoring, to strengthen and improve the quality standardization of the famous and special products; take advantage of market awareness and product reputation background to support and promote the brand strategy of agricultural products; enhance the value-added of agricultural products?increase farmers' income?thereby contributing to resolving issues concerning agriculture, countryside and farmers (p. 54).

Eguillor (2014) argues that at both national and international level, it is expected that GIs will add value to products, increasing their demand and price, and helping to the local development. In Europe, there were more than 700 products protected by GIs, 90% of them came from France, Portugal, Italy, Greece, Spain and Germany

(Cáceres, 2019; Cambra & Villafuente, 2009). In Spain, specifically, the economic value of the traded protected products has increased six times in a period of 18 years (Millán & Morales-Fernández, 2012). All these elements show that using GIs as branding services are crucial to build strategies towards the development of rural areas (Cambra & Villafuente, 2009).

Although TRIPS Agreement presents the basic principles to protect GIs, it does not define the link with the origin or an origin-based quality standard (Cáceres, 2019). This specification is established at the product level, by means of the definition of specifications or rules of use (Marie-Vivien & Biénabe, 2017). It must also be considered that GIs are not only an intellectual property right, but also a policy instrument.

Xing (2015) has argued that intellectual property protection is necessary and legit for intangible cultural heritage as it helps to maintain its economic value so that the group enjoys its property rights. Specifically, GIs are the most convenient protection as it integrates the most with intangible cultural heritage. They both represent regional characteristics, considering natural factors but also human factors; and they determine the non-transferability of rights and a collective subject.

In this context, tea culture appears as an interesting cultural heritage as it has developed cultural dimensions, forming and fostering the global tea culture. According to Li and Chen (2010), "the history of tea collecting and drinking can be traced back to 1100 BC, the Zhou Dynasty" (p. 353). Tea culture is crucial to promote and construct a harmonious society and the tea ceremony "advocates us to choose a sincere attitude of life, to socialize with courtesy, to build a new type of interpersonal relationship with peaceful coexistence […]" (p. 353). From here, tea culture related tourism combines an ecological environment and natural resources, cultural aspects of tea, tea production, among other elements.

When considering GIs and tourism, some studies have shown that if producers are able to incorporate tourism activities to their GI strategies, sales can increase even more. For example, through the integration of gastronomic routes related to the protected products. In Argentina and Spain, the number of tourists has increased as they demand more information regarding the origin of the goods, as they prefer local products and their quality (Barrera, 1999, 2006; Millán & Morales-Fernández, 2012). Another important element is that GIs attract new infrastructure investment as a way of improving transport and communication in rural areas, for example, when even hotels and train tours have been incorporated to boost GI related tourism (Cambra & Villafuente, 2009).

Referring to tea GIs and tourism, Suh and MacPherson (2007) conducted a study for the Boseong green tea in South Korea, stating that when the local government decided to position this industry as an engine of regional development, it applied a comprehensive innovation plan base on initiatives such as acquiring GIs to boost product quality. In the end, the GI enhanced the image of the product and increased the general public's awareness of the region. The fields covered with tea leaves has appeared as background in movies, TV shows, etc. In fact, the number of tourists visiting the region increased, representing 300% of increase of tourists in the Boseong area. The GI has increased production, improved prices and stimulated tea-related industries. Therefore, GIs can not only play an important role for product marketing, but also for place marketing. From here, as well as in other countries, the government has developed a variety of tea-related tourism activities such as the green tea festival, a green tea resort, etc.

Xingdong (2017) argues that GIs help to maintain a good ecological environment. Promoting the use of GI products does not only contribute to spread and protect excellent traditional folk customs and arts, but they also contribute to the development of ecological agriculture, ecological tourism, cultural tourism and others. This will also encourage the development of urbanization in rural areas, as well as the development of agricultural industrialization.

As Huang, Tuan, and Wongcha (2014) have argued, since the opening-up of China, economic activities have been reformed in rural areas. Leisure agriculture and rural tourism are considered the global sunrise industry. The China Council has stated that this economic activity needs to be developed to expand rural full employment in both the suburban and rural areas. In this context, tea culture has become crucial for rural tourism in China. The development of tea culture tourism has enriched the rural tourism, understood China's long tea culture history and driven local economic sustainable development (Ya & Qi, 2014).

III. Chinese Protection of Geographical Indications

The protection of GIs was implemented in 1995 in China, with five different types of protection. Nowadays, GIs are protected by means of a dual system as they can be registered as collective and certification trademarks (Xiaobing & Kireeva, 2007). There is also a third protection for agri-food products enacted by the Ministry of Agriculture. When China joined the World Trade Organization (WTO), some changes were introduced to the Trademark Law of the People's Republic of China, referring to GIs protection, as a separate type of trademark. Besides, at the same time, a sui generis system was incorporated in China. Therefore, it can be said that China has three ways of protecting GIs (Sun et al., 2013):

(1) The geographical indication trademark registration of the State Administration for Industry and Commerce (SAIC).

(2) The geographical indication product protection of the General Administration of Quality Supervision, Inspection and Quarantine (AQSIQ) (sui generis)

(3) The agricultural product geographical indication registration of the Ministry of Agriculture (MOA).

According to the State Administration for Industry and Commerce of the People's Republic of China (SAIC), 2697 GIs trademarks had been registered by the end of 2014, more than 85% of them are used for agro-products (Yuanhua, Wei, & Nabi, 2016).

a. Trademark system

This is the earliest system used in China, similar to the one used in the United

States. Chinese Trademark Law did not distinguish GIs from other common signs, so they could be trademarks as long as they did not deceive consumers. In 2001, after China was admitted to the WTO, the Trademark Law from 1993 was amended, introducing certification and collective marks as a way of protecting GIs. In Article 16 (2) (Berti, 2017; Xiaobing & Kireeva, 2007; Yuanhua et al., 2016):

Where a trademark includes a geographical sign that does not describe the location or the origin of the goods in question, the term causes confusion among members of the public and shall be refused registration. Its use as a trademark also shall be prohibited. However, where a registration has been obtained in goodwill, such registration shall continue to be valid. The geographical sign referred to in the above paragraph means that it is the place of origin on the goods at issue and that the special qualities, reputation or other characteristics of the goods are primarily determined by the natural conditions or other humanistic conditions of the geographical location involved (p. 1).

In this case, the applicant must submit a set of documents certifying the qualification of the product. Applicants should also grant the means to supervise the quality of the product. Article 4 of the measure states that a society, an association or any other organization applying for the registration of a GI as a collective mark shall be composed of members from within the region indicated by the geographical indication (Berti, 2017; Xingdong, 2017; Yuanhua et al., 2016). It must be added that in China, GIs do not only refer to a product that is made in a certain geographical area, it also denotes natural and human factors involved in the production of a good; this is known as appellation of origin in other countries. This protection is mostly seen as a defensive protection against the misuse of the geographical trademark by unlawful competitors.

b. Sui generis

The most significant provisions in this case are the "Provisions for the Protection of Geographical Indication Products", an administrative ruling that has been examined and approved by the AQSIQ on May 16, 2005. It includes the Geographical Indications of Goods (Registration and Protection) Act, No. 48 of 1999 (Berti, 2017; Yuanhua et al., 2016). These measures represent a system of protection like the one used in European countries. This system is important mostly to certify to customers the authenticity of the geographical claim and the connection between the specific geographical region and the quality of the product.

Article 10 of the Provision states that the applicant must submit the government's proposal explaining the limits of the place of origin of the product, as well as the technical documentation (it may include the physical, chemical or sensory characteristics of the product and their relationship with the natural and human factors of the place of origin). After the process is completed, if other producers are interested in using the GI label on their products, they must apply for an authorization with the local Quality and Technical Supervision Bureau or Entry-Exit Inspection and Quarantine Bureau, presenting a certificate arguing that the products concerned originate from the GI area (Lin & Lian, 2018; Xingdong, 2017). If accepted, producers can label their products using the following symbol:

c. Agricultural product

This system started in 2008 with the "Measures for the Administration of Geographical Indications of Agricultural Products", an order issued by the Ministry of Agriculture (Berti, 2017). It is based on Trademark Law, but similar to sui generis, only for agricultural products: such as vegetables, cereals, fruits, oil, tea, herbal medicines, handicrafts, flowers, etc. It does no protect wine, vinegar, ceramics, jade, knitting, silk, etc.

As stated in article 2 of the Measures, a Geographical Indication of Agricultural Products refers to:

special agricultural product indications which are named by territorial names and are meant to tell that the indicated agricultural products are from a specific area and that the quality and major characteristics of the products mainly lie in the natural and ecological environment as well as cultural and historical factors of the area (Berti, 2017).

Therefore, the suitable products for the registration are only the ones that coincide with the name of the geographical area where they are produced. In this case, applicants can only be cooperative economic organizations of farmers and industrial associations. After that, producers within the area must present a certificate to the association in order to legitimately use the GI, including the quantity of product that could be labelled as a GI (Berti, 2017; Xiaobing & Kireeva, 2007). The following symbols is used: 8

IV. Tea protection in the Zhejiang Province: Hangzhou's Longjing Tea

China has demonstrated a rich tea culture that has been elaborated over time. The link between tea quality and origin is widely recognized among Chinese consumers, but it has also developed an international reputation. Chinese government invests in the standardization of tea plantations, pest control and green-prevention technology. Besides, a marketing threshold was implemented for tea companies to improve their production processes in order to improve product quality. China's tea production and consumption have grown from 2013 to 2018 as figure 1 and 2 show.

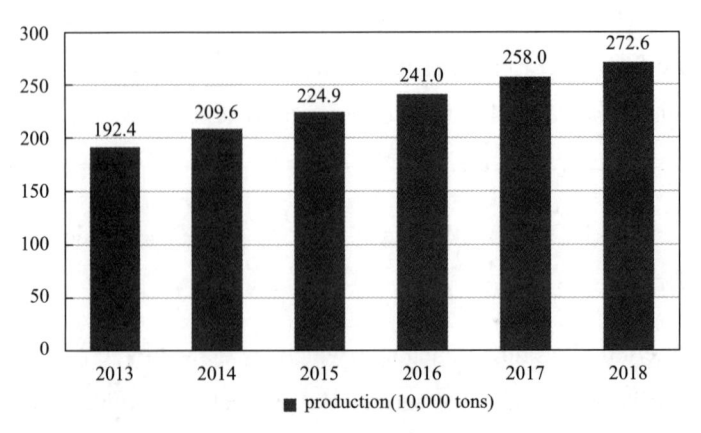

Year	Production (10,000 tons)
2013	192.4
2014	209.6
2015	224.9
2016	241.0
2017	258.0
2018	272.6

Figure 1 China's tea production 2013 - 2018 9

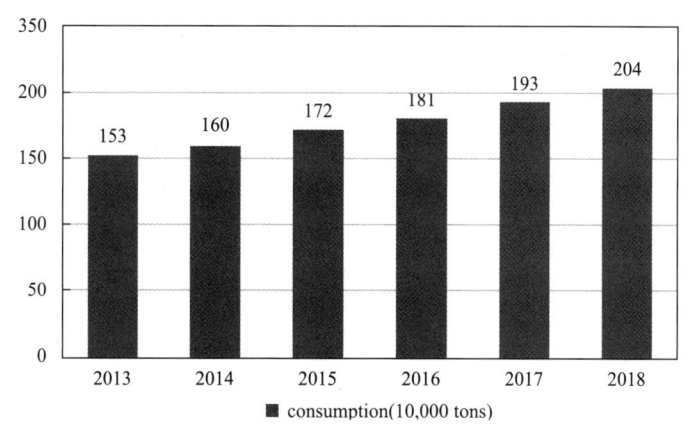

Figure 2 China's tea consumption 2013 - 2018

Zhejiang province is an important producer of tea and even a major export base of green tea in China (Sun et al., 2013). In 2015, it was ranked sixth in the distribution of tea plants, fourth in tea production, and first in tea exports (Liu, 2015). Therefore, tea is now a new bright spot of economy for the current rural areas and agriculture in mountains areas of Zhejiang's province. For this, tea has become an important element to increase the agricultural efficiency and farmer's income. The total size of tea fields in Zhejiang is 1,430,000 hectare (approximately), and 120,000 tons are produced (O-Chanet, 2017). There are 85% of green tea and the other 15% are black and oolong teas.

The protection of tea in Zhejiang province started with the GI product system in 1999. Longjing tea was the first to obtain the treatment of origin product in 2001, and the fourth national GI product in China (Sun et al., 2013). By 2012, the former State Bureau of Quality Supervision, Inspection and Quarantine, had already protected GIs on 8 kinds of tea from Zhejiang Province:

Table 1 Geographical Indication products in Zhejiang province (Sui generis protection)

Ranking approved	Approval time	Geographical indication prolucts	The scope of protection of geographical indication products
4	2001.10.26	Longjing tea	In Zhejiang Province, east from Hupao and Maojiabu, west to Yangfumiao, Longmcnkan and Hejiacun, southfrom Shejing and Fushan, North to Laodongyue and Jinyujing, with a total area of 168 square kilometres
70	2004.04.06	Anji white tea	The current administrative regions under the jurisdiction of Anji County
117	2004.12.13	Wuniu Zao tea	The current administrative regions under the jurisdiction of Yongjia County
325	2007.03.20	Kaihua Duzhong tea	The current administrative regions under thc jurisdiction of Kaihua County
422	2008.03.14	Songyang tea	The current administrative regions under the jurisdiction of Songyang County
435	2008.05.08	Jiande Bao lea	The current administrative regions under the jurisdiction of 9 towns and subdistrict offices in Jiande City (Xin anjiang Street, Yangxi Street, Genglou Street, Xiaya Town, Yangcunqiao Town, Qantan Town, Meicheng Town, Sandu Town and Da yang Town)
665	2010.05.24	Huiming tea	The current administrative regions under the jurisdiction of Jingning She Autonomous County
816	2010.12.31	San Bei Xiang tea	The current administrative regions under the jurisdiction of Taishun County

Source: Sun et al. (2013)

The registration of GI trademarks for tea in Zhejiang province started in 1995 by the SAIC. By 2012, they had registered 22 trademarks:

Table 2 Geographical indications as trademarks in Zhejiang province

Name of trademark	Registrant
Anji white tea	Tea Station of Anji County Bureau of Agriculture
Linhai Panhao tea	Linhai Specialty Technology Extension Station

Contd

Name of trademark	Registrant
Jiangshan Lvmudan tea	Jiangshan Specialty Technology Extension Station
Yuyao Pubu Xianming tea	Yuyao Pubu Xianming Tea Association
Jingshan tea	Jingshan Tea Industry Management Association of Yuhang District in Hangzhou City
Dafo tea	Xinchang Famous Tea Association
Putuofo tea	Tea Industry Association of Putuo District in Zhoushan City
Cangnan Cuilong tea	Agricultural Sociely of Cangnan County
Panan Yunfeng tea	Pan'an Tea Industry Association in Zhejiang Province
Shengzhou Zhu tea	Shengzhou Tea Industry Association
Longjing tea	Cash Crop Administralion, Zhejiang Provincial Department of Agriculture
Tonglu Xueshui Yunlv tea	Tonglu Xucshui Yunlu Tea Industry Association
Jiande Bao tea	Jiande Quality and Quantity Measurement Monitoring Center
Kaihua Longding tea	Kaihua Bureau of Specialty (Bureau of Tea)
Mogan Huangya tea	Comprehensive Agricultural Service Center in Moganshan Town of Deqing County
Tianmu Qingding tea	Linan Tea Industry Association
Qiandao Yuye tea	Chunan Tea Industry Association
Tiantaishan Yunwu tea	Tiantai Specialty Technology Extension Station
West Lake Longjing tea	Longjing Tea Industry Association of West Lake District in Hangzhou City
Xiandu Sunfeng tea	Jinyun Tea Industry Associalion
Songyang Yinhou tea	Songyang 'Tea Industry Association

Source: Sun et al. (2013) 11

The registration of GI agricultural products of the Ministry of Agriculture started in 2008. By 2012, MOA had registered 7 kinds of tea under this system in Zhejiang Province:

Table 3   Agricultural products geographical indications of tea in Zhejiang province

Name of product	Designated protection scope of the place of origin	Applicant
Changxing Zisun tea	Shuikou Township, Jiapu Town, Xiaopu Town, Meishan Town, Baijian Township, Longshan Street, Zhicheng Town, Lincheng Town, Si'an Town, Erjieling Township, Wushan Township, Heping Town, Lijiagang Town, Hongqiao Town and state - run farms and stations in Changxing County, 15 towns and 92 villages in total.	Changxing Tea Industry Association
Taishun San Bei Xiang tea	36 townships and towns (Luoyang Town, Baizhang Town, Liufeng Township, Songyang Township, Pengxi Town, Shiyang Town, Wanpai Township, Xianren Township, Xiaocun Town, Sixi Town, Fengyang Township, Hengkeng Township, Jiufeng Township, Yuehu Township, Fengwen Township, Yayang Town, Guihu Town, Xuexi Township, Baoyang Township, Siqian Town, Zhuli Township, Fengmen Township, Xinpu Township, Huangqiao Township, Beipai Township, Nanyuan Township, Lingbei Township, Sankui Township, Xiyang Township, Xiahong Township, Da'an Township, Zhouling Township and Yangxi Township) and 205 villages in Taishun County	Taishun Tea Industry Association
Qiandao Yinzhen tea	16 townships, towns and streets (Lijia Town, Datong Town, Hangtou Town, Shouchang Town, Genglou Street, Xin'anjiang Street, Yangxi Street, Xiaya Town, Lianhua Town, Yangcunqiao Town, Dayang Town, Meicheng Town, Sandu Town, Qiantan Town and Qintang Township) and 84 villages in Jiande City	Qiandao Yinzhen Tea Cooperative in Jiande City
Yuyao Pubu Xianming tea	All administrative villages in Yuyao City	Yuyao Pubu Xianming Tea Association
Tianmu Qingding tea	15 townships and towns (Taihuyuan Town, Xitianmu Township, Gaohong Town, Yuqian Town, Zaoxi Town, Taiyang Town, Qianchuan Town, Leping Township, Changhua Town, Heqiao Town, Tuankou Town, Longgang Town, Qingliangfeng Town, Daxiagu Town and Daoshi Town) and 78 administrative villages in Tianmu District of Lin'an City	Lin'an Tea Industry Association
Tonglu Xueshui Yunlu tea	9 townships and towns (Xinhe Township, Zhongshan Township, Baijiang Town, Hecun Township, Fenshui Town, Yaolin Town, Hengcun Town, Fuchunjiang Town, Fengchuan Town) and 59 villages in Tonglu County	Xueshui Yunlu Tea Industry Association in Tonglu County
Putuofo tea	Putuo Mountain, Shenjiamen Street, Donggang Street, Goushan Street, Zhanmao Street, Zhujiajian Street, Taohua Town, Liuheng Town and Dengbu Township in Putuo District of Zhoushan City; Chengdong Street, Huannan Street, Jiefang Street, Changguo Street, Yancang Street, Lincheng Street, Baiquan Town, Ganlan Town, Maqiao Town, Xiaosha Town, Cen'gang Town, Shuangqiao Town, Jintang Town and Beichan Township in Dinghai District; Gaoting Town, Dongsha Town, Daidong Town, Daixi Town, Qushan Town, Changtu Town and Xiushan Township in Daishan County	Agricultural Society of Zhoushan City

Source: Sun et al. (2013)

Longjing tea, also called dragon well tea, is a type of green tea that has over 1200 years old. It grows in the surrounding area of West Lake in Hangzhou, Zhejiang province, thanks to the fertile land, multiple high mountains and good climate. It is considered the best tea (1) among the top 10 famous tea in China. Longjing Tea is divided into Shi (Lion,), Long (Dragon,), Yun (Cloud,) and Hu (Tiger,) due to its different geographical origin, indicating the plantations of Shifeng, Longjing, Yunqi and Hupao (China Discovery, 2018). Tea makers in Zhejiang produced 24,000 tons of Longjing tea in 2014 (Mengxing, 2015).

It is believed that in Qing dynasty, the Emperor Qianlong (1711-1799 AD) visited Hangzhou and when he went to Longjing Shifeng and learned the tea-picking, his follower told him his queen mother was ill. After he returned to Beijing, his mother smelt the fragrance of the Longjing Tea and after drinking the water with the tea, she felt better (China Discovery, 2018). There is also a local legend for tourists referring to the name Longjing: there was a clean spring running in the village in ancient time, which seemed the water granted by the Chinese dragon. So, people put a carved dragon well head and one day a geomancer felt the magic spring after drinking and he suggested the villagers did a well for drinking. Finally, they named the well "Longjing (Dragon Well)" (China Discovery, 2018).

There are villages that have developed their economic activities surrounding tea-related tourism. For example, the Longjing village is the place of origin of Longjing Tea. Nowadays, it is not only the residence of over 800 people, but also there are growing plantations of near 800 acres of Longjing Tea. It is a place for tourists where they can visit the tea gardens, the Hugongmiao Temple at Shifeng and the National China Tea Museum.

The Trademark Office of the State Administration for Industry and Commerce approved the registration of "Longjing Tea" by the Zhejiang Agricultural Technology Promotion Center as a geographical indication certification trademark in 2008, seven years later the recognition of GI origin product (HKTDC, 2009; Mengxing, 2015). In 2014, the Center canceled the rights of 35 companies that were planning to use the "Longjing Tea" trademark, mainly because they did not apply for the reuse after the authorization expired. By 2015, 352 companies had the right to use the trademark. Besides, the Center applied to register the trademark in 43 countries and received the registration certificate from the Madrid system for the international registration of marks, as well as approval notices from other countries including Spain, Italy, Germany and the United States (Mengxing, 2015). Regarding the Longjing Tea GI product, 172 companies were using the GI by 2012 (Table 1).

V. Cultural Heritage and Geographical Indications as a Driver for Tourism Development

As it can be read in the China National Tea Museum in Hangzhou (Weber, 2018):

Tea is one of China's major contributions to mankind and world civilization. China is the origin of the tea tree and the first country to discover and use tea. The tea industry and tea culture started from the drinking of tea. Over thousands of years, as the custom of tea penetrated more and more deeply into Chinese people's lives, tea culture has been steadily enriched and developed as part of the age-old national culture and a gem of traditional oriental culture. Today, as a worldwide beverage, tea serves as a tie of deep affection between Chinese and people in other parts of the world (p. 149).

This link between Chinese tea culture and other parts of the world can be reflected in tourism development. In this context, GIs help to promote the inheritance of ethnic culture and its economic development (Xingdong, 2017). GIs can have a positive impact on tourism as the general public's awareness of quality tea in the region increases, helping to boost both product and place marketing. China, especially in Zhejiang Province, has developed a strong tourism related to tea culture based on entertainment, with activities for all the family; education, with the China National Tea Museum in Hangzhou; spiritual wellbeing and outdoor spaces, with relaxing landscapes; and harmonious interior spaces, with teahouses and traditional tea ceremonies.

The GIs for tea in Zhejiang, under the three systems mentioned, represent the natural factors of the province, such as soil type, weather conditions, tea varieties; but also, human factors such as the tea making history, legends of Chinese culture, the history of cultivation, etc. Government agencies in Zhejiang have carried out campaigns to supervise the quality of Longjing tea and the use of the trademark in the legal production areas of the tea, so that its characteristics are maintained and tourists are attracted (Mengxing, 2015). The Zhejiang provincial industrial and commercial administration bureau noted that the successful registration of the "Longjing Tea" GI trademark has helped to establish the exclusiveness of the use of the "Longjing" name (HKTDC, 2009). Regarding process and market access, after Longjing Tea was recognized as a GI, the price of Xihu Lonjing increased by 10% more than other teas between 2000 and 2005. It reached 100 yuan/kg as compared to the 23 yuan/kg for the average price of tea in 2005 (ITC, 2009).

According to the information gathered during field trips in Longjing Village and the visit at the China National Tea Museum in Hangzhou, it can be argued that the intangible cultural heritage of Longjing Tea and tourist-related activities have been cultivated and developed for years. For example, it was included in the world's intangible cultural heritage list on traditional craftmanship of green tea UNESCO passed Convention for the Protection of Intangible Cultural Heritage in 2003. This is also related with the fact that the State Council issued "Views on the Strengthening China's Intangible Cultural Heritage Protection" in 2005, with the aim to rescue and protect its intangible cultural heritage. From here, the traditional craftmanship related to Zhejiang's tea has been exploited: traditional production techniques, traditional music, etc., elements that tourists can experience when visiting different villages.

Longjing village, located at the southwestern side of West Lake, is promoted as the place where tourists will breath clean air with a special scent of tea. Tourists can go to the Hugongmiao Temple to see the "eighteen Emperor Tea Trees", the place from which Emperor Qianlong picked tea leaves for his mother, and see trees living for more than 250 years. There is also the Longjing Mountainous Park with a garden of 130 acres, with tourism attractions such as drinking Longjing Tea in the hundred-year old teahouse, see the process of roasting tea, be part of the tea ceremony or "appreciate the skill of making a cup of tea that expresses the tea spirits of purity, elegance, sincerity and harmony in China" (China Discovery, 2018). There is also the Meijiawu Village, located at the western part of West Lake, that was visited by the former Prime Minister Zhou Enlai; and the Longwu Tea Village, located at the southwestern side of West Lake, closed to the Zhejiang National Tourist Resort. Longwu Village is known as a "natural oxygen bar", thanks to its 666 m2 tea fields with good eco-environment. There are also stores selling Longjing Tea for tourists in these villages, where they can buy souvenirs.

Longjing Village has been reconstructed into a tourist destination: the houses have been rebuilt using the Jiangnan style, well known for overhanging eaves and counterforts. This transformation has been financed by the government, producers and villagers (Chen, 2009). Furthermore, local tea growers run tea farms and hire people depending on the season. On average, their net income is more than 50 RMB each year. In fact, families join to sell Longjing tea together. It is pretty common that even urban residents from Hangzhou want to live in Longjing Village to experience the calm landscape and tea traditions of a rural life. Regarding marketing strategies, the village committee provides the packaging and anti-counterfeiting labels to the tea producers.

These villages also develop special programs for tourists who want to get even more immersed into tea culture. The programs are called "Dragon Well Tea Culture Exploration Programs", in which tourists can visit the Longjing Tea fields, then take a bamboo basket to pick tea leaves with the local tea growers and live the complete tea experience. Then, tourists can see how tea leaves are dried, taste the tea and participate in the performance of the tea ceremony. Finally, they can enjoy a lunch with local dishes.

Besides, Tea Culture Expos are prepared for tourists in Hangzhou. These are three-month tea carnivals that highlight the making, tasting and history of Longjing Tea. According to the information gathered during field trips, tourist see in the expos the opportunity to experience exquisite tea and explore the story behind Longjing tea. They can also see every step in making and brewing tea.

Finally, tourists can visit the China National Tea Museum, where they can see a comprehensive overview of the historical rituals, customs and styles of tea by means of videos, reports and ancient materials, enjoying tea tasting throughout the tour.

From here, it is important to highlight some deficiencies of the current systems to protect GIs, that can also affect the development of tea-related tourism. First, sometimes companies use the Longjing Tea trademark without authorization. For example, the company Kakoo Tea Co in Jiangu province was sued by the Zhejiang Agricultural Technology Promotion Center, as its unauthorized use had a bad effect on the original brand. In this case, the Center asked government agencies to investigate and punish companies that sell fake "Longjing Tea" as they can deceive consumers. Second, as different institutions manage GIs considering diverse laws, some conflicts may arise between organizations that use the term because it was protected under a different legislation. Nevertheless it may still affect product's reputation and deceive consumers (Yuanhua et al., 2016).

Third, sometimes the cost of GI protection increases as applicants must spend more than needed and they have to apply for two or more management organizations. Besides, the administrative functions of SAIC, AQSIQ and MOA overlap, wasting administrative resources (Yuanhua et al., 2016). Lastly, but very important, it is the fact that the coexistence of laws and regulations may confuse consumers, diluting the effect of the identification of GIs. Fourth, sometimes tea growers and producers give the labels to dealers who will just put the symbol on tea products that are not produced in that place of origin and sell the product at a higher price. Furthermore, the disorganized procedures in distribution makes it difficult to trace back to the source of tea and certify its quality, once again, deceiving consumers.

VI. Final Remarks and Policy Recommendations

During the past years we have seen how the concept of "new luxury" has developed as consumers' preferences have shifted from quantity to quality. In this context, it has become more important to know about the history and cultural aspects surrounding a product and how marketing strategies and services associated to those strategies represent that quality. From here, geographical indications can lead to higher-value added products, protecting consumers as it provides certified information regarding the product quality. These GIs will also help to identify and promote the cultural heritage of specific regions as the quality of the product is linked to that origin.

Acknowledging the limitations of a case-study methodology and the scope of the gathered information during the field trip conducted in Hangzhou, it can be concluded that GIs have been incorporated in Zhejiang Province, strengthening tea culture and encouraging its tourism and economic development. GIs have been understood as policy instruments since additional marketing and tourism strategies have been developed, showing a constant collective work between producers, public agencies, and also consumers who have recognized and preferred this product among others. Therefore, tea, as a representation of intangible cultural heritage, will continue its development.

Even though the Longjing Tea case has been more successful, when comparing the Chinese system to Chile in terms of promoting tourism activities, some main differences can be seen. In the Longjing Tea case, after the introduction of the GI system, the image of the tea has been enhanced, it is recognized by the people who work in certain stores or people at the Tea Museum, but as well as the Chilean case (Cáceres, 2019), the general public or even some tea growers do not recognize the term or the label that should be added to the product. In the Chinese case, prices and production levels have increased since the GI registration due to marketing reinforcement and constant campaigns from growers and government institutions to maintain the quality of tea, but in the Chilean case there is not the same support from public institutions. Besides, in the Chilean case, there is not a clear correlation between GIs and tourism development as producers think that only the registration of the GI will be necessary to have a successful product. Their lack of resources and collaborative efforts have made very difficult to overcome this issue.

However, there are other GIs for tea in China that are not correctly using the protection as China does not have a strict administration of GIs. This leaves to associations the costs of inspection to make sure that other product is not deceiving consumers. So even though there is a lot of public support for the development of tea culture-related tourism, it will depend on the different organizations and how they work together to implement a successful quality campaign.

Regarding policy recommendations, more coordination is needed among institutions as it seems necessary to review the systems used so that the activities among institutions do not overlap and the registration of a GI does not end up being a confusing process for organizations and consumers. Besides, more information must be provided to the general public to understand the intangible cultural heritage of tea GIs, so that they can recognize the products and ask for the specific label.

Finally, it must be highlighted that due to the policy implications of this type of research, more research is needed. This paper presents the findings for a specific case, the Longjing Tea in Hangzhou. However, future comparative studies may help to understand how tea GIs can improve and impact tourism development, especially when focusing on concepts such as leisure tourism, not only in other regions of China, but also in other countries.

References

Barrera, E. (1999). Las Rutas Gastronómicas: Una estrategia de desarrollo rural integrado.

Barrera, E. (2006). Rutas alimentarias. Una estrategia cultural para el desarrollo rural mexicano. Patrimonio Cultural y Turismo(15), 68-86.

Berti, R. (2017). The Protection of Geographical Indications under Chinese Law (Publication no. 10.13140/RG.2.2.35633.6896). Retrieved September 10, 2019, from ResearchGate

Cáceres, J. (2019). Intellectual property rights as branding services for exports value-adding: an analysis of Chile's 'Sello de Origen' programme. International Journal of Intellectual Property Management, 9(3/4), 315-341.

Cambra, J., & Villafuente, A. (2009). Denominaciones de Origen e Indicaciones Geográficas: Justificación de su empleo y valoración de su situación actual en España. . Cajamar: Caja Rural Intermediterránea.

Chen, W. (2009). From Tea Garden to Cup: China's Tea Sustainability Report (pp. 83). Beijing: Social Resources Institute.

China Discovery. (2018). Longjing Tea Plantations – Brand-new Try in Nature & Chinese Tea Culture. Retrieved September, 2019, from https://www.chinadiscovery.com/zhejiang/hangzhou/longjing-tea-plantations.html

Eguillor, P. (2012). Programa Sello de Origen: protección de los productos típicos chilenos. Santiago: ODEPA.

Eguillor, P. (2014). Indicaciones Geográficas: una herramienta de diferenciación (pp. 7): ODEPA.

HKTDC. (2009). Longjing Tea Approved for Trademark Registration. Business Alert - China. from http://info.hktdc.com/alert/cba-e0902d-2.htm

Huang, C.-M., Tuan, C.-L., & Wongcha, A. (2014). Development Analysis of Leisure Agriculture–A Case Study of Longjing Tea Garden, Hangzhou, China. APCBEE Procedia, 8(2014), 210 - 215.

ITC. (2009). Guía de Indicaciones Gográficas: Vinculación de los Productos con su Origen. Ginebra: Centro de Comercio Internacional-ITC.

Li, Z., & Chen, M. (2010). The Construction of Chinese Tea Culture Tourism Landscape. China Academic Journal Electronic Publishing House, 3.

Lin, Q., & Lian, Z. (2018). On Protection of Intangible Cultural Heritage in China from the Intellectual Property Rights Perspective. Sustainability, 10(12), 4369.

Liu, Z. (2015). Overview of tea industry in China.

Marie-Vivien, D., & Biénabe, E. (2017). The Multifaceted Role of the State in the Protection of Geographical Indications: A Worldwide Review. World Development, 98, 1-11.

Mengxing, S. (2015). Company sued for use of 'Longjing' trademark. Retrieved September, 2019, from http://www.chinadaily.com.cn/cndy/2015-04/15/content_20435898.htm

Millán, G., & Morales-Fernández, E. (2012). Denominaciones de Origen Protegidas (DOP) y Turismo Gastronómico: Una Relación Simbiótica en Andalucía. Gran Tour: Revista de Investigación Turística, 101-121.

Neilson, J., Wright, J., & Aklimawati, L. (2018). Geographical Indications and value capture in the Indonesia coffee sector. Journal of Rural Studies, 59, 35-48.

O-Chanet. (2017). ea production in Zhejiang province. Retrieved October, 2019, from http://www.o-cha.net/english/teacha/distribution/teaproduction.html

Rawat, P. (2017). Unfolding geographical indications of India: A brief Introduction International Journal of Advanced Research and Development, 2(5), 497-508.

Suh, J., & MacPherson, A. J. A. (2007). The impact of geographical indication on the revitalisation of a regional economy: a case study of 'Boseong'green tea. 39(4), 518-527.

Sun, Z., Xiong, W., Wang, S., & Zhong, X. (2013). Protection of Geographical Indication Intellectual Property of Tea in Zhejiang Province. Asian Agricultural Research, 5(1), 51-54, 58.

Weber, I. (2018). Tea for Tourists: Cultural Capital, Representation, and Borrowing in the Tea Culture of Mainland China and Taiwan. Academic Turistica, 11(2), 12.

WIPO. (2017). Geographical Indicaions: An Introduction. Geneva: WIPO.

Xiaobing, W., & Kireeva, I. (2007). Protection of geographical indications in China: conflicts, causes and solutions. The Journal of World Intellectual Property, 10(2), 79-96.

Xing, X. (2015). The Intellectual Property Protection of Intangible Cultural Heritage. Paper presented at the 3rd International Conference on Education, Management, Arts, Economics and Social Science, Shadong.

Xingdong, Z. (2017). Problems and Suggestions for the Construction of China's Geographical Indication System. Academics, 2(Feb. 2017), 313 - 321.

Ya, F., & Qi, Z. (2014). Tea Cuture in Sichuan Rural Tourism the Development of Research. Paper presented at the The 14th Landscape Architectural Symposium of China, Japan and Korea.

Yin, R. K. (2011). Applications of case study research: sage.

Yuanhua, Z., Wei, S., & Nabi, G. (2016). The Legal Protection of China's Geographical Indications in the Context of TRIPS Agreement. International Journal of Business and Social Science, 7(2), 99-105.

格鲁吉亚国家博物馆的中国陶瓷

纳蒂亚 【格鲁吉亚】
格鲁吉亚国家博物馆东方艺术系　策展人

在格鲁吉亚国家博物馆[1]的各个分馆里保存着珍贵的中国陶瓷文物，研究人员正在对这些文物进行分期研究。这些藏品大部分保存在沙尔瓦·阿米拉纳什维利美术馆的东区，但在格鲁吉亚国家博物馆的其他分馆中则保存相对较少。美术馆东区收藏的部分中国瓷器被转移至现有的博物馆，有些是在不同时期从个人手中购入。通过这些藏品，我们可以从中观察中国瓷器从过去到现在的阶段性发展和趋势。我们的藏品几乎每个时代都有保存，最重要的是，通过许多不同类型的文物，我们再次深刻认识到了藏品的重要性。

众所周知，中国是闻名世界的陶瓷生产中心和主要的陶瓷出口国。这一领域中所有最重要的藏品发现都起源于此，包括瓷器的发明——许多世纪以来，这是世界上人们一直在探索的奥秘。因此，几个世纪以来，中国在这个领域持续保持龙头地位，其不仅对邻国，如日本或韩国，甚至对所有东欧国家的陶瓷生产都产生了重大影响。

中国陶器是博物馆远东藏品的重点，瓷器为其代表。最早期的藏品历史可以追溯到十三至十四世纪。图一是一组非常独特和出彩的藏品组，是塞拉东瓷盘（瓷器发现编号为 sxm/ag 3085、3087、3088、3089、3367、3086）[2]，其在艺

1　格鲁吉亚国家博物馆是若干国立博物馆的总称，创建于2004年，由11个博物馆组成。
2　见本书第333页图一。

和历史研究方面都极具价值。著名摄影师亚历山大·罗伊纳什维利（Alexander Roinashvili）从达吉斯坦的塔尔科夫斯基家族（Tarkovsky family of Dagestan）手中买下了这些瓷器作品，以此作为个人收藏。这些藏品后来成为国宝，现存于格鲁吉亚国家博物馆（National Museum of Georgia），是镇馆之宝。

青瓷是一种绿色釉质单色瓷器，产于公元十世纪的中国，有珍贵软玉的特殊替代品之称。在中国，没有比软玉更完美、更精巧、更美丽的天然物质了，其美誉人所共知。这也归功于它的神奇特性和用途。青瓷和软玉一样，在中国古代家喻户晓，直到出口海外后，其受欢迎程度超过了软玉[1]。

众所周知，中国青瓷发展的巅峰时期是宋朝（960-1279），而在元朝（1279—1368）和明朝（1368—1644）期间，中国大师创制了青瓷之最。

亚历山大·罗伊纳什维利所收藏的瓷盘现保存在我们的博物馆里，其品质厚实，色泽为浅绿色；它们的历史可以追溯到十三至十四世纪，时间线上对应宋元时期。这些藏品大多数底部和边缘都饰有植物装饰，有些具有波纹的壁面和彩绘的边缘。此外，要确定瓷釉的年代相当困难，因为在不同国家的不同时期，甚至在中国，人们经常试图复制早期的美丽瓷釉，但都没有成功。然而，早期的青瓷，其釉面的质量、色调的渐变、植物和几何装饰所呈现的效果与众不同，很容易被辨识。

馆内有6块保存状况佳的青瓷盘。据报道，其仅呈现出轻微裂迹，主要是裂缝和修补痕迹。

在人们的认知里，亚历山大·罗伊纳什维利是一位了不起的人物，多年来，他一直在高加索、俄罗斯和近东这些地方收集藏品并对它们的情况进行详细分享。近年来，有很多关于他藏品的文章，许多研究和展览都聚焦于这位格鲁吉亚首位摄影师的生活和工作。值得注意的是，在国家陶瓷博物馆的众多藏品中，那些最精美、一流的藏品正是由他收集而来，其中包括24件来自中国和日本的陶器：盘子、平底锅、水壶等[2]。

明代（1368—1644）的瓷器中有3件是亚历山大·罗伊纳什维利的收藏品，这些藏品在用途、形式或艺术装饰方面都是无与伦比的。

明代被公认为是中国瓷器历史的顶峰，主要体现在该时期精美的青花瓷上。这些青花瓷所描绘的风景、马、凤凰、龙、鱼或奇异的植物都采用了真实和超现

1　Demurishvili. 2017. pp.74-75.
2　Mamatsashvili, Koshoridze, Dgebuadze. pp.143, 146, 150-152, 154-155.

实的手法，运用了令人惊叹的工艺。自明朝（十六世纪）以来，彩绘这种工艺已被广泛使用于陶器制作上，尽管人们普遍认为钴釉陶器是代表该时期艺术美学的名片。十六世纪青花瓷其中一个代表作是"垦地"（sxm/ag 1173；图2）[1]。在格鲁吉亚西蒙·贾纳夏博物馆中世纪考古藏品里（A 546），保存着一个形态略微不同的"垦地"，它的历史也可以追溯到明代。

"垦地"是一只大象形态的杯子。其喉部细而高，以一只非常逼真的棕褐色大象的头尾为特色。这种创作形态的历史可以追溯到十五世纪，即明朝时期的中国瓷器生产中，并且这种工艺在国外市场上也取得了成功，其功能主要在于装饰。在十六到十七世纪，"垦地"在伊朗也非常受欢迎。伊朗人是最早、也是最成功的中国瓷器制造商之一，他们在当地陶瓷制作中创立并采用了糖色，这种技术和艺术表现都非常接近中国的原始风格。

东方收藏品中的"垦地"饰有釉下钴画，其嘴唇周围有铜带装饰，这种形态表明该物品是出口到伊朗的。众所周知，从中国出口的陶瓷装饰着类似的纹饰。由此可见，塔尔科夫斯基的家人从伊朗得到了"垦地"，而多亏了亚历山大·罗伊纳什维利，这件罕见的瓷器才能得以作为藏品保存于格鲁吉亚国家博物馆。

十六世纪瓷器的代表作有茶壶（sxm/ag 1132；图3）[2]和杯子（sxm/ag 1133），其特色为釉下彩绘。这些藏品不仅仅是塔尔科夫斯基·罗伊纳什维利（Tarkovsky Roinashvili）系列的珍宝，也是整个东方藏品的瑰宝。亚历山大·罗伊纳什维利也尤其强调了它们的重要性。他对瓷碗进行了描述："碗和茶壶以明朝独有的艺术剧目特色进行装饰，即孔雀和奔跑者，通常以花卉装饰为背景。"

值得注意的是，明朝时期的陶器大都存放在博物馆的东方宝库中，这再次深度说明了这些藏品的重要性。

高加索博物馆所收藏的中国陶器藏品是独一无二的（该博物馆的法定继承人是格鲁吉亚国家博物馆）[3]。在这些藏品中，有一件是青瓷（sxm/ag 1124；图4）[4]，三件是彩绘钴（sxm/ag/998、693、1049；图5、6、7）。档案研究证实，这四件藏品[5]都来自著名的阿德比尔清真寺，该清真寺是伊朗的宗教中心（1502—1736）[6]。众所

1　见本书第333页。
2　同上。
3　高加索博物馆——格鲁吉亚的第一个博物馆，1852—1918。
4　见本书第333页。
5　同上。
6　Demurishvili. 2008. pp.249-250.

周知，萨法维统治在伊朗政治生活中特别重要。萨法维王朝的传奇祖先萨菲·阿德·丁（Safi Ad Din, 1252—1334）就葬在阿尔德比勒（Ardebil），16世纪时在其陵墓周围修建了一座宏伟的建筑群。这个祭仪建筑群的一部分也就是所谓的"China khane"——一个专门存放中国瓷器的地方。

在萨法维王朝统治者的直接监督下，这里汇聚了极其丰富且最珍贵的瓷器藏品，以及独特手稿、纺织品等藏品，并作为礼物送给清真寺，该清真寺被认为是伊朗的宗教神学中心。这些藏品来自不同的时期，其源自外交礼物、大量名人的捐献和战利品。中国瓷器在阿德比尔的宝藏中有着特殊的地位。这里保存着中国瓷器中的杰出作品，这亦是中国元朝瓷器一直能够引起各类旅行者和学者兴趣和赞美的原因。德国旅行家和外交官亚当·奥利留斯、意大利传教士皮埃特罗·德拉·瓦尔、法国商人和旅行家让·巴蒂斯特·塔弗尼耶、英国民族志学家詹姆斯·弗雷泽等人都为我们提供了这方面的相关介绍。当地人讲述了中国可汗藏品的故事，他们是历史学家和占星家莫拉·贾拉尔、著名的史学家伊斯坎达尔·贝格·孟希以及其他人。

萨法维王朝（1736年）灭亡后，阿德比尔不再拥有此前的特权和荣耀，在整个十八至十九世纪时期，阿德比尔一直是各种战争的战场，其中包括波斯—奥斯曼战争和俄罗斯—波斯战争。这从后续瓷器的收藏地上可以了解到：中国元朝瓷器被洗劫一空，部分宝藏被毁，而最终保留下来的藏品如今被储存于伊朗及全世界不同的博物馆里。

馆内所保存的1903—1918年时期的中国陶器来自阿德比尔，是由高加索博物馆馆长、著名研究人员阿尔·卡兹纳科夫和该博物馆的雇员、考古学家维·谢尔科夫尼科夫在1910年对伊朗的一次考古探险中发现的。其被发现的细节不详。

经过对相关材料的考察，可以确定塞拉东花瓶的年代为十三世纪（元朝时期），而所谓的青花瓷碟则是十四至十六世纪的明朝时期。重要的是，这组瓷器中有两件都印有萨法维王朝最著名的代表人物——沙阿·阿巴斯大帝（1571—1629）的个人印章。

中国陶瓷博物馆藏品中的真正明珠是独特的钴彩瓷盘，即所谓的凤凰装饰盘。这个碟子在东方藏品中是一件罕见的中国瓷器（sxm/ag 2359；图8）[1]，由沙尔瓦·阿米拉纳什维利美术馆于1976年从圣彼得堡著名的收藏家S.哈努卡耶夫手中购入。

---

[1] 见本书第333页。

除了上述提及的藏品盘,博物馆还从 S. 哈努卡耶夫那里一起购入了三件十八世纪的藏品:两个灯笼(sxm/ag 2357、2358)和一个盘子(sxm/ag 2360)[1]。

众所周知,自明朝末年以来,中国的大量出口贸易收入得益于瓷器业。十六世纪末,中国瓷器的主要出口国是西班牙和葡萄牙;自十七世纪以来,荷兰—印度公司开始垄断,向欧洲供应大量瓷器,因为欧洲是中国瓷器的主要消费国。

清朝(1644—1911)标志着陶瓷工业的新崛起。从出口量惊人的增长以及陶瓷领域引入的许多艺术和技术革新可见一斑。在这方面,我们应该特别关注清朝康熙皇帝(1661—1722)统治的时代。康熙年间,瓷器保留了明代的特色,其重点运用象征和重复旧设计。青花瓷依旧是非常受欢迎的瓷器,尽管当时也出现了一种制作蓝色单色的新方法:在单色瓷上,用刷子或竹管注入颜料之前,会先涂上钴。在许多情况下,经过烘烤后,蓝色表面被涂上了金色。东方藏品保留了蕴含这种技术的一些藏品,比如博物馆旧藏品中的一个中型碗(sxm/ag 1135;图9),历史可追溯到十八世纪初。杯子的蓝色表面与不对称的、朴素的、带有金色的花卉装饰完美搭配,这清楚地表明,这一时期瓷器的艺术装饰风格带有非常愉快和自由的表现特色。这里摒弃了典型的明朝时期的平衡和极度对称的构图方案,以艺术风格的表现取而代之,倾向于愉悦和自由的现实主义绘画。然而,这并不影响瓷器的价值,相反,它代表了中国瓷器生产在康熙时代创造了新高度的辉煌。这既包括出口量的惊人增长,也包括在瓷器生产中引入的许多艺术和技术革新,尤其是陶瓷。

清朝时期的青花钴彩瓷器中,有一件独特的藏品,是带有花卉图案的精美花瓶(sxm/ag 90;图10)[2],在该年代是将其放置在乾隆皇帝(1735—1796)御座前的坡脚上。这件藏品当时是在景德镇(中国东南部)的皇家工厂所制。

在被莫斯科东方文化博物馆收藏之前,这件花瓶一直被列入东方藏品名单之中[3]。该花瓶以其精细的外观、极其精致和匀称的特色而著称,而其艺术装饰则沿袭了明代传统的风格化的花朵、水果和几何图案。

十六世纪盛行的多色画从清朝时期,特别是康熙皇帝统治时期开始复苏,在整个十七至十八世纪,它是中国瓷器生产的主要焦点。

在十七至十八世纪,玫瑰色和绿色珐琅绘画在欧洲和东方得到广泛应用,以其

---

1 Demurishvili. 2015. p.75.

2 见本书第333页。

3 众所周知,苏联的博物馆经常提供临时和永久使用的藏品。格鲁吉亚国家博物馆的东方藏品列出了从其主要博物馆永久转移的东方物品,包括大量中国展品。

无限的色调层次和数千种变化著称。在欧洲科学文献中，以绿色和玫瑰色染料为主的多色釉制成的瓷器物品为绿色系和玫瑰色系瓷器。大约在同一时期，他们创造了一种以黑色为主的盘子。这种瓷器在欧洲国家也很流行，被称为"黑色系"[1]。

清朝时期的瓷器在艺术装饰方面也发生了重大变化。新的趋势是在陶器上描绘风俗场景，其中描绘的穿着传统服装的中国人通常出现在室内。通常情况下，色彩奇幻的风景图案和风俗场景都绘制于一个容器上。看起来是很奇怪，但对世界其他国家的人们来说，特别是对欧洲，这非常具有异国情调。

值得注意的是，从十八世纪起，中国瓷器生产中出现了另一项重要的创新——深受顾客喜欢的铭文。铭文通常具有专用的或表示归属的含义。在陶器的正面绘制祖传的纹章、首字母和旗帜也很受欢迎。这一创新很好地反映了欧洲和东方消费者新时代的品味和精神。

在整个十八世纪，中国大城市广州，当时是唯一的对外贸易开放港口，其流向全世界的瓷器数量最大。如果说在清朝早期，中国瓷器仍保留着其最鲜明的特点——形式和装饰的完整性，那么自十八世纪末以来，情况发生了一些变化：此时，中国的瓷器制造业正在逐渐失去其作为世界市场主要瓷器供应商的特权地位。自1709年以来，欧洲相继开设瓷器制造厂，与中国形成了明显的竞争。此外，中国瓷器出口的增长水平也明显下降。

十九世纪的中国陶器生产水平有所下降，主要是由于国家政治局势动荡。相应地，欧洲瓷器从那个时期开始取而代中国并得到推广，成为陶瓷史上的最新阶段。

博物馆东方藏品中保存的清代陶瓷，主要是十八至十九世纪的出口瓷器。伊朗市场的瓷器正是这批藏品中最大的一组藏品。

众所周知，在伊斯兰世界中，中国文化受到高度重视。自九世纪以来，中国陶器对伊斯兰陶瓷的发展产生了重大影响；十三世纪以来，中国的装饰图案出现在了伊朗的灯饰上。根据沙阿·阿巴斯一世（1587—1629）的命令，中国移民者被流放到伊斯法罕，以恢复和发展伊朗的陶瓷生产。值得注意的是，中世纪后期的伊朗陶艺在形式和艺术装饰方面受到了中国瓷器的影响。在十七世纪，这种影响发展演变成了抄袭。法国珠宝商和旅行者让·沙尔丁在十七世纪曾三次前往伊朗，并保存了关于该国文化和存在的重要信息。他报道了中国瓷器在伊朗国王和

1　Sullivan. pp.242-244.

伊朗贵族圈阶层的流行情况[1]。

中国出口至伊朗的各类器皿，可以从两个主要方面辨认出：这些器皿会采用丰富的黄金装饰，并刻有阿拉伯语或波斯语的铭文。鉴于其重要性和艺术意义，我们可以聚焦于伊朗卡贾尔王室（1789—1925）下令制作的两件藏品：盘子（sxm/AG3859；图11）和碗（sxm/ag3858；图12）[2]。就其艺术风格而言，它们属于所谓的玫瑰色系工艺。这些藏品是博物馆于1985年从格鲁吉亚公民阿扎德·侯赛因埃芬迪耶娃手中购入，它们的艺术装饰基于相同的艺术表现形式。在以蝴蝶、花朵（主要是玫瑰）和鸟类图案的金色背景上，装饰性的卡通画呈现了中国人日常生活和山水画构成的场景。这两件藏品上都刻有波斯铭文。碗上和盘子上的铭文都是波斯语，即所谓的"Nasta'liq"（自十四世纪以来在伊朗特别著名和流行的伊斯兰书法风格之一）。

铭文中标明的农历迁徙日期"1297"时间线上对应于公元1880年（更准确地说，是从1879年12月15日到1880年12月3日这段时间）。

卡贾尔王朝的代表人物马苏德·米尔扎·泽尔勒·苏丹（1850—1918）的名字不仅在伊朗非常有名，而且在国外学术文献和研究资料中也可以经常见到。卡贾尔王子马苏德·米尔扎是马赞达拉、阿斯塔拉巴、戈尔根、塞姆南和达姆甘地区的总督。从1865年到1870年，马苏德·米尔扎一直担任伊斯法罕总督一职。

根据研究可知，这些碗和盘子来自于一套大型餐具的一部分。不幸的是，如今这套餐具仍散落在不同国家的博物馆中或被私人收藏。其中在埃尔米塔奇博物馆（俄罗斯）、莫斯科东方艺术博物馆（俄罗斯）、巴库（阿塞拜疆）等地可观赏到这套餐具的其他部分。

在西蒙·贾纳夏博物馆（格鲁吉亚国家博物馆）的东方藏品中，还保存着另一件独特的中国出口瓷器藏品——这只碗，可能也是卡贾尔统治者纳赛尔·丁·沙阿（Nasser ad Din Shah）和他的两个儿子，即前文提及的马苏德·米尔扎和他的兄弟沙阿·穆扎法尔·阿德丁的大型晚餐餐具套装的一部分，上面有他们的肖像和铭文（图13a、b、c）[3]。后续证实了此藏品制作的客户也是伊朗王室。这再次证明了伊朗对中国瓷器的兴趣有多大。

在格鲁吉亚的博物馆和私人收藏中，如此丰富和重要的伊朗收藏再次突显了格鲁吉亚和东方世界之间在历史和文化关系中的广泛贸易。一方面，这是格鲁

---

[1] 高加索博物馆——格鲁吉亚的第一个博物馆，1852—1918。
[2] 见本书第333页。
[3] 见本书第333页。

吉亚与东方国家之间数世纪以来政治经济和文化关系的结果，另一方面也清楚地表明，中国商品在伊朗和格鲁吉亚都非常受欢迎。通过对这些瓷器的研究表明，当时购买瓷器的不仅是王室，还有贵族和中产阶级公民。继博物馆仓库中为伊朗制造的出口器皿之后，还有大量为欧洲制造的瓷器，颜色特别丰富，有蝴蝶、花朵和风俗画。各种中国瓷器出口产品也吸引了人们的注意（sxm/ag 3756、4052、2622、2131、3885、3045、2963、2967、3164、3165、2970、e2623、727、26242634、4109、3778、2638、2652、1140、4130、2649、2831、2832 等）。这些藏品的历史大多可以追溯到十八至十九世纪，其中一些是从美术馆前身博物馆的东方藏品中继承下来的，一些则是第比利斯公民在二十世纪80年代购入的。

博物馆里有大量且有趣的东方藏品，比如所谓的佛教陶瓷，它们以小样品的形式陈列，其年代可追溯到十八世纪末至十九世纪。

众所周知，十七至十八世纪的中国雕塑着重于细节，装饰细致，表现手法干练且写意。值得注意的是，正是在这一时期，中国古代传统的佛教祭祀雕像面貌发生了变化：1743年颁布的一项法令规定了佛教神像及其肖像的样式。该法令规定，由于满洲统治贵族承认藏传佛教，因此必须按照藏族的渊源制作佛教神像。这一变化主要影响了青铜神像的造型，以及木雕、石雕或陶瓷雕塑。青铜神像尽管发生了这些变化，但仍然保留了传统艺术的一些风格特征，而陶瓷雕塑则大大简化了；蚀刻装饰和如上所述的图形示意图（2187、2809、2834、4049、2625）都受到了影响。

值得注意的是，在十八世纪至二十世纪，佛教神像尽管具有邪教意义，但在欧洲国家却广受欢迎，在那里，它不是一种邪教，而是一种异国情调。其中一件突出的藏品就是馆内所收藏的瓷器佛像，即所谓的瓷器。有一个广泛流传的版本，就是著名的布袋佛（sxm/ag2187；图14）[1]是未来弥勒佛转世的；弥勒佛面带微笑，其动作形态表现为常被孩子们围着和手拿麻袋。这尊雕像被认为是一件来自中国的出口商品。一般来说，中国人会指着布袋佛的肚子祈求宽恕。这一传统已传播到世界上许多国家。这就是为什么在其他信仰的人的家庭中通常会看到这尊快乐的神明。

因此，在研究了格鲁吉亚国家博物馆的沙尔瓦·阿米拉纳什维利美术馆东方宝库中的中国瓷器藏品后，可以得出结论：这些藏品都是非常有价值的宝藏。它们体现了中国陶瓷生产的特点，及其在国内外的作用和重要性，因为正如前所述，中国的瓷器对欧洲或亚洲陶瓷的发展产生了深远的影响。该系列藏品以其多样的

---

1 见本书第333页。

原始艺术装饰和陶器而闻名。

  基于这些有趣且重要的收藏品属性，可按照时间和风格来对这些展品进行分类研究，以达到能够确定中国陶器生产发展的特点、总体艺术趋势及其历史文化价值的目的。这些藏品无疑值得在未来给予特别的关注，促进更广泛的科学研究和发现更多其他类似宝藏。

图一

图二

图三

图四

图五

图六

图七

图八

图九

图十

图十一

图十三

图十四

图十二

Chinese Ceramic in the Georgian National

Natia Demurishvili / Georgia

Oriental Art Department of Georgian National Museum/Curator

Important and valuable artifacts of Chinese ceramics are preserved at the various museums of the Georgian National Museum[1] storages, which are being studied in stages.[2] Most of this collection is kept at the Eastern Department of the Shalva Amiranashvili Fine Arts Museum, and relatively few are distributed in other structures of the Georgian National Museum. Part of the collection of Chinese ceramics from the Eastern Department of the Art Museum is transferred pre-existing museums, and some are purchased from individuals at different times. The collection allows us to observe the stages and trends of Chinese ceramics from the past to the present day. Our collection is preserved in almost every era, and most importantly, many different types of artifacts that once again emphasize the importance of the collection.

It is widely acknowledged that China was the world-famous center of ceramics production and the main exporter of ceramics. This is where all the most important

---

1 The National Museum of Georgia is the largest museum association in the country. It was created in 2004 and combines 11 museums
2 Demurishvili. 2003. pp.92-99; Demurishvili. 2005. pp. 165-178; Demurishvili. 2008. pp. 249-253.

discoveries in this field originate, including the invention of porcelain, the secret of which the world has been trying to unravel for many centuries.Therefore, China has maintained for centuries the right of a fashion legislator for the world in this field, and has had a major impact not only on neighboring Japan or Korea, but also on the production of ceramics in all Eastern and European countries.[1]

The Chinese pottery group forms the core of the museum's Far East collection and is mainly represented by porcelain vessels. The earliest exhibits date to the XIII-XIV centuries. This is a completely unique and distinguished group, 6 plates of so called Seladon Porcelain (inv. number sxm/ag 3085, 3087, 3088, 3089, 3367, 3086) which are of particular interest in both artistic and historical value. The famous photographer Alexander Roinashvili bought them from the main Tarkovsky family of Dagestan for his own collection, which later became a national treasure and is now the pride of the National Museum of Georgia. (pic.1).[2]

Celadon – glazed monochrome, greenish-colored porcelain in the X century was produced in China as a peculiar alternative to precious nephrites. As it is known, in China there was no more perfect, subtle and beautiful natural material than Nephrites. It was also attributed to its magical properties and used as a cult purpose. Celadon, like Nephritis, was very common in ancient China, and after exporting overseas, the popularity of this beautiful monochrome surpassed Nephritis.[3]

It is well-known that the peak of Chinese celadones coincides with the reign of the Song dynasty (960-1279), but during the Yuan (1279-1368) and Ming (1368-1644) dynasties, Chinese masters made the best porcelain of celadon.

The plates of Alexander Roinashvili's collection, preserved in our museum, are thick, light green and date from the XIII-XIV centuries that coincides with the reign of the Song and Yuan dynasties. Most of them are adorned with plant ornaments on

---

1   Кречатова, Вестфален. с.4.
2   Mamatsashvili, Koshoridze, Dgebuadze.p. 143.
3   Demurishvili. 2017.pp.74-75.

the seabed and edges. Some feature corrugated walls and festooned edges. By the way, dating caladones is quite difficult, as in different times in different countries and even in China itself, they have often tried to copy the beautiful saladones of the early salads and to no avail. However, the early pottery of celadon, the quality of the glaze, the tonal gradations, the peculiarity of the performance of the herbal and geometric ornament is distinctive and easily recognizable.

The condition of all six of our celadon plates is satisfactory. Only minor injuries are reported, mainly in the form of cracks and patches.

As it is well known, Alexander Roinashvili is truly amazing person and great patriot, has been collecting items for many years in the Caucasus, Russia and the Near East, detailing and describing them. Much has been written about his collection in recent times, and numerous studies and exhibitions have been devoted to the life and work of the first Georgian photographer. It is noteworthy that the finest, first-rate specimens of the National Museum of Ceramics are precisely collected by Al. Roinashvili, including 24 items of Chinese and Japanese pottery: plates, pans, jugs and more.[1]

Porcelain utensils from the Ming era (1368-1644) are from Al. Roinashvili's collection, totally three items, although, have no equal in terms of performance, form or artistic decoration.

The Ming era is recognized as the peak of Chinese porcelain history; this fact is first of all conditioned by the beautiful item of so-called blue-and-white porcelain of this period. The real and surreal landscapes, horses, phoenixes, dragons, fishes, or strange plants depicted on them are implemented using amazing craftsmanship. Since the Ming Dynasty (XVI century), pottery has been widely used in polychrome paintings, although cobalt glazed pottery has been widely regarded as the visit card of the artistic aesthetics of the era. A prominent example of the blue-and-white porcelain of the XVI century is the so-called Kendi(sxm/ag 1173.pic. 2).A

---

[1] Mamatsashvili, Koshoridze, Dgebuadze.pp. 143,146,150-152, 154-155.

slightly different form of kendi is preserved in the old and current foundation of the medieval archaeological collections of the Simon Janashia Museum of Georgia (A 546), which also dates to the Ming epoch.

Kendi is an elephant-like cup. This vessel, which has a thin, high throat, is distinguished by a very realistically executed tan elephant head and tail. This form dates from the XV century, in the Ming era, in Chinese porcelain production and has been successful in the foreign market, where it mainly applies only to decorative function. In XVI-XVII cc. Kendiwas very popular in Iran as well. The Iranians, as one of the first and most successful fabricators of Chinese porcelain, also took and established candy in local ceramics, which is very close to the Chinese original in technical and artistic performance.

Kendiin the oriental collection is decorated with a underglaze cobalt painting and bronze belt around the lip, which indicates that the item was exported to Iran. There, as is well known, Chinese export ceramics were often adorned with similar decorative details. We think that Tarkovsky's family got the kendi from Iran, while thanks to Al. Roinashvili, this rare vessel was preserved in the collection of the National Museum of Georgia.

Excellent examples of XVI century porcelain are teapot (sxm/ag 1132. pic. 3) and cup (sxm/ag 1133) with underglase cobalt painting. They are not only pearls of Tarkovsky-Roinashvili collection, but also of the Oriental collection in general. Their significance is particularly emphasized by Al. Roinashvili too. He wrote about the bowl: "чашка, украшена разными павлинами, очень изящной работы". Both the bowl and teapot are richly decorated with an artistic repertoire characteristic of the Ming era: peacocks and runners, usually presented in the backdrop of a floral ornament.

It is noteworthy that the pottery of the Ming dynasty period is widely presented in the oriental storages of the museum, which again emphasizes the importance of the collection.

Completely unique specimens of Chinese pottery are in our collection from the famous Caucasus Museum, the legal successor of which is the National Museum of Georgia.[1] From this collection, one attribute of Celadon (sxm/ag 1124; Fig. 4), three painted cobalt (sxm/ag/ 998, 693, 1049 /fig. 5,6,7) attributes' and archival research confirmed that all four specimens are from the collection of famous Ardebil's mosque, the religious centre of Sefevid Iran (1502-1736).[2] As it is known, the Safavid rule is particularly important in Iran's political life. The legendary ancestor of the Safian dynasty, Safi Ad-Din (1252-1334), is buried right in Ardebil, around whose mausoleum a grand architectural complex was built in the XVI century. Part of this cult complex was the so-called China khane too—a special depository of Chinese porcelain.

The richest and most precious collection of porcelain, as well as a library of unique manuscripts, textiles, etc., were collected here under the direct supervision of Safavid rulers as a gift to the Mosque, which was considered as a religious-ideological center of Iran . The collection was filled in different periods and was riched with diplomatic gifts, lots of celebrity contributions and trophies.Chinese porcelain had a special place in the treasures of Ardabil. Here were preserved true masterpieces of Chinese porcelain. That is why China-Khane porcelain deserved the interest and admiration of travelers and scholars of all time. German traveler and diplomat Adam Ollarius, Italian missionary Pietro Della Vale, French merchant and traveler Jean-Baptiste Tavernier, English ethnographer James Fraser and others provide us notes about that. Locals tell the story of China-Khane's collection - historian and astrologer Molla Jalal, of the famous Iskandar Beg Munshiand others.[3]

After the fall of the Safavid dynasty (1736) Ardabil loses its former privilege and glory, and throughout the XVIII-XIX centuries has been a battleground for various battles, including the wars of the Persian-Ottoman and Russian-Persian

---

1 Caucasus Museum - the first museum in Georgia1852-1918
2 Demurishvili. 2008.p. 249-250.
3 DemuriSvili. 2008. p.250.

wars. This was reflected in the subsequent fate of the porcelain collection: China-Khane was looted, part of the treasure was destroyed and what they were able to save is today stored in different museums of Iran and throughout the world.

Chinese Ardebil pottery we preserved in 1903-1918 were discovered by the Director of the Caucasus Museum, a renowned researcher, Al. Kaznakov and an employee of the same museum, archaeologist V. Shelkovnikov during an archaeological expedition to Iran in 1910. The details of the extraction are unknown.

Considering the parallel material, we have dated the Seladon vase from the XIII century (Yuan dynasty period) and the dishes so called blu and white, from the XIV-XVI century to the Ming dynasty. It is important that two of these group of porcelain wares, are with the personal stamp of Shah Abbas the great (1571-1629), the most famous representative of the Safavid dynasty: "Bande-i Velayat Abbas Bar Ashtane Yeh Shah Safi Wakf Namud /'Abbas, slave of the king of sovereign power [i.e., 'Ali, the first Shi'ite imam], made endowment [of this] to the threshold of the Shah Safi" (Banda-ye shāh-e welāyat Abbās waqf bar āstāna-ye Shāh Safī nemūd)".[1]

The real pearl of the Museum of Chinese ceramics collection is the unique procelain plate with cobalt painting, so-called plate with phoenix decor. This dish, which is a rare type of Chinese porcelain (sxm/ag 2359.pic.8), among other oriental items, was purchased by the Fine Arts Museum of Shalva Amiranashvili, from the famous St. Petersburg's collector S. Khanukaev in 1976.

In addition to the up mentioned plate, the Museum purchased from S. Khanukaen three items dated of XVIII century: two lanterns (sxm/ag 2357, 2358) and one plate (sxm/ag 2360).[2]

---

[1] The text was read and translated by the professor GrigolBeradze.
[2] Demurishvili. 2015. p. 75 .

As it is known since the last years of the Ming dynasty, China gained a major income from porcelain industry. By the end of the 16th century, the major exporters of porcelain were Spain and Portugue, and since the 17th century, the Dutch Ost-Indian company became monopolistic, supplying Europe with the largest porcelain batches since Europe is known to be a major consumer of Chinese porcelain.

The era of the Manchurian dynasty of Qing (1644-1911) marked the new rise of the ceramics industry. This includes both the incredible growth in export volumes and the many artistic and technical innovations introduced in ceramics, in particular in ceramics. In this regard, we should particularly highlight the era of the ruling Emperor of the Qing Dynasty, Kangxi Emperor(1661-1722). During the reign of Kangsxi porcelain preserves the traditions of the Ming dynasty, which was characterized by a special love for symbolism and repetition of old design. Blue and white porcelain is still popular, though a new way of making blue monochromes has emerged: On the monochromes, cobalt will be applied before brushing with brush or bamboo tube injection. In many cases, after roasting, the blue surface was painted with gold. The Oriental collection preserves some of the artifacts of this technique, though we chose to use a medium-sized bowl from the museum's old collection dating back to the beginning of the 18th century (sxm/ag 1135. Fig. 9). The blue surface of the cup is perfectly matched by the asymmetrical, plain, floral decor with gold, which clearly shows that the artistic decoration of the porcelain of this period is characterized by a very delightful and free performance. The balanced and extremely symmetrical composition scheme for the typical Ming period is rejected here and, instead of artistic stylization, is preferred to delightful and free, realistic drawing. However, this does not detract, on the contrary, it represents the brilliance of Chinese porcelain production at a new height at the time of the Kangxi era. This includes both the incredible growth in export volumes and the many artistic and technical innovations introduced in production of porcelain, in particular in ceramics.

A distinctive specimen of the blue-and-white cobalt-painted porcelain of the Qing dynasty period is a wonderful vase with floral motifs. (sxm/ag 90.pic.10) on the sloping foot of the Qianlong Emperor (1735-1796). It is manufactured at the Imperial Factory of JINGDEZEN(South East China).

The vase has been listed in the Oriental Collection since 1954. before it was in the collection of the Museum of Oriental Culture in Moscow.[1] The vase is distinguished by its subtlety of performance, remarkably sophisticated and proportionate. Artistic décor adorns Ming dynasty period traditions with stylized flowers, fruits and geometric faces.

The polychrome painting spread in the XVI century was revived from the time of the Qing dynasty, in particular the reign of Emperor Kangxi, and throughout the XVII-XVIII century it was the main focus of Chinese porcelain production.

In the XVII-XVIII centuries, rose and green enamel painting were widely distributed throughout Europe and the East with their infinite tonal gradations and thousands of variations. Porcelain articles made of green and rose dye dominated by polychrome glaze in European scientific literature are referred to as the green family and rose family porcelain. Around the same time they create a dishes with dominated black color. Such porcelain was also very popular in European countries and was called as black family.[2]

The artistic décor of the Qing period porcelain where's also undergoes significant changes. The new trend was to depict genre scenes on pottery, where the Chinese people depicted in traditional garments were usually present in the interior. Often the landscape motifs and genre scenes of the fantastic colors were placed on a single vessel. All of this, of course, is strange and, at the same time, very exotic for the world, and especially for Europe.

---

1 The museums of the Soviet Union, as is well known, often provided collections for both temporary and permanent use. The Oriental Collection of the National Museum of Georgia lists eastern items permanently transferred from major Russian museums, including quantities of Chinese exhibits.
2 Sullivan .p.242-244.

It is noteworthy that from the XVIII century another important innovation in Chinese porcelain production was introduced - the customer's preferred inscription. Often the inscription was dedicated or denoting belonging. Ancestral coats of arms, initials and flags were also popular on the pottery facade. This innovation reflected well the taste and spirit of a new era for both European and Eastern consumers.

Throughout the XVIII century, China's largest city, Canton, which was at that time the only open port for foreign trade, flowed the largest porcelain quantity throughout the world. And if at an early stage of the Qing dynasty Chinese porcelain still retains its most distinctive feature - integrity of form and décor, the situation has changed somewhat since the end of the XVIII: At this time, China's porcelain manufacturing industry is losing its privileged position as a major porcelain supplier to the world market. Since since 1709 in Europe, one after another was opened porcelain manufactures, which were significant competition with China. moreover, that the level of Chinese porcelain export growth with significantly decreased.

Thus, the level of Chinese pottery production in the 19th century declined somewhat, largely due to the volatile political situation of the country. Accordingly, he was replaced with European porcelain, which has been promoted from that period and created the latest stage in the history of ceramics.

The ceramics of the Qing period preserved in the Museum's Oriental collection are mainly represented by export porcelain vessels from the XVIII-XIX centuries. Porcelain for Iran market are particularly the largest group of this collection.

It is well known that in the Islamic world, Chinese culture was highly valued. Chinese pottery had great impact on the development of Islamic ceramics since the 9th century; Chinese ornamental motifs appear on the Iranian tiles from the 13th century. It is also known that by the order of Shah Abbas I (1587-1629) Chinese settlers were exiled to Isfahan for the revival and development of ceramics production in Iran. It is noteworthy that late medieval Iranian ceramic is under influence of Chinese porcelain in terms of form and artistic decoration. In the seventeenth century this influence grew into copy making. French jeweler and traveler Jean Chardin, who travels to Iran three times in the 17th century and preserves important information about the culture and existence of this country, reports on the popularity of Chinese porcelain at the door of the Shah and the Iranian aristocratic circles.[1]

We can identify Chinese export vessels made for Iran in a variety of forms in two main respects: They are richly adorned with gold and have inscriptions in Arabic or Persian. According to the importance and artistic significance, it can be emphasized two items produced by the order of the Iranian Qajar Royal Family (Qajar Dynasty -1789 – 1925): Plate (sxm/ag 3859. Picture 11) and cup (sxm/ag3858 .Pic. 12). By its artistic style they belong to the so called Rose family. The items were purchased by the museum in 1985 from a citizen of Georgia Azad Hussein's Effendieva. Artistic decoration of the items are based on the common artistic scheme. the decorative cartouches presents scenes from Chinese everyday life and landscape compositions on the neutral golden background with butterflies, flowers (mostly roses) and birds. Persian inscription is performed on both of items too. Inscriptions on the bowl, as well as on the plate are done in Persian in the so-called "Nasta'liq" (since the 14th century one of the Islamic calligraphic style that was especially famous and popular in Iranian world). Persian text of the inscription (reads from bottom to top): "Farmayesh-e Hazrat-e As'ad, Amjad, Arfa', Ashraf, Vala, Sultan Mas'ud Mirza Yamin al-Dowleh Zell-e Sultan, 1297".

Translation: "[Made by] order of His Imperial Highness, the Most Fortunate, the Most Glorious, the Highest and Noblest Sultan Mas'ud Mirza Yamin ad-Dowleh Zell-e Sultan, 1297".

---

1 Arapova, Rapoport. pp.25-36.

The lunar Hijra date 1297, indicated in the inscription, corresponds to the year 1880 A.D.

(more precisely to the period from 15 December 1879 to 3 December 1880 AD).

The name of the representative of the Qajar dynasty, Mas'ud Mirza Zell-e Sultan (1850-1918) is very famous not only in Iranian but in foreign sources and scholarly literature as well. Qajar prince Mas'ud Mirza was a governor of Mazandaran, Astarabad, Gorgan, Semnan and Damghan. from 1865 till 1870, Mas'ud Mirza remained as governor of Isfahan.

As we have learned from our research, the bowls and plate are part of a large diner set, that, unfortunately, is still segregated and scattered in museums or private collections in different countries. We found other parts of the service in the Hermitage museum (Russia), Moscow's Museum of Oriental Art (Russia), Baku (Azerbaijan) etc.

In the Oriental collections of Simon Janashia Museum (Georgian National Museum) another distinctive specimen of Chinese export porcelain is preserved the cup, presumably also a part of a large dinner set by Qajar ruler Nasser ad-Din Shah and his two sons—already upmentioned Massoud Mirza and also his brother, Subsequently—Shah Muzaffar ad-Din, with their portraits and also with inscriptions. (Pic. 13a, b, c). The latter confirms that the client in this case is also the royal family of Iran. This is yet another proof of how big Iran's interest in Chinese porcelain was.

Such rich and significant Iranian collections in Georgia, at museums and in private collections underline once again wide trade- historical and cultural relations between Georgia and oriental world. This, on the one hand, is the result of centuries-old political-economic and cultural relations between Georgia and oriental countries, and on the other hand, it clearly indicates that Chinese goods in Iran and also in Georgia were very popular. Examination of these items reveals that porcelain customers were not only the royal family but also the aristocracy and middle-class citizens. Following in the footsteps of the export vessels made for Iran in the museum storages are numerous porcelain made for Europe with exceptionally rich colors, butterflies, flowers and genre compositions. A variety of Chinese porcelain export products will also attract attention. (sxm/ag 3756, 4052, 2622, 2131, 3885, 3045, 2963, 2967, 3164, 3165, 2970, e2623, 727, 2624,2634, 4109, 3778, 2638, 2652, 1140, 4130, 2649, 2831, 2832, etc.). Most of these items date back to the XVIII-XIX centuries, some of which were inherited from the precursor museums' oriental collection of the Museum of Fine Arts, some acquired by Tbilisi citizens in the 1970s and 1980s.

There is a large, but potentially interesting group of oriental collections like so-called Buddhist ceramics that are presented as small plastic samples and are dated by late 18th-19th century.

As it is known, Chinese sculpture of XVII-XVIII centuries is characterized by detail, meticulous decoration and dry, schematic manner of performance. It is noteworthy that it was during this period that the ancient traditional look of Buddhist cult statues changed in China: a decree, issued in 1743, mandated the statues of Buddhist deities statues and their iconography. The decree made it compulsory to make Buddhist deities according to Tibetan origins, as the Manchurian ruling aristocracy recognized Tibetan Buddhist Buddhism. This change primarily affected bronze cult plastic, along with wood, stone, or ceramic sculpture, but if bronze cult, despite these changes, still retains some of the stylistic features of traditional art, ceramic sculpture has become significantly simplified; The impact that has been shown above Etch Decoration and Schematic of Figures (etc. 2187, 2809, 2834, 4049, 2625).

It is noteworthy that in the XVIII-XX centuries, Buddhist plastic, despite its cult significance, was widely popular in European countries, where it was not a cult but an exotic one. A striking example of this is the porcelain Buddha, preserved in our collection, the so-called porcelain. Well-being Buddha - Budai (sxm/ag2187. Pic. 14)is one of the widespread versions of the reincarnation of the future Buddha-

Maitreya, the great and the smiling, often surrounded by children or holding hands with a sack. We think this statue is an export item. As a rule, the Chinese refer to Buddha's (Japanese version, Hotei) belly and ask for mercy. This tradition has spread to many countries around the world. This is why this cheerful deity is usually encountered in families of people of other faiths.

Thus, having studied the specimens of Chinese ceramics preserved in the Oriental repositories of the Shalva Amiranashvili Museum of Fine Arts in the National Museum of Georgia, we can conclude that our collection is a very valuable and valuable material. It introduces the peculiarities of Chinese ceramics production, its role and importance both domestically and abroad, since, as noted, China's porcelain has had a profound impact on the development of European or Asian ceramics. We think that the collection is remarkable for its variety of original artistic decor and pottery.

The attribution of this very interesting and important collection - the study of which we were able to group these exhibits in chronological and stylistic terms-allowed us to identify the features of the development of Chinese pottery production, general artistic trends and its historical-cultural values. We briefly present the results of the current study in this article. We think this collection will undoubtedly deserve special attention in the future for its wider scientific study and for the discovery of additional parallel material.

References

Demurishvili N. "Cinuri faifuris koleqcia. *Narkvevebi, VIII.Akademikos Shalva Amiranashvilis saxelobis xelovnebis saxelmwifo muzeumi,* Tbilisi, 2003 (Demurishvil N., The collection of Chinese porcelain, Tbilisi, 2003)

2005 Demurishvili N , "Iranisa da Chinetis ekonomikur-Kulturuli urtiertobis istoriisatvis" , *Narkvevebi X, Shalva Amiranashvilis saxelobis xelovnebis saxelmwifo muzeumi,* Tbilisi, 2005 (Demurishvili N., For the History of cultural-economical relatuionships of Iran and China, Tbilisi, 2005)

2015. Demurishvili N.Ucnobi Masalebi Sakartvelos erovnuli muzeumis Shalva amiranashvilis saxelobis xelovnebis Muzeumidan.

Koleqcioneri Khanukaevi. Iv. Javakhishvilis saxelobis Tbilisis saxelmwifo Universiteti.

Humanitarul MecnierebaTa f-ti. "Humanituruli Kvlevebi" . Tbilisi. 2015 (Demurishvili N., unknown materials from Shalva Amiranashvili Fine Arts Museum, Tbilisi, 2915)

Demurishvili N. Dzveli Chinetis Khelovneba. Tbilisi, 2017 (Demurishvili N., Antient Art of China, Tbilisi, 2017).

Mamatsashvili L., Koshoridze I., Dgebuadze M. *Alexander Roinashvili da misiMuseumi*.T bilisi, 2015

(Mamatsashvili L., Koshoridze I., Dgebuadze M., Alexander Roinashvili and his Museum, Tbilisi, 2015)

mehdi bamdadi (Mehdi Bamdad). hijris XII, XIII da XIV saukuneebis iranis cnobil moRvaweTa biografiebi. t. IV. Teirani. 1347/1968. Mehdi Bamdad , XII, XIII and XIV cc. The

Biographies of Iranian public Figures. IV, Teheran, 1347/1968. (On Persian Language)

Арапова Т.Б., Рапопорт И. В.К истории культурных связей Ирана и Китая XVI – XVIII в в .

Искусство и археология Ирана . Москва. 1971.Arapova T, Rapoport I, K istoriss Kulturnix Cviazei

Irana i Kitai XVI – XVIII vv. Iskusstbo i Arxeologia Irana. Moskva, 1971

КречатоваМ. Н., ВестфаленЭ.Х.Китайский фарфор. Москва. 1947.Krechatova M, Vestfalen

E.Kitaiskiifarfor. Moskva, 1947

Demurishvili N. Two Chinese bowls from the Chini-khana of Ardabil.*Journal ofPersianate Studies*. vol.

1.n. 2. Leiden.2008.

Nadler D. *China to Order, Focusing on the XIXth Century and Surveying Polychrome Export Porcelain Produced During the Qing Dunasty (1644-1908)*. Paris.2001.

Nadler D. *China to Order, Focusing on the XIXth Century and Surveying Polychrome Export Porcelain Produced During the Qing Dunasty (1644-1908)*. Paris. 2005.

Sullivan M. The Arts of China. London.1984.

Pope J.A., *Chinese Porcelain from Ardebil shrine*, Washington, D.C., 1956

Canby Sh. R., *Shah Ȧbbas –the remaking of Iran,* British Museum Press, 2009

http://www.iranicaonline.org/articles/ardabil#pt4ARDABĪL *(*I- History of Ardab ī l *written by* C. E. Bosworth;

II- Modern Ardab ī l *written by* X. de Planhol; III - Monuments of Ardab ī l *written by* M. E. Weaver ; IV - Ardab ī l Collection of Chinese Porcelain written by M. Medley)

吉利公司在阿根廷的业务发展

何塞 【阿根廷】

阿根廷文化与社会研究中心　博士/国立科尔多瓦大学　教授

本研究的目的是分析和描述吉利作为一家汽车制造企业在浙江经济发展背景下的成长，以及该公司最近在阿根廷的业务扩张。研究分为三个部分：首先，我们将研究吉利诞生的经济环境；也就是说，我们将回顾浙江省的经济发展以及杭州作为创新和高科技产品生产城市的建设。其次，我们将考察吉利的历史及其发展与经济动态的关系。最后，我们将分析吉利在阿根廷的业务，并考虑该公司在南美国家发展的未来前景。本研究使用了来自中国国家统计局（NBSC）和阿根廷汽车经销商协会（ACARA）的统计数据、公开的新闻报道、吉利公司的出版物和专业文献等。

一　浙江省的成功发展和杭州科技创新城的建设

浙江省是吉利诞生之地，杭州市是吉利迈出第一步的地方。从这个意义上说，为了更好地了解汽车公司的发展，有必要回顾公司创建的环境。

改革开放以来，浙江的发展令人瞩目。用何显明教授（2019）的话说，浙江是一个经济快速增长、率先消除贫困的省份，在"绿色经济"发展中处于前列。这样，浙江在发展数量和质量上都发生了变化。

数量上的转变体现在经济事务上取得的成功结果。20世纪50年代至70年代末，浙江几乎没有得到国家投资（Shi and Ganne, 2009）；在中央计划经济情况下，这些投资是该省发展的基本条件。然而，从1978年改革开放初期开始，该省开始腾飞。从这个意义上讲，1978年至2017年，浙江GDP增长了418倍，人均GDP增长了278倍（表1）。

表1　　　　　　　　　浙江省GDP和人均GDP

年	国内生产总值（以不变价格计算为1亿元人民币）	人均国内生产总值（RMB）
1978	123	331
1993	257	4469
2003	9705	10542
2017	51768	92057

资料来源：国家统计局，《中国统计年鉴》（2008，2018）；Yuan（2019，p. 41）

1978年至1993年，全省国内生产总值适度增长；直到1992年后，浙江的经济才开始快速增长。从2003起，习近平在省委书记任期内，全省经济持续高速增长（图1）。当我们观察人均GDP的演变时，对GDP增长的观察也保持不变（图2）。

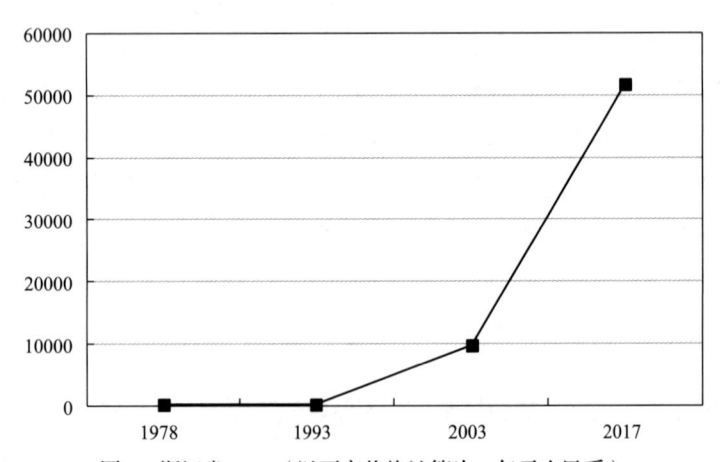

图1　浙江省GDP（以不变价格计算为1亿元人民币）

资料来源：国家统计局，《中国统计年鉴》（2008，2018）；Yuan（2019，p. 41）

多年来，不同经济部门对GDP构成的贡献发生了变化。第一产业始终处于边缘地位，其贡献随时间呈下降趋势；这一点很容易理解，因为浙江是一个相对较小的省份，它的大部分领土都是山脉[1]。

---

[1] 此外，2003年启动的经济增长加快了城市化进程，增加了工业所占的空间，这些工业促进了人口增长，给农田带来了更大的压力。

图 2　浙江省人均 GDP（RMB）

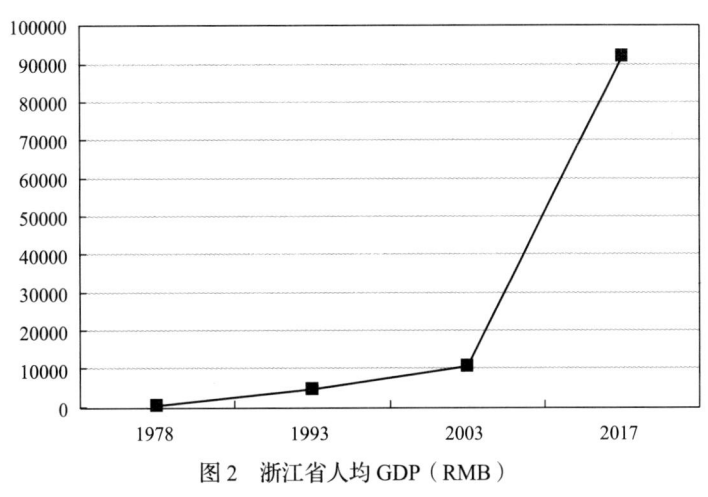

资料来源：国家统计局，《中国统计年鉴》（2008, 2018）；Yuan (2019, p. 41)

长期以来，第二产业一直是该省经济增长的支柱。然而，它对 GDP 的贡献在 2008 年开始呈下降趋势，与 21 世纪初以来第三产业的上升趋势形成对比。因此，2014 年，第三产业在浙江省 GDP 中的参与度首次高于第二产业，这种动态一直保持到今天（表 2 和图 3）。

表 2　　　　　　　　　浙江省按行业划分的 GDP 构成（%）

年	第一产业	第二产业	第三产业
1998	12.7	54.3	33
1999	11.8	54.1	34.1
2000	11	52.7	36.3
2001	10.3	51.3	38.4
2002	8.9	51.1	40
2003	n/a	n/a	n/a
2004	7.3	53.8	39
2005	6.6	53.4	40
2006	5.9	54	40.1
2007	5.3	54	40.7
2008	5.1	53.9	41
2009	5.1	51.8	43.1
2010	4.9	51.6	43.5

续表

年	第一产业	第二产业	第三产业
2011	4.9	51.2	43.9
2012	4.8	50	45.2
2013	4.8	49.1	46.1
2014	4.4	47.7	47.8
2015	4.3	46	49.8
2016	4.2	44.9	51
2017	3.7	42.9	53.3

资料来源：国家统计局，《中国统计年鉴》(2000, 2001, 2002, 2003, 2005, 2007, 2008, 2009, 2010, 2011, 2012, 2013, 2014, 2015, 2016, 2017, 2018)

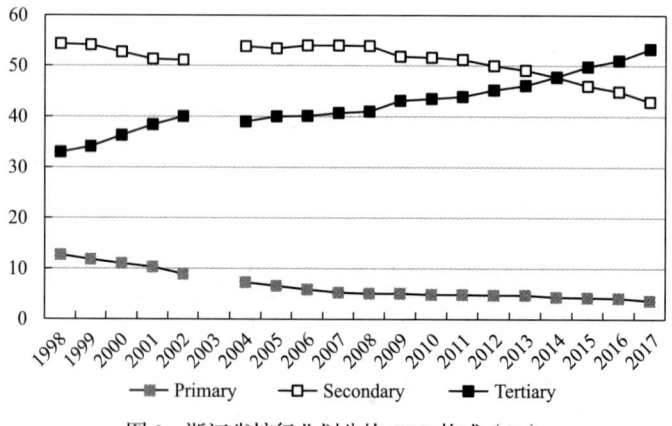

图3 浙江省按行业划分的GDP构成（%）

资料来源：国家统计局，《中国统计年鉴》(2000, 2001, 2002, 2003, 2005, 2007, 2008, 2009, 2010, 2011, 2012, 2013, 2014, 2015, 2016, 2017, 2018)

第三产业的表现可以用银行、金融和咨询活动、科技、交通和电子商务的增长来解释（Xu, 2019, p.4）。这些活动清楚地代表了浙江自2003年以来生产状况的变化，我们称之为"质变"。

2003年以来，浙江经济转型的基础（从数量和质量上衡量）是实施一项名为"八八战略"的全面发展计划。该战略包括鼓励八项优势和推广八项措施，旨在改变该省的生产格局——质量转型。从这个意义上讲，解释"八八战略"可以同时描述浙江的经济发展。

首先,"八八战略"就是要利用浙江的制度优势,积极推动不同类型产权经济的发展,确保公有制的主导地位,完善社会主义市场体系(Xu, 2019, p. 1)。

第二点是利用浙江的地理位置,加强与上海的关系,并在长江三角洲的开发中进行合作(Xu, 2019, p. 1)。上海在金融领域已经有了巩固的地位。这样,通过金融活动和对洋山国际深水港的控制,上海将成为推动长江三角洲发展的火车头。另一方面,浙江和邻近的江苏省在长江三角洲的角色是生产和出口货物,因为两者都有大量的公司,而且很多活动都来自私营企业(Ho, 2012)。

第三,该计划旨在利用众多省级产业的优势,加快以制造高附加值商品为重点的新型工业化道路的建设(Xu, 2019, p. 1)。在这方面,"浙江模式"汇集了许多有助于独特的省级经济发展的因素。继中国银行业协会副会长杨在平(Yang, 2012)之后,以下五个要素定义了"浙江模式":

1. 面向个人。面向人民的制度安排,即加强国家和公共服务的行政能力,这被视为私营经济发展的基础(Yang, 2012)。作为这一点的一个例子,可以考虑"五水共理"的理念,包括处理废水、控制洪水、排放积水、保证供水和节约用水(Xu, 2019, p. 2)。

2. 优先发展民营经济的决定。浙江的经济发展更多的是由私人推动,而不是国家投资;在这方面,一些作者认为,浙江经济发展的特点和优势在于民营经济的发展,而民营资本是浙江投资的主要驱动力(Huang, 2013; Xu, 2012, p. 10)。例如,2012年非公有制经济的生产占全省生产总值的90%(Yang, 2012),到2013年,私营经济贡献了60%的税收(仅吉利集团当年就缴纳了大约85.87亿元的税收),创造出80%以上的出口和90%以上的新就业岗位(Xu, 2012, p.145)。

3. 省内小企业数量众多。截至2012年,全省共有56.9万家小企业,占全省企业总数的97%,占浙江省工业总产值的56.3%(Yang, 2012)。为国内市场生产产品,尤其是出口产品的众多小公司的存在,一直是"浙江模式"(Lu, 2007)的主要特征[1]。然而,这些小企业在获得融资方面面临困难,他们不能获得国家信贷,因为不符合必要的要求,而且上海金融服务是面向大型国家或跨国公司的。这样一来,一方面,私人融资对这些小企业的发展至关重要;另一方面,杭州市已将自己定位为上海的一个互补性区域金融中心,服务于中小企业的需求(Xia, 2010)。

---

[1] 浙江模式的另一个显著特征是中国人对这些众多公司的所有权,这一点与"江苏模式"形成了对比(Lu, 2007)。

4. 浙江商人。根据 Yang（2012）的说法，如果没有一批具有特殊才能并学会利用稀缺资源发展业务的活跃企业家，该地区的经济发展就不可能实现。Jin Pingnu（2006）也认同这一观点，他认为，在浙江经济发展的主要原因中，应该考虑特定的人口特征：开拓精神和创业精神，经商和长期工作的倾向，"时间"和机会概念的强烈印记——今天能做的事就不能明天做——以及实用性。

5. 产业集群的存在。浙江几乎所有城市都有一个或多个由众多小公司组成的产业集团，推动了当地的工业化进程。继 Shi 和 Ganne（2009）之后，浙江可以确定三个不同的产业集群发展区域：第一个区域位于浙江省北部，那里的产业集群具有非常动态的特点，总部位于杭州和宁波的大公司和高科技集团脱颖而出，萧山的纺织生产和余姚的塑料生产也非常突出。第二个区域包括台州和温州[1]：这里大约有十个不同的产业，例如鞋、衣服、打火机和眼镜制造等[2]。第三个区域包括金华、衢州和丽水：产业集群较新，地区较不发达，集中生产一些较低生产成本的消费品。

第四，利用城乡协调发展加快城乡一体化。再次提醒一下，浙江省是中国陆地面积最小的省份之一，其大部分区域都是山区，几乎没有可供开发的自然资源。从这个意义上讲，随着人口的不断增长，城市化和农业同时扩张的空间受到限制，这两个空间的协调发展是非常必要的。

第五，提出利用全省生态优势建设"绿色浙江"。建设"绿色浙江"战略意味着该省环境发展的第一步，因为环境保护必须与建设"生态浙江"和"美丽浙江"联系起来。在这方面，2014 年 5 月，浙江省在中共十三届五中全会做出了建设"美丽浙江"的决定，这意味着生态工业发展，即"绿色消费"，宜居生态社区和优美生态环境的持续资源可用性开发。

第六，促进该省海洋和山区资源的开发，使其成为新的经济增长点。

第七，抓住浙江的环境优势，积极推进建设。

第八，确立了利用浙江的人文优势，通过科技振兴浙江，使浙江成为一个文化强省。

21 世纪第二个十年伊始，通过实施"四大建设"和"四个转变、三大行动"，"八八战略"的基本支柱得到了更新和延续。"四大建设"涉及推进大平台、大产

---

[1] 温州的特点是私营企业数量众多，正是这座城市激发了"浙江模式"的概念。

[2] 例如，到 2001 年，温州制造的鞋占中国总市场的 20%，打火机占 90%，剃须刀占 60%（Shi and Ganne, 2009）。

业、大项目、大公司建设。"大平台"建设包括规划和发展 14 个工业区（包括大江东）[1]，改善现有工业园区，推进科技创新基地建设。建设"大产业"，就是要培育具有竞争优势的产业，使之成为强大的企业和高附加值的制成品生产商[2]；从这个意义上讲，11 个主要行业的发展是有特权的——其中包括汽车行业，其主要省级参考是吉利——以及 9 个新兴战略行业——生物、物联网、新能源、具有替代能源的汽车等。此外，促进了制造业和服务业的融合。实施"大项目"涉及基础设施项目的开发，以促进发展和激活建设。最后，"大公司"意味着培育能够在地区舞台上扮演领导者角色的强大公司（Yuan, 2019, p. 69-72）。

至于"四个转变、三大行动"，这四个转变包括：一是改革全省产业结构，有利于发展高质量、低资源消耗、高创新能力和高附加值制成品生产的高效产业，取代不符合这些特征的行业。这项政策被称为"腾笼换鸟"[3]。第二个变化涉及将工业机器人纳入生产，以缓解劳动力短缺的压力，降低工资成本，提高劳动生产率。这一战略通常被称为"以机器代替人"。第三个变化意味着通过重新设计和重建城市空间、工厂、建造高层住宅和开发地下城市空间来优化空间利用，以"节约土地"，解决该省日益严重的土地短缺问题。最后，第四个变化旨在通过促进电子商务来扩大市场（Yuan, 2019, p. 74-76）。

"三大行动"旨在通过以下方式深化省级生产结构的转型：首先，支持浙江省已跻身全国龙头企业行列的企业的发展。反过来，要实现这一目标，就要刺激企业的创新能力，支持它们的全球化，保证它们获得信贷、减税和充足的能源供应（这一战略被称为"培育知名企业"）。其次，鼓励国内外市场发展消费者满意度高的知名品牌，被称为"培育知名品牌"。最后，还建议培训具有创新能力的企业管理和技术人员，培训企业家个人，并与大学和研究机构密切合作（Yuan, 2019, p. 77-78）。

作为该省变革的一部分，杭州占据了特殊地位，这是该省自 2003 年以来实施变革的一个明显例子。从这个意义上讲，这座城市一方面被确立为高端商品的

---

[1] 大江东是位于杭州的一个工业园区。它已经成为浙江省汽车工业的基地，吉利、长安福特、广汽和东风等不同的工厂已经在那里落户（Fang, Shen and Lai, 2018）。

[2] 如上所述，浙江的产业结构以小企业的存在为特征，因此，生产力分散，创新能力低（Yuan, 2019, p. 69）。

[3] 这个想法最早是在 2003 年提出的，涉及"在笼子里腾出空间"来饲养吃得少、产蛋多、飞得高的"好鸟"："吃得少"意味着公司消耗的资源更少；"多下蛋"，企业获得高经济回报；"飞得高"意味着公司有能力长期发展（Yuan, 2019, p. 74）。

生产中心，在这里创造了大江东工业区的良好形象[1]。杭州目前已将精力投入九个关键行业的工业发展：电子信息，这是2016年收入最高的行业，其特点是设计和制造芯片，并提供电子金融解决方案[2]；高端设备制造：飞机部件、蒸汽、燃气和水力涡轮机、空分设备等的生产[3]；电动汽车：杭州是首批推广电动汽车的试点城市之一；生物医学；能源节约、环境保护和新能源[4]：在这一领域，有生产水力发电、光伏和LED设备等的公司；软件和信息服务、软件开发和电子商务[5]；云计算和大数据；工业设计：杭州拥有国家级工业设计中心、52个省级中心和91个市级中心，员工约1万人；物联网：专注于视频监控、射频硬件、通信、网络等的产品制造[6]（杭州市政府信息办公室，2018）。

另一方面，杭州将自己定位为创新中心。为此，浙江海外高层次人才海创园于2010年7月落成，并于2011年12月更新为未来科技城（FSTC）——于2012年1月2日正式开放（Xu, 2019, p. 259-260）。这个"城市"有三个支撑平台，其中一个是"梦想小镇"。后者旨在通过互联网相关创新促进城市经济发展，并被视为中国智能发展的互联网孵化中心。随着浙江信息经济的快速发展，以及阿里巴巴集团互联网公司的成立，梦想小镇在其发展中备受青睐。从这个意义上说，梦想小镇是一个由政府部门推动的增长型项目，但通过与初创企业、风险投资行业、阿里巴巴集团等与创新相关的非国家行为者的沟通，梦想小镇是中国公共和私营部门为促进智能经济而共同努力的典范项目（Argyriou, 2019, p. 198）。

除未来科技城之外，还创建了青山湖科技城、城西科技创新走廊等发展空间，并于2017年底宣布创建紫金港科技城。从这个意义上说，市政府希望到2020年吸引400家高科技公司和45家科研院所（China Daily, 2017）。

这些"城市"的目标是创建技术开发和创新中心，将来自中国和世界各地的科学家、技术人员和科技公司集中在这些中心。按照这些思路，未来科技城项目的驱动力是通过人才和创新产业来整合资源的开发（Argyriou, 2019, p. 198）。在这种情况下，未来科技城的一个中心目标是在信息经济、生物医学、新能源和金

1　除大江东工业区外，杭州还有六个园区：富阳经济技术开发区、杭州城西科技创新产业集群、杭州国家高新区、杭州余杭经济技术开发区、杭州经济技术开发区、萧山经济技术开发区。
2　在那里运营的一些公司有东通和硅烷微电子。
3　该领域的公司有西子航空、杭州锅炉集团、杭茶集团和杭州汽轮机集团。
4　比亚迪在这里工作。吉利还建立了技术研发中心，目标是制造电动汽车。
5　在那里运营的公司包括阿里巴巴、网易杭州网络和海康威视数字。
6　在那里运营的公司有海康威视、大华科技、霍利科技和利达。

融服务等战略领域重新安置高质量的外国人才和专业人员。

到目前为止，通过根据不同的政府发展战略，"八八战略""四大建设""四大变化""三大行动"，我们已经能够描述该省的经济增长和未来发展前景。因此，我们考虑了吉利发展为汽车公司的情景。接下来，将重点关注该公司的发展，以及该省经济动态与该公司所走道路之间的联系点。

二 浙江经济发展背景下"吉利"的建立与发展

吉利汽车集团（Geely Automotive Group，简称 GAG）的历史可以追溯到 1984 年，该集团的创始人李书福开始进入商界，他利用自家的院子和家人的资助，建立了一家冰箱配件厂。由于没有获得许可证，该工厂后来不得不关闭，仍由当地政府接管。当李书福决定创立吉利时，所采用的吉利取义中国传统的"吉利"之意。1993 年他的工厂开始生产摩托车。由于没有获得许可证，他只能依托嘉陵摩托车拥有的许可证生产；到 1998 年，他的工厂达到 35 万台。李书福的梦想是制造汽车，这也需要拿到营业执照。

20 世纪 80 年代，中国政府制定的汽车行业产业政策侧重于国有企业（SOE）和外国公司组建合资企业（JV）。直到 20 世纪 90 年代末，对私人投资的禁令才被解除。从那时起，这些公司在生产摩托车或电子产品的工厂改造后开始生产乘用车。吉利就是其中之一。

在经历了不同的业务之后，李书福从 1998 年开始专注于开发一家新的汽车公司。他获得了制造小型汽车的许可，并在浙江开设了一家工厂（Anderson, 2012, p. 141）。1998 年 8 月 8 日，吉利制造的第一辆汽车"海清"顺利下装配线[1]。然而，这些车的质量不好。根据李书福的说法，前三批车没有上市，直接被丢弃了（Milne, 2014）。

吉利创始人说，汽车制造是一项复杂的任务，如果要生产高质量的汽车，挑战更大。因此，该公司的新战略是生产廉价汽车，让一部分人能够购买第一辆汽车并支付费用。在此之前，中国汽车行业一直被合资企业垄断，汽车生产主要面向高端市场。此外，有学者指出，合资企业在中国销售的汽车价格通常比国际市场的价格高出三四倍。在这方面，吉利坚持专注于廉价汽车市场的战略：自 2000 年以来，吉利销售的汽车价格低于 4 万元人民币。2004 年，在一汽集团子公司天

---

[1] 选择第 8 个月的第 8 天来展示新车是基于中国文化传统，因为数字 8 被认为是好运的象征。

津一汽生产的夏利车型（售价为3.18万元）的竞争下，吉利将价格降至2.9万元，设定历史最低价格。

自2001年中国加入WTO后，大公司和合资企业享有特权的汽车行业保护性发展政策开始改变，吉利成为第一家获得汽车制造证书的私营企业。2003年，该公司与中国光大银行签署了战略合作协议，并将其销售和行政总部迁至杭州，同年8月，该公司在海外销售了第一辆汽车。

公司的增长令人鼓舞。然而，要走增长之路，就必须拥有更大的资本，而这是该公司所缺的。吉利于2005年开始在香港证券交易所上市交易。根据Anderson（2012），吉利2009年从高盛获得了3亿3400万美元的投资。

2006年，吉利进入新阶段之前的最后一步是收购英国锰铜23%的股份，成为公司的主要股东（Anderson, 2012）。几年后的2013年，吉利收购了整个公司。按照这些思路，吉利继续在英国投资相关业务，这些业务的中心是经典的伦敦出租车。通过这种方式，2014年收购绿宝石汽车公司的交易被添加到锰铜公司的购买中，以便将该公司开发的有关电动汽车和减排的技术应用到新出租车的制造中。此外，吉利还投资在考文垂为伦敦电动汽车公司（LEVC）建造了一座新工厂，为此吉利获得了英国前首相、时任伦敦市长鲍里斯·约翰逊（Boris Johnson, 2015）的赞扬。吉利持有英国锰铜股份之后继而成为公司的主要股东。两家公司在中国成立了一家新的合资企业，以生产标志性的伦敦黑色出租车，该出租车现在以SKD[1]的形式从中国出口，在英国组装（Anderson, 2012, p. 145）[2]。

自2007年以来，该公司通过提高产品质量和技术，改变了其最初制造廉价汽车的战略，从而开启了2.0时代。这一变化的关键是逐步从低成本战略转向产品差异化战略。因此，吉利开始打造三个子品牌：帝豪、全球鹰和上海英伦（Zhan, 2018, p. 6）。除了生产的汽车质量的预期变化外，2.0阶段的特点是促进出口和海外投资（对外投资意味着建设新工厂和收购公司）。从这个意义上说，我们认为，

---

[1] SKD（Semi-Completely Knocked-down，半完全拆卸）是一种交付车辆装配套件的方式，与CKD（Completely Knocked Down，完全拆卸）不同。从CKD套件中获得新车只涉及其零件的组装，SKD套件在开发前照灯、座椅、塑料零件、玻璃等方面需要额外的工作。后一种形式通常用于遵守原产地证书和避税。

[2] 英国锰铜公司于1973年收购了BSA（Birmingham Small Arm Company）。BSA曾于1954年收购了传统的黑色出租车制造商伦敦出租车公司（London Taxi Company，也称为Carbodies）。因此，吉利在收购锰铜股份时，也加入了伦敦出租车公司。自2017年以来，伦敦出租车公司被称为伦敦电动汽车公司（London EV Company，LEVC）。

吉利"全球布局"的开始是出于两个原因：一方面，根据新的战略计划，通过收购公司获得新的技术和诀窍；另一方面，建设新的汽车装配厂，以进入不同的市场，避免第三国通常对进口产品施加的税收负担。在出口方面，吉利首先进入了东南亚、中东和北非国家，这些国家的内部竞争和需求较少（在能源消耗、减排和车辆安全方面）。此外，吉利还打算增加在欧亚地区的销量，比如在俄罗斯和白俄罗斯等国，这也是因为该地区的一些国家在2015年成立了欧亚经济联盟[1]。

为了巩固在这些地区的市场地位，吉利在不同国家投资建设了汽车装配厂。在这方面，吉利于2007年在印度尼西亚建立了一家工厂，开始供应国内和南亚市场。2005年在马来西亚进行的投资失败后，首次尝试覆盖这一地理区域。在那里，马来西亚前总理马哈蒂尔在与IGC集团签署制造、组装和出口汽车的协议后表示，中国汽车将接管当地市场，并要求所有生产的汽车出口，排除了在该国修建核电站的可能性（Wang, 2019, p. 11）。因此，马来西亚政府消除了任何可能威胁当地公司宝腾的竞争（Perusahaan Otomobil Nasional Bhd）（China Daily, 2006）。2012年，吉利与GBAuto（Ghabbour Group）签署协议，在埃及建立一家工厂，用于组装CKD套件的汽车，年生产能力为30000辆。除了覆盖埃及市场，该公司还希望从新工厂向北非和中东地区供货（Embassy of the People's Republic of China in the Arab Republic of Egypt, 2012）。2015年，吉利与世界上最大的采矿机械制造公司之一的Belaz以及当地零部件制造商联盟（SOYUZ）在白俄罗斯成立了一家合资企业Belgee，目的是组装汽车，在白俄罗斯的同一个市场销售，并出口到俄罗斯和乌克兰。这项投资在欧洲国家是一个里程碑，因为Belgee成为该国第一家汽车装配厂（在此之前，那里只生产农业和机械车辆）（Resiale Viano, 2019），除了建造新工厂，在2006年获得锰铜的参与权后，吉利于2009年重新投资收购外国公司：它收购了澳大利亚公司DSI（传动系统国际公司），这是世界第二大自动变速器制造商。这笔交易的成交价为4022万美元（Reuters, 2009）。因此，这家中国公司获得了专门知识和新技术，以提高其车辆的质量，这是2.0时代的主要目标。2010年，ZGHG完成了对福特之前拥有的沃尔沃汽车部门的收购，获得了包括制造厂和研发中心在内的所有有形和无形资产，以及10000多项专利（Zhan, 2018）。在这一点上，应该澄清的是，交易是由ZGHG进行的，而不是GAG公司——在香港证券交易所

---

[1] 2013年是吉利出口额创纪录的一年，达到118871辆，占公司总销售额的22%；这些出口产品的主要目的地包括俄罗斯、埃及、沙特阿拉伯、伊朗和乌克兰（Wang, 2019）。

上市和制造汽车的那家公司。ZGHG 是一家由李书福持有 90% 股份的公司。此外，截至 2012 年，ZGHG 拥有 GAG 50.97% 的股份。因此，李书福控制着 GAG 和沃尔沃，但 GAG 并未参与沃尔沃收购的交易（Anderson, 2012）。李书福说"沃尔沃是沃尔沃，吉利是吉利"，沃尔沃的运营独立性保持不变（Tie, 2019）。

吉利与沃尔沃合作的关键是 2013 年成立的中国—欧洲汽车技术公司（CEVT），这是吉利位于哥德堡子公司的研发中心[1]。CEVT 的开发资金来自拥有知识产权的吉利，但沃尔沃在技术和安全方面的经验贡献了知识。此外，鉴于沃尔沃在该市的历史地位、CEVT 与沃尔沃技术、沃尔沃信息技术等工业资产以及哥德堡大学和查尔默斯大学建立的密切关系，该工厂的位置也有其优势（Yakov, et al., 2019）。

通过这种方式，吉利获得了高端核心技术，提高了研发能力，也为品牌的强化做出了贡献。尽管沃尔沃品牌得以在高端汽车领域占据一席之地，但吉利品牌仍在廉价汽车领域发挥作用。对这家瑞典公司的收购证明了吉利在提高汽车质量和安全性方面的新战略。李书福表示："我们已经实现了收购沃尔沃的梦想，但这并不是我们计划的终点，这只是一个起点。"（Fang and Leung, 2010）

2014 年 4 月，吉利宣布将退出 2.0 时代，进入 3.0 时代。3.0 时代的目标是通过"为每个人打造精致汽车"的提议来打造品牌。因此，该公司开始将该品牌细分为五款车型：专注于微型车市场的"熊猫"、专注于小型车市场的"金刚"、专注于低端紧凑型运动型多用途车（SUV）市场的"愿景"、专注于中档轿车的"博瑞"，以及专注于紧凑型 SUV 的"博越"（Zhan, 2018）[2]。

在 3.0 时代的背景下，吉利于 2017 年推出了其新品牌领克（LYNK & CO），该品牌由来自 20 多个国家的 2000 多名工程师在吉利欧洲研发中心开发，并基于沃尔沃和吉利联合开发的 CMA 平台（Zhan, 2018）。虽然吉利瞄准大众市场，但领克打算将自己定位为高端品牌（Geely Group, n/d）。

在这一新阶段，吉利的海外投资与前一阶段的战略保持一致。从这个意义上

1　该公司的目标是开发一个最先进的模块化平台，即紧凑型模块化体系结构（CMA），该平台将允许开发新一代沃尔沃和吉利 C 系列汽车，与福特福克斯或奥迪 A3 车型（Yakov, et al., 2019, p. 66）相当。模块化平台允许品牌从单一基地开发新车型，节省时间和新开支。

2　吉利生产的车型通常根据销售地区的不同而有不同的名称：Panda（也称为吉利 LC 或 Gleagle GX2）；金刚（也称吉利 MK 或英伦 EC6）；愿景（也称吉利远景、格里格尔 FC 或格里格尔 GC7）；Borui（也称为 Emgrand GT）；博悦（又名 Emgrand NL-3、吉利 NL-3、吉利阿特拉斯、吉利 Emgrand X7 Sport、质子 X70）。

说，该公司继续其在亚洲市场的存在和获取新技术的意图。

2017年，吉利汽车（Geely Automotive）收购了宝腾（Proton）49.9%的股份，马来西亚政府为了避免竞争，阻止了吉利在该国的投资。通过收购宝腾，吉利还获得了莲花公司（Lotus Company）51%的股份[1]。

同年，吉利继续参与能够为其提供技术的不同公司。吉利以32.7亿美元收购了瑞典投资公司Cevian Capital持有的AB沃尔沃8.2%的股份，由此，这家中国公司参与了全球第二大卡车制造商（Resiale Viano, 2019）。此外，吉利在同一年收购了美国初创企业Terrafugia，这显然是对未来的投资。Terrafugia由麻省理工学院的毕业生于2006年创立，致力于飞行汽车的开发（Terrafugia, 2017）。

2018年，吉利再次撼动了汽车市场，就像他在2010年收购沃尔沃时那样，这一次是收购了戴姆勒9.7%的股份（Zhou, 2019）。该交易引起了德国政府的警惕，德国政府表示将"密切关注"中国在德国的投资，理由是中国打算获得欧洲的技术创新（Berría, 2019）。按照这些思路，德国经济部长宣布，他们应该保持警惕，因为尽管德国对投资开放，但德国不应该被用来支持其他国家产业政策的利益（Resiale Viano, 2019）。除上述交易外，两家公司还设计成立了一家合资企业生产智能电动汽车，该汽车应于2022年上市（Daimler, n/d）。此外，吉利和戴姆勒之间的合作关系不仅专注于电动汽车本身的开发。还旨在联手应对优步和谷歌在电动汽车市场的前沿阵地（Taylor and Shirouzu, 2019）。

总结吉利的海外业务如表3所示。

表3　　　　　　　　2007—2018年吉利外国投资

年份	国家	目的	公司名称
2007	印尼	新建工厂	
2009	澳大利亚	收购公司	DSI
2010	瑞典	收购公司	Volvo
2012	埃及	新建工厂	
2013	英格兰	收购公司	Manganese Bronze
2014	英格兰	收购公司	Emerald Automotive

---

[1] 1996年，宝腾收购了英国著名运动和赛车品牌莲花汽车的大部分股份，莲花汽车由科林·查普曼于1952年创立。

续表

年份	国家	目的	公司名称
2015	英格兰	新建工厂	
2015	白俄罗斯	新建工厂	
2017	马来西亚	收购公司	Proton
2017	美国	收购公司	Terrafugia
2017	瑞典	收购公司	Volvo Trucks
2018	德国	收购公司	Daimler

ZGHG 目前在中国有 12 个生产基地[1]，在美国、英国、埃及、白俄罗斯和印度尼西亚有 30 个工厂，名称为吉利汽车或沃尔沃（Wang, 2019, p. 10）；位于杭州（吉利）、宁波（吉利）、哥德堡（吉利和沃尔沃）、哥本哈根（沃尔沃）、上海（沃尔沃）和考文垂（LEVC）的研发中心；洛杉矶、哥德堡、巴塞罗那和上海的设计中心。ZGHG 拥有超过 80000 名员工，包括 50000 名 GAG 员工、31000 名沃尔沃员工和 1000 名 LEVC 员工（Geely Group, n/d）。

通过对吉利资产的描述，我们可以衡量该公司的增长，并感知其决定在产品的技术规模上进步的坚定程度。吉利对全球汽车行业正在经历的时代变化并不陌生，并正在努力适应它。这方面的一个例子是与戴姆勒建立的最后一次合作关系。

从这个意义上看，该公司在电动汽车的设计和制造方面起步较晚。然而在研发领域，到 2018 年，它在全球已有 10000 名员工（Zhan, 2018, p. 22-23）。除研究任务外，该公司还拥有吉利商用车（GCV），这是一家新能源电动和混合动力商用车公司，为吉利在该领域的两个品牌提供支持：前述的 LEVC 和远程汽车（Geely Group, n/d）。

目前，吉利正在努力实现"2020 战略"的目标，由 2016 年度 GAG 制定的"李书福同志基金会成立第三十周年庆典"为背景，目标是到 2020 年生产 200 万辆汽车，这一数字似乎接近实现（表 4）。

---

[1] 分别是台州临海和台州路桥（台州）、宁波杭州湾和宁波春晓（宁波）、上海、成都（四川）、张家口（河北）、济南（山东）、湘潭（湖南）、宝鸡 y 晋中（山西）、贵阳（贵州）（Zhan, 2018, p. 24-25）。

表4　　　　　　　　　吉利：汽车年产量和世界排名

年份	产量	世界排名	年份	产量	世界排名
2017	1,950,382	15	2010	802,319	20
2016	1,266,456	19	2009	330,275	27
2015	999,802	21	2008	220,955	31
2014	890,652	21	2007	216,774	37
2013	969,896	20	2006	207,149	33
2012	922,906	21	2005	149,532	32
2011	897,107	21	2004	91,744	41

资料来源：International Organization of Motor Vehicle Manufacturers, 2019

那么，吉利怎么能在这么几年内成为全球汽车制造商呢？

一是公司创始人李书福的领导，二是浙江的社会文化背景。如果没有李书福的活力和胆识，吉利将难以生存。这是由于其在企业中的创业精神和坚持不懈的品格。从这个意义上说，这位商人在国内外都被视为出身于农村地区普通家庭的人，他凭借自己的努力创造了自己的实业，在西方赢得了"中国亨利·福特"和"亚洲埃隆·马斯克"的绰号（Berría，2018）。李书福的这种创业精神在很大程度上归功于浙江省的文化传统，例如，一些人认为吉利的创始人具备了浙江人的冒险基因（Wu, 2017, p. 50）[1]。

"创业精神"理念存在于浙江居民中，并在该省人口中构成了一个非常强烈的身份特征。从这个意义上说，一些技能，如知道如何面对风险、坚忍不拔、适应环境和对"机会"的感知，以及其他特征，形成了个人发展自身的共同氛围，这种环境有助于消除或减轻某些社会信念的负担，例如在从事不同的业务后不能成功的"失败"。

第二个因素是经济环境。我们在第一节中提到了该省的巨大经济增长，这种经济增长还伴随着代表人口的汽车消费的增加。从表5中可以看出，过去10年，浙江省的汽车保有量高于中国东部沿海最发达省份的其他地区（除了2010年和2012年，广东省略高于浙江省），且远高于中国所有地区的汽车总消费量。

解释消费增长的原因必须从人口规模、购买力的提高和城市化的增长中找到。此外，正如Zhan（2018）所言，汽车是地位和财富的象征，从社会习俗来看，

---

[1] 同样，娃哈哈集团创始人宗庆后也被认为是该省企业家精神的代表（Wu, 2017, p. 50）。

拥有房子和汽车是年轻人结婚的条件,因此没有任何迹象表明未来汽车消费会减少。从这个意义上讲,建设小康社会也意味着建设"汽车社会"。为了实现这一目标,国务院于2017年发布的《汽车行业中长期规划》支持汽车企业的扩张、强化和跨境整合(Zhan, 2018)。因此,GAG从这种不断增长的需求中受益,尤其是从那些首次接触汽车的人那里,而ZGHG通过沃尔沃已经能够满足高端汽车的需求。

第三个因素是政府支持,李书福在成立汽车公司初期面临困难,但这些限制来自中央政府为中国汽车行业设计的战略。在吉利成立初期,台州地方政府是吉利的重要合作伙伴,以低于市场价格的价格出售土地使用权,并给予免税;作为补偿,当地政府受益于创造就业机会和增加税收(Anderson, 2012)。

三　吉利在阿根廷的现状与展望

在中国政府倡导的"走出去"政策和公司在全球投资的背景下,吉利公司于2016年底通过乌拉圭公司(Grupo Fiancar)进入阿根廷市场。"中国吉利"进入阿根廷的谈判始于2013年,由于阿根廷政府更迭直到2016年,吉利品牌才得以进入该国,但直到2017年8家经销商开业,该公司才正式开始运营(Perfil, 2018)。

首批抵达阿根廷的吉利车型是LC、GC5和Emgrand轿车,2017年6月,在布宜诺斯艾利斯汽车展厅,两款新车型Emgrand X7 Sport(SUV)和Emgrand GS(Crossover)亮相(Geely Argentina, 2019)。

2016年随着吉利的加入,在阿根廷有了三家中国汽车制造商,另外两家是奇瑞和力帆。随后来自中国的众多汽车公司纷纷加入:2017年的福田、众泰以及2018年的北汽、DFSK、DFM、JMC、比亚迪和江淮汽车。在两年多的时间里,中国汽车制造商纷纷涌入阿根廷,各种中国汽车品牌的到来是通过进口商和当地代表实现的,就像奇瑞这个第一家在阿根廷销售汽车的中国汽车制造商,也是通过当地的公司Socma开展贸易。

吉利公司在阿根廷的销售与其他中国汽车制造商类似,即通过当地进口商运作,其目标是占有廉价汽车市场。从这个意义上讲,2016年,在阿根廷销售的五款最便宜的汽车中,有吉利LC和奇瑞QQ。2018年,这两款车都是最便宜的,吉利LC是市场上第二便宜的车型,仅次于大众Up(Ámbito Financiero, 2016b;2018)。

除了专注于经济型汽车以获得市场份额外,吉利的战略还专注于售后服务。吉利阿根廷分公司总经理费德里科·马约拉(Federico Mayora)表示,进军阿根廷市场的战略是建立一个从北到南、从东到西的网络,这样吉利的阿根廷买家就可以在阿根廷各地获得官方服务的支持并能购买到吉利的原装零部件,这样就可以在全国范围内使用吉利生产的汽车工作和进行家庭旅行,而不必担心车辆出现任何问题时无法获得援助(Perfil,2018)。

阿根廷消费者起初不愿意购买中国汽车,因为他们担心这些汽车的质量。打破这一障碍,赢得消费者信心是吉利面临的主要挑战。补充一点,阿根廷虽然不是经济最发达的国家之一,但在汽车制造方面有着悠久的传统:它是拉丁美洲领先的汽车生产商之一,与巴西和墨西哥一道,在那里有世界主要汽车公司的工厂——福特、通用汽车、大众汽车、菲亚特、雷诺、日产、丰田和本田。从这个意义上说,阿根廷消费者对他们期望从新车中获得的好处提出了要求,并愿意为此买单。

在吉利进入阿根廷之初,该公司的目标是巩固自己作为该国最畅销的中国品牌的地位,并希望在乌拉圭组装汽车,为阿根廷和巴西市场提供服务;当然也不排除能在阿根廷进行直接投资建厂(Argentina Autoblog, 2016)。然而,2019 年,在经济危机的背景下,汽车消费量大幅下降——与 2018 年相比,0 公里汽车专利下降了 45%(Argentina Autoblog, 2016),产量随着需求的减少而下降,工厂产能闲置、开始裁员。在这方面,到了 9 月,许多进口品牌都在重新考虑它们在阿根廷的存在——其中大多数在一个月内售出的汽车不超过 10 辆——有可能将几个品牌集中在少数人手中。例如,北汽和福田的进口商、商人雨果·贝尔卡斯特罗(Hugo Belcastro)承认正在就保留吉利品牌进行谈判(Alonso, 2019)[1]。除了需求下降之外,下一年年(2020 年 1 月)还将对进口汽车征收新税[2]。此外,官方汽车进口商和分销商商会(Cidoa,西班牙语缩写)宣布,这将使许多进口品牌的经营面临风险。受影响的品牌包括许多中国公司,比如吉利(TNAutos, 2019)。

---

1 其他公认的中国汽车进口商包括 Grupo Socma(奇瑞、江淮和 DFSK)和 Grupo CarOne(哈弗、长安和长城)。

2 从那天起,批发价在 130 万比索(公众约 170 万比索,约 2.6 万美元)和 240 万美元(公众约 310 万比索,约 4.9 万美元)之间的车辆将缴纳 20% 的税费。

表 5　　　　吉利在阿根廷的销量与其他中国汽车品牌的比较

品牌	2017（辆）	份额（%）	2016（辆）	份额（%）
吉利	518	0.1	3	—
奇瑞	6250	0.7	3779	0.5
力帆	1841	0.2	405	0.1

资料来源：ACARA，2018。

在表 5 中可以看到奇瑞在阿根廷有着更多的优势，是中国汽车销售的领导者，其次是力帆。根据吉利阿根廷分公司（2019）的数据，2018 年公司在阿根廷销售了 1500 台汽车，这意味着 2018 年的销售额比 2017 年增长了约 200%。然而，尽管中国制造的汽车在阿根廷的销量正在增长，但它们在汽车总销量中的份额仍然非常有限，接近 1%[1]。

随着吉利公司 23 家经销商遍布阿根廷全国，秉持在危机背景下致力于销售经济型汽车以及专注于售后服务的持续战略，吉利在阿根廷的销售额可能会大幅提高。但是仍需密切监测人们购买力的恢复指标，如果增长乏力，营销增长可能会很缓慢。因此，进口企业必须具备足够的经济实力，在希望经济复苏的同时维持现状；此外，吉利必须关注新政府关于进口的经济政策；最后，它必须继续努力，以消除影响阿根廷人对中国汽车的先入为主的观念[2]。

四　结论

本文详细讨论了吉利的案例。我们能够观察到该公司的发展，尤其是在其 1.0 阶段（1997—2007）是如何得到地方和省级政府的支持和政治支持的，这为该公司的大发展铺平了道路。成为行业龙头企业后，吉利开始在"走出去"政策背景下得到中央政府的支持。这样，在 2.0 阶段（2007—2014），该公司开始通过建设新工厂和收购现成公司的方式进行海外投资。从而获得了国外技术，以实现"技术飞跃"，并发展新的科研机构，哥德堡的 CEVT 就是一个例子。这也符合政府鼓励扩大技术规模的战略。由此吉利开始了其 3.0 时代，继续通过增加参与或收购外国公司来获取新技术，但现在专注于与电动汽车开发和减排相关的技术，这

---

[1] 在阿根廷经济危机加剧之前，中国在阿根廷的汽车进口商希望到 2019—2020 年达到 2% 的市场份额。

[2] 2018 年，吉利为其车辆提供了 5 年或 15 万公里的保修。

是新公司车型中应用的关键方面。因此，一方面，吉利将自己置于全球汽车发展的前沿；另一方面，它将其商业战略与中国政府旨在减少车辆污染和废气排放的政策相协调，从而为"绿色浙江"的发展做出贡献。

本文还分析了吉利在阿根廷的经验。这家中国公司近年来才开始在南美国家的业务，但仅通过车辆出口实现的，没有登记投资，近期也没有投资计划。吉利于2016年进入阿根廷，当时该国在继2001年经济危机之后开始经历最大的经济危机之一，这直接影响了汽车市场。在这种情况下，我们认为进口商等待需求复苏的能力至关重要，因为我们知道，在稳定的条件下，阿根廷汽车市场非常活跃。继续押注于廉价汽车行业可能是一个不错的策略，尤其是当考虑到开始摆脱经济危机的消费者时。然而，必须严格遵守阿根廷国家政府关于进口的政策，这一因素将直接影响进口汽车的价格，从而使其难以在经济型汽车领域竞争。在这种情况下，如果阿根廷的需求复苏，可以考虑在邻国乌拉圭进行投资，在那里组装吉利汽车，这些汽车可以进入阿根廷，从而享受南方共同市场保证的区域生产税收优惠——乌拉圭也将是进入巴西市场的跳板。总而言之，我们认为，吉利在中期内必须面对的另一个挑战是，要想用自己的车型征服需求旺盛的阿根廷消费者，仅靠价格和售后服务是不够的，它必须为汽车提供更高的质量/技术/安全性和舒适性。

The Development of Geely and the Expansion of its Business in Argentina

Jose Maria Resiale Viano /Argentina

Argentina Center for Research and Studies on Culture and Society (CIECS)-CONICET/PhD. Scholarship holder; National University of Córdoba/Professor

The objective of this essay is to analyze and describe the development of Geely as an automotive company in the context of the economic development of Zhejiang Province, as well as the recent expansion of the company's business in Argentina. The work is subdivided into three sections: first, we will study the economic environment in which Geely was born; that is, we will review the economic development of Zhejiang Province and the construction of Hangzhou as a city of innovation and production of high-tech goods. Second, we will consider Geely's history and the relationship between its development and the economic dynamics of the province. Finally, we will analyze Geely's career in Argentina and consider the company's future prospects in the South American country.

To achieve these objectives we have worked with statistical data from the National Bureau of Statistic of China (NBSC) and the Association of Automobile Dealers of the Argentine Republic (ACARA), press articles, company publications, and specialized literature.

I. The successful development of Zhejiang Province and the construction of Hangzhou as a city of technology and innovation

Zhejiang Province is the land where Geely was born, and Hangzhou City was the home where the company took its first steps. In this sense, in order to better understand the development of the automotive firm, it is necessary to review the environment in which the company was created. The development of Zhejiang has been impressive since the beginning of the Reform and Opening-Up period; In the words of Professor He Xianming (2019), Zhejiang has been a province of rapid economic growth, the first to eliminate poverty, and it is at the forefront in the development of the "green economy". In this way, Zhejiang has been transformed both quantitatively and qualitatively. The quantitative transformation can be appreciated when we consider the successful results in economic matters. Between 1950 and the late 1970s Zhejiang received little state investment (Shi and Ganne, 2009); these investments were a fundamental condition for the development of the province when the central planning of the economy was absolute. However, from the Reform period started in 1978, the province began to take off. In this sense, between 1978 and 2017 the Zhejiang GDP multiplied by 418 times, and the GDP per apita by 278 (Table 1).

Table 1   Zhejiang GDP and GDP per capita

Year	GDP (100 mill.RMB. At constant price)	Per Cápita GDP (RMB)
1978	123	331
1993	257	4469
2003	9705	10542
2017	51768	92057

Own elaboration. Source: NBSC China Statistical Yearbook (2008, 2018); Yuan (2019, p. 41)

Between 1978 and 1993 the GDP of the prov nce increased moderately; it was only after Deng Xiaoping's visit in Shen Zhen that Zhe Jiang's economy began to grow faster. Since 2003, during the tenure of Xi Jinping as provincial Party Secretary, it can be seen the sustained provincial economic growth at high rates taking place. (Graph 1). The same observations on GDP growth are sustained when we observe the evolution of per capita GDP (Graph 2).

Graph 1　Zhejiang GDP (100 mill. RMB. At constant price)

Own elaboration. Source: NBSC, China Statistical Yearbook (2008, 2018); Yuan (2019, p. 41)

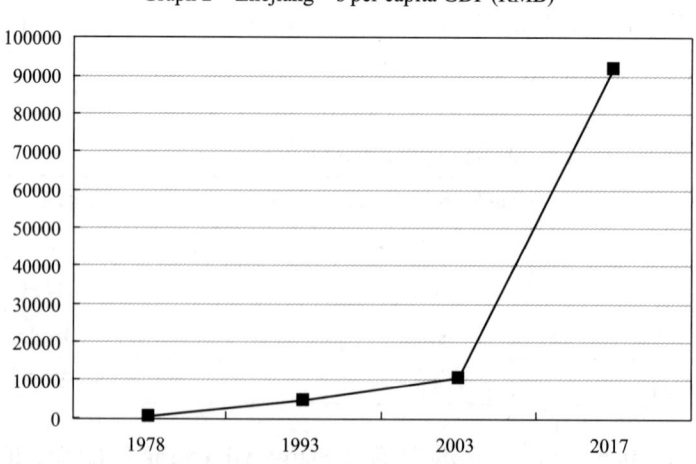

Graph 2　Zhejiang's per capita GDP (RMB)

Own elaboration. Source: NBSC, China Statistical Yearbook (2008, 2018); Yuan (2019, p. 41)

The contribution of the different sectors of the economy to the composition of the

GDP has changed over the years. The primary sector always occupied a marginal place, and its contribution followed a downward trend over time; this can be easily understood if we consider that Zhejiang is a relatively small province and that much of its territory is crossed by mountains.[1] The secondary sector has been the pillar of the economic growth of the province for a long time; however, its contribution to GDP began to follow a downward trend in 2008, contrasting with the upward trend experienced by the tertiary sector since the beginning of the new century. Thus, in 2014 for the first time the participation of the tertiary sector in the Zhejiang GDP was superior to the secondary sector, and this dynamic has been maintained until today (Table 2 and Graph 3).

Table 2 Composition of the Zhejiang GDP by sector (%)

Year	Primary	Secondary	Tertiary	Year	Primary	Secondary	Tertiary
1998	12.7	54.3	33	2008	5.1	53.9	41
1999	11.8	54.1	34.1	2009	5.1	51.8	43.1
200o	11	52.7	36.3	2010	4.9	51.6	43.5
2001	10.3	51.3	38.4	2011	4.9	51.2	43.9
2002	8.9	51.1	40	2012	4.8	50	45.2
2003	n/a	n/a	nl/a	2013	4.8	49.1	46.1
2004	7.3	53.8	39	2014	4.4	47.7	47.8
2005	6.6	53.4	40	2015	4.3	46	49.8
2006	5.9	54	40.1	2016	4.2	44.9	51
2007	5.3	54	40.7	2017	3.7	42.9	53.3

Own elaboration. Source: NBSC, China Stat stical Yearbook (2000, 2001, 2002, 2003, 2005, 2007, 2008, 2009, 2010, 2011, 2012, 2013, 2014, 2015, 2016, 2017, 2018).

The performance of the tertiary sector can be explained by the increase in banking, financial and consulting activities, science and technology, transport and e-commerce (Xu, 2019, p.4). These activities clearly represent the change in the

---

[1] In addition, the economic growth initiated in 2003 accelerated the urbanization process and increased the space occupied by the industries that, added to the population growth, put more pressure on the farmland.

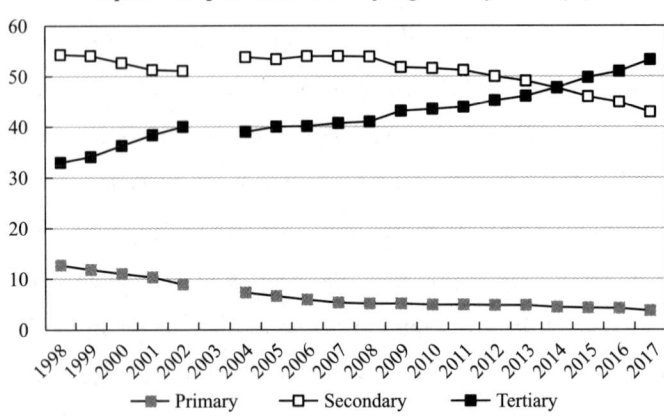

Graph 3: Composition of the Zhejiang GDP by sector (%)

Own elaboration. Source: NBSC, China Statistical Yearbook (2000, 2001, 2002, 2003, 2005, 2007, 2008, 2009, 2010, 2011, 2012, 2013, 2014, 2015, 2016, 2017, 2018).

productive profile of Zhejiang since 2003, which we have decided to call "qualitative changes". The basis for the economic transformation of Zhejiang from 2003, measured in both quantitative and qualitative terms, was the implementation of a comprehensive development plan called "Eight-Eight Strategy".

The Strategy consisted in the encouragement of eight advantages and the promotion of eight measures, which would end up changing the productive profile of the province qualitative transformation. In this sense, to explain the Eight-Eight Strategy allows us to describe at the same time the economic development of Zhejiang.

First, the Eight-Eight Strategy sought to take advantage of the Zhejiang institutions to actively promote the development of the economy with different types of property, ensuring that public property remains dominant and that the socialist market system is improved (Xu, 2019, p. 1).

The second point was to take advantage of the geographical location of Zhejiang in order to strengthen relations with Shanghai and to cooperate in the exploitation of the Yangzi River Delta (Xu, 2019, p. 1). In this way, Shanghai would be the locomotive that would boost the development of the Yangzi River Delta through the financial activity and control of the Yangshan International Deepwater Port. On the other hand, the role of Zhejiang and the neighboring province of Jiangsu in the Yangzi Delta would be the production and export of goods, because both have a large number of companies based there and a lot of activity stemming from private companies (Ho, 2012).

Third, the plan was to take advantage of the presence of the numerous provincial industries in order to accelerate the construction of a new industrialization path focused on the manufacture of goods with greater added value (Xu, 2019, p. 1). In this regard, the "Zhejiang Model" brings together many of the elements that contribute to the distinctive provincial economic development. Following Yang Zaiping (2012), vice president of the China Banking Association, five are the elements that define the "Zhejiang Model":

1. The orientation towards individuals: institutional arrangements oriented to the people, that is, the strengthening of the administrative capacities of the State and public services, which are considered as the basis for the development of the private economy (Yang, 2012). As an example of this point, the idea of "the governance of five types of water" could be considered, which consisted of treating wastewater, controlling flooding, discharging accumulated water, guaranteeing water supply and saving water (Xu, 2019, p. 2).

2. The decision to prioritize the development of the private sector of the economy: Zhejiang's economic development was due more to a private impulse than to state investments; In this regard, some authors argue that the characteristic and advantage of Zhejiang's economic development has been the development of the private economy, and that private capitals were the main driving force behind the investments made in Zhejiang (Huang, 2013; Xu, 2012, p. 10). For example, the production of the non-public sector accounted for 90 percent of the 2012 provincial Gross Product (Yang, 2012), and by 2013 the private economy contributed with 60 percent of the taxes collected (only the Geely Group paid in taxes for about 8587 million RMB that year, approximately), more than 80 percent of exports and over

90 percent of new jobs created (Xu, 2012, p.145).

3. The large number of small enterprises located in the province: By 2012 there were 569,000 small businesses representing 97 percent of the total companies in the province, and accounting for 56, 3 percent of Zhejiang industrial production (Yang, 2012). This presence of numerous small companies that produce for the domestic market and, especially, for export, has been the main feature of the "Zhejiang Model" (Lu, 2007).[1] However, these small businesses have faced difficulties in obtaining financing, as long as they cannot access state credits because they do not meet the necessary requirements, and given the fact that Shanghai financial services are destined for large national or multinational companies. In this way, on the one hand, private financing has been fundamental for the development of these small firms; on the other hand, the city of Hangzhou has positioned itself as a complementary regional financial center of Shanghai, serving the needs of small and medium-sized enterprises (Xia, 2010).

4. Zhejiang businessmen: According to Yang (2012), the economic development of the region would not be possible without a group of active entrepreneurs who have special talents and have learned to develop their businesses with scarce resources. This point of view is also shared by Jin Pingnu (2006), who argues that among the main reasons for the economic development of Zhejiang, specific population traits should be considered: the pioneer and entrepreneurial spirit, the predisposition to trade and to permanently work, a strong imprint of the concepts of "time" and opportunity what can be done today cannot be done tomorrow -and practicality.

5. The existence of industrial clusters: practically all cities in Zhejiang have one or more industrial groups made up of numerous small companies that have promoted the local industrialization process. Following Shi and Ganne (2009), three different areas of cluster development can be identified in Zhejiang: the first is

---

1 Another distinctive feature of the Zhejiang Model is the Chinese ownership of these numerous companies, an aspect that contrasts, for example, with the "Jiangsu Model" (Lu, 2007).

located in the north of the province and the clusters present there are characterized by being very dynamic; there, the big companies and high-tech groups based in Hangzhou and Ningbo stand out, as well as textile production in Xiaoshan and plastics in Yuyao. The second area covers Taizhou and Wenzhou;[1] here there are about ten different sectors of activity, such as shoes, clothes, lighters and glasses manufacturing, among others.[2] The third area includes Jinhua, Quzhou and Lishui: the clusters are more recent, the region is less developed and they concentrate on the manufacture of consumer goods that require lower production costs.

The fourth point of the Eight-Eight Strategy was to take advantage of coordinated urban and rural development to accelerate integration between city and countryside. It is convenient to remind again that Zhejiang is one of the smallest provinces in China in terms of land area, that much of its territory is crossed by mountains and that it has few natural resources to exploit. In this sense, with a growing population and a space that limits the simultaneous expansion of urbanization and agriculture, the coordinated development of both spaces is extremely necessary.

Fifth, the Strategy proposed the use of the ecological advantage of the province to build a "Green Zhejiang".

The strategy of building a "Green Zhejiang" implies the first step in the environmental development of the province, as environmental protection must be linked to the construction of an "ecological Zhejiang" and a "beautiful Zhejiang". In this regard, in May 2014, at the Fifth Plenary Session of the Thirteenth Party Committee of Zhejiang Province, the decision was made to build a "beautiful Zhejiang", which implied an ecological industrial development, the "green consumption", sustained resource availability development of livable ecological communities and a beautiful ecological environment (Qi, 2019, p. 197).

---

1 Wenzhou is characterized by the large number of private firms, and it was the city that inspired the concept of "Zhejiang Model".
2 As an example, by 2001, shoes made in Wenzhou accounted for 20% of the total Chinese market, lighters for 90% and shavers for 60% (Shi and Ganne, 2009).

Point number six of the Strategy was to promote the exploitation of marine and mountain resources in the province so that they become new sources of economic growth.

Seventh, it was intended to seize Zhejiang's environmental advantages to actively boost construction.

Finally, the eighth point established the use of the human advantages of the province to rejuvenate Zhejiang through science and technology, and turn the province into a culturally strong region.[1]

At the beginning of the second decade of the 21st century, the fundamental pillars of the Eight-Eight Strategy were updated and continued through the implementation of the "Four major constructions" and the "Four changes and three well-knows actors". "Four major constructions" involved promoting the construction of large platforms, large industries, large projects and large companies. The construction of "large platforms" consisted of planning and developing fourteen industrial zones among which Dajiangdong is counted[2], improving existing industrial parks and promoting the construction of bases to carry out scientific and technological innovation tasks. Building "large industries" meant fostering the development of industries with competitive advantages to turn them into strong companies and producers of high value-added manufactures;[3] in this sense, the development of 11 main industries was privileged among which was the automotive industry and whose main provincial reference is Geely and 9 emerging strategic industries

---

1 Here we can find an antecedent of the idea of "National Rejuvenation", which will be recovered by Xi Jinping when he assumed as General Secretary of the CPC years later. In this regard, on November 29, 2012, Xi launched the idea of the "Chinese dream of national rejuvenation" during a visit to the exhibition of the National Museum of China entitled The Road to Rejuvenation.
2 Dajiangdong is an industrial park located in Hangzhou. It has become the base of the automotive industry in Zhejiang Province, and different factories such as Geely, Changan Ford, GAC and Dongfeng are already installed there (Fang, Shen and Lai, 2018).
3 As mentioned above, the industrial structure of Zhejiang was characterized by the existence of small businesses; therefore, the productive forces are dispersed and have a low capacity for innovation (Yuan, 2019, p. 69)

biology, internet of things, new energy, cars with alternative energy, among others In addition, the merging between the manufacturing and the service industries was promoted. Executing "large projects" involved the development of infrastructure projects in order to promote development and activate construction. Finally, "large companies" meant the fostering of the development of strong companies able to play the role of leaders in the regional arena (Yuan, 2019, pp. 69-72).

As for the "Four changes and three well-knows actors", the four changes consisted of: first, reforming the industrial profile of the province, favoring the development of efficient industries with high quality and low resource consumption, high capacity for innovation and production of manufactured goods with high added value, replacing industries that do not meet these characteristics—this policy is known as "vacating the cage to change birds"[1]. The second change involves the incorporation of industrial robots into production in order to relieve the pressure of labor shortages, to reduce wage costs and to improve labor productivity a strategy commonly referred to as "replacing people with machines". The third change meant to optimize the use of space through the redesign and reconstruction of urban space, factories, the construction of high-rise housing and the exploitation of underground urban space, in order to "save land" and combat the growing land shortage of the province. Finally, the fourth change aimed at expanding the market by means of promoting e-commerce (Yuan, 2019, pp. 74-76).

"Three well-knows actors" meant to deepen the transformation on the provincial productive profile by, first, to support the development of Zhejiang's companies already included among the nation's leading enterprises. This was in turn to be accomplished by means of providing stimulus to the enterprises innovative capacities, propping-up their globalization and guaranteeing credit access, tax cuts and sufficient energy provision for them (this strategy was known as

---

1 This idea was first proposed in 2003, and involved "making space in the cage" to raise "good birds" that eat less, lay more eggs and fly high: "eat less" meant that companies consume less resources; "lay more eggs" that companies get high economic returns; and "fly high" meant that companies have the ability to develop in the long term (Yuan, 2019, p. 74).

"cultivating known enterprises"). Secondly, to encourage the development of well-known brands both in the domestic and the foreign market with a high consumer satisfaction degree was known as "to cultivate well-known brands". Finally, it was also proposed to train exports in corporate management and technical staffs with innovation abilities, to train entrepreneur individuals and to work closely with universities and research institutions (Yuan, 2019, pp. 77-78).

As part of the transformations that took place in the province, Hangzhou occupied a privileged place, and it is a clear example of the transformations that have been implemented in the province since 2003. In this sense, the city was established, on the one hand, as a center for the production of high-end goods, where the creation of the Dajiangdong industrial area as a good.[1] Hangzhou has currently channeled its energies into the industrial development of nine key sectors: 1. electronic information, a sector that reported the most revenue for 2016 and characterized by designing and manufacturing chips and providing solutions for electronic finance;[2] 2. manufacture of high-end equipment: production of aircraft parts, steam, gas and hydraulic turbines, air separation equipment, etc.[3]; 3. electric vehicles: Hangzhou is among the first pilot cities to promote electric vehicles[4]; 4. biomedicine; 5. conservation of energy, protection of the environment and new energies: in this segment we find firms that produce hydroelectric power, photovoltaic and LED devices, etc.; 6. software and information services, software development and e-commerce[5]; 7. cloud computing and big data; 8. Industrial design: Hangzhou has a state-level industrial design center, 52 provincial-level centers and 91 municipal-

---

1 In addition to Dajiangdong industrial area, there are six other parks in Hangzhou: Fuyang Economic and Technological Development Zone, Hangzhou Chengxi Technology Innovation Industry Cluster, Hangzhou National High-Tech Zone, Hangzhou Yuhang Economic and Technological Development Zone, Hangzhou Economic and Technological Development Area, and Xiaoshan Economic and Technological Development Zone.
2 Some companies that operate there are Eastcom and Silan Microelectronic.
3 Some companies in this field are Xizi Aviation, Hangzhou Boiler Group, Hangcha Group and Hangzhou Steam Turbine Group.
4 BYD works here. And Geely has built technology research and development centers with the goal of manufacturing electric cars.
5 Some companies that operate there are Alibaba, NetEase Hangzhou Network y Hikvision Digital.

level centers, employing approximately 10,000 workers; and 9. Internet of things: manufacture of products focused on video surveillance, radio frequency hardware, communication, networks, etc.[1] (Information Office of Hangzhou Municipal Government, 2018).

On the other hand, Hangzhou has positioned itself as an innovation center. In this regard, the Zhejiang Overseas High-level Talents Innovation Park was inaugurated in July 2010 and in December 2011 the park was updated to Future Sci-Tech City (FSTC) officially opened on January 2, 2012 (Xu, 2019, p. 259-260). This "city" has three support platforms, among which is "Dream Town". The latter was designed to promote the economic development of the city through Internet-related innovation, and has been thought of as an Internet incubation center for intelligent development throughout China. Dream Town has been favored in its development by the rapid growth of the information economy of Zhejiang as well as by the installation of Alibaba Group Internet Corporation. In this sense, Dream Town is a growth-oriented project promoted by government authorities, but in communication with non-state actors related to innovation, such as startups, venture capital industries, the Alibaba Group, etc. In this way, Dream Town represents an exemplary project of joint efforts made by the public and private sectors of China in order to promote the smart economy (Argyriou, 2019, p. 198).

In addition to FSTC, other development spaces such as Qingshan Lake Science and Technology City and Chengxi Sci-Tech Innovation Corridor were created, and the creation of Zijiangang Sci-Tech City was announced towards the end of 2017; in this sense, the city authorities hoped to attract 400 high-tech companies and 45 scientific research institutes by 2020 (China Daily, 2017). The objective of these "cities" is to create centers of technological development and innovation, concentrating there scientists, technicians and technology companies from China and the world; along these lines, the FSTC project is driven by the idea of articulating the development of resources with talented people and innovative

---

1   Some companies that operate there are Hikvision, Dahua Technology, Holley Technology y Lierda

industries (Argyriou, p. 2019, 198). In this context, a central objective of FSTC is the resettlement of high-quality foreign talent and professionals in strategic areas such as information economics, biomedicine, new energy and financial services. So far, by organizing the information based on the different government development strategies —Eight-Eight Strategy, Four major constructions and Four changes and three well-knows actors, we have been able to describe the economic growth of the province and the future development prospects. Thus, we have considered the scenario in which Geely has developed as an automotive company. Next, we will focus on the development of the company and the points of contact between the economic dynamics of the province and the path followed by the company.

II. Origin and development of Geely in the context of Zhejiang economic development

The history of Geely Automotive Group (GAG) dates back to 1984, when its founder, Li Shufu, began to enter in the business world by establishing a factory of accessories for refrigerators using the funds that he had managed to gather through his photographic studio and contributions of family members; however, after not obtaining the permits to carry out this activity, the factory had to close its doors and remained in the hands of the local government. (Zhou, 2019, p. 28; Qiu and Xu, 2016, p. 102; Anderson, 2012, p. 139). It was there when Li decided to found Geely, whose name is similar to the Chinese word "luck" (吉利). Li's next step, in 1993, was to start manufacturing motorcycles; nevertheless, as he was not licensed to do so, he started producing under the license that Jialing Motorcycle possessed; by this token he had manufactured 350,000 units by 1998 (Zhou, 2019, p. 27). However, Li's dream was to make cars, a task for which he also needed to have a license that he did not possess.

The industrial policy for the automotive sector by the central government during the 1980s was focused on the formation of Joint Ventures (JV) between state-owned enterprises (SOEs) and foreign companies. Only towards the end of the 1990s, the ban on private investment was lifted. From then on, some companies emerged later known as "the young tigers" emerged, which began to produce passenger vehicles after the conversion of their factories producing motorcycles or electronic products. Among these companies was Geely (Luo et al, 2006, pp. 36-40).[1]

After going through different businesses, Li Shufu finally began to concentrate his work on the development of a new automotive company from 1998 and he was able to obtain permission to build small cars and opened a factory in Zhejiang (Anderson, 2012, p. 141). The first car manufactured by Geely, the Haiqing, left the assembly line on August 8, 1998;[2] however, the cars were of poor quality and for that reason, according to Li's words, the first three lots did not go on sale and were directly discarded (Milne, 2014).

The founder of Geely warned that the manufacture of a car was a complex task, and the challenge was greater if it was intended to produce a high quality vehicle. Therefore, its new strategy was to produce cheap vehicles accessible to a sector of the population that was beginning to be able to have their first car and pay for it. Until that time, the Chinese automotive industry was monopolized by the JVs and the production of cars was targeted at the high-end market. Moreover, as Zhan (2018, p. 5) argues, the prices of cars sold by JVs in China were generally three or four times higher than those of the international market. In this line, Geely persisted with the strategy of focusing on the cheap car segment: since 2000 Geely sold cars below 40,000 RMB and, in 2004, under the competition of the Xiali model -manufactured by Tianjin FAW, a subsidiary of FAW Group-which sold for 31,800 RMB, Geely lowered its prices to 29,000 RMB, setting a historic minimum price (Qiu and Xu, 2016, p. 103).

The policy of protected development of the automotive industry that privileged large companies and JVs began to change from 2001 on when China joined the WTO, and Geely became the first private company to obtain a certificate for car

---

1 Among the "young tigers" stand out, on the side of private companies, Geely, Lifan, BYD, Bird and Aux; and on the side of state companies, Chery and Brillance.
2 The choice of day 8 of month 8 to present the new vehicle is framed in the Chinese cultural tradition, because the number 8 is considered a symbol of good fortune.

manufacturing. In 2003 the company signed a strategic cooperation agreement with China Everbright Bank and moved its sales and administration headquarters to Hangzhou, and in August of the same year it sold its first car abroad.

The company's growth was encouraging; nevertheless, to follow the path of growth it was necessary to have a larger capital, which the company did not have. In this regard, Geely began trading on the Hong Kong stock exchange in 2005 and, according to Anderson (2012, p. 142), in 2009 it also received an investment of 334 million dollars from Goldman Sachs.

In 2006, Geely's last step before entering a new stage, defined by the company as Era 2.0, was the acquisition of the 23 percent share of the UK-based Manganese Bronze Holding, thereby becoming the main shareholder of the company. Both companies created a new JV based in China in order to manufacture the iconic London Black Taxi, which is now exported from China in the form of SKD[1] for assembly in the United Kingdom (Anderson, 2012, p. 145).[2] Years later, in 2013, Geely acquired the entire company. Along these lines, Geely continued to invest in Britain in related businesses whose center was the classic London taxi. In this way, the acquisition of the Emerald Automotive startup in 2014 was added to the purchase of Manganese, in order to apply the technology developed by this company regarding electric vehicles and emission reduction to the manufacture of the new Taxi (ZGHG, 2014); besides, Geely invested in the construction of a new plant for LEVC in Coventry, an event for which Geely received the praise of the current British Prime Minister, Boris Johnson, then mayor of London (LEVC, 2015).

---

1 SKD (Semi-Completely Knocked-down) is a way in which the kits for the assembly of vehicles are delivered and it differ from the CKD -Completely Knocked Down-. While obtaining a new vehicle from a CKD kit only involves the assembly of its parts, a SKD kit requires additional work in the development of headlights, seats, plastic parts, glass, etc.; this last form is usually used to comply with certificates of origin and avoid taxes.
2 Manganese Bronze acquired BSA (Birmingham Small Arm Company) in 1973. BSA had previously bought the London Taxi Company (also called Carbodies) in 1954, the traditional black taxi manufacturer. Hence, when Geely acquired a stake in Manganese, it also acceded to London Taxi Co. Since 2017, London taxi is called London EV Company (LEVC).

Since 2007, the company transformed its initial strategy of manufacturing cheap cars by improving the quality and technology of its products, thus beginning the 2.0 Era. The key in this change was to gradually move from a strategy guided by low costs to a strategy of product-differentiation; hence, Geely began to build three sub-brands: Emgrand, Gleagle and Shanghai Yinglun (Zhan, 2018, p. 6).

In addition to the intended change in the quality of the vehicles produced, the 2.0 stage is characterized by the boost to exports and investments abroad (outward investment meant both the construction of new factories and the acquisition of companies). In this sense, we believe that the beginning of Geely's "global go" was stimulated for two reasons: on the one hand, to obtain new technologies and know-how through the acquisition of companies, in line with the new strategic plan; on the other hand, to build new vehicle assembly plants in order to reach different markets and to avoid the tax burdens that are usually applied by third countries to imports.

With regard to exports, Geely first entered in the countries of Southeast Asia, the Middle East and North Africa, regions with less inner competition and requirements (regarding energy consumption, emission reduction and vehicle safety). Besides, Geely also intended to increase sales in the Eurasian region, in countries like Russia and Belarus – also given that some countries in this region formed in 2015 the Eurasian Economic Union.[1]

In tune with the intention of consolidating itself in these regional markets, Geely invested in the construction of vehicle assembly plants in different countries. In this regard, Geely built in 2007 a factory in Indonesia, which started supplying the domestic and South Asian markets. The first attempt to cover this geographical area came with the failed investment attempted in Malaysia in 2005. There, after signing the agreement with IGC Group to manufacture, assemble and export cars, former Malaysian Prime Minister Mahathir said that the Chinese cars would take over the

---

[1] 2013 was the record high-year in Geely's export, reaching 118,871 vehicles representing a 22 percent of the company's total sales; among the main destinations of these exports were Russia, Egypt, Saudi Arabia, Iran and Ukraine (Wang, 2019, p. 12-14).

local market, and demanded that all vehicles produced be exported, a circumstance that led to dismiss the possibility of building the plant in that country (Wang, 2019, p. 11). Thus, the Malaysian government eliminated any competition that could threaten the local firm, Proton (Perusahaan Otomobil Nasional Bhd) (China Daily, 2006). In 2012 Geely signed an agreement with GB Auto (Ghabbour Group) to build a plant in Egypt for assembling cars from CKD kits, with a production capacity of 30,000 vehicles per year. In addition to covering the Egyptian market, from the new plant it was hoped to supply North Africa and the Middle East (Embassy of the People's Republic of China in the Arab Republic of Egypt, 2012).

Geely established in 2015 a joint venture in Belarus, Belgee, together with Belaz, one of the largest mining machinery manufacturing companies in the world, and SOYUZ – a local manufacturer of spare parts-, with the aim of assembling cars to be sold in the same Belarusian market and to export them to Russia and Ukraine. This investment was a milestone in the European country, given the fact that while Belgee became the first car assembly factory in that country, (until then, only agricultural and mechanical vehicles were produced there)(Resiale Viano, 2019)

Aside from the construction of new plants, in 2009 Geely returned to invest in the acquisition of foreign companies after the participation obtained in Manganese Bronze in 2006: it acquired the Australian company DSI (Drivetrain Systems International), the second largest automatic transmissions world manufacturer. The transaction would have been made for $ 40.22 million (Reuters, 2009). By this token, the Chinese company achieved know-how and new technologies to improve the quality of its vehicles, the primary objective of the 2.0 Era.

In 2010 ZGHG completed the purchase of the Volvo automobile division previously owned by Ford, receiving all physical and intangible assets including manufacturing plants and R&D centers and more than 10,000 patents (Zhan, 2018, p. 6). At this point, it should be clarified that the transaction was made by ZGHG and not by GAG -the company that is listed on the Hong Kong stock exchange and manufactures automobiles; ZGHG is a company owned in a 90 per cent share by Li Shufu; in addition, ZGHG had the 50.97 percent of GAG by 2012. Consequently, Li controls GAG and Volvo, but GAG was not involved in of Volvo's purchase (Anderson, 2012, p. 147). In this line, Li Shufu said that "Volvo is Volvo and Geely is Geely"; besides, the Volvo's operational independence has remained unchanged (Tie, 2019).

The key facilitating infrastructure in the cooperation between Geely and Volvo was the creation in 2013 of China Euro Vehicle Technology (CEVT), a subsidiary research and development center of Geely located in Gothenburg.[1] The financing for CEVT's development came from Geely -which owned intellectual property rights-, but knowledge was contributed by Volvo's experience in technology and security; in addition, the location of the plant has its advantages given the historic presence of Volvo in the city, the close relationship established by CEVT with industrial assets such as Volvo Technology, Volvo Informations Technology, and with the universities of Gothenburg and Chalmers (Yakov, et al., 2019, p. 65).

In this way, Geely acquired high-end core technology and improved its research and development capacity, but also contributed to the strengthening of the brand; while the Volvo brand allowed to gain presence in the high-end car segment, the Geely brand remained functional in the cheaper cars segment. Thus, the acquisition of the Swedish company evidences Geely's new strategy of growing in quality and safety of vehicles; In this regard, Li Shufu said: "We have fulfilled our dream of acquiring Volvo, but that is not the end of our plan; it is only the starting point" (cit. in Fang and Leung, 2010).

In April 2014, Geely announced that it was leaving Era 2.0 behind to enter Era 3.0. The goal of Era 3.0 was to build the brand with the proposal to "make refined cars

---

1   The company's objective was to develop a state-of-the-art modular platform, the Compact Modular Architecture (CMA), that would allow the development of the new generation of Volvo and Geely C-segment vehicles - comparable to the Ford Focus or Audi A3 models- (Yakov, et al., 2019, p. 66). Modular platforms allow brands to develop new car models from a single base, saving time and new expenses.

for everyone". Thus, the company began fragmenting the brand into five models: the "Panda" focused on the mini-car market, the "King Kong" in the small car market, the "Vision" in the market for low-end compact sport utility vehicles (SUV), the "Emgrand Borui" focused in the mid-range sedan, and the "Emgrand Boyue" in compact SUVs (Zhan, 2018, p. 6).[1]

In the context of Era 3.0, Geely launched in 2017 launched its new brand, LYNK & CO, which was developed by more than 2000 engineers from more than 20 countries in the Geely European R&D center and is based on the CMA platform developed jointly by Volvo and Geely (Zhan, 2018, p. 7). While Geely is aimed at the mass market, LYNK & CO intends to position itself as a premium brand (Geely Group, n/d). The Geely investments abroad continued in this new stage in line with the strategy of the previous stage; in this sense, the company continued with its intentions to gain presence in the Asian market and to acquire new technologies. In 2017, Geely Automotive acquired the 49.9 percent share of Proton, that company for which the Malaysian government had blocked Geely's investments in the country to avoid competition. With the acquisition of Proton, Geely also achieved a 51 percent stake in the Lotus Company.[2]

In the same year, Geely continued adding participation in different companies that could provide it with technology. Geely paid $ 3,270 million for 8.2 percent of AB Volvo, which was in the hands of Cevian Capital, a Swedish investment firm; thus, the Chinese company achieved participation in the second worldwide truck manufacturer (Resiale Viano, 2019). In addition, in a clear bet to the future, Geely acquired the American startup Terrafugia in the same year; Terrafugia was founded by graduates of the Massachusetts Institute of Technology in 2006, and

---

1 The car models produced by Geely are often referred to differently according to the region where they are sold: Panda (also called Geely LC or Gleagle GX2); King Kong (also called Geely MK or Englon EC6); Vision (also called Geely Yuanjing, Gleagle FC or Gleagle GC7); Borui (also called Emgrand GT); Boyue (also called Emgrand NL-3, Geely NL-3, Geely Atlas, Geely Emgrand X7 Sport, Proton X70).
2 In 1996 Proton had acquired the majority share of Lotus Cars, the famous British sports and racing car brand founded by Colin Chapman in 1952.

was devoted to the development of flying cars (Terrafugia, 2017). In 2018, Geely shook the automotive environment again in the same way that he did when it acquired Volvo in 2010; on this occasion, the reason was the acquisition of the 9.7 percent of Daimler's shares (Zhou, 2019, p. 27). The transaction raised alert in the German government, which expressed that it would have "a watchful eye" on the Chinese investments in Germany arguing that China intended to access the European technological innovations (Berría, 2019). Along these lines, the Minister of Economy of the Teutonic country declared that they should be vigilant, because although Germany is open to investments, Germany should not be used to favor the interests of other countries' industrial policies (Resiale Viano, 2019). In addition to the aforementioned transaction, both firms devised the formation of a JV to manufacture Smart electric vehicles that should be available for sale in 2022 (Daimler, n/d). Besides, the partnership between Geely and Daimler is not only focused on the development of electric cars per se. It is also aimed at joining forces to face the Uber and Google outposts in the electric cars market (Taylor and Shirouzu, 2019).

To summarize Geely's operations abroad, we have constructed the following scheme (Table 3):

Table 3 Geely Foreign Investment, 2007-2018

Year	country	Purpose	company
2007	Indonesia	Construction of a new factory	
2009	Australia	Acquisition of company	DSI
2010	Sweden	Acquisition of company	Volvo
2012	Egypt	Construction of a new factory	
2013	England	Acquisition of company	Manganese Bronze
2014	England	Acquisition of company	Emerald Automotive
2015	England	Construction of a new factory	
	Belarus	Construction of a new factory	
2017	Malaysia	Acquisition of company	Proton

Contd

Year	country	Purpose	company
	United States	Acquisition of company	Terrafugia
	Sweden	Acquisition of company	Volvo Trucks
2018	Germany	Acquisition of company	Daimler

Own Elaboration.

Summing up, we can say that ZGHG currently has 12 production bases in China,[1] and factories in the United States, United Kingdom, Egypt, Belarus and Indonesia -under the name of Geely Automotive or Volvo -(Wang, 2019, p. 10); R&D centers in Hangzhou (Geely), Ningbo (Geely), Gothenburg (Geely and Volvo), Copenhagen (Volvo), Shanghai (Volvo) and Coventry (LEVC); design centers in Los Angeles, Gothenburg, Barcelona and Shanghai. ZGHG has more than 80,000 employees, including 50,000 in GAG, 31,000 in Volvo and 1,000 in LEVC (Geely Group, n/d). This account of Geely's assets allows us to measure the growth of the company and perceive the firmness with which it has decided to advance in the technological scale of its products. In this sense, Geely is no stranger to the changing times that the automotive industry is experiencing worldwide, and is trying to adapt to it; an example of this is the last partnership established with Daimler.

In this sense, the company began to work relatively late in the design and manufacture of electric cars, for example, BYD started in 2008; However, it is not sparing any effort, and by 2018 it had 10,000 employees worldwide only in the R&D areas (Zhan, 2018, p. 22-23). In addition to the research tasks, the company owns Geely Commercial Vehicle (GCV), a new energy –electric and hybrid- commercial vehicle firm acting as support for two of Geely's brands in this segment: the aforementioned LEVC and Yuan Cheng Auto (Geely Group, n/d).

Currently, Geely is on track to meet the objective of the "20200 Strategy", formulated by the GAG in 2016 in the context of the celebrations for the 30th

---

[1] These plants are: Taizhou Linhai and Taizhou Road and Bridge (Taizhou), Ningbo Hangzhou Bay and Ningbo Chunxiao (Ningbo), Shanghai, Chengdu (Sichuan), Zhangjiakou (Hebei), Jinan (Shandong), Xiangtan (Hunan), Baoji y Jinzhong (Shanxi), Guiyang (Guizhou) (Zhan, 2018, p. 24-25).

anniversary of the foundation of ZGHC by Li Shufu; the objective is to produce 2 million vehicles by 2020, a figure that seems to be close of being achieved (Table 4).

Table 4 Geely: Vehicle production per year and world ranking position.

Year	Production	World Ranking	Year	Production	World Ranking
2017	1,950,382	15	2010	802,319	20
2016	1,266,456	19+	2009	330,275	27
2015	999,802	21	2008	220,955	31
2014	890,652	21	2007	216,774	327
2013	969,896	20	2006	207,149	33
2012	922,906	21	2005	149,532	32
2011	897,107	21	2004	91,744	41

Own elaboration. Sources: International Organization of Motor Vehicle Manufacturers, 2019

Now, how could Geely became a global automotive player in so few years? The answer to this question must be found in a combination of different factors.

The first is the leadership of the firm's founder, Li Shufu, and the socio-cultural context of Zhejiang. As Anderson (2012, p. 148) argues, it would be difficult to argue that Geely would exist in the absence of Li Shufu's energy and audacity. This is due, to the entrepreneurial and persistent character of Li in businesses, whose end result has been the success of his company. In this sense, the businessman is seen nationally and abroad as a man who was born from a modest family in a rural area and created an economic empire thanks to his own effort, earning in the West the nickname of the "Chinese Henry Ford" and the "Asian Elon Musk" (Berría, 2018). This entrepreneurial spirit of Li is largely attributed to the cultural tradition of Zhejiang Province; for example, some argue that the founder of Geely carries with him the adventurous genes of the people of Zhejiang (Wu, 2017, p. 50).[1] Some authors have gone further, and argue that the "entrepreneurial spirit" of the people

---

1 Similarly, Zong Qinghou, founder of the Wahaha Group, is also considered a representative of the entrepreneurial spirit of the province. (Wu, 2017, p. 50)

of Zhejiang can be traced back to the Tang dynasty (Yang, 2012). Beyond the fact that this last statement is very hard to verify, the truth is that the "entrepreneurial spirit" idea is present in the inhabitants of Zhejiang and constitutes a very strong identity feature in the population of the province. In this sense, some skills such as knowing how to live with risks, the perseverance, adaptation to circumstances, and the perception of "opportunity", among other characteristics, form a common atmosphere within which individuals develop themselves; therefore, this environment helps to extinguish or lessen the burden of some social convictions, such as the "failure" after not being able to succeed in different businesses undertaken.

The second factor is the economic context. We stated in our first section the great economic growth of the province, and this economic growth was also accompanied by an increase in the consumption of vehicles on behalf of the population. As can be seen in Table 5, car ownership in Zhejiang Province over the past 10 years has been higher than in the rest of the most developed Eastern Coastal Chinese provinces–except for the years 2010 and 2012, where it was slightly surpassed by Guangdong province-and it has been well above the general consumption of cars in all China.

The reasons explaining the growth of consumption must be found in the size of the population, the improvement in purchasing power, and in the urbanization growth. In addition, as Zhan (2018, pp. 10-11) expresses, the cars are a status and wealth symbol; judging by social customs, young people pretend to marry and have a house and a car, so nothing suggests that vehicle consumption will decrease in the future. In this sense, the construction of a moderately prosperous and well-off society also implies the construction of a "car society"; to achieve this end, the medium and long-term plan for the automotive industry launched in 2017 by the State Council has supported the expansion, strengthening and cross-border integration of automotive companies (Zhan, 2018, p. 9). Thus, GAG has benefited from this growing demand, especially from those who access a vehicle for the first time, while ZGHG through Volvo has been able to meet the demand for high-end cars.

III. Geely in Argentina: present and perspectives

Within the context of the Go Global policy promoted by the Chinese government and the company's expansion around the world, Geely entered the Argentine market at the end of 2016, through the Uruguayan company Grupo Fiancar. The negotiation process for the arrival of the Chinese brand began in 2013, but it was only able to enter the country three years later, after the governmental change which took place in 2015.[1]

With the entry of Geely, three were the Chinese automakers with a presence in Argentina in 2016, along with Chery and Lifan. However, numerous firms from the eastern country were arriving: JMC, Foton, Zotye and DFM in 2017, and BAIC, DFSK, DFM, JMC, BYD and JAC in 2018. Thus, in a little more than two years there was a flood of Chinese automakers in the country, a circumstance that can be explained by the changes in Argentine economic policy referred above. The arrival of the various Chinese vehicle brands occurred through importers and local representatives, in the same way that Chery, the first Chinese automaker to sell cars in Argentina, had acted through the local firm Socma -property of Grupo Macri-eight years before. Geely's behavior in Argentina is similar to the rest of the Chinese automakers in the country: it acts through local importers and its goal is to conquer the cheap car segment. In this sense, in 2016, among the five cheapest cars sold in Argentina were the Geely LC and the Chery QQ. In 2018 both vehicles were among the least expensive, the Geely LC being the second cheapest model in the market, only behind the Volkswagen Up (Ámbito Financiero, 2016b; 2018). In addition to focusing on economic vehicles to gain market share, Geely's strategy

---

[1] While the second Cristina Kirchner (2011-2015) administration was characterized by a strong control of imports (through the imposition of high tariffs, import prohibition of certain products and difficulties in obtaining dollars to pay for imports), the government of Mauricio Macri (2015-2019) was characterized by an opening perspective, with a rapid deregulation of exchange controls and the elimination of import restrictions taking place.

was also focused on after-sales services; along these lines, Federico Mayora, General Manager of Geely Argentina, expressed that the strategy to land in the Argentine market was to set up a network from north to south and from east to west, so that the Argentine buyer of Geely can have an official service backup and original parts of Geely available throughout Argentina, so that he can make its work or family trips throughout the country without worrying about assistance in case of having any problem with the vehicle (Perfil, 2018). This last point is very important, because Argentine consumers are reluctant to buy Chinese vehicles on the basis of the prejudice that these cars are of poor quality. Breaking that barrier and gaining consumer confidence is the main challenge Geely faces. It is convenient to add that Argentina, despite not being among the most economically developed countries, has a vast tradition in the manufacture of cars: it is one of the leading producers of vehicles in Latin America -along with Brazil and Mexico-and it has the presence there of factories of the main automotive companies worldwide –Ford, General Motors, Volkswagen, Fiat, Renault, Nissan, Toyota and Honda-. In this sense, Argentine consumers are demanding regarding the benefits they expect to receive from a new vehicle, and are willing to pay for it. At the beginning of Geely's journey through Argentina, the company's objective was to consolidate itself as the best-selling Chinese brand in the country, with the possibility of refloating the assembly of cars in Uruguay to provide the Argentine and Brazilian market from there, not ruling out even possible direct investments also in Argentina (Argentina Autoblog, 2016). However, by 2019 the scenario is completely different; in a context of economic crisis, vehicle consumption has been drastically reduced -a 45% drop in 0km car patents compared to 2018-(Argentina Autoblog, 2019), the production has fallen in line with the reduction in demand, and in the factories the idle capacity and the personnel suspensions increase altogether. In this line, by September many of the imported brands were rethinking their presence in the country -most of them had not sold more than 10 vehicles in the month-, with possibilities of concentrating several brands in few hands; For example, businessman Hugo Belcastro, importer of BAIC and Foton, acknowledged being in negotiations to keep also the Geely brand (Alonso, 2019).[1] In addition to the drop in demand, new levies for imported cars will come into force next year (January 2020).[2] Moreover, the Chamber of Official Importers and Distributors of Automotive (Cidoa, acronym in Spanish) announced that this would put the activities of many imported brands at risk; among the affected brands are many of the Chinese firms, including Geely (TNAutos, 2019).

Chery, with more tradition in the country, is a leader in sales as far as Chinese cars are concerned, followed by Lifan. We lack more recent data, but according to Geely Argentina (2019), in 2018 1500 units of the brand circulated throughout the country; this would mean that in 2018 sales increased approximately 200 percent compared to 2017. However, despite the fact that Chinese car sales are growing, their share in total vehicle sales is still very limited, approaching 1 percent.[3]

Finally, we can say that with the presence of 23 dealers throughout the country, a commitment to economic cars—in a context of crisis -and with the persistent strategy focused on after-sales services, the marketing of Geely in the country could prosper; however it will be first necessary to closely monitor the recovery of the population's purchasing power, which if it happens, can be slow; therefore, the importing firm must have sufficient economic capacity to sustain the structure for a while hoping for the recovery of the economy; in addition, Geely must be attentive to the economic policy of the new government regarding imports; and, third, it must continue to work in order to combat the preconceptions that weigh on Chinese cars.[4]

---

1. Other recognized Chinese vehicle importers include the Grupo Socma (Chery, JAC and DFSK) and Grupo CarOne (Haval, Changan and Great Wall).
2. From that day on, vehicles with wholesale price from 1,300,000 pesos (about 1,700,000 pesos to the public, 26,000 dollars, approx.) will pay a 20 percent tax, and from $ 2,400,000 (about 3,100,000 pesos to the public, 49,000 dollars approx.) a 35 percent tax.
3. Before the deepening of economic crisis in the country, Chinese vehicle importers in Argentina hoped to reach 2 percent of the market by 2019-2020
4. In this sense, in 2018 Geely offered a guarantee of 5 years, or 150,000 kilometers, on its vehicles.

IV. Final Considerations

In the first section of this study we addressed the economic growth of Zhejiang, and we found that it started from the Reform and Opening-up period. In this sense, we reviewed the characteristics of this growth through of the "Eight-Eight Strategy", the "Four major constructions" and the "Four changes and three well-knows actors". In addition, we considered that the particular economic performance of the province resulted in the formation of the so called "Zhejiang Model", in which private companies play a preponderant role, without however being the State role secondary or neglecting. Along these lines, we also considered the emphasis placed on continuing this economic growth through the development of science, research, technology and environmental care; and we pointed out that Hangzhou city is a good example of this. At this point, we must also note that this choice for economic development based on science and technology corresponds to the joint work between the private and public sectors. In line with the above-stated, we discussed Geely's case. In this way, we were able to observe how the development of the company, especially in its stage 1.0 (1997-2007) had the backing and political support of the local and provincial governments, a circumstance that paved the way for the great growth of the company. After becoming a leading company in the sector, it began to be supported by the central government in the context of Go Out policy; in this way, coinciding with Stage 2.0 (2007-2014), the company began to invest abroad by means of both the installation of new factories and acquisition of already existing companies. This last point allowed Geely to acquire fundamental foreign technology to carry out the "technological leap" and develop new

scientific research institutes—the CEVT in Gothenburg is an example of this, also in line with the government's strategy of encouraging an increase in the technological scale. Thus, Geely began its 3.0 Era continuing the policy of acquiring new technologies by adding participation or acquiring foreign companies, but now focusing on technologies linked to the development of electric vehicles and emission reduction, key aspects to be applied apply in the new company's models; thus, on the one hand, Geely places itself at the forefront of automotive developments worldwide; on the other hand, it harmonizes its business strategy with the policies of the Chinese government aimed at reducing pollution and gases emitted by vehicles, thereby contributing with the development of a "Green Zhejiang". Finally, we considered Geely's experience in Argentina. The arrival of the Chinese firm in the South American country has been recent, and this arrival has occurred through the export of vehicles, not registering investments -and they are not planned in the near future-. Thus, Geely entered Argentina in 2016, when the country began to experience one of the biggest economic crises after having left behind that of 2001, an aspect that directly affected the automotive market. In this scenario, we believe that the ability of importers to wait for demand recovery will be essential, knowing that in conditions of stability the Argentine car market is very dynamic. Continuing to bet on the cheap vehicle sector can be a good strategy, especially when thinking about consumers who begin to leave behind an economic crisis. However, the national government's policy regarding imports will have to be closely followed, a factor that would directly influence the prices of imported cars and, therefore, make it difficult to compete in the economic vehicles section. Given this scenario, if Argentina's demand recovers, it would be possible to think about investments in the neighboring country of Uruguay to assemble there the Geely vehicles that could enter Argentina and thereby enjoy the tax benefits that MERCOSUR assures for regional production—Uruguay also would be the springboard to enter the Brazilian market. To conclude, we believe that another challenge that Geely will have to face, in the medium term, is to be able to conquer the demanding Argentine consumer with their models and, for this, price and after sales services will not be enough; it will have to provide greater quality / technology / safety and comfort in cars.

References

Alonso, H. (October 23, 2019) Importadores de autos buscan salir del país por caída de ventas, Ámbito Financiero. Available: https://www.ambito.com/economia/

autos/importadores-autos-buscan-salir-del-paiscaida-ventas-n5061339

Ámbito Financiero (December 20, 2016a) Desembarca nueva marca china. Available: https://www.ambito.com/edicion-impresa/desembarca-nueva-marca-china-n3966435).

Ámbito Financiero (December 26, 2016b) Avanzada: ya dos de los diez modelos de autos más baratos son chinos. Available: https://www.ambito.com/edicionimpresa/avanzada-ya-dos-los-diez-modelos-autos-mas-baratos-son-chinos-n3967087)

Ámbito Financiero (January 10, 2018) Duro inicio de 2018: ya no quedan autos de menos de $200.000-. Available: https://www.ambito.com/edicion-impresa/duro-inicio2018-ya-no-quedan-autos-menos-200000-n4008914)

Anderlini, J. (March 28, 2018) Chinese tycoons have to play the connections game, Financial Times. Available: https://www.ft.com/content/2e9c859c-31b6-11e8-b5bf23cb17fd1498

Anderson, G. (2012). Designated drivers. How China plans to dominate the global auto industry. Singapore: John Wiley & Sons.

Argentina Autoblog (December 13, 2016) Apuntes del lanzamiento de Geely Argentina. Available: https://autoblog.com.ar/2016/12/13/apuntes-del-lanzamiento-degeely-argentina/

Argentina Autoblog (October 3, 2019) La Argentina se desploma en el ranking de ventas de autos por habitante. Available: https://autoblog.com.ar/2019/10/03/la-argentina-se-desploma-en-el-ranking-de-ventas-de-autos-por-habitante/

Argyriou, I. (2019). The smart city of Hangzhou, China: the case of Dream Town Internet Village, in: Anthopoulos, L.(Ed). Smart City Emergence. Cases from around the world. Amsterdam: Elsevier, 195-218.

Asociación de Concesionarios de Automotores de la República Argentina

(ACARA) (2018). Yearbook 2017.

Berría, C. (March 20, 2018). Cómo Li Shufu, el hijo de un granjero chino, logró convertirse en dueño de Geely, la mayor accionista de Mercedes-Benz, BBC Mundo. Available: https://www.bbc.com/mundo/noticias-43404785

China Daily (November 2, 2017). New sci-tech city to promote innovation in Hangzhou city. Available: http://subsites.chinadaily.com.cn/regional/zhejiang/201711/02/c_151412.htm

China Daily (September 28, 2006). Geely to make cars in Indonesia. Available: http://www.chinadaily.com.cn/business/2006-09/28/content_698874.htm

Daimler (n/d). Joint Venture with Geely. Daimler and Geely Holding form global joint venture to develop smart. Available: https://www.daimler.com/company/joint-venturewith-geely.html

Embassy of the People's Republic of China in the Arab Republic of Egypt (October 22, 2012). The assembling plant for Geely cars launched in Egypt. Available:

Fang, Y. and Leung, A. (August 1, 2010). China's Geely completes Volvo buy. Reuters. Available: https://www.reuters.com/article/us-geely/chinas-geely-completes-volvo-buyidUSTRE66S1TC20100802

Geely Argentina (2019). Available: https://geelyargentina.com/

Geely Automotive Group (2019). Available: http://global.geely.com/

Geely Group (n/d). Available: https://www.geely.cl

He, X. (September 9, 2019). Government reform and "sharing" development. Lecture given at the Zhejiang Gongshang University.

Ho, L. (October 25, 2012). Xi Jinping's time in Zhejiang: doing the business, South China Morning Post. Available: https://www.scmp.com/news/china/article/1068825/chinas-leadership-transition-xijinpings-time-zhejiang

Huang, Y. (2013). A Study on Utilization Efficiency of Non-state-owned Investment to Regional Economy. A Case Study of Zhejiang Province. Singapore: International Conference on Management Innovation and Business Innovation, 15, 160-164.

Information Office of Hangzhou Municipal Government (2018). Available: http://www.ehangzhou.gov.cn//

International Organization of Motor Vehicle Manufacturers (2019). Available: http://www.oica.net/

Jin, P. (2006). The study of culture of supporting Zhejiang economic development. Zhejiang. (Master Thesis). Zhejiang University of Technology.

LEVC (March 6, 2015), Geely to invest £250m in new London Taxi site to develop next-generation green cab. Available: https://www.levc.com/corporate/news/geely-toinvest-250m-in-new-london-taxi-site-to-develop-next-generation-green-cab/ -Li, R. (2015). Empirical research about effect of economic growth on employment based on Hangzhou city. Changsha: 3rd International Conference on Education, Management, Arts, Economics and Social Science.

Lu, X. (2007). Comparison of "Zhejiang model" and "Jiangsu model" of China and encouragement of endogenous export-oriented strategy in developing countries. Network Ideas. Available: http://www.networkideas.org/feathm/mar2007/PDF/Lu_Xia.pdf

Luo, J., Roos, D. and Moavenzadeh, J. (2006). The Impact of Government Policies on Industrial Evolution: The Case of China's Automotive Industry. (Master Thesis in Technology and Policy), Massachusetts Institute of Technology, Cambridge.

Milne, R. (April 6, 2014) How a photographer became China's answer to Henry Ford. Financial Time. Available: https://www.ft.com/content/e83a97f2-bb2a-11e3-948c00144feabdc0

NBSC. China Statistical Yearbook, from 2000 to 2018. Available: http://www.stats.gov.cn/english/Statisticaldata/AnnualData/

Perfil (June 28, 2018) Geely, autos que llegaron para quedarse en Argentina. Available: https://www.perfil.com/noticias/tecnologia/geely-autos-que-llegaron-paraquedarse-en-argentina.phtml

Qi, Z. (2019). Ecology: clean, clearwaters and lush mountains, "Gold and Silver Mountain", in: Liu, Y., Huang, Q. and Wang, J. (Ed.) Chinese dream and practice in Zhejiang-General Report Volume, Singapore: Springer.

Resiale Viano, J. M. (2019) La industria automotriz china en el nuevo siglo: consolidación local y expansión hacia nuevos mercados (2004-2019), in: Santillán, G. and Mina, F. (eds.). El Noreste Asiático en el escenario contemporáneo. Córdoba. 172-Reuters (March 28, 2009). China's Geely to pay up to $40 mln in DSI purchase. Available: https://www.reuters.com/article/geely/chinas-geely-to-pay-up-to-40-mln-indsi-purchase-idUSHKG6622220090328

Shi, L. and Ganne, B. (2009). Understanding the Zhejiang industrial clusters:Questions and re-evaluations. Asian Industrial Clusters, Global Competitiveness and New Policy Initiatives. World Scientific, 239-266.

State Council Information Office (2018). Xi's Huzhou trip: The birth of "Two Mountains" theory. Available:http://english.scio.gov.cn/topnews/2018-05/08/content_51175998.htm

Taylor, E. and Shirouzu, N. (March 28, 2019). Daimler to develop Smart brand together with Geely. Reuters. Available: https://www.reuters.com/article/us-daimlergeely-electric/daimler-to-develop-smart-brand-together-with-geely-idUSKCN1R90NG

Terrafugia (November 13, 2017). Zhejiang Geely Holding Group completes acquisition of Terrafugia, Inc. Available: https://terrafugia.com/2017/11/13/zhejiang-geely-holdinggroup-completes-acquisition-of-terrafugia-inc/

Tie, C. (2019). Research on Geely Group's cross-cultural integration strategy in the perspective of comparative management. Shenzhen: 2019 International Conference on Education, Management, Economics and Humanities.

TN Autos (December 24, 2019) Cuáles son las 22 marcas de autos que podrían irse del país por la Ley de Solidaridad Social. Available: https://tn.com.ar/autos/lo-ultimo/cuales-son-las-22-marcas-de-autos-que-podrian-irse-del-pais-por-la-ley-de-solidaridad-social_1020903

Wang, X. (2019). Analysis of Geely Group's location selection for transnational operation. (Master Thesis), Lanzhou: Lanzhou University of Finance and Economics.

Wu, X. (2017). From the experience of Li Shufu, we can see the evolution of a Chinese entrepreneur. Resource Recycling, 50-51

Xia, H. (2010). Study on the Relationship between Financial Development and Economic Growth of Zhejiang Province. (Master Thesis in Regional Economy). Zhejiang, College of Economic and Managment, Zhejiang Normal University.

Xu, J. (2019). Zhejiang economic development and the chinese dream. In: Pei, C. and Xu, J. (Ed.). Chinese dream and practice in Zhejiang-Economy, Singapore: Springer.

Yakob, R., Nakamura, H. R. and Ström, P. (2018).Chinese foreign acquisitions aimed for strategic asset-creation and innovation upgrading: The case of Geely and Volvo Cars. Technovation, 70/71, 59-72.

Yang, Z. (May 17, 2012). Zhejiang model gets a boost from "banking bess". China.org Available: http://www.china.org.cn/opinion/2012-05/17/content_25408564.htm

Yuan, L. (2019); Economy: pressure-induced change, active guidance, en: Liu, Y., Huang, Q. and Wang, J. (Ed.). Chinese dream and practice in Zhejiang-General

Report Volume, Singapore: Springer.

ZGHG (February 28, 2014) Emerald Automotive Acquired By Zhejiang Geely Holding Group. Available: http://zgh.com/media-center/news/20140228_1/?lang=en

Zhan, J. (2018). Research on the development strategy of Geely Automobile Group. (Master Thesis) Beijing: Capital University of Economics and Business

Zhou, Y. (2019). China Geely Group development path from perspective of trade barriers. Shandong Textile Economy, 1, 26-28.

中国在巴西投资的机会

马睿婷 【巴西】
圣保罗大学　法学博士 / 联邦参议院监管、经济、商业和商业法　立法顾问

罗杰里奥 【巴西】
圣保罗大学　研究生 / 新卡尔达斯学院　教授

中国已成为世界上最大的经济体，但仍有内部挑战需要克服[1]。

20世纪80年代初，中国开始改革，以适当满足扩大公共服务覆盖面的需要，以及其他政治目标，保持中央政府的主导地位并给予当地政府、公共机构和企业更多的自主权。20世纪90年代以来，中国开始了以市场为导向的公用事业改革，引入竞争机制，改革管理体制，试行资本多元化方案[2]，推广吸引外资的方式。

"中国在1995年由全国人大、电力部和交通部共同发布的《关于批准外商投资特许经营试点项目有关问题的通知》（BOT通知）中，特许经营首次获得了合法地位。该通知指出，能源和通信等基础设施是发展的瓶颈。除了鼓励外商通过中外合资经营企业、中外合作经营企业和外商独资企业进行投资外，国家还计划采用BOT的方式来建设外商投资试点项目。"[3]

1　Shen, Dajun. Access to Water and Sanitation in China: History, Current Situation and Challenges. UNDP: Human Development Report Office, 2006. http://hdr.undp.org/sites/default/files/shen_dajun.pdf.
2　Wei, Yan. Regulating Municipal Water Supply Concessions. Springer Berlin Heidelberg. Edição do Kindle.
3　Wei, Yan. Regulating Municipal Water Supply Concessions. Springer Berlin Heidelberg. Edição do Kindle.

在某种程度上，外资参与中国公共事业，尤其是污水和配水行业的时间比巴西在这方面早。2002年，公用事业特许经营项目的经验被引入中国的行政实践中，并与合同一起成为领先的法律模式。

下表中详细说明了私营和外国资本在这些领域的参与情况。

表一　　　　　　　　中国供水行业私人参与门槛 *

项目	民营投资	外国投资
水工业所有权		
水厂	是	是
水网	法律法规没有明确规定	是的，但国有企业持有控股权
水资产转让	是	是
供水行业的运营	是	是
强制性合资企业		
水厂	否	否
水网	私人参与仅限于国内私营部门的参与	是
拥有特许权的权利		
水厂	是	是
水网	是	是
特许权的可转让性	受限	受限
土地使用权的法律约束	否	否
税收优惠	否	否
征用的条件	公共利益	公共利益
从当地国际来源获得融资的可能性	是	是

*（Wei, Yan. *Regulating Municipal Water Supply Concessions* (p. 35). Springer Berlin Heidelberg. Edição do Kindle）

特许权通过授权书、政府命令、特许权合同、政府命令下的项目实施协议、资产转让协议或管理权转让协议、购水协议、合资企业合同或公司章程以及委托合同的方式授予[1]。法律标准由有权授予特许权的市政当局确定。

目前，围绕着加强问责制的需要而提出的批评越来越多，并提出了许多方法，

1　Wei, Yan. Regulating Municipal Water Supply Concessions. Springer Berlin Heidelberg. Edição do Kindle.

以完善对特许权的管束。例如，2005 年，《关于加强市政公用事业监管的意见》强调了市政府和省级政府的监督作用，需要完善特许权法以及公用事业法规的能力建设。

在一些作者看来，中国将受益于一个更清晰的法律框架，即政府和私人实体之间的合同，这些实体更希望参与污水和供水行业。对于这些作者来说，如果中国司法部门对这些合同采取更明确和适当的方法，以及更透明和参与性更强的污水和供水政策，最后，根据法律赋予国有企业（State Owned Enterprises）无论是否是合资企业，或在污水和供水合同中起主导作用的私人行为者相应的管理责任，就能更好地解决效率和缺乏问责的问题。

表二　　　中国私人参与污水处理和供水行业的法律法规现状

参数	分析
适用范围	城市供水、供气、供热、公共交通、污水处理、垃圾处理等（《办法》2004）：（1）供水、供气、供热；（2）污水和固体废物处理；（3）城市轨道交通和其他公共交通；（4）市政府确定的其他城市基础设施（北京，2005）
签约机构	直辖市、市和县政府的市政公用事业主管部门（《办法》2004）、区县政府的市政公用事业主管部门以及由直辖市和区县政府（北京，2005）、市政府（深圳，2005）指定的部门。在实践中，市政府通常作为一个整体协调所有相关部门，并负责整个项目。不管具体的承包权限如何，市政府都有最终决定权。
特许权的形式（BOT、TOT 等）	"特许权"定义下的安排形式是什么？参见（深圳，2005），包括 BOT、TOT、提供服务的委托和法律法规规定的其他形式。
	在中国，除特许权合同外，还可通过多种方式授予特许权。曾有人总结，在实践中，至少有八种方式被用来授予特许权：（1）授权书（深圳，2005）；（2）政府命令（如上海大昌水厂项目）；（3）特许权合同（如成都第六水厂 BOT）；（4）根据政府命令的项目实施协议；（5）资产转让协议或管理权转让协议；（6）购水协议；（7）合营合同或者章程；（8）委托合同。
特许权的排他性	关于是否授予独家经营权没有明确规定，但（深圳，2005）除外，它明确规定，在同一行业中，应授予两个或两个以上运营商独家经营权，但受行业性质或地区条件限制的情况除外。然而，在实践中，总是由特许经营者获得专有权。
赔偿条款	（北京，2005）第 32 条规定："在符合公共利益的前提下，政府可以收回特许权、终止特许协议、征用特许经营的城市基础设施，或指示特许公司提供公共产品或服务，但应按照特许协议进行赔偿。"这意味着补偿协议是保护投资者的先决条件。

续表

参数	分析
特许经营商选择的可预见性	这已在第3部分中讨论过。目前最大的问题是，特许公司的选择或多或少受到主管官员的控制，对选择方法和程序的规定也很模糊。
客观监管规则	城市供水行业受相关部门的监管，如建设部（自2008年后改为住房和城乡建设部）、财政部和水利部。尚未制定独立的法规。监管职能在一定程度上仍与所有权结构相结合。在重庆的案例中，合资特许公司和重庆水务集团直接受市政府监管，而非上述任何行政部门。
与其他法律的一致性	除了一些专门管理供水行业的法律法规外，许多管理外国投资的法律法规也会影响供水行业。到目前为止，规范管理特许权的最高法律效力和临时文件是建设部2004年发布的《办法》，根据《行政许可法》第1554条的规定，该文件可能与地方法规的适用性相冲突。
特许权合同的可谈判性：水价和收益率	从沈阳和兰州的选定案例中我们可以看出，政府当局和特许公司之间就合同条款进行的谈判是非常有保障的。
法院或仲裁裁决的可执行性	特许权合同的法律性质目前仍在辩论中，这给行政或民事法庭的索赔带来了困难。有关特许权的法庭案件相当有限。实践中的争议更可能通过谈判解决，仲裁条款会在特许权合同中规定，并在特许权立法中给出建议。

随着城市地区的高速增长，中国地方社会在社会层面经历了深刻的变化，随之而来产生了许多影响这些地区基础设施的问题，尤其是环境卫生。自1978年改革开放以来，中国社会的各个领域都在经历着日益增长的城市化和现代化现象。到2008年底，中国的城市化率已达到人口的45.7%。

历史上中国人口生活在农村地区，那里的经济活动基本上以农业为基础。其人口因开始有公民到城市寻找更好的生活条件而流失[1]。这些家庭对传统耕种投入的管理并没有考虑到最基本的健康保护，这也造成了农村人口的身体健康问题。

值得注意的是，在中国的边远城市，公共厕所没有遵守卫生和质量标准，因为这些人的教育水平并不高，他们在该领域的工作需要时间和精力[2]。

---

[1] ALVES, Frederick Fagundes and TOYOSHIMA, Silvia Harumi. Disparidade Socioeconomica e fluxo migratorio chines: interpretacao de eventos contemporaneous Segundo os classicos do desenvolvimento. Rev. econ. contemp. [online]. 2017, vol.21, n.1 [cited 2019-12-28], e172115. http://www.scielo.br/scielo.php?script=sci_arttext&pid=S1415-98482017000100203&lng=en&nrm=iso>. Epub June 26, 2017. ISSN 1415-9848. http://dx.doi.org/10.1590/198055272115.

[2] THE WORLD BANK. Fourth rural water supply and sanitation project. 1999. http://documents.worldbank.org/curated/en/929021468746703340/pdf/multi-page.pdf.

在农村地区，中国政府在发展经济的同时也意识到需要解决这个问题。通过提供教育和与当地社区、党组织、妇联和卫生机构[1]的合作减少因不正确使用和处理水而导致的患病率，并传授提高生活质量的方法。因此，针对这些卫生行为，以上团体采取行动，旨在减少污染。

尽管取得了巨大成就，根据世界银行的报告，中国661个城市中约有60%仍然面临季节性缺水，超过100个城市有严重的水资源短缺问题。中国仍在改进污水处理和供水模式。

根据国际经验，中国的供水行业一直被政府垄断。因此，中国正面临着几乎相同的缺点和挑战，如低效率、高成本和各种浪费，这导致了几乎相同的路径：体制和法律改革以及向私人投资开放。

与巴西一样，中国的供水企业由地方政府管理，出现了许多对官僚主义和低效问责制、腐败和办事拖延的投诉。

中国各级政府之间的职责存在重叠，对这些机构的工作也没有明确的定义，但卫生和供水方面的法律组织结构图和理论框架遵循了2002年《中华人民共和国水法》[2]和1984年《中华人民共和国水污染防治法》(1996年、2008年和2018年修订，于2018年1月1日生效)[3]中规定的原则。

在中国，私营部门参与基础设施融资和服务管理效仿了深圳市的成功特许经营模式，在具有独立监管和运营职能的指导下，其合同期限规定为30年。

合资企业的创建使私人资本成为可能，但其总是受到中国公共机构的监督，特别是受到国务院监管和管理委员会的监管。通常情况下，企业对这些公司的控制权仍在中国合作伙伴手中，让他们控制和指导投资以及服务的执行。

"中国经济经历了根本性的变化，从完全依赖很少有外国投资和国际贸易的国有和集体企业，转变为混合经济，完全商业化的国有和私营企业发挥越来越大的作用。私营部门对供水行业的参与反映了经济中这些更广泛的变化，并将继续

---

1 The World Bank. Fourth rural water supply and sanitation project. 1999. http://documents.worldbank.org/curated/en/929021468746703340/pdf/multi-page.pdf.

2 Chinese Government's Official Web Portal. Water Law of the People's Republic of China (Order of the President No.74). http://111.13.45.139/laws/2005-10/09/content_75313.htm

3 Xinhuanet. 2017. China revises law on water pollution prevention and control. http://www.xinhuanet.com//english/2017-06/27/c_136399271.htm>

努力加深经济市场化。"[1]

基础设施 PPP 特许权有多种形式，在中国，如合同、合作合同、建设—自有—运营（BOO）、建设—转让—运营（BTO）、建设—自有—运营—转让（BOT/BOOT）、综合附加、购买—建设—运营（BBO）和租赁—建设—运营（LBO）。然而，BOT 合同正在逐渐盛行。"中国政府已逐渐意识到，BOT 模式是基础设施项目的一种良好融资方案，是与私营部门分担技术和金融风险的有效方法"。[2]

正如我们所看到的，中国特许经营的法律和市场环境仍在不断发展，这表明公用事业部门存在着固有的挑战，如污水和供水、大量的沉没投资，以及对普及饮用水和污水处理服务以促进发展的强烈要求。

考虑到中国城市中心的规模及其多样化工业的复杂性，在普及供水和卫生服务方面取得的突出进展是一项更为显著的成就。这无疑是与巴西建立有前途的经济伙伴关系的一个表率，巴西现在愿意追求其基本生态服务的普及。

正如上述在巴西联邦参议院咨询委员会小组主导下完成的研究报告所述：

"根据对环境服务领域主要国际参与者（美国、欧盟、印度、中国、韩国、日本以及东南亚国家）自由化承诺时间表的分析（模式 3 商业存在，其汇集了该领域最大的服务），环境服务的开放程度相对较高。"

对于巴西和那些允许国家垄断公共服务发展和管理的国家来说，即使不是宪法规定的，也面临着对管理规范的挑战。举个例子，我们将讨论基本的卫生服务，也就是传统的环境服务。

"基本卫生设施"一词在 1988 年《宪法》中有双重含义：第 21 条第 100 款规定联邦有权制定城市发展准则，包括城市地区的住房、卫生和交通；第 200 条第 IV 款规定统一卫生系统的职能是参与制定和实施基本卫生行动；第 20 条第 III 款和第 VI 款以及第 26 条第 I 款涉及联邦和各州对水资源的控制，区分了水资源本身的属性和联邦的水力发电潜力属性，尽管州和市政府通过收取开采权使用费或对其开发的财政补偿来参与。1997 年 1 月 8 日的第 9433 号法律将水定义为一种领域商品，其使用取决于联邦或州公共权力的授予。

---

[1] ZHENG, Xiaoting; JIANG, Yi and SUGDEN, Craig. People's Republic of China: Do Private Water Utilities Outperform State-Run Utilities? https://www.adb.org/sites/default/files/publication/190682/eawp-05.pdf

[2] Yang, J., Nisar, T., & Prabhakar, G. (2017). Critical success factors for build–operate–transfer (BOT) projects in China. The Irish Journal of Management, 36(3), 147-161. https://doi.org/10.1515/ijm-2017-0016

据估计，巴西的基本卫生部门（生产和分配污水收集、清除和处理）每年产生约 70 亿美元的收入，因此有资格成为资本利益的来源。然而，政府扩大这项服务供应及改善其环境质量还有很大的提升空间。

为了普及服务，联邦政府在 1998 年估计，到 2010 年需要投资约 442 亿雷亚尔，分配如下：67 亿雷亚尔用于供水，220 亿雷亚尔用于污水收集，99 亿雷亚尔用于污水处理，74 亿雷亚尔用于资产置换。这些投资每年大约相当于 GDP 的 0.36%，被认为是无法实现的目标，因为投资率在 1970 年代为 GDP 的 0.34%，1980 年代为 0.28%，1990 年为 0.13%。

据皮特森（Petersen and Brancher）数据显示，供水行业对维持人口健康具有战略重要性，面临的主要挑战有：

1）注意力缺陷集中在低收入阶层和欠发达地区；
2）由于物理方面（泄漏）和商业方面（无测量）造成的供水服务损失；
3）供应时断时续；
4）收集的污水 90% 是新鲜的或未经处理排入河流、泉水或土壤；
5）污水雨水收集系统的使用；
6）对用户缺乏足够的关注（服务不足，科室和投诉及维修处理不力）；
7）根据 1997 年第 9433 号法律建立的国家资源管理体系迫切需要将卫生部门与国家资源管理体系相结合，这意味着与流域管理层之间的关系既为经济用途的资金筹集者，也为受体体内废水的最终处置者。

这些作者还列举了私人资本参与环卫部门的各种形式（行政或管理合同、租赁、战略伙伴关系、部分或全部特许权、出售国有公司或市政卫生设施的控制权）。

鉴于巴西国家经济和社会发展银行（BNDES）在其国家卫生政策中提出的目标，即 96% 的家庭用水、65% 的污水收集和 44% 的污水处理，增加私人股本参与这些服务的运营似乎是不可避免的。虽然巴西与世贸组织关于服务业横向和纵向安排的任命时间表没有重大限制，但 1993 年 6 月 21 日第 8666 号《招标和合同法》规定了国家产品和服务的优惠幅度。因此，巴西面临的巨大监管挑战就是有效地监管服务部门，以允许更多的私人或外资企业进入。

"导致最终确定部门监管的工作（技术性的，但也是政治性的）应该提前进行，最好是在本轮谈判之前进行。国际谈判代表没有办法在不确定的情况下同意是否推进国家的最大利益，或是尽可能放纵，增加国家之间的趋同和谈判进展的机会。"[1]

对于私人和外国资本来说，巴西是一个很有前途的基础卫生设施和供水市场。中国在巴西市场有这方面的经验，尽管它可能面临经验丰富的国际参与者的竞争。借鉴阿瓜斯迪林多亚市的经验，中国应该把重点放在那些公私合作在卫生方面可能会产生连带效应的城市和地点，在这些地方有着中国可能有兴趣投资的其他行业，如旅游业或其他基础设施项目。这可能会使中国获得必要的展示效果，向巴西地方当局展示其高度专业化的专业知识，而这通常是分析竞争性项目的一个决胜标准。

目前的疫情使巴西当局更加迫切地需要改善社会的公共卫生条件。巴西的政治环境良好，公共卫生方案因其对基本人权和环境保护的服务而受到高度关注。

---

[1] SIMON, Clarita Costa. Bens e Servicos Ambientais nas Agendas Legislativa e da Diplomacia Comercial: do nominalismo ao pragmatismo. Textos para Discussao 145. Nucleo de Estudos e Pesquisa da Consultoria Legislativa. Senado Federal. https://www12.senado.leg.br/publicacoes/estudos-legislativos/tipos-de-estudos/textos-para-discussao/td-145-bens-e-servicos-ambientais-nas-agendas-legislativa-e-da-diplomacia-comercial-do-nominalismo-ao-pragmatismo. pp. 30-34.

The Opportunities for Chinese Investment in Brazil

Clarita Costa Maia / Brazil

PhD. student in International Law from the University of São Paulo LL.M Business Law and Intellectual Property Law, UC Berkeley Federal Senate Legislative / Consultant on Regulatory, Economic, Commercial and Business Law

Rogério Do Nascimento Carvalho / Brazil

PhD. student in Latin American Integration Program from the University of São Paulo /Lawyer and Professor at Faculdade de Caldas Novas - Goiás

China has become the largest economy in the world, but there are internal challenges to be overcome[1]. In the early 1980s, China started its reform in order to properly meet the need for a larger coverage of public services, among other politics goals, keeping the orientation from the central government, by granting the municipalities and the public agencies and enterprises more authonomy. And since the 1990s, China has started a market-oriented reform of public utilities, introducing competition mechanisms, reforming management systems and experimenting

---

1 Shen, Dajun. Access to Water and Sanitation in China: History, Current Situation and Challenges. UNDP: Human Development Report Office, 2006. http://hdr.undp.org/sites/default/files/shen_dajun.pdf.

capital diversification[1], promoting ways to attract foreign capital.

In China, concessions first received legitimacy in the Circular on Questions Concerning the Ratification of Pilot Foreign Invested Concession Projects (BOT Circular) in 1995, which was co-issued by the NPC, the Ministry of Electricity, and the Ministry of Communications. The circular stated that infrastructures, such as energy and communications, are the bottlenecks of development.Asides from encouraging foreign investments through Sino-foreign equity joint ventures, Sino-foreign cooperative joint ventures and wholly foreign-owned enterprises, the state planned to adopt BOTs to build pilot foreign-invested projects[2].

In a way, the foreign capital participation in public utilities in China, notably in the sewage and water distribution sectors, are more long-lived than in Brazil.In the year 2002, concession projects experiences for public utilities were introduced in the Chinese administrative praxis and remain to be the leading legal model along with contracts.

Yan Wei provides the following table detailing the participation of private and foreign capitals in the sectors:

Itens	For private participation	For foreign investors
Ownership of water industry		
Water plants	Yes	Yes
Water networks	Not clearly specified in laws and regulations.	Yes, but state-owned enterprises hold the controlling shares
Water asset transfer	Yes	Yes
Operation of water supply industry	Yes	Yes
Obligatory joint venture		
Water plants	No	No
Water networks	Private participation is only for the involvement of the domestic private sector.	Yes

---

1 Wei, Yan. Regulating Municipal Water Supply Concessions. Springer Berlin Heidelberg. Edição do Kindle.
2 Wei, Yan. Regulating Municipal Water Supply Concessions. Springer Berlin Heidelberg. Edição do Kindle.

Contd

Itens	For private participation	For foreign investors
Entitlement to hold concessions		
Water plants	Yes	Yes
Water networks	Yes	Yes
Transferability of concession	Restricted	Restricted
Legal constraints for land-use rights	No	No
Tax incentives	No	No
Conditions for expropriation	Public interest	Public interest
Availability of financing from local international sources	Yes	Yes

Diagram 2.2 Threshold for private participation in China's water supply sector Wei, Yan. Regulating Municipal Water Supply Concessions (p. 35). Springer Berlin Heidelberg. Edição do Kindle.

Concessions can be granted by means of letters of authorization, government orders, concession contracts, project implementation agreement per government orders, asset transfer agreements or management rights transfer agreements, water purchase agreements, joint venture contracts or articles of association, and delegation contracts. The legal standard is defined by the municipality competent in granting the concession.

In the current days, critics around the need to enhance their accountability are on the rise and many techniques are suggested in order to refine the concessions discipline. For instance, in 2005, the Opinions on Strengthening the Regulation of Municipal Public Utilities emphasized the supervisory role of the municipal and provincial governments, the need to improve concession laws, and capacity building for utility regulations[1].

For some authors, China would benefit from a clearer legal framework for the contracts among government and private entities that want to explore specially its sewage and water supply sectors. For those authors, the efficiency and lack

---

1　Wei, Yan. Regulating Municipal Water Supply Concessions. Springer Berlin Heidelberg. Edição do Kindle.

of accountability shortcomings would be better addressed by a more clear and appropriate approach of the Chinese Judiciary to those contracts, as well as with a more transparent and participative sewage and water supply politics and, finally, with granting to the State Owned Enterprises (SOE), in joint venture or not, or the private actors with the lead in sewage and water supply contracts of the corresponding managerial responsibilities in accordance with the laws.

The state of the art of the legal discipline of private participation in sewage and water distribution sectors in China is summarized by Wei in the following table:

Parameters	Analysis
Scope of application	Urban water supply, gas supply, heat supply, public transport, sewage treatment, garbage disposal, etc. (Measures 2004) (1) water supply, gas supply, heat supply; (2) sewage and solid waste disposal; (3) urban rail transit and other public transportation; (4) other urban infrastructure determined by the municipal government (Beijing 2005)
Contracting authorities	The authority in charge of municipal utilities in the governments of "municipalities directly under State Council", cities and counties. (Measures 2004) The authority in charge of municipal utilities, government at district and county level, as well as departments designated by the governments of "municipalities directly under State Council", districts or counties. (Beijing 2005) and municipal government (Shenzhen 2005) In practice, the municipal government often as a whole entity coordinates all related departments and is responsible for the whole project. Regardless of the specific contracting authority, the municipal government has the final say.
Forms of concession (BOT, TOT, etc.)	What forms of arrangements are under the definition of a "concession"? This is listed in Shenzhen 2005. They are BOT, TOT, service provision delegation and other forms provided in laws and regulations.
	In China, concessions are granted through many ways in addition to concession contracts. It was once summarized that at least eight ways are used to grant concessions in practice.They are: (1) letters of authorization (Shenzhen 2005), (2) government orders (e.g. Shanghai Da Chang Water Plant Project), (3) concession contracts, (e.g. Chengdu No. 6 Water Plant BOT), (4) project implementation agreement per government orders, (5) asset transfer agreements or management rights transfer agreements, (6) water purchase agreements, (7) joint venture contracts or articles of association, and (8) delegation contracts.

Contd

Parameters	Analysis
Exclusivity of the concessionary right	There are no clear provisions on whether exclusive rights are granted, except in Shenzhen 2005 which clearly specifies that in the same industry, two or more operators shall be granted exclusive rights except when restricted by the nature of the industry or regional conditions. However, in practice, it is always the exclusive right obtained by the concessionaire.
Compensation clauses	In Beijing 2005, Article 32 stipulates that: "subject to the public interest, the government may take back a concession, terminate the concession agreement, expropriate the concessionary urban infrastructure or instruct concessionaire to provide public goods or services, but should compensate compensate in accordance with concession agreement." This implicates that the pre-agreement on compensation is the prerequisite for investor protection.
Foreseeability of concessionaire selection.	This has been discussed in Chap. 3. The greatest issue at present is that the concessionaire selection is more or less controlled by the officers in charge, and there are vague provisions on the selection methods and process.
Objective regulatory rules	The urban water industry is under the regulation of relevant departments, like the MOC (Ministry of Housing and Urban-rural Development since2008), Ministry of Finance, and MWR. Independent regulations have not been developed. The regulatory functions, to some extent, are still combined with the ownership structure.52 In the Chongqing case, the joint venture concessionaire and Chongqing Water Group are directly under the regulation of the municipal government rather than any of the administrative branches listed above.
Consistency with other laws	Asides from several laws and regulations that specifically govern the water supply sector, many laws and decrees that govern foreign investments also affect the water industry. Up to the present, the highest legal force and ad hoc document that regulates concessions is Measures 2004, which was issued by the MOC, and may conflict with local ordinances on applicability according to the Administrative License Law, Article 1554.
Negotiability of concession contracts: water prices and rates of return	From selected cases in Shenyang and Lanzhou, we can see that negotiation on contract terms between the government authority and the concessionaire is very much guaranteed.
Enforceability of court or arbitral determinations	The legal nature of a concession contract is currently still under debate, which causes difficulties with claims in the administrative or civil tribunal. Court cases on concessions are quite limited. Disputes in practice are more likely to be resolved through negotiation and the arbitral clause is always specified in a concession contract and recommended in concession legislations.

Chinese local societies have experienced profound changes in its social layers, as there is the high growth of urban regions and, with them, issues that affect the infrastructure of these localities, notably sanitation. Since the Reform and Open Policy in 1978, China is experiencing growing phenomenon of urbanization and modernization in all realms of its society. By the end of 2008, China's urbanization rate reached 45.7% of the population.

Historically, the Chinese population lived in rural areas where basically economic activity was based on agriculture, began to lose citizens who went to cities in search of better living conditions [1]. However, the tradition of these families with the management of inputs for cultivation did not take into consideration the rudimentary health protection, which also caused diseases in the rural population.

It is noteworthy to add that in the cities furthest from China, public toilets did not follow standards of hygiene and quality, since the educational level of the population that did not have regular access to high-level studies because their work in the field required time and dedication[2].

In the rural area, the Chinese government, as it helped the nation's economic development, also realized the need to address this issue by offering education and partnerships with bodies linked to the local community, the communist party, the women's league and health[3] in order to reduce the rate of diseases caused by incorrect use and disposal of water, as well as to teach procedures to improve the quality of life. Therefore, actions aimed at contemplating hygienic behaviour, where these groups acted, have been responsible for reducing contamination.

---

1 ALVES, Frederick Fagundes and TOYOSHIMA, Silvia Harumi. Disparidade Socioeconomica e fluxo migratorio chines: interpretacao de eventos contemporaneous Segundo os classicos do desenvolvimento. Rev. econ. contemp. [online]. 2017, vol.21, n.1 [cited 2019-12-28], e172115. http://www.scielo.br/scielo.php?script=sci_arttext&pid=S1415-98482017000100203&lng=en&nrm =iso>. Epub June 26, 2017. ISSN 1415-9848. http://dx.doi.org/10.1590/198055272115.
2 THE WORLD BANK. Fourth rural water supply and sanitation project. 1999. http://documents.worldbank.org/curated/en/929021468746703340/pdf/multi-page.pdf.
3 THE WORLD BANK. Fourth rural water supply and sanitation project.1999. http://documents.worldbank.org/curated/en/929021468746703340/pdf/multi-page.pdf.

Despite its great accomplishments, and according to a World Bank report around 60 percent of China's 661 cities still face seasonal water shortages, and over 100 cities have severe water constraints and China considers itself still improving its model of sewage and water distribution.

Mirroring the international experience, the water supply sector in China has been monopolized by the government. And, as such, is facing almost the same shortcomings and challenges such as low efficiency, high costs and wastes, which are leading to almost the same paths: institutional and legal reforms and opening up to private investment.

Like in Brazil, the Chinese water supply enterprises are managed by local governments and many complains emerged concerning bureaucratic and inefficient accountability, corruption and slowness of the public machine.

There is an overlap of responsibilities between the different levels of government in China, as well as an absence of clear definitions on the performance of these bodies, but the legal organization chart and theoretical framework on sanitation and water supply follow the principles set out in the 2002 Water Law[1] and the 1984 Water Pollution Prevention and Control Act, revised in 1996, 2008 and more recently in 2018, which entered into force on January 1, 2018[2].

In China, private sector participation in infrastructure financing and service management is modelled after the successful concession in Shenzhen City, under the guidance of having separate regulatory and operational functions, and whose term of contract was stipulated in 30 (thirty) years.

The creation of a joint venture, whereby private capital is made possible, but always under the supervision of Chinese public bodies, in particular controlled by

---

1　CHINESE GOVERNMENT'S OFFICIAL WEB PORTAL.Water Law of the People's Republic of China (Order of the President No.74).http://111.13.45.139/laws/2005-10/09/content_75313.htm
2　XINHUANET. 2017. China revises law on water pollution prevention and control. http://www.xinhuanet.com//english/2017-06/27/c_136399271.htm>

the State Council committee for regulation and management. Normally, corporate control of the companies remains with the Chinese partners, giving them control and direction of investments and the execution of the service.

The PRC economy has undergone fundamental change as it transformed from relying completely on state-owned and collective enterprises with little foreign investment and international trade, to a mixed economy where fully commercialized state-owned and private enterprises play an increasing role. Private participation in the water sector has reflected these broader changes in the economy and is likely to remain tied to efforts to further marketize the economy[1].

Infrastructure PPPs concessions take many forms, in China such as contract, cooperative contract, Build-Own-Operate (BOO), Build-Transfer-Operate (BTO), Build-(Own)-Operate-Transfer (BOT/BOOT), Wrap Around Addition, Buy-Build-Operate (BBO), and Lease-Build-Operate (LBO). BOT contracts, however, is becoming somewhat prevailing. "The Chinese government has gradually realised that the BOT model is a sound financing technique for infrastructure projects, and it is an effective method to share the technical and financial risks with private sector"[2].

As we see, the concessions legal and market environment in China is still evolving, which points out to the inherent challenges of the public utilities sector in which there is a natural monopoly, such as sewage and water distribution, great amount of sunk investment and also great urge to universalize the access to potable water along with sewage services in order to promote development.

The outstanding progress of the People's Republic of China in the universalization of its water supply and sanitation services is an even more remarkable achievement considering the magnitude of its urban centres and the complexity of its diversifying

---

1 ZHENG, Xiaoting; JIANG, Yi and SUGDEN, Craig. People's Republic of China: Do Private Water Utilities Outperform State-Run Utilities?https://www.adb.org/sites/default/files/publication/190682/eawp-05.pdf
2 Yang, J., Nisar, T., & Prabhakar, G. (2017). Critical success factors for build–operate–transfer (BOT) projects in China. The Irish Journal of Management, 36(3), 147-161. https://doi.org/10.1515/ijm-2017-0016

industry. It is certainly an extraordinary sign of a promising economic partnership with Brazil, which is now willing to pursue the universalizing its basic ecological services.

As stated by a above mentioned study concluded under the auspices of the Brazilian Federal Senate Advisory Board Study Circle:

From the analysis of the liberalization commitment schedules of the main international players in the field of environmental services(United States, European Union, India, China, Republic of Korea, Japan and United Nations Association countries Southeast Asia) – in mode 3 (commercial presence), which brings together the largest services in this area – the area of environmental services is relatively significantly opened.

For Brazil and the countries that allow the state monopoly of the development and management of public services, meets a normative, if not constitutional, challenge.Just to illustrate, we will deal with the basic sanitation services, considered traditional environmental services.

The term 'basic sanitation' is doubly contained in the 1988 Constitution: in the art. 21, item XX, which determines that it is the Union's competence to institute guidelines for urban development, including housing, sanitation and transport urban areas; and in art. 200, item IV, which provides the function of the Unified Health System participate in policy formulation and implementation of basic sanitation actions.Articles. 20, III and VI, and 26, I, deal with the control of waters by the Union and the States, distinguishing between the property of water itself and that of its hydroelectric potential – of Union, although States and Municipalities participate through the receipt of royalties or financial compensation for their exploitation. The Law No. 9,433 of January 8, 1997, in turn, defined water as a domain good whose use depends on the granting of federal or state public power.

It is estimated that the basic sanitation sector in Brazil (production and distribution sewage collection, removal and treatment) generates annual revenues of approximately US$ 7 billion, thus qualifying it as a source of capital interest. Nevertheless, the government's ability to expand supply for this service, as well as its environmental quality, seems remote.

For the universalization of services, the federal government estimated, in 1998, the need of investments of around R$ 44.2 billion by 2010, distributed as follows: R$ 6.7billion for water supply; R$ 20.2 billion for sewage collection; R $ 9.9billion for sewage treatment and R $ 7.4 billion for asset replacement. Those investments correspond approximately 0.36% of GDP in annual terms and are considered unattainable goals because of the history of the investment rate 0.34% of GDP during the 1970s, 0.28% in the 1980s and 0.13% in 1990.

This sector, of strategic importance for the maintenance of the population's health, faces the main challenges, according to Petersen and Brancher:

1) Attention deficit concentrated in lower income brackets and less developed regions;

2) Losses in water services due to physical aspects (leaks) and commercial (no measurement);

3) Supply intermittently;

4) 90% of collected sewage is discharged fresh or untreated suitable into rivers, springs or soil;

5) The use of the sewage rainwater collection system;

6) Lack of adequate attendance to users (deficient services, sections and poor handling of complaints and repairs); and

7) High need for integration of the sanitation sector with that of against the national resource management system established by Law No. 9,433 of 1997, which implies a relationship between with basin management both as a fundraiser for

economic use, as well as in the final disposal of effluents in receptor bodies.

The same authors cite various forms of private capital participation in the sanitation sector (administration or management contract, lease, strategic partnership, partial or full concessions, sale of control of state companies or municipal sanitation).

Increasing private equity participation in the operation of these services seems unavoidable in view of the goal of the National Development Economic and Social Organization (BNDES), included in its National Sanitation Policy, to 96% of homes with water, 65% of sewage collection and the treatment of 44% of the collected sewage. Although the appointment schedule of Brazil's horizontal and vertical arrangements with the WTO regarding services do not have significant restrictions, the Bidding and Contracts Law, Law No. 8.666, of June 21,1993, deals with margins of preference for national products and services. The large Brazil's regulatory challenge is therefore to regulate the service sector efficiently to allow for greater private or foreign.

The exercise - technical but also political - leading to the finalization of sectoral regulation should be advanced, preferably ahead of the current Negotiations Round. There is no way for the international negotiator to agree on an uncertainty as to whether or not the best interests of the country are advancing, or indulge as much as possible, increasing the chances of convergence between countries and progress in negotiations[1].

Brazil isa promising market in basic sanitation and water distribution for private and foreign capital. China has experience in the Brazilian market in this niche although it might face the competition of experienced international players.What

---

1 SIMON, Clarita Costa. Bens e Serviços Ambientais nas Agendas Legislativa e da Diplomacia Comercial: do nominalismo ao pragmatismo. Textos para Discussao 145. Nucleo de Estudos e Pesquisa da Consultoria Legislativa. Senado Federal. https://www12.senado.leg.br/publicacoes/estudos-legislativos/tipos-de-estudos/textos-para-discussao/td-145-bens-e-servicos-ambientais-nas-agendas-legislativa-e-da-diplomacia-comercial-do-nominalismo-ao-pragmatismo. pp. 30-34.

China should focus, profiting from the experience of Águas de Lindoia, are those municipalities and locations in which the PPP on sanitation might generate spin-over effects on other sectors in which Chinese actors might also have interest on investing, like tourism or other infrastructure projects. It might grant to China the necessary showcase effect to demonstrate to the Brazilian local authorities its highly specialized expertise, which is usually a tiebreaker criterion in the analysis of competing propositions.

The current pandemia made even more urgent for the public authorities to enhance the sanitary conditions of the Brazilian society as a hole. The political momentum is favourable and the agenda of public sanitation in Brazil attracts natural sympathies for its high service to basic human rights and environmental protection.

中国－阿根廷旅游合作发展战略

贡萨洛 【阿根廷】

弗雷罗大学拉丁美洲中国政治经济研究中心 教育主任／
亚洲—拉美关系研究员

一 中国出境旅游市场情况

近十年来，中国出境旅游人数逐年增加，中国出境旅游市场正处于快速发展阶段，未来发展潜力巨大。随着相关旅游政策的出台，旅游者消费能力的提升，旅游需求更加多样化和个性化，出境游经营者应加强旅游产品的精细化和多元化设计，细分旅游市场，进行差异化经营。

据联合国世界旅游组织（2019）统计，2017 年，中国出境旅游消费支出约 2580 亿美元，占全球市场份额的 19.2%，已连续六年排名世界第一。与此同时，中国出境游客数量不断增长，2018 年达到 1.49 亿，比 2017 年增长 14.7%。由此可见，中国出境游市场将继续呈现稳定增长态势，海外消费将保持全球领先地位。

从地域分布来看，出境游客主要分布在广东、北京、上海、浙江、江苏、山东等沿海发达省份，这些省份经济发达，居民可支配收入较高。从城市分布来看，主要分布在居民人均收入较高的一线和二线发达城市。

1. 中国出境旅游热潮
- 2018 年，中国大陆居民持有的有效普通护照达到 1.3 亿本。
- 2019 年最新的亨氏护照指数显示，入境时持有中国护照的免签证国家已达 74 个。出境国家和地区范围进一步扩大。

图 1　中国出境游客分布前 10 名地域

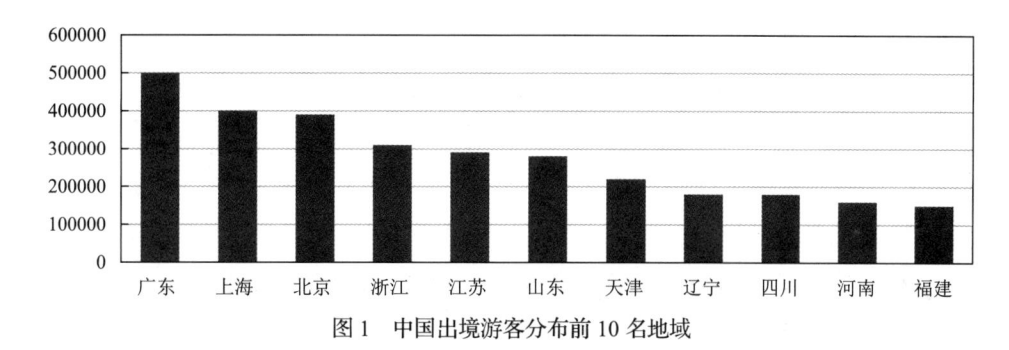

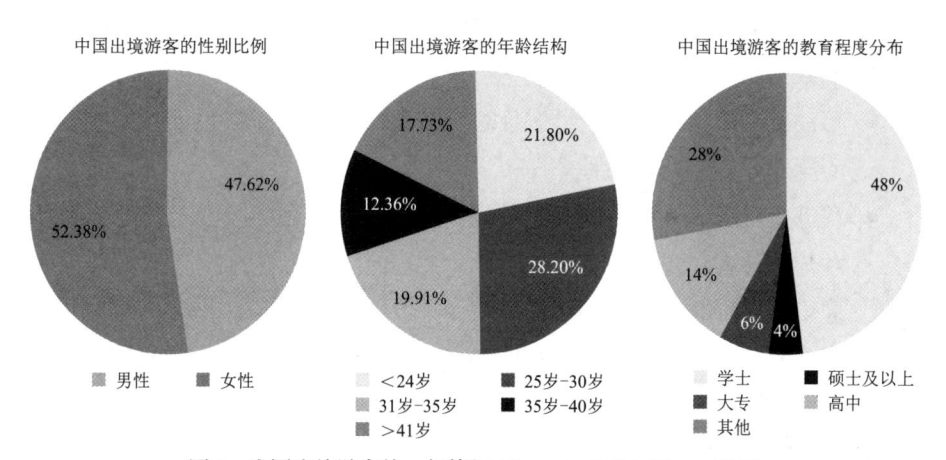

图 2　中国出境游客的一般特征 (Hongxiu, 2014; Xiang, 2013)

- 中国与周边国家、欧美国家有着良好的外交环境。比如 2018 中欧旅游年、2019 中国太平洋岛屿旅游年等。随着与俄罗斯、东欧和南美友好交流合作的不断加强，签证政策趋于简化和宽松。
- "一带一路"倡议促进了中国和沿线国家之间的合作，这些合作已扩展到北非和南非中部。

2. **中国旅游业增加国民收入，促进宏观经济发展**

- 居民收入水平显著提高：2018 年，国家统计局公布，居民人均可支配收入达到 28228 元人民币（4091 美元），较去年同期名义增长 8.7%。
- 旅游业对 GDP 的贡献持续上升：2018 年，中国旅游业占 GDP 的 11.04%，对相关产业有显著拉动作用。
- 旅游业有效地刺激了就业：到 2018 年，旅游业实现直接就业 2826 万人，旅游直接和间接就业 7991 万人，占全国总人口的 10.29%。

3. 主要消费群体的变化

- 80 后和 90 后成为主要消费者：80 后和 90 后成为主要工作人口和消费人口，他们的消费观念起代际驱动作用。
- 旅游消费频率增加：旅游消费已成为重要的日常消费，消费性旅游的频率和消费金额迅速增加。
- 新旅游接受度高：个性化、趣味性、体验性、新鲜性、消费升级，促进出境旅游发展。
- 全球和平指数显示，中国主要出境目的地国的和平指数处于较高水平。

4. 新技术和旅行便利性

- 移动终端的利用率加快了信息的传播和流动，打破了地域限制，增强了不同地方之间的连通性。
- 移动支付国际化：以支付宝和微信支付为代表的移动支付已经走向海外，并与全球各地的海外目的地商户达成合作。芝麻信用的信用体系已开始应用于海外租车等消费场景。
- 语音助手、语音翻译、智能旅行助手和其他技术改善了出境旅行的体验。

二　阿根廷旅游目标市场分析

阿根廷是中国国外旅游市场的远程目的地，没有直飞航班，通常需要飞行 30 小时，票价从 7 到 15 万元人民币不等。基于这种情况，我们认为中国的目标市场应该是具有较高消费能力，同时具有丰富旅游经验的中高端游客。这些经验丰富的游客通常对旅游质量有很高的要求。以下是具体的目标市场细分。

1. 有孩子的家庭

在出境旅游的过程中，有孩子的家庭更加关注目的地的人文内涵，希望为孩子提供开阔视野、学习外语的机会。因此，海外度假休闲自驾游可以独立安排，或以具有一定教育功能的教育旅游产品为主要兴趣点。

2. 年轻夫妇

年轻夫妇一般具有较高的审美水平和审美要求，喜欢有强烈的视觉冲击力和以 KOL（意见领袖）为主导的新旅游目的地和少数民族风情。特别旅游项目，包括岛屿旅游、冰雪旅游、摄影旅游等，是他们的重点关注。未来，年轻夫妇将成为有孩子家庭的新成员，这可能会引领家庭旅行的潮流。

3. 95后和00后

95后和00后的新兴力量开放活跃，更加注重旅行的个性化和差异化，追求个人满意度，甚至愿意为满意的服务或体验支付额外费用。他们对短视频和移动广播应用的大量使用表明，他们的社交方式发生了一些变化。他们更喜欢快乐的内容分享和陌生人社交。对二次元的热爱也可能是他们旅行的重要动力。朝圣之旅、IP打卡和追随偶像将是他们此行的关键主题和重要组成部分。

4. 有经验的独立旅行者

中国的独立旅行者主要在互联网发达和日益成熟的在线旅游市场的帮助下设计线路、在线消费和分享旅行经历。每个独立旅行者平均都去过1.45个国家，而有经验的独立旅行者甚至平均去过7个以上的国家。除了东南亚等热门出境目的地外，经验丰富的中国独立游客还进一步前往非洲和南美等地，探索未知领地。

此外，独立旅行者的人均支出和旅行时间高于其他游客。海外目的地中最昂贵的目的地是冰岛、斐济和新西兰，超过1.8万元人民币。在新西兰，独立游客的平均旅行时间最长，可达12天。第二个是美国、澳大利亚、摩洛哥、土耳其、西班牙和英国，它们的天数为10天及以上。许多前往欧洲的独立旅行者将申请申根签证，并在旅途中访问多个国家。

5. 高收入游客

中国高收入游客普遍拥有更多的社会财富和卓越的消费能力，平均每年家庭消费总额为173万元（约25万美元），其中高端游客消费在100万至300万元（约15—43万美元）之间，具有很强的消费能力和积极的消费态度。80%的高收入游客将海外旅游视为家庭年度消费计划的一部分。

中国出境旅游呈现出巨大的区域差异，主要旅游市场是一线城市，如上海、北京、广州、深圳。此外，一些新兴重要城市，如武汉、成都等出境旅游增长较快。

上海、深圳、北京、广州、杭州、武汉、天津、南京、成都和苏州已成为出境游十大热门出发城市。其中，上海、深圳、北京、广州和杭州占中国游客总数的51.49%。与此同时，武汉、苏州等新一线城市的出境游客数量也得到了大幅提升。随着新一线城市居民收入的提高，越来越多的市民选择出国旅游，拓宽视野。

三　产品开发

基于以上对目标市场的分析，我们对阿根廷旅游资源进行了总体规划。总的来说，阿根廷的自然旅游产品是吸引中国游客最重要的产品类型。在自然旅游的基础上，我们可以进行体育、探险、亲子、教育、科研等相关的产品体系。

1. 巴塔哥尼亚（Patagonia）

巴塔哥尼亚是南美一个非常重要的旅游目的地，旅游资源丰富，旅游业发达，旅游度假形式多样。它已经成为一个有吸引力的整体目的地。有必要对巴塔哥尼亚品牌进行统一的营销推广、规划和设计。

- 总体定位：高端自然旅游度假目的地。
- 目标市场：中国市场的自然探险游客、年轻背包客、高收入家庭度假者。
- 产品设计：埃尔卡拉特法（El Calatefa）冰川观光、探险、家庭游；乌斯怀亚（Ushuaia）冬季冰雪之旅、夏季自然探险；安哥斯度拉村（Villa la Angostura）和巴里洛切（Bariloche）高端度假旅游、狩猎探险和自然旅游。
- 营销策略包括：

网络营销：建立巴塔哥尼亚旅游中文网站、微信和微博账号，与中国主要社交媒体合作传播巴塔哥尼亚旅游图片和视频。

渠道合作：与中国主要的在线旅行社（OTA）、传统旅行社合作，为巴塔哥尼亚自然旅游和度假产品的销售提供奖金和奖励。

专业群体：通过中国自然探险俱乐部、汽车自驾游俱乐部、婚恋交友平台、亲子教育社区、高收入家庭俱乐部，推广巴塔哥尼亚旅游线路和品牌。

节目推广：与中国知名真人秀节目、网络名人直播平台、节目制作团队合作，巴塔哥尼亚旅游真人秀节目可在中国知名频道制作播出。

跨国合作：通过特殊的旅游签证政策和旅游线路设计，与智利等周边国家合作，推广巴塔哥尼亚旅游品牌。

（1）埃尔卡拉特法岛

埃尔卡拉特法以佩里托·莫雷诺（Perito Moreno）冰川而闻名，但在中国市场上，了解这座冰川的游客并不多，一旦他们身临其境，他们就会对这座冰川的壮观深感震惊。因此，冰川景观的宣传非常重要。

首先，我们可以选择与专业摄影师以及网络名人合作，宣传冰川视频、照片和其他视觉图像。

第二，在中国，自然旅游爱好者深入传播和推广科学教育知识，结合探险、邮轮、攀岩、徒步等活动提高体验。

三是亲子旅游市场深度旅游产品的设计，结合科研教育、亲子娱乐等要素，邀请资深旅游爱好者进行推广。

第四，与传统旅行社和在线旅行社、携程等中国国际旅行社合作，推广巴塔哥尼亚自然旅游线路，其中以佩里托·莫雷诺冰川为主要产品。

（2）乌斯怀亚（Ushuaia）

乌斯怀亚冰雪资源十分独特，气候宜人，冬季降雪量丰富，气温零下2度左右，非常适合冰雪旅游。在北半球的冬季，冰雪旅游目的地的温度非常低，平均低于零下15度，甚至更低。温度过低会给游客带来不舒服的体验。

首先，乌斯怀亚冬季较高的温度对中国市场具有吸引力，适合在中国7月和8月的暑假期间进行淡季家庭滑雪和冰雪旅行。特别是，一些高收入家庭可以在7月和8月获得更长的假期，带孩子去阿根廷度假，在夏天滑雪，体验世界末日的独特魅力。

其次，乌斯怀亚的夏天与北半球的冬天重合。可以推广国家公园和近极地地区的夏季自然旅游、家庭教育和体育产品，以吸引年轻的中国游客、家庭游客和自然游客。

第三，作为南极洲的极地考察中转站，它还可以提高乌斯怀亚作为"世界末日"的品牌知名度。

第四，在会展旅游方面，在现有酒店和会展中心设施的基础上，加大在中国市场的推广力度，吸引部分企业奖励旅游、会展、高端论坛等。

（3）巴里洛切和安哥斯度拉村

巴里洛切和安哥斯度拉村是阿根廷和南美著名的度假胜地，建成了许多高端度假设施，如精品酒店、水疗中心、滑雪板、游艇、游轮、国家公园、旅游小镇等，拥有丰富的雪山、草原、湖泊等资源。中国度假游客可以在这里体验一站式的高端度假服务。对于中国游客，可以推广以下产品：

- 高端游客的一站式度假套餐

中国的度假小镇建设才刚刚开始，像巴里洛切和安哥斯度拉村这样成熟的度假服务和设施在中国还很少。因此，我们应该在中国市场树立高端度假的品牌形象，举办"T20"峰会等一系列论坛，进行权威认证和品牌推广，形成小镇联盟共同推动市场。

- 狩猎旅游

由于枪支管理的限制，中国市场上的狩猎产品较少，尤其是猎鹿。猎鹿是中国清代一项独特的狩猎运动。对于现代中国游客来说，猎鹿充满了神秘的高端感觉。巴里洛切的狩猎场为中国度假游客提供野生鹿狩猎，这可以创造一个非常独特的度假品牌，并成为一个独特的有吸引力的产品。

- 自然旅游

该地区湖泊和雪山资源丰富，通过游艇、游轮、皮划艇、登山、徒步、露营、国家公园研究、亲子教育等户外活动，我们可以提供高品质的度假和自然旅游产品。通过自然旅游产品在中国市场吸引高收入，度假体验质量要求更高的人群。这些产品可以与专业自然旅游机构、俱乐部和OTA、高收入群体合作推广和销售。

2. 布宜诺斯艾利斯（Buenos Aires）

作为阿根廷首都，布宜诺斯艾利斯是外国游客进入该国的主要门户城市，它也是中国游客前往阿根廷的必经目的地。布宜诺斯艾利斯的城市景观、探戈、足球、美食、博物馆、街道、广场和教堂已成为主要景点。作为一个典型的城市旅游目的地，该地区的旅游产品需要设计和推广，作为阿根廷旅游的起点或终点，与阿根廷北部和南部地区相结合。

- 足球旅游

布宜诺斯艾利斯的足球主题之旅。河床竞技足球俱乐部、博卡青年俱乐部是阿根廷最著名的两个足球俱乐部，对足球爱好者非常有吸引力。除了观光旅游，它还可以与中国城市建立友谊联盟，组织中国青少年参加足球夏令营、冬令营等。

- 城市旅游

粉色之家、五月广场、纪念碑、天主教堂、博物馆、历史街区等城市景观，通过微信、微博、豆瓣、小红书等渠道进行传播和分享，评选出十大必游景点进行推广。

- 文化旅游

探戈、葡萄酒、美食体验。通过探戈表演、葡萄酒博物馆、露天集市、美食节和十大餐厅选择，将阿根廷文化传递给游客，鼓励他们参与探戈作坊、品酒、美食制作等活动，为游客提供更深入的体验，并鼓励他们通过微信等社交媒体分享经验和获奖。

3. 米西奥斯省 (Misiones Province)

（1）伊瓜苏瀑布 (Iguazu Falls)

伊瓜苏瀑布是一个很受欢迎的旅游景点，全年都有许多游客前来游览。这些瀑布位于巴西和阿根廷边境，占据伊瓜苏河沿岸一英里多的地方。伊瓜苏国家公园分为巴西和阿根廷两部分。该公园是联合国教科文组织世界遗产，两国都致力于保护其美丽景观。这些美丽的瀑布被称为世界自然奇观之一。

伊瓜苏瀑布对中国家庭游客、自然游客、探险游客和度假游客具有强烈的吸引力。

- 自然旅游

通过微信、小红书、豆瓣等社交平台，推广伊瓜苏瀑布的自然风光、瀑布景观、鸟类和动物丛林资源，吸引人们探索。

- 丛林探险

在游览伊瓜苏瀑布的基础上，人们对热带雨林有着强烈的好奇心。因此，对于中国游客的探险、科研、教育、亲子和体育，针对家庭和年轻游客的丛林旅游产品有可能延长游客的停留时间。在伊瓜苏瀑布的体验可以得到加深。

- 丛林赌场

中国游客往往对赌场有着特殊的热情，伊瓜苏瀑布凭借热带雨林和联合国教科文组织世界遗产的优势资源，通过丛林赌场品牌创造特殊的赌场形象和体验，吸引中国度假游客。

（2）世界遗产

阿根廷的圣伊格纳西奥米尼、圣安娜、罗雷托和圣母玛利亚艾尔马约尔村是耶稣会传教定居点，它们是17世纪和18世纪在瓜拉尼土著社区建立的令人印象深刻的遗迹。这些幸存下来的遗迹反映了耶稣会在南美洲的经历。在那里，定居点出现了一个独特的空间、经济、社会和文化关系体系。

- 文化旅游

作为联合国教科文组织的世界遗产，位于米西奥内斯省的圣伊格纳西奥米尼遗址可以组织一条与伊瓜苏瀑布相连的旅游线路，以吸引中国游客在参观世界自然遗产后参观世界文化遗产。通过节日活动、展览教育、工作坊等产品，增进中国游客对这里文化的了解和体验。

（3）莫肯瀑布，唐恩里克公园 - 生物圈亚博蒂

亚博蒂生物圈是南美第二大雨林，是理想的自然生态旅游目的地，拥有丰富的科研、教育和勘探资源。但由于地理位置远离主要机场和城市，对于长途游客来说，迫切需要改善其交通便利性。该地区适宜的旅游形式有：

- 丛林生态酒店

依托土著和当地社区，在该地区修建了生态酒店，导游与这些酒店合作，为游客提供丛林探险、徒步旅行、运动、瀑布等活动。生态酒店与当地社区紧密结合，为游客提供独特的体验，对中国游客具有吸引力。此外，丛林资源加工的农产品也是一种独特的旅游纪念品。

- 科学研究

亚博蒂生物圈作为热带雨林生态保护的典范，具有很高的科研价值。因此，与中国大学和研究机构合作建立研究站和生态观测站，对区域生态的可持续发展具有积极意义。通过举办论坛和会议，生物圈亚博蒂的生态旅游品牌可以得到很好的推广。

（4）波萨达斯市（Posadas City）

作为米西奥内斯省的省会城市，波萨达斯市美丽的城市风光和与乌拉圭接壤的地理位置可以考虑发展边境旅游、会议和展览旅游。通过在乌拉圭免税区购物和观光，可以吸引中国会议和展览游客，并在展览外安排参观伊瓜苏瀑布和圣伊格纳西奥遗址世界遗产线路。

四 "你好中国"计划

为了欢迎中国出境游客，帮助阿根廷酒店和旅游企业做好进入新市场的准备，有必要启动"你好中国"计划。该计划旨在为阿根廷旅游业提供深入调查和专业建议，帮助他们了解中国游客，制定中国市场营销策略和计划，为中国游客提供满意的服务。

1. 作用

"你好中国"计划的主要作用总结如下：

- 进行市场调查并发布研究报告，以了解中国市场的行为、需求、未来趋势、市场特征；
- 为提高阿根廷酒店和旅游业的服务质量、业务流程和客户满意度提供专

业咨询；
- 为具有中国旅游服务专业知识和指导的一线员工提供文化意识培训，确保中国客人受到适当的欢迎和服务。了解文化差异可以带来更好的客户体验；
- 为阿根廷的目的地提供销售渠道、品牌、促销活动、活动、定价、产品设计方面的营销策略，并帮助他们在中国市场进行推广；
- 联系中国旅游投资者和在阿根廷的项目评估，介绍两国之间的投资和商业机会；
- 主办峰会、会议、活动、展览、会议，以鼓励两国之间的商业、学术和政治合作。

2. 营销策略

"你好中国"计划可能是阿根廷整体国家品牌战略的营销。营销策略包括以下工作：

- 制作一个推广阿根廷旅游的品牌视频：根据中国目标市场的特点，选择视频中的内容，通过适当的渠道分发视频，并收集中国观众的反馈。
- 建立在线推广平台：网站、社交媒体账户、旅游社区讨论和在线旅行社广告，以推广阿根廷的目的地。在这些渠道中介绍内容和更新主题，并鼓励信息在网上流动。
- 在目标市场进行线下推广：使用户外广告、电梯屏幕、创意 flash 活动和其他推广活动，提高阿根廷品牌的公众认知度。
- 举办促进阿根廷旅游业发展的会议和论坛："T20论坛"、"旅游投资会议"等相关峰会和论坛，增加政府、投资者、商业伙伴、媒体等利益相关者的宣传和支持。

五　结论

综上所述，在分析了中国出境旅游市场的情况和阿根廷潜在增长的具体目标后，我们可以说，中国旅游业在阿根廷有着美好的未来。中国出境旅游的巨大增长和阿根廷的接待率仍然很低，呈现出一幅互补性很强的全景图。为了实现这一目标，有必要制定具体的战略。

因此，我们在本报告中对阿根廷的主要目的地、它们的优势和劣势进行了调查，以吸引中国公众。这是一个关键工具，可以推动制定一项具体计划（即"你好中国"计划）的提案。

通过深入的实地研究，开发一个名为"你好中国"的项目将有助于作为推广本报告中分析的阿根廷目的地的框架。我们认为，阿根廷和中国利益相关者之间的联系对于互惠互利、互补发展以及对两国经济都有利的中期计划非常重要。

随着阿根廷加入"一带一路"倡议、签署签证便利协议以及双边关系的改善，都将对贯彻落实《阿根廷报告》所制定的战略、确保中国旅游业的发展起到积极的作用。旅游业可以成为两国双边关系中的一个关联领域。旅游业是全球增长最快的经济活动之一（2018年为6%），它创造了更多的直接和间接就业机会。最后，与南美地区其他国家共同制定这一战略具有重要意义。从这个意义上说，向中国主要的旅行社提供包括南美最著名的旅游景点的行程，将是非常重要的。

Strategies for the Development of China-Argentina Tourism Cooperation

Gonzalo Anibal Tordini / Argentina

Center for Chinese Political and Economic Studies in Latin America of Flores University / Education Director; Asia- Latin America Relations / Chairman, Researcher

I. Introduction to China's Outbound Tourism Market

In the past 10 years, the number of Chinese outbound tourists has increased year by year, and China's outbound travel market is in the stage of rapid development and has great potential in the future. With the introduction of tourism-related policies, the upgrading of tourists' consumption capacity and the more diversified and individualized tourism demand, outbound travel operators strengthen the refinement and diversified design of tourism products, and subdivide the tourism market for differentiated operation.

According to the statistics of the United Nations World Tourism Organization (2019), China spent about 258 billion US dollars on outbound travel in 2017, accounting for 19.2 percent of the global market share, and has become the largest country in the world for the six consecutive years. At the same time, the number of

Chinese outbound tourists continued to grow, reaching 149 million in 2018, an increase of 14.7 percent over 2017. Thus it can be seen that China's outbound travel market will continue to show a stable growth trend, overseas spending will maintain a global lead.

In terms of geographical distribution, outbound tourists are mainly distributed in Guangdong, Beijing, Shanghai, Zhejiang, Jiangsu, Shandong and other coastal developed provinces, these provinces are economically developed, residents have a higher disposable income. In terms of the city distribution, mainly distributed in the first-tier and second-tier developed cities, in which the residents have high per capita income.

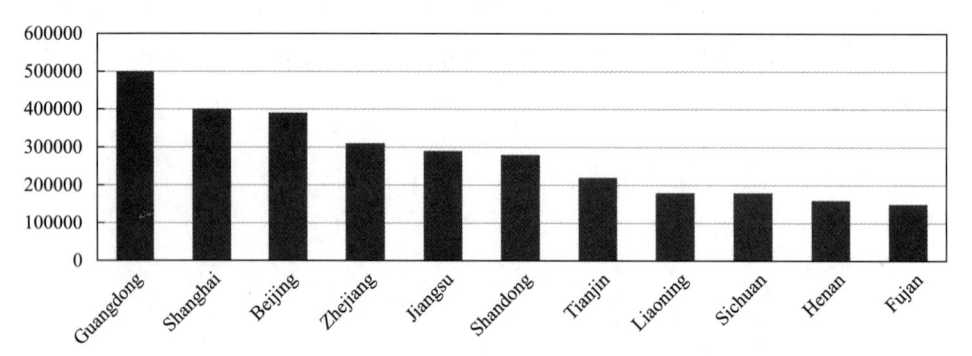

Figure 1   General Characteristics of Chinese Outbound Tourists

Elaborated by the author (based on References)

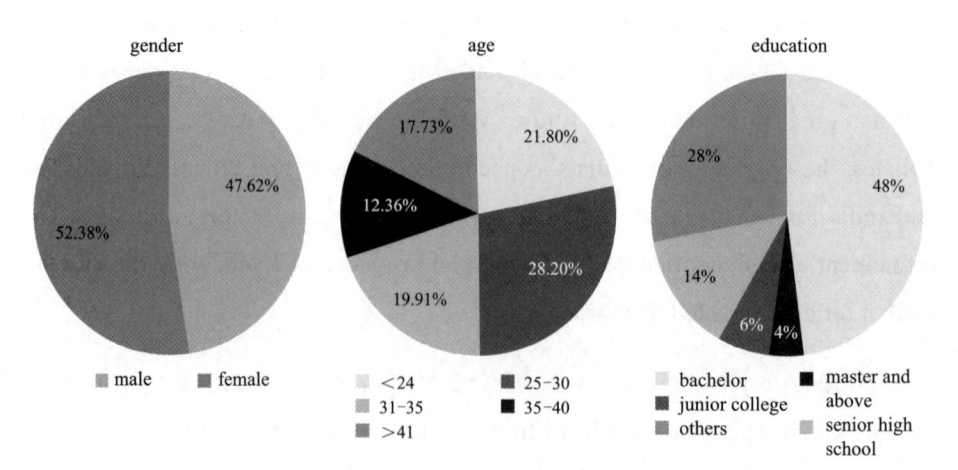

Figure 2   Educational Distribution of Chinese Outbound Tourists

Elaborated by the author (Hongxiu, 2014; Xiang, 2013)

1.1 China's outbound tourism boom

- In 2018, the number of valid ordinary passports held by mainland Chinese residents reached 130 million.

- The latest Heinz passport index in 2019 shows that the number of visa-free countries with Chinese passports on arrival has reached 74. The scope of outbound countries and regions has been further expanded.

- Diplomatic environment: China has good diplomatic environment with neighboring countries, European and American countries. Many diplomatic efforts have bloomed the outbound tourism: 2018 Central European Tourism Year, 2019 China Pacific Island Tourism Year, etc. With the improving friendly exchanges and cooperation with Russia, Eastern Europe and South America, visa policies tend to be simplified and loose.

- Belt and Road Initiative promotes cooperation between China and countries along the route, which has been extended to North Africa and central South Africa.

1.2 The increase in national income and the promotion of macroeconomic development by tourism in China

- The income level of residents increased significantly: in 2018, the National Bureau of Statistics announced that the per capita disposable income of residents reached 28,228 CNY (USD4,091), an increase of 8.7 percent in nominal terms over the same period last year.

- The contribution of tourism to GDP continues to rise: in 2018, China's tourism accounted for 11.04% of GDP, which has a significant pulling effect on related industries.

- The tourism industry has effectively stimulated employment: by 2018, the tourism industry has achieved direct employment of 28.26 million people, tourism direct and indirect employment of 79.91 million people, accounting for 10.29% of the total population of the country.

1.3 The major consumer population changes

- The 80s and 90s generation become the main consumer: the 80s and 90s become the main working population and consumer population, and their consumption concept plays an intergenerational driving role.

- The frequency of tourism consumption increases: tourism consumption has become an important daily consumption, and the frequency of consumer tourism and the amount of spending have increased rapidly.

- High acceptance of new tourism: personalized, interesting, experiential, fresh, consumption upgrading to promote the development of outbound tourism.

- The global peace index shows that the peace index of China's main outbound destination countries is at a high level.

1.4 New technologies and travel convenience

- The utilization rate of mobile terminal accelerates the dissemination and flow of information, breaks the regional restriction and enhances the connectivity between different places.

- The internationalization of mobile payment: mobile payment represented by Alipay and WeChat Pay has gone overseas and has reached cooperation with overseas destination merchants throughout the world. The credit system of sesame credit has begun to be applied to consumption scenarios such as renting cars abroad.

- Voice assistant, voice translation, intelligent travel assistant and other technologies improve the experience of outbound traveling.

II. An Analysis of Argentine Tourism Target Market

Argentina is a long-distance destination for the Chinese market. There is no direct flight, usually takes 30 hours. The ticket price ranges from CNY 150,000 to CNY 70,000. Based on this situation, we think that the target Chinese market should be a medium-and high-end tourists with higher consumption ability, but also rich in travel experience. These experienced tourists usually have high tourism quality requirements. Specifically, these are the following target market segmentation.

2.1 Market Types

2.1.1 Families with kids

In the process of outbound travel, families with kids pay more attention to the humanistic connotation of the destination, hoping to provide their children with an opportunity to broaden their horizons and learn a foreign language. Therefore, the overseas self-driving tour for vacation and leisure can be arranged independently, or the educational tourism products with certain educational function, are their main interest points.

2.1.2 Young Couples

Young couples generally with a high aesthetic level and aesthetic requirements, like to have a strong visual impact and KOL led by the new tourist destination and minority popularity. Special tourism projects, including island tours, ice and snow tours, photography tours and so on, are their focus. And young couples will become new members of families with kids in the future, which may lead the trend of family travel.

2.1.3 95s & 00s

The 95s & 00s, the new forces are open and active, pay more attention to the individualization and differentiation of travel, pursue personal satisfaction, and are even willing to pay extra fees for their satisfactory services or experiences. Their high use of short video and mobile radio applications indicates that there have been some changes in the way of their socialization. They prefer delighted content sharing and strangers socializing. The love of quadratic elements can also be an important driving force for them to travel. Pilgrimage trips, IP punch in, and following idols will be a key theme and an important part of their trip.

2.1.4 Experienced Independent Travelers

Chinese independent travelers mainly make decisions, spend and share their journey online, and start a trip with the help of the developed Internet and the increasingly mature online tourism market. On average, each independent travelers has traveled to 1.45 countries, while experienced independent travelers have traveled more than seven countries averagely. In addition to popular outbound destinations such as Southeast Asia, experienced Chinese independent tourists have gone further to those minority destinations such as Africa and South America to explore unknown territory.

In addition, the per capita expenditure and travel time of independent travelers are higher than other tourists. The most expensive destination of overseas destinations is Iceland, Fiji and New Zealand, with more than CNY 18,000. Independent tourists have the longest average travel time in New Zealand, up to 12 days. The second is the United States, Australia, Morocco, Turkey, Spain and the United Kingdom, which are 10 days and above. Many independent travelers to Europe will apply for Schengen visas and visit multiple countries at journey.

2.2 High-income Tourists

Chinese high-income tourists generally have more social wealth and outstanding consumption ability, the average annual total household consumption is 1.73 million Yuan (approx. 250 thousand USD), of which more than 1 billion high-end tourists spend between 1 million to 3 million Yuan (approx. 150-435 thousand USD), with very strong consumption capacity and positive consumption attitude. 80 per cent of the high-income tourists regard tourism as part of the family annual consumption plan.

The average annual travel expenditure of high-end tourists in China is 380,000 Yuan (55,000 USD), more than 50% of which spend 310,000-500,000 Yuan

(45,000-72,500 USD) on traveling, and 8% of super-high-end tourists spend more than 1 million Yuan (145,000 USD) on traveling. During the trip, the average shopping expenditure of Chinese high-end tourists is 220,000 Yuan (32,000 USD), and 5% of super-high-end tourists even spend more than 500,000 Yuan (72,500 USD) on shopping. Cosmetics, local specialties, luggage, clothing accessories and so on have become the most popular products among Chinese high-end tourists (McKinsey&Company 2018; World Tourism Cities Federation 2018).

China's outbound tourism shows great regional differences, the main tourist markets are first-tier cities, such as Shanghai, Beijing, Guangzhou, Shenzhen, in addition, some emerging important cities, such as Wuhan, Chengdu and other outbound tourism growth faster.

Shanghai, Shenzhen, Beijing, Guangzhou, Hangzhou, Wuhan, Tianjin, Nanjing, Chengdu and Suzhou have become the top ten popular departure cities for outbound travel. Among them, Shanghai, Shenzhen, Beijing, Guangzhou and Hangzhou account for 51.49% of the total number of tourists in China. At the same time, the number of outbound tourists in the new first-tier cities such as Wuhan and Suzhou has also been greatly improved. with the improvement of the income of the residents of the new first-tier cities, more and more citizens choose to travel abroad and broaden their horizons.

III. Product Development

Based on the above analysis of the target market, we have made a general planning of Argentine tourism resources. Generally speaking, Argentina's natural tourism products are the most important product type to attract Chinese tourists. On the basis of natural tourism, we could carry on a product system with sports, adventure, parent-child, education, scientific research and other related products.

3.1 Patagonia

Patagonia is a very important tourism destination in South America, which is rich in resources, developed in tourism and mature in various forms of tourism vacation.

It has become an attractive overall destination. It is necessary to carry out unified marketing promotion, planning and design of Patagonia brand.

- Overall positioning: high-end natural tourism and vacation destinations

- Target market: natural adventure tourists, young backpackers, high-income family vacationers in the Chinese market

- Product design: El Calatefa glacier sightseeing, adventure, family tour; Ushuaia winter ice and snow tour, Ushuaia summer natural adventure; Villa la Angostura and Bariloche high-end vacation tour, hunting adventure and natural tour

- Marketing strategy:

Online marketing: build Patagonia Travel Chinese website, WeChat and Weibo accounts, and work with major social media in China to disseminate pictures and videos of Patagonia Travel;

Channel cooperation: in cooperation with China's major OTA, traditional travel agencies, give bonus and awards to sell Patagonia natural tourism and holiday products;

Professional groups: through China's natural adventure club, car self-driving travel club, marriage and dating platform, parent-child education community, high-income family club, to promote Patagonia tourism routes and brands;

Program promotion: in cooperation with famous Reality Show programs, network celebrity live broadcast platform and program production group in China, the tourism Reality Show program of Patagonia can be produced and broadcast on famous channels in China.

Transnational cooperation: cooperate with Chile and other neighboring countries to promote Patagonia tourism brand through special tourist visa policy and travel route design.

3.1.1 El Calafate

El Calatefa is famous for Perito Moreno Glacier, but in the Chinese market, there are not many tourists who know the glacier, and once they really visit, they are deeply shocked by the grandeur of the glacier. Therefore, the propaganda of glacier scene is very important.

First, we can choose to work with professional photographers, as well as online celebrities, to promote Glacier videos, photos and other visual images.

Second, in China, natural tourism enthusiasts carry out in-depth dissemination and promotion of scientific and educational knowledge, combined with exploration, cruise, rock climbing, hiking and other activities to improve experience.

Third, the design of deep tourism products in parent-child tourism market, combined with scientific research education, parent-child entertainment and other elements, invited KOL to do promotion.

Fourth, cooperate with traditional travel agencies and OTAs, China International Travel Service such as trip to promote Patagonia natural tourism routes, in which Perito Moreno Glacier should be the main product.

3.1.2 Ushuaia

The ice and snow resources of Ushuaia are very unique, the climate is pleasant, the snow quantity is abundant in winter, the temperature is about 2 degrees below zero, so it is very suitable for ice and snow tourism. In winter in the northern hemisphere, the temperature of ice and snow tourist destinations is very low, with an average of less than 15 degrees below zero, or even lower. Too low a temperature creates a uncomfortable experience for tourists.

First, the higher winter temperatures in Ushuaia are attractive to the Chinese market, and are suitable for off-season family skiing and ice and snow travel during the summer vacation of July and August in China. In particular, some high-income families can get longer holidays in July and August to take their children on vacation trips in Argentina, ski in the summer, and experience the unique charm at the end of the world.

Second, Ushuaia's summer coincides with the northern hemisphere's winter. It promotes summer natural tourism, family education and sports products in national parks and near polar regions. It can attract young Chinese tourists, family tourists and natural tourists.

Third, as a polar exploration transit station to Antarctica, it can also enhance the brand awareness for Ushuaia as 'the End of the World'.

Fourth, in the aspect of convention and exhibition tourism, based on the existing hotel and convention and exhibition center facilities, we should also increase the promotion in the Chinese market, attract some enterprises to reward tourism, exhibition and convention, high-end forums, and so on.

3.1.3 Bariloche & Villa la Angostura

Bariloche&Villala Angostura is a famous resort in Argentina and South America. It has built a lot of high-end resort facilities, such as boutique hotels, SPA, skis, yachts, cruise ships, national parks, tourist towns, etc. With abundant resources such as snow mountain, grassland and lake, Chinese holiday tourists can experience one-stop high-end holiday service here. For Chinese tourists, the following products can be promoted:

- One-stop vacation package for high-end tourists

The construction of holiday towns in China has just started, and there are few mature vacation services and facilities similar to Bariloche&Villala Angostura in China. Therefore, we should establish the brand image of high-end vacation in the Chinese market, hold a series of forums such as "T20" summit, carry out authoritative certification and brand promotion, and form a small town alliance to promote the market together.

- Hunting tourism

Due to gun management constraints, there are fewer hunting products in the Chinese market, especially deer hunting. Deer hunting was a unique hunting sport in the Qing Dynasty in China. For modern Chinese tourists, deer hunting is full of mysterious high-end feelings. Bariloche's hunting grounds offer wild deer hunting among Chinese holiday tourists, which can create a very unique holiday brand and become a unique attractive product.

- Natural tourism

The area is rich in lakes and snow mountain resources, through the out-door activities such as yacht, cruise ship, kayaking, mountaineering, hiking, camping, national park research, parent-child education and other products, we can provide high-quality vacation and natural tourism products. Through natural tourism products to attract high income in the Chinese market, holiday experience quality requirements are higher. These products can be promoted and sold in cooperation with professional natural tourism institutions, clubs and OTA, high-income groups.

3.2 Buenos Aires

As the capital of Argentina, Buenos Aires is the main gateway city for foreign tourists to enter the country. It is also a must-come destination for Chinese tourists to Argentina. Buenos Aires's urban landscape, tango, football, gourmet food, museums, streets, squares and churches have become the main attractions. As a typical urban tourism destination, tourism products in this region need to be designed and promoted as the starting or ending point of Argentine travel in combination with the northern and southern regions of Argentina.

- Football Tourism

Buenos Aires's football theme tour. River Plate Club & Museum, Club Atlético Boca Juniors are two of the most famous football clubs in Argentina, which are very attractive to football enthusiasts. In addition to sightseeing tours, it can also establish friendship league with China cities, organize Chinese teenagers to participate in football summer camps, winter camps and so on.

- Urban Tourism

The Pink House, May Plaza, Monument, Catholic Church, Museum, Historical Street and other urban landscapes are combined with famous restaurants, bars, riverside, wharf, park green space and other urban leisure facilities to form urban sightseeing and leisure routes, through WeChat, Weibo, Douyin, Xiaohong Book and other channels to spread and share, select the top ten must visit and promote these scenic spots.

- Culture Tourism

Tango, wine, gourmet experience. Pass on Argentine culture to tourists through tango performances, wine museums, open-air bazaars, food festivals, and top 10 restaurant selections, and encourage them to participate in activities such as tango workshops, wine tasting, gourmet production, etc., to provide more in-depth experience for tourists, and to encourage them to share their experiences and receive awards through social media such as WeChat.

3.3 Misiones Province

3.3.1 Iguazu Falls

Iguazu Falls is a popular tourist attraction that are visited by many travelers throughout the year. These falls are located along the border of Brazil and Argentina and are positioned over a mile along the River. Iguazu National Park is split between both Brazil and Argentina. The park is a UNESCO World Heritage Site and both bordering nations are devoted to preserving its beauty. These beautiful falls are known as one of the great natural wonders of the world.

Iguazu Falls has a strong appeal to Chinese family tourists, natural tourists, adventure tourists and vacation tourists.

- Natural tourism

Through WeChat, Xiaohongshu, Douyin and other social networking platforms, the natural scenery, waterfall landscape, bird and animal jungle resources of Iguazu Falls can be popularized to attract people to explore.

- The jungle adventure

On the basis of the sightseeing of the Iguazu Falls, people have a strong curiosity about the tropical rain forest. Therefore, for the exploration, scientific research, education, parent-child and sports of Chinese tourists, it is possible to extend the stay time of the tourists for the jungles tourism products targeting on the family and the young tourists. And the experience at Iguazu Falls can be improved.

- Jungle Casino

Chinese tourists tend to have special enthusiasm for casinos, and Iguazu Falls relies on the advantage resources of the Rainforest and UNESCO World Heritage to create a special casino image and experience with the Jungle Casino brand to attract Chinese holiday visitors.

3.3.2 Patrimonio de la Humanidad

San Ignacio Miní, Santa Ana, NuestraSeñora de Loreto, and Santa María la Mayor in Argentina are the impressive remains of Jesuit Mission settlements established in the 17th and 18th centuries on lands originally occupied by Guarani indigenous communities. The properties' surviving ruins depict the experience of the Society of Jesus in South America, where there emerged a singular system of spatial, economic, social, and cultural relations in the settlements.

Culture Tourism

As an UNESCO World Heritage, San Ignacio Ruins are located in Misiones Province can organize a tourist route with Iguazu Falls, to attracts Chinese tourists to visit a World Cultural Heritage site after visiting the World Natural Heritage site. Through festival activities, exhibition education, workshops and other products to enhance the understanding and experience of Chinese tourists to the culture here.

Moconá Falls, Don Enrique Park - Biosphere Yabotí, as the second largest rainforest in South America, Biosphere Yabotí is an ideal natural ecotourism destination, rich in scientific research, education and exploration resources. But the location is far from the main airport and city, so for long-distance tourists, there is an urgent need to improve the convenience of transportation. The suitable forms of tourism in this area are:

- Eco Hotel of the jungle

Relying on indigenous and local communities, Eco Hotel has been built in the area, guides cooperate with these hotels to provide tourists with jungle exploration, hiking, sports, waterfall and other activities. Eco Hotel, which is closely integrated with the local community, provides a unique experience for tourists and is attractive to Chinese tourists. In addition, the agricultural products processed by jungle resources are also a unique tourist souvenir.

- Scientific research

As a model of tropical rainforest ecological protection, Biosphere Yabotí has high scientific research value. Therefore, the establishment of research stations and ecological observation stations in cooperation with Chinese universities and research institutions is of positive significance to the sustainable development of regional ecology. By holding forums and conferences, Biosphere Yabotí 'ecotourism brand can be promoted very well.

3.3.3 Posadas City

As the capital city of Misiones Province, Posadas City's beautiful urban scenery and geographical location along the border with Uruguay can be considered for the development of border tourism, convention and exhibition tourism. Through shopping and sightseeing in Uruguay's duty-free zone, Chinese convention and exhibition tourists can be attracted, and visits to the Iguazu Falls & San Ignacio Ruins World Heritage route can be arranged outside the exhibition.

IV. "Hello China" Scheme

In order to welcome Chinese outbound tourists and help Argentinian hotels and tourism enterprises to get ready to the new market, it is necessary to initiate "Hello China" Scheme. This scheme aims at providing in-depth investigation and professional suggestions for Argentinian tourism business, help them understand Chinese tourists, work out the marketing strategies and plans on Chinese market, and provide satisfying services to Chinese tourists.

4.1 Functions

The main functions of "Hello China" scheme are summarized as the followings:

- Conduct market investigation and publish research report to understand the behavior, demand, future trend, market characteristics of Chinese market;

lConduct professional consulting for the improvement of service quality, business procedure, customer satisfaction for hospitality and tourism industry in Argentina;

- Provide cultural awareness training for front-line employees with the professional knowledge and instructions of serving for Chinese tourism ensure that Chinese guests are welcomed and served properly. Understanding cultural differences can lead to a better customer experience;

- Provide marketing strategy in sells channels, branding, promotion activities, events, pricing, product design for destinations in Argentina, and help them to promote in Chinese market;

lConnect Chinese investors in tourism and the project evaluation in Argentina, to introduce investment and business opportunities between the two countries;

lHost summit, conference, event, exhibition, convention to encourage business, academic, political cooperation between the two countries.

4.2 Marketing strategy

"Hello China" Scheme could be a marketing for the overall national branding strategy for Argentina. The marketing strategy includes the following efforts:

- Produce a branding video to promote Argentina tourism: on the basis of the characteristics of the target marketing in China, select the content in that video and distribute the video through the appropriate channels and collect feedback from the Chinese audience.

- Establish online promotion platform: a website, social media account, travel communities discussion and OTA advertising to promote destinations in Argentina. Introduce content and update topics among these channels and encourage the flowing of the information online.

- Conduct offline promotion in the target markets: use out-door advertisement, elevator screens, creative flash activities, and other promotion activities to increase the public awareness of Argentina brand.

- Hold conference and forum to promote Argentina tourism: "T20 Forum", "Tourism Investment Conference" and other related summits and forum to increase the publicity and support from government, investors, business partners, media, and other stakeholders.

V. Conclusions

To conclude, and after analyzing the situation of both China's outbound Tourism Market and the specific target with potential growth in Argentina, we can state that there is an excellent future for Chinese tourism in Argentina. The huge growth of outbound tourism in China, and the still low reception in Argentina, presents a panorama of great complementarity. To achieve this objective, it is necessary to develop a specific strategy.

Therefore, we did an investigation in this report on the main Argentine Destinations, their strengths and weaknesses, with possible interest in the Chinese public. This serves as a key tool to move forward with a proposal for the development of a specific plan that we can call "Hello China plan."

The development of a program called "Hello China" would help as a framework for the promotion of the Argentine destinations analyzed in this report, through a thorough field study. We believe that associativity between Argentine and Chinese stakeholders is important for the mutual benefit, complementary development and a medium-term plan that benefits both economies.

In the near future, the incorporation of Argentina to the Belt and Road Initiative, visa facilitation agreements, and the improvement in the bilateral relationship will have great importance to carry out the strategies developed in our report and to ensure that the development of the Chinese tourism has a positive effect in Argentina. The tourism industry can become a relevant field in the bilateral relationship between our countries. Tourism is one of the economic activities that is growing most globally (6% in 2018) and that generates more direct and indirect jobs. Finally, it is important to develop the strategies together with other countries of South American region. In this sense, it will be significant to foster a strategy in order to offer to main Chinese travel operators itineraries that include most prominent tourist attractions in South America.

References

Chinese tourists: Dispelling the myths. McKinsey&Company. New York, 2018

Hurun Research Institute. Chinese Luxury Traveler Report. Shanghai, 2016

Liu Guojun, Wang Liancheng. Library History Research [M]. Beijing: Higher Education Press, 1979:15-18, 31.

Reima Suomi &Hongxiu Li. Profiling Chinese outbound tourist: an empirical survey. Department of Management and Entrepreneurship Turku, School of Economics University of Turku. Finland, 2014.

World Tourism Cities Federation. Market Research Report on Chinese Outbound Tourist Consumption (2017-2018). Beijing, 2018.

World Tourism Organization. 12th UNWTO/PATA Forum on Tourism Trends and Outlook – The Future of Tourism. Guilin, 2019.

Xiang, Yixian. The Characteristics of Independent Chinese Outbound Tourists. Tourism Planning & Development, 2013. 134-148, 10.

通过旅游发展尼中关系

戴韦 【尼泊尔】
尼泊尔教育与科技部　秘书

一　导言

1. 尼泊尔的旅游业

旅游是指人们为了休闲、商务或其他目的，连续但不超过一年前往并停留在其通常环境之外的地方的活动。旅游业是一个以服务为导向的行业，被认为是尼泊尔最大的外汇和收入来源。世界旅游组织（World Tourism Organization）对旅游业的定义更为笼统，它"超出了人们对旅游业的仅限于假日活动的普遍看法"，而是人们"为了休闲、商务或其他目的，连续但不超过一年时间前往并停留在他们通常环境之外的地方"。

尼泊尔拥有丰富的古老文化，与世界上最引人注目的风景相映成趣，是一片充满发现和独特体验的土地。对于重视真实和迷人体验的心胸开阔的人来说，尼泊尔是理想的目的地。来自世界各地的人们来到这里，都将陶醉于未被触及和未被发现的事物中，希望揭开它们的面纱。

尼泊尔所拥有无与伦比的多样性，从潮湿的特莱丛林到世界最高峰的雪山，这意味着其提供的活动范围非常广泛。徒步旅行、登山、在壮观的风景中漂流，这仅仅是尼泊尔最著名的三件事。各种各样的活动，如大象马球和穿越喜马拉雅山脉的轻型飞行，都表明在尼泊尔人充满想象力。尼泊尔有15个国家公园和野生动物公园（其中两个被联合国教科文组织认定为非物质文化遗产），是地球上仅存的能看到亚洲犀牛和皇家孟加拉虎的地方之一。

对许多人来说，尼泊尔最大的吸引力在于它的人民。尼泊尔传统多样性和尼泊尔人著名的热情好客的确是它如此特殊的一个主要原因。从偏远的山村到中世纪的山城和加德满都山谷的古城，尼泊尔人民总是充满热情。游客前来体验尼泊尔美食的浓郁而独特的风味，那些美食是用爱和浓郁的风味烹制而成，或者加入全年的众多节日一起进行庆祝。事实上，节日的数量比一年中的天数还多，世界上没有其他地方能像尼泊尔那样举办如此多的庆祝活动。

旅游业是尼泊尔经济的支柱之一，它也是外汇和收入的主要来源。尼泊尔拥有世界上最高的10座山中的8座，是登山者、攀岩者和寻求冒险的人的热门目的地。尼泊尔的印度教、佛教和其他文化遗产以及一年四季的晴朗天气，也是非常吸引人的地方。

尼泊尔是拥有世界上最高峰珠穆朗玛峰的国家，也是乔达摩佛祖蓝毗尼的诞生地。登山和其他类型的冒险旅游和生态旅游对游客来说有很大的吸引力。全国各地还有其他重要的宗教朝圣场所，供不同教派和宗教的信徒参观。

尼泊尔的主要旅游活动包括荒野和冒险活动，如山地自行车、蹦极、攀岩和爬山、远足、徒步旅行、观鸟、山地飞行、超轻型飞机飞行、滑翔伞和热气球飞越喜马拉雅山脉，还可以通过木筏、皮划艇或独木舟和丛林探险去探索水道，尤其是在特莱地区。

除了外国游客，国内游客访问尼泊尔不同地区的趋势也在增加。在自然、文化、历史和民族多样性的诱惑下，人们越来越活跃，尼泊尔将有能力改变该国的整体社会经济地位。因此，当地产品和服务水平在促进旅游业方面发挥着关键作用，从而促进国家的经济繁荣。

2. 尼泊尔旅游业发展趋势

20世纪50年代末，尼泊尔制定了旅游计划和政策。1959年，法国人乔治·勒布雷克（George Lebrec）编制的《尼泊尔旅游组织总体规划》是第一个旅游规划。自1962年以来，旅游部开始对来尼泊尔的外国游客进行统计。1967年，旅游局隶属于工商部。传说"Manjushree"是第一位访问尼泊尔的游客。

尼泊尔旅游业在过去50年中取得了良好的发展，游客数量从1962年的6179人增长到2010年的6202867人。自1962年初以来，除1965、1981、1984、1989、1993、2000、2001、2002、2005和2008年外，前往尼泊尔的外国游客数量每年都在增加。

1962年的游客人数为6179人，十年后1972年达到52930人，增长了8.6倍。同样，在随后的几十年中，1982、1992和2002年，游客总数分别增加了175448、334353和275468人，与1962年相比，每十年分别增加28.4倍、54.1倍和44.6倍。2010年，游客人数达到6202867人，比2009年增长了18.2%，比1962年初增长了98倍，是2010年以前尼泊尔游客人数最多的一年。尼泊尔旅游局在2018年1月至12月期间登记了1173072名游客的入境记录。其中，969287名游客通过飞机访问尼泊尔，203785名游客通过陆路访问尼泊尔。这比2017年的940218人次增长了24%。尼泊尔旅游局认为，如果2020年有更多的国际机场准备就绪，尼泊尔将接待更多的游客。

尼泊尔的游客人数虽然在大多数情况下呈现出稳定的趋势，但也表现出相对的停滞和波动。例如，1965年，由于巴基斯坦和印度之间的紧张关系，游客人数减少了1.5%。1978年至1982年期间，由于尼泊尔的民主运动和石油危机，导致旅游业相对停滞不前。1989年，由于尼泊尔和印度之间的贸易和过境争端，游客人数有所下降。1993年以来尼游客人数下降的原因可能有很多：比如签证费的增加、有限的航空座位容量、泰国和菲律宾航空公司的飞机事故、加德满都日益严重的污染及其国际宣传缺乏，洪水、山体滑坡，尤其是在马丹·班达里去世后多次罢工和"班达"造成的破坏等。在2000年、2001年和2002年，尼泊尔的游客人数持续下降，原因是1999年12月24日，一架印度航空公司的飞机在从加德满都飞往德里的途中被劫持，之后许多印度游客前往泰国、新加坡、马来西亚，而不是尼泊尔。同样，由于泰国曼谷素万那普国际机场的罢工，2008年的游客人数减少了5.0%。因此，内部和外部干扰都对尼泊尔的游客入境有很大影响，虽然尼泊尔可能无法控制外部因素，但如果我们真的想稳定发展旅游业，就应该管理和控制内部因素。

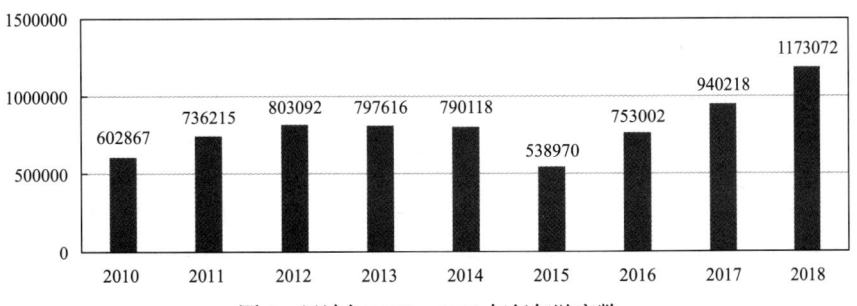

图 1　尼泊尔 2010—2018 年每年游客数

二　尼泊尔与中国的旅游关系

1. 尼中关系史

尼泊尔和中国之间的关系根深蒂固。尼泊尔有幸在历史上就与中国建立了密切的关系，这种关系已经逐渐发展并扩展到影响普通民众日常生活的所有可以想象的领域——社会经济、文化、宗教、工业、能源、环境、旅游、过境贸易和商业往来。这种关系建立在相互信任、尊重、理解和合作的基础上。历史上，这种关系表现在双方著名僧侣艰苦的朝圣之旅，他们为了寻求共同的文化、文明和宗教遗产，穿越喜马拉雅山脉进行艰难的旅行。公元 6 世纪，布列库提公主与松赞干布的婚姻关系进一步丰富了这种关系，使得佛教在中国传播。接下来是 13 世纪艺术家阿拉尼科（Araniko）的旅程，他在元朝统治时期在各地以宝塔的形式建造了一系列尼泊尔工艺的杰出建筑。

1955 年 8 月 1 日，尼泊尔和中国建立了正式外交关系。尼中关系的特点是平等、和谐共处、友谊长存、全面合作。此外，尼泊尔坚定地奉行一个中国政策，也承诺不允许自己的领土被用于任何针对中国的敌对活动。两国关系的特点是友好、理解、相互支持、合作和尊重对方的敏感性。两国对和平共处五项原则的理想有着坚定的信念。两国高层定期互访对进一步巩固两国互利关系发挥了重要作用。

2. 中国对尼泊尔旅游业的贡献

2018 年，尼泊尔接待中国游客 153602 人次，同比增长 46.8%。根据尼泊尔旅游局的数据，2018 年中国游客占外国游客总数的 13.09%。尼泊尔正在开展的"2020 年访问尼泊尔"活动对外国游客的显著增长起到了推动作用，这为实现"2020 尼泊尔旅游年"的目标提供了坚实基础。中国是尼泊尔第二大外国游客来源地。2019 年第一季度，中国游客在外国游客榜上高居榜首。尼泊尔政府已从 2016 年 1 月 1 日起免除中国游客的签证费。www.welcomenepal.cn 是尼泊尔旅游局为方便中国游客而推出的中文版网站。中国政府宣布 2017 年为尼泊尔旅游促进年。五家中国运输公司和京拉铁路的建设是中国游客的主要交通方式。尼泊尔与中国的拉萨、西安、成都、昆明、广州和香港建立了直接空中连接。

中国正在帮助修建通往安纳普纳环线徒步旅行路线的门户博卡拉机场和乔达姆佛陀出生地蓝毗尼机场。2015 年发生毁灭性地震后，中国为尼泊尔重建提供了 30 亿人民币，用于互选的 25 个重大项目。为感谢中国对尼泊尔经济发展的帮助和倡议，2017 年 5 月 12 日，尼泊尔和中国之间签署了"一带一路"倡议下的合作谅解备忘录。

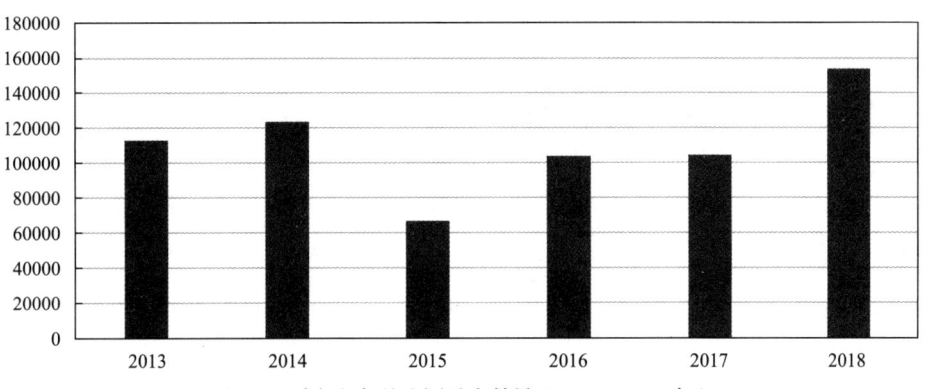

图 2　尼泊尔每年的中国游客数量（2013—2018 年）

3. 高层正式访问和联合声明

应尼泊尔总统班达里的邀请，中华人民共和国主席习近平于 2019 年 10 月 12 日至 13 日对尼泊尔进行了国事访问。访问期间，习主席会见了班达里总统，与总理奥利举行了会谈，并出席了班达里总统举办的欢迎宴会。在热烈亲切的气氛中，两国领导人就双边关系和共同关心的地区和国际问题深入交换了意见，达成了广泛共识。

双方对两国 1955 年建交以来，中尼关系经受住国际形势的变化，持续、稳定、健康发展表示满意，这为不同规模的国家之家建立了和平共处的模式。双方确认，两国关系具有平等、和谐共处、世代友好、全面合作的特点。

中国和尼泊尔以"一带一路"倡议为契机，全面深化各领域互利合作，谋求共同繁荣，致力于维护地区和平、稳定和发展。中尼双边关系进入新阶段。双方决定在和平共处五项原则、《联合国宪章》和睦邻友好原则的基础上，将中尼长期友好的全面合作伙伴关系提升为长期友好、共同发展、共同繁荣的战略合作伙伴关系。

双方同意坚持相互尊重对方独立、主权和领土完整，相互尊重彼此核心利益和重大关切。双方将坚持睦邻友好政策，深化全面合作，实现互利共赢，共同谋求稳定与发展。

尼方重申坚定奉行一个中国原则，承认台湾是中国领土不可分割的一部分，西藏事务是中国内政，坚决不允许在尼泊尔领土上进行任何反华活动。中方重申坚定支持尼泊尔维护国家独立、主权和领土完整，坚定支持和尊重尼泊尔根据本国国情自主选择的社会制度和发展道路。

中方祝贺尼泊尔实现历史性、划时代的政治变革，经济社会快速发展。相信尼泊尔人民将团结一致，继续朝着"桑里达尼泊尔，苏基尼泊尔"（"繁荣尼泊尔，幸福尼泊尔"）的愿景前进，以实现政治稳定、社会和谐和经济快速发展。中方表示愿意继续与尼方就治理经验进行交流。

尼泊尔向中华人民共和国成立七十周年表示祝贺，对中国七十年来的奇迹般的成就表示钦佩，衷心祝愿习近平在中国特色社会主义思想指引下迈向新的时代，中国人民将继续为实现两个一百年目标而奋斗，把中国建设成为富强、民主、文明、和谐、美丽的社会主义现代化伟大国家。

双方强调，高层接触对双边关系的发展具有特别重要的意义。双方同意保持高层互访势头，深化政治互信，扩大各级政府部委、立法机构和政党之间的交流与合作。

双方同意加强"一带一路"倡议下的合作谅解备忘录，以加强连通性，包括港口、道路、铁路等重要组成部分；跨喜马拉雅多维互联网络总体框架内的航空和通信，以期对尼泊尔的发展议程做出重大贡献，包括尽早脱离最不发达国家行列，到2030年成为中等收入国家，并在同一日期实现可持续发展目标。

双方回顾了2018年6月21日两国在铁路项目合作上签署的《莫乌协议》，同意开展2019年10月13日在莫乌签署的可行性研究，为跨境铁路的建设奠定了重要基础。双方还重申了在加德满都—博卡拉—蓝毗尼铁路项目上扩大合作的承诺。

双方欢迎樟木（Khasa）港重新开放和恢复货运功能，并将优化吉隆（Kerung）港的功能，尽早开放黎子（Neching）港，并在边境尼泊尔一侧建设必要的基础设施。

双方将继续执行《尼泊尔利用中国西藏公路货运议定书》和《过境运输协定议定书》。在保持阿拉尼科公路长期运营条件的基础上，双方同意优先合作，逐步对该公路进行升级改造。中方表示愿意启动修缮西亚夫鲁贝西－拉苏瓦加迪（Syaphrubesi-Rasuwagadhi）公路。

双方认识到加强两国间互联互通的重要性，同意积极合作开展吉隆至加德满都公路沿线隧道建设的可行性研究。

中方注意到尼泊尔方面对科西公路基马坦卡－勒古瓦加特（Kimathanka-Leguwaghat）段的建造要求，并同意在今后的合作计划中考虑该项目，并要求尼泊尔方面提交详细建议。

双方重申致力于研究合作的可能性，如2018年6月21日在北京发表的联合声明所述，以开发尼泊尔的三条南北走廊，即戈西经济走廊、甘达基经济走廊和卡纳利经济走廊，旨在创造就业机会，改善当地生活，刺激经济增长和发展。

中方将为培训尼泊尔铁路、公路、隧道工程、内河航运等领域的技术人才提供援助。

双方欢迎两国民航当局就扩大航权安排达成共识，鼓励两国航空公司在该框架下开展/运营更直接的航空服务。双方将密切配合，加快博卡拉国际机场的建设，使其早日投入运营。双方对中尼跨境光缆的成功商业运营表示满意，并同意进一步加强信息通信领域的互利合作；双方同意加强在贸易、旅游、投资、产能、改善民生等经济领域的合作，促进共同发展。

在中尼经贸联委会框架下，双方将成立由秘书/副部长级官员或其指定人员领导的投资合作工作组和贸易工作组，以促进双边投资和贸易。中方欢迎尼方参加2019年11月在上海举行的第二届中国国际进口博览会全国展览。

双方将就加强两国贸易关系进行全面讨论。中方将采取积极措施，扩大尼泊尔对华出口。中方将考虑为尼泊尔建立多功能实验室提供技术支持，并开展必要的合作，使塔塔帕尼边防检查站全面投入使用。尼泊尔将为中国银行在尼泊尔开设分行和其他金融服务提供便利，以促进两国之间的贸易和投资。双方将尽早完成《过境运输协定议定书》实施的内部程序，并尽最大努力尽早实施。

双方对签署《尼泊尔向中国出口柑橘类水果植物卫生要求议定书》表示欢迎，并同意尽早签署关于食品安全进出口合作的谅解备忘录，将按照"企业主导、尊重商业原则、坚持市场导向、遵循国际惯例"的原则，继续开展产能和投资合作。

根据中华人民共和国国家能源局与尼泊尔能源、水利和灌溉部于2018年6月21日签署的能源合作谅解备忘录，双方将充分发挥中尼能源领域合作联合实施机制（JIM）的作用，在水电、风电、太阳能、生物质能等新能源和电网领域开展交流与合作，双方同意共同实施中尼电力合作计划，并在一年内完成。双方同意将该计划作为下一步双边电力合作的重要参考，并推动其实施。

尼方对中方在尼泊尔发展努力中提供的宝贵支持，以及2015年地震后为尼泊尔重建提供的及时、自发和慷慨的支持深表感谢。

中国政府将继续向尼泊尔经济社会发展提供力所能及的援助，重点加强在改善民生领域的合作。

中方高度重视尼方建立多学科马丹班达里科技大学的愿望，以表达对已故人民领袖马丹班达里的敬意，并将在尼方选择合适地点后尽早给予支持。双方将根据中方实地考察工作组提交的报告继续讨论。中方愿加快加德满都供水水质改善工程。中方注意到尼泊尔关于综合发展的建议，包括在尼泊尔喜马拉雅地区安置分散的人口。中方愿与尼泊尔一方分享经验，并考虑就该建议进行合作。

双方认识到珠穆朗玛峰是中尼友谊的永恒象征，将推动在不同领域的合作，包括应对气候变化和保护环境。他们将共同宣布珠穆朗玛峰的高度并进行科学研究。

双方对《中华人民共和国政府和尼泊尔政府关于边界管理制度的协议》的签署表示满意，该协议将提高双方的边界管理和合作水平。双方同意加强执法机构在信息交流、能力建设和培训方面的合作。未来3年，中国每年将为尼泊尔执法人员提供100个培训名额。为促进安全领域的合作，双方将继续加强在安全人员互访、联合演习和培训、防灾减灾和人员培训等方面的合作。

双方同意在教育、文化、旅游、传统医学、媒体、智库和青年等不同层面促进交流与合作。中方将向尼方提供100个孔子学院奖学金。中方支持尼方举办2020年访尼活动，欢迎尼方参加在华举办的旅游博览会，愿为尼泊尔在华旅游推广提供便利。中方将在尼泊尔举办第九届中国文化节和第四届加德满都文化论坛，继续鼓励中国文化中心和孔子学院推动中尼文化交流与合作。双方欢迎中国南京与尼泊尔加德满都、中国西安市和尼泊尔布特瓦尔市发展友好城市关系。

中方同意尼泊尔在中国四川省成都市设立总领事馆。

双方同意振兴两国现有机制，进一步加强关系，推进各领域互利合作。

双方同意加强在联合国等多边论坛上的合作，维护发展中国家的共同利益。双方就在地区问题上促进合作、加强合作交换了富有成果的意见，同意在共同关心的问题上相互支持。双方表示坚定致力于多边贸易体制，致力于实现更开放、更包容、更平衡、利益共享的经济全球化。

习近平主席在中华人民共和国成立七十周年的历史性时刻，对尼泊尔进行国事访问，标志着中尼关系进入新的时代，是两国友好合作史上的一个重要里程碑。

中方对尼泊尔政府和人民的热情友好接待表示衷心感谢。

4. 尼泊尔和中国签署和交换的文书清单

尼中双方在中国国家主席习近平国事访问期间签署并交换了各种谅解备忘录。尼泊尔和中国之间签署和交换的文书清单如下：

① 尼泊尔政府和中华人民共和国政府关于边界管理制度的协定。

② 尼泊尔政府与中华人民共和国政府关于治理能力建设交流与合作的谅解备忘录。

③《尼泊尔和中华人民共和国刑事司法协助条约》。

④ 尼泊尔与中国关于萨加玛塔山（珠穆朗玛）保护合作的谅解备忘录。

⑤ 尼泊尔国家计划委员会与中华人民共和国国家发展和改革委员会关于推进产能投资合作重点项目的谅解备忘录。

⑥ 尼泊尔驻成都总领事馆换文。

⑦ 尼泊尔基础设施和交通运输部与中华人民共和国交通运输部关于中尼跨境铁路项目可行性研究的谅解备忘录。

⑧ 尼泊尔加德满都都市与中华人民共和国南京市建立友好城市关系协议。

⑨ 尼泊尔布特瓦尔市与中华人民共和国西安市建立友好城市关系的协议。

⑩ 尼泊尔政府卫生和人口部与中华人民共和国国家中医药管理局关于中医药合作的谅解备忘录。

⑪ 尼泊尔内政部与中华人民共和国应急管理部关于减灾和应急合作的谅解备忘录。

⑫ 中华人民共和国最高人民检察院与尼泊尔总检察长办公室合作备忘录。

⑬ 尼泊尔大学与中国孔子学院总部在特里布凡大学成立孔子学院的协议。

⑭ 尼泊尔政府农业部与中华人民共和国海关总署关于从尼泊尔向中国出口柑橘类水果的植物检疫要求议定书。

⑮ 尼泊尔政府工业、商业和物资部与中华人民共和国商务部关于成立贸易联合工作组的谅解备忘录。

⑯ 援尼泊尔地震监测网项目交付验收证书。

⑰ 尼泊尔财政部与中华人民共和国商务部关于成立投资合作工作组的谅解备忘录。

⑱ 尼泊尔财政部与中国国际开发合作署关于隧道建设合作的谅解备忘录。

⑲ 换文购买边境安全设备和办公设备。
⑳ 援尼泊尔加德满都河谷市政供水改善项目可行性研究会议纪要。

三 结论

尼泊尔将庆祝"访问尼泊尔年"并认为这将增加对旅游业的投资，探索中国企业投资尼泊尔风景名胜区、酒店和旅行社的模式。尼泊尔需要开通更多从北京、上海、广州、深圳、杭州、南京、成都、西安和拉萨到尼泊尔加德满都的直飞航班，以方便来自中国各地的游客。旅游从业人员应接受足够的培训，以达到国际标准。尼泊尔需要在人口超过1000万的中国主要城市打开"旅游窗口"，包括发放宣传书籍、播放视频以及推出特殊商品。与此同时，尼泊尔政府应为高中生和大学生组织高水平的研究项目，以交流技术和技能。建议尼泊尔和中国优先实施"一带一路"倡议合作备忘录，以加强互联互通，包括跨喜马拉雅多维互联网络框架内的港口、公路、铁路、航空和通信。

Development of Nepal-China Relationship Through Tourism

Devi Prasad Upadhaya / Nepal

Ministry of Education, Science and Technology (Nepal) / Secretary

I. Introduction

1.1 Tourism in Nepal

Tourism is the activities of people traveling to and staying in places outside their usual environment for leisure, business or other purposes for not more than one consecutive year. It's a service-oriented industry that is considered largest source of foreign exchange and revenue for the country. The World Tourism Organization defines tourism more generally, in terms which go "beyond the common perception of tourism as being limited to holiday activity only", as people "traveling to and staying in places outside their usual environment for not more than one consecutive year for leisure and not less than 24 hours, business and other purposes".

Nepal with rich ancient cultures set against the most dramatic scenery in the world, is a land of discovery and unique experience. For broad minded individuals who value an experience that is authentic and mesmerizing, Nepal is the ideal destination. People from around the world come and revel in the untouched and the undiscovered thus uncovering themselves.

It is unsurpassed that the sheer diversity Nepal boasts from steamy jungle of Terai to the icy peaks of the world's highest mountains, means that the range of activities on offer. Trekking, mountaineering, rafting in spectacular scenery are just three things Nepal is most famous for. Activities as diverse as Elephant Polo and a micro-light flight through the Himalayas show that in Nepal, the only boundary imagination. With 15 National & Wildlife Parks (two are UNESCO Heritage sites) Nepal is one of the last places on earth that one can spot the Asiatic rhinoceros and the Royal Bengal tiger.

For many, Nepal's greatest attraction is its people. The traditions and famous hospitality of its many different groups are indeed a major part of what makes Nepal so special. From remote mountain villages to medieval hill-towns and the ancient cities of the Kathmandu Valley, the people of Nepal are always welcoming. Tourists Come and experience the strong and unique flavors of Nepalese cuisine, prepared with love and a depth of flavor or join in and celebrate at one of the many festivals year-round. In fact, with more festivals than days of the year, there is nowhere else in the world that can offer as many festivities as Nepal.

Tourism is one of the mainstays of Nepalese economy. It is also a major source of foreign exchange and revenue. Possessing 8 of the 10 highest mountains in the world, Nepal is a hot spot destination for mountaineers, rock climbers and people seeking adventures. The Hindu, Buddhist and other cultural heritage sites of Nepal, and around the year fair weather are also strong attractions.

Nepal is the country of the Mount Everest, the highest mountain peak in the world, and the Birthplace of Gautama Buddha- Lumbini. Mountaineering and other types of adventure tourism and ecotourism are important attractions for visitors. There are other important religious pilgrimage sites throughout the country for the followers of various sects and religions.

Nepal's major tourist activities include wilderness and adventure activities such as mountain biking, bungee jumping, rock climbing and mountain climbing, trekking, hiking, bird watching, mountain flights, ultralight aircraft flights, paragliding and hot air ballooning over the mountains of the Himalaya, hiking and mountain biking, exploring the waterways by raft, kayak or canoe and jungle safaris especially in the Terai region.

In addition to foreign tourists, there is an increasing trend of internal tourists visiting different parts of Nepal. Given the growing commotion of people, lured by the natural, cultural, historical, and ethnic diversity, Nepal is capable of transforming the overall socio-economic status of the country. Hence, use of local products and skills play a pivotal role in promoting tourism that can lead to economic prosperity of the country.

1.2 Trends of Tourism Development in Nepal

Tourism plan and policy was made in Nepal in late 1950s. "General Plan for the organization of Tourism of Nepal" prepared by French national, George Lebrec, in 1959 was the first tourism plan. Since 1962, the Tourism Department has started maintaining statistics of the foreign tourist coming to Nepal. In 1967, Tourism Department came under Ministry of Industry and Commerce. Legends say "Manjushree" is the first tourist ever visiting Nepal.

Sound growth has been recorded in Nepal's tourism industry in the past five decades with the number of tourists visiting the country growing from 6,179 in 1962 to 6,02,867 in the year 2010. The number of foreign visitors to Nepal has been increasing every year since the beginning year, 1962, except in the years 1965, 1981, 1984, 1989, 1993, 2000, 2001, 2002, 2005 and 2008.

The tourist arrival in 1962 was 6179 and after a decade in 1972 it reached 52,930, which was an increase by 8.6 times. Similarly, in the following decades in 1982, 1992 and 2002 the total number of tourist arrivals increased 1,75,448, 3,34,353 and 2,75,468 respectively which was an increase by 28.4, 54.1 and 44.6 times respectively in every decade in comparison to the year 1962. In the year 2010, the number of tourists reached 6,02,867 by recording a growth of 18.2 percent over 2009 which was the highest figure of tourist arrival in Nepal until the year 2010. The total number of tourist arrivals 6,02,867 in the year 2010 reached 98 times increase in comparison to the beginning year 1962. Nepal Tourism Board registered a tourist arrival record of 1,173,072 arrivals between January-December 2018. Out of them, 969,287 tourists visited Nepal via air and 203,785 tourists came via land. That is a growth of 24 percent with that of 940, 218 tourist arrival in 2017. Nepal Tourism Board believes that it would be able to bring more tourists to Nepal if more international airports are ready by 2020.

Tourist arrivals in Nepal, despite showing a steady trend on most occasions have also shown relative stagnancy and fluctuations. For example, the number of tourist arrivals decreased by 1.5 percent, in 1965, due to tension between Pakistan and India. There has been a relative stagnancy during the period 1978-82 due to the democracy movement in Nepal and oil crisis which led to decline in world tourism low. Tourist arrivals declined in the year 1989 due to trade and transit dispute between Nepal and India. Decline in tourist arrivals in 1993 may be attributed to a host of reasons viz. like the increase in Visa fees, limited air seat capacity, THAI and PIA aircraft accidents, increasing pollution in Kathmandu and its international publicity, lack of promotional activities abroad, destruction caused by floods and landslides and numerous strikes and 'Bandha' as a part of political unrest particularly after the death of Madan Bhandari. In the years 2000, 2001 and 2002 there was a continuous decrease in tourist arrivals in the country and it is attributed to the hijacking of an Indian Airlines aircraft on 24 December 1999 on route to Delhi from Kathmandu attracting many Indian tourists to visit Thailand, Singapore, Malaysia rather than Nepal. Maoist insurgency and unnecessary 'Bandhas' directly affected tourism. Similarly, tourist arrival was decreased by 5.0 in 2008 due to the strike in Suvarnabhumi International Airport, in Bangkok, Thailand. Thus, both internal and external disturbances highly influenced tourist arrival in Nepal and though Nepal may not have much control over externalities, we should manage and control internal factors if we really want to develop tourism steadily.

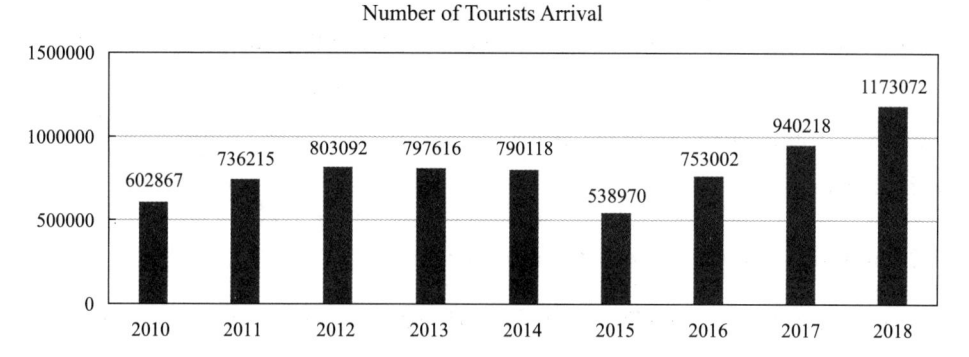

Number of Tourists Arrival

Year	Number
2010	602867
2011	736215
2012	803092
2013	797616
2014	790118
2015	538970
2016	753002
2017	940218
2018	1173072

II. Nepal China Relationship through Tourism

2.1 History of Nepal China Relationship

The relation between Nepal and China is very deep rooted. Nepal has the proud privilege of having a close relationship with China from the very early stage of history, which has gradually developed and expanded into all conceivable sectors affecting the daily life of the common people – socio-economic, cultural, religious, industrial, energy, environmental, Tourism, trade transits and commerce in recent days. This relationship is based on mutual trust, respect, understanding, and cooperation. Historically, this relationship is marked by arduous pilgrimages made by celebrated monks on both sides who made formidable travels across the Himalayas in quest of our common cultural, civilizational and religious heritage. The relationship was further enriched by the nuptial relationship of Princess Bhrikuti with Songtsen Gampo, in the 6th century, culminating into spread of Buddhism in China. This was followed by the journey of Artist Araniko in 13 century who built a chain of outstanding edifices of Nepalese craftsmanship in the form of Pagoda at various places during the reign of Yuan dynasty.

On 1 August 1955, a formal diplomatic relationship between Nepal and China was established. Nepal-China relationship is characterized by equality, harmonious coexistence, ever-lasting friendship and comprehensive cooperation. Furthermore,

Nepal is firmly committed to One China policy and is also committed not to allow its soil to be used for any inimical activities against china. The relations between the two countries have been marked by friendliness, understanding, mutual support, cooperation and respect for each other's sensitivities. Both countries have relentless faith on the ideals of the Five Principles of Peaceful Co-existence. Regular exchange of high-level visits has played an important role in further consolidating our mutually beneficial relations.

2.2 Contribution of China in Nepali Tourism

China contributed 153,602 tourists in 2018 with a rise of 46.8 percent compared to 2017. The share of Chinese visitors in total foreign tourists stood at 13.09 percent in 2018, according to NTB. This remarkable growth in foreign visitors has given boost as Nepal is working on "Visit Nepal 2020" campaign. This has prepared astound and solid platform to achieve the target of Visit Nepal Year 2020. China is second largest source of foreign tourists to Nepal. In early quarter of 2019, Chinese tourist topped the chart of foreign tourists. The Government of Nepal has waived Visa Fees for the Chinese Tourist effective from 1 Jan 2016. www.welcomenepal.cn is launched by Nepal Tourism Board in Chinese language for efficiency and easiness of Chinese Tourists. Chinese government announced 2017 as Nepal Tourism promotion year. Five Chinese carriers and construction of the Beijing-Lhasa railroad are the main modes of transportation for Chinese tourists. Direct air-link of Nepal with Lhasa, Xian, Chengdu, Kunming, Guangzhou and Hong Kong SAR of China is established.

China is helping to airports in Pokhara, gateway to the Annapurna Circuit trekking trail, and in Lumbini, the birthplace of Gautam Buddha. Following the devastating earthquakes of 2015, China provided 3 billion Yuan on Nepal's reconstruction to be used in mutually selected 25 major projects. Acknowledging China's help and initiative for economic development of Nepal, signing of the Memorandum of Understanding on Cooperation under the Belt and Road Initiative was done on 12 May 2017 in Kathmandu between Nepal and China.

Number of Tourists Arrival

Number of Chinese Tourists

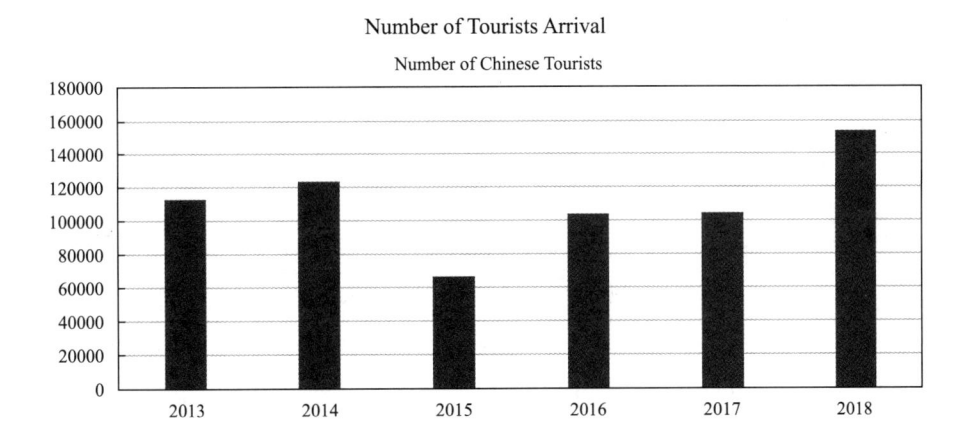

2.3 High Level Official Visit and Joint Statement

At the invitation of Rt. Hon. Bidya Devi Bhandari, President of Nepal, H.E., Xi Jinping, President of the People's Republic of China, paid a state visit to Nepal from 12 to 13 October 2019. During the visit, President Xi met with President Bhandari, held talks with Prime Minister K. P. Sharma Oli and attended the welcoming banquet by President Bhandari. In a warm and cordial atmosphere, leaders of the two countries reached broad understanding through in-depth exchange of views on bilateral relationship and regional and international issues of common concern.

1. The two sides expressed satisfaction over the fact that since the establishment of diplomatic relations between the two countries in 1955, China-Nepal relationship has withstood changes of the international situation and has been growing in a consistent, steady and healthy manner, which sets a model of peaceful coexistence between the countries of different size. Both sides recognized that the bilateral relationship between the two countries is characterized by equality, harmonious coexistence, ever-lasting friendship and comprehensive cooperation.

China and Nepal take the Belt and Road Initiative as an opportunity to deepen mutually beneficial cooperation in all fields in a comprehensive manner, jointly pursue common prosperity and dedicate themselves to maintaining peace, stability and development in the region. The bilateral relationship between China and Nepal has entered a new phase. Both sides decided to, on the basis of the Five Principles of Peaceful Coexistence, Charter of the United Nations and principles of good neighborliness, elevate China-Nepal Comprehensive Partnership of Cooperation Featuring Ever-lasting Friendship to Strategic Partnership of Cooperation Featuring Ever-lasting Friendship for Development and Prosperity.

2. The two sides agreed to respect each other's independence, sovereignty and territorial integrity, and respect and accommodate each other's concerns and core interests. The two sides will adhere to good neighboring policy and deepen overall cooperation in a win-win manner, so as to achieve mutual benefit and pursue stability and development together.

The Nepali side reiterated its firm commitment to One China policy, acknowledging that Taiwan is an inalienable part of the Chinese territory and Tibet Affairs are China's internal affairs, and the determination on not allowing any anti-China activities on its soil. The Chinese side reiterated its firm support to Nepal in upholding the country's independence, sovereignty and territorial integrity, and its firm support and respect to Nepal's social system and development path independently chosen in the light of Nepal's national conditions.

3. The Chinese side congratulated Nepal on the historic and epoch-making political transformation and its rapid economic and social development. It is believed that the Nepali people would unite as one and keep marching towards the vision of 'Samriddha Nepal, Sukhi Nepali' ('Prosperous Nepal, Happy Nepali'), so as to achieve political stability, social harmony and rapid economic development. The Chinese side expressed willingness to continue interacting with the Nepali side on the experience of governance.

The Nepali side congratulated on the 70th Anniversary of the Founding of the People's Republic of China and expressed its admiration to China's miraculous achievement in development over the past 70 years and sincerely wished that under the guidance of Xi Jinping Thought on Socialism with Chinese Characteristics for a New Era, the Chinese people would keep striving to realize the two centenary goals and build China a great modern socialist country that is prosperous, strong, democratic, culturally advanced, harmonious, and beautiful.

4. Both sides underlined that high-level contacts are of special importance to the development of bilateral relations. The two sides agreed to maintain the momentum of high-level visits, deepen political mutual trust and expand exchanges and cooperation between government ministries, departments, legislatures and political parties at all levels.

5. The two sides agreed to intensify implementation of the Memorandum of Understanding on Cooperation under the Belt and Road Initiative to enhance connectivity, encompassing such vital components as ports, roads, railways, aviation and communications within the overarching framework of trans-Himalayan Multi-Dimensional Connectivity Network with a view to significantly contributing to Nepal's development agenda that includes graduating from LDC at an early date, becoming middle income country by 2030 and realizing the SDGs by the same date.

The two sides, while recalling the MoU signed between the two countries on 21 June 2018 on Cooperation in Railway Project, agreed to conduct the feasibility study as outlined in the MoU signed on 13 October 2019, which will lay an important foundation to launching the construction of the Cross-Border Railway. Both sides also reiterated their commitment to extend cooperation on Kathmandu-Pokhara-Lumbini Railway Project.

The two sides welcomed the reopening and the restoration of the freight functions of the Zhangmu(Khasa) port and will optimize the functions of the Jilong(Kerung) port and open the Lizi(Nechung) port at the earliest possible time and build necessary infrastructure on the Nepali side of the border.

Both sides would keep implementing the Protocol concerning the Utilization of Highway in Tibet, China by Nepal for Cargo Transport and the Protocol to the Agreement on Transit Transport. On the basis of maintaining the long-term operational condition of the Araniko Highway, both sides agreed to cooperate on upgrading and reconstructing the highway on a priority basis in a step by step manner. The Chinese side conveyed its readiness in initiating the repair of Syaphrubesi-Rasuwagadhi Highway.

Realizing the importance of enhanced level of connectivity between the two countries, the two sides agreed to proactively cooperate on the feasibility study for the construction of the tunnels along the road from Jilong(Kerung) to Kathmandu.

The Chinese side noted the request made by the Nepali side for the construction of Kimathanka-Leguwaghat section of the Koshi Highway and agreed to consider this project in future cooperation plan and requested the Nepali side to submit a detailed proposal.

The two sides reiterated their commitment to undertake study on the possibility of cooperation, as reflected in the Joint Statement issued in Beijing on 21 June 2018, for the development of the three North-South corridors in Nepal, namely Koshi Economic Corridor, Gandaki Economic Corridor and Karnali Economic Corridor in order to create jobs and improve local livelihood, and stimulate economic growth and development.

The Chinese side will extend assistance for training Nepali technical human resources in the fields of railway, road and tunnel engineering as well as inland waterway and shipping.

Both sides welcomed the consensus reached by the civil aviation authorities of the two countries on expanding the air rights arrangements, under the framework of which the airlines of both countries are encouraged to launch/operate more direct air services. Both sides will coordinate closely to speed up the construction of the Pokhara International Airport so that it would start operation at an early date.

The two sides expressed satisfaction over the successful commercial operation of China-Nepal cross-border optical fiber cable and agreed to further strengthen cooperation on information and communications for mutual benefit.

6. The two sides agreed to strengthen cooperation in various fields of economy including trade, tourism, investment, capacity of production and improving people's livelihood so as to promote mutual development.

Under the framework of China-Nepal Joint Commission on Economy and Trade, the two sides will establish a working group on investment cooperation and a working group on trade led by secretary/vice minister-level officials or their designates so as to facilitate bilateral investment and trade. The Chinese side welcomed the Nepali side to participate in the National Exhibition of the Second China International Import Expo to be held in Shanghai in November 2019.

Both sides will hold comprehensive discussions with a view to strengthening trade relations between the two countries. The Chinese side will take positive measures to expand Nepal's export to China. The Chinese side will consider providing technical support for the establishment of a multifunctional laboratory in Nepal and extend necessary cooperation to make Tatopani Frontier Inspection Station at Larcha fully functional. Nepal will facilitate the Chinese banks to open their branches and other financial services in Nepal with a view to facilitating trade and investment between the two countries. Both sides will complete their internal procedure at the earliest time for the operationalization of the Protocol to the Transit Transport Agreement and try their best to implement it at an early date.

Both sides welcomed the signing of the Protocol on Phytosanitary requirements for the Export of Citrus Fruits from Nepal to China and agreed to conclude MoU on Cooperation on Import and Export of Food Safety at the earliest.

The two sides will continue cooperation on production capacity and investment according to the principles of "dominated by enterprises, respecting business principles, adhering to market-orientation and following international common practice".

On the basis of the Memorandum of Understanding on Energy Cooperation between the National Energy Administration of the People's Republic of China and the Ministry of Energy, Water Resource and Irrigation of Nepal signed on 21st June 2018, both sides will bring into full play the Joint Implementation Mechanism (JIM) on China-Nepal Cooperation in energy sector, to carry out exchanges and cooperation in the fields of hydropower, wind power, solar power, biomass energy and other kinds of new energy as well as grid system, etc. Both sides agreed to jointly carry out China-Nepal Electric Power Cooperation Plan and complete it within one year. Both sides agreed to take this Plan as an important reference for the next step of bilateral electric power cooperation and promote its implementation.

The Nepali side extended its deep appreciation to the Chinese side for the valuable support it has been providing in Nepal's development efforts and for the timely, spontaneous and generous support extended to Nepal's reconstruction after the earthquake in 2015.

The Chinese government will continue to provide assistance to Nepal's economic and social development within its capacity with an emphasis on strengthening cooperation in the field of improving people's livelihood.

The Chinese side attached great importance to the aspiration of the Nepali side to establish a multidisciplinary Madan Bhandari University for Science and Technology as a mark of respect to People's Leader Late Madan Bhandari and will extend support at the earliest date after the Nepali side chooses suitable site for the University. Both sides will continue their discussion on the basis of the report to be submitted by the site visit working group of the Chinese side.

The Chinese side is willing to expedite the project of improving the quality of supplied water in Kathmandu.

7. The Chinese side noted Nepal's proposal on Integrated Development, including resettlement of scattered population in the Himalayan Region of Nepal. The Chinese side is willing to share experiences and consider cooperating with the Nepali side on this proposal.

8. Recognizing that Mount Zhumulangma(Sagarmatha) is an eternal symbol of

the friendship between China and Nepal, the two sides will promote cooperation in different fields, including addressing climate change and protecting the environment. They will jointly announce the height of mount Zhumulangma(Sagarmatha) and conduct scientific researches.

9. Both sides expressed satisfaction with the signing of the Agreement between the Government of the People's Republic of China and the Government of Nepal on Boundary Management System, which will improve the level of boundary management and cooperation for both sides. They were also satisfied with signing the Treaty on Mutual Legal Assistance in Criminal Matters and expressed hope for an early conclusion of the Treaty on Extradition. The two sides agreed to strengthen cooperation between the law enforcement agencies on information exchanges, capacity building and training. In the next 3 years, China will offer 100 training opportunities to the Nepali law enforcement officers each year. With a view to promoting cooperation in security sector, the two sides will continue to strengthen cooperation in the exchange visits of the security personnel, joint exercises and training, disaster prevention and reduction and personnel training.

10. The two sides agreed to promote exchanges and cooperation in education, culture, tourism, traditional medicine, media, think tanks and youth at different levels. The Chinese side will offer the Nepali side 100 Confucius Institute Scholarships. The Chinese side supports the Nepali side to hold the activity of Visit Nepal Year 2020, welcomes the Nepali side to participate in the travel marts held in China and is willing to facilitate Nepal's promotion on tourism in China. The Chinese side will hold the 9th China Festival and 4th Kathmandu Cultural Forum in Nepal and continue to encourage the Chinese Cultural Center and the Confucius Institute to promote China-Nepal cultural exchanges and cooperation. The two sides welcomed that Nanjing of China and Kathmandu of Nepal, Xi'an city of China and Butwal Sub-Metropolitan city of Nepal had developed friendship-city relations.

11. The Chinese side consented to the establishment of Nepal's Consulate General in Chengdu, Sichuan Province of China.

12. Both sides agreed to revitalize the existing mechanisms between the two countries to further strengthen relations and advance mutually beneficial cooperation in various fields.

13. Both sides agreed to strengthen cooperation in the United Nations and other multilateral fora and safeguard common interests of developing countries. Both sides exchanged fruitful views on promoting collaboration and strengthening cooperation in regional issues and agreed to support each other on matters of mutual interests. The two sides expressed firm commitment to the multilateral trading regime and work for a more open, inclusive and balanced economic globalization with shared benefits.

14. Both sides held that President Xi Jinping's state visit, on the historic occasion of the 70th anniversary of the founding of the People's Republic of China, to Nepal marked the beginning of a new era in China-Nepal relations and served as an important milestone in the history of friendly cooperation between the two countries. The Chinese side would like to extend its sincere gratitude to the Government of Nepal and its people for their warm and friendly reception.

2.4 List of Instruments Signed and Exchanged between Nepal and China

Nepal and China have signed and exchanged various agreements and memorandum of understandings (MoUs) during the State Visit of Chinese President Xi Jinping. The list of instruments signed and exchanged between Nepal and China are:

1. Agreement between the Governments of Nepal and the People's Republic of China on the Boundary Management System

2. MoU between the Governments of Nepal and the People's Republic of China on the Exchanges and Cooperation on Governance Capacity Building

3. Treaty between Nepal and the People's Republic of China on Mutual Legal Assistance in Criminal Matters

4. MoU on Mount Sagarmatha(Zhumulangma) Protection Cooperation between Nepal and China

5. MoU on Promoting Key Projects of Investment and Cooperation on Productive Capacity between the National Planning Commission of Nepal and the National Development and Reform Commission of the People's Republic of China

6. Exchange of Note for Setting up a Consulate General of Nepal in Chengdu

7. MoU between the Ministry of Physical Infrastructure and Transport of Nepal and the Ministry of Transport of the People's Republic of China on Feasibility Study of China-Nepal Cross-Border Railway Project

8. Agreement between Kathmandu Metropolitan City of Nepal and Nanjing City of the People's Republic of China on the Establishment of Sister-City Relationship

9. Agreement between Butwal Sub-Metropolitan City of Nepal and Xi'an City of the People's Republic of China on the Establishment of Sister-City Relationship

10. MoU on Cooperation on Traditional Medicine between the Ministry of Health and Population of the Government of Nepal and the National Administration of Traditional Chinese Medicine of the People's Republic of China

11. MoU between the Ministry of Home Affairs of Nepal and the Ministry of Emergency Management of the People's Republic of China Regarding Cooperation in Disaster Risk Reduction and Emergency Response

12. MoU on Cooperation between the Supreme People's Procurator of the People's Republic of China and Office of the Attorney General of Nepal

13. Agreement between Tribhuvan University of Nepal and Confucius Institute Headquarters of China on the Establishment of Confucius Institute at Tribhuvan University

14. Protocol of Phytosanitary Requirements for the Export of Citrus Fruits from

Nepal to China between Department of Agriculture of the Government of Nepal and General Administration of Customs of the People's Republic of China

15. MoU between the Ministry of Industry, Commerce and Supplies of the Government of Nepal and the Ministry of Commerce of the People's Republic of China on the Establishment of Joint Working Group on Trade

16. Delivery and Acceptance Certificate for the China-Aid Earthquake Monitoring Network Project in Nepal

17. MoU on Establishment of Investment Cooperation Working Group between the Ministry of Finance of Nepal and the Ministry of Commerce of the People's Republic of China

18. MoU between the Ministry of Finance of Nepal and China International Development Cooperation Agency on Tunnels Construction Cooperation

19. Exchange of Letter for Border Security Equipment and Office Equipment

20. Minutes of Meeting for Feasibility Investigation of China-Aid Municipal Water Supply Improvement Project in Kathmandu Valley of Nepal

III. Conclusion

As Nepal is going to celebrate 2020 as visit Nepal year, it has to increase the investment in tourism. It has to explore the pattern of Chinese enterprises investing in Nepali scenic spots, hotels and travel agencies. More direct flights from Beijing, Shanghai, Guangzhou, Shenzhen, Hangzhou, Nanjing, Chengdu, Xi'an and Lhasa to Kathmandu, Nepal needs to open to facilitate tourists from different parts of China. Tourism practitioners should be trained enough to meet international standards and criteria. Tourist window needs to open in major Chinese cities with the population of more than 10 million, including publicity books, videos and special commodities. High-level research projects for high school and college students should be organized to exchange technology and skills. Nepal and China have to prioritize the implementation of the MoU on Cooperation under the BRI (Belt and Road Initiative) to enhance connectivity, which includes ports, roads, railways, aviation and communications in the framework of the Trans-Himalayan Multi-Dimensional Connectivity Network.

References

Shrestha, H., & Shrestha, P. (2012). Tourism in Nepal: A Historical Perspective and Present Trend of Development. Himalayan Journal of Sociology and Anthropology, 5, 54-75. https://doi.org/10.3126/hjsa.v5i0.7039

Bhattarai, Sundar Nath, Nepal-China Relationship: Its intrinsic attributes, Kathmandu, Makalu Publication House (2018), ISBN: 978-9937-622-87-5.

Sangroula, Yubraj, South Asia-China Geo-Economics, Bhaktapur, Lex & Juris Publication (2018), ISBN: 978-9937-0-5236-8

China's New Leadership: The Fifth Generation, Kathmandu, China Study Center, (2013) (https://www.cscnepal.org.np), ISBN: 978-9937-8147-1-3

Workshop on China-Nepal-India Economic Corridor (CNIEC) Feasibility and Approaches, Kathmandu, China Study Center, (2017) (https://www.cscnepal.org.np), ISSN: 2467-9542

Government of Nepal, Ministry of Foreign Affairs Singha Durbar, Kathmandu, Nepal. (https://mofa.gov.np/Nepal-china-relations/)

First Year of China's Diplomacy Under the New Leadership, Kathmandu, China Study Center, (2013-14) (https://www.cscnepal.org.np), ISBN: 978-9937-8147-2-0

Friendship Journal of Nepal-China Studies, Kathmandu, China Study Center, (2016) (https://www.cscnepal.org.np), ISSN: 2467-9542

Nepal Tourism Statistics 2018, Government of Nepal, Ministry of Culture, Tourism and Civil Aviation (2019), (https://www.welcomenepal.com)

https://www.nepalisansar.com/tourism/2018-nepal-tourist-arrivals-reaches-magical-1-million-mark/

科特迪瓦的中资企业案例研究

阿里妈咪 【科特迪瓦】
费利克斯·胡弗埃·博伊尼大学　研究员

在过去十年中，通过直接投资、合同项目和贸易，中国在科特迪瓦的商业参与度迅速增长。2014年至2016年间，中国与科特迪瓦间的贸易增长了800%。中国已成为科特迪瓦的第三大贸易伙伴。

总部位于科特迪瓦的中国商会（CCEC）注册的中资企业约有40家，分布在多个领域，包括饮用水供应、阿比让港扩建工程、国家电网扩建工程、光纤网络和水电站大坝的建设。

本文收集了科特迪瓦人对这些公司的看法并分析了其形成的原因。

一　研究方法

虽然我们注意到在科特迪瓦运营的中国公司有国有企业（SOE）、私营企业（POE）和混合型中资公司，但我们的研究仅关注在以下领域运营的中小型和大型公司，即：农业、采矿、能源、住房和建筑。关注这些部门，主要是因为它们具有生态和社会敏感性。

本研究在上述4个行业中各选择了6家公司，也就是选择了在科特迪瓦经营的大约40家中资公司中的24家公司。其依据是这些公司在这些行业中拥有举足轻重的影响力，其中有15家是在科特迪瓦具有竞争力的公司。在8个月的时间内（从2019年9月到2020年4月），我们采访了1200名在科特迪瓦中资公司工作的科特迪瓦人，还采访了 48 名社区委员会负责人（关键线人访谈），他们来自不同的地理区域以及这些公司所在的社区。

由于受访者被告知所收集的数据仅用于研究目的，因此他们将在报告中得到匿名保护，我们在本文中仅披露对研究结果进行上下文分析所需的最低数量的细节。由于本研究涉及认知分析，定性数据收集方法（包括焦点小组讨论、访谈和参与/观察）和定量研究（基于各种形式的调查）都被用来揭示思想和观点的趋势。访谈包括半结构化讨论和调查。本项研究参考了相关期刊文章、书籍和科特迪瓦领导人发表的演讲。

本文从以下几方面来衡量当地人对中资企业的看法：(i) 中资企业在中国的声誉；(ii) 服务和/或制造产品的质量；(iii) 企业社会责任；(iv) 就业实践。

二　研究局限性

必须指出，我们没有足够的时间来观察这些公司的行为，也没有时间与他们的高层管理人员建立信任关系，导致存在一些受访者信任度低的潜在问题，以及访谈结论可能有矛盾。因此，这篇论文不是为了得出一个最终结论，而是抛砖引玉，让读者参与关于中资企业在科特迪瓦和整个非洲存在的热烈讨论。

三　研究发现

1. 对中资企业声誉的看法

正如沃瑟曼（Wasserman：2012）所说，从总体角度来看，中资企业在非洲的存在通常被视为一种完全的二元关系：要么是一种剥削和掠夺，要么是一种发展伙伴。科特迪瓦的情况也不例外。我们在本研究框架内采访的科特迪瓦人对在科特迪瓦经营的中资公司的声誉有着复杂的感受，这些公司的形象好坏参半。我们对总部位于科特迪瓦的中资企业声誉的调查结果很好地反映了这种对比。调查结果显示，**47%** 的看法描绘了这些公司良好的正面形象，而 **53%** 的看法是负面的。

中资企业的支持者不仅将其视为替代欧洲和美国在当地市场主导地位的实体，还将其视为向一个经济陷入困境的国家提供援助的企业。支持者进一步指出，这些公司与许多当地同行进行了一种双赢的经济合作。

这种正面的形象受到了媒体助长的相对消极看法的挑战，那些观点认为位于科特迪瓦的中资企业没有为促进当地经济做出贡献，也没有促进国内竞争对手的发展，因为他们不断向当地市场供应从中国进口的廉价商品 (Carmody, 2011; Fergus, 2013; Kofi, 2014)，而不是支持当地的创造力和创业精神。还有一些认为中资企业在扩大生产能力方面的政策缺乏明确而详细的当地发展计划（包括对当地科特迪瓦员工的专业培训），也缺乏传授技能和经验的计划。中资企业也因没有给那些优秀的当地员工足够的在其中国总部接受进一步的专业培训的机会而受到批评。

2. 对中国制造的服务和/或产品质量的看法

对中资企业提供的服务和产品质量的认知调查是在年龄在 15 至 49 岁之间的人群中进行的。在对中资企业产品质量的采访中，我们看到了一幅复杂的图景，其中消费者购买力低以及刺激他们订购或购买中国产品的误导性广告等促进了人民消费。

我们的调查显示，在对中国产品消费的增长中，有 87% 以上的服务消费或产品是由位于科特迪瓦的中资企业生产或从中国进口的。这些产品从重型农业机械到家用电器无所不包。

受访者的普遍共识是，中资企业提供了在当地市场销售的欧美商品的替代品。虽然美国产品在科特迪瓦国民的"消费偏好"排行榜上名列前茅，但重要的是，正如我们的调查结果所证明的那样，居民的消费偏好已经从"法国产品"迅速转变为"中国产品"。事实上，超过 57% 的目标人群偏爱美国产品，24% 偏爱中国产品，19% 偏爱法国产品。声称偏好中国服务和产品并愿意订购、使用或购买这些服务和产品的受访者表示，他们认为这些服务/产品的质量可以接受，并认为平均价格可以承受。

采访显示，那些放弃中资企业产品的科特迪瓦国民的看法主要针对中资产品的耐用性较差。事实上，一些受访者明确表示，其中一些产品质量低劣，要么对人体健康有害，要么不太环保。

值得一提的是，一些受访者只从当地媒体听说过中国产品的质量，这些媒体要么由西方媒体集团所有，要么由西方人或当地人经营而由欧洲或美国的上级控制。然而，这些媒体往往——或许更多的时候——并没有传达中资企业产品的正面形象。

从这个角度来看，我们可以指出，中国产品/服务在当地市场上的一个主要问题是，它们没有强大的媒体宣传活动跟进来改变当地消费者的认知和购买决定。

换句话说，中资企业制定的营销政策在纸面上可能是明确的、意图很好的，但如果它不结合当地实际情况，就无法有效解决当地媒体对中国商品的"抨击"。

3. 对科特迪瓦中资企业社会责任的看法

本节探讨在科特迪瓦的中资企业的声誉如何受到其企业社会责任政策的影响。研究建议这些公司可以在更大程度上提高其在客户、消费者、东道主国社区和国民中的声誉的方式开展企业社会责任活动。

在本研究的框架内，企业社会责任应该通过"世界可持续发展商业理事会"（WBCSD 2004）提出的广义定义来理解，它将企业社会责任定义为"企业践行致力于经济的可持续发展的承诺，与员工及其家庭、东道主社区和整个社会合作，提高他们的生活质量。"基于这一定义，企业社会责任（CSR）与企业声誉之间存在关联，消费者、客户和东道主社区往往将企业的价值观和声誉与其CSR政策联系起来。

大多数接受采访的公司都强调他们重视参与社区建设。他们自豪地展示了自己的一些社区活动成果，其中包括修建或翻新道路、学校、5个卫生设施和市场，并向孤儿院、青年或妇女组织捐款。然而，我们的调查显示，60%受访的东道主社区不认可中资企业对社区请求的回应。超过70%的社区称，公司对社区的回应对社区的凝聚力的提升产生了负面的影响，有时甚至忽视了对环境的尊重和保护。因此，在科特迪瓦的许多地区，东道主国社区与中国公司都有过紧张关系。

调查进一步显示，在大多数情况下，除少数设有公共关系部门的大公司，中资企业对东道主国社区请求的回应大多是非正式的。

大多数接受调查的企业都缺乏明确的书面的企业社会责任书以及与所在社区保持沟通的正式规定。他们与这些社区的关系往往没有纳入任何计划；往往是非正式、个人化和随意的，经常是出于对地方当局或社区领导人的呼吁的反应，而这些呼吁并不总是社区真实和迫切的需求。

4. 对中资企业就业实践的看法

总体而言，接受采访的员工（在中国公司工作）认为，中国经理对当地国家劳工政策和法律的认识较低。57%的受访者表示，他们不满意中资企业有关劳动条件的管理政策。他们明确表示，管理者无视劳动法赋予工人的权利。这些权利包括结社自由、加入工会的权利，以及在安全环境中获得公平工资的权利。53%的受访工人强调，大多数工人没有在国家社会保障局（CNPS）登记，因为他们没有签订书面雇用合同。因此，这些工人往往被迫在没有医保和社保的情况下工作。75% 的受访者指出，中资企业对科特迪瓦的文化和社会习俗方面认识不足。他们认为，这些企业的经理们会拒绝与生活和文化事件（婚姻、死亡、出生和其他文化活动）有关的休假。这些受访者对工人培训、安全和公司简介方面政策缺失表示了一定程度的不满。他们还认为，公司不提供激励员工的措施。

四　结论和建议

本研究的主要调查结果提出了科特迪瓦国民对在科中资公司的看法，并基于公司声誉、产品和服务质量、企业社会责任和就业实践等因素探讨了这些看法。这项研究揭示了这些观念背后的原因，旨在帮助中资企业更好地了解其经营地当地文化背景，从而改善其形象和影响。该研究调查了在科特迪瓦经营的约 40 家在中国商会注册的中资企业中的 24 家，还有 15 家科特迪瓦人拥有的同行公司，以及 48 名来自这些公司运营区域和社区的社区委员会负责人。

1. 中资企业的声誉

本研究不是试图评估中资企业在科特迪瓦的总体影响，而是了解科特迪瓦人对这些企业声誉度看法的主要原因。

中国产品的质量（低质量商品的生产和销售，加上当地市场充斥着廉价产品）、企业社会责任和就业实践被认为是建立"科特迪瓦国民对在科经营的中资企业印象"的最主要因素。这些因素是造成这些公司的声誉的基础。

除上述因素外，媒体还在塑造公众对在科中国公司的看法和态度方面发挥着关键作用。不良或不公平的报道确实扮演了重要角色，受访者认为它们主要提供了关于中资企业正面或负面的形象。毋庸置疑，将媒体宣传作为这些公司改善形象和声誉战略的核心应该是头等大事。

2. 中资企业的服务和产品质量

大多数位于科特迪瓦的中国公司从中国进口低成本商品，并在当地市场转售。这些公司销售的廉价但劣质的商品受到低收入人群的青睐。但是，与这些商品相关的误导性和不真实的广告仍然是一个问题。事实上，虽然消费者承认这些商品是资金有限的科特迪瓦人创业的垫脚石，但他们感到经常被与这些商品有关的欺骗和虚假宣传所误导。

不仅是误导性广告欺骗了消费者，并引发了对中资企业的产品服务和产品质量的负面认知，而且存在西方或本地人拥有或经营的媒体的影响，这些媒体受欧洲或美国高级别的控制，传达并延续对中国产品/服务的偏见和刻板印象，并影响消费者的认知和购买决策。

除非中资企业通过强有力的媒体宣传支持其商品的营销，或者赞助当地媒体纠正这些偏见，否则很难改变当地人对这些商品质量的看法。他们的营销政策可能在纸面上很明确，用意也很好，但只要不结合实际情况，就无法有效应对当地媒体对中国商品的"抨击"。

3. 关于企业社会责任

大多数接受采访的中资企业都强调了他们的社区参与，并自豪地展示了他们对东道主社区的支持（包括社区工作和捐款）。然而，在大多数情况下，上述工作的受益者不认可这些公司对社区所做的工作，因为这种回应通常是非正式的、个人的（并不总是表达社区真实和迫切的需求），并且是在特定的情况下发生的。

明智之举是建立一个专门负责公共关系的部门，制定明确的书面CSR（企业社会责任）政策，并制定与东道主社区保持沟通的正式政策。事实上，良好的社区关系对在科特迪瓦做生意至关重要，在非洲其他地方也是如此。在科特迪瓦的特定环境中，如果当地人支持在社区安家的公司，他们就更有可能变得友好和合作。最重要的是，正式的公共关系部门是减少偏见和改善运营环境的关键工具。

4. 对中资企业就业实践的看法

尽管中国工人和中国管理者被视为非常守时，在他们的工作领域技术也非常熟练，对他们的员工也被视为诚实可靠，但在中国公司的科特迪瓦员工中存在一种看法，即中国管理人员和经理人的利益高于员工福利。

科特迪瓦员工对中国管理者及其中国同事的沟通方式持批评态度。他们认为，中国管理者及其中国同事在建立人际关系之前非常重视工作，最终导致公司员工之间缺乏联系。在中资企业的雇佣关系和领导层管理的所有方面中，受访者对劳动条件最为挑剔，他们强调了一个事实，即公司的许多员工不是根据书面合同雇佣的，剥夺他们享受社会福利的权利，以及工人经常在应休假的时候被拒绝。

对中资企业雇佣行为的认知意味着科特迪瓦工人和他们的中国同事在对待工作的认知上存在文化差异。事实上，虽然中国工人和管理者非常重视结果，把工作放在首位，但科特迪瓦人更重视培养他们与同事之间的人际关系，这导致了这两种不同的"工作"观和从业实践成见之间的文化冲突。

毫无疑问，文化在对从业实践的认知中起着至关重要的作用。如果中资企业的管理者鼓励中国工人和他们的科特迪瓦同事更多地互动，学习彼此的语言和文化习俗，定期举办关于文化与工作实践之间关系的研讨会，将有助于减少或避免工作场所的误解。

本研究揭示了一些对科特迪瓦人关于中资企业的看法和观念有很大影响的因素，这些观念形成了他们对中国经济参与的看法。中资公司在科特迪瓦和其他有类似文化背景和管理模式的发展中国家开展业务时，这些研究结果也阐明了一些更具建设性和可持续发展的可能路径。

Local's Perceptions of Chinese Economic Engagement in Africa: Case Study of Chinese-owned Companies Operating in Côte d'Ivoire (West Africa)

Gbane Alymamy / Côte d'Ivoire

University Felix Houphouet Boigny/Economic PhD. student and Junior Researcher

China's business engagement in Côte d'Ivoire has grown rapidly in the past decade through direct investment, contract projects and trade. Trade between China and Côte d'Ivoire grew by 800% between 2014 and 2016. China has become Côte d'Ivoire's third largest trade partner. There are about 40 Chinese-owned companies registered with Côte d'Ivoire-based Chinese Business Chamber of Commerce (CCEC) and which are present in various sectors, including drinking water supply, the Abidjan harbor extension construction works, the extension of national electricity grid, optic fiber networks and the construction of hydroelectric dam. What follows is an exposé of how Ivorians perceive these companies, and the reasons of their perceptions are exposed and discussed.

I. Research Methodology

While we acknowledge the existence of Chinese State-Owned Enterprises (SOE) and Privately Owned Enterprises (POE) and hybrid Chinese-owned companies operating in Côte d'Ivoire, our research focuses only on small, medium and large companies operating in the following fields: (i)-agriculture; (ii)-mining; (iii)-energy; (iv)-housing and construction. We focus on these sectors, mainly because they are ecologically and socially sensitive.

For this research, 6 companies were selected in each of the 4 sectors mentioned above. Then, in total, 24 companies over approximately 40 Chinese-owned companies operating in Cote d'Ivoire were selected, on the basis of their having a commanding and large presence in these sectors, along with 15 rival companies owned by Ivorian nationals. Within a 8-month period (from September 2019 to April 2020), we interviewed a total of 1200 Ivorians national working for Chinese-owned companies in Côte d'Ivoire and we also interviewed 48 heads of Communities' Councils (key-informant interviews) from the geographical areas and the communities were these companies are based.

As the respondents were told that the data collected are to be used only for research purposes, and that their anonymity would be protected in the research write-up, we are therefore only disclosing the minimum amount of detail needed to contextualize our findings throughout this paper. As this research is concerned with a perception analysis, both qualitative data collection methods (including focus group discussions, interviews and participation/observations) and quantitative research (based on various forms of surveys) were used to uncover trends in thought and opinions, and dive deeper into the problem. Interviews consisted of semi-structured discussions plus a survey. For this research, journal articles, books and speeches by Ivorians leaders were consulted.

The following categories have been identified to measure locals' perception of Chinese-owned companies: (i) Reputation of Chinese-owned businesses in the country; (ii) Quality of services and or products manufactured; (iii) Corporate social responsibility ; (iv) Employment practices.

II. Limitations

What follows is a presentation of the findings about Ivorian nationals' perception towards Chinese-owned businesses. It is important to point out the fact that we did not have enough time to observe practices within these companies ; neither did we have time to build trust with their top managers ; leading to potential issues of low trust in some interviewees, and possible inconsistency of interview sets. Then. We present this paper not as a presentation of final conclusions but as a means to engage readers in the vibrant ongoing debates about the presence of Chinese-owned companies in Cote d'Ivoire and all over Africa.

III. Key Findings

1. Perception of the Reputation Of Chinese-Owned Businesses

As Wasserman (2012) argues, from a general perspective, the presence of Chinese-owned businesses in Africa is often viewed in stark binary terms: as either an exploitative, predatory force or a development partner. The Ivorian context makes no exception. Ivorian nationals we interviewed in the framework on this study have mixed feelings about the reputation of Chinese-owned companies operating in Côte d'Ivoire. These companies have attracted a mixture of favorable and unfavorable images. This contrast is well captured by the results of our survey on the perception of the reputation of Côte d'Ivoire-based Chinese-owned businesses which reveal that 47% of perceptions portray a favorable positive image of these companies, while 53% are negative.

Proponents for Chinese-owned companies not only see them as entities providing an alternative to the European and American dominance of the local markets, but also as businesses bringing an aid to a country struggling with its economy. Proponents have further argued that these companies have entered a kind of economic win-win cooperation with many of their local counterparts.

This positive image is challenged by a relatively negative perception, not only fueled by media but also, based on the beliefs that Côte d'Ivoire-based Chinese-owned companies do not contribute to foster local economy and boost national rival companies as they keep flooding the local markets with cheap goods imported from China (Carmody, 2011; Fergus, 2013; Kofi, 2014), instead of supporting local creativity and entrepreneurship.

Some of these beliefs are also based on the ideas that the policies of Chinese-owned companies, regarding the expansion of their production capability, lack a clear and detailed local development plan, including professional training for local Ivorian employees, and the absence of a plan to transfer skills and experience. Chinese-owned companies are under critics for not giving enough opportunities to those excellent locals working for them to further their professional training at their headquarters of in China.

2. Perception of Quality of Services and or Products Manufactured by Chinese-Owned Companies

The survey on the perception of the quality of services and products offered by Chinese-owned companies was carried out on a population whose age varies between 15 and 49 years. The picture that emerged from the interviews on the quality of products manufactured by Chinese-owned companies is a complex one in which aspects such as consumers' low purchasing power and the misleading advertising to encourage and push them to order or buy Chinese products play a pivotal role.

The growth in Chinese products' consumption is supported by our investigations which revealed that more than 87% of the population uses or consumes services or products manufactured either by Chinese companies based in Côte d'Ivoire and run by Chinese nationals or products imported from China. These products run from heavy agricultural machines to household appliances.

The general consensus among interviewees is that Chinese-owned companies offer an alternative to European and American goods sold on local markets. While American products top the list of consumption preferences' of Ivorian nationals, it is important to point out the fact that there has been a quick shift from consumption preferences' from French products to Chinese products, as evidenced by the results of our survey.

Indeed, more than 57% of the targeted population have a preference for American products, 24% for Chinese products and 19% for French products.

Interviewees who claimed preferences for Chinese services and products, and who are willing to order, use or buy them, said that the find the quality of these services/products acceptable, and considered the average price affordable.

Interviews revealed that the main argument supporting the perception of those Ivorian nationals who turn their back to products manufactured by Chinese-owned companies is that of the sustainability of the products. Indeed some interviewees explicitly stated that some of these products were of poor quality, either harmful for human health or not so eco-friendly.

It is however important to mention that, some of the respondents had only heard of the quality of Chinese products from local media either owned by Western-based media groups and or run by Westerners or locals that are under the controlled of Europe or US-based hierarchical superiors. These media, often, however – and perhaps more often than not – do not convey a positive image of products manufactured by Chinese-owned companies.

From this perspective, one of the major problems that we can point out concerning with Chinese products/services offered on local markets is that their are not accompanied with strong media advertising campaign to change local consumers' perception and change their purchasing decision. In other words, the marketing policy set by Chinese-owned companies may be clear and well-intentioned on paper, but as long as it does not integrate ground realities, it could not effectively address the 'bashing' of Chinese goods in local media.

3. Perception of Cote D'Ivoire-Based Chinese-owned Companies Corporate Social Responsibility

This section examines how the reputation of Côte d'Ivoire-based Chinese-owned companies is influenced by their CSR policies. It exposes whether CSR activities are carried out by these companies in a such a way that they enhance their reputation with clients, consumers, host communities and populations, to a much greater extent.

In the framework of this research, CSR should be perceived or comprehended through the broad definition proposed by the World Business Council for Sustainable Development (WBCSD 2004), which defined CSR as "the commitment of a business to contribute to sustainable economic development, working with employees, their families, the local community and society at large to improve their quality of life." Based on this definition, needless to say there is a correlation between corporate social responsibility (CSR) and the reputation of businesses and that consumers, clients and host communities very often relate companies' value and reputation to their CSR policy.

Most of the companies interviewed emphasized their community engagement. They proudly exhibited some of their community works which include building or renovating roads, schools, health facilities and markets and donating money to sponsor orphanages and youth or women organizations.

Yet, our survey revealed that 60% of host communities interviewed disagreed with Chinese-owned companies' response to community requests. More than 70% of these communities described the companies' community response as having a corrosive effect on community consolidation and strengthening, and sometimes as a response that overlooks respect and protection of the environment. As a result, in many regions of Côte d'Ivoire, host communities experienced strained relations with Chinese-owned companies.

The survey further revealed that in most cases, Chinese-owned companies' response to host communities' request is occurred mostly in an informal way, except in the case of a handful of large companies that have public relations departments.

A majority of the businesses surveyed, lacked a clear written CSR policy and a formal policy on maintaining communication with host communities. Their relationships with these communities are very often, not built into any plan; they are very informal and personal and occurred situationally, in response to requests from local authorities or community leaders who do not always express communities' real and pressing needs.

4. Perception of Employment Practices of Chinese Businesses

In general, employees (working in Chinese-owned companies) interviewed felt that Chinese managers have a low awareness of national employment policies and laws. 57% of these interviewees said they were dissatisfied with the managerial policy of Chinese-owned companies regarding labor conditions. They explicitly stated that managers ignore employment laws and rights that empower workers. These include freedom of association, the right to join a trade union, and the right to work for a fair wage in a safe environment. 53% of the workers interviewed emphasized the fact that most of the workers are not registered with the National Social Security Agency (CNPS), since they are not hired on the basis of a written contract. As a consequence, these workers are often obliged to work without health care or social services.

75% of the interviewees pointed out the fact that Chinese-owned businesses have a low awareness of unwritten governance factors such as cultural and social practices in Côte d'Ivoire. They felt that managers of these businesses turn their back to leaves related to life and cultural events (marriage, death, birth and other cultural events). A degree of bitterness was expressed among these interviewees about the lack of policy regarding worker training and safety and carrier profile. They also felt that companies do not provide incentives to motivate workforce.

IV. Conclusion and Recommendations

This research presents the key findings about the perceptions of Ivorian nationals on Chinese-owned companies based in Côte d'Ivoire. It explores these perceptions on the basis of factors such as the reputation of the companies, the quality of their products and services, their corporate social responsibility and employment practices. This research exposes the reasons underlying these perceptions with the aim to help Chinese-owned companies better understand the local cultural context in which they operate in order to improve both their image and impact. It surveyed 24 companies over approximately 40 Chinese-owned companies operating in Cote d'Ivoire and registered with the Chinese Business Chamber of Commerce (CCEC); 15 rival companies owned by Ivorian nationals; 1200 Ivorian nationals working as employees at Chinese-owned companies and 48 heads of Communities' Councils from the geographical areas and the communities were these companies operate.

1. On the Reputation Of Chinese-Owned Businesses

Rather than attempting to evaluate Chinese-owned companies' overall impact in Côte d'Ivoire, this study captures Ivorian nationals' perceptions of the main drivers of these companies' reputation.

The quality of Chinese products (the production and sale of low-quality commodities coupled with flooding local markets with cheap products), Corporate Social Responsibility and employment practices are seen as factors contributing the most to building the perceptions' of Ivorian nationals on Chinese-owned companies operating in Côte d'Ivoire. These factors lay the very foundations of the reputation of these companies.

Beyond the above mentioned factors, media also plays a pivotal role in shaping public perception of, and attitudes towards Chinese-owned companies operating in Côte d'Ivoire. There is indeed a poor or unfair media coverage of key factors the respondents believed primarily provided them with a positive or negative image of China-owned companies. Needless to say that putting media support at the heart of the strategy of these companies to improve their image and their reputation should be a top priority.

2. On the Quality of Services and or Products Manufactured by Chinese-Owned Companies

Most of Côte d'Ivoire-based Chinese-owned companies import low-cost goods from China and resell them on local markets. The cheap but low quality goods sold by these companies in Cote d'Ivoire are preferred by the low income populations. But, the misleading and untruthful advertisement associated with these goods remain a problem. In fact, while consumers acknowledge that these goods serve as a stepping-stone for Ivorian nationals with limited funds, to start their own businesses, they felt misled by deceitful and false propaganda that are very often associated with the goods.

It is not just misleading advertising which deceives the consumer and provokes a negative perception of the quality of services and products manufactured by Chinese-owned companies. There is also the influence of media, owned or run by Westerners or locals that are under the controlled of Europe or US-based hierarchical superiors, which convey and perpetuate biases and stereotypes about Chinese products/services and influence consumers' perception and purchasing decision.

Unless Chinese-owned companies support the marketing of their goods with a strong media campaign or unless they sponsor local media to correct these biases, they could hardly change locals' perception of the quality of these goods. Their marketing policy may be clear and wellintentioned on paper, but as long as it does not integrate ground realities, it could not effectively address the 'bashing' of Chinese goods in local media.

3. On Corporate Social Responsibility

Most of the Chinese-owned companies interviewed emphasized their community engagement and proudly exhibited their support to host communities (including community works and money donations). Yet, people supposed to be the beneficiaries of these works, most of the times, disagree with companies' response to community requests, as this response is very often informal, personal (do not always express communities' real and pressing needs) and occurs situationally.

Establishing a department dedicated to public relations, with a clear written CSR (Corporate Social Responsibility) policy and a formal policy on maintaining communication with host communities would be a wise move. In fact, good community relations are essential to doing business in Côte d'Ivoire, likewise elsewhere in Africa. In the Ivorian particular context, if locals sympathize with companies implanted in their neighborhoods, they are more likely to become pleasant and cooperative. Above all, a formal public relations department is a critical tool for reducing biases, prejudices and improving the operating environment.

4. Perception of Employment Practices of Chinese-owned Businesses

Though Chinese workers and Chinese managers are seen as very punctual, skilled in their field of work and perceived as honest and reliable towards their employees, there exists a perception among Ivorian nationals, employees of Chinese-owned companies, that Chinese managers priorities results over the employees' welfare.

Ivorian employees are critical of the communication style of Chinese managers and their Chinese colleagues who they think put a heavy emphasis on work before building interpersonal relationships culminating in a lack of bonding between workers at the companies. Of all aspects of employment practices and leadership management of Chinese-owned companies, the interviewees were most critical of the labor conditions, with an emphasis on the fact that and that many workers at the companies are not hired on the basis of an written contract, depriving them of the benefit of social services and the fact that workers are very often denied leaves, even when they deserve it.

The perception of employment practices of Chinese-owned companies implies a cultural difference in how work is perceived between Ivorian workers and their Chinese coworkers. Indeed, while Chinese workers and managers heavily priorities results and put work first and foremost, Ivorian nationals put a higher value in nurturing interpersonal relationships between them and their fellow coworkers, this resulting in a cultural clash between these two different outlooks on the subject of "work" and biases about employment practices.

Culture undoubtedly plays a crucial role in the perception of employment practices. If managers of Chinese-owned companies encourage Chinese workers and their Ivorian colleagues to interact more and learn each other languages and cultural practices and if they conduct periodic workshops on the relationship between culture and work engagement, they will arguably help reduce or avoid workplace misunderstandings.

The findings of this research reveal factors that have a great influence on Ivorian's perceptions and views of Chinese-owned operating in their country and which shape their view of China's economic engagement. The findings implicitly identify potential avenues for more constructive and sustainable engagement with these companies in Côte d'Ivoire and in other developing countries with similar cultural framework and governance conditions.

References

Abidjan.net. 2020. "Les relations Chine -Côte d'Ivoire se trouvent à leur meilleur niveau de l'histoire". https://news.abidjan.net/h/667912.html (Posted on 1/4/2020), Consulted on June16, 2020. AIP -Agence Ivoirienne de Presse-2017. "Le DG de CRBC s'explique sur les affrontements entre des Chinois et des ouvriers ivoiriens à Odienné", culled from :

https://aip.ci/le-dg-de-crbc-sexplique-sur-les-affrontements-entre-des-chinois-et-des-ouvriersivoiriens-a-odienne/ (Published on 06/04/2017) Albert, Eleanor. 2017. "China in Africa." https://www.cfr.org/backgrounder/china-africa Anton, Petersson. 2018. Perceptions of Chinese influence in Sub-Saharan Africa, Jönköping University, 29p. Bijian, Zheng. (2005). China's 'Peaceful Rise' to Great Power status. Foreign Affairs, 84(5 [Sep/Oct

2005]), p. 18-24. Boness, C. M., Louw, L., & Mayer, C-A. 2017. Perceptions of Chinese and Tanzanian employees regarding intercultural collaboration. SA Journal of Human Resource Management, 15, 1-12. Retrieved from https://sajhrm.co.za/index.php/sajhrm, on January 18, 2020. Carmody, Pádraig, 2011. The New Scramble for Africa. Polity Press. 240p. Chen, Chien-Kai. 2016. CHINA IN AFRICA: A THREAT TO AFRICAN COUNTRIES? Strategic Review for Southern Africa, 38(2), 100-122. Retrieved from http://www.up.ac.za/en/political-sciences/article/19718/strategic-review-for-southern-africa.

Fergus, S. 2013. China & Africa: A review of media coverage. The Politics Reader. Retrieved from http://politics-reader.blogspot.com/2013/06/china-africa-review-ofmediacoverage.html. Fraternité Matin. 2017. "Affaire bagarre Odiennéka-Chinois" : Les autorités font triompher le dialogue". From : https://www.fratmat.info/article/75091/64/affaire-bagarre-odienneka-chinois-les-autorites-font-triompher-le-dialogue (Published on 04/25/2017). French, Howard. 2014. China's second continent. New York: Alfred A. Knopf. Goretti Nassanga & Sabiti Makara. 2014. "Perceptions of chinese presence in Africa as reflected in the African Media : Case study of Uganda". Presented at the International Conference China and Africa Media, Communications and Public Diplomacy in Beijing, 2014. 14p. Info Ivoire. "Faut-il craindre un péril chinois en Côte d'Ivoire : Investissements et coopération internationale?". http://www.infoivoire.net/master.php?mod=une&un=3427 (Published on 04/18/2017), Consulted on March 18, 2020. Jiang, Wenran. 2009. "Fuelling the Dragon: China's Rise and its Energy and Resources Extraction in Africa." The China Quarterly 199:585-609. Kissinger, Henry. 2011. On China. New York: The Penguin Press.

Koffi, Alle. 2014 . Africa: Minerals for Manufacturing -Towards a Bolder China

Strategy. Retrieved from http://allafrica.com/stories/201406022546.html?viewall=1 (Published on June 2nd, 2014). Le Monde. 2019. "Côte d'Ivoire : au port d'Abidjan, les Chinois voient grand". From :

https://www.lemonde.fr/afrique/article/2019/04/02/cote-d-ivoire-au-port-d-abidjan-les-chinois-voient-grand_5444573_3212.html (Published on 4/02/2019) Park, Yoon Jung. 2013. Perceptions of Chinese in Southern Africa: Constructions of the "Other" and the Role of Memory. African Studies Review, 56(1), 131-153. Retrieved from

https://www.cambridge.org/core/journals/african-studies-review.

Sautman, Barry, Yan Hairong. 2009. "African Perspectives on China–Africa Links." The China Quarterly 199 : 728-759. Strauss, Julia C. 2009. "The Past in the Present: Historical and Rhetorical Lineages in China's Relations With Africa." The China Quarterly 199: 777-795. Strauss, Julia C., Martha Saavedra. 2009. "Introduction: China, Africa and

Internationalization", The China Quarterly 199: 551-562. Sun, Yan. 2014. "China's Aid to Africa: Monster or Messiah?". https://www.brookings.edu/opinions/chinas-aid-to-africa-monster-or-messiah/. The People's Republic of China State Council. 2005. China's peaceful development road. Beijing : The PRC State Council. The People's Republic of China Embassy in Côte d'Ivoire's Website. "Les relations sinoivoiriennes". http://ci.china-embassy.org/fra/zkgx/. Consulted on July 21, 2020. Wasserman, Hermann. 2014. Reporting China in Africa: Media Discourses on Shifting Geopolitics. Kindle Edition. Xavier, Aurégan. 2014. "Géopolitique de la Chine en Cote d'Ivoire", Carnets de géographes [En ligne], 7 | 2014, From : http://journals.openedition.org/cdg/394 (Published on 12/1/2014).

阿根廷和中国的"全面战略伙伴关系"研究

艾丽卡 【阿根廷】

阿根廷外交部中国事务处　处长/拉努斯国立大学　教授

一　引言

2014年7月，中国国家主席习近平对阿根廷进行国事访问。在克里斯蒂娜·费尔南德斯（Cristina Fernandez）执政期间，中国与阿根廷建立了全面战略伙伴关系。在毛里西奥·马克里（Mauricio Macri）担任阿根廷总统（2015年12月）后，两国决定继续深化这一关系。

本文旨在描述这一战略伙伴关系自2015年12月至今取得的主要成就，并对阿中双边关系的现状提供一个全面的看法。

二　阿中"全面战略伙伴关系"的建立

为了建立更加公正合理的国际体系，维护两国及发展中国家整体利益，阿中两国于2014年7月决定为双边关系注入新的动力。

因此，在2014年中国国家主席习近平国事访问的框架下，两国签署了《关于建立全面战略伙伴关系的联合声明》，这标志着两国双边关系在过去十年中进入了一个新阶段。"全面战略伙伴关系"是中国与其他国家之间最重要的伙伴关系之一（例如，在拉丁美洲国家中，巴西、秘鲁、墨西哥、委内瑞拉和智利也与中国有这种关系）。

中阿全面战略伙伴关系自建立以来，一直在追求以下目标：1.巩固自主发展；

2. 在双方的优先主题上相互支持；3. 制定联合行动计划；4. 通过两国常设委员会（2013 年成立）协调行动；5. 协作经济合作与协调战略对话（2013 年成立）的会议；6. 通过附加值促进双边贸易更加平衡；7. 建设基础设施；8. 整合产业链；9. 在金融方面合作；10. 协调联合国改革和全球经济治理行动；11. 支持中国与拉美和加勒比国家的合作；12. 签署关于政治、经济和文化问题的新协议。

三 自 2015 年 12 月以来中阿全面战略伙伴关系主要成果

自全面战略伙伴关系建立以来，中阿双边关系展现出强大韧性和充满活力。尽管克里斯蒂娜·费尔南德斯和毛里西奥·马克里来自不同的政党，对阿根廷的一些政策可能有不同的看法，但对与中国的双边关系都坚定支持。从这个意义上讲，两国加强了互信，在许多领域取得了丰硕成果，保持了合作与战略协作。

2015 年 12 月至今的主要成就如下表。

表 1   中阿全面战略伙伴关系主要成就

高层互信的建立	高层交流	11 次
	高级别会议	5 次
高产和经济领域	签订主要协议 10 项	
投资领域	15 家中国公司宣布投资 19 个项目，共计 141.3 万美元	
教育和文化领域	提供对方国学生奖学金等	
国防与安全方面	每年进行军事交流	
体育方面	在足球领域合作	

2014 年签署了 2014—2018 年的路线图，称为"联合行动计划"，详细阐明了双边和多边关系的主要领域。该文件主要侧重于政治、社会、经济、贸易、科技和国际合作。2018 年 12 月签署了关于 2019—2023 年新的"联合行动计划"。阿根廷和中国在全球议程的核心问题上有着相似的观点，如自由贸易、气候变化和发展中国家面临的共同问题。2017 年 6 月，阿根廷成为亚洲基础设施投资银行的"潜在成员"。马克里总统参加了 2018 年在约翰内斯堡举行的金砖国家与新兴市场和发展中国家合作（EMDC）第二次会议。2018 年，阿根廷副总理出席了在智利圣地亚哥举行的第二届中国与拉丁美洲国家共同体部长级会议。2018 年在布宜诺斯艾利斯，中国在阿根廷外交和宗教部主办了为拉共体成员国官员举行的首

次中国融资培训班。阿根廷自 2017 年以来一直支持"一带一路"倡议：2017 年，马克里 (Macri) 总统出席了北京第一次"一带一路"论坛，外交部部长豪尔赫·富里耶 (Jorge Faurie) 出席了 2019 年在北京举行的第二届"一带一路"论坛。2018 年 12 月，阿根廷和中国发表"一带一路"联合公报，宣布全面战略伙伴关系可延伸到"一带一路"倡议，两国同意在"一带一路"倡议框架下，推动两国企业在第三市场合作。该声明还包括在 2019—2023"联合行动计划"（2018 年 12 月签署）中。

四 潜力和困难

阿中关系非常重要，潜力巨大。对阿根廷来说，中国代表机遇。中国是阿根廷的第二大贸易伙伴，也是基础设施融资的主要来源之一。两国央行之间签署了互换协议，阿根廷出口产品有可能进入中国市场。阿根廷也可以为中国提供体育、旅游和教育等服务。

然而，阿根廷和中国的关系也存在一些困难。阿根廷面临的主要问题是双边贸易逆差不断增加。为了改善这种状况，应该缩短地理和文化距离。一方面，北京是距离布宜诺斯艾利斯较远的首都，因此应该增加两国间更多的联通。例如，在不久的将来签署一项协议，通过共享代码创建直飞航班，这将具有非常积极的意义。另一方面，阿根廷和中国在处理关系时可能有不同的文化方式。两国将共同思考如何进一步改善地理和文化差异。

五 结论

阿中关系非常重要且潜力巨大。两国应共同思考如何进一步改善地理和文化差异。

尽管 2015 年 12 月阿根廷执政党发生了变化，但与中国的双边关系并未受到影响。因此，全面战略伙伴关系（2014 年建立）得到了加强。

从这个意义上说，自 2016 年 12 月以来，两国互信不断加强，在许多领域取得了丰硕成果，保持了合作与战略协调。

笔者相信，阿中全面战略伙伴关系将继续发展。

Current situation of the "Strategic Comprehensive Partnership" between Argentina and China

Erika Imhof/Argentina

Ministry of Foreign Affairs, Argentina/Chief of the China Desk

I. Introduction

In July 2014, during the state visit of the Chinese President, Xi Jinping, to Argentina, China and Argentina established a Strategic Comprehensive Partnership during the Argentine government of Ms. Cristina Fernandez. After the assumption of Mr. Mauricio Macri as the President of Argentina (December 2015), both countries have decided to continue deepening it.

This paper aims to describe the main achievements of this strategic partnership from December 2015 to date, and to provide a comprehensive view about the current situation of the bilateral relations between Argentina and China.

II. Establishment of the "Strategic Comprehensive Partnership" between Argentina and China

With the objective of building a more just and reasonable international system, safeguard the interests of both countries and safeguard the common interests of developing nations, Argentina and China decided to give a new impetus to the bilateral relationship in July 2014.

For that reason, in the framework of the state visit of Chinese President, Xi Jinping, to Argentina in 2014, both countries signed the "Joint Declaration for the establishment of an Strategic Comprehensive Partnership". That was the beginning of a new stage in the bilateral relations built over the previous decade. A "Strategic Comprehensive Partner" is one of the most important partnerships between China and other countries (for example, among Latin American countries, Brazil, Peru, Mexico, Venezuela and Chile have also this relation with China).

Since its establishment, the Comprehensive Strategic Partnership between Argentina and China has been pursuing the following aims: 1. To consolidate autonomous development, 2. To support each other in the priority themes of each part, 3. To develop joint action plans, 4. To coordinate measures through the PermanentBinationalCommission (established in 2013) 5. To coordinate meetings of the Strategic Dialogue for Cooperation and Economic Coordination (established in 2013), 6. To promote a more balanced bilateral trade by added value, 7. To build infrastructure, 8.To integrate industry chain, 9.To cooperate in finance, 10.To coordinate actions for the UN reform and global economic governance, 11.To support the cooperation between China and Latin America and the Caribbean countries, and 12.To sign new agreements on political, economic and cultural issues.

III. Main accomplishments of the Strategic Comprehensive Partnership between China and Argentina from December 2015

From the establishment of the Strategic Comprehensive Partnership the bilateral relationship between China and Argentina is intense and very dynamic. Although Ms. Cristina Fernandez and Mr Mauricio Macri are from different political parties and may have different views about some Argentine policies, the bilateral relation with China has remained solid and strong. In this sense, mutual trust has been strengthen, fruitful results in many areas have been achieved and cooperation and strategic coordination has been maintained between the two countries.

The following main achievements from December 2015 can be listed as examples:

1. Building mutual trust

(a) Travel and visits: relevant high-level exchanges took place (Presidents-met 5 times, Foreign Ministers, Ministers, etc.), parliamentary authorities held 4 annual meetings through the mechanism of parliamentary political dialogue, several provincial and municipal exchanges has also took place. (b) High level meetings were also held: the Permanent Binational Commission held a meeting in 2017 in Beijing and the Strategic Dialogue for Cooperation and Economic Coordination held 4 annual meetings.

2. Obtaining fruitful results in many areas

(a) Commercial and Economic issues: Negotiations to allow Argentine products to enter in the Chinese market were intensified. In 2019 were signed the following documents: The Protocol on Inspection, Quarantine and Veterinary Health Requirements for Pork Import and Export between China and Argentina was signed in Beijing on April 24 2019 in Beijing. The Protocol on the Entry of Bulk Honey in Batches was signed on 19 March 2019 in Buenos Aires. Main Protocols signed between 2017 and 2018: (i) Fresh cherries (12/2018), (ii) Equine foot alignment protocol (11/ 2018), (iii) Sheep meat and goat meat (11/2018), (iv) Bovine semen and embryos (09/2018); (v) Chilled beef frozen with and without bone (05/2018); (vi) Bovine pancreatic products for industrial use (05/2018); (vii) Greendried peas (02/2018); (viii) Blueberries (12/2017); (ix) Grapes (05/2017).

(b) Investments: Flows of Chinese Direct Investment in Argentina have presented a fluctuating trajectory. In 2016, there was a stock of US $618 million which represented a decline of 6.5% from the previous year. According to the information provided by the Argentine Agency for Investment and International Trade (AAICI) since December 2015 to December 2017, a total of 15 Chinese companies announced 19 investment projects for $1.413 million for the period. The main sectors are industrial goods, renewable energy, oil and gas, telecommunications, culture and education.

(c) Educational and Cultural Exchange: (i) Ministers of Education from Argentina and China gives 40 scholarships to help Argentine and Chinese students pursue postgraduate studies every year, (ii) A Chinese Cultural Center in Argentina is to be established in the near future (an agreement was signed in 2017), (iii) A joint cultural program was signed for the period 2019-2023 with the main objective to promote exchanges of artists and cultural heritage protection. (iv) In December 2018 an agreement for mutual recognition of universities degrees was signed with the main objective to promote higher education in the other country. (v) An assistant program for languages has been created (vi) People to people exchanges (including think tank cooperation) are common and widely promoted.

(d) Defense and Security: (i) China donated quality equipment for the Argentine security forces, (ii) Military exchanges have been taken place every year(iii) Argentine upgraded the rank of the Defense Corps in Beijing.

(e) Space Cooperation: (i) An antenna for the exploration of outer space was constructed in Argentina (Neuquen Province). (ii) A radio telescope for San Juan Province is being building.

(f) Nuclear Cooperation: The construction of a nuclear power plant in Argentina is under negotiation.

(g) Sports: The cooperation in soccer has been deepening (an agreement was signed in 2017 and Argentina received football players from China for a training program in 2018);

(h) Other areas of cooperation: environment, technical cooperation, Antarctic cooperation, health, tourism, science and technology.

3. Maintaining strategic coordination and cooperation

(a) Strategic planning: A road map for the period 2014-2018 was signed in 2014, called the Joint Action Plan, which detailed the main areas of bilateral and multilateral relations. The document is mainly focus on political, social, economic, trade, science and technology and international cooperation. A new Joint Action Plan for 2019-2023 was signed in December 2018.

(b) Coordination and exchange in multilateral institutions and mechanisms: Argentina and China share similar views on the core issues of the global agenda, such as free trade, climate change and common issues of developing countries. Argentina became a "prospective member" of the Asian Infrastructure Investment Bank in June 2017. President Macri participated in the second meeting of the BRICS Plus cooperation with emerging markets and developing countries (EMDCs) in Johannesburg in 2018.

(c) Forum for the Community of Latin American and Caribbean countries (CELAC) and China: In 2018, the Deputy Prime Minister of Argentina attended the Second Ministerial Conference of China and the Community of Latin American Countries in Santiago, Chile. In 2018, China held the first China Financing Training Course for officials from CELAC member countries in Buenos Aires host by the Argentine Ministry of Foreign Affairs and Worship.

(d) The Belt and Road Initiative: Argentina has been supporting the Belt and Road Initiative since 2017: President Macri attended the First Belt and Road Forum in Beijing in 2017 and the Ministry of Foreign Affairs, Jorge Faurie, attended the Second one in Beijing in 2019. In December 2018, Argentina and China issued a joint communique announcing that the Strategic Comprehensive Partnership is extendable to the Belt and Road Initiative and both countries agreed to promote joint actions for cooperation between enterprises of the two countries in third markets under the framework of the Belt and Road Initiative. This statement was also included in the Joint Action Plan 2019-2023 (signed in December 2018).

IV. Potentiality and difficulties

The relationship between Argentina and China is very important and has great potential. For Argentina, China represents an opportunity. It is our second trading partner and it is one of the main sources for financing infrastructure. We signed swap arrangements between central banks, and it is possible to put argentine exports into the Chinese market. Argentina can provide services like sports, tourism and education.

However, Argentina and China's relationship has also some difficulties. The main problem for Argentina is the increasing negative balance of the bilateral trade. In order to improve the situation, both geographical and cultural distance should be shortened. In one hand, Beijing is the capital that it is located more far away from Buenos Aires. For that reason, more connectivity should be improved. For instance, it will be very positive to sign an agreement to create direct flights through share codes in the near future. On the other hand, Argentina and China may have a different cultural approach for conducting ties. Both countries would consider how to further improve geographical and cultural differences together.

V. Conclusion

The relationship between Argentina and China is very important and has a great potential. However, both countries would consider how to further improve geographical and cultural differences together.

Although there was a change in the ruling party of Argentina in December 2015, the bilateral relation with China has not been affected. Therefore, the Strategic Comprehensive Partnership (established in 2014) has been strengthened.

In this sense, since December 2016 mutual trust has been strengthen, fruitful results in many areas have been achieved and cooperation and strategic coordination has been maintained between the two countries.

Argentina will have national elections on October 2019. Beyond the results, it is expected that the Strategic Comprehensive Partnership between Argentina and China will keep growing.

乌拉圭和中国：共建之路

帕马拉 【乌拉圭】
乌拉圭中国门户网站　创始人、翻译

一　门户网站"中国乌拉圭"：我们是谁

门户网站"中国乌拉圭"的创立来源于合作伙伴葆拉·德·圣地亚哥（本文作者）和玛丽亚·M. 苏佩维列（María Supervielle）的共同热情以及都想研究和分享所拥有的中国知识和经验。葆拉·德·圣地亚哥在中国生活了几年，在那里学习文化和语言，玛丽亚·M. 苏佩维列也在中国学习了几年，包括拿到她的中国研究专业的硕士学位。

我们确信，当我们生活在美洲南端地区，并把中国作为乌拉圭及该地区的主要商业伙伴和日益重要的参与者时，就不能忽视对中国的改革开放和技术发展的研究。

在庆祝乌中建交 30 周年之际，我们与中国驻乌拉圭大使馆建立了牢固而密切的关系，不仅在推广文化活动上，而且在有关"一带一路"倡议的官方和商业活动上进行合作。

因此，与玛丽亚·苏佩维列一起，我决定从文化的角度建立理解的桥梁。我们最初共同创建"中国乌拉圭"，目标是成为一个新闻门户网站，涉及所有与中国有关的新闻。我们将所有信息收集在一起，以动态的方式供读者学习和阅读。我们开发了自己的网页 www.portalchina.com.uy。

后来，我们开始在位于边缘社区的公立学校工作，那里的学生往往没有重要机会。我们组织研讨会，鼓励年轻人学习和思考关于中国的文化。

意识到儿童和年轻人对中国和中国文化知之甚少，我们下一步的工作主要是在公立学校开设有关中国古代文化、历史和语言的讲习班。我们发现了年轻学生对中国和中国语言的兴趣和积极的学习态度。

基于拓宽对中国了解的愿景，我们开始与当地同中国合作的其他机构建立联系和交流。向他们学习并与他们合作，这也有助于改进我们在开发更深入内容研讨会方面的工作。

门户网站"中国乌拉圭"还提供以客户为导向的服务，如为私营企业提供与中国建立业务关系的建议，以及提供翻译服务。

今天，门户网站"中国乌拉圭"参与了乌拉圭和该地区所有与中国有关的文化活动。我们也被邀请参加关于拉丁美洲的小组讨论。作为门户网站"中国乌拉圭"，我们的目标是在两种文化之间建立理解的桥梁。

知识是一种重要而有力的工具，我们的目标是让我们的年轻一代在有关中国事务、中国企业和中国研究方面有更多的工作机会。

二 乌拉圭和中国：30 年的关系

乌拉圭最近庆祝了与中国建交 30 周年。我们参加了不同的活动，向有兴趣的商人和潜在投资者推介两国，邀请他们访问"中国—乌拉圭"。

乌拉圭举办了许多活动，目的是促进乌拉圭成为拉丁美洲商业、物流和技术中心以及基础设施、农业综合企业和企业服务投资的目的地。优质商品和服务的出口供应地也在目标定位之中。

在北京，乌外交部长还签署了一项协议，使乌拉圭成为南大西洋和南美共同市场中第一个加入"21 世纪海上丝绸之路"的国家。

2017 年是乌拉圭和中国战略伙伴关系实施的第一年，该伙伴关系是 2016 年底乌拉圭总统塔巴雷·巴斯克斯 (Tabaré Vázquez) 对中国进行国事访问时达成的。

可以说，双边议程的各个方面都得到了加强，特别是与文化、旅游、教育、科学和合作有关的问题得到了加强。

我国与中国外交关系的关键一年可以定义为 2017 年，因为两国战略规划多元化，不再主要集中在经济方面，更加注重文化交流，这对于理解两国关系至关重要。

中国文化部副部长是 2017 年访问乌拉圭的第一位高级官员。在他的访问之际，两国签署了文化加强协议，明确了文化领域的合作，加强了乌拉圭和中国之间 2016—2020 年文化领域合作的执行计划。

按照这些方针，在优先开展文化交流的战略伙伴关系和旨在加强这方面关系的具体战略双边文书框架内，乌拉圭驻华大使馆在 2017 年优先开展了四项工作。

首先，与前几年一样，继续实现文化活动倍增和多样化的目标，以及艺术家、运动员和政府部门在中国推广乌拉圭文化方面的参与。

其次，使馆也集中精力去各地举办活动，以接触到更广泛的中国公众。除北京和上海外，大使馆还参加了在香港、澳门、成都、天津、三亚、哈尔滨等地开展的活动。从这个意义上说，乌拉圭在中国 10 多个城市举办了年度盛会的大规模推广活动。11 月 30 日至 12 月 2 日在埃斯特角举行的中拉工商峰会，创下了中国企业家参与数量的记录。

第三，通过接触，激发乌拉圭艺术家与中国同行之间的交往。为此，除了组织和支持特定活动外，还与大学、美术馆、博物馆、新闻界、文化和相关专家建立学术和专业交流平台。

乌拉圭驻华代表还致力于为两国建交 30 周年庆典而开展的文化活动和国别推广工作。上述活动有短期、中期和长期目标。在短期内，可以确定具体的文化和体育赛事的实现。在这一领域，2017 年，开展了来自不同艺术领域的活动，包括电影、音乐、造型艺术、舞蹈等。

2018 年文化和体育活动安排可归类为中期目的，旨在让更多来自两种文化的相关代表参加，以更好地庆祝两国建交 30 年。

在长期目标方面，值得强调的是，中国文化机构在与同行交流中给予了大力支持，同时中乌艺术家之间也相互支持。

"我们乌拉圭驻华大使馆的成员计划继续在这方面工作，以加深两国之间的文化交流。毫无疑问，为了增进相互了解，这种类型的交流将继续多样化和扩大，以促进各级（国家和省政府、学术、艺术、社区）的文化联系，因此，交流活动需要更多的准备和研究时间。"[1]

自门户网站"中国乌拉圭"成立以来，我们发展了多种多样的战略联盟，如：青年促进理解、跨太平洋、奥特大学联盟等。

---

1 费尔南多·卢格里斯：《建交 30 周年框架下乌拉圭在华文化概况》。

三　洛斯·皮诺斯·卡萨瓦莱松基金会：通往中国

在蒙得维的亚的卡萨瓦莱社区，只有 3% 的人口接受了义务中等教育。在这种背景下，创新实践对于鼓舞和激励学生至关重要。中专学校以项目为基础，运用灵活的学习计划和评估方法来开发课程。教育过程以学生的兴趣为中心，并伴随着创新过程的基础设施设计，允许开发与 STEAM (科学、技术、工程、艺术和数学) 思维相关的项目。在这项工作中，介绍了学生的教学过程。

洛斯·皮诺斯·卡萨瓦莱松基金会是一个教育中心，一个由私人和公共资金资助的私人管理机构。这里有儿童俱乐部、青年中心和职业培训课程。

"中国乌拉圭"和洛斯·皮诺斯（Portal China & Los Pinos）

洛斯·皮诺斯是一个在乌拉圭蒙得维的亚周边为处于极为弱势的儿童、青少年和年轻人提供陪伴的组织。

2018 年，门户网站"中国乌拉圭"开设了中国文化入门课程和普通话在线学习模式课程。

中国文化和语言通过动漫和其他含有中国意味的漫画传入乌拉圭。

由于所处的社会环境，学生通常很少接触其他语言，他们没有前期的知识来支持与新语言相关的新学习。

在这个意义上，训练者设计了一个激励计划来鼓励学生。通过进行激励性演讲和设立以视听材料为基础的讲习班，以创建一个适当的学习框架。

由于乌拉圭是中国的主要出口目的地。对于那些社会关系很少的学生来说，学习普通话是进入劳动力市场的一个竞争优势。

实施加速儿童和青少年心理发展过程的活动，这些活动以具体思想为基础，允许基于基本现实的投资，以了解社会和经济动态。

洛斯·皮诺斯用基于项目的学习方法。这些项目来自两个领域：社会科学和 STEAM。在职业高中 STEAM 项目的框架内，他们有实验和机器人技术的必修课程。

此外，洛斯·皮诺斯还有劳动技能培训课程，包括为期 5 个月的劳动培训课程，提供就业安置。这些课程适用于 17 岁至 24 岁之间没上学或没有工作的年轻人。职业培训中心的课程包括机械操作员、机械维修工人、物流、客服、自动化、实验室操作员。2018 年，有 120 名年轻人参与，105 人进入劳动力市场。2019 年，将有 260 人参加。我们把入学人数增加了一倍，因为需求量很大。

当我们开始了解乌拉圭的学术课程时，我们发现其中没有关于中国的语言或文化方面的官方研究。直到 2018 年 8 月，蒙得维的亚的第 47 高中和拉瓦莱哈省首府米纳斯市的第 3 高中才被选中在学校里开设普通话课程。

来自中国的两名教师抵达乌拉圭，负责讨论模式的课程教学。这些课程不是强制性的，也不在大纲之内。这源于我国与中国之间的谈判与合作，这种支持也体现在教育领域，这个"亚洲巨人"提供就业和奖学金。

由于中国在该地区变得越来越重要，作为乌拉圭的主要商业伙伴和战略盟友，我们意识到关于中国社会研究和经济技术发展的知识成为我们了解中国和"一带一路"倡议相关性的优先事项。我们明白，应该付出更多努力来实现高质量的教育和与中国建立长久关系的合作。

文化在"一带一路"的主动性中起着重要作用，文化交流是社会多方面加强合作和尊重的基础。

四 结论

学术和文化交流在"一带一路"框架内不断增多具有重要意义，因为它有助于加深国家间的了解，促进与中国的合作。

学生们可以通过思考并意识到另一种文化的存在，学习一种新的语言来反思自己的文化，从而为个人和职业发展创造新的机会。

我们在洛斯·皮诺斯基金会的经历对研究学生的意识、动机和学习意愿方面都很感兴趣。我们相信乌拉圭的课程大纲可以做很多改进，以建立一座相互理解的桥梁，引导我们在奖学金和学术交流方面达成更好平衡。

在人们密切关注中国不断进步的技术发展和商业的时代，我们相信，我们与中国的最佳关系是建立在相互尊重、协作和共同努力的基础上，以实现互利共赢的伙伴关系，促进共同发展。

Uruguay and China: Still much more Road to Build Together

Paula De Santiago / Uruguay

Portal China Uruguay / Co-Founder, translator

I. Portal China Uruguay: Who We Are

Portal China Uruguay is an uruguayan institution that started with a shared passion among its partners: Paula De Santiago and Maria M. Supervielle. Both of us wanted to study and share the knowledge and experiences we had with China: Paula De Santiago had lived in China for several years and studies culture and language there and Maria M. Supervielle had studied several years including her masters degree on China Studies.

We are convinced that living in the southern cone of america and having China as the main comercial partner and increasingly relevant actor in Uruguay and in the región, studies about China and its reforming , opening up and technological development could not be ignored.

We have developed a strong and close relationship with the Chinese embassy in Uruguay to work cooperately on promoting not only cultural but also official events related to Belt and Road Initiative and the business relationship between Uruguay and China after celebrating the 30 years of diplomatic relationships anniversary.

As a result, together with María Supervielle, we decided to build a bridge of understanding from a cultural perspective. We co-created Portal China Uruguay as portal news initially. We aimed to be a news portal concerning all the news that dealt with China in the región. We gather all the information together, for readers to learn and to read in a very dynamic way. We developed our own web page www.portalchina.com.uy.

Later on, we started working in public schools located in marginal neighborhoods where students might grow with no major opportunities. We organize workshops and encourage young people to learn and reflect about this distant and amazing culture.

Our next steps were based mainly on developing workshops on Chinese ancient culture, history and language in public schools realizing how little knowledge children and young people had about China and chinese culture. Though we discovered the interest amongst young students and the positive attitude they had towards China and its language.

Our vision to broad then our knowledge on China drove us to start building our networking and Connections with other institutions working with China in the region. Learning from them and working cooperatively, help us to improve our work in developing high content workshops.

Portal China Uruguay also provides customer oriented services such as advice to private enterprises on building business relationships with China, and translations.

Today Portal China Uruguay is present in all the cultural activities concerning China in Uruguay and if posible in the region. We rare invited to participate in panels of discussion around Latin America. As Portal China Uruguay, we understand that our aim is at building bridges of understanding between both cultures.

Knowledge is a key powerful tool, and we aim at empowering our young generations to have more labor opportunities related to China matters, China enterprises and studies.

Since Portal China was founded, we developed quite a diverse range of strategic alliances, such as Youth For Understanding, Cruzando el Pacifico, Universidad ORT, Red China / América Latina.

II. Uruguay and China: 30 Years of Relations

Uruguay has recently celebrated 30 years of uninterrupted international relations with China. Participating in different events and promoting both countries to eager businessmen and potential investors to visit China and Uruguay.

Many activities were organized aiming to promote Uruguay as a gateway to Latin America and a business, logistics and technology hub, as well as a destination for investments in infrastructure, agribusiness and corporate services. The exportable offer of quality goods and services was also positioned.

In Beijing, the Minister of Foreign Affairs also signed an agreement by which Uruguay became the first country in the South Atlantic and Mercosur to enter the Maritime Silk Route of the 21st Century, a Chinese initiative known as Belt and Road.

"2017 was the first year of the implementation of the Strategic Association in Uruguay and China, reached at the end of 2016 on the occasion of the State Visit of the Uruguayan President, Dr. Tabaré Vázquez, to the People's Republic of China.

It could be said that all aspects of the bilateral agenda were reinforced and especially those issues related to culture, tourism, education, science and cooperation were strengthened.

One year hinge for the diplomatic relations between our country and China could be defined to the year 2017 since the strategic planning between the two was diversified and ceased to concentrate mainly on the economic aspects to give greater attention to cultural exchanges, fundamental for the understanding of the villages.

The Vice Minister of Culture of China was the first high-level authority to visit Uruguay during the past year. On the occasion of his visit, the Cultural Strengthening Agreement was signed between the two countries that established a clear sheet of cooperation in the cultural sphere, which came to reinforce the Executive Plan for Cooperation in the field of Culture that exists between Uruguay and China for the period 2016-2020.

Along these lines, within the framework of a Strategic Partnership that privileges cultural exchanges and bilateral instruments that introduce a concrete strategy, aimed at strengthening the relationship in this regard, four lines of work were prioritized from the Uruguayan Embassy in China during 2017.

First, and as in previous years, work continued to achieve the objective of multiplying and diversifying activities, cultural and the presence of artists, athletes, and authorities concerning the cultural promotion of Uruguay in China.

Second, the Embassy concentrated heavily on decentralizing activities, generating events outside of Beijing, which would reach a wider spectrum of the Chinese public. In addition to Beijing and Shanghai, it participated in activities carried out in Hong Kong, Macao, Chengdu, Tianjin, Sanya, Harbin, among others. In this sense, the great presence of Uruguay in more than 10 Chinese cities in which mass promotion activities of the event of the year were held, which was the China-LAC Business Summit that took place in Punta del Este between the November 30 and December 2, and that had an absolute record of participation of Chinese entrepreneurs.

Third, contact was stimulated interpersonal between Uruguayan artists and their Chinese counterparts. For this, in addition to organizing and supporting specific events, efforts were made to establish academic and specialized exchange platforms, with universities, art galleries, museums, press, cultural and related experts.

The representation of Uruguay in China was also dedicated to the planning of cultural activities and country promotion for the celebration of the 30th anniversary of diplomatic relations between the two countries, to be celebrated as of February 3, 2018. Said lines of action have short, medium and long term objectives. In the short term, the realization of specific cultural and sporting events can be identified. In this area, during 2017, events from the different artistic branches were presented, including cinema, music, plastic arts, dance, among others.

The planning of the calendar of cultural and sports activities 2018 can be classified as a medium-term purpose, which aims to include more exponents relevant from both cultures to best celebrate the three decades of diplomatic ties of the two countries.

On the other hand, with regard to long-term goals, it is worth highlighting the great support received from the Chinese cultural institutions that allowed the exchange with our counterparts, as well as the same mutual support between artists from China and Uruguay.

It is the intention of those of us who are part of the Uruguayan Embassy in China to continue working in this line, in order to deepen cultural exchanges between the two countries. Without a doubt, to greater mutual knowledge, this type of contacts will continue to diversify and amplify, to stimulate a cultural relationship at all levels (national and provincial government, academic, artistic, community) and thus, joint activities that require more preparation and research time." Fernando Lugris, Ambassador of Uruguay in Beijing. Extract from Overview of Uruguayan Culture in China under the framework of the 30th anniversary of Diplomatic Relations.

III. Fundation Los Pinos Casavalle : Open to China

In the Casavalle neighborhood of Montevideo, compulsory secondary education ends only 3% of the population. In this context, innovative practices are of vital importance to conquer and motivate students. The technological secondary school develops its classes based on projects and with agile methodologies of planning and evaluation of learning. The educational process centered on the interests of the students and with an infrastructure design that accompanies the innovation process, allows the development of projects linked to STEAM thinking. (Science, Technology, Engineering, Arts and Mathematics) In this work, the pedagogical process that the students went through is presented.

Fundacion Los Pinos Casavalle is an educational center, a private management institution financed with private and public funds. Where a children's club, a youth center, and a job training courses are available.

Los Pinos, is an organization that accompanies children, adolescents and young people in situations of high vulnerability in the periphery of Montevideo, Uruguay.

During 2018, Portal China Uruguay, developed an introductory workshop course on Chinese Culture and an e-learning mode course on mandarin.

Chinese culture and its language come to Uruguay especially through Anime and other comics that transmit part of what China implies.

Students who are usually very little exposed to other languages because of the social context in which they live do not have previous knowledge that support for new learning related to a new language.

In this sense, the trainers designed a motivation plan that stimulated the students. By giving motivational talks, and a workshop based on audiovisual material, it was possible to create an adequate framework for learning.

Since Uruguay has as main export destination China. The aim for learning mandarin is a competitive advantage for students who have very few social links to enter the labor market.

Implementing activities that accelerate the process of psychic development in children and adolescents who are anchored in the concrete thought, allows to invest on a basic reality for the understanding of the social and economic dynamism.

The technological high school works with the methodology of Project-Based Learning. The projects are from two areas: Social Sciences and STEAM (science, technology, engineering, art and mathematics). Within the framework of the STEAM projects in the technological high school, they have compulsory curricular spaces of experimental and robotic technology.

In addition, Los Pinos has Labor Training Courses. They are 5-month labor training courses with job placement. It is for young people between 17 and 24 years old who do not study or work. The courses of the job training center are Industrial Operator, Industrial

Maintenance, Logistics, Customer Service, Automation, Laboratory Operator. In 2018, 120 young people participated and 105 were inserted into the labor market. In 2019, 260 will participate. We double the enrollment because they are in high demand. The courses of the job training center are Industrial Operator, Industrial Maintenance, Logistics, Customer Service, Automation, Laboratory Operator.

Once we started exploring the uruguayan academic curricula, we found out that not official Chinese studies concerning language or culture are included.

But it was until October 2018, that two high schools No. 47 of Monte video and the No. 3 of the city of Minas, capital of the department of Lavalleja, were chosen to have mandarin in the schools.

Two teachers from China arrived in Uruguay and are in charge of teaching the courses that are taught in workshop mode. These courses are not mandatory nor will they be within the curriculum.

This arises from the negotiations and cooperation that exists between our country and China and that such support is also given in the educational area, where jobs and scholarships are offered by the Asian giant.

Since China has become increasingly relevant in the región, as the main comercial partner for Uruguay and a strategic ally, and we realized that knowledge about China social studies, and economic technological development becomes a priority for us to understand the relevance of China and the Belt and Road Initiative. We understand that much more effort should be done to achieve high quality education and cooperation for long lasting relationship with China.

Culture plays an important role in the Belt and Road Initiative, as cultural exchange is the foundation through which multinational cooperation and respect can be strengthened in many aspects of our society.

IV. Conclusions

Since academic and cultural exchange have been increasing within the frame of BRI with great importance because it helps deepening understanding between countries and promoting cooperation with China.

Students are opened to reflect about their culture by reflecting and becoming aware of the existence of another culture, and by studying a new language that will generate new opportunities both personal and professional development.

Our experience in Foundation Los Pinos has been interesting in terms of interest, awareness, motivation and will to learn. And we believed that many improvements in the Uruguayan curricula can be done, to build a bridge of mutual understanding that will lead us to work better twinning agreements for scholarships and academic exchanges.

In times where people seem to be paying closed attention to china's ever advancing technology development and business, we believed that the best relationship we can have with China is one based on mutual respect, collaborative and collective work to achieve a win-win partnership for mutual development.

通过旅游促进中肯民间外交和跨文化交流

茹丝 【肯尼亚】

内罗毕大学孔子学院　讲师

一　肯尼亚外交政策

肯尼亚外交政策的基础和宗旨是建立一个"和平、繁荣和具有全球竞争力的肯尼亚"。肯尼亚的外交政策试图通过创新的外交方式来展示、促进和保护肯尼亚在世界各地的利益和形象。肯尼亚希望通过外交来实现几个国家目标,包括保护主权和领土完整、促进一体化和促进经济繁荣。全球化导致了国际经济和社会体系网络的出现,这种网络既有积极的影响,也有消极的一面。日益激烈的国际竞争导致许多国家提高了经济和社会福利。肯尼亚寻求在复兴的非洲中发挥主导作用,强烈寻求一个更强大的非洲,能够应对其面临的挑战,并确保可持续发展。外交政策的主要目标包括促进肯尼亚的经济繁荣,展示肯尼亚的形象和声誉。在处理外交任务和外交关系方面,肯尼亚推进了对外关系,与中国和其他发展迅速的亚洲国家签订了双边协议。外交政策基于五个相互关联的支柱,包括环境外交、文化外交、和平外交、侨民外交和经济外交。肯尼亚一直致力于提升与中国的旅游、经济合作和交流项目,来提高其经济水平和树立良好形象。

二　"肯尼亚愿景2030"和中国两个百年目标

"肯尼亚愿景2030"是"一个来自全国各地的利益攸关方的全方位、全面参与的协商进程,旨在确定肯尼亚人希望在2030年实现的目标"。这一愿景基于三个支柱：经济、政治和社会。"愿景 2030"提出了一项长期发展蓝图，力求在 2030 年将肯尼亚转变为一个新型工业化、中等收入、生活质量高的国家。它还寻求促进清洁、安全的环境和高品质的生活。经济和宏观支柱旨在促进经济福祉，并在其他经济活动中带来与旅游、进口、技术专家和外国直接投资相关的利益（Baah & Jauch, 2009）。

社会经济转型的基础是基础设施、能源、土地改革和人力资源开发。经济支柱集中在旅游业、农业、制造业和金融服务业。与中国有关的旅游业增长使肯尼亚及其邻国的整体经济受益。肯尼亚的旅游业立足于这个国家在世界地图上的战略地位。肯尼亚已有投资在亚洲宣传肯尼亚旅游，特别是在与中国相关方面的目的地。还投资开发以度假城市为重点的海岸，并实现了更高的旅游收入（Kaminsky，2017）。创造新的高价值的利基产品以及吸引高端国际连锁酒店仍然是增加中肯旅游经济的途径之一。

中国的两个百年目标侧重于发展经济，使之成为世界上增长最快、规模最大的经济体。中国的最终目标是保持经济增长，包括减少政府官僚作风、提高效率和减少特殊利益集团的权力。2019 年中国百年奋斗目标是建设富强、和谐、民主、文明的社会主义现代化模范国家。中国还计划在 2021 年中国共产党成立 100 周年之际，使 2010 年的人均收入数字翻一番。中国共产党（2021 年）和中华人民共和国成立（2049 年）这两个百年纪念日显示了中国领导层在促进社会、经济和政治发展方面的决心和勇气。中国继续以农业、工业、交通、手工业和商业为主要目标，鼓励和促进经济增长。中国投资于培育与包括中国在内的国际伙伴共享的文化和科学发展。通过经济外交，中国寻求实现技术自给自足，同时试图在关键行业获得优势。两个百年目标部分是由"一带一路"倡议推动的，这是一项面向世界各地战略伙伴的万亿美元投资项目。过去五年中，肯中关系显著加强（Onjala，2008）。例如，中国已成为肯尼亚仅次于世界银行(World Bank)的第二大贷款国，向肯尼亚提供了 5570 亿肯尼亚先令的贷款，而世界银行的贷款为 5810 亿肯尼亚先令。中国的两个百年目标侧重于在非洲投资，以期与成员国建立密切伙伴关系。2013 年中国提出"一带一路"倡议代表了中非关系的高水平发展，肯尼亚走在了中非关系的前列。中国正在帮助世界各国提高其公民的生活水平，肯尼亚是与这个亚洲巨人合作的主要国家之一。

三 通过"一带一路"倡议振兴国家产业

肯尼亚是中国"一带一路"倡议的受益者之一，它受益于通过贷款来修建公路和桥梁。"一带一路"推动了多条公路、铁路和其他基础设施的建设，加强了两国之间的关系。基础设施不足阻碍了非洲和肯尼亚的发展，也突显了基础设施的建设在开发公司之间建立工作关系的必要性。Madegwa（2019）认为肯尼亚从"一带一路"倡议的总体方案中获益匪浅。交通基础设施的建设提高了连通性，并降低了从蒙巴萨到该国内陆的运输成本。由于肯尼亚的国内生产总值主要由农业活动支撑，因此向新市场的农产品运输得到了加强，从而改善了该国的经济。"一带一路"基础设施的实施继续促进肯尼亚和东非共同体其他成员国的区域贸易和经济发展，包括布鲁迪、卢旺达、埃塞俄比亚、乌干达和刚果民主共和国。中国的"海上丝绸之路"倡议通过肯尼亚促进了非洲和亚洲之间的联系，将该国置于发展路线图上（Leung, Au, & Law，2015）。

"一带一路"倡议面临的挑战是：投入大，一些国家无法偿还贷款，导致关键资产的收回困难。肯尼亚政府每月向中国路桥公司支付1000万美元来运营这条铁路。肯尼亚打算在未来几年里支付5.39万亿肯尼亚先令，否则它将失去蒙巴萨港。失去一些关键资产的前景也促使许多肯尼亚人和其他非洲国家对"一带一路"的参与感到担忧。

四 肯尼亚文化外交战略与中肯民间外交

肯尼亚文化外交是肯尼亚外交政策的重要组成部分，是五大相互关联的外交支柱之一。肯尼亚的文化遗产非常丰富，一个国家拥有多种多样的文化。肯尼亚在文化外交上投入了大量资金，任命了总统级别的文化大使，以在现有肯尼亚品牌上建立比较优势，向世界宣传肯尼亚的国家形象，并就肯尼亚人的价值观和愿望发出清晰和一致的信息。文化外交还要求发展项目，突出肯尼亚外交战略中所有五个相互关联的支柱。

文化战略有四个目标，实施后将促进文化外交。例如，战略目标一谈到尊重和承认肯尼亚人民的文化多样性和遗产。该目标旨在通过增进对肯尼亚人民及其文化的了解，促进对该国文化多样性的了解，促进将文化、体育和艺术作为庆祝文化多样性的工具，并加强肯尼亚文化认同。文化目标的实现是通过媒体宣传该国的正面形象，使用肯尼亚的手工艺品、绘画和歌曲以及其他独特的标识。通过与中国的交流项目，以及在肯尼亚（在很大程度上，在非洲）举办的中国商品和服务交易会，促进对肯尼亚文化多样性的理解（Yang, Wall, & Smith, 2008）。

肯尼亚文化外交的第二个目标是促进文化交流和伙伴关系。因此，第二个目标是通过加强双边和多边关系、促进国内和国际文化交流以及推广肯尼亚文化产品来实现的。肯尼亚对包括中国在内的其他国家的文化外交的第三个目标是通过加强与中国和其他国家的文化接触来促进全球文化间对话（Sun, 2015）。该目标通过举办肯尼亚食品展、图片展、现场活动、书展、肯尼亚电影和肯尼亚文化周等方式实现。中国曾先后参加过贸易交易会，这些交易会后来也延伸成为文化交易会。

肯尼亚文化外交的第四个目标是促进体育和艺术外交，展示肯尼亚男女运动员。肯尼亚和中国有交流项目，以促进文化理解。中国和肯尼亚一直在推动高等院校之间的文化交流项目。例如，肯尼亚的主要大学都设有孔子学院，那里有交流项目。在这种情况下，中肯关系得到加强。通过让运动员参加足球、艺术（绘画、雕刻和音乐等）和文化活动等体育运动，加强了体育、艺术和文化方面的合作关系（Hofmann et al., 2007）。第五个目标是加强对斯瓦希里语作为大陆和全球语言的承认。斯瓦希里语是东非人的母语，以肯尼亚和坦桑尼亚为主。通过与高等教育机构的合作，肯尼亚在肯尼亚和整个东非推广斯瓦希里语作为交流工具。中国推广学习斯瓦希里语的机构以及肯尼亚推广学习普通话的机构，进一步促进了两国的文化外交。

五 中肯民间外交与肯尼亚旅游

肯尼亚外交政策文件中提出的五大外交支柱推动了肯尼亚与中国的接触。五大外交支柱还促进了两国之间的旅游业，重点放在两国可以交流文化的关键领域。Gadzala（2009）表示，两国之间的友好关系促进了中国企业家进入肯尼亚当地产业，包括家庭手工业。不断扩大的贸易、投资和援助的重点是促进肯尼亚人和中国人民的互动。通过两国的旅游业，两国公民寻求促进可持续经济发展和促进贸易的机会。中国中小企业的迅速崛起为肯尼亚中小企业和大企业提供了专业技术，促进了经济和文化旅游（Suntikul, Tang & Pratt, 2012）。中国的中小企业冲击了肯尼亚的非正规行业，造成了贸易失衡和零售商人的不满。民间外交吸引了个别中国商人在内罗毕市中心的商场和街道上进行贸易，这表明了两国之间的联系程度。环境和经济外交促进了广泛的旅游业，在过去五年中，肯尼亚从中国游客那里获得的国外收入增长了15%。在肯尼亚投资建立四五星级酒店、中餐馆和聚焦中国的旅游公司等旅游项目，表明两国旅游业的前景越来越广阔。中国在肯尼亚旅游业（以及其他行业）的投资不断增加，加剧当地行业中小企业的竞争，由于来自中国的廉价商品，肯尼亚一些企业被挤出了市场。

六　中国游客在肯尼亚的影响及面临的问题

随着中肯双边协议的建立，在肯尼亚和整个东非的中国游客数量有所增加。政府和私人投资者从旅游业中获得收益，整个旅游业也受益于中国游客，因为他们带来了外汇的增加，并且旅游渠道沿线增加了许多就业和零售业务机会。提供中国产品和服务的旅游公司也有所增加，包括北京、广州、上海、香港和深圳等中国大型旅游城市旅游套餐。同样的旅游热情也体现在为中国游客提供穿越肯尼亚的许多旅游景点的旅行套餐。

肯尼亚的旅游业仍然是第三大外汇收入来源。由于环境因素，旅游收入略有下降。影响肯尼亚旅游业的挑战之一是旅游产品质量的退化和恶化带来的影响。肯尼亚的旅游业在选举期间受到了政治稳定、恐怖分子（青年党）造成的不安全、不可持续的旅游业发展和全球经济衰退等方面的挑战。旅游业的环境影响是广泛的，因为一个地区的行为可能会影响其他许多地区的旅游业。例如，茂集水区的森林砍伐影响了马拉河的水位，而马拉河维系着世界闻名的从肯尼亚到坦桑尼亚的动物大迁徙。干涸的河流对肯尼亚马萨伊马拉和安博塞利野生动物保护区的旅游业带来了挑战。

由于肯尼亚传统上一直在营销现有旅游目的地，因此有一种趋势是，景点的集中营销会导致环境退化。游客集中的地方，海滩受到污染，海洋物种受到不利影响，珊瑚礁遭到破坏。旅游目的地的持续破坏导致游客人数减少。由于体制薄弱、管理不善、腐败以及政治和行政能力不足，收回遭破坏的旅游景点，缓解景点遭到破坏的努力受到阻碍。

在文化遗产中，可以看到一些肯尼亚人接受了中国的工艺品、风格和生活方式。例如，受到中国人民喜爱的武侠片在肯尼亚很受欢迎。中国体育项目深受肯尼亚年轻人喜爱，体现了对中国传统文化的接受。学习普通话以及其他形式的中国文化（烹饪、服装和工业）表明两国文化内容的交流不断增加。

七 经济和文化影响

在过去十年中，中国对肯尼亚经济发展的影响有所增加。据观察，自齐贝吉总统执政以来，肯尼亚一直依赖东方（即中国）提供经济支持。两国签署双边贸易协定后，从东方获得的商品和服务大幅增加，来自同一地区的游客和投资者数量也有所增加。受中国经济影响，肯尼亚的进口翻了一番，但对中国的出口几乎没有变化。肯尼亚继续与中国同行接触，开拓新市场，尤其是牛油果和园艺产品等农产品（Gadzala，2009）。

中国人民的文化外交和影响力体现在肯尼亚的许多方面，包括基础设施的建筑、丰富的中国菜以及与肯尼亚同行共享的其他文化产品。肯尼亚继续从中国借鉴许多生活方式，包括在商务、娱乐和相互交流中使用普通话。

在肯尼亚，内罗毕大学、肯雅塔大学等相继成立孔子学院，中国文化在肯尼亚得到广泛传播。肯尼亚成为中国文化和普通话的传播中心（Řehák, 2016）。肯尼亚也有越来越多的斯瓦希里语教师到中国机构教授斯瓦希里语。在交流项目中，许多肯尼亚人开始教授斯瓦希里语，以加强两国之间的贸易，从而促进了牢固的双边关系。中国文化中心在东非的集中，促进了许多人对汉语的兴趣，加强了两国的利益。

八 如何应对挑战，进一步发展中肯两国的民间外交

民间外交面临的挑战之一是两国签署的双边贸易协定的性质。在大多数情况下，即使项目在肯尼亚或其他非洲国家实施，所提供的贷款也是基于中国法律。当涉及双边协议时，外交主要面临腐败指控、挪用资金和政府高级官员通常涉及的非法行为（Leung, Au, & Law, 2015）。中国经济外交的合法性之一是将所有贷款安排都基于中国国际经济贸易仲裁委员会（Sun，2015）。这限制了肯尼亚在与中国打交道时讨价还价和获得公平交易的自由。当该条款规定仲裁应在北京进行时，各国就失去了主动权和谈判自由。解决这一挑战的方法是采用对两国都有利的中立法律。例如，在英国等中立国家进行仲裁，或适用国际货币基金组织或世界银行等国际金融组织推动的贸易法。

经济外交面临的另一个挑战是，许多国家接受中国的巨额贷款，并将其用于支付贷款国的承包商和材料购置费。例如，肯尼亚从中国借款，这些钱被用来从中国购买商品、服务和技术。

在实施发展项目方面，两国需要加强合作。例如，建议对项目进行联合评价

和规划。这样就可以消除多余的预算资源，最大限度地减少浪费。

九 结论

近年来，由于发达国家争相与非洲国家开展双边贸易，肯中关系有所改善。民间外交塑造了肯尼亚基础设施投资的性质，以及肯尼亚与中国的关系。中国在肯尼亚的融资和外交面临的挑战之一是，所有协议和合同都要以中国法律为基础。两国的经济外交、文化外交、环境外交、和平外交和侨民外交都有所增加（Scheyvens，2007）。两国之间的经济旅游业也得到了促进，以至于中国游客涌入肯尼亚。两国人民继续分享文化发展和促进经济社会发展的基础设施项目。肯尼亚愿景 2030 以及中国的双百年目标的重点是促进经济发展。总之，民间外交促进了两国间的旅游业。当两国签署双边协议时，经济旅游、环境旅游和其他形式的旅游将得到推广。改善贸易协定的政策实施确保了未来光明的民间外交（Scheyvens，2007）。

Promoting People-to-People Diplomacy and Cross Cultural Interaction between China and Kenya through Tourism

Ruth Njeri Wangui / Kenya

Confucius Institute at the University of Nairobi / Lecturer

1. Introduction to Kenya Foreign Policy

The Kenya foreign policy is fueled by the mission of having a "peaceful, prosperous and globally competitive Kenya." The foreign policy tries to project, promote as well as protect Kenya's interests and image across the world through having innovative diplomacy. Diplomacy has been used to achieve several national objectives, including protecting sovereignty and territorial integrity, promoting integration, and advancing economic prosperity. The phenomenon of globalization has led to the emergency of an international network of economic and social systems that have both positive and negative effects. The increased international competition has led to many countries promoting their economic and social wellbeing. Kenya seeks a lead role in the renewed Africa Renaissance with a strong quest for a stronger Africa that is capable of addressing the challenges it faces as well as ensuring sustainable development. Among the leading objectives of the foreign policy includes advancing economic prosperity of Kenyans and projecting her image and prestige. In dealing with foreign missions and relations, Kenya has advanced her foreign relations to enter into bilateral agreements with China and other Asian countries that have developed fast. The foreign policy is based on five interlinked pillars that include environmental diplomacy pillar, cultural diplomacy pillar, peace diplomacy pillar, diaspora diplomacy pillar and economic diplomacy pillar. Kenya has invested in promoting tourism, economic cooperation and exchange programs with China to enhance her economy and project good image.

2. Kenya Vision 2030 and China Bi-Centennial Goals

The Kenya Vision 2030 is an all-inclusive and fully participatory stakeholder consultative process from all parts of the country in an effort to determine what Kenyans would want to be achieved by 2030. The vision is based on three pillars, economic, political and social. The vision 2030 presents a long-term development blue-print that seeks to transform Kenya into a newly industrializing, middle-income country with high quality of life by 2030. It also seeks to promote clean, secure environment and promote high quality life. The economic and macro pillar seeks to advance the economic wellbeing, and bring in benefits related to tourism, imports, experts and foreign direct investments among other economic activities (Baah & Jauch, 2009).

The foundations for socioeconomic transformation are anchored in infrastructure, energy, land reforms, and human resource development. The economic pillar of the economy focuses on tourism, agriculture, manufacturing and financial services. Tourism, in relation to China, has increased benefiting the whole economy of Kenya and her neighbors. Tourism in Kenya is anchored on the fact that the country is strategically placed on the world map. In relating to China, the country has invested in marketing the destination in Asia and specifically in China. The country has invested in developing the coast focusing on resort cities, and achieving higher tourist revenues (Kaminsky, 2017). Creating new high value niche products as well as attracting high-end international hotel chains remains one of the approaches to increase Sino-Kenya economic tourism.

The Chinese bi-centennial goals focus on development of her economy and raising to the world most growing and largest economy. China's ultimate goal is to have sustaining economic growth encompassing the reduction of government bureaucracy, improved efficiency, and reducing the power of special interests. The China centenary goal to be achieved by 2019 is that the county will be strong, harmonious, democratic, civilized and a model modern socialist country. The country also aims at doubling the 2010 per capita income figures by 2021 when the founding Communist Party of China will be celebrating the first centenary of its existence. The two centenaries, one for the Communist Party of China (in 2021) and the one for the establishment of the People's Republic of China (in 2049)s show the determination and inspiration of the Chinese leadership in promoting social, economic, and political development. Chine has continued to encourage and promote economic growth through agriculture, industry, transportation, handicrafts and commerce as the main targets. The country has invested in nurturing cultural and scientific developments that are shared with international partners, including China. Through economic diplomacy, China has seen sought to exercise technological self-sufficiency while trying to gain superiority in key industry. The bi-centennial goals are partly driven by the Belt and Road Initiative, a trillion-dollar investment project projected to strategic partners across the world.

The last five years have seen Kenya-China increasing their ties significantly (Onjala, 2008). For instance, China has assumed the second largest lender to Kenya after World Bank, having loaned the country Ksh. 557 billion against the latter's 581 billion. The Chinese Bi-centennial goals focus on investing in Africa to the level of establishing close partnerships with member countries. The birth of the Chinese BRI (Belt and Road Initiative) in 2013 represented an advanced level of relationship between China and Africa, Kenya being at the forefront. China is helping countries across the world to improve the living standards of their citizens, with Kenya being among the leading countries in cooperating with the Asian giant. The cases of Sri Lanka losing her port for 99 years to China points to the need for the African countries to ensure they agree to sustainable asset financing.

3. Reviving Countries' Industries through the Belt and Road Initiative

Kenya is one of the beneficiaries of the Chinese Belt and Road Initiative where it has benefited through the loans advanced to build roads and bridges. The CBRI has facilitated construction of several roads, railway lines and other infrastructure that has strengthened the relationship between the two countries. Infrastructure deficit has held Africa and Kenya back, underlining the need to create working relationship among other development corporations. Madegwa (2019) concludes that Kenya has a lot to gain from the overall scheme of Belt and Road Initiative. The construction of the transport infrastructure has increased connectivity as well as reducing the transport cost from Mombasa into the interior of the country. Since Kenya's GDP is largely supported by agricultural activities, transportation of produce to new markets is enhanced, improving the economy of the country. The implementation of the BRI infrastructure has continued to promote regional trade and economic development in Kenya and the other members of East African Community, including Burudi, Rwanda, Ethiopia, Uganda and DRC (Congo). The Chinese initiative of "Maritime Silk Road" has promoted connection between Africa and Asia through Kenya, putting the country on the roadmap of development (Leung, Au, & Law, 2015).

The challenge of the Belt and Road Initiative is that it is expensive and some countries have failed to pay the loans, leading to repossessing of key assets. Kenyan government pays $10 million in every month to the China Road and Bridge Corporation (CRBC) to run the railway. Kenya intends to pay the Ksh. 5.39 trillion over the course of years, failure to which it will lose her Mombasa port. The prospects of losing some key assets has also pushed many Kenyans and other African countries to fear the BRI engagements.

4. Kenya Cultural Diplomacy Strategy and Sino-Kenya People-to-People Diplomacy

Kenyan cultural diplomacy is enshrined in the Kenya Foreign Policy, forming one of the five inter-linked pillars of diplomacy. Kenya's cultural heritage is enormous with diverse cultures captured in one country. Kenya has invested heavily on the cultural diplomacy where it has appointed cultural ambassadors at presidential levels to build comparative advantage on the existing Kenyan brand, propelling Kenya's national image to the world and projecting clear and consistent messages on the values and aspirations of the Kenyans. The cultural diplomacy also calls for development of projects that catapult all the five interlinked pillars in the Kenya's diplomacy strategy.

The cultural strategy has four objectives that when implemented promote cultural diplomacy. For instance, strategic objective one talks about respecting and recognizing cultural diversity and heritage of the Kenyan people. The objective is used for promoting an understanding of the country's cultural diversity through enhanced understanding of the Kenyan people and their culture, promoting the use of culture, sports and arts as a tool of celebrating cultural diversity, and strengthening Kenyan cultural identity. The cultural objective is implemented through having media to promote a positive image of the country, using Kenyan artifacts, paintings and songs among other unique identifiers. The aspect of promoting an understanding of the cultural diversity has been promoted by exchange programs with China, as well as trade fairs for Chinese goods and services in Kenya (and to a great extent, Africa) (Yang, Wall, & Smith, 2008).

The second objective of the Kenya's cultural diplomacy is promoting cultural exchanges and partnerships. The second objective is thus achieved by strengthening bilateral as well as multilateral relations, promoting domestic and international cultural exchanges, and promoting Kenyan cultural products. The third objective of the cultural diplomacy of Kenya to other countries including China is promoting global intercultural dialogue that is achieved by enhancing cultural contacts with

China and other nations (Sun, 2015). The objective is achieved by among others, having Kenyan foods fairs, photo exhibitions, field events, book exhibitions, Kenyan movies, and Kenyan cultural weeks. China has severally participated in trade fairs that also turn out to be cultural fairs by extension.

The fourth objective of the Kenyan cultural diplomacy is promoting sports as well as art diplomacy where Kenyan sportsmen and women (including athletes) are showcased. Kenya and China have had exchange programs in a bid to promote cultural understanding. China and Kenya have been promoting cultural exchange programs with major collaboration among the higher institutions of learning. For instance, Confucius Institutes are available in major Kenyan universities where exchange programs happen. In this case, the Sino-Kenyan relationships are strengthened. Strengthening partnerships in sports, arts and culture has been advanced by having athletes participate in such sports like football, art (paintings, carvings, and music among others) and cultural events (Hofmann et al., 2007). The fifth objective is to strengthen the recognition of Kiswahili as a continental and global language. Swahili language is a native language of East Africans with Kenya and Tanzania having majority of speakers. Through cooperation with institutions of higher learning, Kenya has marketed Swahili as a tool of communication when in Kenya and across East Africa. The Chinese institutions promoting leaning of Swahili as well as the Kenyan institutions promoting learning of Mandarin further promote the cultural diplomacy of the two countries.

5. Sino-Kenya People-to-People Diplomacy and Tourism in Kenya

The five diplomacy pillars presented in the Kenyan Foreign Policy Document have driven the Kenya's engagement with China. The five diplomacy pillars have also promoted tourism between the two countries, focusing on the key areas where the two can exchange cultures. Gadzala (2009) indicated that the cordial relationship between the two countries has promoted the entry of Chinese entrepreneurs into Kenya's local industries, including *jua kali* sector. The spanning trade, investments and aid focus on the promoting interactions of the Kenyans and the Chinese people. Through the tourism inspired by the two countries, the citizens of the two countries seek opportunities to foster sustainable economic development and boost trade. The rapid rise in the Chinese Small and Medium Enterprises (SMEs) has seen export of expertise to Kenyan SMEs and large corporations, contributing to economic and cultural tourism (Okello, Kenana, & Kieti, 2012). China's SMEs have stormed the Kenya's informal sectors, causing trade imbalance and dissatisfaction among the retail traders. The case of people-to-people diplomacy has attracted individual Chinese businessmen to trade in downtown malls and streets in Nairobi, showing the extent of the bonding between the two countries. The environmental and economic diplomacy has promoted a wide range of tourism that has seen Kenyan foreign earnings from Chinese tourists shift by 15% in the last five years (Suntikul, Tang & Pratt, 2016). The establishment of tourism investments like four- and five-star hotels in Kenya, Chinese restaurants and tour companies focusing on China point to the increasing tourism prospects between the two countries. The increasing Chinese investment in tourism (and to an extend in other sectors) in Kenya has increased competition for the local industry SME players, pushing some out of the market due to cheap goods from China.

6. Influence of Chinese Tourists in Kenya and Problems Faced

The establishment of Sino-Kenya bilateral agreements has seen an increase in the number of Chinese tourists in Kenya and across the East Africa. The tourism sector has benefited from Chinese visitors as it has led to increased foreign exchange, with government and private investors gaining income from the industry (Okello, Kenana, & Kieti, 2012). The tourism industry has also benefited from the many opportunities in employment and retail businesses along the tourist channels. The country has also seen an increase in tour companies offering Chinese products and services, including packages for Beijing, Changzhou, Shanghai, Hong Kong and Shenzhen among other big tourist cities in China (Kaminsky, 2017). The same zeal of tours has also been seen where Chinese tourists are offered packages to travel and traverse many tourist attractions in Kenya (Suntikul, Tang & Pratt, 2016).

Tourism in Kenya remains the third largest foreign exchange earner. There has been a slight decrease in the earnings from tourism due to environmental factors. One of the challenges influencing tourism in Kenya is the degradation and deterioration affecting the quality of tourism products. Tourism in Kenya has suffered challenges related to political stability during electioneering period, insecurity arising from terrorists (Al-Shabaab), unsustainable tourism development and global economic recession are common. The environmental impacts of tourism are widespread as an act in one region can affect tourism in many other parts. For instance, deforestation in Mau catchment area has affected the water levels in River Mara that supports the famous world beast migration from Kenya to Tanzania. The drying rivers present a challenge to the existence of tourism in Kenya's Masaai Mara and Amboseli game reserves.

Since Kenya has had a tradition of marketing the existing tourist destinations, there is a tendency to perpetuate concentration of the attractions promoting environmental degradation (Kaminsky, 2017). Where there are concentrated tourists, beaches are polluted, marine species adversely affected and coral reefs destroyed. The continued destruction of the tourist destinations lead to reduced tourist numbers. The mitigation efforts to reclaim the destroyed tourist attractions are constrained by weak institutions, mismanagement, corruption and inadequate political and administrative capacities.

Cultural heritage is seen where Kenyans have adopted some of the Chinese artifacts, styles, and ways of life. For instance, the Chinese martial arts films are popular in Kenya, advocated for by the Chinese people. Chinese sports that many of Kenyan youths are adopting, showing adoption of the Chinese heritage. The learning of the mandarin as well as other forms of Chinese culture (cuisine, attire and industry) show the increasing exchange of the cultural components of the two countries.

7. Economic and Cultural Influence

The Chinese influence on economic development in Kenya has increased over the last one decade. It has been observed that since the reigns of President Kibaki, the country has continuously depended on the East (read China) for economic support. The signing of bilateral trade agreements between the two countries has seen a leap in the goods and services vouched from the east as well as an increase in the number of tourists and investors from the same region. Economic influence from China has seen Kenyan imports doubling with little change in the exports to the former. Kenya has continued to engage the Chinese counterparts in opening new markets, especially for the agricultural products like avocados and horticultural produce (Gadzala, 2009).

The cultural diplomacy and influence from the Chinese people is seen in many fronts in Kenya, including the architecture of the infrastructure, the rich Chinese cuisine as well as other cultural artifacts shared with the Kenyan counterparts. Kenya has continued to borrow from China many ways of life, including adopting the mandarin language for business, entertainment and mutual understanding.

The Chinese culture has been exemplified in many platforms in Kenya, with the establishment of the Confucius Institutes at the University of Nairobi and at Kenyatta University among other institutions. The centers act as transmission centers for the Chinese culture and mandarin language (Řehák, 2016). Kenya has also seen an increase in the number of Swahili teachers moving to teach the language in Chinese institutions. The exchange programme has seen many Kenyan nationals moving to teach Kiswahili to enhance trade between the two countries, hence fostering strong bilateral ties. The focus of Chinese cultural centers in East Africa has promoted development of mandarin language interest among many individuals, promoting the interests of the two countries.

8. Challenges and Further Development of Sino-Kenya People-to-People Diplomacy

One of the challenges arising from the people-to-people diplomacy is the nature of the bilateral trade agreements signed between the two countries. In most cases, the loans given are based on the Chinese laws even when the project is implemented in Kenya or other African countries. The diplomacy is mostly faced with allegations of corruption when bilateral agreements are involved, misappropriation of funds and illegalities that are usually covered by senior government officials (Leung, Au, & Law, 2015). One of the legalities of the Chinese economic diplomacy is the basing all loan facilities on the China International Economic and Trade Arbitration Commission (Sun, 2015). This limits Kenya's freedom to bargain and get fair deals when dealing with China. When the clause states that the arbitrations should be done in Beijing, countries lose their right and freedom to bargain. Solution to the challenge would be applying a neutral law that can favor both countries. For instance, doing arbitration in a neutral country like United Kingdom, or applying trade law promoted by international financial organizations like IMF or World Bank.

Another challenge of the economic diplomacy experienced is the aspect of many countries taking huge Chinese loans and spending it to pay the contractors and materials from the loaning country. For instance, Kenya borrows from China then it uses the money to buy goods, services and technology from China.

There is need for strong cooperation between the two countries when it comes to execution of development projects. For instance, joint evaluation and planning of projects is recommended. This allows for removing excess budgeted resources minimizing wastage.

9. Conclusion

The Kenya-Sino relations have improved in the recent past owing to the fact that developed countries are scrambling for bilateral trade with African countries. The people-to-people diplomacy has shaped the nature of Kenya's investment in infrastructure as well as her relations to China. One of the challenges of the Chinese financing and diplomacy in Kenya is the basing of all agreements and contracts on the laws of China. The two countries have seen an increased economic diplomacy, cultural diplomacy, environmental, peace and diaspora diplomacy (Scheyvens, 2007). Economic tourism is also promoted between the two countries to the extent that Kenya has seen an influx of Chinese tourists. People from the two countries have continued to share cultural developments and infrastructural projects promoting economic and social developments. The Kenyan Vision 2030 as well as the Chinese Bi-Centennial goals focus on promoting economic development. In conclusion, the people-topeople diplomacy has promoted tourism between the two countries. Economic tourism, environmental tourism and other forms of tourism are promoted when the two countries embrace bilateral agreements. Improving policy implementations for trade engagements ensures bright and future people-to-people diplomacy (Scheyvens, 2007).

References

Baah, A. Y., & Jauch, H. (2009). Chinese investments in Africa. *Chinese Investments in Africa: A Labour Perspective*, 35.

Gadzala, A. (2009). Survival of the fittest? Kenya's jua kali and Chinese businesses. *Journal of Eastern African Studies*, *3*(2), 202-220.

Ghai, J. (2019). Is Kenya a beneficiary or victim of Chinese Belt and Road Initiative? Retrieved from https://www.katibainstitute.org/is-kenya-a-beneficiary-or-victim-ofchinese-belt and-road-initiative/

Hofmann, K., Kretz, J., Roll, M., & Sperling, S. E. B. A. S. T. I. A. N. (2007). Contrasting perceptions: Chinese, African, and European perspectives on the China-Africa summit. *Internationale Politik und Gesellschaft*, *2*, 75-90.

Kaminsky, A. (2017). *The Chinese Safari: A New Tourist Gaze in Kenya's Tourism Industy* (Doctoral dissertation).

Leung, R., Au, N., & Law, R. (2015). The recent Asian wave in tourism research: The case of the Journal of Travel & Tourism Marketing. *Asia Pacific Journal of Tourism Research*, *20*(1), 1-28.

Madegwa, D. (2019). China Belt and Road can drive Kenya growth. Retrieved from https://www.businessdailyafrica.com/analysis/letters/China-Belt-and-Road-can-drive Kenya-growth/4307714-5084598-m13abgz/index.html

Okello, M. M., Kenana, L., & Kieti, D. (2012). Factors influencing domestic tourism for urban and semiurban populations around Nairobi National Park, Kenya. *Tourism analysis*, *17*(1), 79-89.

Onjala, J. (2008). A scoping study on China-Africa economic relations: The case of Kenya.

Řehák, V. (2016). China-Kenya Relations: Analysis of the Kenyan News Discourse. *Modern Africa: Politics, History and Society*, *4*(2), 85-115.

Scheyvens, R. (2007). Poor cousins no more: valuing the development potential of domestic and diaspora tourism. *Progress in Development Studies*, *7*(4), 307-325.

Sun, X. (2015). *Chinese FDI: A study of the impact of Chinese infrastructure investments in Kenya, Africa* (Doctoral dissertation, Columbia University).

Suntikul, W., Tang, C., & Pratt, S. (2016). An exploratory study of Chinese tourists on Kenya safari tours. *Journal of China Tourism Research*, *12*(2), 232-251.

Yang, L., Wall, G., & Smith, S. L. (2008). Ethnic tourism development: Chinese Government Perspectives. *Annals of Tourism Research*, *35*(3), 751-771.

中欧关系——"17+1"机制下的中国与西巴尔干关系比较分析

桑亚 【塞尔维亚】

塞尔维亚共和国政府 顾问

一 导言

21 世纪初，尤其是在 2008 年全球金融危机之后，当世界上大多数经济体都游走在衰退边缘或处在衰退的震中面临其影响时，越来越多的欧洲国家和非国家行为体开始将北京视为潜在的合作伙伴[1]。尽管中国和欧盟自 2003 年以来就建立了全面的战略伙伴关系，但欧洲国家直到欧洲危机期间才开始对北京作为伙伴的地位产生信心，当时中国帮助其克服了市场波动，并表现出极高的协作水平[2]。在帮助欧盟的同时，中国保护了自身的出口市场，这是新技术和设备的来源，也是最大的外国投资来源之一。中国希望通过这些方式防止欧盟作为维护多极世界角色重要地位被削弱[3]并展示中国在解决全球问题上是一个"负责任的大国"。

在欧元区危机期间，中国向欧洲提供的援助使中国能够更深入地发展与欧洲国家的关系。高层互访增多，贸易合作加强，中国对外直接投资增加，签署了多项伙伴关系协议。这种方法的成功还得益于中国在世界上"软实力"的更大投射

---

[1] 2001 年，中国拥有 2100 亿美元的外汇储备，此后外汇储备开始快速增长，2018 年底达到 3057 亿美元。

[2] Song Tao, "Kineska pomoć Evropi", Politika, 2012.

[3] 同上。

（建立孔子学院、文化中心、科学交流、熊猫外交等），中国对外投资和援助模式的推广，以及周恩来20世纪50年代提出的原则——相互尊重国家主权、平等、双赢和不干涉别国内政的原则。

2013年，中国国家主席习近平提出了"一带一路"倡议，旨在通过陆路和海路连接欧亚大陆的两个经济发达地区（西欧和中国东部）。该倡议包括中国过去在古丝绸之路沿线实施的零星小型项目，以及与沿线国家的现有合作机制，包括中国与中东欧国家的合作机制（所谓的"16+1"机制或"17+1"机制）。这一机制对中国极其重要，因为它是改善与中欧和东欧国家合作关系的框架。

中东欧国家在"17+1"机制下与中国的合作在双边和多边层面上进行，但也意味着中国与其中某些地区，如东南欧的合作。它突出了巴尔干半岛的一部分，欧盟为该部分设计了一个特殊的政治名称——西巴尔干，由五个非欧盟国家组成：塞尔维亚、黑山、波斯尼亚和黑塞哥维那、北马其顿和阿尔巴尼亚。在过去十年中，自2009年欧洲危机开始以来，西巴尔干地区一直在寻求通过双边和上述合作机制改善与中国的关系。他们中的一些国家在这条道路上走得快一些（塞尔维亚），而另一些国家走得慢一点，往往受到不稳定的内部局势、政府变化和各种外部因素的阻碍。

本研究的基本假设是，尽管美中关系发生了变化，但在未来一段时间内，西巴尔干国家与中国之间的合作将会加强。

在过去一段时间里，关于中国与西巴尔干国家关系的研究主要集中在合作的积极和消极方面。本研究侧重于在"17+1"机制下对中国与西巴尔干国家的关系以及影响其关系动态的因素进行比较分析。作者在研究过程中回答了以下问题：自欧洲危机开始以来，中国与西巴尔干国家的关系如何？什么因素会影响他们关系的动态？这些关系的未来是什么？该研究将使用相关学术和政策文件、官方声明以及来自美国、中国、欧洲和其他国际媒体的新闻。此外，作者还与美国、欧洲和中国官员、分析人士、研究人员、记者和商人进行了正式和非正式的采访和对话，这些人直接参与了中欧关系的各个方面，这些采访和对话充实了本研究内容，增加了可信度。

二 "17+1"机制下中国与西巴尔干的关系

为了改善与16个中东欧国家的关系和已有的合作，北京于2012年建立了

"16+1"机制。随着时间的推移，中国与中东欧国家在各个领域建立了许多合作的体制机制，在各个领域的合作都取得了进展：加强双边贸易、双向投资、基础设施合作，深化财政金融合作，各领域专家进行交流[1]。

迄今为止，中东欧国家和中国已举行了9次经贸论坛和8次总理政治峰会[2]。在2019年5月于杜布罗夫尼克举行的论坛上，希腊成为该机制的第17个新成员，其名称改为"17+1"[3]。2012年，作为对该机制的支持，北京设立了一个初始资本为（10+3）亿美元的投资基金，用于振兴和建设中东欧地区的基础设施，以及支持中国企业积极参与该地区的公私合作和私有化进程。在2013年中国国家主席习近平提出"一带一路"倡议后，"17+1"机制以及此前在该地区实施的所有项目都成为该倡议的重要组成部分。大多数中东欧国家已在该倡议范围内与中国签署了合作备忘录，一些国家已成为亚洲基础设施投资银行（Asian Infrastructure Investment Bank）的成员，该机构成立于2015年，旨在支持该倡议[4]。

"17+1"机制中一个特别重要的区域是东南欧，它代表着中国与中欧和西欧之间的"桥梁"。在该地区，中国与西巴尔干五国的合作尤其有趣，因为它们不是欧盟成员国。2009年欧洲危机爆发后，西巴尔干国家与其他中东欧国家一样，很快采取了"向东开放"战略，积极吸收来自中国的投资[5]。政治、经济、文化和其他关系同步发展，首先是双边层面，然后是自2012年以来在"17+1"机制内的多边层面[6]。重要的是，与欧盟成员国不同，西巴尔干国家可以在没有布鲁塞尔干预的情况下自行决定与北京的合作。这首先意味着，它们自己做出外交政策决定，在与外国投资者达成协议时，不受适用欧盟法规义务的约束。然而，它们的独立性受到欧洲一体化进程的限制，所有西巴尔干国家都将欧洲一体化进程宣布为其外交政策目标，并提到在加入这一国际组织之前，外交政策决定和立法与欧盟条例的逐步协调。此外，在吸引中国投资方面，对它们有利的一个积极论点是，由于与欧盟签订了稳定与结盟协议，这些国家有能力将其产品出口到一个巨

1　Wen Jiabao, "Strenghthen Traditional Friendship and Promote Common Development", The China-CEE Economic Forum, Budapest, 25 June 2011.
2　布达佩斯（2011年）、华沙（2012年）、布加勒斯特（2013年）、贝尔格莱德（2014年）、苏州（2015年）、里加（2016年）、布达佩斯（2016年）、索非亚（2018年）、杜布罗夫尼克（2019年）。
3　COASI, 20th EU-China Summit report, Beijing, 2018.
4　波兰、匈牙利、希腊和塞尔维亚为成员国，捷克共和国和罗马尼亚为候选国。
5　Sanja Arežina, *China in Europe*, Institute of European Studies, Belgrade, 2018, p. 147.
6　在中欧和东欧地区的17个国家中，12个是欧盟成员国，其余5个正在加入欧盟——三个是成员国候选国（塞尔维亚、黑山和马其顿），两个有志成为候选国（波黑）。

大的欧盟市场。

由于这些好处，以及积极参与吸引中国资本，近年来在西巴尔干地区已经完成了一些投资基金项目。其中大部分资金来自优惠贷款，这是中国对外援助的一种重要形式，与中国资本向国外市场出口的"走出去"政策密切相关。然而，在过去两年中，这些国家也吸引了大量中国的外国直接投资，帮助它们为长期存在财务问题、雇佣大量员工的公司找到了战略合作伙伴。

三 影响中国与西巴尔干关系的因素

中国与西巴尔干国家的关系受到不同因素的影响，尤其是中国在 21 世纪作为解决全球问题的国际贡献者尤为重要。作为联合国安理会常任理事国之一、一个核大国、最大的外汇储备持有者和联合国维和部队派遣国，中国的声音在国际上具有重大影响力。因此，世界上大多数国家倾向于与北京建立、保持并努力加强良好关系，这也适用于西巴尔干地区。

第二个因素是西巴尔干国家与中国传统上的良好关系。作为东方集团的一部分，在苏联于 1949 年承认中华人民共和国后不久，这个地区的所有国家也跟着承认了中国[1]。然而，虽然当时大多数是共产主义国家，但除了外交关系外，只有阿尔巴尼亚与中国有政党关系。20 世纪 70 年代末，中国与阿尔巴尼亚断绝党际关系，与南斯拉夫联盟共和国建立了关系，这一时期南斯拉夫联盟共和国为中国的改革提供了最大的支持。随着冷战的结束，以及共产主义政权的倒台（以及 SFR 南斯拉夫的解体），西巴尔干国家开始奉行以西方为主导的外交政策，将促进欧洲—大西洋一体化作为其外交政策目标之一。中方对此表示支持，首先考虑到在各自欧洲政策的决策过程中需要伙伴参与。

影响中国与西巴尔干国家关系的第三个重要因素是该地区良好的地理位置和接近欧盟市场。也就是说，由于中国在过去几十年里的强劲经济扩张，特别是在 2008 年全球金融危机之后，通过"一带一路"倡议，中国使其有可能向世界各地的市场以及欧洲市场注入过剩资本。在这方面，西巴尔干地区是"一带一路"项

---

1 冷战期间，中、东欧国家属于苏联势力范围。中国科学家使用了"欧亚国家"或"苏联和东欧阵营"的名称，以确定这些国家的地缘政治特征。随着冷战的结束，当转型和欧洲化开始时，他们的身份从"欧亚国家"转变为"欧洲国家"。许多中国机构，如文化部、中共中央对外联络部、商务部和一些研究机构，继续将中东欧国家部分或全部列入欧亚国家名单。中国与这些国家的关系不是面向俄罗斯，而是面向欧洲。（刘作奎 .op.cit, p. 3）

目海上部分的一个地理连接点，位于希腊与中欧和西欧之间。自 2009 年以来，中国中远集团一直在希腊参与比雷埃夫斯港的运营。因此，中国产品通过海运从中国抵达比雷埃夫斯港，然后通过公路和铁路（10 号走廊）进一步经过北马其顿、塞尔维亚和匈牙利运输到中欧和西欧。

此外，西巴尔干地区是一个预备基地，中国企业可以在那里获得按照欧洲标准运营的经验，但没有更强大的欧盟竞争或更大的监管压力。在中国海外工程有限责任公司（COVEC）未能在柏林和华沙之间修建高速公路之后，这一点尤为重要。与中国公司相对应的是，这些国家拥有直接和优先进入整个欧盟市场的便利、更低的税收、合格的低收入劳动力，以及提供国家担保以获得优惠贷款的能力，而欧盟成员国无法做到这一点。

第四个因素是，西巴尔干国家需要新的资本来填补全球金融危机和欧元区危机期间大多数欧洲国家经济和金融能力减弱所造成的投资真空。欧元区危机期间，发达欧洲国家缺乏资金，这是该地区国家转向与中国合作以吸引尽可能多资金的一个重要原因。在中美"贸易战"的背景下，特别是在中国不附加任何条件的金融资源的情况下，这一因素更加突出。与有能力使用结构性和凝聚力基金的欧盟成员国不同，西巴尔干国家有非常重要的机会从中国银行获得 10—20 年的无条件优惠贷款，利率为 2%—4%，宽限期为 3—7 年。

影响中国与西巴尔干国家关系的第五个重要因素是与欧盟的关系。具体而言，中国希望与布鲁塞尔建立良好的伙伴关系，主要是因为它们都希望建立一个基于多边主义的更平衡的国际秩序。此外，中国和欧盟是重要的贸易伙伴，每天的贸易额约为 15 亿欧元。鉴于中美之间自 2018 年 3 月以来爆发的"贸易战"，欧盟市场对于中国产品的出口和中国投资非常重要，这一点对北京来说非常重要。然而，在 2012 年 "16+1" 机制建立后，布鲁塞尔官员的一些声明表明，欧盟越来越多地将这一机制视为"特洛伊木马"，中国通过后门进入欧盟并将其分裂为东西两部分。因此，中东欧国家在与中国签订经济协议时被建议不要"违反欧盟规定"，并向西巴尔干国家发出了关于使用中国优惠贷款的警告，因为它们可能陷入"债务陷阱"[1]。这样，欧盟的双重标准政策使这些国家在与旧成员国的关系中处于从

1　United States Senate, "Senators' Letter to Michael Pompeo and Steven Mnuchin", 2018.

属地位，而旧成员国在与中国签订协议和吸引中国投资时没有收到类似的警告[1]。然而，应该记住，欧盟才是西巴尔干国家的最大投资者和援助者。虽然由于投资来源多样化的需要，中国在这一地区的投资不断增长，但目前还不能说中国的投资数量能够与来自欧盟的投资数量相匹配。尽管这些年来中国投资的数量有所增加，特别是在塞尔维亚，但它们仍然主要是中国银行提供的优惠贷款，用于资助西巴尔干国家的大型项目。

为了防止对中国加强与中东欧和西巴尔干地区合作的敌意，中国官员在声明中一直表示，这是发展地区经济的一种合作方式，是平等、相互尊重、互利、共同发展的，双方共同致力于推进中欧关系。他们认为，中国与这些地区的关系不是试图实施"征服和统治"战略，而是另一座中国"通往欧洲的桥梁"，这首先应该成为加强与欧盟关系的途径[2]。与此同时，中东欧国家的官员强调，他们的意图不是组成一个反对欧盟的集团，而是按照欧盟规则行事。此外，在实践中，这些国家在吸引中国投资方面的竞争越来越激烈，这也正在激起布鲁塞尔方面的负面反应。

第六个重要因素是与美国的关系，这可能是影响中国与西巴尔干国家关系的最大因素。作为保证众多盟国安全的全球性大国，美国有能力将其外交政策立场强加于世界其他国家。与巴拉克·奥巴马总统任期不同，当时中国是一个共生伙伴（"中美共同体"）[3]，唐纳德·特朗普总统的上台改变了现有的"中国是合作伙伴"的观念，变成了"中国是潜在的竞争对手"。当美国开始与中国进行"贸易战"时，美国国务卿迈克·蓬佩奥（Mike Pompeo）给了盟国一个机会，表明他们有多大意愿在世界各地追求美国的利益。华盛顿呼吁布鲁塞尔打击冷酷无情的中国贸易，减少中国对欧洲大陆敏感高科技技术的收购。这导致欧盟开始阻止中国公司收购某些安全敏感公司，并寻求加快在欧洲市场引入保护措施（欧盟外国直接投资筛选机制、国际公共采购工具、劳工和生态标准的改善等），以限制中国资本的进入，

---

1 这方面的例子是，欧盟委员会在 2012 年就波兰打算在能源问题上与中国进行单方面合作向波兰发出警告，而在同一问题上，布鲁塞尔在 2013 年没有作出反应，当时德国、英国、奥地利和意大利采取了单方面行动。

2 这方面的例子是，中国坚持希腊留在欧元区内，不削弱欧盟在全球经济中的地位。新华社，中央委员会关于全面深化改革重大问题的决定（全文），第 7 章，第 26 点，2013 年。

3 Nial Ferguson, "Not two countries, but one: Chimerica", The Telegraph, 4 March 2007.

尤其是在安全敏感部门[1]。此外，布鲁塞尔更进一步，在 2019 年 3 月将中国称为"系统性竞争对手和经济竞争对手"。2017 年 8 月，中国领导层为加强对资本退出欧盟的控制而引入的此类布鲁塞尔政策和限制性措施，导致中国在欧盟市场的投资从 2016 年的 370 亿欧元减少到 2017 年的 291 亿欧元和 2018 年的 173 亿欧元[2]。然而，就巴尔干半岛西部国家而言，在同一时期，中国的投资额和开通的项目数量都有增加的趋势，这些资金都来自中国银行的优惠贷款。

四 中国与西巴尔干关系比较分析

近年来，美国对中国的负面言论不断加强，导致人们对与中国合作的看法发生了负面的变化，尤其是欧盟成员国。然而，仍有相当多的欧洲国家将与这个遥远的亚洲国家的合作置于外交议程的重要位置。这些国家大多位于西巴尔干地区，中国与该地区开展双边合作，并在"17+1"机制框架内开展合作。基于上述影响中国与该地区各国关系的因素，在本节中，我们将阐述中国在过去几年中与每个西巴尔干国家的关系动态。

塞尔维亚和中国自 2009 年以来一直保持着战略伙伴关系，并在 2012 年得到深化，然后在 2016 年达到全面战略伙伴关系的水平。自签署战略伙伴关系以来，由于高层互访频繁，政治关系稳步发展。"17+1"机制和国际合作的"一带一路"论坛的建立，使两国总理每年都能在双边访问的基础上相互交流。2014 年，贝尔格莱德在"17+1"机制下主办了总理峰会和经济贸易论坛。此外，塞尔维亚还被选为该机制基础设施项目秘书处所在地和亚洲投资基础设施银行成员。特别重要的是，中国支持在国际组织框架内接受将科索沃作为塞尔维亚的成员。科索沃于 2008 年单方面宣布独立，尽管根据联合国安全理事会第 1244（1999）号决议，它是联合国在南斯拉夫联邦共和国和随后的继承国塞尔维亚共和国内临时管理的领土。

良好的政治合作为经济合作提供了基础。与世界上大多数国家一样，塞尔维亚与中国存在贸易逆差，但在中国兽医和植物检疫证书方面也有一些显著的好处。

---

1 US Embassy in Georgia, National Security Strategy of the United States of America, 2017; Jeff Smith, "China's Belt and Road Initiative: Strategic Implications and International Opposition", The Heritage Foundation, 2018.
2 Thilo Hanemann et al., *Chinese FDI in Europe: 2018 trends and impact of new policies*, Papers on China, Merics, 2019, https://www.merics.org/en/papers-on-china/chinese-fdi-in-europe-2018.

因此，最大的塞尔维亚公司可以向中国市场出口草药和动物产品。塞尔维亚吸引了大量中国投资，最显著的是收购了钢铁厂"斯梅德雷沃"、科珀矿业公司和冶炼厂"博尔"，建造了兹伦贾宁的轮胎厂、洛兹尼察的汽车零部件厂、博尔查的工业园。对中国公司来说，塞尔维亚有可能向欧盟和俄罗斯市场免税出口，这一点极为重要。除了中国的投资，塞尔维亚还从进出口银行获得了大量资金，这些资金以优惠条件用于实施许多基础设施项目。最重要的项目是匈牙利—塞尔维亚铁路重建项目，该项目包括塞萨洛尼基—布达佩斯铁路线的一部分，多瑙河上的"米哈伊洛—普宾"大桥，奥布雷诺瓦茨—乌布公路，拉伊科瓦茨—勒吉格公路，苏尔契因—奥布雷诺瓦茨公路，普雷利纳—波泽加公路，普瑞立那—波热加公路，以及贝尔格莱德绕道的建设。此外，还从进出口银行获得了能源项目的优惠贷款：振兴 TPP "Kostolac B"等。到目前为止，塞尔维亚已从中东欧国家投资基金中提取了约 60 亿美元（其中投资超过 20 亿美元），在所有项目完成后，有可能达到 100 亿美元。

与中国的文化合作也非常重要。除了位于贝尔格莱德和诺维萨德的两所孔子学院外，塞尔维亚还在北京开设了一个文化中心，而贝尔格莱德中国文化中心的建设预计将于 2019 年底/2020 年初完成。这个文化中心对塞尔维亚来说非常重要，因为欧洲只有巴黎一个中国文化中心，是在 20 世纪 70 年代开设[1]。贝尔格莱德中小学和大学都教授汉语。

黑山（离开塞尔维亚和黑山国家联盟后）和中国自 2006 年建交以来，进行了良好和全面的合作，并不断升级，最终于 2013 年签署了《友好合作协定》[2]。近年来，高级别（总理）会晤主要在"17+1"机制框架内举行，另外在 2014 年 2 月索契冬奥会和 2014 年 8 月南京夏季青年奥运会等其他国际赛事期间双方也举行了会谈[3]。

这个西巴尔干国家与中国也存在贸易逆差。黑山的外国直接投资流入很少，主要是中国资本通过优惠贷款进入该国。中国进出口银行为从保利科技集团购买四艘船舶提供了优惠贷款[4]。此外，该贷款还被批准用于修建从巴尔到博尔贾尔—斯莫科瓦茨—马特舍沃的一段道路，这引发了 16 名美国参议员的负面评论，他

1　*Mondo*, "Kineski kulturni centar – 'najlepša zgrada' ", 20 July 2017.
2　中华人民共和国外交部，"中国和黑山"，2013 年。
3　Ambasada NR Kine u Crnoj Gori, "Istorija bilateralnih odnosa NR Kine i Crne Gore", 28 October 2016.
4　*Ekapija*, "Vlada Crne Gore kupuje dva trgovačka broda kineske proizvodnje", 2 November 2009.

们在 2018 年 8 月致函美国国务卿迈克·蓬佩奥和美国财政部长史蒂文·姆努钦，警告他们黑山和其他国家（巴基斯坦、斯里兰卡和吉布提）可能因中国贷款导致的不可持续债务而面临问题[1]。

文化合作也是黑山与中国关系的一个重要方面。在中小学开设汉语课程，同样黑山大学设立的孔子学院也有汉语教学。

波斯尼亚和黑塞哥维那与中国的合作在很大程度上是由"17+1"机制推动的，该机制基本上是最高官员访问的唯一论坛。然而，近年来，波黑对中国人的投资越来越有吸引力。

中国的对外直接投资非常少，但中国银行为波斯尼亚和黑塞哥维那的各种项目提供了更优惠的贷款，如建设 TPP "Stanari"、TPP "Tuzla"、巴尼亚卢卡到姆利尼什特的公路。值得注意的是，TPP "Stanari" 是波斯尼亚和黑塞哥维那第一个按照欧盟环境保护指令（2001/80/EC）运行的能源设施[2]。

文化合作通常在"17+1"机制的框架内运作。目前小学和中学以及位于萨拉热窝和巴尼亚卢卡的两所孔子学院教授汉语。

由于马其顿拥有高质量的镍铁材料，北马其顿对中国市场的出口量远远高于该地区其他国家。中国的直接投资很少，大部分是中国银行在优惠条件下贷款的项目。在这方面，涉及中国公司的最重要项目是在特雷斯卡河峡谷建造科兹贾克水电站。此外，大量中国资金被指定用于修建两条公路——西部基切沃—奥赫里德公路和东部米拉迪诺维奇—什蒂普公路[3]。2014 年 12 月，在贝尔格莱德举行的"17+1"总理峰会上，马其顿总理尼古拉·格鲁耶夫斯基与中国总理李克强签署了关于修建布达佩斯至塞萨洛尼基快速铁路的协议。为了实现该项目，马其顿政府从中国购买了六列客车。

在文化合作方面，北马其顿对中国非常重要，因为"17+1"机制的文化合作协调中心位于斯科普里。孔子学院于 2011 年在斯科普里成立，在这里，北马其顿人民有机会学习汉语。

自 2009 年签署《关于深化传统友好关系的联合声明》以来，阿尔巴尼亚和

1　Wen Jiabao, "Strengthen Traditional Friendship and Promote Common Development", The China-CEE Economic Forum, Budapest, 25 June 2011.
2　Uroš Ačanski, "Kina: novi igrač na evropskom terenu", *Biznis & finansije*, 3 December 2013.
3　Martin Kraljevski, "Kineski kapital u Makedoniji: skupe autoceste i kreditiranje korupcije", *Bilten*, 10 April 2015.

中国一直保持着良好的政治关系。因此，两国之间的贸易逐年增加，目前中国是阿尔巴尼亚五大经济伙伴之一。此外，两国还在文化、教育、科技、农业、体育、广播电视以及国际论坛等领域开展合作。中国在阿尔巴尼亚的直接投资并不多。其中最重要的一项是 Geo Jade Petroleum Corp. 收购了加拿大石油公司（Banker's Petroleum），该公司在阿尔巴尼亚运营，包括帕托斯马林泽和库科瓦油田[1]。此外，中国光大有限公司通过地拉那的特蕾莎修女机场特许权收购了该公司，权限直至 2027 年[2]。关于中国的优惠贷款，连接阿尔巴尼亚和马其顿的阿尔伯公路就是在此基础上修建的。此外，中国的中矿资源勘探有限公司在阿尔巴尼亚成立了一个子公司，该公司正在与阿尔巴尼亚地质研究所合作进行矿山建设和地质测试。中国还对阿尔巴尼亚农业部门进行了大量投资。

近年来，文化合作有了显著发展。在地拉那建立了一所孔子学院，让更多的公众学习汉语。此外，阿尔巴尼亚对发展与中国的旅游合作非常感兴趣。在这方面，阿尔巴尼亚旅游组织在西巴尔干地区非常活跃。

五 结语

本研究的出发点是加强中国在欧洲市场的存在，这是中国经济加速发展的结果，也是继续保持高经济增长、满足国内市场对重要资源的需求和国内产品分销新市场的需要，所有这些都是为了提高公民的生活水平，保持中国共产党的执政地位。中国在世界上的影响力不断增加，导致中国的利益与世界主要大国，尤其是美国的利益重叠。这导致美国对北京的负面态度加剧，并采取了措施旨在减少中国在美国领土上政治和经济的存在。负面言论已经从美国转移到了欧洲，在那里，欧盟主要国家正越来越多地开始显示出一种倾向，即通过对外国投资，尤其是中国投资采取保护性措施，削弱中国在其市场的存在，也削弱了中国在欧盟单一市场中的存在。考虑到欧盟对潜在成员国的压力将会加大，而且如果它们希望沿着加入欧盟的道路前进，也需要对欧盟的决定表现出合作和团结，预计它们也会采取类似行动。

---

1 Liu, Zuokui, "The Pragmatic Cooperation between China and CEE: Characteristics, Problems and Policy Suggestions", Working Paper Series on European Studies, Institute of European Studies, Chinese Academy of Social Sciences, Vol. 7, No. 6, 2013, p. 3

2 这方面的例子是，欧盟委员会在 2012 年就波兰打算在能源问题上与中国进行单方面合作向波兰发出警告，而在同一问题上，布鲁塞尔在 2013 年没有作出反应，当时德国、英国、奥地利和意大利采取了单方面行动。

本文概述了与中东欧地区性合作方式的优势和劣势，以及在加强与中国的双边合作（政治、经济、文化等）的背景下，区域性解决方法提供的机遇。特别强调了在改善区域基础设施方面开展合作的重要性，因为优质道路是更多外国直接投资和加强贸易合作的基础。这将使该地区有机会成为一个交通和通信枢纽，方便转运货物，更快地运输到奥地利、德国、乌克兰等其他欧洲目的地。

在研究过程中，确定了影响西巴尔干国家与中国合作的因素。大多数因素对西巴尔干地区与中国的关系具有积极影响，只有少数因素具有消极影响。因此，如果西巴尔干国家能够利用一切有利于它们的因素，它们就处于改善与中国合作的理想地位。对这些国家过去几年与中国关系的比较分析可以看出，它们已经在这样做，而且时间对它们有利。

迄今已完成数十个联合项目，其中许多项目对西巴尔干国家具有战略重要性。这些项目的价值几乎超过了中东欧投资基金为此目的指定的金额。不过，目前的合作还可以进一步加强。在这方面，西巴尔干国家的基本利益之一应该是增加对中国市场的出口。由于这些国家的出口能力很差，而且针对中国市场稀缺产品的个别出口谈判进展非常缓慢，几乎没有取得明显的成果，它们应该通过政治参与"17+1"机制，把自己作为北京的合作伙伴，并达成政治协议。中国政府可以起草一份中国市场所需的产品清单，这样就可以找到农产品和动物产品的销售场所。说到出口，重点可能放在中国西部，要记住，东部省份已经有来自美国和西欧的公司的强大竞争。在这方面，至关重要的是，西巴尔干国家应共同努力，向中国的大市场出口尽可能多的产品。此外，中国应更多地了解该地区各国的困境主要是冒着欧洲一体化进程放缓的风险，以加强与中国的合作。希望能将西巴尔干公司进入中国市场的门槛降到最低。因此，这是各国领导人最大的责任，只有齐心协力，他们才能将力量的源泉转化为成功的智慧——从而实现各自的利益和目标。

Sino-European Relations - Comparative Analysis on Sino-Western Balkans Relations within "17+1" Mechanism

Sanja Arežina / Serbia

Government of the Republic of Serbia / Counselor

I. Introduction

At the beginning of the 21st century, and especially after the Global Financial Crisis of 2008, when most of the world's economies were facing its effects in the lobby or at the very epicenter of the recession, a growing number of European national and non-state actors began to perceive Beijing as a potential partner for cooperation.[1] Although there has been a comprehensive strategic partnership between China and the EU since 2003, European countries was only during the Eurocrisis began to gain confidence in Beijing as a partner, when China helped them to overcome market volatility and showed extremely high levels of solidarity.[2] While helping the EU, China has protected its export market, a source of new technology and equipment and one of the largest sources of foreign investment. In doing so, it

---

[1] In 2001, China held 210 billion dollars in foreign exchange reserves, after which they began to grow rapidly, reaching 3,057 billion dollars at the end of 2018.
[2] Song Tao, "Kineska pomoć Evropi", *Politika*, 2012.

has reduced its ability to suffer losses itself, at the same time aspiring to open up the European market for Chinese investment and authorizing European officials to ease arms trade restrictions and sensitive high-tech products that are necessary for the new national economic model and achieve the "Chinese dream" in 2049 (Zhongguo Meng).[1] Through such behavior, China wanted, above all, to prevent the weakening of the EU as an important actor in safeguarding the multipolar world,[2] demonstrating that it represents a "responsible great power" (Fuzeren de Daguo) in solving global issues, which it has been asked for years ago.[3]

The assistance it provided to Europe, during the Eurozone crisis, enabled China to develop relations with European countries more intensively. The exchange of high-level visits has increased, trade cooperation has been enhanced, Chinese foreign direct investment has increased, and numerous partnership agreements have been signed. The success of this approach was further aided by a larger projection of the "soft power" of China in the world (the establishment of a Confucius Institutes, cultural centers, scientific exchanges, panda diplomacy, etc.), the promotion of the Chinese model of foreign investment and assistance, and Zhou Enlai's principles from the 1950s – mutual respect for states sovereignty, the principle of equality, win-win and non-interference in the internal affairs of other states.

Progress in cooperation has continued following the promotion of "One Belt, One Road" initiative (Yidai Yilu) by Chinese President Xi Jinping in 2013, which aims to link the two economically developed parts of Eurasia (Western Europe and and the eastern part of China) by land and sea. This initiative included sporadic smaller projects implemented in the past by China along the ancient Silk Road route, as well as existing mechanisms for cooperation with countries along the road, including

---

1 In November 2012, at the Third Plenum of 18th Congress, President Xi Jinping mentioned the vision of the "Chinese Dream" , which he subsequently clarified as the accomplishment of a large number of internal reforms agreed in the Program of 60-point. Gong Weibin, *Chinese Experience of Development*, Lecture, Seminar "China's issues" , Chinese Academy of Governance, Beijing, 23 November 2013.
2 COASI, 20th EU-China Summit report, Beijing, 2018.
3 Sanja Arežina, *China in Europe*, Institute of European Studies, Belgrade, 2018, p. 147.

the Mechanism of Cooperation between China and the Central and Eastern European Countries (the so-called "16+1" Mechanism or "17+1" Mechanism). This Mechanism is extremely important to China because it is a framework for improving cooperation with the Central and Eastern European (CEE) countries, with which China developed very good relations.

The cooperation of CEE countries with China, within the "17+1" Mechanism, takes place at bilateral and multilateral level, but also implies the cooperation of China with certain regions located in this area, such as Southeast Europe. It highlights the part of the Balkan Peninsula for which the European Union has devised a special political name – the Western Balkans – which consists of five non-EU countries: Serbia, Montenegro, Bosnia and Herzegovina, North Macedonia and Albania. During the last ten years, since the start of the Eurocrisis in 2009, the Western Balkans have sought to improve their relations with China, bilaterally and through the aforementioned cooperation mechanism. Some of them were moving faster along this path (Serbia), while others were going slower, often hindered by an unstable internal situation, changes in government and various external factors.

In the past period, researches on the relationship between China and the Western Balkans countries have focused mainly on the positive and negative aspects of cooperation. This research focuses on a comparative analysis of relations between China and the Western Balkans countries, within the "17+1" Mechanism, and the factors that influence the dynamics of their relationship. The author answers the following questions during the research: What is China's relationship with the Western Balkans countries since the beginning of the Eurocrisis? What factors affect the dynamics of their relationship? What is the future of these relationships? The research will use relevant academic and policy documentation, official statements and news from US, Chinese, European and other international media. Also, for the sake of authenticity, the research was enriched by formal and informal interviews and conversations the author had with US, European and Chinese officials, analysts, researchers, journalists and businessmen, who were directly involved in various aspects of Sino-European relations.

II. Relationship between China and Western Balkans within the "17+1" Mechanism

In order to improve relations and pre-existing cooperation with 16 Central and Eastern European countries, Beijing established the "16+1" Mechanism in 2012. In the course of time, numerous institutional mechanisms for cooperation in various fields were developed between China and the CEE countries, in which cooperation progressed in all segments: strengthening bilateral trade, two-way investment, infrastructure cooperation, deepening fiscal and financial cooperation and exchanging experts in various fields. [1]

So far, 9 economic and trade forums and 8 political summits of the prime ministers of Central and Eastern European countries and China have been held. [2] At the last forum, held in Dubrovnik in May 2019, Greece became the new 17th member of the Mechanism whose name was changed to "17+1". [3] In 2012, as support to the Mechanism Beijing established an Investment Fund with an initial capitalization of 10+3 billion dollars, which was spent to revitalize and build infrastructure in the CEE region, as well as to support Chinese companies for active participation in public-private partnerships and privatization processes in this region. After Chinese President Xi Jinping promoted the "One Belt, One Road" initiative in 2013, the "17+1" Mechanism has become an integral part of it, along with all the projects previously implemented in this region. Most CEE countries have signed memorandums of cooperation with China within this initiative, and some have become members of the Asian Infrastructure Investment Bank, an institution established in 2015 to support the initiative. [4]

---

1 Wen Jiabao, "Strengthen Traditional Friendship and Promote Common Development", The China-CEE Economic Forum, Budapest, 25 June 2011.
2 In Budapest (2011), in Warsaw (2012), in Bucharest (2013), in Belgrade (2014), in Suzhou (2015), in Riga (2016), in Budapest (2016), in Sofia (2018), in Dubrovnik (2019).
3 Emilian Kavalski, "China's '16+1' Is Dead? Long Live the '17+1'", The Diplomat, 29 March 2019.
4 Poland, Hungary, Greece and Serbia are members, while Czech Republic and Romania are candidate countries.

A particularly significant region within the "17+1" Mechanism is Southeastern Europe, which represents a "bridge" between China and Central and Western Europe. Within this region, China's cooperation with the five Western Balkan countries is particularly interesting, having in mind that they are not EU members. After the beginning of the Eurocrisis in 2009, the Western Balkan countries, like other Central and Eastern European countries, very quickly adopted the "Open to the East" strategy, actively absorbing investments that come from China.[1] Political, economic, cultural and other relations have been developed simultaneously, first at the bilateral level and then multilaterally within the "17+1" Mechanism since 2012.[2] Of great importance was the fact that, unlike EU member countries, Western Balkans countries could make their own decisions on cooperation with Beijing, without the intervention of Brussels. This means in the first place that they make their own foreign policy decisions and are not subject to the obligation to apply EU regulations when concluding deals with foreign investors. However, their independence is limited by the process of European integration, which all Western Balkan countries have proclaimed as their foreign policy goal, and refers to the gradual harmonization of foreign policy decisions and legislation with EU regulations, up to the date of their accession to this international organization. Also, a positive argument in their favor when it comes to attracting Chinese investment is the fact that these countries, thanks to the stabilization and association agreements with the EU, have the ability to export their products to a huge EU market.

Thanks to these benefits, as well as active involvement in attracting Chinese capital, a number of investment fund projects have been completed in the Western Balkans in recent years. Most of them are financed by preferential loans, which represent a significant type of China's foreign assistance and closely linked to the

---

1 Liu Zuokui, "The Pragmatic Cooperation between China and CEE: Characteristics, Problems and Policy Suggestions", Working Paper Series on European Studies, Institute of European Studies, Chinese Academy of Social Sciences, Vol. 7, No. 6, 2013, p. 3

2 Of the 17 countries in the CEE region, 12 are EU member countries, while the remaining five are in the process of accession - three are candidates for membership (Serbia, Montenegro and Macedonia), while two are aspiring to become candidates (Bosnia and Herzegovina and Albania).

"going out" policy of exporting Chinese capital to foreign markets (Zou Chūqù). However, in the last two years, these countries have also attracted a number of Chinese foreign direct investments, which have helped them to find strategic partners for companies that have long-standing financial problems and employ a large number of people.

III. Factors affecting relations between China and the Western Balkans

China's relations with the Western Balkans countries are influenced by a number of different factors, most notably the importance of China in the 21st century as an international contributor to solving global problems. As a permanent member of the UN Security Council, a nuclear power, the largest holder of foreign exchange reserves and a UN peacekeeping contributor, its voice has great weight internationally. Consequently, most countries in the world tend to establish, preserve and work to strengthen good relations with Beijing, which also applies to the Western Balkans region.

The second factor is the traditionally good relations of the Western Balkan countries with China. Namely, all the countries of this region, as part of the Eastern Bloc, did so soon after the Soviet Union recognized the PR China in 1949.[1] However, at that time, although most of them were communist countries, only Albania had party relations with China in addition to diplomatic relations. In the late 1970s, China broke off party relations with Albania and established with the SFR Yugoslavia, which during this period provided the greatest support for Chinese

---

1 During the Cold War, the CEE Countries belonged to the Soviet sphere of influence. Chinese scientists have used the name "Eurasian States" or "Camp of the Soviet Union and Eastern Europe" for these countries to identify their geopolitical character. With the end of the Cold War, when the transformation and europeanization started, their identity changed from the "Eurasian countries" to "European countries". Many Chinese institutions such as the Ministry of Culture, the International Department of the Central Committee of the CPC, the Ministry of Commerce and some research institutions continue to place the CEE Countries into the Eurasian countries list partially or in their entirety. China's relationship with these countries is not oriented towards Russia, but towards Europe. Liu Zuokui, *op. cit*, p. 3.

reforms. With the end of the Cold War, following the fall of communist regimes (and the breakup of the SFR Yugoslavia), the Western Balkan countries are beginning to pursue a foreign policy predominantly West oriented, promoting Euro-Atlantic integration as one of their foreign policy goals. China is supporting them in this, having in mind, first and foremost, the need for partners in the decision-making process within their respective European policies.

The third significant factor affecting China's relations with the Western Balkan countries is the region's good geographical position and proximity to the EU market. Namely, because of its strong economic expansion over the past few decades, and especially after the Global Financial Crisis of 2008, China has made it possible to place surplus capital to markets around the world, as well as to the European market, thanks to the "Belt and Road" initiative. In this regard, the Western Balkans region is a geographical link, within the maritime component of this project, between Greece, where the Chinese company COSCO has been involved in the operation of the Port of Piraeus since 2009, and Central and Western Europe. Thus, Chinese products arrive by sea from China to the Piraeus port, and are then transported further by road and railway (Corridor 10) through North Macedonia, Serbia and Hungary to Central and Western Europe.

In addition, the Western Balkans region is a form of preparatory ground on which Chinese companies gain experience in operating in accordance with European standards, but without stronger EU competition or stronger regulatory pressure. This is especially significant after the failure of the Chinese company COVEC to build a highway between Berlin and Warsaw. It corresponds to Chinese companies that these countries have direct and privileged access to the entire EU market, lower taxes, qualified low-income labor, and the ability to provide state guarantees in order to receive preferential loans, which EU member countries are unable to do.

The fourth factor is the Western Balkan countries' need for fresh capital to fill the investment vacuum created by the weakening economic and financial capacity of most European countries during the Global Financial Crisis and the Eurozone Crisis. The lack of funding in developed European countries amid the Eurozone crisis is an important reason why countries in the region have turned to partnering with China in order to attract as much funding as possible. This factor is even more pronounced in the context of a "trade war" between China and the US, which is reflected in 2/3 of the global market, especially given that China provides no strings attached financial resources. Unlike EU member countries that have the ability to use Structural and Cohesion Funds, the Western Balkan countries have a very significant opportunity to get no strings attached preferential loans from Chinese banks for 10-20 years at 2-4% interest rate and 3-7 year grace period.

The fifth important factor affecting China's relations with the Western Balkan countries is relations with the European Union. Specifically, China wants to have good partnerships with Brussels, primarily because they share a desire for a more balanced international order based on effective multilateralism. In addition, China and the EU are significant trading partners, with around 1.5 billion euros in daily trading. The European Union market is very important for exporting Chinese products and placing Chinese investment, which is very important for Beijing given the "trade war" that has existed between the US-China since March 2018. However, after the establishment of the "16+1" Mechanism in 2012, some statements by Brussels officials indicated that EU was increasingly perceiving this mechanism as a "Trojan horse" and another in a series of Chinese attempts to enter the European Union through a back door and divide it into the East and the West. Therefore, CEE countries were advised not to "violate EU regulations" when concluding economic agreements with the China, and a warning was issued to Western Balkan countries regarding the use of preferential Chinese loans, due to the possibility of being in a "debt trap".[1] In this way, the EU's double standards policy places these countries in a subordinate position in relations to the old member countries,

---

1 United States Senate, "Senators' Letter to Michael Pompeo and Steven Mnuchin", 2018.

which did not receive similar warnings when entering into agreements with China and attracting Chinese investment.[1] However, it should be borne in mind that the European Union is the largest investor and donor to the Western Balkan countries. Although China is increasingly present in this area, due to the need to diversify its sources of investment, it cannot yet be said that the number of Chinese investments can match the amount of investment coming from the EU. Although their numbers have increased over the years, especially with regard to Serbia, they are still mostly preferential loans given by Chinese banks to finance larger projects in the Western Balkan countries.

In order to prevent animosity towards strengthening China's cooperation with the CEE and Western Balkans, Chinese officials have always stated in their statements that the aim of this type of cooperation is to develop a regional approach, based on equality and mutual respect and benefit, mutual development and mutual effort, advance relations between China and Europe. According to them, China's relationship with these regions is not an attempt to implement the "conquer and rule" strategy, but another Chinese "bridge to Europe", which, above all, should serve as a way to strengthen relations with the European Union.[2] At the same time, officials from CEE states stressed that their intention was not to form a bloc against the EU, but to act in accordance with EU rules. Moreover, in practice, these countries are increasingly rival among themselves attracting as much Chinese investment then they are provoking negative reactions from Brussels.

The sixth significant factor, that perhaps most influences China's relations with the Western Balkan countries, is relations with the US. As the largest global power

---

1 The example for this is a warning which the European Commission gave to Poland in 2012 regarding its intent to unilaterally cooperate on the energy issues with the PR China, while on the same issue Brussels did not react in 2013, when Germany, the United Kingdom, Austria and Italy acted unilaterally. Sanja Arežina, *op. cit*, 248.
2 The example of this is the Chinese insistence that Greece remains within the Eurozone not to weaken the EU's position in the global economy. *Xinhua*, "Zhonggong zhongyang guanyu quanmian shenhua gaige ruogan zhongda wenti de jueding (quanwen) [Central Committee's Decision on Major Issues Concerning Comprehensively Deepening Reforms (full text)]", Chapter 7, Point 26, 2013.

that guarantees security to many allies, the US are in a position to impose their foreign policy positions on other countries in the world. Unlike President Barack Obama's tenure, when China was a symbiosis partner ("Chimerica")[1], President Donald Trump's rise to power changed the existing perception of "China as a partner" to "China as a potential rival". When the US began a "trade war" with China, US Secretary of State Mike Pompeo gave the opportunity to the Allies to show how willing they were to pursue US interests around the world. Washington has called on Brussels to combat the unfeeling of Chinese trade with a view to reducing the takeover of sensitive hi-tech technologies on the European continent. This led the European Union to start blocking the acquisition of certain security-sensitive companies by Chinese companies and seek to accelerate the introduction of protective measures in the European market that would restrict the entry of Chinese capital, especially in security-sensitive sectors (EU Screening Mechanism for Foreign Direct Investment, International Public Procurement Instrument, Improvement of Labor and Ecological Standards, etc.).[2] In addition, Brussels went one step further and referred to China in March 2019 as a "systemic rival and economic competitor". Such Brussels policies and restrictive measures introduced by the Chinese leadership in August 2017 to increase controls on the exit of capital from the country have resulted in a reduction of Chinese investments in the European Union market from 37 billion euros in 2016 to 29.1 billion euros in 2017 and 17.3 billion euros in 2018.[3] However, when it comes to the Western Balkan countries, in the same period, there is a tendency to increase the number of Chinese investments and started projects for which funds are obtained through preferential loans from Chinese banks.

---

1 Nial Ferguson, "Not two countries, but one: Chimerica", *The Telegraph*, 4 March 2007.
2 US Embassy in Georgia, National Security Strategy of the United States of America, 2017; Jeff Smith, "China's Belt and Road Initiative: Strategic Implications and International Opposition", The Herirage Foundation, 2018.
3 Thilo Hanemann et al., *Chinese FDI in Europe: 2018 trends and impact of new policies*, Papers on China, Merics, 2019, https://www.merics.org/en/papers-on-china/chinese-fdi-in-europe-2018.

IV. Comparative Analysis on Sino-Western Balkans Relations

The strengthening of US negative rhetoric about China in recent years has led to a change in the negative perception of cooperation with China, which most European countries, especially EU member countries, have had. However, there are still significant number of European countries that put cooperation with this far-flung Asian country high on their diplomatic agenda. Most of these countries are located in the Western Balkans region, with which China cooperates bilaterally and within the framework of the "17+1" Mechanism. Based on the above factors that influence China's relations with the countries of this region, in this section we will explain the dynamics of relations which China has had individually with each Western Balkan country in the last few years.

Serbia and China have had a strategic partnership since 2009, which deepened in 2012 and then reached the level of a comprehensive strategic partnership in 2016. Since the signing of the strategic partnership, political relations have steadily progressed, thanks to the high level of high-level visits that have been exchanged. The establishment of the "17+1" Mechanism and the Belt and Road Forum for International Cooperation enabled the presidents and prime ministers to see each other on an annual basis, beyond bilateral visits. Belgrade hosted the Summit of the prime ministers and the Economic and Trade Forum under the "17+1" Mechanism in 2014. Also, Serbia has been selected to be the seat of the Secretariat for Infrastructure Projects of this mechanism and a member of the Asian Investment Infrastructure Bank. Particularly very significant is the Chinese support that Serbia receives within the framework of international organizations concerning membership of Kosovo, which unilaterally declared independence in 2008, although under UN Security Council resolution 1244 (1999) it is a provisionally administered UN territory within the FR Yugoslavia and then within the successor states – the Republic of Serbia.

Good political co-operation provided a good basis for economic co-operation. Serbia, like most countries in the world, has a trade deficit with China, but also has some significant benefits when it comes to the Chinese veterinary and phytosanitary certificates. As a result, the largest Serbian companies can export their herbal and animal products to the Chinese market. Serbia has attracted a large number of Chinese investments, most notably the purchase of Steel Mill "Smederevo", Coper Miner and Smelter "Bor", construction of a tyre factory in Zrenjanin, car parts factory in Loznica, an industrial park in Borča, etc. It is extremely important for Chinese companies that Serbia has the possibility of duty-free exports to the EU and Russian markets. In addition to Chinese investments, Serbia has received significant funding from Exim Bank under preferential conditions for the implementation of numerous infrastructure projects. The most significant projects are the Reconstruction Project of the Hungarian-Serbian Railway, which should be part of the Thessaloniki-Budapest railway link, the "Mihajlo Pupin" bridge over the Danube, the Obrenovac-Ub highway, the Lajkovac-Ljig highway, the Surčin-Obrenovac highway, the Preljina-Pozega highway, the Pozega-Boliari highway and the construction of the bypass around Belgrade. Also, preferential loans were obtained from Exim Bank for energy projects: revitalization of the TPP "Kostolac B", etc. So far, Serbia has withdrew about 6 billion dollars from the CEEC Investment Fund (of which investments are over 2 billion dollars), with a tendency to reach 10 billion dollars after all the projects have been completed.

Cultural cooperation with China is also very significant. In addition to the two Confucius Institutes located in Belgrade and Novi Sad, Serbia has opened a Cultural Center in Beijing, while the construction of the Chinese Culture Center in Belgrade is expected to be completed in late 2019/early 2020 at the same location where the former Embassy of the PR China was located before it was demolished during the 1999 NATO bombing. The importance of this cultural center for Serbia is great, bearing in mind that there is just one more Chinese Culture Center in Europe, Paris, which opened in the 1970s.[1] Chinese is taught in primary and secondary schools, as well as at the University of Belgrade.

---

1 *Mondo*, "Kineski kulturni centar –'najlepša zgrada'" , 20 July 2017.

Since 2006, when diplomatic relations were established (after leaving the State Union of Serbia and Montenegro), Montenegro and China have had good and comprehensive cooperation, which they have constantly upgraded, which resulted in the signing of the Friendship and Cooperation Agreement in 2013.[1] In recent years, high-level (Prime Minister) meetings have taken place mainly in the framework of the "17+1" Mechanism, as well as in other international events such as the Winter Olympics in Sochi in February 2014 and the Summer Youth Olympics in Nanjing in August 2014.[2]

This Western Balkan country also has a trade deficit with China. There is very little inflows of foreign direct investment in Montenegro, mainly Chinese capital entering the country through preferential loans. China's Exim Bank granted preferential loans for the purchase of four ships from Poly Technologies Group.[3] Also, the loan was approved for the construction of a section of the road from Bar to Boljare Smokovac-Mateševo, which sparked negative comments from 16 US senators who in August 2018 sent a letter to US Secretary of State Mike Pompeo and US Secretary of the Treasury Steven Mnuchin warning them of a problem Montenegro and other countries (Pakistan, Sri Lanka and Djibouti) may have due to the unsustainable debts caused by Chinese loans.[4]

Cultural cooperation is also an important aspect of Montenegrin relations with China. Chinese is taught in primary and secondary schools, as well as at the Confucius Institute established at the University of Montenegro.

Bosnia and Herzegovina's co-operation with China is largely driven by the "17+1" Mechanism, which is essentially the only forum for top official visits. However, in recent years Bosnia and Herzegovina has become an increasingly attractive investment destination for the Chinese.

1　Ministry of Foreign Affairs of the PR China, "China and Montenegro", 2013.
2　Ambasada NR Kine u Crnoj Gori, "Istorija bilateralnih odnosa NR Kine i Crne Gore", 28 October 2016.
3　*Ekapija*, "Vlada Crne Gore kupuje dva trgovačka broda kineske proizvodnje", 2 November 2009.
4　United States Senate, op. cit.

There is very small amount of Chinese foreign direct investment, but there are more preferential loans granted by Chinese banks for various projects in Bosnia and Herzegovina, such as construction of TPP "Stanari", construction of TPP "Tuzla", highway from Banja Luka to Mliniste, etc. It is important to note that the TPP "Stanari" is the first energy facility in Bosnia and Herzegovina that operates in accordance with the EU directives on environmental protection (2001/80/ EC).[1]

Cultural cooperation generally operates within the framework of the "17+1" Mechanism. Chinese is taught in primary and secondary schools as well as in two Confucius Institutes, located in Sarajevo and Banja Luka.

North Macedonian exports to the Chinese market are much higher than in other countries in the region because Macedonia has high quality ferronics. There is little Chinese direct investment, most of them are projects that have been loaned by Chinese banks under preferential conditions. In this regard, the most important project involving Chinese companies is the construction of the Kozjak hydroelectric plant in the Treska river canyon. Also, considerable Chinese funds were earmarked for the construction of the two highway – the western Kičevo–Ohrid and the eastern Miladinovci–Štip.[2] At the Summit of the prime ministers of "17+1", held in Belgrade in December 2014, the Macedonian Prime Minister Nikola Gruevski signed an agreement on building a fast railway from Budapest to Thessaloniki with Chinese Prime Minister Li Keqiang.[3] In order to realize this project, the Macedonian government has purchased six passenger trains from China Railway Rolling Stock Corporation's.[4]

Regarding cultural cooperation, North Macedonia is very important for China,

---

1 Uroš Ačanski, "Kina: novi igrač na evropskom terenu" , *Biznis & finansije*, 3 December 2013.
2 Martin Kraljevski, "Kineski kapital u Makedoniji: skupe autoceste i kreditiranje korupcije" , *Bilten*, 10 April 2015.
3 *China Military Online*, "Chinese premier highlights infrastructure projects with CEE countries" , 18 December 2014.
4 *Asia Times*, "China in the Balkans: Macedonia, Albania seek Beijing's funds for projects", 11 July 2016.

because the seat of a Cultural Cooperation Coordination Center of "17+1" Mechanism is in Skopje. The Confucius Institute was opened in Skopje in 2011, in which the North Macedonian people have the opportunity to learn Chinese.

Albania and China have had good political relations since 2009, when the Joint Statement on deepening traditional friendly relations was signed. As a result, trade between the two countries has been increasing year by year, and China is today among Albania's five largest economic partners. In addition, the two countries also cooperate in the fields of culture, education, science and technology, agriculture, sports, radio and television, as well as within international forums. There are not many Chinese direct investments in Albania. One of the most significant is the takeover of Canadian oil company Banker's Petroleum, which operates in Albania, including the Patos-Marinze and Kucova oil fields, by Geo-Jade Petroleum Corp.[1] Also, Chinese company Everbright Limited acquired through concession the airport Mother Teresa in Tirana until 2027.[2] With regard to Chinese preferential loans, the Arber highway was built thanks to them, linking Albania with Macedonia. In addition, the Chinese company Sinomine Resource Exploration has established a daughter company in Albania, which is working on the construction of mines and geological tests in cooperation with the Albanian Geological Institute. China also invests heavily in the Albanian agricultural sector.

Cultural cooperation has developed significantly in recent years. A Confucius Institute was founded in Tirana where wider public can learn Chinese. In addition, Albania is extremely interested in developing tourism co-operation with China. In this regard, Albanian tourism organizations are very present in the Western Balkans region.

V. Concluding Remarks

The starting point of this research was to strengthen China's presence in the European market, which is a consequence of its accelerated economic development

---

1 *Oil & Gas Journal*, "Geo-Jade acquiring Bankers Petroleum", 22 March 2016.
2 Everbright, "China Everbright Limited Acquired Tirana International Airport", 25 April 2016.

and the need to continue to maintain high economic growth, satisfy the needs of the internal market for vital resources and new markets for the distribution of domestic products, all with the aim of improving the standards of its citizens and keeping the Communist Party of China in power. China's increased presence in the world has led to overlapping Chinese interests with those of the world's leading powers, above all the US. This has led to a strengthening of negative attitudes towards Beijing and the introduction of measures aimed at reducing China's political and economic presence on US territory. From the US, negative discourse has shifted to Europe, where leading EU countries are increasingly beginning to show a tendency to diminish China's presence in their markets, but also in the EU's single market, by introducing protective measures for foreign investments, especially Chinese. Similar moves is expected from potential member states, bearing in mind that Brussels' pressure on them will intensify, and that if they wish to advance on the European Union's path, they will need to show co-operation and solidarity with the Brussels' decisions.

At the beginning of the research, the relations between the Western Balkan countries and China is defined within the framework of the "17+1" Mechanism. The advantages and disadvantages of cooperation with the CEE region are outlined, as well as the opportunities offered by the regional approach in the context of strengthening bilateral cooperation (political, economic, cultural, etc.) with China. The importance of joint co-operation in improving regional infrastructure was particularly emphasized, given that quality roads are the basis for more foreign direct investment and greater trade co-operation. This would give the region the opportunity to become a transport and communications hub for convenient reloading and faster transport to other European destinations such as Austria, Germany, Ukraine, etc.

During the research, the factors that influence the Western Balkan countries' cooperation with China were identified. Summarizing them, it was concluded that most factors have a positive impact on the Western Balkan region's relations with

China, and that only a minority of them have a negative impact. Therefore, it was concluded that the Western Balkan countries are in an ideal position to improve cooperation with China if they are able to exploit all the factors that go in their favor. However, a comparative analysis of these countries' relations with China over the last few years gives the impression that they are already doing so and that time is working in their favor.

Several dozen joint projects have been completed so far, many of which are of strategic importance to the Western Balkan countries. The value of these projects has almost exceeded the funds earmarked for this purpose in the CEE Investment Fund. Nevertheless, the cooperation so far can be further enhanced. In this regard, one of the basic interests of the Western Balkan countries should be the increase exports to the Chinese market. Since these countries have poor export capacities, and individual export negotiations on products that are lacking in the Chinese market are proceeding very slowly and give barely visible results, they should impose themselves as partners in Beijing through political participation in the "17+1" Mechanism and achieve political agreement. The Chinese government could draw up a list of products needed for the Chinese Market, where a place for the agricultural and animal products would be found. When it comes to exports, the focus could be on the Western China, bearing in mind that there is already strong competition in eastern provinces from the companies from the US and Western Europe. In this regard, it is crucial that the Western Balkan countries work together to export as many products as possible to the large Chinese market. Also, Chinese leaders would show more understanding of the difficult position of the countries of the region, primarily risking a slowdown in the European integration process to strengthen co-operation with China. They should show a willingness to put to the minimum limit for the entry of the Western Balkans companies to the Chinese Chinese market. Therefore, it is the greatest responsibility of the leaders of the countries, because they should show with their support and participation awareness that only together, they can turn sources of power into successful smart power strategies – and thus achieve the individual interests and goals.

References

Ačanski Uroš, "Kina: novi igrač na evropskom terenu", *Biznis & finansije*, 3 December 2013, http://bif.rs/2013/12/kina-novi-igrac-na-evropskom-terenu/ #sthash.xu3CfkRT.dpbs.

Ambasada NR Kine u Crnoj Gori, "Istorija bilateralnih odnosa NR Kine i Crne Gore", 28 October 2016, http://me.chineseembassy.org/mon/zhgxs/ t1411160.htm.

Arežina Sanja, *China in Europe*, Institute of European Studies, Belgrade, 2018.

Asia Times, "China in the Balkans: Macedonia, Albania seek Beijing's funds for projects", 11 July 2016, http://www.atimes.com/article/china-in-the-balkans-macedonia-albania-seek-beijings-help-in-building-infrastructure.

China.org, "China, Macedonia Normalize Relations", 19 June 2001, http://china.org.cn/english/2001/Jun/14858.htm.

China Military Online, "Chinese premier highlights infrastructure projects with CEE countries", 18 December 2014, http://english.chinamil.com.cn/news-channels/today-headlines/2014-12/18/content_6275101.htm.

COASI, 20th EU-China Summit report, Beijing, 2018.

Ekapija, "Vlada Crne Gore kupuje dva trgovačka broda kineske proizvodnje", 2 November 2009, http://www.ekapija.com/website/sr/page/269472/Vlada-Crne-Gore-kupuje-dva-trgovapercentC4percent8Dka-broda-kineske-proizvodnje.

Everbright, "China Everbright Limited Acquired Tirana International Airport", 25 April 2016, http://www.everbright165.com/NewsDetails/all/2016/3701?IR=false.

Global Policy Forum, "China Vetoes", 25 February 1999.

Ferguson Nial, "Not two countries, but one: Chimerica", *The Telegraph*, 4 March 2007, www.telegraph.co.uk/comment/personal-view/3638174/Not-two-countries-but-one-Chimerica.html.

Gong Weibin, *Chinese Experience of Development*, Lecture, Seminar "China's issues", Chinese Academy of Governance, Beijing, 23 November 2013.

Kavalski Emilian, "China's '16+1' Is Dead? Long Live the '17+1'", The Diplomat, 29 March 2019, https://thediplomat.com/2019/03/chinas-161-is-dead-long-live-the-171.

Liu Zuokui, "The Pragmatic Cooperation between China and CEE: Characteristics, Problems and Policy Suggestions", Working Paper Series on European Studies, Institute of European

Studies, Chinese Academy of Social Sciences, Vol. 7, No. 6, 2013, http://ies.cass.cn/webpic/web/ies2/en/UploadFiles_8765/201311/2013111510002690.pdf.

Martin Kraljevski, "Kineski kapital u Makedoniji: skupe autoceste i kreditiranje korupcije", *Bilten*, 10 April 2015, http://www.bilten.org/ ?p=6040.

Ministry of Foreign Affairs of the PR China, "China and Montenegro", 2013, http://www.fmprc.gov.cn/mfa_eng/wjb_663304/zzjg_663340/xos_664404/gjlb_664408/Montenegro_664680.

Mondo, "Kineski kulturni centar – 'najlepša zgrada'", 20 July 2017.

Oil&Gas Journal, "Geo-Jade acquiring Bankers Petroleum", 22 March 2016, http://www.ogj.com/articles/2016/03/geo-jade-acquiring-bankers-petroleum. html.

Smith Jeff (2018): China's Belt and Road Initiative: Strategic Implications and International Opposition. The Herirage Foundation, https://www.heritage.org/asia/report/chinas-belt-and-road-initiative-strategic-implications-and-international-opposition.

Song Tao, "Kineska pomoć Evropi", *Politika*, 2012, http:// www.politika.rs/rubrike/Svet/Kineska-pomoc-Evropi.lt.html.

The State Council of the PR China, "Joint statement between China and Macedonia", 5 December 2007, http://www.gov.cn/misc/2007-12/05/ content_826315.htm.

Thilo Hanemann et al., *Chinese FDI in Europe: 2018 trends and impact of new policies*, Papers on China, Merics, 2019, https://www.merics.org/en/papers-on-china/chinese-fdi-in-europe-2018.

United States Senate, "Senators' Letter to Michael Pompeo and Steven Mnuchin", 2018, https://www.perdue.senate.gov/imo/media/doc/IMF%20China%20Belt%20and%20Road%20Initiative%20Letter.pdf.

US Embassy in Georgia, National Security Strategy of the United States of America, 2017, https://ge.usembassy.gov/2017-national-security-strategy-united-states-america-president.

Wen Jiabao, "Strenghthen Traditional Friendship and Promote Common Development", The China-CEE Economic Forum, Budapest, 25 June 2011.

Xinhua, "Zhonggong zhongyang guanyu quanmian shenhua gaige ruogan zhongda wenti de jueding (quanwen) [Central Committee's Decision on Major Issues Concerning Comprehensively Deepening Reforms (full text)]", Chapter 7, Point 26, 2013.

"梦"在阿中两国文学中相似性之比较

穆成功 【埃及】
开罗爱资哈尔大学语言与翻译学院汉语言文学系　助理教授

一　引　言

梦与占梦在阿拉伯传统文化与中国传统文化中都占有较高地位。虽然在阿拉伯文字中,"梦"以真实梦和乱梦其中一词为指称之,而中文中,"梦"是一个字,并且经历了形态上的转变,但两者意义的内涵与外延从古至今都有着惊人的相似性。在不同历史、宗教、语言等文化背景下,根据梦的不同种类,阿中两国形成了各自的释梦方法与涉梦理论,甚至都产生了职业占梦师。

"梦"是难以把握的,但也是不可或缺的。可以说,"梦"既是一种心灵体验的活动,更是一片神秘莫测的领地。没有人敢说"梦"是可有可无的,因为尽管其虚无缥缈,但却是司空见惯、真实可见的。也正是因为梦与人的生存不可分离,所以在阿拉伯与中国浩如烟海的文学作品中,"梦"也始终是文人们热衷的话题。那么为什么大多数的文人们会将"梦"作为其作品中很重要的部分呢?那就不能不提到文学中"梦"的作用。当然,"梦"有积极作用也有消极影响,如现代人就会认为"梦"影响了人的睡眠质量,但这是否为事实,又不得而知,所以其消极的一面是可以略而不谈的。而作为阿拉伯文学与中国文学中很重要的古代文学中的"梦"是应该给予重视的,探讨其作用不仅可以为后人研究阿拉伯文学与中国文学提供另一种视角,也能促进当今梦文学的发展。

阿中两国的传统梦文学的作用无论在"梦"这一文学主题中，还是在梦文学所记录、描写的与梦境相关的各类活动中，都具有极为相似的形式。阿中两国古代梦文学中具有极其相似的"梦"之作用主要有三：表示寓意即训诫、表示抒情、表示讽刺与嘲笑。笔者将从《一千零一夜》与其他古代阿拉伯诗歌，以及先秦两汉文学及唐传奇中选择一些与"梦"有关的作品，以此作为示例，从而将阿拉伯与中国古代文学中"梦"的这三大作用呈现出来。

二 "梦"在阿中两国文学中相似含义的比较研究

1. "梦"的寓意

《一千零一夜》中的《破产巴格达商人因梦变富》是一个补梦的故事：有一位富有的巴格达商人，他因追求奢靡的生活而破产。有一天他梦见在埃及某个地区有一个宝藏。在几次梦见这一场景后，他决定去埃及寻宝。当他到达埃及时已经身无分文，进入了一个小教堂休息。商人并不知道此前恰有一些盗贼将偷盗而来的赃物藏在了该教堂里。当警察赶来的时候，盗贼已跑，于是警察把商人抓进了监狱。警察把商人带去见法官，法官问他为什么偷东西，商人说自己并不是本地人，也没偷东西，只因反复做一个关于宝藏的梦而来到了埃及。法官听完大笑说，你真是一个傻瓜，为了这种荒诞的梦而来埃及寻找藏宝！真是太可笑了！我有几次梦见巴格达某个宅院的花园里有一个喷泉，里有很多藏宝，但我从来不信。最后法官给了商人一点路费，让他返回巴格达并劝他不要相信这些。法官却不知道他梦见的巴格达人的宅院，竟正好是这个商人的家。商人回家后就从花园的水泉旁挖出了藏宝，又成为了富人[1]。

这种故事的真正寓意在于，对人们来说真实的珍宝就是自我的存在，而每个人应该寻找自己内在的天赋，这些天赋才是他真正的无价之宝。

在中国，"文以载道"的传统的影响是深远的，不仅影响了文人的创作，该传统也在一定程度上影响着民间文学。在中国古代文学中，"梦"也有暗含寓意及训诫的，如《左传·宣公十五年》就是一个极具教化意义的例子。

初，魏初，魏武子有嬖妾，无子。武子疾，命颗曰："必嫁是。"疾病，则曰："必以为殉。"及卒，颗嫁之，曰："疾病则乱，吾从其治也。"

---

[1] 《一千零一夜》，《破产巴格达商人因梦变富》，刘晓菲译，北京文艺出版社2013年版，第167页。

及辅氏之役，颗见老人结草以亢杜回，杜回踬而颠，故获之。夜梦之曰："余，而所嫁妇人之父也。尔用先人之治命，余是以报。"

这则故事是带有很强的教化性的，这主要体现在启发人们要懂得报恩。而在此处教导世人"报恩"的人却是鬼神。也许这与中国"敬鬼神"的观念是分不开的。在这则故事中，魏颗曾经救下了父亲的小妾，以此得到小妾的父亲前来报答他，帮他挡住了杜回。小妾的父亲在梦里告诉魏颗，正是因为他执行其父亲清醒时候的话，所以才报答他。由此可知这并不是简单地标榜知恩图报的观念，关键还有一点就是：人在做任何决定时，都应该保持清醒。这也就教导人们要拥有清醒的头脑。尽管后面的一层教化义是以"托梦的形式"转达的。

2．"梦"中抒情

抒情的文学作品最常见于诗歌，比如诗人常常通过诗歌，来表达对情人强烈的思念。

阿拉伯最伟大的诗人伊本·哈泽穆·阿勒-安达卢斯（Ibn-Ḥazm Al-Andalusi，994—1064），他在其著作《鸽子的脖圈》（Tawqu Al-Hamamatu）"知足篇"里撰写了睡眠中见其情人之梦，并以诗歌的形式陈述了这个梦。很多具有虔诚信仰者（指苏菲派信徒）因不想中断自己向真主祷告与做礼拜等宗教的义务，而不愿睡觉，伊本·哈泽穆却认为爱情与思念最有能力让恋爱中的人合不上眼睛，从而脱离睡眠的世界。而另一方面，恋爱中的人也控制不住自己，希望能够入睡，从而在梦中看见且享受情人的身影。在此，他希望入睡的主要目的是为了能够跟情人约会。在此，伊本·哈泽穆说：

"情人的身影来访了又脆弱又可怜的我，如不是情人的身影来访，我就不睡觉。"[1]

《一千零一夜》中有三个女孩在玩，她们赌谁能说出最美的诗歌，就赢得三百蒂娜尔（Dinar，是古代伊拉克的货币）。三个女孩都说到抒情的梦诗歌[2]。

---

[1] Imam Abu Muhammad Ali Ibn Saeed Ibn Hazm Alandalusi, interpreted by Hasan Kamil Sayrafi. *The Ring of the Dove*. Cairo: Hijazi Press, 1950:99.

[2] Anonymous. *One Thousand and One Nights*, the third part, revised according to the edition of Bulaq Press. Cairo: Alsaeidia Press, 1935:205.

大女孩说："我吃惊的是他在我梦中来到我的床边，而若是他在清醒时来访将使我更吃惊。"

　　第二个女孩说："我唯有在梦中见了他的身影，而对他说：你好！欢迎！"

　　小女孩说："我牺牲自己与家人只为每夜见到他，而他有比香水更香的口水。"

　　三个女孩的抒情诗词丰富多彩，内涵很深。第一个，是渴望在梦中能见其情人，而见到情人之事使她吃惊并为此感到开心，但其实上她更渴望在现实中与他在一起。第二个，是说只在梦中见到了情人的身影，但他们之间只有打招呼而已。这两位的诗歌说明情人在现实生活中根本没有跟他们交往。第三个，她说的诗歌内涵很丰富，她不仅说明了她和情人的交往，而且赞美了情人的神香，更证明她和情人在现实与梦中的交往，展现了《一千零一夜》中古代女人对爱情强烈的渴望、对诗歌的学习，充满了智慧和卓越的文化。故事中的诗歌呈现了三个女孩试图以幽默的方式写诗的场景。

　　人们对于梦的理解总是从"虚幻"开始的。而正是因为"梦"本身的虚幻性，从而与文学作品的"虚幻性"往往能一拍即合。生活中的不如意在政治开明、思想自由的时代是可以大胆发言的，但在思想受到严格控制的时代，有些情感必须学会隐藏，以此才能保全身家性命。所以，在这时候，"梦"就会成为文人在其创作中的一种情感寄托，这种情感看似荒谬，实为真实。中国的大多数古人对梦都有一种特殊而无法言说的情感，因为他们不仅可以凭借其所塑造的梦境得到一时的满足，同时也使得其情感得到了一个发泄口，甚至可以以"梦"来承载他们的种种盼望与期待。

　　如"熊罴梦"就有中国古代人们"渴望生子添丁的吉祥寓意"[1]，王安石的《思王逢原》中就有这样一句：贤者宜有后，固当梦熊罴。又如"梦兰"故事："燕姞梦天使予已兰曰：'余为伯鯈？余而祖也，是以为而子。'"[2] 最后，燕姞真的为郑文公生了一个儿子，为之取名为"兰"。可以说，在这样的一些文学作品中，作者以"梦"来寄托情感是最为恰当的。当美"梦"成真带给人的是无比的欣喜，

1　刘艳：《先秦两汉占梦现象的文化考察》，陕西师范大学2012年博士论文，第21页。
2　[清]阮元校刻：《十三经注疏》，《春秋左传正义》卷二十一，中华书局出版社1980年版，第1868页。

而若只是"梦一场",那也不会有太大的遗憾,毕竟比现实要美好得多。人类表达情感的方式是多种多样的,但在一些中国古代文人心目中,"梦"恰恰是其期盼的最好依托之所在。

3. "梦"表示讽刺与嘲笑

(1) 讽刺与嘲笑在古代和现代阿拉伯文学中占了很大的空间。阿拉伯世界文学与文化里,当人面临最可恶的灾难与坏事时候,就往往采用嘲讽的形式,所以古话说:"最邪恶的事情是那些让人发笑的坏事与灾难"。在诗歌和散文中最特别的是用"梦"的形式来表示讽刺与嘲笑。

例如,阿拉伯阿巴斯时代的一个诗人叫巴沙尔·伊本·布尔德(Bashar ibn-Bourd,公元784卒年),他去见朋友,一副不高兴的样子,朋友们问他原因,他回答说,他的一匹驴已死,昨晚梦见了它,巴沙尔问了它为什么走得这么早,我对你不好吗?那匹驴用诗歌的形式给巴沙尔讲其爱情故事说:"我喜欢上了一头在阿斯巴海尼(Al-Asbahani)的门前遇见的母驴,它跟我分手,我因难过而死了。"它在描写母驴的美丽时就说:

"它有柔嫩的脸,就像阿勒施法冉尼的脸一样。"

朋友们问诗人巴沙尔说:阿勒施法冉尼"Al-Shefarani"是什么意思。巴沙尔说:"我怎么知道呢?这是公驴最奇怪的地方。如你们碰见它,自己问此事吧。"这就是一头公驴爱情故事的悲惨的结局。借用公驴的这种梦来实现讽刺的目的[1]。

(2) 中国古代文学中除了"载道"的作品比较丰富之外,还有一类作品是不容忽视的,那就是讽喻文学。中国古代文人都有一份投身政治的炽热情怀,"学而优则仕"是当时有抱负的文人的普遍观念。然而当统治者暴虐无道,文人也会愤而拍案,于是就会涌现出许多的讽刺文学作品。而值得注意的一点是,"梦"是中国古代讽喻文学作品中的催化剂。所以以"梦"来达到文人的讽喻无道政治的目的比较盛行,"梦"既能让人产生虚实相生的感悟,更能让人顿悟政治的黑暗。当一觉醒来,"梦"烟消云散,但脑海中的感悟却会萦绕不去。

唐传奇对中国小说的发展贡献很大,当代的学者们对唐传奇也带有浓厚的兴

---

[1] Bashar Ibn Bourd, interpreted by Muhammad al-Tahir ibn Ashur. *Poems of Bashar Ibn Bourd*. Cairo: Translation, Writing and Publishing Committee Press, 1966:214.

趣。而其中被当代学者发现的一个亮点就是：唐传奇中的梦文学的存在。唐代传奇作品是不被唐代的正统文人所看好的，但却渗透着耀眼的光芒而被当代中国文坛所认可，如其中的《枕中记》、《南柯太守传》等，既是梦文学的代表之作，也是被看作是讽喻文学的典型作品。下面笔者仅《南柯太守传》这一则传奇故事为例，来阐述"梦"在中国古代文学中的讽刺作用。

> 贞元七年九月，因沉醉致疾。时二友人于坐扶生归家，卧于堂东庑之下。二友谓生曰："子其寝矣。余将秣马濯足，俟子小愈而去。"生解巾就枕，昏然忽忽，仿佛若梦。见二紫衣使者，跪拜生曰："槐安国王遣小臣致命奉邀。"生不觉下榻整衣，随二使至门。见青油小车，驾以四牡，左右从者七八，扶生上车，出大户，指古槐穴而去……周生暴疾已逝，田子华亦寝疾于床。生感南柯之浮虚，悟人世之倏忽，遂栖心道门，绝弃酒色。后三年，岁在丁丑，亦终于家。时年四十七，将符宿契之限矣……[1]

该传奇故事篇幅比较大，但读来很有启发意义。"南柯一梦"不仅是故事主人公淳于棼的，也是当时贫穷士子的人身写照，更是身处同样困境的千千万万的读书人的。该故事把封建社会污浊的官场比作"蚁穴"，把在仕途上竞相奔走的庸碌之辈喻为"蚁聚"，这是极具嘲讽意味的。同时该文以梦作为构思的中心，梦境实为淳于棼想象生活的写照，梦中的繁华更是与现实世界里的冷漠形成了鲜明的对比，真幻交织，从而让世人真正领悟了何为"南柯一梦"。而文末李肇的四句"贵极禄位，权倾国都，达人视此，蚁聚何殊！"更是发人深省。

三 结论

在阿拉伯与中国古代文学中"梦"是一个不可忽视的关键要素。它的作用甚至远远不只是教化、讽刺、寄托情感以及优化结构，同时它还是批判社会、表达美好理想以及对现实世界中自然美的赞美时不可或缺的一个工具。可以说，正是因为阿拉伯与中国的古代文学中有"梦"的存在，才让人们更加热爱这些文学作品捧在手心。

---

[1] 林骅、王淑艳编：《唐传奇新选》湖北教育出版社2004年版，第91-100页。

虽然在阿中两国的不同文学作品中，梦境有着不同的目的与功能，但可以看出阿中两国的文学作品在中体现这些目的与功能却极其相似。因此，本文分析了细读《一千零一夜》这一部阿拉伯民间文学作品以及其他诗歌中的梦境故事，并将其与《唐代传奇》和《太平广记》等中国古典著作中所记录的梦文学题材作比较。我发现两国梦文化已对两国梦境文学产业的影响很大。从上文看出，阿中两国传统梦文学的作品中展现了"梦"的三大作用，即表示寓意即训诫、抒情、讽刺与嘲笑。笔者在对阿中古代文学梦文学的作用比较后，发现在阿中传统梦文学中所记录的助于缓解心理问题的活动、借用为批评社会的功能、用于批评政权等，上述的阿中梦文学的作用具有相似的表现形式。有鉴于此，对梦文学的研究成果表明中世纪阿中两国人民不仅仅在政治、贸易方面取得联系，而且阿中两国文明在文化与文学上也存在潜在联系。

参考文献

《一千零一夜》，刘晓菲译，北京文艺出版社 2013 年版。
《十三经注疏》，《春秋左传正义》卷二十一，中华书局出版社 1980 年版。
林骅、王淑艳：《唐传奇新选》，湖北教育出版社 2004 年版。
刘艳：《先秦两汉占梦现象的文化考察》陕西师范大学博士论文，2012 年。
杨乃乔，乐黛云顾问：《比较文学概论》，北京大学出版社 2014 年版。
刘文英、曹田玉：《梦与中国文化》，人民出版社 2003 年版。
杨伯峻：《春秋左传注》（第二册），北京中华书局 1981 年版。
方爱华：《唐代小说中的占梦文化研究》新疆师范大学博士论文，2015 年。

Dream in Arabic and Chinese Literature: A Comparison of the Similarities

Nageh Mohamed Ibrahim Mohamed Taha / Egypt

Al-Azhar University, Faculty of Languages and Translation, Department of Chinese Language and Literature / Assistant Professor

I Introduction

Dreams and the divination of dreams occupy a high position in both Arab traditional culture and Chinese traditional culture. Although in Arabic, the "dream" can be divided into "AL-RU'YA" (real dream) and "AL-HULMU" (chaotic dream), while in Chinese, " 梦 " ("dream") is a Chinese character, and the character has undergone morphological changes, the connotation and extension of the meanings of "dream" in Arabic and Chinese have been strikingly similar from ancient times to the present. Against different historical, religious, linguistic and other cultural backgrounds, according to different types of dreams, the Arabs and the Chinese have formed their own methods of interpreting dreams and dream-related theories, and both of them have professional dream diviners.

A dream is difficult to grasp, but it is also indispensable. It can be said that a "dream" is not only an activity of spiritual experience, but also a mysterious territory. No one dares to say that "dreams" are dispensable, because although they are illusory, they are common and visible. It is precisely because dreams are inseparable from human existence that "dreams" have always been a hot topic among literati in the vast literary works of Arabia and China. So why do most literati regard the "dream" as an important part of his/her works? For this question, we have to understand the role of the "dream" in literature. Of course, the "dream" has both positive and negative effects. For example, modern people will think that a "dream" affects the quality of a person's sleep, but whether this is true or not is unknown. So its negative side can be ignored. The "dream" in ancient literature, which is very important in Arab literature and Chinese literature, should be paid attention to. The discussion of its role will not only give another perspective to future generations in their study of Arab literature and Chinese literature, but it will also promote the development of today's dream literature.

The role of traditional dream literature in China and Arab countries is very similar in both the literary theme of the "dream" and in various activities related to dreams recorded and described in dream literature. There are three functions of the "dream" that are very similar in the ancient dream literature of China and of Arab countries: expressing morals and admonition, expressing lyricism, expressing irony and ridicule. I will choose some works related to the "dream" from the One Thousand and One Nights and other ancient Arab poems, as well as the literature of the pre-Qin and Han Dynasties and the Tang legends, taking them as an example, so as to show these three functions of the "dream" in ancient Chinese literature and in Arab literature.

II The Three Functions of the "Dream" in the Dream Literature of China and Arab Countries

2.1 Using the "dream" to express morals and admonition

2.1.1 We have found that in these literatures, dreams can be repetitive or complementary. For example, when one person dreams of the first part of a story, while another person dreams of the second part, the two people's dreams complement each other to form a complete dream, which can be called the "complement-dream". Another kind of dream is that the dreams of two dreamers are the same, which can be called the "same-dream". When two dreamers meet, they can not only complete the content of their dream, but they can also make the content very clear, so as to uncover the riddle in the dream.

There is a well-known complement-dream story, Bankrupt Baghdad Businessman Becoming Rich by Dreams in the *One Thousand and One Nights* (Alf Laylah wa Laylah). In the story, there was a very wealthy Baghdad businessman who went bankrupt because of his extravagant life. One day, he dreamed that there was a treasure in a certain area of Egypt. After dreaming about this scene several times, he decided to visit Egypt to discover it. When he arrived in Egypt, he was penniless and went to a small church to rest. Unexpectedly, just before he arrived, some thieves hid stolen goods from the church, and when the police arrived, the thieves had run away, so the police arrested and imprisoned the businessman. The police took the businessman to the judge, and the judge asked him why he had stolen from the church. The businessman said that he was not a local citizen and he hadn't stolen anything, and he explained that he had come to Egypt because he had repeatedly dreamed about a treasure. After hearing that, the judge laughed and said, "What a fool you are to come to Egypt for the hidden treasure just because of this absurd dream! How ridiculous!" " I dreamed several times that there was a fountain in the garden of a house in Baghdad, where there were many hidden treasures, but I never believed it." Finally, the judge gave the businessman a little money for going back to Baghdad and asked him not to believe these dreams. But the judge didn't know that the house in Baghdad he had dreamed of happened to be the businessman's home. After returning home, the businessman dug up the hidden treasure from the fountain in the garden and became a rich man again[1].

The connotation and value of this kind of story lie in teaching us that the real

---

[1] Anonymous author: One Thousand and One Nights [M], Bankrupt Baghdad Businessman Becoming Rich by Dreams, translated by Liu Xiaofei, Beijing: North Literature and Art Publishing House, 2013, p. 167.

treasure for people is inherent, and everyone should look for his own inner talent, which is his real priceless treasure.

2.1.2 The influence of the Chinese tradition of "writings for conveying truth" is far-reaching. It not only influenced the creation of the upper-class literati, but also dominated the lower-class literature to a certain extent. In ancient Chinese literature, using the "dream" to express moral truths and admonition is also obvious. For example, the Chronicle of Zuo: the Fifteenth Year of Xuangong's Reign is an example of the significance of great enlightenment, and more importantly, it can be regarded as part of dream literature.

In the early Wei Dynasty, Wei Wuzi had a concubine who didn't have any children. When Wei Wuzi was ill, he instructed Wei Ke: "After I die, you must ask her to remarry." When he was critically ill, he said: "She must be sacrificed for my death!" When Wei Wuzi died, Wei Ke allowed the woman to remarry, and he explained "My father was muddled when he was seriously ill, so I followed what he instructed me to do when he was clear-headed." During the Fushi battle, Wei Ke saw an old man tie grass into a knot to trip the enemy general Du Hui. Du Hui tripped and fell to the ground, so he was captured. At night, Wei Ke dreamed of an old man talking to him, "I am the father of the woman whom you allowed to remarry. I repaid you for following the command made by your father when he was clear-headed."

This story is highly instructive, in that it admonishes people to repay kindness. However, the subject teaching people "gratitude" here is a ghost. It is the "ghost" that can better let people know such a truth. Perhaps, this is also closely associated with the Chinese culture of "respecting ancestors and ghosts". In this story, Wei Ke once saved his father's concubine, and consequently affected the ghost of the concubine's father to repay him and help him capture Du Hui. The concubine's father told Wei Ke in his dream that it was because he had followed his father's words given when his father was still clear-headed that he had then helped him out of appreciation. What this story highlights is not only the concept of remaining grateful and repaying for others' kindness, but also the key point that everyone should stay clear-headed when making any decisions. It teaches people to keep a clear mind. Although the latter enlightenment is conveyed by "talking in a dream", it is more readable.

It is precisely because this story has a "dream" as the theme that it is easier for people to remember it and understand the truth of gratitude. Using the "dream" to explain the author's thought is more effective and more authentic, because "ghosts, fairies" and "dreams" are closely related.

2.2 Using the "dream" to express lyricism

2.2.1 Literary works indicating lyricism are most common in poems. Poets often express their strong yearning for their lovers through poems. A poet once stated: "Although seeing the figure of his lover in a dream can satisfy his desire for seeing her, it is not a warm feeling, it only comforts his strong memory." This phenomenon exists in both ancient and modern poetry.

The greatest Arab poet Ibn Hazem Al-Andalusi, born in 994-died in 1064 AD), wrote a poem to state the dream of seeing his lover in the article "Contentment" in his book The Ring of the Dove (Tawqu Al-Hamamatu). When many devout believers (Sufism believers) don't want to sleep because they don't want to interrupt their religious obligations including praying to God and worshiping, Ibn Hazem thinks that "love" and "missing" are the most capable of keeping people in love from sleeping. On the other hand, people in love cannot help missing their lovers, so they hope to fall asleep, so that they can see their lover's figure in their dreams. The main purpose for them to fall asleep is to be able to associate with their lovers. For which, Ibn Hazem said:

"The lover's figure visited me, who is fragile and pitiful. I wouldn't sleep if it wasn't for the lover's figure."[1]

In The Story of Women and Their Poetry Told by Asmayi to Harun Al-Rashid,

---

1 Imam Abu Muhammad Ali Ibn Saeed Ibn Hazm Alandalusi, interpreted by Hasan Kamil Sayrafi. *The Ring of the Dove*. Cairo: Hijazi Press, 1950:99.

three girls were playing, so they began to bet that whoever could compose the most beautiful piece of poetry would win three hundred Dinars (the currency of Ancient Iraq). All the three girls composed lyrical dream poems[1].

The oldest girl composed, "I was surprised that he came to my bed in my dream, and if he came to me when he was awake, I would be even more surprised."

The middle girl composed, "I can only see his figure and greet him in my dreams by saying Welcome to visit!"

The little girl composed, "I sacrificed myself and my family to see him every night. What follows me in my dream is his saliva more fragrant than any perfume."

The lyric poems of the three girls are rich and colorful, and their connotation is deep. The first girl was eager to meet her lover in her dream, and seeing her lover surprised her and made her happy. But in fact, she was more eager to be with him in reality. The second poem expresses the fact that the girl can only see her lover in her dream and say hello. The poems of the two girls show that their lovers do not associate with them at all in real life. The third poem has rich connotation. She not only explained her communication with her lover, but also praised her lover's perfume and saliva, and proved her communication with her lover in reality not only in dreams. The One Thousand and One Nights shows the ancient women's strong desire for love and their study of poetry, full of wisdom and excellent culture. The poems in the story present the scene of three women trying to write poems in a humorous way.

2.2.2 People's interpretations of dreams always begin with an "illusion". It is precisely because of the illusion of the "dream" itself that dreams can often coincide with the "illusory nature" of literary works. Disappointments in life can speak out boldly in the era of political openness and ideological freedom, but in the era under strict ideological control, some emotions must be hidden in order to save literati's

---

[1] Anonymous. *One Thousand and One Nights*, the third part, revised according to the edition of Bulaq Press. Cairo: Alsaeidia Press, 1935:205.

lives. Therefore, in this situation, the "dream" becomes an emotional sustenance of literati in their creation. This kind of emotion seems absurd, but it is real. Most ancient people in China have a special and unspeakable emotion about dreams, because they can not only get a temporary satisfaction by virtue of the dreams they create, but they also obtain an outlet for their emotions, and even carry their hopes and expectations within the "dreams".

For example, "xióng pí ru meng" (dreaming of a giant bear) has the auspicious meaning of "having more children" for ancient Chinese people[1], and there is the following sentence in Wang Anshi's poem Missing Wang Fengyuan: "A sage should have offsprings, so he will dream of a giant bear." Another example is the story of the "orchid dream": "One day, Yan Ji dreamed that an angel gave her orchids and said, 'I'm Bo Xiu, I'm your ancestor, so I come here to help you have your own children.'"[2] Finally, Yan Ji really gave birth to a son for Zheng Wengong, and named him "Lan" (Orchid). It can be said that in some of these literary works, it is most appropriate for the author to express his feelings through "dreams". When a "dream" comes true, it brings people great joy, and if it is just a "dream", there will be no great regret, after all, it is much better than reality. There are always many ways for human beings to express their emotions, but in the minds of some ancient Chinese literati, the "dream" is precisely the best carrier for their wishes.

2.3 Using the "dream" to express irony and ridicule

2.3.1 Irony and ridicule have occupied a large space in ancient and modern Arab literature. In Arab world literature and culture, the most abominable disasters and evils will be realized in an ironic way, so the old saying goes: "The evilest things and disasters are those that make people laugh". The greatest special example in poetry and prose is the use of the "dream" to express irony and ridicule.

1　Liu Yan. Cultural Investigation of Dream Divination in Pre-Qin and Han Dynasties [D]. Shaanxi: Shaanxi Normal University, 2012, p. 21.

2　[Qing] Ruan Yuan proofreading: Thirteen Classic Explanatory Notes and Commentaries [M], *Chun Qiu Zuo Zhuan Zheng Yi*, volume XXI, Beijing: Zhonghua Book Company Press, 1980, p. 1868.

For example, a poet named Bashar ibn-Bourd (died in 784 AD) in the Arab Abbasid Dynasty went to see his friends. He looked unhappy, and friends asked him why. He replied that one of his donkeys had died, and he dreamed of it last night. Bashar asked it why it left so early. Had he treated it badly? The donkey told Bashar its love story in the form of poetry, saying, "I fell in love with a female donkey I met in front of the door of Al-Asbahani. It broke up with me, and I was so sad that I died." When describing the beauty of the female donkey, it said:

"It has a tender face, just like the face of Al-Shefarani."

His friends asked the poet Bashar, "What does Al-Shifarani mean?" Bashar said, "How should I know? This is the strangest thing about this male donkey. If you meet it, ask yourself about it." This is the tragic ending of the love story of a donkey. Through the dream of the donkey, the purpose of allegory is achieved.[1]

2.3.2 Besides the abundant works for conveying truth, in ancient Chinese literature, there is another kind of work that cannot be ignored, that is, allegory literature. Ancient Chinese literati were all zealous about participating in politics. The idea that "officialdom is the natural outlet for good scholars" was very common in the aspiring literati at that time. However, when the rulers were tyrannical and unscrupulous, the literati would be angry and indignant, so a mass of satirical literary works would emerge. It is worth noting that the "dream" is a baking powder in Chinese ancient allegory literature. Therefore, it is scenery for literati to use the "dream" to satirize immoral politics. The "dream" can not only make a person have the feeling of virtual reality, but it can also make people have an insight into the darkness of politics. When you wake up, the "dream" disappears, but the feeling will linger on in your mind.

Tang legends have made great contributions to the development of Chinese novels, and contemporary scholars are also very interested in Tang legends. One of

---

1 Bashar Ibn Bourd, interpreted by Muhammad al-Tahir ibn Ashur. *Poems of Bashar Ibn Bourd*. Cairo: Translation, Writing and Publishing Committee Press, 1966:214.

the highlights discovered by contemporary scholars is the dream literature in those legends. Works regarding Tang legends were not favored by orthodox scholars of the Tang Dynasty, but they are permeated with dazzling light, and are recognized by contemporary Chinese literary circles, such as The Pillow Story and The Governor of the Southern Tributary State, which are not only representative works of dream literature, but also typical works of allegory literature. Below, I only take The Governor of the Southern Tributary State as an example to illustrate the satirical role of the "dream" in ancient Chinese literature.

One day in September of the seventh year of Zhenyuan's Reign, Chunyu Fen was sick because he was drunk. At this time, his two friends lifted him from his seat and wanted to take him home. Then, he was lying under the porch in the east of the guest room. His two friends said to him, "You'd better have a rest now. We'll feed the horses and wash our feet here until you feel better." Chunyu Fen took off his turban and fell asleep. At this moment, he felt in a daze, as if he were having a dream. He saw two emissaries dressed in purple, bowed down to him and said, "The King of Huai'an Kingdom sent us to invite you to our country". Chunyu Fen got up, adjusted his clothes and followed the two messengers to the door. He saw a black carriage with four horses and seven or eight attendants beside it. They helped Chunyu Fen into the carriage, which went out of the gate and headed for the hole of the old locust tree… Zhou Bian died of an acute illness, and Tian Zihua was also ill in bed. Chunyu Fen sighed with emotion for the illusion of his dream, and thus learned that life is just a fleeting moment, so he believed in Taoism and quit sensuality. Three years later, it was the year of Ding Chou. He died at home at the age of 47, just in line with what his father had said in his dream letter.[1]

This legend story is quite long, but it is instructive to read. The Nanke Dream is not only the story of the hero Chunyu Fen, but also the personal portrayal of the poor literati at that time, as well as the mirror of the life of thousands of intellectuals

---

1 Lin Hua and Wang Shuyan, ed.: New Selections of Tang Legends [M]. Hubei: Hubei Education Press, 2004, pp. 91-100.

who were in the same predicament. The story compares the dirty officialdom of feudal society to an "ant nest" and the mediocre people who are racing to run into an official career to an "ant assembly", which is extremely ironic. At the same time, this story takes the dream as the conception center, and the dream is actually a portrayal of Chunyu Fen's imaginary life. The colorful experience in the dream is in sharp contrast with the indifference seen in life in the real world, making reality and fantasy intertwined, so that a reader can truly understand what "a dream in Nanke" is. At the end of the story, as Li Zhao's poem says: "To be a high dignitary, with power, outweighs all officials in the capital, if a reader is intelligent enough, he/she may understand that there is no difference between these and a dream in the nest of ants!" What a thought-provoking poem.

III Conclusion

The dream is an element that cannot be ignored in both ancient Arab and Chinese literature. Its function is far more than educating, satirizing, expressing emotion and optimizing structure. At the same time, it is also an indispensable tool for criticizing society, expressing beautiful ideals and praising natural beauty in the real world. It can be said that it is the existence of "dreams" in the ancient literature of Arabia and China that makes people love these literary works.

Although dreams have different purposes and functions in different literary works of Arabia and China, we can see that the literary works of Arabia and China are very similar in terms of the embodiment of these purposes and their functions. Therefore, in this paper, I have compared the dream stories in the One Thousand and One Nights, an ancient piece of folk literature, and other poetry collections, with those recorded in Chinese classical works such as the Tang Legends and the Tai Ping Guang Ji. I have found that the dream culture of the two civilizations has had a great influence on their dream literature. From the above research, it can be seen that in the works of the traditional dream literature of Arabia and China, the three functions of the "dream" have been demonstrated, that is, to express morals & admonition, lyricism, irony & ridicule. After comparing ancient Arab and Chinese dream literature, I found that in the traditional dream literature of Arab-Chinese literature, in order to realize the above three functions, they all adopted very similar forms of expression: using the "dream" to relieve psychological problems, using the "dream" to criticize society and using the "dream" to criticize political power. In view of this, the results of my research on dream literature imply that the people of Arab and Chinese civilizations in the Middle Ages not only got in touch with each other in politics and trade, but also had potential connection of their cultures and literature.

References

Chinese literature

[Arab] Anonymous author. One Thousand and One Nights [M]. Translated by Liu Xiaofei. Beijing: North Literature and Art Publishing House, 2013:167.

[Qing] Ruan Yuan proofreading: Thirteen Classics Explanatory Notes and Commentaries [M], Chun Qiu Zuo Zhuan Zheng Yi, volume XXI, Beijing: Zhonghua Book Company Press, 1980, p. 1868.

Lin Hua and Wang Shuyan, ed.: New Selections of Tang Legends [M]. Hubei: Hubei Education Press, 2004, pp. 91-100.

Liu Yan. Cultural Investigation of Dream Divination in Pre-Qin and Han Dynasties [D]. Shaanxi: Shaanxi Normal University, 2012.

Arabic references

Imam Abu Muhammad Ali Ibn Saeed Ibn Hazm Alandalusi, interpreted by Hasan Kamil Sayrafi. The Ring of the Dove. Cairo: Hijazi Press, 1950: 99.

Anonymous. One Thousand and One Nights, the third part, revised according to the edition of Bulaq Press. Cairo: Alsaeidia Press, 1935:205.

Bashar Ibn Bourd, interpreted by Muhammad al-Tahir ibn Ashur. Poems of Bashar Ibn Bourd. Cairo: Translation, Writing and Publishing Committee Press, 1966:214.

Auxiliary references

Yang Naiqiao, consulted by Le Daiyun. Introduction to Comparative Literature [M]. Beijing: Peking University Press, 2014.

Liu Wenying and Cao Tianyu: Dreams and Chinese Culture [M]. Beijing: People's Publishing House, 2003.

Yang Bojun: Notes to Chun Qiu Zuo Zhuan [M] (Volume II). Beijing: Zhonghua Book Company Press, 1981.

Fang Aihua. A Study of Dream Divination Culture in the Novels of the Tang Dynasty [D]. Xinjiang: Xinjiang Normal University, 2015.

东汉中期皇帝行幸长安初探

彭暮雷 【德国】

明斯特大学汉学系暨东亚研究所　博士研究生、助理教授

一　绪论

建武元年十月，镇守洛阳的朱鲔在刘秀军队的包围下宣布投降。刘秀已经于六月即皇帝位了，后人通常以其谥号称之为光武帝。光武帝的即位意味着东汉的开始。光武帝攻下了洛阳之后，立即将其定为汉朝的新都[1]。

光武帝定都洛阳时，关中还不属于他能控制的地区，这也许可以解释，为何他没有选择长安作为首都。即使后来光武帝的军队平定了关中，包括长安，光武帝及其后代依旧没有考虑迁都长安，这极有可能是由下列三个主要原因造成的[2]。

第一，王莽严重低估了匈奴的实力，从而导致了关中地区的安全受到威胁[3]。

第二，由于关中地区生产的粮食不足以供给长安的消耗，因此每年都需要通过漕运运送大量的粮食。洛阳位于中国的中心，离越来越重要的山东地区也较近，就地理位置而言，洛阳拥有较大的优势[4]。

1　记载于范晔：《后汉书》，中华书局 1973 年版，1.22-25。
2　长安被赤眉破坏是光武帝定都洛阳之后的事情，因此 Victor Xiong 和廖伯源认为长安残破不是选择洛阳为首都的主要原因之一；参阅 Victor Cunrui Xiong, *Capital Cities and Urban Form in Pre-Modern China*: *Luoyang, 1038 BCE to 938 CE*，Routledge 2017，p. 32；廖伯源：《论东汉定都洛阳及其影响》，《史学集刊》2010 年第 3 期，第 21-22 页。
3　参阅 Rafe de Crespigny: *Fire over Luoyang*：*A History of the Later Han Dynasty 23–220 AD*，Brill 2016，p. 20。
4　参阅廖伯源：《论东汉定都洛阳及其影响》，第 22 页。

第三，定都洛阳是由于光武帝遵从了谶书的预言[1]。

显而易见，洛阳有其特定的优势，但规模较小的洛阳在不少方面依旧比不上昔日的长安。在洛阳为官的官员之中肯定也有怀念繁华的长安生活的[2]。

洛阳为东汉的首都，据此，长安对东汉朝政而言还有何意义？虽然已有部分学者对此进行了讨论，但相关的论述并不系统且全面。到目前为止可以总结为两个重要的意义，即：军事意义以及统治的正统性。在军事方面，当时的长安是抵抗羌族的一个军事重镇；在正统性方面，位于长安附近的十一陵[3]则彰显了西汉王朝与东汉王朝之间一脉相承的关系[4]。

光武帝逝世之后，他的后代明帝、章帝、和帝、安帝、顺帝和桓帝也均特地行幸过一次长安[5]。虽然每位皇帝的行程不尽相同，可是也有一些不变的地方：由于十月为"高祖定秦之月"[6]，他们都于十月出发前往长安；主要的目的地不是长安而是高庙和十一陵。根据《后汉书》的记载，明帝、章帝、和帝、安帝还会祭祀西汉之大臣，例如安帝"以中牢[7]祠萧何、曹参、霍光"[8]；章帝和安帝也"遣使者祠太上皇于万年"[9]。此外东汉皇帝行幸长安时还习惯宴请三辅的高官并且赐予当地官员或百姓谷[10]。

二 东汉皇帝在位期间何时行幸长安？

皇帝为何行幸长安？较为简单的答案是西汉皇帝的十一陵在长安附近。因此

---

1 参阅廖伯源：《论东汉定都洛阳及其影响》，第23页。
2 最著名的例子是班固撰写的《西京赋》；见于严可均（校辑）《全上古三代秦汉三国六朝文》，中华书局1999年版，第602-604页。
3 十一陵是指高祖长陵、惠帝安陵、文帝霸陵、景帝阳陵、武帝茂陵、昭帝平陵、宣帝杜陵、元帝渭陵、成帝延陵、哀帝义陵、平帝康陵；西汉皇帝的十一座陵墓。参阅范晔《后汉书》，1.48。
4 参阅马雪芹《东汉长安与关中平原》，《中国历史地理论丛》2000年第2期，第190-193页。
5 记载于《后汉书》，2.104；3.144；4.172-173；5.240；6.267；7.306。
6 范晔：《后汉书》，95.3130。
7 中牢包括羊、豕两种动物；参阅《汉书》，中华书局1973年版。
8 范晔：《后汉书》，5.240。
9 范晔：《后汉书》，3.144；5.240。
10 《后汉书》记载，除了安帝以外，行幸长安之皇帝都有赐予谷；参阅《后汉书》，2.104；3.144；4.172；6.267；7.306。马雪芹认为东汉皇帝行幸长安赐予钱粮"对恢复和发展关中地区的经济起到了一定的促进作用"，《东汉长安与关中平原》，第190页。东汉皇帝行幸长安十分罕见，因此笔者认为赐予钱粮之经济促进作用极小，况且皇帝行幸长安的目的也不在发展关中地区而在强调皇帝之正统性。

东汉皇帝即位时非去祭拜不可。不过并非所有的东汉皇帝在即位后很快行幸长安，有的会等好几年才前往长安，其原因不一[1]。

中元二年二月，光武帝晏驾，明帝即位，次年定年号为永平[2]。永平二年十月"甲子，西巡狩，幸长安，祠高庙，遂有事于十一陵。历览馆邑，会郡县吏，劳赐作乐。十一月甲申，遣使者以中牢祠萧何、霍光。帝谒陵园，过式其墓[3]。进幸河东，所过赐二千石、令长已下至于掾史，各有差。癸卯，车驾还宫"[4]。其后的皇帝行幸长安时均参照了明帝的行程。明帝等了三十二个月才出发去长安，这也许是因为其遵守"三年之丧"的礼法，按照礼法，其需要等待二十五个月，但由于"高祖定秦之月"的传统，明帝又等待了七个月[5]。明帝即位时已成年，不需他人临朝摄政，因此他可以很自由地把行幸长安当作一种上任访问。

章帝为何在其即位的第八年（建初七年）才出发行幸长安，笔者目前无法很好地解释。但也许存在如下可能：章帝对明德马太后非常恭顺[6]。章帝或许是在马太后逝世后，居三年之丧，然后才出发行幸长安的[7]。

和帝即位于章和二年，当时皇帝才十岁，因此窦皇太后临朝[8]。永元三年春正月"皇帝加元服"[9]；冬十月皇帝"行幸长安"[10]。对和帝而言，加元服和行幸长安具有特殊的意义，因为和帝离开洛阳就意味着摆脱窦太后严格的监督和控制，终于能够以一个成年皇帝的身份与臣民近距离接触沟通。窦太后或许因其允许皇帝出发去长安而后悔，因为她曾派她的哥哥大将军窦宪"与车驾会长安。及宪至，尚书以下议欲拜之，伏称万岁。棱正色曰：'夫上交不谄，下交不黩[11]，礼无人臣称万岁之制。'议者皆惭而止。"[12]此时坚持皇帝才是真正的天子的韩棱后来协助和帝灭

1　马雪芹有列出中期皇帝行幸长安的所有事情，可惜没有做任何分析；参阅马雪芹《东汉长安与关中平原》，第191-192页。
2　范晔：《后汉书》，1.85；2.99。
3　"式"是表示敬意的意思，后汉纪用"轼"字；参阅袁宏《后汉纪》，中华书局2005年版。
4　范晔：《后汉书》，2.104。
5　参阅陈立撰《白虎通疏证》，《新编诸子集成》中华书局1994年版，第507-509页。
6　参阅记马太后与章帝的通信往来，记载于范晔《后汉书》，10.411-412。
7　明德马太后死于建初四年六月；章帝建初七年十月行幸长安。参阅范晔《后汉书》，10.414；3.144；16.917。
8　参阅范晔《后汉书》，4.165。
9　范晔：《后汉书》，4.171。
10　范晔：《后汉书》，4.172。
11　阮元：《十三经注疏》卷1《周易》，艺文印书馆2001年版，8.13A（第171页）。
12　记载于韩棱的传记；范晔：《后汉书》，45.1535。

除了窦氏家族[1]。和帝正式对抗窦氏可能就从其行幸长安开始。

和帝晏驾，殇帝早夭，延平元年八月安帝即皇帝位，和熹邓太后临朝[2]。邓太后临朝终生，太后死后，安帝才亲政。直至那时皇帝才出发行幸长安，而且是等到皇太后逝后三年多才出发。因此安帝即位十八年才行幸长安[3]。

顺帝行幸长安是在其皇位已经很稳固的时候（永和二年）。顺帝离开洛阳一个多月，长安就发生了地震，皇帝便回了洛阳[4]。

桓帝初即位时，梁氏掌握大权，梁太后临朝。梁太后逝世后，大将军梁冀与其妹妹梁皇后女莹仍然控制朝廷的所有事务[5]。延熹二年秋七月"皇后梁氏崩"[6]，桓帝借机于八月剥夺了梁冀的权力，梁冀自杀[7]。桓帝亲政还不到两个月，他就决定要行幸长安，以此彰显其皇位的正统性[8]。桓帝在长安时还封其最重要的大将单超为车骑将军[9]，行幸长安对桓帝而言很明显是一种凯旋。

三 结论

虽然光武帝定都洛阳时，长安便失去了汉朝最重要城市的地位，但由于皇帝仍然以长安及位于长安附近的十一陵作为宣示其统治正统性的重要地点，于是皇帝行幸长安变成了一种传统。由于每一位皇帝的政治状况大不同，其当时的政治权力亦不一样，行幸长安对不同的皇帝也有不同的意义。尽管如此，皇帝行幸长安均有展示其实力和巩固皇位之作用。东汉皇帝在长安巡幸的地方及做的事情也都是为了这样的一个目的：在正统性方面，东汉皇帝会利用西汉皇帝来显示其已经被祖先认同，因此东汉皇帝祭拜十一陵和高庙是必要的。而身为明君亦应当尊敬忠诚的大臣，故而东汉皇帝还祭祀萧何、曹参和霍光，并宴请在关中地区的官员。此外皇帝还以祭祀太上皇、赐予百姓粮食来表现其孝顺慈悲之心。

虽然东汉中期皇帝行幸长安之旅程总体一致，但细察皇帝即位期间的何时行

1　范晔：《后汉书》，45.1535。
2　范晔：《后汉书》，5.204。
3　范晔：《后汉书》，5.240。
4　范晔：《后汉书》，6.267。是否有地震是值得怀疑的，或许是官员托词召回皇帝。
5　Rafe de Crespigny, "The Harem of Emperor Huan: A Study of Court Politics in Later Han," *Papers of Far Eastern History* Vol. 12, 1975, pp. 5-11.
6　范晔：《后汉书》，7.304。
7　范晔：《后汉书》，7.304-305。
8　范晔：《后汉书》，7.306。
9　范晔：《后汉书》，7.306。

幸长安可以看出一些有趣的差别。明帝、章帝及顺帝行幸长安是在其已经占有不可争议的、稳固的皇位时，他们以行幸长安宣示其权力，故而均在合乎礼制的时间前往旧都。安帝和桓帝直到亲政后才出发去长安：安帝等了约四十个月，而桓帝则在灭除梁氏家族后即刻前往，因此桓帝行幸长安很明显是一种凯旋。和帝行幸长安时，窦太后还临朝，故和帝是一个特例；他并未通过行幸长安这个方法来彰显其皇位的正统性，而是以行幸长安向臣民展示自己已经成年，不需要依赖皇太后临朝。行幸长安对和帝而言极为重要，具有特殊的意思，因为前往长安是和帝抵抗窦氏家族的重要开端。

Emperors Travelling to Chang'an in Mid Eastern Han-Dynasty

Alexander Brosch / Germany

University of Münster, Institute of Sinology and East Asian Studies / PhD. student, Assistant Professor

I. Introduction

In the tenth month of the first year of the reign-era jianwu, Zhu You, who was guarding Luoyang at that time, proclaimed surrender under the pressure of Liu Xiu's troops. Four months before, Liu Xiu had already taken the title of Emperor and is now better known by his posthumous name Emperor Guangwu ("the arbitrating Emperor"). Emperor Guangwu's accession to the throne marks the beginning of the Eastern Han-Dynasty. When he took possession of Luoyang, Emperor Guangwu immediately established it as the Han-Dynasty's new capital.[1]

At the time Emperor Guangwu decided to make Luoyang his capital, he was not yet in control of the Guanzhong-area around Chang'an, which is why not choosing Chang'an as capital was a natural decision. Later Emperor Guangwu's troops conquered the Guanzhong-area, including Chang'an. Nevertheless Emperor

---

[1] See Fan Ye: Hou Han shu, 2008 edition of Zhonghua shuju, 1.22-25.

Guangwu and his successors did not consider moving to the former capital Chang'an. The three main reasons for Luoyang are the following:[1]

- Wang Mang adopted an arrogant attitude towards the Xiongnu-tribes, jeopardizing the safety of the Guanzhong-area. [2]

- The amount of grain produced in the Guanzhong-area was not sufficient to saturate the demands from the capital Chang'an's inhabitants. Great amounts of grain had to be brought into Guanzhong by ship. Luoyang was situated in the central part of China and therefore comparatively close to the ever more important Shandong-area, which is why Luoyang did not have this problem. [3]

- It was also based on prognostications that Emperor Guangwu decided to make Luoyang the capital. [4]

Luoyang obviously had its benefits, but was slightly smaller in size than Chang'an and could not compare with the former capital in terms of bustle. Among the countless officials serving the court in Luoyang there surely were many who reminisced about the vibrant life in Chang'an.[5]

The question, what kind of importance Chang'an had during the Eastern Han-Dynasty with its capital Luoyang is still waiting to be investigated in detail. Two aspects which helped Chang'an keep some importance are its meaning in terms of military and legitimation. On the one hand, Chang'an played a significant role as a

---

1 The destruction of Chang'an by the red eyebrow troops happened after Emperor Guangwu had decided on Luoyang, which is why Victor Cunrui Xiong and Liao Boyuan believe that this was not one of the main reasons to choose Luoyang as capital. See Victor Cunrui Xiong: Capital Cities and Urban Form in Pre-Modern China: Luoyang, 1038 BCE to 938 CE, 2017 edition of Routledge, p. 32; Lun Donghan ding du Luoyang ji qi yingxiang by Liao Boyuan, Shixue jikan, No. 3, 2010, pp. 21-22.
2 See Rafe de Crespigny: Fire over Luoyang: A History of the Later Han Dynasty 23–220 AD, 2016 edition of Brill, p. 20.
3 See Lun Donghan ding du Luoyang ji qi yingxiang by Liao Boyuan, p. 22.
4 See Lun Donghan ding du Luoyang ji qi yingxiang by Liao Boyuan, p. 23.
5 The most famous example is Ban Gu's Rhapsody of the Western Capital; Yan Kejun: Quan Shanggu Sandai Qin Han Sanguo Liuchao wen, 1999 edition of Zhonghua shuju, pp. 602-604.

stronghold against the Qiang-tribes. On the other hand, the eleven grave mounds[1] of the emperors of the Western Han-Dynasty were located near Chang'an and represented a key location for the Eastern Han-Dynasty's emperors who saw the earlier emperors as their forebearers.[2]

After Emperor Guangwu had passed away, his successors Emperor Ming, Emperor Zhang, Emperor He, Emperor An, Emperor Shun and Emperor Huan all traveled to Chang'an once during their respective reign-periods. Although the itinerary differed from emperor to emperor, some parts were fixed. Surely because the tenth month was "the month that Gaozu pacified the Qin"[3], they all left for Chang'an during the tenth month. The most important destinations also remained the same for every emperor: It was not Chang'an city, but the ancestral temple of Gaozu and the aforementioned eleven grave mounds.

The Hou Han shu records that Emperor Ming, Emperor Zhang, Emperor He and Emperor An also presented offerings to the most merited loyal officials of the Western Han-Dynasty, for example Emperor An "used a medium set of animals[4] to give as an offer to Xiao He, Cao Can and Huo Guang" [5]; the Emperors Zhang and An also "dispatched an envoy to make offerings to the Supreme Exalted One at Wannian" [6] Furthermore the emperors of the Eastern Han-Dynasty made it a custom to invite the high officials of the region to a feast when visiting Chang'an and beyond that grant the regional officials or even the commoners a

---

1 "Eleven grave mounds" refer to the graves of the Emperors Gaozu, Hui, Wen, Jing, Wu, Zhao, Xuan, Yuan, Cheng, Ai and Ping. See Fan Ye: Hou Han shu, 1.48.
2 See Donghan Chang'an yu Guanzhong pingyuan by Ma Xueqin, Zhongguo lishi dili luncong, No. 2, 2000, pp. 190-193.
3 Fan Ye: Hou Han shu, 95.3130.
4 "A medium set of animals" consists of a sheep and a pig; see Ban Gu: Han shu, 1973 edition of Zhonghua shuju, 7.225.
5 Fan Ye: Hou Han shu, 5.240.
6 Fan Ye: Hou Han shu, 3.144; 5.240. The "Supreme Exalted One" is Emperor Gaozu's father.

certain amount of grain. [1]

II. When during their respective reign-periods did the emperors set out for Chang'an?

If one were to ask the question why the emperors of the Eastern Han-Dynasty travelled to Chang'an, a rather superficial answer would be that the eleven grave mounds were near Chang'an. Therefore, every emperor of the Eastern Han had to go and pay his respects when ascending the throne. But not all emperors of Eastern Han-Dynasty travelled to Chang'an immediately after they became emperor; for differing reasons some even waited for several years until they set out.[2] These reasons are to be explored in the following.

In the second year of the reign-era zhongyuan Emperor Guangwu passed away and Emperor Ming ascended the throne. Emperor Ming set yongping as the name of the next reign-era. In the tenth month of the second year of the reign-era yongping "on a jiazi-day, the Emperor went westwards on an inspection tour, travelled to Chang'an, made offerings at the ancestral temple of Emperor Gaozu and subsequently did sacrificial service at the eleven grave mounds. [He] visited every hall and town, assembled the officials from the commanderies and counties, granted rewards and let music play. On the jiashen-day of the eleventh month [the emperor] sent an envoy to use a medium set of animals to give as an offer to Xiao He and Huo Guang. When the emperor payed his respect to the grave mounds, he

---

1 The Hou Han shu records that apart from Emperor An every Emperor visiting Chang'an handed out grain to low officials of poor people; see Fan Ye: Hou Han shu, 2.104; 3.144; 4.172; 6.267; 7.306. Ma Xueqin believes that the handing out of grain "had a certain accelerating function concerning the recovery and development of the Economy of the Guanzhong-area"; Donghan Chang'an yu Guanzhong pingyuan by Ma Xueqin, p. 190. The emperors very seldom visited Chang'an, therefore the author is convinced that this accelerating function was barely even existing; furthermore, the Emperors' purpose of travelling to Chang'an was not to strengthen the Guanzhong-area but to emphasize their imperial legitimation.

2 Ma Xueqin lists all the imperial journeys to Chang'an during Mid Eastern Han-Dynasty, but unfortunately does not do any analysis; Donghan Chang'an yu Guanzhong pingyuan by Ma Xueqin, pp. 191-192.

passed the resting places in an honoring posture."[1] "[The Emperor] further visited the Hedong-area and everywhere he passed by, he granted the 2000 shi-officials, the leading officials, down to the minor officials [rewards], according to their rank. On the guimao-day the imperial carriage returned to the palace."[2] When planning their journeys to Chang'an, the succeeding emperors based their respective itinerary on Emperor Ming's example.

Probably because he respected the "three year mourning period"[3], Emperor Ming waited for thirty two months before he set out for Chang'an. When ascending the throne Emperor Ming was already of full age and did not have to rely on a regent dowager, therefore he was in a position to decide on an inaugural visit to Chang'an freely.

Emperor Zhang waited until the eighth year of his reign period (the seventh year of the reign-era jianchu) before he set out for Chang'an. To detect reasons for this decision is quite a difficult task. Emperor Zhang always kept a deferential attitude towards the Empress Dowager Ma. He might have spent three years in mourning after the Empress Dowager passed away and perhaps went on his journey to Chang'an only after the mourning period had ended.[4]

Emperor He ascended the throne in the second year of the reign-era zhanghe. He was a minor of ten sui at that time, hence the Empress Dowager Dou acted as regent.[5] In the first month of the third year in the reign-era yongyuan, "the Emperor took the cap of manhood"[6]; in the tenth month the Emperor "travelled

---

1 The Hou Han ji version has shi "軾", meaning "to hold on to the front bar in respect" instead of shi "式"; see Yuan Hong: Hou Han ji, 2005 edition of Zhonghua shuju, 9.168.
2 Fan Ye: Hou Han shu, 2.104.
3 See Chen Li [Editor]: Baihutong shuzheng, Xinbian zhuzi jicheng, 1994 edition of Zhonghua shuju, pp. 507-509.
4 Empress Dowager Ma died in the sixth month of the forth year of the reign-era jianchu; Emperor Zhang travelled to Chang'an in the tenth month of the seventh year; see Fan Ye: Hou Han shu, 10.414; 3.144; 16.917.
5 See Fan Ye: Hou Han shu, 4.165.
6 Fan Ye: Hou Han shu, 4.171.

to Chang'an"[1]. By leaving Luoyang Emperor He could free himself of the rigid surveillance and control the Empress Dowager Dou was exercising and moreover, present himself as a grown-up emperor who would be more than able to rule. Therefore, taking the cap of manhood and travelling to Chang'an were key steps to reigning on his own terms. The Empress Dowager Dou might have regretted her decision to allow the emperor his journey to Chang'an. She sent her brother, the Grand General Dou Xian, to meet the imperial carriage in Chang'an. When [Dou] Xian arrived, the imperial secretaries and their adjuncts mentioned in a discussion that they want to visit him and in bowing wish him ten thousand years. [Han] Leng rectified their behaviour saying: "In intercourse with the higher you don't flatter, in intercourse with the lower you don't show greed[2]; in the rites there is no principle of wishing a subject ten thousand years." The discussants were all ashamed and discontinued [to speak about it]. [3] Han Leng, who had insisted here that only the emperor is the rightful ruler and should be honored in imperial fashion, later assisted the young emperor with the elimination of the Dou family clan. [4] Emperor He's resistance against the stronghold of political power by the Dou clan might well have started with his journey to Chang'an.

When Emperor He passed away and Emperor Shang died young, Emperor An ascended the throne in the eighth month of the first year in the reign-era yanping. Since he was a minor as well, the Empress Dowager Deng acted as regent. She continued to reign until her own death, which therefore was the point of time Emperor An started to reign on his own. Only after the Dowager had died – not even directly, but after three more years – did Emperor An travel to Chang'an. Legally the emperor was already on the throne for eighteen years before he visited the former capital.[5]

---

1 Fan Ye: Hou Han shu, 4.172.
2 This is a passage from the book of changes; see Ruan Yuan 阮元 (edit.): Shisanjing zhu shu 1: Zhou yi, 2001 edition of Yiwen yinshuguan, 8.13A (p. 171).
3 This is recorded in the biography of Han Leng. Fan Ye: Hou Han shu, 45.1535.
4 See Fan Ye: Hou Han shu, 45.1535.
5 See Fan Ye: Hou Han shu, 5.240.

Emperor Shun set out for Chang'an when his reign was already quite consolidated (in the second year of the reign-era yonghe). After Emperor Shun had already left Luoyang for over one month, an earthquake was reported and he hurried back to the capital. [1]

When Emperor Huan ascended the throne, members of the Liang clan held supreme power and the Empress Dowager Liang acted as regent. Later, when the Empress Dowager had passed away, Grand General Liang Ji and his younger sister, the Empress Nüying, still managed to keep control over the imperial court.[2] In the seventh month of the second year of the reign-era yanxi "the Empress Liang passed away"[3]. Emperor Huan immediately took the chance to strip Liang Ji of his power which resulted in Liang Ji killing himself.[4] After just two months in control Emperor Huan decided to travel to Chang'an and show off his undisputed sovereignty.[5] While staying in Chang'an Emperor Huan furthermore established his most important comrade in arms Chan Chao as General of chariots and the cavalry[6]. Quite obviously, the journey to Chang'an was kind of a triumphal procession for Emperor Huan.

III. Conclusion

When Emperor Guangwu made Luoyang the capital, Chang'an lost its position as the most important city in the Han-empire. But because the emperors of the Eastern Han-Dynasty still thought of Chang'an and the eleven imperial grave mounds of the Western Han as important places for dynastic legitimation, travelling to Chang'an became tradition. The political situation changed from emperor to emperor and the political power of the emperors varied. Therefore, visiting Chang'an carried

---

1 See Fan Ye: Hou Han shu, 6.267. One may wonder whether there even was an earthquake or if the officials just needed an excuse to call back the emperor.
2 See The Harem of Emperor Huan: A Study of Court Politics in Later Han by Rafe de Crespigny, Papers of Far Eastern History, No. 12, 1975, pp. 5-11.
3 Fan Ye: Hou Han shu, 7.304.
4 See Fan Ye: Hou Han shu, 7.304-305.
5 See Fan Ye: Hou Han shu, 7.306.
6 See Fan Ye: Hou Han shu, 7.306.

a different meaning for each of the emperors. Even though, visiting Chang'an normally fulfilled the function of showing the emperor's strength and consolidating his position as ruler. The places the emperors visited and the things they did during their journeys to Chang'an were designed to fulfill such a function as well: For legitimation purposes the emperors travelled to the eleven grave mounds and used these resting places of the emperors of Western Han-Dynasty to show that they are acknowledged by their ancestors. A benevolent and strong emperor should also show respect towards loyal subjects. Therefore, the emperors of Eastern Han made offerings to Xiao He, Cao Can and Huo Guang and furthermore invited the officials of the Guangzhong-region to feast together. In addition, the emperors showed their filiality and mercy by making offering to the Supreme Exalted one and handing out grain to the people.

Although the itinerary of the emperors travelling to Chang'an during Mid Eastern Han-Dynasty were basically the same, one can still observe some interesting differences regarding the motivation to travel to Chang'an when looking at the time the emperors set out for the former capital. The Emperors Ming, Zhang and Shun travelled to Chang'an when their reign was undisputedly consolidated. They showed their powerful sovereignty by visiting Chang'an and just chose a date fitting the rules of propriety. The Emperors An and Huan waited until power over the court was in their own hands before they set out for Chang'an; Emperor An even waited for another period of time. Emperor Huan planned his journey as soon as he had eliminated the Liang clan around Liang Ji. His journey to Chang'an basically was a triumphal procession.

Because the Empress Dowager Dou still acted as regent when Emperor He set out for Chang'an, he can be seen as the exception. He did not use the journey to Chang'an as a method to show his undisputed sovereignty, but rather to present himself as an adult who is able to rule without any support by the Empress Dowager or anyone else. For Emperor He the journey to Chang'an was a greatly important step in his resistance against the Dou clan. This should not be underestimated.

References

班固：《汉书》，中华书局 1973 年版。

陈立：《白虎通疏证》，新编诸子集成，中华书局 1994 年版。

范晔：《后汉书》，中华书局 1973 年版。

廖伯源：《论东汉定都洛阳及其影响》，《史学集刊》2010 年第 3 期。

马雪芹：《东汉长安与关中平原》，《中国历史地理论丛》2000 年第 2 期。

阮元：《十三经注疏》卷 1《周易》，艺文印书馆 2001 年版。

严可均（校辑）：《全上古三代秦汉三国六朝文》，中华书局 1999 年版。

袁宏：《后汉纪》，中华书局 2005 年版。

Rafe de Crespigny. *Fire over Luoyang：A History of the Later Han Dynasty 23–220 AD*. Brill , 2016.

Rafe de Crespigny, "The Harem of Emperor Huan: A Study of Court Politics in Later Han," *Papers of Far Eastern History*, 1975(12).

Victor Cunrui Xiong, *Capital Cities and Urban Form in Pre-Modern China: Luoyang, 1038 BCE to 938 CE*, Routledge, 2017.

试论《周易》"贞"字的含义和用法

鲍葛薇·安吉塔 【拉脱维亚】
拉脱维亚大学亚洲研究系　副教授

一　语义

"贞"字在《周易》中出现 111 次[1]（全文共 5016 个字），通常显示占卜的结果或提供建议、如何评估形势、如何行动。该字包含两个部首："贝"部意思为贝壳——古代金钱的象征；"卜"部，指甲骨文上的线条——一种占卜过程。因此，就产生了这样一种解释——支付先知，以便进行占卜（许慎，2002, p. 206, p. 412）。然而，中国考古学家发现，在甲骨文上，这个汉字以另一种形式出现，即"鼎"，一种器皿，一种用来雕刻预言结果的祭器。在鼎上面加了部首卜，表示占卜过程，后来才演变出单独"贞"[2]。

考虑到该字可能隐含的不同语法和词汇形式，原始象形文字可能还具有以下含义：请求神谕、建议占卜、占卜过程、吉祥占卜等。此类服务必须有足够报酬，问题必须是相关的和真诚的。这就是为什么后来在儒家伦理语境中，该字的意义与同音字"真"联系在一起的原因。道教哲学中的"真"概念表示真理、现实、原始状态，以及达到圆满和返璞归真。"贞"和"真"这两个字可能有共同的起源，因为它们的文字结构也有相似之处[3]。

1　在中国命理学中，这个数字象征着创造阳能量的顶峰。
2　侯乃峰、丁原植：《〈周易〉文字汇校集释》，台湾古籍出版有限公司 2009 年版。
3　赵逸之：《汉字探索——"贞"与"真"》[EB/OL]. 华韵国学网. 深圳大学端阳社，2007—2014. https://www.hygx.org/thread-53736-1-1.html, 2019-12-28。

在卦1（乾）的卦辞中共有四个字[1]，最后一字是贞。在这个卦中，所有的爻都是长横（阳爻），代表天的光明、强大、活跃和创造力。在《文言》中[2]，这些字与"四德"有关，其中，"贞"的意思是"坚持，完成工作所必需的"[3]。孔子的弟子子夏在《子夏传》中，借助同音字"正"来解释"贞"——正确、诚实、真实[4]。魏国哲学家王弼[5]，声称第一卦中的"贞"在各种关系中都意味着"信任"[6]。但唐代研究者李鼎祚[7]评注称，它与有助于有效行动的"知识"有关[8]。宋朝儒家思想家程颐[9]，在《程氏易传》将"贞"定义为"万物的圆满或宝库"[10]。

卦2（坤）有六条双短横（阴爻），象征着大地的温和、软弱、受纳和被动。贞出现在卦辞的开头和结尾。起初，这四个字与卦1中的相同，只有"贞"被"牝马"一词与其他字隔开。在篇尾，有一个短语共包含三个字："安"、"贞"、"吉"。可以得出这样的结论，在这个卦中，"贞"与贞洁和贞操等女性美德相结合，带来了和平与幸福。在其他一些古籍资料中，这个字也有类似的解释。在《周书·谥法》中，"贞"的意思是"清纯，守贞"[11]。在司马迁的《史记·甲单列传》中，"贞女子，一女不嫁二夫"[12]，这意味着在丈夫去世后，女子对死者保持忠诚，不再结婚。

从这两个例子中可以推断，"贞"可以与坚持、诚实、正义、智慧、信任、忠诚等良好品质联系起来，也可以与贞节和童贞等女性特定的美德联系起来。文中确实有很多地方是这样理解"贞"的，并与"丈人""君子"或"妇""女"这些字一起被提到。然而，在某些情况下，贞也与其他人一起出现，例如"弟子""幽人""童仆"或"武人"。

奇怪的是，在卦1中，"贞"表示积极和创造性地发展，只出现一次。但在

1　元亨利贞。These and all other quotes from "Zhou yi" are taken from 易经［周易］原文 [EB/OL]. 易学网，2011.https://www.eee-learning.com/article/571, 2019-12-28。
2　这是儒家学者在公元前一千年写的"十翼"注释之一。它解释了前两个卦。
3　易经［周易］原文 [EB/OL]. 易学网，2011.https://www.eee-learning.com/article/571, 2019-12-28。
4　元，始也。亨，通也。利，和也。贞，正也。
5　王弼、韩康伯注，孔颖达疏；《周易正义》，《十三经注疏》，中华书局1979年版。https://www.eee-learning.com/article/643, 2019-12-28
6　元则仁也，亨则礼也，利则义也，贞则信也。
7　李鼎祚. 四库全书经部：易类：周易集解 [EB/OL]. 易学网，2011.http://www.eee-learning.com/book/481, 2019-12-28
8　言君法五常 [..] 仁义礼智信 [..] 贞为事干，以配于智。
9　汉典：重编国语辞典修订本 [EB/OL]. http://www.zdic.net/, 2019-12-28。
10　贞者，万物之成，万物之收藏。
11　清白守节曰贞。
12　贞女不更二夫。

卦 2 中，它被提到了五次，而且明显地与困境、邪气和女性的弱点相关。很清楚，它不可能总是具有占卜过程、吉祥、正义等传统意义。在卦 2 中，"贞"听起来更像是在危险或灾难的情况下的提醒或警告。此外，在卦文 9 第 6 行的一个短语中有三个字——"妇贞厉"，这并不意味着一个积极的结果。但卦 32 第 5 行说，"贞妇人吉夫子凶"。

二　中国学者的文章

现代中国学者对《周易》中"贞"一字的不同分析方法和意义进行了深入研究。在这里，我只会提到那些与上文中所提观点不同的观点。张荣贵赋予以下含义：为，定，专一，一心一意[1]。她提到了分析《周易》文本的几种可能的方法，例如：矛盾转化法、阴阳平衡法、循序渐进法[2]。张认为，尽管周代的一些汉字可能有多种含义，但它们在文本中应该主要用于一种含义，而一个汉字的含义变化应该有一个非常重要的原因，其与上下文密切相关。

张耀天和崔瑞认为"贞"的原意通常是一种褒义：表示当前的良好状态，表示未来的有利决定和行动；向占卜者询问更多问题可能会有所帮助。两位作者还认为，"贞"的意思是"问占卜者问题"，但假设一个强制性的先决条件应该是一个正直的意图和一个适当的问题。此外，他们同意，在某些情况下，"贞"可能意味着"持续而不改变，保持稳定而不变化"[3]。

王化平对比了不同考古文献，筛选出"贞"的三个主要含义：卜问、正命和坚固。他还赞同"贞"字代表着一种正常、稳定、不变的状态。此外，王根据其他早期文献给出了一长串可能的解释：当、精诚、常、成就[4]。据他说，贞字还可能表达问卜者的期望，即超自然力量会给他们带来吉利，给他们带来好的结果和运气[5]。

本文同意王化平的观点，认为将"贞"字译为"卜问"没有什么道理。这个概念显示了当前占卜过程的结果，是对当前询问的回答，而不是敦促一个人进一步询问和安排另一个占卜。在中国古代，占卜是一件非常重要的事情，是一个复

---

[1]　张荣贵:《释疑〈周易〉之"贞"》,《江苏大学学报》2010 年第 4 期。
[2]　同上。
[3]　张耀天、崔瑞:《易学"贞"字在断定逻辑系统下的研究》,《长江工程学院学报》2009 年第 4 期。
[4]　王化平:《〈周易〉之"贞"》,《江苏大学学报》2010 年第 4 期。
[5]　王化平:《〈周易〉之"贞"》,《江苏大学学报》2010 年第 2 期。

杂的过程，需要专门的准备、精确安排时间、单独的地点，也许还需要大量的金钱。这不是每个人都能做到的。

学者朱兴国发现"贞"的"卜问"这个意思在其他早期的古籍中也找不到。他认为这是后来的说法。像卜、兆、占、蓍、龟、筮这些字与占卜问题或占卜过程的关系比贞更密切。但他赞同"贞"字含有对神力的虔诚和信仰。他将"祯"字作为"贞"的同义词，意思是"吉祥、吉祥"（带有一个左偏旁"示"），寓意"神圣精神""神圣崇拜"或"牺牲"[1]。

三 卦辞中的"贞"字

在实际应用（占卜、武术、医学、天象等）中，卦的顺序和排列可能会有所不同，具体取决于所使用的方法。通常选择一两个卦来描述一种情况或回答一个问题。卦辞和卜辞包含两个可思考的层面：1）通常以格律的形式和形象的比喻来描述特定的情景和事件（就像民歌一样）；2）对卜辞的判断和如何应对提出建议[2]。但在传统的《周易》文本中，有一个固定的 64 卦。每卦包括一幅卦象、卦名和卦辞，以及六爻。

本节将在卦辞的语境中探讨"贞"字，一方面，指的是经典注释《序卦》（Xu gua）给出的含义和关系；另一方面，分析"贞"字在卦文中的判断。"贞"出现在 38 个卦辞中，只有 26 个卦辞没有提到它。这里给出了前两个和后两个卦作为分析示例。

卦 1（乾）描绘了宇宙的开始、活跃的力量（天、日等）。在这里，贞在创世过程中表现出严谨、正直和高效。

相反，卦 2（坤）显示了弱、暗、冷、被动、接收（地、月）。天地就像夫妻一样，共同创造了世界上的一切事物和生命（天地之间，人类世界就诞生了）。在这里，贞与女性特质相关联（跟随，面朝西边，月出之地，内敛，谨慎），只有这样，才能实现和平与幸福。

卦 62（小过）建议人们专注于实际的日常事务，而不是规划伟大的事情。在这种情况下，贞是一种与生俱来的美德，自我克制。一个人必须谦逊节俭，并做出妥协。

---

1 朱兴国，卜辞"贞"字及相关问题新论 [EB/OL]. 中国社会科学院历史研究所，先秦史研究室，2007. http://www.xianqin.org/xr_html/articles/jgyj/465.html, 2019-12-28。
2 黄玉顺：《易经古歌考释》，巴蜀出版社 1995 年版。

卦 63（既济）显示了完美和幸福。尽管一个人必须继续努力，"贞"字还是敦促人们要细心、严谨和自信。即使在和平与繁荣的时代，智者也会思考未来的发展和可能的复杂情况。

可以得出结论，"贞"字几乎会遇到各种情况，无论是吉是凶。在很大程度上，这个字与应该积极向好的发展有关。这可能同时适用于男性和女性特征，但在大多数情况下，性别没有具体指明。在一些卦辞中，贞与困难、危险或困境有关。

因此，"贞"字在不同的情况下有不同的程度、不同的强度以及不同的作用。在一种情况下，它是吉祥的，但在另一种情况下，它可能是不受欢迎的，甚至是不可能的。例如，刚毅和自信一般是好的品质，但如果一个人过于自信，用武力将自己的意志强加给他人，并试图达到目的，而不考虑权力和地区影响力的失衡，这种坚持可能会失败并带来厄运。

四 "贞"与爻辞的关系

在不同的情况下，与具体卦爻的关系可以非常清楚地观察到贞的不同含义。卦爻位置会使该词的用法有很大不同。有些地方，它偏向于阴（弱、温和、小、阴等），而在另一些地方，它更偏向于阳（强、硬、大、阳等）。

第 1 行是发展的开始，在这里谨慎和克制是好的，因此，贞出现在阴爻中的频率更高。总的来说，这一阶段的发展进程非常有利。贞与不幸只有一例相关。

第 2 行位于下卦的中间。在这里，也希望获得阴性的特征和行为，这就是为什么贞出现在阴爻辞中多达 7 次。然而，中间偏下的位置也适合对应的阳（用正面的词语提到了 4 次）。在第二行中，它指出谦逊、中庸、内敛、深沉，以及相信有权势和智慧的人。

随着第 3 行中困境的出现，下卦已经达到顶点甚至过度，而且下一行将从下卦的内部（小、私人）发展转变为在上三字组中另一个完全不同的外部事物范围（大、全局）。这原本是阳（奇数）的位置，但在这一阶段，过度的坚持、自我主张、硬度和太多的力量是不吉利的（在阳爻中，与贞有关的否定词出现 7 次）。一个人不能超越极限，但要非常谨慎，以便为即将到来的变化做好准备。

第 4 行仍然指出了一个困境。在这里，贞字 4 次伴随不吉利的话。然而，这是一个真正行动的开始，因此，阳的特点（如决心、正义、毅力、坚定等）带来了相当好的结果。

第 5 行通常被视为卦中的"王",它位于上三角形的中心。这是一个阳(奇数)数,对于一个积极、强壮和聪明的人来说,这个高位置是非常合适的,所以"贞"经常在阳爻中显示出积极的作用(3 次)。这不是一个黑暗、软弱、被动和有邪恶势力的地方,因此在阴爻中,"贞"的消极影响达到最大(出现 5 次负面词语)。尽管如此,还是有一些例外,比如"贞"为小人物带来好运,但为大人物带来不幸;为女人带来吉祥,为男人带来不利。这意味着,有时候,即使是领导人,也应该培养女性的柔情、妥协、处事温和,以及接近弱者和下人。此外,让女性和年轻人当领导也并非不可能。

在第 6 行中,"贞"已经主要与过度的权力或自私联系在一起,它在阳爻中出现了 4 次负面含义。在这里,与阴关联的特征克制、自省和收敛得以推荐(2 次好的预测)。

如果计算贞在阴爻(− −)和阳爻(——)中出现的次数,那么结果表明,贞在阳爻(——)中使用的次数最多,为 4—10 次,但在阴爻(− −)中使用的次数最少。但在这两种情况下,在吉祥而强大的第五爻中,"贞"字的次数几乎相同。

中国儒学的传统研究主要将"贞"解释为男人的积极特征(统治者、父亲、丈夫)。但是,如上所述,《周易》列举了许多例子(其数量甚至排在前五位),在这些例子中,具有阴性品德如温柔、忍让被认为是正确的,而非像阳那样直接和强硬。在《周易》中,这两个对立物只是位置不同而已,它们只是在力量和功能上有所不同,并不存在孰轻孰重的问题。此外,在实际应用中,没有特定的卦序,它们与自然现象一样处于绝对平衡状态。

五 与其他词语的关系

将"贞"与其他字结合起来看,可以观察到两种类型的含义,即正面和负面的:

1)与运气、和平、积极发展的关系(正面):

可贞

利居贞

贞吉[1]

---

[1] 这句话最常出现,在整篇文章中出现了 35 次。

利永贞

元永贞

安贞吉，等。

2）与困难、厄运、痛苦的关系（负面）：

贞凶

贞吝

贞厉

贞疾

艰贞

不可贞，等。

一般来说，"贞"指的是令人向往的东西——良好的品质或幸福。在这些情况下，传统儒家和道家的解释相当准确地揭示了其含义。然而，有不少表达与困难或非人所愿之境有关。为了澄清这些片段的含义，我特别关注了这些困境之情况。下面是一个详细分析的例子。对于其他卦，只给出总括性结论。

在卦3第五行，贞的含义变得模棱两可，因为有一定的前提条件才能获得吉祥的结果。爻辞曰：小贞吉，大贞凶。不同的评论和翻译[1]对其解释如下：

象传："现在还不是采取行动的时候。"[2]

王弼[3]："对于小人物的行为是吉祥的。对于大人物的则是不吉利的。"[4]

李鼎祚[5]："建议在第四行中寻找伴侣（妻子），而不是在第二行中追求遥远的目标。"[6]

李光地[7]："可能是小事情。而不可能是大事情。"

唐颐[8]："小雨[9]带来好运，大雨带来坏运气。"[10]

1　来源按时间顺序列出，从最早的中文评论开始，最后是最新的西方翻译。
2　易经［周易］原文 [EB/OL]. 易学网，2011.https://www.eee-learning.com/article/571, 2019-12-28。
3　Wang Bi (3.cent.).
4　王弼、韩康伯注，孔颖达疏：《周易正义》，《十三经注疏》，中华书局1979年版，https://www.eee-learning.com/article/643, 2019-12-28。
5　Li Dingzuo (8.cent.).
6　李鼎祚："四库全书经部：易类：周易集解" [EB/OL]. 易学网，2011.http://www.eee-learning.com/book/481, 2019-12-28
7　李光地（1642—1718）。
8　当代学者。
9　上三角形代表水或雨。
10　唐颐：《图解易经智慧宝典》，台北华威国际出版社2013年版。

James Legge[1]："只要坚定和正确，在小事上就会有好运；（甚至）在大事上会有邪恶。"[2]

Richard Wilhelm[3]："小坚持带来好运，大坚持带来厄运。"[4]

Julian K. Shchutsky[5]："小事坚定——祝你好运。大事上的坚定——倒霉。"[6]

Geoffrey Redmond："对于小事，占卜是吉祥的；对于大事，占卜是不祥的。"[7]

当代学者的翻译，由 J.DeKorne 编辑[8]：

Rudolf Ritsema："小的考验：重要。大的考验：隐患。"

Edward L. Shaughnessy："小事吉，大事凶。"

Wu Chung："宜成小事，难成大业。"

"贞"这个词的直译是很困难的。它在很大程度上取决于给定的情况，也取决于上面提到的与其他词语的搭配。此外，周朝没有断句法，所有的汉字都是一个接一个写的。直到后来，中国学者才添加了标点来分隔意群、短语或句子。根据断句的不同，内容解释可能会有很大差异。例如：

勿用永贞。

勿用。永贞。

丧其童仆。贞厉。

丧其童仆贞。厉。

贞疾。

贞。疾。

妇贞厉。

1　1815-1897.

2　Legge J. (transl.). Sacred Text Archive, The I Ching [EB/OL]. http://www.sacred-texts.com/ich/index.htm, 2019-12-28.

3　1873–1930.

4　Wilhelm R. (transl.). I Ging: Text und Materialien [M]. Köln: Diederichs, 1986: 38.

5　Юлиан К.Щуцкий (1897-1938).

6　Щуцкий Ю. К. (пер.).Конфуций: Уроки мудрости: Китайская Классическая "Книга Перемен" [M]. Москва: Эксмо, 2008: 615.

7　Redmond G, *The I Ching (Book of Changes): A Critical Translation of the Ancient Text* [M]. London: Bloomsbury, 2017: 78.

8　DeKorne J. (ed.). The Gnostic Book of Changes [EB/OL]. http://www.jamesdekorne.com/GBCh/GBCh.htm, 2019-12-28.

妇。贞。厉。
妇。贞厉。

中国学者吴辛丑根据西方语法规则分析《周易》文本，将"贞"的功能定义为主语、宾语或谓语。他认为用该方法可以区分不同的意思[1]。主要是他给出了"卜问"的动词含义，将贞之前和之后的词作为宾语短语的直接间接宾语进行分析，宾语短语可以由名词、动词、形容词等组成[2]。诚然，《周易》中的词语是紧密相连的，它们的意义是相互依存的，但它们也取决于卦图所代表的情况。

汉语在词和短语中的划分仍然是一个非常有争议的问题，因为学者和评论家往往根据自己的经验和论证，对它们进行不同的划分。因此，我支持朱兴国的观点，即最好将"贞"作为一个独立的单元来对待，而不是与其他词或短语结合[3]。另一种选择是，按照熊谊华[4]的建议，只给出文本中的语音转录，并在各自的注释中添加完整的解释。

六　结论

在《周易》中，"贞"这个字有不透明的、多层次的用法；原始文本（即使有经典注释的帮助）并不能在每个地方揭示这个词的确切含义。每个读者和评论家都可以根据自己的经验和知识，以不同的方式分配含义。"意义不能被视为固定的或静态的，而是不断演变的。它产生于相互竞争的概念之间不断协商的过程。"也许，一个人不应该追求自然原本的真相，而应该对这些相互竞争的解释进行审视，这些解释结合起来产生最终的意义[5]。

《周易》是一个处处充满辩证法智慧，恒常变化的系统；它有助于产生无限的新含义和解释。它谈论变化，其本身也在变化，敦促读者记住真理并非唯一，在不断变化的循环中分析对立面，并为新的挑战做好准备。

《周易》的文字、意义和结构经过几千年的演变，现在已经为汉语词汇和日

1　吴辛丑：《〈周易〉"贞"字结构分析》，《华南师范大学学报》2003 年第 6 期。
2　吴辛丑：《〈周易〉"贞"字结构分析》，《华南师范大学学报》2003 年第 6 期。
3　朱兴国．卜辞"贞"字及相关问题新论 [EB/OL]．中国社会科学院历史研究所，先秦史研究室，2007. http://www.xianqin.org/xr_html/articles/jgyj/465.html, 2019-12-28
4　熊谊华：《〈周易〉中"贞"的英译探折》，《湖北函授大学学报》2016 年第 11 期。
5　Turner C., Critical Legal Thinking: Jacques Derrida: Deconstruction [EB/OL]. http://criticallegalthinking.com/2016/05/27/jacques-derrida-deconstruction/, 2019-12-28.

常表达奠定了基础。现在，当这本书进入西方社会，出现了众多译本之后，词义会继续发生更多的变化，以适应现实情况和西方人的心理。

　　法国语法学家雅克·德里达（Jacques Derrida）说，单词的存在是通过"在一个分类中发挥作用，因此构成一个系统的差异性"[1]。《周易》的真正价值在于读者能够发现新的机会，将词语整合成新的链条和关联。"贞"字甚至并不意味着一组明确的含义，而是一种不受时间和空间限制的广阔、多维度的体验，从而打开了理解宇宙和永恒本质的大门。

1　Derrida J., Spivak G. Ch. (transl.) *Of Grammatology* [M]. Baltimore: John Hopkins Press, 1976: 109.

Meaning and Usage of the Word ZHEN 貞 in the "Book of Changes"

Baltgalve Agita / Latvia

Department of Asian Studies, University of Latvia / Associate Professor

I. Semantics

The character ZHEN 貞 appears in the text 111 times[1] (out of the total 5016 characters), usually showing the result of the divination or giving advice, how to evaluate the situation, how to act. The pictogram contains two radicals: 贝 a shell – an ancient symbol of money and 卜 lines on oracle bones – the divination process. Hence the explanation was derived – to pay the prophet, in order to perform the divination (Xu Shen, 2002, p. 206, 412). However, Chinese archeologists have found out that on oracle bones this character appeared in another form as 鼎 a cauldron – a sacrificial vessel where results of prophesies were engraved. The radical 卜 was added on the top of 鼎, indicating the divination process, only later the separate character 貞 evolved.[2]

Taking into account different grammatical and lexical forms that could have been

---

[1] In Chinese numerology, this number symbolizes the culmination of the creative yang energy.
[2] 侯乃峰、丁原植:《〈周易〉文字汇校集释》, 台湾古籍出版有限公司 2009 年版。

implied in this symbol, the original pictogram may also have had the following meanings: asking the oracle, advisable to do divination, divination as a process, auspicious divination etc. The payment for such kind of service had to be adequate, and the question had to be relevant and sincere. This is the reason why later, within the context of Confucian ethics the meaning of the character was associated with the homonym *zhen* 真 (true, real). In Daoism philosophy the concept *zhen* 真 indicates truth, reality, primordial state, as well as attainment of perfection and realization of truth. These two characters may have had a common origin, for similarities can be observed also in their graphical structure 貞 and 真 .[1]

In the judgment of Hexagram 1 (*qian* 乾) there are four characters (four words)[2], the last of them is ZHEN. In this hexagram, all lines are unbroken (*yang*) and indicate to the bright, powerful, active and creative force of the heaven. In the commentary "Wen yan" 文言[3] these words are associated with "four virtues" (*si de* 四德) where ZHEN means "persistence, necessary for completing the work".[4] Zixia, the disciple of Confucius, in his commentary "Zi xia zhuan" 子夏传 explains ZHEN with a help of the synonym *zheng* 正 meaning – correctness, honesty, truthfulness[5]. Wang Bi 王弼[6], philosopher of Wei state, claims that ZHEN in the first hexagram means "trust" in all kinds of relationships.[7] But the researcher of Tang Dynasty Li Dingzuo 李鼎祚[8] commentary says that it is related to "knowledge"

1　赵逸之:《汉字探索——"贞"与"真"》[EB/OL]. 华韵国学网 . 深圳大学端阳社 , 2007—2014. https://www.hygx.org/thread-53736-1-1.html, 2019-12-28

2　元亨利贞。These and all other quotes from "Zhou yi" are taken from 易经［周易］原文 [EB/OL]. 易学网 , 2011. https://www.eee-learning.com/article/571, 2019-12-28.

3　This is one of "Ten Wings" commentaries, written by Confucian scholars in 1st mil. BC. It gives explanations for the first two hexagrams.

4　易经［周易］原文 [EB/OL]. 易学网 , 2011. https://www.eee-learning.com/article/571, 2019-12-28

5　元 , 始也。亨 , 通也。利 , 和也。贞 , 正也。

6　王弼 , 韩康伯 , 孔颖达 . 周易正义 [EB/OL]. 十三经注疏 . 中华书局 , 1979. https://www.eee-learning.com/article/643, 2019-12-28

7　元则仁也 , 亨则礼也 , 利则义也 , 贞则信也。

8　李鼎祚 . 四库全书经部 : 易类 : 周易集解 [EB/OL]. 易学网 , 2011. http://www.eee-learning.com/book/481, 2019-12-28

that helps to act effectively[1]. Cheng Yi 程颐 [2], Neo-Confucian thinker from Song Dynasty, in his commentary (*Cheng shi yi zhuan* 程氏易传) defines ZHEN as "fulfillment or storehouse of all things"[3].

Hexagram 2 (*kun* 坤) has six broken (*yin*) lines that symbolize the mild, weak, receptive and passive energy of the earth. ZHEN appears both the beginning and in the end of the judgment. At first, there are the same four words as in Hexagram 1, only ZHEN is separated from others by the phrase "female horse (mare)" (*pin ma* 牝马). At the end of the text, there is a phrase that contains altogether three words: "peace" (*an* 安), ZHEN and "auspicious" (*ji* 吉). It is possible to conclude that, in this hexagram, ZHEN brings peace and happiness in combination with feminine virtues, such as virginity and chastity. In several other classic sources, the word has a similar explanation. In "Documents of Zhou" (*Zhou shu* 周书 : *Shi fa* 谥法) it is said that ZHEN means "innocent and pure, preserving the chastity"[4]. In "Records of Historian" by Sima Qian (*Shi ji* 史记 : *Jia dan lie zhuan* 甲单列传) it is said that "a woman with ZHEN does not change two men"[5] which means that after the death of her husband she remains faithful to the deceased and never marries again.

From these two examples it infers that ZHEN can relate to such good qualities as persistence, honesty, justice, wisdom, trust, loyalty, as well as to specifically feminine virtues, such as chastity and virginity. There are indeed many places in the text where ZHEN is understood in this way and is mentioned together with words "strong man" (*zhang ren* 丈人), "gentle man" (*jun zi* 君子) or "wife" (*fu* 妇), "woman" (*nv* 女). However, in some cases, ZHEN also appears with other persons, for example, "younger brother" (*di zi* 弟子), "hermit" (*you ren* 幽人), "servant boy" (*tong pu* 童仆) or "warrior" (*wu ren* 武人).

1 言君法五常 [...] 仁义礼智信 [...] 贞为事干，以配于智。
2 汉典：重编国语辞典修订本 [EB/OL]. http://www.zdic.net/, 2019-12-28
3 贞者，万物之成，万物之收藏。
4 清白守節曰贞。
5 贞女不更二夫。

It is peculiar that in Hexagram 1, where ZHEN indicates a positive and creative development it appears only once. But in Hexagram 2, it is mentioned five times, obviously relating to a problematic situation, the influence of evil forces or the feminine weakness. It is quite clear that it cannot always have the traditional meaning of divination process, auspiciousness, righteousness etc. In Hexagram 2, ZHEN sounds rather like a reminder or warning in the case of danger or calamity. Furthermore, in Hexagram 9, Line 6 in one phrase there are three words – "woman, ZHEN, danger" (nv zhen li 妇贞厉) that could hardly imply a positive result. But Hexagram 32, Line 5 says, "ZHEN, wife, auspicious, husband, inauspicious." (*zhen fu ren ji fu zi xiong* 贞妇人吉夫子凶)

II. Articles by Chinese Scholars

Modern Chinese scholars have done thorough researches regarding different methods of analyses and meanings of the word ZHEN in the "Book of Changes". Zhang Ronggui（张荣贵） gives the following meanings: *wei* (为 becoming, activity), *ding* (定 stability), *zhuan yi* (专一 single-minded, concentrated), *yi xin yi yi* (一心一意 whole-heartedly).[1] She mentions several possible approaches in analysing the text of "Zhou yi", e.g.: Transformation of contradictions (*mao dun zhuan hua fa* 矛盾转化法), Balancing of Yin and Yang (*yin yang ping heng fa* 阴阳平衡法), Gradual processeding forwards (*xun xu jian jin fa* 循序渐进法).[2] Zhang maintains that even though some characters may have had several meanings during Zhou time, still in the text they should have been used mostly in one meaning, and the shift of the meaning of one character should have had a very substantial reason, closely related to the context.

Zhang Yaotian（张耀天）and Cui Rui（崔瑞）explain that the original meaning of ZHEN is generally a positive affirmation: an expression of an excellent state at present, of favorable decisions and actions in the future; it may be beneficial for asking the diviner further questions. The two authors also consider the meaning of

---

1　张荣贵:《释疑〈周易〉之 "贞"》,《江苏大学学报》, 2010 年第 4 期。
2　Ibid.

ZHEN to be the "asking diviner a question", however, assuming that an obligatory prerequisite should be an upright intention and a proper question. Furthermore, they agree, that in some cases ZHEN may mean "continuing without changes, maintaining stability without movements".[1]

Wang Huaping 王化平 compares results of archeological findings of different text versions. He singles out three main meanings of ZHEN: "asking divination question" (*bu wen* 卜问), " proper livelihood" (*zheng ming* 正命) and "consistency" (*jian gu* 坚固). He also agrees that ZHEN indicates a regular, stable, not changing state of affairs. Further Wang gives a long row of possible interpretations based on other early texts: "appropriateness" (*dang* 当), "sincerity" (*jing cheng* 精诚), "regularity" (*chang* 常), "accomplishment" (*cheng jiu* 成就).[2] According to him ZHEN may also express expectations of inquirers that supernatural powers will be auspicious to them and give them good answer and good fortune.[3]

The author of this article agrees with the opinion of Wang Huaping that the translation of ZHEN as "asking divination question" does not make much sense. This concept shows the result of the present divination process, an answer the present inquiry rather than to urge one to further inquiries and the arrangement of another divination. In ancient China the divination was a very important matter, a complicated process that required special preparation, exact timing, seperate venue and perhaps also rather serious finances. It could not be done by everyone once in a while.

The scholar Zhu Xingguo (朱兴国) has found out that this meaning of ZHEN (to ask diviner a question 卜问 *buwen*) can not be found in other early classical text, either. He assumes that it is of a later origin. Such characters as *bu* 卜, *zhao* 兆, *zhan* 占, *shi* 蓍, *gui* 龟, *shi* 筮 were more related to the divination question or process than ZHEN. But he agrees that ZHEN could show sincere trust and belief

---

1　张耀天，崔瑞. 易学"贞"字在断定逻辑系统下的研究 [J]. 长江工程学院学报，2009, 20 (4): 5-6.
2　王化平：《〈周易〉之"贞"》,《江苏大学学报》, 2010 年第 4 期。
3　王化平：《〈周易〉之"贞"》,《江苏大学学报》, 2010 年第 2 期。

in the power of the oracle. He gives *zhen* 祯 as a synonyme for ZHEN, meaning "auspicious, propitious" (with an additional radical 示 of the "sacred spirit", "sacred cult" or "sacrifice" on the left side).[1]

III. ZHEN in Judgments of Hexagrams

Sequence and arrangement of hexagrams in practical applications (divination, martial arts, medicine, astrology, etc.) can vary, depending on the method used. Usually one or two hexagrams are chosen to describe a situation or to answer a question. Words of hexagrams and lines contain two thinkable layers: 1) descriptions of specific situations and happenings, often in rhythmic form with picturesque comparisons (just like folk songs), and 2) judgments with words of divination and suggestions on how to deal with the situation.[2] But in the traditionally inherited text of "Zhou yi" there is a fixed chain of 64 hexagrams (or chapters). Each chapter includes one hexagram graph, hexagram name and judgment, as well as words of six lines.

In this chapter the word ZHEN will be explored in the context of hexagram judgments, on one hand, referring to meanings and relationships as given by the classical commentary "Sequence of Hexagrams" (Xu gua 序卦), on the other hand, analyzing ZHEN in the text of hexagram judgments. ZHEN appears in 38 hexagram judgments, and only 26 hexagram judgments do not mention it. First two and last two hexagrams are given as analyses example here. Hexagram 1 (*qian* 乾) depicts the beginning of the universe, the active force (heaven, sun etc.). Here, ZHEN indicates rigor, integrity and efficiency in the creation process.

Hexagram 2 (*kun* 坤) shows the opposite – weak, dark, cold, passive, receiving (earth, moon). Earth and heaven like husband and wife together create all things and beings of the world (and between them the human world arises). Here, ZHEN is associated with feminine qualities (following in the back, turning to the west, where the moon rises, hiding its beauty, behaving cautiously), only then it is possible to

---

1　朱兴国．卜辞"贞"字及相关问题新论 [EB/OL]．中国社会研究院历史研究所，先秦史研究室，2007. http://www.xianqin.org/xr_html/articles/jgyj/465.html, 2019-12-28

2　黄玉顺:《易经古歌考释》，巴蜀出版社1995年版．

achieve peace and happiness.

Hexagram 62 (*xiao guo* 小过) recommends people to focus on practical everyday things without planning great things. In these circumstances, ZHEN is an innate virtue, self-restraint. A person has to be humble and frugal, and to make a compromise.

Hexagram 63 (*ji ji* 既济) shows perfection and happiness, however, even here a man must continue his efforts, ZHEN urges to thoroughness, rigor and self-confidence. Even in times of peace and prosperity, wise people think about the future development and possible complications.

It can be concluded that ZHEN is to encounter in almost any kind of situation, be it an auspicious case or a time where forces of darkness dominate. For the most part, the word relates to a positive development that should be continued. This may apply both to masculine and feminine characteristics, but in most cases gender is not specified. In some hexagram judgments, ZHEN is associated with difficulties, danger or problematic situations.

It follows that ZHEN have various degrees, greater or lesser strength, as well as different effects under different circumstances. In one situation it is auspicious, but in another it may be unwanted or even impossible. For example, rigidity and self-confidence are mostly good qualities, but if someone is too confident, imposes his will on others with force, and tries to achieve goals without consideration about the out balancing of power and influence zones, this kind of persistence may fail and bring misfortune.

IV. ZHEN Relations to Words of Lines

Different connotations of ZHEN in different situations can be very clearly observed in relations to definite lines of hexagrams. The usage of this word differs greatly in relation to the hierarchical positions of lines. In some positions it is more favorable for yin (weak, gentle, small, feminine etc.), and in others – for yang (strong, hard, large, masculine etc.).

Line 1 is the very beginning of the development, here it is good to be cautious and self-restrained, and therefore, ZHEN appears in yin lines more often. Overall, this phase of the development process is highly auspicious. ZHEN is related to misfortune just one case.

Line 2 is in the middle of the lower trigram. Here, it is also preferable to acquire yin characteristics and behavior, and that is why ZHEN appears in yin lines as much as 7 times. However, the lower center position is also rather beneficial for the yang counterpart (mentioned in positive phrases 4 times). In Line 2 it points to humility, modesty, stabilizing of inner virtues, fundamental planning, and trusting powerful and wise ones.

With Line 3 problematic circumstances set in. The lower trigram has reached culmination or even excess, besides, the next line is going to be a change from the inner (small, private) development of the lower trigram to a quite another scope of outer matters (big, global) in the upper trigram. This is originally a position for the yang energy (odd number), but an excessive persistence, self-assertion, hardness and too much power in this phase are inauspicious (in yang lines negative words related to ZHEN appear 7 times). One must not exceed limits, but be very cautious, in order to prepare for coming changes.

Line 4 still points out to a difficult situation. Here, ZHEN appears with inauspicious words 4 times. However, it is the beginning of a real action, and therefore, characteristics of yang energy (such as determination, righteousness, perseverance, firmness etc.) bring a fairly good result.

Line 5 is usually seen as "the king" of the hexagram, it is in the center of the upper trigram. This is a yang (odd) number, and the high position is really appropriate for an active, strong and wise person, so ZHEN quite often shows a positive effect in yang lines (3 times). This is not a place for dark, weak, passive and evil forces, so in yin lines ZHEN amounts to the greatest negative result (appearing

5 times with negative words). Still, there may be exceptions when ZHEN brings fortune for small ones, but misfortune for big ones; when it is auspicious for women, but inauspicious for men. This means that sometimes it is advisable even for leaders to cultivate feminine tenderness, to compromise, to act mildly and to approach weaker and lower ones. Besides, it is not impossible to have a woman or a youngster as a leader, as well.

In Line 6 ZHEN is already predominantly associated with excessive power or selfishness, it appears 4 times in negative connotations in yang lines. Here, restraint, reflection and moderation according to yin features are recommended (good prediction 2 times).

If one counts the number of ZHEN appearances in yin (broken) and yang (unbroken) lines, then it turns out that it is most often used in yang line 4 – 10 times, but the least in yin line 4 – 1 time. It appears seldom in yang line 1 – 3 times and often in yin line 2 – 11 times. But the auspicious and powerful line 5 has nearly the same number of ZHEN in both cases.

Chinese traditional commentaries by Confucian scholars mainly interpret ZHEN as a positive feature for a man (ruler, father, husband). But, as seen above, "Zhou yi" lists numerous cases (even in the leading 5th position) where it is right to be mild and yielding like *yin*, not straightforward and hard like *yang*. In "Zhou yi" both opposites only take up different positions, they differ regarding force and functions, but no one of both is less important or less worthy than the other. Besides, in the practical application there is no specific order of hexagrams, they are in absolute balance, just like natural phenomena.

V. Relations with Other Words

Looking at the ZHEN in phrases together with other words, one can observe two types of connotations – positive and negative:

1) Relation with luck, peace, positive development (positive):

- possible, ZHEN (*ke zhen* 可貞)

- advantage, to reside, ZHEN (*li ju zhen* 利居貞)

- ZHEN, auspicious (*zhen ji* 貞吉)[1]

- advantage, lasting, ZHEN (*li yong zhen* 利永貞)

- beginning, lasting, ZHEN (*yuan yong zhen* 元永貞)

- peace, ZHEN, auspicious (*an zhen ji* 安貞吉) etc.

2) Relation with difficulties, bad luck, misery (negative):

- ZHEN, inauspicious (*zhen xiong* 貞凶)

- ZHEN, misery (*zhen lin* 貞吝)

- ZHEN, danger (*zhen li* 貞厲)

- ZHEN, illness (*zhen ji* 貞疾)

- difficulties, ZHEN (*jian zhen* 艱貞)

- not possible, ZHEN (*bu ke zhen* 不可貞) etc.

Generally ZHEN refers to something desirable – good qualities or happiness. In these cases, traditional Confucian and Daoist interpretations reveal the meaning quite accurately. However, there are not a small number of expressions where ZHEN relates to difficulties or where it is not desirable. In order to clarify meaning of these fragments, the author paid special attention to such problematic situations. Below there is one example of a detailed analyses. For other hexagrams only summarized conclusions will be given.

In Hexagram 3, Line 5 the meaning of ZHEN becomes ambiguous, because there are definite preconditions for an auspicious result. Line words say: **small ZHEN**

---

1   This phrase can be encountered most often, 35 times in the whole text.

auspicious, big ZHEN inauspicious (*xiao ZHEN ji, da ZHEN xiong* 小贞吉 , 大贞凶). Different commentaries and translations[1] explain this phrase as follows:

- "Image commentary" (*Xiang zhuan* 象传): "It is not the time for action, yet."[2]

- Wang Bi[3]: "For actions of small ones it is auspicious. For works of great men – inauspicious."[4]

- Li Dingzuo[5]: "It is advisable to look for the partner (wife) in Line 4, not to aspire for the distant goal in Line 2."[6]

- Li Guangdi[7]: "Possible small things. Big things not possible." (Li Guangdi, 2011)

- Tang Yi[8]: "Small rain[9] brings good luck, big – bad luck."[10]

- James Legge[11]: "With firmness and correctness there will be good fortune in small things; (even) with them in great things there will be evil."[12]

- Richard Wilhelm[13]: "Small persistence brings good luck, big – bad luck."[14]

- Julian K. Shchutsky[15]: "Firmness in the small things – good luck. Firmness in

---

1   Sources are listed chronologically, starting from earliest Chinese commentaries and ending up with recent Western translations.
2   易经［周易］原文 [EB/OL]. 易学网 , 2011. https://www.eee-learning.com/article/571, 2019-12-28
3   Wang Bi (3.cent.).
4   王弼 , 韩康伯 , 孔颖达 :《 周易正义 》,《 十三经注疏 》中华书局 1979 年版 , https://www.eee-learning.com/article/643, 2019-12-28
5   Li Dingzuo (8.cent.).
6   李鼎祚 : "四库全书经部 : 易类 : 周易集解" [EB/OL]. 易学网 , 2011.http://www.eee-learning.
7   李光地（ 1642—1718 ）。
8   当代学者。
9   The upper trigram symbolizes water or rain.
10 唐颐 :《 图解易经智慧宝典 》, 台北华为国际出版社 2013 年版。
11 1815-1897
12 Legge J. (transl.). Sacred Text Archive: The I Ching [EB/OL]. http://www.sacred-texts.com/ich/index.htm, 2019-12-28.
13 1873–1930 .
14 Wilhelm R. (transl.). I Ging: Text und Materialien [M]. Köln: Diederichs, 1986: 38.
15 Юлиан К.Щуцкий (1897-1938)

big things – bad luck."[1]

- Geoffrey Redmond: "For minor matters divination auspicious; for major ones, ominous."[2]

- Rudolf Ritsema: "The small, Trial: significant. The great, Trial: pitfall."

- Edward L. Shaughnessy: "Little determination is auspicious, great determination is inauspicious."

- Wu Chung: "Conditions suitable for limited progress but detrimental for great undertakings."

A literal translation of the word ZHEN is very problematic. It depends highly on the given situation and also upon other words, mentioned in the phrase. Moreover, in Zhou Dynasty there were no syntactic marks, all characters were written one after another. Only later, Chinese scholars added dots for separating ideas, phrases or sentences. Content interpretations can vary greatly depending on the division of characters. For example:

- *Wu yong yong zhen.* 勿用永貞。Not necessary a lasting persistence.

    Wu yong. Yong zhen. 勿用。永貞。Don't handle. Lasting persistence.

l*Sang qi tong pu. Zhen li.* 丧其童仆。貞厉。Lose own servant boy. Confidence in danger (*or*: confidence in spite of danger, confidence is dangerous).

Sang qi tong pu zhen. Li. 丧其童仆貞。厉。Lose own servant boy's trust. Danger.

- Zhen ji. 貞疾。Confidence in illness (*or*: confidence is illness).

    Zhen. Ji. 貞。疾。Confidence. Illness.

---

1 Щуцкий Ю. К. (пер.). Конфуций: Уроки мудрости: Китайская Классическая "Книга Перемен" [M]. Москва: Эксмо, 2008: 615.
2 Redmond G. The I Ching (Book of Changes): A Critical Translation of the Ancient Text [M]. London: Bloomsbury, 2017: 78.

- Fu zhen li. 妇貞厉。Wife's virtues are dangerous.

  Fu . Zhen. Li. 妇。貞。厉。Wife. Confidence. Danger.

  Fu. Zhen li. 妇。貞厉。Wife. Confidence in danger.

Chinese scholar Wu Xinchou 吴辛丑 analyses "Zhou yi" text according to the Western grammar rules, defining the functions of ZHEN as subject, object or predicate. He holds a view that the meaning can be distinguished with this method.[1] Mostly he gives the verbal meaning "to ask diviner a question", analysing words before and after ZHEN as direct of indirect objects of object phrases that can consist of nouns, verbs, adjectives etc.[2] It is true, that words in "Zhou yi" are closely linked to each other, and their meanings are interdependent, however, they also depend on the situation represented by hexagram schemes.

The division of Chinese characters in words and phrases is still a very disputable matter, for scholars and commentators often divide them differently, basing on their own experience and argumentation. Therefore the author of this article supports the view of Zhu Xingguo that it is the best to treat the word ZHEN as a seperate unit, not combining it with other words or phrases.[3] Another option is to give only the phonetical transcription in the text and to add a thorough explanation in respective commentaries, as suggested by Xiong Yihua.[4]

VI. Conclusion

In "Zhou yi" the word ZHEN has non-transparent, multilayered implementations; the basic text (even with the help of Classical commentaries) does not reveal the exact meaning of the word in every place. Every reader and commentator can allocate meanings differently, depending on his or her experience and knowledge. "Meaning cannot be regarded as fixed or static, but is constantly evolving. It arises

---

1　吴辛丑:《〈周易〉"贞"字结构分析》,《华南示范大学学报》2003 年第 6 期。
2　Ibid.
3　朱兴国．卜辞"贞"字及相关问题新论 [EB/OL]．中国社会研究院历史研究所, 先秦史研究室, 2007. http://www.xianqin.org/xr_html/articles/jgyj/465.html, 2019-12-28
4　熊谊华:《〈周易〉中"贞"的英译探折》,《湖北函授大学学报》2016 年第 11 期。

from the constant process of negotiation between competing concepts." Perhaps, one should not pursue the truth of a natural origin, but should rather require the interrogation of these competing interpretations that combine to produce the ultimate meaning.[1]

"Zhou yi" is not a polished, monolithic treatise, but a constantly changing scheme where contradictions are found in every sentence; it is contributing to the emergence of infinite new meanings and interpretations. It talks about changes and is changing itself, urging readers to keep in mind several options of the truth, to analyze opposites in cycles of constant change and to prepare for new challenges.

Characters, their meanings and schemes of "Zhou yi" have been evolving for thousands of years, and now, they have built the bases for Chinese vocabulary and everyday expressions. Now when the book has reached Western society and many translations have been done, meanings of words continue to change even more intensely, adapting to actual realities and to the mentality of Western people.

French grammatologist Jacques Derrida said that words exist through their "functioning within a classification and therefore within a system of differences".[2] The real value of "Zhou yi" consists in the factor that the reader can unfold new opportunities, integrating words into new chains and correlations. The word ZHEN does not even imply a definite group of meanings, but rather a spacious, many-dimensional experience that is not limited in time and space, thus opening the door to understanding the essence of universe and eternity.

1　Turner C. Critical Legal Thinking: Jacques Derrida: Deconstruction [EB/OL]. http://criticallegalthinking.com/2016/05/27/jacques-derrida-deconstruction/, 2019-12-28.
2　Derrida J., Spivak G. Ch. (transl.). Of Grammatology [M]. Baltimore: John Hopkins Press, 1976: 109.

儒家政治思想与新丝绸之路

罗杰里奥 【墨西哥】
墨西哥蒙特雷科技大学　国际关系项目主任

一　引言

20世纪以来,世界经历了前所未有的社会和政治变化,促使各国领导人寻求更好的治理方式。近几十年来,全球相互依存不断加深,外交事务变得越来越重要。中国提出的"一带一路"倡议旨在加强许多国家之间的经济一体化和政治合作并有助于各国间文明交流。

"一带一路"倡议的灵感来自古代丝绸之路——一条连接亚洲和欧洲的陆路贸易路线。自汉朝(公元前206—公元220年),中国开始向中亚派遣官方贸易团,随后它到达了中东、非洲和欧洲。古代丝绸之路有两条贸易路线:陆地和海上。陆路是丝绸之路的起点,几个世纪后,海上航线成为另一个地点。在整个隋唐时期(581—907年),陆地丝绸之路蓬勃发展,它成为一个重要的经济和文化交流区。在宋朝(960—1279年),随着指南针的发明,中国的航海技术得到了发展,海上航线取代了陆路航线,因为它更容易运输货物,也更方便快捷地到达其他地区。

"一带一路",也被称为"新丝绸之路",是一个基础设施互联互通项目,从陆路连接东亚与欧洲("一带"),从海上连接东南亚、非洲和欧洲("一路")。"一带一路"倡议最早由中国国家主席习近平于2013年提出。如今,中国和参与国为实现这一目标进行了大量的共同努力。当前,中国向多个国家注入了大量资金,许多项目都处于起步阶段，全球政治经济相互依存日益明显。

20世纪70年代末改革开放后，中国经历了一个转折点。通过从命令经济或计划经济转向更为市场化的经济，经济实力显著增强，其政治取向采用了新的治理方式，因为它必须适应当时的地缘政治。此外，大约在同一时间，儒家传统有了复兴。经过几十年的边缘化，学术界重新开始讨论儒家传统，中国共产党（CPC）开始将重要的儒家概念引入政治话语中，如小康社会和和谐社会。

本文探讨了"一带一路"发展过程中可能出现的一些潜在问题，旨在说明儒家思想在为这些问题提供更好结果方面的相关性。政府、学者、企业和组织将"一带一路"视为一个激动人心而又复杂的项目。对于这个项目是否真的会让所有参与者受益，或者它是否只会有助于中国成为下一个全球霸权，有着正面和负面的假设。中国政府的目标是保持经济稳定，促进国家的经济繁荣和维护社会政治稳定；这也表明"一带一路"参与经济体将获得可观的收益。本文的结论是，现代儒家思想，特别是其政治方面，可以用来改善国际权力关系，以应对全球相互依存，中国将在21世纪形成和塑造一种新的全球政治文化。

二 转型中的中国

到了20世纪中叶，许多国家将资本主义作为其经济和政治制度。两次世界大战后，经济发展成为社会和政治稳定的基础。各国开始以更大的规模进行贸易，从而必然会在经济上相互依存。总的来说，全球相互依存可被称为全球化——这是一种现代人类经验，在许多方面是有价值的，但在其他方面是有害的。

20世纪70年代末，中国寻求新的发展，实施了多项改革，特别是经济改革，以应对中国在21世纪即将面临的挑战。经济从计划经济转向市场经济，在东部沿海设立经济特区，欢迎外国直接投资。所谓的四个现代化增强了中国的农业、工业、国防和科技水平。在这一时期，中国致力于通过工业化（中国尚未开发的发展领域）改善国内条件，并开始显著推进其现代化进程。

另一个在中国转型中要考虑的重要事项是20世纪80年代中期的教育改革。这为儒学的学术复兴提供了机会。中国学术界的儒家学术受到学者的欢迎，来自海外的华人和非华人学者应邀参加会议，就儒家传统的实用性和价值进行了有趣的辩论[1]。关于儒学的价值和对未来意义的讨论引起了人们的关注，儒学家们开始对这一传统有了更多的信心。不同领域的专家看到了中国的现状如何受到社会行为和模式的广泛影响[2]。同样，政府开始看到投资中国最伟大的文化遗产的好处。

目前，资本的需要和使用是进步和稳定的同义词。中国是世界上最大的经济体之一，正寻求通过"一带一路"倡议，促进经济、政治、社会和文化层面的国际合作。经济上，"一带一路"将促进中国和其他参与经济体之间的贸易往来，促进商品和服务在国际和洲际层面的流动。文化方面，旅游业将得到发展，新的艺术节、博物馆交流、文学比赛和烹饪文化等将促进多元文化的发展，目的是创造文化意识、相互理解和更紧密的多边文化纽带。

中国在20世纪末经历的经济和政治转型在全球范围内产生了影响。中国正在利用其文化、政治和经济实力推动国家进步，并在地缘政治上拥有更好的地位。中国已经成为世界上最强大的国家之一，它有能力在经济合作和政治关系上倡导一种不同的方式。中国可以利用其儒家文化遗产，在发展"一带一路"的同时，提供人道的支持。除了强调提高个人道德品质，善政和维护和平的社会关系是儒家哲学的基本目标。

三 多边合作

任何以贸易为目的连接两个或两个以上国家的基础设施项目都需要政治合作。许多双边和多边贸易协定已经签署并付诸实施，如非洲大陆自由贸易区、北美自由贸易协定、中亚区域经济合作计划、东南亚国家联盟和大湄公河次区域计划等。"一带一路"将是一个新的贸易集团，沿着欧亚大陆延伸，将通过陆海相通，到达东南亚、非洲、中东和西欧。此外，其他没有连接到"一带一路"的国家将参与并受益于该计划的基础设施项目。

沿着一带一路，许多现存的贸易集团和贸易协定将受到影响。经合组织的一份报告指出，"创造和改善'一带一路'的自由贸易区块是'一带一路'的明确

---

1 Umberto Bresciani, *Reinventing Confucianism: The New Confucian Movement* (Taipei Ricci Institute for Chinese Studies, 2001), 30-32, 427-51.
2 Daniel A. Bell, "Exchanges: Reconciling Confucianism and Socialism," *The China Beat Blog Archive 2008-2012* (2010).

目标。"[1] 其目的是加强自由贸易并利用现有贸易路线。为了实现这一目标，需要达成政治协议。政府官员必须与当地以及外国实体、决策者、企业、银行、机构和组织合作，因为需要他们参与并在该计划中发挥重要作用。"一带一路"是一个洲际基础设施项目，将改变世界贸易格局。新的贸易模式将出现并得到发展，希望以明智和和谐的方式进行，以推进区域经济合作。

近几十年来，中国发展了一套成熟的政治和经济关系体系。它与邻国建立了参与、援助、贸易和投资的多边渠道，并试图与地理范围以外的发展中国家建立更好的关系。20世纪，中国是最大的外援受援国之一，而今天，它是最大的援助提供者之一。中国通过最近成立的国家国际开发合作署（CIDCA）向其他国家提供援助和投资，并从中受益。该机构旨在与邻国建立更密切的关系，因为中国的近邻经济和政治稳定符合中国的利益，这也意味着进步和秩序。

中国政府宣称在其外交事务中实行"不干涉政策"，但研究表明，它应该清楚地阐明这一政策的含义，因为对于中国而言，更有创造性和建设性的参与方式正成为帮助其快速增长的必要方式[2]。现在已有70多个国家签署了与"一带一路"相关的协议，中国必须确保该项目运行良好，特别是在易受社会经济不稳定和政治动荡影响的国家。

自世纪之交以来，中国通过财政援助和其他资助计划巩固了其对外关系。一项研究表明，2000年至2014年间，近140个国家从中国官方发展援助和其他官方资金流中获得了基础设施资金，建造了近4300个基础设施项目。数据显示，中国在六个地理区域投资了3500多亿美元，使其成为几个国家最大的单一资金来源。[3] 因此，许多政治领导人质疑中国在为基础设施项目融资或向其他国家提供外援方面的真实意图。中国官员表示，他们希望沿着"一带一路"推动经济繁荣，并倡导全球参与。然而，截至2018年，中国建筑公司已在"一带一路"合同中获得了近3500亿美元的资金，这是"一带一路"投资预期初始成本的三分之一，

---

1 《中国在全球贸易、投资和金融领域的"一带一路"倡议》（OECD，2018），第31页。
2 参见 Chen Zheng, "China Debates the Non-Interference Principle," *The Chinese Journal of International Politics* 9, No. 3 (2016).
3 Axel Dreher et al., "Aid, China, and Growth: Evidence from a New Global Development Finance Dataset," *AIDDATA: A Research Lab at William & Mary* (2017): 1-2.

预计成本会随着"一带一路"的进展而变化。[1] 然而,这并不意味着本地企业不会在其运营中得到任何利益或利润,但这确实表明,许多中国企业家和公司将从此类合同中获利,从而在本国与其他国家的运营之间形成巨大差距。

此外,中国对原材料的需求呈指数级增长,几年后,中国零售市场将成为世界上最大的市场。这就是为什么中国将"一带一路"作为二十一世纪的关键事业之一的其中一个原因。该倡议除了加强旅游和文化交流外,还促进了一带一路走廊的经济繁荣与合作。由于中国对商品和服务的高需求,本国人民将从该倡议中受益。从中国进口原材料和其他资源将更加容易,使中国公司能够轻松生产产品并将其运送到国内外的众多目的地,这不可避免地会创造一个更大的全球市场。

四 儒家思想与商业实践

随着商业世界的发展,人们创造了不同的工业化机制和管理战略来提高生产。在东亚,许多商业实践都与儒家文化有关。例如,儒家思想深植于日本和韩国的商业文化中,代表这两个社会的伦理体系和家庭价值观在很大程度上借鉴了儒家思想的哲学和历史根源。道德和价值观从个人延伸到家庭、朋友圈、同事和社区中的人际关系。日本和韩国的企业实践融合了儒家价值观(和其他地方习俗)和西方形式的企业组织结构[2]。同样,在中国台湾和香港地区以及新加坡也有一些亚洲最发达的经济体,因为这些区域也被认为融合了儒家文化。如今,儒家伦理在商业实践中正得到学者和商业专家的认可和检验,以证明某些儒家价值观如何体现在管理实践中。

一些东亚国家在商业界奉行儒家价值观。儒家思想有一个等级关系体系,在不同的公司中有不同的层次。例如,儒家商业道德的理想是通过精英管理实现职位晋升,管理者鼓励员工之间建立和谐、相互尊重的关系,而不管他们的职位如

---

[1] Lily Kuo and Niko Kommenda, "What Is China's Belt and Road Initiative?" *The Guardian*, 30 July, 2018. Although there is not a definite amount of money appraised for the BRI, some sources estimate there will be an average of US$1-8 trillion invested, see Jonathan E. Hillman, "How Big Is China's Belt and Road," *Center for Strategic and International Studies*, 2018.

[2] Marc J. Dollinger, "Confucian Ethics and Japanese Management Practices," *Journal of Business Ethics* 7, No. 8 (1988); Chong-Yeong Lee and Hideki Yoshihara, "Business Ethics of Korean and Japanese Managers," *ibid*.16, No. 1 (1997); Heungsik Park, Michael T. Rehg, and Donggi Lee, "The Influence of Confucian Ethics and Collectivism on Whistleblowing Intentions: A Study of South Korean Public Employees," *ibid*.58, No. 4 (2005).

何。显然，并不是每个公司都实行这样的做法，有许多公司的职位晋升是通过腐败或关系网等不同手段获得的。

儒学哲学家提出了一种称为"C"理论的综合管理哲学。他认为，道德在个人层面上对个人起作用，以管理自我，而管理则允许人们在制度上与其他同事保持联系，并富有成效。他运用中国的文化传统和哲学，将文化、价值观和哲学融入管理研究，以改进管理实践[1]。"C"理论以"创造力""中心性""变化"和"协调性"四个中文术语为基础，从儒家的角度将理性主义和人文主义管理实践结合起来，目的是培养德行兼备的商业领袖[2]。

也有学者对中国本土价值观与消费者行为和商业模式的关系进行了研究。迈克·汤姆森将儒家思想视为中国本土价值观的核心，但区分了本土价值观和美德。对汤普森来说，"本土价值观已经脱离了其道德根源……指的是非道德的行为或做法"，而美德"则明显与个人和人际的伦理行为有关：勇气、节制、正义和仁爱"。[3]他注意到，在盈利之前，儒家企业家注重正义的商业实践；同样，他认为国有企业试图维持社会稳定，而不是利润最大化。[4]

如今，中国人期望企业家和政府官员对社会负责。儒家理念或美德，包括君子（模范人物）、礼（礼节）、仁（仁）、信（诚）、义（义），可以在商业实践中实施，以达到以下目的：（1）在所有的员工中维持一个受人尊敬的工作环境；（2）将消费者的需要而非利润放在首位；（3）和气生财。尽管儒家传统强调权力的等级制度，但在应用于现代管理实践时，不需要将其视为负面因素。每一个企业、机构或组织都有某种等级制度，需要得到尊重，每一个角色都需要参与者完成，以实现目标。显然，东亚公司所奉行的儒家伦理体系无疑适应了现代商业实践。因此，那些认为儒家思想提出的古代等级制治理或其他方法在今天无法在不同的公司层面上实施的结论是错误的。

五　了解并理解中国人

中国文化和非中国文化能否和谐相处？近几十年来，中国受到许多国家的

1　Chung-ying Cheng, "The 'C' Theory: A Chinese Philosophical Approach to Management and Decision-Making," *Journal of Chinese Philosophy*, No. 19 (1992): 126.

2　同上，第 146-148 页。

3　Mike Thompson, "Signals of Virtue in Chinese Consumerism and Business," *Journal of International Business Ethics* 3, No. 2 (2010): 71.

4　同上，第 74-75 页。

欢迎。它在160多个国家设有大使馆，在世界各地的高等教育机构中设立了大约480所孔子学院。它是许多国家的重要贸易伙伴，其文化和艺术在国际上得到广泛推广。中国作为一个紧密的政治、教育、商业和文化伙伴，让许多国家受益。毫无疑问，与这个亚洲巨人保持良好或积极的关系是有益的。双方可以从经济和技术交流、资源分配、共享医疗进步和集体解决共同问题中获益。

当前富裕的中国已成为其他国家的模范。世界上许多国家都希望像中国一样繁荣。他们希望加强经济建设，改善人民生活，并迅速适应前所未有的社会政治和经济转型。然而，目前还不确定中国是否会在"一带一路"沿线受到欢迎——即使政治领导人已经签署了协议。渐渐地，中国人民将会出现在"一带一路"沿线国家：许多中国公司将会建立起来，他们将会带来成千上万的中国工人，而其他与该项目有关的人将会推广中国的文化、历史和传统。此外，流入的中国产品将会增加，当地企业将与中国新企业展开竞争，而且已经或将会签署大量合同和协议，地方自治团体也有可能采用中国的管理方式。

参与"一带一路"的经济体将以投资和消费本国产品为条件，促进经济增长。随着中国企业的到来，产品可以很容易地被中国人以有竞争力的价格出售。对于本土公司来说，这种竞争可能是有害的。目前，中国公司往往提供同等或更便宜的价格，有时，这些产品的质量还可能更好。因此，这将是中国企业向其他市场拓展的机会。在这方面，如果当地企业想要跟上中国的步伐，他们可能会觉得有必要采用中国的管理策略——这为企业和企业家提供了一个向中国学习或想出新的、更有竞争力的方法的机会之窗。

此外，地方政府也将采取类似的做法。中国政府可以监管参与"一带一路"的中国银行、公司和组织的运作方式，因为它们将被要求不断报告其海外业务。因此，政府掌握着关于这些问题的宝贵信息，必须通过仔细规划来保证经济效益。在中国，这些机构必须遵守政府已经制定的法律法规。在国外，中国政府将拥有很大的决策权，因为它是向其他相关方提供财政激励的最重要提供者之一。因此，中国政府将在书面合同和协议中设置特定的条件，以确保他们的经济愿景和地缘政治战略与他们的世界观一致，而这些文件的设计应该使所有人受益。因此，各国有可能会考虑"中国式"行事方式，接受其中许多条件，缘于发展经济符合他们自身的利益。

要了解中国，就必须了解中国的文化。一般来说，东亚人以集体而非个人的方式看待他们的社会关系。新加坡前总理李光耀（Lee Kwan-Yew）在20世纪90年代发起的著名的亚洲价值观与西方价值观辩论广泛讨论了这个话题。这场辩论使西方世界看到，有多少亚洲新兴经济体正在利用其文化价值观和传统迅速适应曾经由西方列强指导和引导的现代化进程。许多亚洲价值观是基于儒家思想和哲学的。儒家思想倡导尊重、孝顺、人道和正义的价值观。这些价值观是儒家文化固有的，他们越来越意识到不仅需要了解或理解这些价值观，而且需要将其付诸实践。这种做法正在逐步塑造社会伦理和民生，这些都可以很容易地适用在"一带一路"沿线。

儒家思想强调自我修养的必要性，以使自己成长为一个道德高尚的人。一个自我修养的人明白，在任何一个社区都涉及各种责任。一个道德高尚的人应该以身作则，同样地，在更大的社会范围内，以有益的方式行事。大多数在商业运营中使用儒家思想的公司都是东亚公司。然而，将儒家价值观融入非东亚国家的商业实践是可以实现的。许多在儒家文化国家之外开设工厂的东亚公司仍然保持基于其文化价值观和传统的商业战略。然而，为了适应目的地国家或地区的行政或官僚程序，需要进行一些改变或调整。

随着国际贸易和全球化的发展，特别是随着"一带一路"等项目和倡议的发展，商业战略也在不断演变。公司、机构、政府、大学和其他组织制订教育计划，为感兴趣的个人提供在特定国家或地区开展业务的具体方式方法。例如，2006年，伦敦经济学院、清华大学和国家汉办（隶属于教育部）在伦敦成立了孔子商学院。尽管学生们并没有接受严格的儒家哲学或伦理教育，但它确实教会了人们理解中国（和其他东亚国家）商业运作的不同方面。人们接受中国语言和文化培训，以及一些管理和商业交流活动，以更有效地认识中国的商业文化和实践。人们可能会问，学术界、商界领袖和政府官员是否可以鼓励类似的教育项目，并在"一带一路"沿线的商业发展中践行儒家价值观。

六　结论

儒家的政治思想与伦理道德和德治紧密相连。在儒家思想中，治理的艺术应该通过道德权威来实现，并与特定的仪式保持一致，这有助于在政治领导人和社会之间建立一个稳定、和平、和谐的环境。儒家思想是一项古老的传统，虽然没有必要完全抛弃它所建议的传统治理方式，但有必要寻求一种共识，使传统儒家思想能够适应现代伦理制度。尽管各个国家利益有差别，但重要的是"求同存异"在世界各国人民和政府之间建立共识。最终的追求必须是让所有人受益，有共同的目标，并为共同利益而合作。

目前，中国政府正在把"一带一路"倡议作为互利共赢的象征。习近平主席的讲话特别注重和平、发展、民主、正义和公平。随着"一带一路"倡议提供的贸易能力提升，将为许多国家带来经济转型，预计这种经济转型将提高数百万人的生活水平。

与其他国家保持良好的经济和政治关系符合中国政府的利益，因为这将有助于实现其总体国内和国际目标。"一带一路"沿线国家如果想要与中国各种组织建立适当的关系，就必须理解中国。因此，所有参与经济体都必须对中国习俗和文化传统，特别是对儒家思想有一个基本的了解。自20世纪80年代以来，儒学逐渐受到中国学术界重视，逐渐在其政治话语中体现。此外，中国政府已经意识到儒家思想成为海外大众了解中国和中国文化的重要方面。

Confucian Political Ideology and the New Silk Road

Rogelio Leal / Mexico

The Monterrey Institute of Technology and Higher Education / Director of International Relations Program

I. Introduction

The unprecedent social and political changes that the world experienced during the twentieth century have made political leaders to search for better ways of governing. In recent decades, global interdependence has raised, and foreign affairs have become as important as domestic affairs. The twenty-first century will be witness of a new global political culture—one that involves numerous countries and regions—with the rise of China, especially as it develops the Belt and Road Initiative (BRI). This initiative aims to enhance economic integration and political cooperation amid many nations, and it can be useful to harmonise Chinese and non-Chinese cultures.

The BRI was inspired by the ancient silk road, a trading land route linking Asia to Europe. Since the Han dynasty (206 BCE-220 CE), China started sending official trading commissions to Central Asia; subsequently, reaching the Middle East, Africa and Europe. There were two trading routes of the ancient silk road: land and maritime. The land route was the starting point of the silk road, and centuries later, the maritime route became an alternate venue. Throughout the Sui and Tang period (581-907), the land silk road flourished. It became an important economic and cultural exchange zone. During the Song period (960-1279), navigation technology in China was developed with the invention of the magnetic compass, and the maritime route became an alternative to the land route as it was easier to transport goods and it became a convenient way to reach faster other regions.

The Belt and Road, also known as the New Silk Road, is an ambitious infrastructure connectivity project linking East Asia with Europe by land (the "Belt") and with Southeast Asia, Africa, and Europe by sea (the "Road"). The BRI was initially proposed by Chinese President Xi Jinping in 2013, it became one of the three national strategies the following year, and today, numerous joint efforts by China and participating nations to make it happen are in progress. Presently, a massive flow of money is being injected by China into several countries, many projects are in their initial stages, and global political and economic interdependence is becoming more evident.

After the reform and opening of the late 1970s, China experienced a turning point. The economy significantly strengthened by shifting from a command or planned economy to a more market-oriented economy, and its political orientation adopted novel ways of governing as it had to adapt the geopolitics of the time. Moreover, around the same time, the Confucian tradition had a resurgence. Discussions on the Confucian tradition were reopened in academic circles after decades of being marginalised, and the political rhetoric of the Communist Party of China (CPC) started to introduce important Confucian concepts into their political discourses such as *xiaokangshehui* (moderately well-off society) and *hexie shehui* (harmonious society).

This essay explores some potential problems that may arise as the BRI is developed and aims to illustrate the relevance of Confucianism in providing better outcomes for such problems. Governments, scholars, corporations, and organisations take the BRI as an exciting yet complex project. There are both positive and negative suppositions of whether this project will actually benefit everyone involved or if it will only serve for China to become the next global hegemon. The Chinese government aims to maintain a stable economy and to develop the economic prosperity and the social and political stability of the country; likewise, it suggests that BRI participating economies will have comparable benefits. It is concluded that modern Confucianism, especially its political aspects, can be used to ameliorate power relations internationally in response to global interdependence, and that a new global political culture will be formed and shaped by China in the twenty-first century.

II. China in Transition

By the mid-twentieth century, many nations adopted capitalism as their economic and political system. After the two world wars, economic proliferation became the basis for social and political stability. Nation-states began to trade with one another at greater scales, and, subsequently, they were bound to economic interdependence. In general terms, global interdependence can be referred to as globalisation—a modern human experience that has been valuable in many ways and detrimental in many others.

In the late 1970s, China sought new areas of development. The economy was liberalised: it went from a planned economy to a market economy, Special Economic Zones (SEZs) were opened in the east coast, and foreign direct investment was welcomed. The so-called Four Modernisations strengthened Chinese agriculture, industry, defense, and science and technology. This was a period where China aimed to improve its domestic condition through industrialisation—an area of development that China had not yet exploited—and began to significantly advance in its modernisation processes.

Another important item to consider in China's transformation are the educational reforms of the mid-1980s. These provided an opportunity for Confucianism to be reinvigorated academically. Confucian scholarship in Chinese academic circles was celebrated by mainland scholars, and Chinese and non-Chinese scholars from overseas were invited to participate in conferences where interesting debates on the usefulness and value of the tradition were taking place.[1] Scholars of Confucianism began to have more confidence in the tradition, and discussions on its value and significance for the future raised eyebrows. Experts in diverse fields saw how the status quo of China was widely affected by the behaviours and patters of society.[2] Equally, the government started seeing the benefits of investing in China's greatest cultural heritage.

Currently, the need for and use of capital is synonymous to progress and stability. China is one of the largest economies of the world and is seeking to promote international cooperation at economic, political, social, and cultural levels through the Belt and Road Initiative. Economically, the BRI will allow China and other participating economies to improve their trade, and it will facilitate the flow of goods and services at an international and intercontinental level. Culturally, tourism will develop and new arts festivals, museum exchanges, literature competitions, and culinary culture, to name a few, will promote multiculturalism. The aim is to create cultural consciousness, mutual understanding, and closer cultural bonds multilaterally.

The economic and political transformation China experienced in the late twentieth century has had effects at a global scale. China is using its cultural, political, and economic potential to progress as a nation and to have a better geopolitical stand. China has become one of the most powerful nations in the world, and it has the capacity to instigate a different approach to economic cooperation and political relations. Good governance and maintaining peaceful social relationships

---

1 Umberto Bresciani, *Reinventing Confucianism: The New Confucian Movement* (Taipei Ricci Institute for Chinese Studies, 2001), 30-32, 427-51.
2 Daniel A. Bell, "Exchanges: Reconciling Confucianism and Socialism?", *The China Beat Blog Archive 2008-2012* (2010).

are fundamental objectives of the Confucian philosophy in addition to stressing the need to enhance the moral character of individuals.

III. Multilateral Cooperation

Any sort of infrastructural project that connects two or more countries for trading purposes requires political cooperation. Numerous bilateral and multilateral trading agreements have been signed and put into practice such as the African Continental Free Trade Area, the North American Free Trade Agreement, the Central Asia Regional Economic Cooperation Program, Association of Southeast Asian Nations, and the Greater Mekong Subregion Program, to name a few. The BRI will be a new trade bloc stretching along Eurasia that will reach South East Asia, Africa, the Middle East, and Western Europe via land and sea—in addition, other countries not connected to the Belt and Road corridor will participate and benefit from the planned infrastructure projects.

Along the Belt and Road, numerous existing trade blocs and trade agreements will be affected. A report by the OECD states that "creating and improving free trade blocks along the Belt and Road is an explicit objective of the BRI."[1] The intent is to enhance free trade and take advantage of existing trading routes. To accomplish this, political agreements need to be reached. Government officials must work with local and foreign entities—policy makers, businesses, banks, institutions, and organisations—since all partake and play an important role in the initiative. The BRI is an intercontinental infrastructure project that will transform world trade. New trade models will emerge and be developed to advance regional economic cooperation, hopefully in a wise and harmonious way.

In recent decades, China has developed a mature system of political and economic relationships. It has created multilateral channels of participation, aid, trade, and investment with neighbouring countries in addition to trying to establish

---

1 "China's Belt and Road Initiative in the Global Trade, Investment and Finance Landscape" (OECD, 2018), 31.

better relations with developing nations outside its geographical sphere. Last century, China was one of the largest recipients of foreign aid, and today, it is among the largest aid providers. China benefits from providing aid and investing in other countries through the recently formed China International Development Cooperation Agency (CIDCA). This agency aims to cultivate closer relationships with neighbouring countries as it is in the interest of China that its close neighbours are economically and politically stable as this equates to progress and order.

The Chinese government declares it practices a "non-intervention policy" in its foreign affairs, yet studies suggest that it should clearly state what this policy stands for as more creative and constructive ways of involvement on the part of China are becoming necessary to assist in its rapid growth.[1] Now that more than 70 countries have signed agreements in relation to the BRI, China must assure that the project runs well, especially in countries that are susceptible to socio-economic instability and political turmoil.

Since the turn of the millennium, China has solidified its foreign relations through financial aid and other funding programmes. A study shows that between 2000 and 2014, nearly 140 countries received infrastructure funding from the Chinese official development assistance and other official flows creating nearly 4,300 infrastructure projects. The data reveals that more than US$350 billion was invested in six geographical regions, making China the single largest source of finance for several countries.[2] Consequently, many political leaders question the true intentions of China when it comes to financing infrastructure projects or providing foreign aid to other nations. Chinese officials state that they want to promote economic prosperity along the Belt and Road and that the initiative is open for global participation. However, as of 2018, Chinese construction companies have secured nearly US$350 billion in BRI contracts, this is about one-third of the expected initial cost of the

---

[1] See for example, Chen Zheng, "China Debates the Non-Interference Principle", *The Chinese Journal of International Politics* 9, no. 3 (2016).

[2] Axel Dreher et al., "Aid, China, and Growth: Evidence from a New Global Development Finance Dataset", *AIDDATA: A Research Lab at William & Mary* (2017): 1-2.

Belt and Road investment—the estimated costs vary and will shift as the BRI progresses.[1] This, however, does not mean that local firms will not see any benefits or profits reflected in their operations, but it does suggest that many Chinese entrepreneurs and companies will profit from such contracts creating a large gap between Chinese operations and those of other countries.

Furthermore, the need of China for raw materials has augmented exponentially, and in few years, the Chinese retail market will be the largest in the world. This is one of the reasons why China has made the BRI one of its key undertakings of the twenty-first century. The initiative promotes economic prosperity and cooperation along the Belt and Road corridor in addition to reinforcing tourism and cultural exchanges. Due to the high demand of goods and services that China is undergoing, Chinese nationals will benefit from the initiative. It will be easier to import raw materials and other resources to China allowing Chinese companies to easily make products and export them to numerous destinations in and outside China inevitably creating a larger global market.

IV. Confucianism & Business Practices

As the business world develops, different mechanisms of industrialisation and managerial strategies are created to enhance production. In East Asia, many business practices are linked to the Confucian culture. For instance, Confucianism is embedded in Japanese and Korean business culture. The ethical system and family values that represent both societies heavily borrow from the philosophical and historical roots of Confucianism. Ethics and values extend from the individuals to their interpersonal relationships within their families, circle of friends, work colleagues, and the community. Corporate practices in Japan and Korea integrate Confucian values (and other local customs) and Western forms of business

---

1 Lily Kuo and Niko Kommenda, "What Is China's Belt and Road Initiative?" *The Guardian*, 30 July, 2018. Although there is not a definite amount of money appraised for the BRI, some sources estimate there will be an average of US$1-8 trillion invested, see Jonathan E. Hillman, "How Big Is China's Belt and Road," *Center for Strategic and International Studies*, 2018.

organisational structures.¹ The same goes for Taiwan, Hong Kong, and Singapore—some of the most developed economies in Asia—as these societies are considered to be culturally Confucian as well. Today, Confucian ethics in business practices are being recognised and examined by scholars and business experts to demonstrate how certain Confucian values are represented in managerial practices.

Several East Asian countries practice Confucian values in the business world. Confucianism has a system of hierarchical relationships which is used at various levels in different companies. For example, the ideal of Confucian business ethics is that job promotions are achieved through meritocracy and that managers encourage harmonious and respectful relationships among workers regardless of their position. Obviously, not every company implements such practices, there are numerous companies were job promotions are obtained through different means such as corruption or by *guanxi* (network of relationships).

Confucian philosopher Cheng Chung-ying developed and proposed an integrative philosophy of management called the "C" Theory. He believes ethics work for the individual at a personal level, to govern the self, while management allows people to be institutionally connected to other colleagues and be productive. He uses Chinese cultural traditions and philosophy to integrate culture, values, and philosophy into managerial studies for refined management practices.²

Other scholars have researched on the relationship between Chinese indigenous values and consumer behaviours and business patterns. Mike Thomson takes Confucianism as the core of Chinese indigenous values but differentiates between indigenous values and virtues. For Thompson, "indigenous values have become

---

1 See for instance, Marc J. Dollinger, "Confucian Ethics and Japanese Management Practices", *Journal of Business Ethics* 7, no. 8 (1988); Chong-Yeong Lee and Hideki Yoshihara, "Business Ethics of Korean and Japanese Managers", ibid.16, no. 1 (1997); Heungsik Park, Michael T. Rehg, and Donggi Lee, "The Influence of Confucian Ethics and Collectivism on Whistleblowing Intentions: A Study of South Korean Public Employees", ibid.58, no. 4 (2005).
2 Chung-ying Cheng, "The 'C' Theory: A Chinese Philosophical Approach to Management and Decision-Making", *Journal of Chinese Philosophy*, no. 19 (1992): 126.

detached from their ethical origin and...refer to behaviours or practices that are *non-ethical*" whereas virtues "are distinctly concerned with personal and interpersonal ethical behaviour: courage, moderation, righteousness and benevolence."[1] He observes that, before profit making, Confucian entrepreneurs focus on righteous business practices; similarly, he argues that state owned enterprises attempt at maintaining social stability instead of maximising profits.[2]

Today, Chinese people expect entrepreneurs and government officials to be socially responsible. Confucian concepts or virtues including *junzi* (exemplary person), *li* (ritual propriety), *ren* (benevolence), *xin* (sincerity), and, *yi* (righteousness) can be implemented in business practices for (1) maintaining a respectable work environment among all workers, (2) to place consumers' needs and not profits as top priority, and (3) to reduce the ecological blueprint. Although the Confucian tradition emphasizes a hierarchical system of authority, it does not need to be taken as a negative aspect when applied to modern managerial practices. Every business, enterprise, institution, or organisation has some sort of hierarchical system that needs to be respected and every single role fulfilled for the partakers to achieve whatever the objective(s) may be. Obviously, the ethical system of Confucianism that is being practiced in East Asian companies is, certainly, adapted to modern-day business practices. Therefore, it is wrong to conclude that the ancient hierarchical system of governance or other approaches proposed by Confucianism cannot be implemented today at different corporate levels.

V. Greeting and Understanding the Chinese

Can Chinese and non-Chinese cultures live in harmony? In recent decades, China has been welcomed by many nations. It has embassies in more than 160 countries, there are about 480 Confucian Institutes inside institutions of higher education around the world, it is an important trading partner for many nations, and the arts

---

1 Mike Thompson, "Signals of Virtue in Chinese Consumerism and Business", *Journal of International Business Ethics* 3, no. 2 (2010): 71.
2 Ibid., 74-75.

and culture are being widely promoted internationally. Many countries benefit from having China as a close political, educational, commercial, and cultural partner. It is certain that having good or positive relationships with the Asian giant is beneficial. Both parties can benefit from economic and technological exchanges, resource distribution, sharing medical advancements, and tackling common problems collectively.

Due to its present affluence, China has become a model nation for other countries. Many nations worldwide want to be as prosperous as China. They would like to enhance their economy to ameliorate the people's livelihood and rapidly adapt to unprecedented socio-political and economic transformations. However, it is still uncertain whether the Chinese will be positively greeted and welcomed along the Belt and Road corridor—even if political leaders have already signed agreements. Gradually, Chinese people will be physically seen in BRI countries: many Chinese companies will be built, and they will bring along thousands of Chinese workers, and others affiliated to the project will be promoting Chinese culture, history, and traditions. Additionally, the inflow of Chinese products will augment, local businesses will compete with newly established Chinese businesses, and it is expected that local governments may adopt Chinese ways of governing since numerous contracts and agreements have been or will be signed.

Participating Belt and Road economies will be conditioned to invest in and consume their own local products for economic proliferation. With the arrival of Chinese businesses and enterprises, products can be easily sold by the Chinese at competitive prices. For the local companies, this sort of competition can be detrimental. Currently, Chinese companies tend to provide equal or cheaper prices, and at times, these could also be of better quality. Thus, this will be an opportunity for Chinese businesses and enterprises to expand to other markets. In this regard, local businesses may feel obliged to adopt Chinese managerial strategies if they want to keep up with them—allowing a window of opportunity for businesses and entrepreneurs to learn from the Chinese or come up with new and more competitive ways.

Moreover, local governments will take a similar approach. The Chinese government can regulate how the Chinese banks, companies, and organisations that will partake in the BRI operate as they will be required to constantly report their overseas operations; thus, the government holds valuable information on them and must guarantee economic benefits through careful planning. In China, such organisms must abide by the laws and regulations already set by the government. In foreign countries, the Chinese government will have a lot of decision-making power since it is one of the most important providers of financial incentives to the rest of the parties involved. As a result, the Chinese government will place specific sets of conditions in the written contracts and agreements to assert that their economic vision and geopolitical strategy align with their worldview; yet, these documents should be devised to benefit all. So, it is possible that countries will take into consideration the "Chinese way" of doing things as they shall accept many of those conditions because it will be in their interest to advance their economies.

To understand China, it is necessary to understand its culture. Generally, East Asians think of their social relations in a collective rather than an individual manner. This topic was widely discussed by former Prime Minister of Singapore Lee Kwan Yew during the famous Asian vs Western values debate that originated in the 1990s. This debate helped the Western world see how many Asian emerging economies were using their cultural values and traditions to rapidly adapt to the modernisation processes that once were directed and guided by Western powers. Much of the Asian values are based on the ideas and philosophies of Confucianism. Confucianism inculcates values of respect, filial piety, humaneness, and justice. These values are intrinsic to people pertaining to Confucian civilisations, and they are becoming more conscious of the need to not only know or understand them but to put them in practice. Such practices are gradually shaping the social ethic and livelihood of people, and these could be easily adapted along the Belt and Road corridor.

Confucianism emphasises the need for self-cultivation to grow as a morally superior person. A self-cultivated person understands that belonging to any community involves various responsibilities. A morally superior person is expected to lead by example and, similarly, act in ways that that will be beneficial at grater social scales. Most companies that use aspects of Confucianism in their business operations are East Asian. Yet, taking Confucian values into the business practices of non-East Asian nations can be achieved. Numerous East Asian companies that have opened factories outside culturally-Confucian countries still keep the business strategies based on their cultural values and traditions. Some changes or adaptation are, nonetheless, required to acclimatise to or fit in the administrative or bureaucratic processes of the destination country or region.

As international trade and globalisation develop, particularly with projects and initiatives such as the BRI, business strategies evolve. Companies, institutions, governments, universities, and other organisations develop educational programmes to provide interested individuals with specific tools to conduct business operations in particular countries or regions. For instance, the London School of Economics, Tsinghua University, and Hanban (under the Ministry of Education) launched in London a Confucian Institute for Business in 2006. Although students are not strictly taught Confucian philosophy or ethics, it does teach people to understand different dimensions of how business is conducted in China (and other East Asian countries). People are trained in Chinese language and culture and several managerial and business communication activities to recognise more effectively Chinese business culture and practices. One can ask if the academic community, business leaders, and government officials could encourage similar educational programmes and the practice of Confucian values for business development along the BRI.

VI. Concluding Remarks

Confucian political ideology is tied to ethics and virtuous ruling. In Confucianism, the art of governing should be done by means of moral authority and keeping in line with specific rituals that help establish a stable, peaceful, and harmonious environment among political leaders and the society. Although

Confucianism is an ancient tradition, it might not be necessary to fully abandon the traditional ways of governing it suggests, but it is necessary to search for a consensus where those traditional Confucian ways can be adapted to modern ethical systems. Because interests differ, it is important to establish consensuses between the peoples and governments of the world. The ultimate pursuit must be to benefit all, have shared goals, and cooperate in ways for the common good.

Currently, the Chinese government is using the Belt and Road Initiative as a symbol of co-existence and mutual benefit. The conferences of President Xi Jinping seem to be notably motivated by peace, development, democracy, justice, and fairness. With the trading capabilities that the Belt and Road Initiative will offer, social and political challenges along the corridor will emerge. This project will bring about economic transformations for many nations, and with this, it is expected that such economic transformations will elevate the living standards of millions of people.

It is in the interest of the Chinese government to have good economic and political relations with other nations as this will help them achieve its overall domestic and international goals. The nations along the Belt and Road corridor, must understand China in Chinese terms if they want to have proper relations with all the Chinese organisms that will eventually enter the country. Therefore, it is essential for all participating economies to have a basic understanding of Chinese mores and cultural traditions, specifically Confucianism. Since the 1980s, the Chinese government allowed Confucianism to reappear in Chinese academic circles, and gradually, they have used aspects of Confucianism in their political discourses. Also, the government has realised that Confucianism is one of its most valuable cultural heritages, so they have been using it to promote China and Chinese culture overseas.

As the Belt and Road develops, diverse challenges will emerge; these can be tackled by taking into consideration politicised and non-politicised aspects of Confucianism while the BRI begins to take shape. Most modern Confucian discourses exemplify positive features of the tradition that could be applicable today, and the Chinese government can take advantage of these discourses to use Confucian political ideology to serve the necessities of its citizens and of the countries along the Belt and Road corridor. In recent decades, Confucianism has been widely examined, and it reappeared as a source to answer modern socio-political matters. Also, interesting discussions of Confucianism in areas of leadership, managerial practices, and the environment have come up. Confucianism is a philosophical tradition that can guide people to mature as individuals through self-cultivation and create a better environment by establishing harmonious interpersonal relationships.

References

Bell, Daniel A. "Exchanges: Reconciling Confucianism and Socialism?" . *The China Beat Blog Archive 2008-2012* (2010).

Bresciani, Umberto. *Reinventing Confucianism: The New Confucian Movement*. Taipei Ricci Institute for Chinese Studies, 2001.

Cai, Xiang, Xiahui Che, Bangzhu Zhu, Juan Zhao, and Rui Xie. "Will Developing Countries Become Pollution Havens for Developed Countries? An Empirical Investigation in the Belt and Road." *Journal of Cleaner Production* 198 (October 10 2018): 624-32.

Chan, Yuk Wah, and Sin Yee Koh. *New Chinese Migrations: Mobility, Home, and Inspirations*. Routledge, 2017.

Cheng, Chung-ying. "The 'C' Theory: A Chinese Philosophical Approach to Management and Decision-Making." *Journal of Chinese Philosophy*, no. 19 (1992): 125-53.

"China's Belt and Road Initiative in the Global Trade, Investment and Finance Landscape." OECD, 2018.

Dollinger, Marc J. "Confucian Ethics and Japanese Management Practices." *Journal of Business Ethics* 7, no. 8 (1988): 575-84.

Dreher, Axel, Andreas Fuchs, Bradley Parks, Austin Strange, and Michael J. Tierney.

"Aid, China, and Growth: Evidence from a New Global Development Finance Dataset." *AIDDATA: A Research Lab at William & Mary* (2017).

Fukuyama, Francis. "Confucianism and Democracy." *Journal of Democracy* 6, no. 2 (1995): 20-33.

Hall, David L., and Roger T. Ames. *The Democracy of the Dead: Dewey, Confucius, and the Hope for Democracy in China*. Carus Publishing Company, 1999.

Hillman, Jonathan E. "How Big Is China's Belt and Road." *Center for Strategic and International Studies*, 2018.

Kim, Sungmoon. *Confucian Democracy in East Asia: Theory and Practice*. Cambridge University Press, 2014.

Kuo, Lily, and Niko Kommenda. "What Is China's Belt and Road Initiative?" *The Guardian*, 30 July, 2018.

Lee, Chong-Yeong, and Hideki Yoshihara. "Business Ethics of Korean and Japanese Managers." *Journal of Business Ethics* 16, no. 1 (January 01 1997): 7-21.

Li, Peiyue, Hui Qian, Ken W. F. Howard, and Jianhua Wu. "Building a New and Sustainable "Silk Road Economic Belt"." *Environmental Earth Sciences* 74, no. 10 (November 01 2015): 7267-70.

Narins, Thomas P. "Evaluating Chinese Economic Engagement in Africa Versus Latin America." *Geography Compass* 10, no. 7 (2016): 283-92.

Ni, Peimin. "Confucianism and Democracy: Water and Fire? Water and Oil? Or Water and Fish?" . In *Polishing the Chinese Mirror: Essays in Honor of Henry Rosemont, Jr.*, edited by Marthe Chandler and Ronnie Littlejohn, 89-108: Global Scholarly Publications, 2007.

Park, Heungsik, Michael T. Rehg, and Donggi Lee. "The Influence of Confucian Ethics and Collectivism on Whistleblowing Intentions: A Study of South Korean Public Employees." *Journal of Business Ethics* 58, no. 4 (June 01 2005): 387-403.

Sullivan, Jonathan, and Jing Cheng. "Contextualising Chinese Migration to Africa." *Journal of Asian African Studies* 53, no. 8 (2018): 1173-87.

Tan, Sor-hoon. "Democracy in Confucianism." *Philosophy Compass* 7, no. 5 (2012): 293-303.

Thompson, Mike. "Signals of Virtue in Chinese Consumerism and Business." *Journal of*

International Business Ethics 3, no. 2 (2010): 71-79.

Xi, Jinping. "Secure a Decisive Victory in Building a Moderately Prosperous Society in All Respects and Strive for the Great Success of Socialism with Chinese Characteristics for a New Era." In *Delivered at the 19th National Congress of the Communist Party of China*: Xinhuanet.com, 2017.

Zheng, Chen. "China Debates the Non-Interference Principle." *The Chinese Journal of International Politics* 9, no. 3 (2016): 349-74.

丝绸之路上的罗马：关于中古汉语中"拂菻"名称起源的几点思考

冯海城 【马其顿】

翻译

一 历史背景

"拂菻"这一名称在中国文献中首次出现是在《隋书》中，一本关于隋朝（581-618）官方记录的历史书：

> 波斯每遣使贡献。西去海数百里，东去穆国四千余里，西北去拂菻四千五百里，东去瓜州万一千七百里。[1]

学者普遍认为这里提到的"拂菻"一词指的大致是罗马帝国的领土，或者至少指的是东地中海的一半。中国史料中的"拂菻"这个名称取代了更早的名称"大秦"，该名称首次出现在《后汉书》的"西域传"部分[2]：

> 大秦国，一名犁鞬，以在海西，亦云海西国。地方数千里，有四百余城。小国役属者数十。以石为城郭。列置邮亭，皆垩墍之。有松柏诸木百草。[3]

---

[1] 《隋书·卷八十三》。
[2] 范晔（398—445）。
[3] 《后汉书·西域传》, 24。

由于拂菻出现的时间较晚[1]，这个名称也有资格更准确地指代东罗马帝国，即拜占庭。

再说大秦这个名字，其主要来源是《后汉书》记录的甘英于公元97年奉西域都护班超（32-102年）之命出使大秦。

> 和帝永元九年，都护班超遣甘英使大秦，抵条支。[2]

也许更早的文字证据"大秦"[3]这个名字可以在《列仙传》中找到，最早可追溯到西汉末期（公元前206年至公元9年），最迟在西晋（265-317年）期间：

> 后周德衰，乃乘青牛车去，入大秦。[4]

二 尝试解释"拂菻"这个名称

"拂"和"菻"这两个字的发音，在中古汉语中重建的名字通常是 *piət（或 *pʰut）和 *lim[5]，其基本语音结构为：

1）双唇辅音—嗓音—齿音
2）流音—嗓音—鼻音

这种重构可以与当代粤语"拂菻"的发音相比较——fat¹-lam¹。对于这些字符的古汉语发音，舒斯勒（Schuessler）[6]将它们重构为：*phət - *rem。

重建的古汉语地名 *piət-lim 的第二个音节通常被解释为最小形态元素 rom 的语音再现——来自罗马的原始名称，例如拉丁语：Roma，或希腊语：'Ρώμη。

然而，"拂菻"的第一个音节"拂"（ *bat / *piət）出现了一个问题，因为它

---

1 《隋书》于636年完成，距离西罗马帝国于476年崩溃200年。不过，从语言学角度来看，这是无关紧要的，因为在以君士坦丁堡为中心的罗马帝国（现在主要讲希腊语）中，罗马名没有资格被用于自指。

2 《后汉书·西域传》，22。

3 但这并不排除一种可能性，即在这种情况下，这片土地及其名称的最终信息来源也取决于甘英的西行。

4 《列仙传·老子》。

5 Cf. Pulleyblank, Edwin G. *Lexicon of Reconstructed Pronunciation in Early Middle Chinese, Late Middle Chinese, and Early Mandarin*. Vancouver: University of British Columbia Press, 1991; p. 99, p. 194.

6 Schuessler, Axel. *ABC Etymological Dictionary of Od Chinese*. Honolulu: University of Hawaii Press; p. 41, p. 359.

似乎是多余的。为了解释这一点，有人提出它代表一个辅音，通常是来自中亚中间语言的唇音，罗马的名字就是通过这个辅音进入中国的。这个词是在伊朗中部地区的语言中找到的。没错，罗马的名称在那里包含这样一个首辅音：

中古波斯语：hrwm[1]

帕提亚语：frwm

粟特语：ßr'wm

大夏语：fromo

我们提出了另一种在中古汉语中传播罗马名称的模式，其最终形成了以"拂菻"指借"罗马"的名字。

在早期几个世纪，这个名字进入中国的中间语言可能不是某种中古波斯语言，而是一种闪族语言，或者更准确地说是叙利亚语。这种语言，现在我们讨论的是被称为古典叙利亚语的语言，它最初是黎凡特和美索不达米亚地区所说的阿拉姆方言连续体的一部分，是历史悠久的叙利亚北部古城埃德萨周围地区的方言[2]，在《旧约和新约》被翻译成《圣经》后，从公元二世纪一直持续到公元五世纪初，它在国际上引起了广泛关注[3]。《圣经》的叙利亚语译本，即所谓的《别西大译本》（Peshitta）成为所有叙利亚语教堂的官方经文版本，包括东方教会（Church of the East, Ēdtā' d-Madenḥā），叙利亚东正教[4]和安提俄克大主教的梅尔凯特教堂[5]，古典的叙利亚语也获得了教会大臣的官方礼仪和行政语言的地位。

因此，作为"拂菻"（*bat lam/*piət-lim）名称起源的可能解决方案就是：bēth 字面意思是"家"、"住所"，但在上下文中，当与地理术语搭配时，它只意味着"国家"、"王国"（在语义上与汉语"家"相当，比如说"国家"）。有很多这种用法的例子，比如 Bēth Qatrayē，Bēth Sinaye 成为东方教会的中国分教会等。

我们不妨这样假设，"拂"（*bat/*piət）代表叙利亚语单词 *bēth*，而"菻"（*lam/*lim）代表叙利亚语单词 *Romayē* 的词根。通过这种方式，罗马/罗马帝国名称在古汉语中的完整传播路径可以重建为：Roma > 'Pώμη > Bēth Romayē > *bat-lam / *piət-lim。根据语音相近程度，"拂菻"（*bat-lam/*piət-lim）名称中的音节

---

1 这种特殊的形式可以与亚美尼亚语的 -hrom 相比较，并且不排除亚美尼亚语版本的罗马名称是从中波斯语中借用的。

2 土耳其东南部的桑利乌法。

3 Terminus ante quem 是在公元 411-435 年担任埃德萨主教拉布拉。

4 米阿菲斯特教会，经常被其批评者称为雅各布派教会。

5 与占主导地位的希腊人和后来的阿拉伯人共享地位。

*bat/*piət 最好被解释为叙利亚语 bēth 的翻版，它与叙利亚语完全共享语音结构（双唇辅音—人声辅音—牙齿辅音），而不是来自某些中古波斯语言的单一首辅音的代表。

三 名称的传播者

至于谁可能是 Bēth Romaye 这个名字的直接传播者，显而易见，很有可能是东方教会的神职人员和信徒，叙利亚语在该教会中既是礼仪语言，也是行政语言。现有记录充分证实了唐代东方教会（或所谓的"景教"教会）的存在，在中文资料中被称为"景教"。叙利亚语在摩尼教范围内也具有"官方语言"的地位，在唐朝时期也存在于中国。事实上，叙利亚语在唐代的存在已经被敦煌的文字库以及散布在全国各地的碑文所证明。然而，在这里，我们似乎面临着一个按时间顺序排列的难题。东方教会在中国存在的最早记载来自七世纪，即 635 年阿罗本（Āluóběn）和他的手下抵达长安：

> 太宗文皇帝，光华启运，明圣临人，大秦国有上德，曰阿罗本，占青云而载真经，望风律以驰艰险。贞观九祀，至于长安。

正如上文提到的，已知最早提到的"拂菻"，包含在次年完成的《隋书》中。时间跨度确实很小，尽管从理论上讲，《隋书》的编纂者和数据收集者并非不可能通过这些新来的神职人员或叙利亚商人以及其他较早到达中国的入境者，获得有关（东）罗马帝国的信息。

如果有证据证明东方教会在中国存在更早，我们的解释就更加合理。 说到这里，我在公元 5 世纪上半叶杨玄之的《洛阳伽蓝记》中找到了一段奇特的文字，记载了北魏（385—535）洛阳佛教机构的状况：

> 永明寺，宣武皇帝所立也，在大觉寺东。时佛法经像盛于洛阳，异国沙门，咸来辐辏，负锡持经，适兹乐土。世宗故立此寺以憩之。房庑连亘，一千余间。庭列脩竹，檐拂高松，奇花异草，骈阗堦砌。百国沙门，三千余人。西域远者，乃至大秦国。[1]

---

1 《洛阳伽蓝记》，第四卷。

这段经文的奇怪之处在于，它提到了佛教的苦行僧，即沙门，来自大秦，即罗马帝国。然而，罗马帝国几乎没有任何本土佛教僧曾前往中国。因此，如果我们要在《洛阳伽蓝记》中保存这一说法的真实性，则以下假设之一应该是正确的：

1）文中提到的僧侣实际上是佛教徒，但他们并非来自大秦。这意味着，杨玄之所认定他们的来源地是错误的，也许是他在地理上的夸张，因为他们可能来自"遥远的西方"，但这并不像作者所说的那么远，他们最多可能是中亚某个地区的本地人。

2）这些僧侣实际上来自大秦，即罗马帝国。这意味着几乎可以肯定他们不是佛教僧侣，但很可能是基督徒[1]。这意味着作者（或公众）只熟悉外国佛教僧侣，无法理解他们的真正宗教身份。

换句话说，要么我们保存他们的宗教身份，要么我们保存他们的地理身份。然而，如果第二个假设是正确的，那么我们将获得关于基督教神职人员在中国存在的历史记录。由于这要早于唐朝，因此不难想象，上述来源仅记录了基督教僧侣或普通人偶然访问中国的一个例子。从这个角度来看，我们可以看到中国在公元635年正式建立了东方教会的教会组织，而阿罗本（Alopen）到达长安只是代表教会承认在中国已经有一个基督教社区。这需要一项最终建立主教团并形成一个新的教会省的法规。

关于《洛阳伽蓝记》中提到的大秦僧人，不难想象，他们是在罗马东方因基督教论争议（431年的以弗所议会和451年的卡尔西顿议会）而卷入更大动乱的背景下来到中国的。受这种混乱影响最大的地区是罗马黎凡特的讲叙利亚语的土地。关于叙利亚僧侣旅行的记忆保存完好，例如，在埃塞俄比亚教堂中，它回忆起在五世纪后期逃离罗马东部的埃塞俄比亚所谓的九圣徒的定居点，他们基本上建立了埃塞俄比亚的修道院。我们在佐治亚州也遇到过类似的情况，13位亚述神父在六世纪来到高加索后被认为在现在的佐治亚州建立了修道院传统。由于我们提到的神学争议，罗马皇帝芝诺（425–491年在位）于489年关闭了著名的埃德萨学校，该学校的教职人员被怀疑有景教倾向，之后这些僧侣不得不逃往伊朗。总而言之，在五六世纪，有很多讲叙利亚语的僧侣在流动，其中一些人可以通过丝绸之路来到中国，这并不难想象。从时间上看，所有这些事件都与北魏时期相吻合，即杨玄之所说的，大秦的僧人来到中国。

---

[1] 也不太可能是摩尼教教徒。

回到我们讨论的内容。至少可以确定了公元五世纪在中国存在讲叙利亚语的僧侣的合理性，这足以说明在《隋书》中首次提到"拂菻"这个名称之前，这个名称的起源很可能是叙利亚语短语 Bēth Romayē。我们推测"拂菻"这个名字逐渐取代中文资料中的"大秦"而作为罗马帝国的指称原因。"大秦"和"拂菻"的最初使用语境完全不同。在使用"大秦"的情况下，很容易假设这个名称是由甘英或班超发明的，他们是那个时代唯一接近罗马统治地区的中国人。这个名称完全是中国人命名的名称。

而"拂菻"代表了一个由罗马统治地区的当地人或至少来自他们附近的人使用的名称。因此，前者的名称可以被认为是外来语地名，而后者是地名。故"拂菻"的第二个音节是罗马原名的中文译名。唐朝时，他们从"遥远的西方"、靠近（东）罗马帝国的地区涌入，自然而然地，新来者所使用的名称在中国人心中扎下根，而"大秦"则隐退为一个古老而庄严的名称。

Rome on the Silk Road: Some Thoughts on the Origin of the Toponym " 拂菻 "(Fúlǐn) in Middle Chinese

Igor Radev / Macedonia

Translator

I. The Historical Background

The first known mention of the name " 拂菻 "(Fúlǐn) within the corpus of Chinese literature is contained in the *Book of the Suí* (隋书 : Suí Shū), the official historical record of the Suí Dynasty (隋 ; 581-618)[1]:

"波斯每遣使贡献。西去海数百里，东去穆国四千余里，西北去拂菻四千五百里，东去瓜州万一千七百里。"[2]

Ambassadors from Persia regularly make tribute missions. Going to the west from there for hundred *lǐ* is *Hǎishù*, while going to the east for more than four thousand *lǐ* the country of *Mù* is situated. Going in the direction of northwest for four thousand and five hundred *lǐ* is *Fúlǐn*, and going towards the east for one thousand and seven hundred *lǐ* is *Guāzhōu*.

---

1 Completed in 636.
2 《隋书·卷八十三》.

It is generally considered uncontroversial that the appellation *Fúlǐn* as mentioned here was used to refer roughly to the territory of the Roman Empire, or at least to its eastern Levantine half. In this role, *Fúlǐn* in Chinese literary sources supersedes the earlier name *DàQín* (大秦), which occurs for the first time in the *Xīyù-zhuàn* (西域传) section of the *Book of the Later Hàn* (后汉书 : Hòu Hànshū):[1]

"大秦国，一名犁鞬，以在海西，亦云海西国。地方数千里，有四百余城。小国役属者数十。以石为城郭。列置邮亭，皆垩墍之。有松柏诸木百草。"[2]

The Realm of Dà Qín is also called Líjiān. As it is situated to the west of the sea, it is also named the Land of West Sea (Hǎixī). Its territory extends for several thousands of *li*. It contains more than four hundred walled cities. There are several tens of smaller kingdoms under it. The walls of the cities are made of stone. They have established postal relays at intervals, which are all plastered and whitewashed. There are pines and cypresses, as well as many sorts of trees and plants.

Due to the later time of the initial appearance of *Fúlǐn*,[3] this designation is also qualified as to refer more precisely to the Eastern Roman Empire, i.e. Byzantium.

Returning now to the name *Dà Qín*, as primary sources for this name in the *Book of the Later Hàn*, for the most part served the records of the western expedition of Gān Yīng (甘英) launched in 97 AD on the instructions of general Bān Chāo (班超 ; 32-102 AD):

"和帝永元九年，都护班超遣甘英使大秦，抵条支。"[4]

Perhaps an even earlier textual attestation of the name " 大秦 " (*Dà Qín*)[5] we can find in a Daoist text - *Biographies of Holly Worthies* (列仙傳 : Liè Xiān Zhuàn),

---

1 Written by Fàn Yè (范晔 ; 398-445 AD).
2 《后汉书·西域传》, 24.
3 The *Book of the Suí* being being completed in 636, almost two hundred years after the collapse of the Western Roman Empire in 476. Though, from linguistic viewpoint this is irrelevant since the Roman name without any qualifications was used for self-reference in the (now mainly Greek speaking) Roman Empire centered on Constantinople.
4 《后汉书·西域传》, 22.
5 Though this doesn't precludes the possibility that in this case also the ultimate source of information about the existence of this land and its name also depends on Gān Yīng's expedition.

the composition of which is usually dated at earliest in the later years of the Western Hàn (西汉；206 BC – 9 AD) and at the latest during Western Jìn Dynasty (西晋；265-317):

"后周德衰，乃乘青牛车去，入大秦。"[1]

II. Attemptat Explanation of the name " 拂菻 " (Fúlǐn)

The pronunciation of the two characters < 拂 > and < 菻 >, which constitute the name in question is reconstructed in Middle Chinese usually as *piət (or *pʰut) and *lim[2] and with a basic phonetic structure of:

1) Bilabial Consonant – Vocal – Dental Consonant

2) Liquid consonant – Vocal – Nasal Consonant

This reconstruction can be compared with the contemporary Cantonese pronunciation of " 拂菻 " -fat¹-lam¹. Concerning the Old Chinese pronunciation of these characters, Schuessler reconstructs them as: *phət - *rem.[3]

The second syllable of the reconstructed Middle Chinese toponym *piət-lim has been most often interpreted as phonetic rendition of the minimal morphological element rom- from the original name for Rome, e.g. in Latin: Roma, or in Greek: Ῥώμη.

However, the first syllable of " 拂菻 ", i.e. < 拂 > (*bat / *piət) posed a problem, since it seemed redundant. This has been attempted to be explained away by proposing that it represents a consonant, most often labial one from an intermediary language in Central Asia, through which the name for Rome has entered China. The candidate was sought among the Middle Iranian languages, where, true enough, the

---

1 《列仙传·老子》.
2 Cf. Pulleyblank, Edwin G. *Lexicon of Reconstructed Pronunciation_in Early Middle Chinese, Late Middle Chinese, and Early Mandarin*. Vancouver: University of British Columbia Press, 1991; p. 99, p. 194.
3 Schuessler, Axel. *ABC Etymological Dictionary of Old Chinese*. Honolulu: University of Hawaii Press; p. 41, p. 359.

designation for Rome contained such an initial consonant:

Middle Persian: hrwm[1]

Parthian: frwm

Sogdian: ßr'wm

Bactrian: fromo

We, on the other hand, propose another model for the transmission of the name for Rome in Middle Chinese, producing eventually the form of "拂菻" (Fulin).

The intermediary language through which this name entered China in the early centuries of the common era perhaps wasn't some Middle Iranian language, but a Semitic one, or more precisely – Syriac. This language, and now we are talking about what is specifically called – Classical Syriac, originally part of the Aramean dialect continuum spoken all over the Levant and Mesopotamia, as the dialect of the region around the ancient city of Edessa in historical northern Syria,[2] got an international prominence after the Bible (the Old and the New Testament) has been translated into it during a process that lasted from the II Century till the beginning of the V Century.[3] The Syriac translation of the Bible, the so called *Peshitta* became the official version of Scripture for all the Syriac language churches, including the Church of the East: Ēdtā' d-Maḏenḥā), the Syrian Orthodox Church[4] and the Melkite Church of the Antiochian Patriarchate,[5] classical Syriac also obtaining the status of official liturgical and administrative language of ecclesiastical chancelleries.

Thus, as a possible solution for the question concerning the origin for thename < 拂菻 > (*bat-lam / *piət-lim) to be Bēth Romayē, where bēth literally denotes

---

1 This particular form can be compared with the Armenian - *hrom*, and it is not excluded that the Armenian version of the name for Rome is a borrowing from Middle Persian.
2 Sanliurfa in southeastern Turkey.
3 *Terminus ante quem* is the serving of Rabbula as a bishop of Edessa 411-435 AD.
4 The miaphisite Church, referred often by its detractors as the Jacobite Church.
5 The miaphisite Church, referred often by its detractors as the Jacobite Church.

"home", "abode", but contextually when paired with geographic terms, it means simply a "state", "realm" (semantically comparable with the role of the Chinese "家", as in "国家"). We have many examples of such usage, like Bēth Qatraye,[1] Bēth Sinayē for the ecclesiastical province of China of the Church of the East etc…

If we accept this hypothesis, then < 拂 >(*bat/*piət) represents the Syriac word *bēth*, while < 菻 > (*lam/*lim) represents the root of the Syriac word *Romaye*. In this way, the full transmission path of the name for Rome / Roman Empire in Middle Chinese we would reconstruct as: Roma > ʻΡώμη > Bēth Romayē> *bat-lam / *piət-lim. Based on phonetic closeness, the syllable *bat / *piət in the name < 拂菻 > (*bat-lam / *piət-lim) is better accounted for as a rendition of the Syriac bēth, with which it completely shares the phonetic structure (bilabial consonant – vocal – dental consonant), rather than as a representation of a single initial consonant from some Middle Iranian language.

III. Carriers of the Name

As to who might have been the direct human transmitters of the name Bēth Romaye, the obvious candidate is the clergy and the laity of the Church of the East, where Syriac served both as liturgical and administrative language. The presence of the Church of the East (or so called "Nestorian" Church), designated in Chinese language sources as "景教" (Jǐngjiào) during Tang Dynasty era is copiously confirmed by the available record. Syriac also had the status of the "official language" within the confines of the Manichean religion, also present in China at the time of the Tang Dynasty. In fact, the presence of the Syriac language in Táng China is attested by a corpus of texts from Dunhuang, as well as epigraphic monuments scattered across the country. Yet, here it seems we are confronted with a chronological conundrum. The earliest record for the presence of the Church of the East in China comes from the VII Century, namely the arrival of Alopen (阿罗本 :Āluóběn) and his men in Chángān in 635:

---

1 Sharing the status with the dominant Greek and later Arabic.

The cultured emperor Taizong causedsplendor and prosperity, and he treated the people as behoofs an enlightened and sagelike. There was a Worthy in thekingdom of Dàqín, called Āluóběn. As he had interpreted the azure clouds, he then loaded the truthful scriptures, observed duly the tunes of the wind and hadthus overcome all the difficulties so as to arrive in Chángān in the ninth year of Zhēnguān (i.e. 635).

On the other hand, the earliest known mention of *Fúlǐn*, as we have already said, is contained within the *Book of the Suí* completed the following year. The time span seems very narrow indeed, though it wouldn't be theoretically impossible for the compilers and data gatherers for the *Book of the Suí* to get information on the (Eastern) Roman Empire either through these newly arrived clerics, or perhaps through Syriac merchants and other arrivals that had come to China on an earlier date.

A better shot at plausibility we would have if there was some evidence for even earlier presence of the Church of the East in China. Speaking of that, I managed to find a curious passage from the *Record of Buddhist Establishments in Luòyáng* 《洛阳伽蓝记》 written by Yáng Xuànzhī (杨衒之) somewhere in the first half of V Century, recording the state of the Buddhist institutions from the Northern Wèi (385-535) era Luòyáng.

The Yǒngmíng monastery, which was established by Emperor Xuānwǔ, is located to the East of Dàjué monastery. At that time the scriptures of the Buddha's Dharma and the Buddhist images were very popular in Luòyáng, and Śramaṇas from foreign lands carrying staffs and sutras all gathered in this propitious land. Shìzōng built this monastery in order to house them. Rows of tall bamboos grew in the courtyard and lofty pine trees touched the eves of the roof. Strange flowers and exotics plants grew abundantly around the stairway.

Śramaṇas from hundred a land, more than three thousand of them were there. From the extreme west, even from *Dàqín* they came.

What is so strange about this passage, is that it mentions Buddhist ascetics, i.e. Śramaṇas as having come from *Dàqín*, that is to say the Roman Empire. Well, hardly there would have been any native Buddhist monks in the Roman Empire that could have made their way to China. So, if we are to save the veracity of this claim in the *Record of Buddhist Establishments in Luòyáng* either one of the following suppositions should be true:

1) The monks in questions were really Buddhists, but they didn't come from *Dàqín*. This would mean that the identification of their place of origin by Yáng Xuànzhī was mistaken, perhaps a geographic hyperbole on his part, in the sense that though they might have come from the "far West", still this was not as far as the author claims, at most they could have been natives of some area of Central Asia.

2)The monks really had come from *Dàqín*, i.e. the Roman Empire. The import of this would be that they were almost certainly not Buddhist monks, but most probably Christian. This could only mean that the author (or the general public for that matter) being familiar only with Buddhist foreign monks, failed to comprehend their true religious identity.

In other words, either we save their religious identity or we save their geographic identity. If, however, the second hypothesis is true, then we would have obtained a first historical record about Christian clerics being present in China. Since this predates the Táng Dynasty, then it is not inconceivable to suppose that the said source recorded just one instance of what could have been a regular occurrence of Christian monastics or laymen visiting China on occasions. From this perspective, we could see the formal establishment of an ecclesiastical structure of the Church of the East in 635 AD in China with the arrival to Chánga'ň of Alopen simply a recognition on the behalf of the Church that in China there was already a Christian community that needed a regulation with an eventual establishment of an episcopal see and forming a new ecclesiastical province.

Concerning the monks from *Dàqín* mentioned in the *Record of Buddhist*

Establishments in Luòyáng, it is not far fetched to imagine that they made their way to China within the context of the larger turmoil that engulfed the Roman East as a consequence of the Christological controversies connected with the Council of Ephesus of 431 and the Council of Chalcedon from 451. The most affected areas from this confusion were the Syriac speaking lands of the Roman Levant. It suffices to remember that a great movement of monks was started at that time as a result of persecution and the general nature of these theological disputes. The memory about travelling Syriac monks is well preserved, for example, in the Ethiopian Church that recalls the settlement of what it calls the Nine Saints in late V Century in Ethiopia fleeing from the Roman East, and who basically established Ethiopian monasticism. Similar case we have in Georgia with the Thirteen Assyrian Fathers who after coming to the Caucasus in the VI Century are credited with establishing the monastic tradition in what is now Georgia. As a consequence of the theological controversies we mentioned, Roman Emperor Zeno (r. 425 – 491) closed in 489 the famed School of Edessa, whose staff were suspected of Nestorian leanings, after which its scholar monks had to flee to Sassanid Iran. All in all, we have a lot of Syriac speaking monks on the move during the V and VI Century, and it is not beyond imagination that some of them could have made their way to China traveling on the Silk Road. And chronologically, all these events coincide with the time span of the Northern Wèi Dynasty, when, according to Yáng Xuànzhī monks from *Dàqín* came to China.

Returning now to our basic topic. Having established at least the plausibility of Syriac speaking monks being present in China in V Century, that it is to say sufficiently before the writing of the first mention of the name "拂菻" (Fúlĭn) in a Chinese source the *Book of the Suí*, it gives credence to the likelihood that the origin of this name is the Syriac phrase Bēth Romayē . As a finishing note, we could make some suppositions on why gradually the name "Fúlĭn" replaced "Dàqín" in Chinese sources as a referent of the Roman Empire. The contexts of the original start of use of "Dàqín" and "Fúlĭn" are completely different. In the case of "Dàqín" it is easy to suppose that this name was invented by Gān Yīng or Bān Chāo, who were the only Chinese of the era to have travelled relatively close to territories under Roman sway. This name is a completely Chinese one.

On the other hand, "Fúlǐn" represents a name communicated by persons who were either natives of lands under Roman rule or at least originated near them. Thus, the former name could be considered an exonym, while the latter is an endonym. As such, the second syllable of "Fúlǐn" is a Chinese rendition of the original name for Rome. During the Táng Dynasty, when there was an influx of people coming from the "far west", areas close to the (Eastern) Roman Empire it was only natural that among the Chinese populace to take root the name which the newcomers themselves used while "Dàqín" was relegated to the status of venerable archaicity.

References

Deeg, Max. "The 'Brilliant Teaching': The Rise and Fall of 'Nestorianism'

(Jingjiao) in Tang China." Japanese Religions 31: 91-110, 2006.

Di Cosimo, Nicola. Maas, Michael. (ed.) *Empires and Exchanges in Eurasian Late Antiquity - Rome, China, Iran, and the Steppe, ca. 250-750.* Cambridge: Cambridge University Press, 2018.

Gillman, Ian and Hans-Joachim Klimkeit. *Christians in Asia before 1550.* Ann

Arbor: University of Michigan Pres,1999.

Hirth, Friedrich. *China and the Roman Orient: Researches into their Ancient and Mediaeval Relations as Represented in Old Chinese Records* (reprint ed.). Leipzig, Munich, Shanghai, & Hong Kong: Georg Hirth; Kelly & Walsh, (1939) [1885].

Johnson, Scott Fitzgerald. 2017. "Silk Road Christians and the Translation of

Culture in Tang China." Studies in Church History 55: 15-38.

Moule, A. C. Christians in China before the year 1550. London: Society for

Promotion of Christian Knowledge, 1930.

Pelliot, Paul. *L'inscription nestorienne de Si-Ngan-Fou*. Edited with Supplements by Antonino Forte. Roma, Paris (Italian School of East Asian Studies Epigraphical Series 2 / Collège de France, oeuvres posthumes de Paul Pelliot),1996.

Pulleyblank, Edwin G. *Lexicon of Reconstructed Pronunciation_in Early Middle Chinese, Late Middle Chinese, and Early Mandarin*. Vancouver: University of British Columbia Press, 1991.

Schuessler, Axel. *ABC Etymological Dictionary of Od Chinese*. Honolulu: University of Hawaii Press.

Les provinces de l'extérieur vues par l'Église-mère, in P.G. Borbone et P. Marsone (éd.), Le christianisme syriaque en Asie centrale et en Chine , Paris, Geuthner 2015, pp. 121-159.

Li Tang and Winkler, Dietmar W. (ed). *Winds of Jingjiao - Studies on Syriac Christianity in China and Central Asia*. Wien: LitVerlag, 2016.

Пигулевская, Нина В. *Культура сирийцев в средние века*. Москва: Наука, 1979.

Takahashi, Hidemi. 2004. Syriac as a Vehicle for Transmission of Knowledge across Borders of Empires. Horizon, 29-52.

中国在法律全球化中的作用：为共同繁荣立规

伊丽莎维塔　【乌克兰】

乌克兰敖德萨州立大学　教授

一　中国在法律全球化和治理中的行动

全球化现象及其对文化和法律制度的影响是巨大的。自 21 世纪初以来，为了进一步整合和提高竞争力，国家和超国家政府开始实施全球规则，催生了法律全球化[1]。

在全球化时代，开放、联通、共享和共赢等理念将逐渐成为现代国家外交政策的关键要素。

中国积极参与法律全球化的形成，自中国政府首次为中国企业制定"走出去"战略以来，将企业对外扩张作为国家未来经济发展的一项重大战略举措[2]。

如今，中国在法律规范和实践的全球化中发挥了自己的作用。

首先，形成了与"一带一路"沿线国家在生态环境保护领域全面开放合作的新格局。

该倡议具有一个全球项目的特点，包含两个倡议精神和行动：

1. 新的"丝路经济带"，主要以陆地为基础，预计将连接中国与中亚、东欧

---

[1] 法律全球化（法律全球化）可以定义为跨国法律结构和话语在世界范围内沿着广度、强度、速度和影响的维度发展。Terence C. Halliday and Pavel Osinsky. Globalization of Law. *Annual Review of Sociology* Vol. 32 (2006), pp. 447-470.

[2] Wang H., Miao L. (2016) "Going Global Strategy" and Global Talent. In: China Goes Global. Palgrave Macmillan Asian Business Series. Palgrave Macmillan, London , p.144.

和西欧；

2."21世纪海上丝绸之路"倡议，这是一个以海洋为基础的项目，旨在将中国南部沿海连接到地中海、非洲、东南亚和中亚。马新民[1]认为这项倡议"……呼吁各国在协商、贡献和分享利益的原则上开展海洋合作，共同应对风险和挑战。中国倡导国际合作，在国际航运、海洋科学研究、海洋环境保护、海上安全保障等领域取得了丰硕成果"。

显然，尽管中国是一个中等收入发展中国家，但中国仍然是世界经济发展的主要驱动力。国际货币基金组织驻华代表团2019年第四条磋商讨论的最新数据显示了这一趋势："2019年和2020年，中国的经济增长预计将分别放缓至6.2%和6.0%，因为计划中的政策刺激部分因为美国最近提高对中国2000亿美元进口商品的关税造成的负面影响被抵消了。随着经济向更高水平发展，到2024年，增长预计将逐渐放缓至5.5%，并迈向可持续发展的态势。2019年，总体通胀预计将上升至2.3%，反映出食品价格上涨。考虑到贸易紧张局势可能进一步升级，近期前景仍然特别不确定"[2]。

中国财富快速增长的历史是以对外贸易为基础的，外交政策与国内的外国居民密切相关。布兰科·米拉诺维奇教授解释说，中国在很长一段历史时期，要么被外国殖民军队入侵，要么被外国人管理通常为国民从事的活动（预算、贸易政策、教育）；或者是因为外国人享有治外法权（不受中国法院审判），或者是因为他们统治了该国的部分地区，或者最后是因为中国有大量外国人（无论是作为人道主义工作者、传教士、技术专家，还是军事顾问）参与其生活。由于大国与中国之间的密切联系，中国的内部政治史既是一部与外国人打交道的历史，也是一部关于中国内部政治的历史[3]。

第二，中国积极参与实现2030年可持续发展议程的17项可持续发展目标。

1　Xinmin Ma, "China and the UNCLOS: Practices and Policies", in *The Chinese Journal of Global Governance*, Vol.5., I.1, 2019, P.9.
2　IMF Press Release #19/196, available at: https://www.imf.org/en/News/Articles/2019/06/05/pr19196-china-imf-staff-completes-2019-article-iv-mission
3　Branko Milanovic. History Without Ideology. A Review of Robert Bickers' "Out of China", *Global Policy Journal*, 01 August 2019, Available at :https://www.globalpolicyjournal.com/blog/01/08/2019/history-without-ideology-review-robert-bickers-out-china]

为了实现可持续发展目标，中国政府发布了《实施议程的国家计划》（2016年）[1]。

第三，中国作为一个负责任的大国，在"一国两制"的实践中，把城市规划作为发展战略的一个重要环节来抓。例如，2019年2月，中央政府颁布了《粤港澳大湾区发展规划纲要》。

二 全球化城市与世界：改革开放时代的上海

为了理解中国政府的行动对法律全球化的重要性，我们可解读《上海2035》这份极具影响力法律文件的精髓。作为第一个远至2035年的特大城市总体规划，以及中国共产党第十九次全国代表大会后国务院批准的第一个总体规划，其作用具有示范性。这份文件全面贯彻落实中国共产党第十九次全国代表大会精神，把习近平新时代中国特色社会主义思想作为指导思想，全面贯彻和落实发展新时期中国特色社会主义的基本政策[2]。

然而，从地理上和战略上讲，上海并不位于中国的中心——上海是一个超级国际金融中心，一个在经济、文化和环境保护方面具有影响力的全球性城市。值得强调的是，上海与世界其他地方有着多种关系。

据潘光教授[3]统计，从1933年到1941年，上海接收了近3万名逃离纳粹迫害和大屠杀的欧洲犹太人。除了那些离开上海前往其他国家的难民，到1941年12月日本轰炸珍珠港时，这座城市已经收容了2万至2.5万名犹太难民。潘光教授引用了西蒙·维森塔尔大屠杀研究中心的数据，根据该中心的数据，上海作为一个城市接收的犹太难民数量超过了加拿大、澳大利亚、新西兰、南非和印度几个国家的总和。

由于国际化的推进，从1978年到1989年春天，上海发生了巨大的经济变化，成为国际金融中心。

1990年，中国政府宣布启动邓小平提出的浦东开发和进一步开放项目。该项

---

1 Qin Tianbao, Hou Fang. China's National Plan on Implementation of the 2030 Sustainable Development Goals: from the Perspective of National Performance of Multilateral Environmental Agreements., in *Journal of Vasyl Stefanyk Precarpathian National University* http://jpnu.pu.if.ua vol. 5, no. 2 (2018), 55-66.

2 Available at: http://www.shanghai.gov.cn/newshanghai/xxgkfj/2035004.pdf

3 Pan Guang. Shanghai: a Heaven for Holocaust Victims. In The Holocaust and the United Nations Outreach Programme, P.65, available at: https://www.un.org/en/holocaustremembrance/docs/pdf/chapter6.pdf

目为上海与伦敦、纽约、东京和巴黎等全球城市一起参与国际经济对话提供了平台。自1992年至今，上海一直被称为经济发展中心。

如今，《2017—2035年上海总体规划》提出了上海成为卓越的国际城市的15年长期目标。到2020年，上海将获得全球影响力，成为科技中心。此外，上海将保持强大的文化、生态、海洋全球影响力城市地位。

《2017—2035年上海市总体规划》由上海市人民政府组织编制并获国务院批准。它是上海辖区内城市规划、建设和管理的依据和正式文件，是指导上海未来发展的重要文件，是实现"城市，让生活更美好"的发展蓝图。

"城市，让生活更美好"最初是作为2010年世博会的主题出现的，展示了上海这次展览的理念。2010年世博会是中国第一届世博会，也是有史以来规模最大的一届世博会。2010年10月16日，世博会在一天内参观人数达到100多万。

回顾世博会的历史，值得一提的是，上海市人民政府在"十二五"规划中将世博会博物馆（WEM）项目列为重大文化设施建设项目。该项目于2010年11月23日启动，当时上海市人民政府和国际展览局（BIE）在法国巴黎正式签署了《世博博物馆合作备忘录》，将世博博物馆定义为BIE唯一的官方博物馆和授权文件中心。

WEM选址在15-02街区，即原上海世博会园区文化博览区的第15个社区，北至龙华路东侧，南至巨门路，西至15-01街区，东至蒙自路。占地面积4公顷，总建筑面积46550平方米，总开放管理面积90580平方米。建筑高度为34.8米（地上6层，地下1层）。WEM于2013年12月底开工，是上海新的文化地标。

今天，世博会博物馆通过世博会展馆和一般的地方展览来展示中国对世界城市的看法。世博会激发了文化旅游的灵感，吸引了大批观众——游客在一个城市里周游世界。

从历史上看，中国博物馆与包括乌克兰在内的欧洲和后苏联国家有着密切的经济、政治和文化联系。目前，中乌文化经济合作正在蓬勃发展。

2019年4月25日至27日，在北京举行的第二届"一带一路"国际合作高峰论坛（BRF）上，乌克兰代表团提出了一个联合项目组合：发展港口基础设施、替代能源设施、修建公路和桥梁、发展铁路和机场设施、高科技、航空航天、农产品加工方面的合作。乌克兰寻求在乌克兰工业现代化方面开展合作，并建立联合生产设施。在论坛期间，乌克兰代表团同意签署乌克兰政府和中国政府之间的投资协议，总金额为 3.4 亿美元，将在克里门舒格建造一座横跨第聂伯河的大桥。乌克兰将积极参与乌中一带一路倡议路线图的制定[1]。

根据第二次 BRF 的可交付成果清单，乌克兰将参与 BRF 框架下的多边合作机制。中国国家美术馆和来自 18 个国家的 21 家美术馆或主要美术机构，包括俄罗斯、韩国、希腊、白俄罗斯、哈萨克斯坦、越南、斯里兰卡、乌克兰、立陶宛、保加利亚、孟加拉国、匈牙利、土耳其、摩尔多瓦、亚美尼亚和波兰，联合成立了丝绸之路国际艺术博物馆和画廊联盟[2]。

乌克兰将受益于博物馆和博览会的最佳体验和效果，以及它们对主办城市的影响和实现社会目标的结果，例如：

- 提升人民的文化信心，
- 完善法律全球化的历史基础，
- 推动爱国运动——例如，世博博物馆是为中国赢得荣誉的爱国骄傲。

三 中国智慧、互利和给发展中国家指南

全球治理体系的改革需要注入新的力量。何亚非[3]认为，中国在国内治理方面的成功将为全球治理带来东方资源和中国智慧。

美国有研究人员认为，中国"一带一路"的初步政治成果具有启发性。签署"一带一路"倡议的国家名单很长，而且还在不断增加，因为它表达了发展中国家的希望和愿望。随着许多国家变得更加富裕，它们的利益已经从满足人类的基本需求发展到能源、电力、贸易和投资等问题。中国通过提供大量政府融资、双边合作以及承诺快速交付项目，利用了这些利益。中国之所以成功，主要是因为它愿意承担其他投资者没有承担的风险，无论是合法的还是非法的。在很多情况下，中国的提议不仅是最佳选择，而是发展中国家的唯一选择[4]。

---

1 КовальО. Новий етап ініціативи "Поясу та шляху", «Україна-Китай» №2(16), 2019, c.17, available at: http://sinologist.com.ua/wp-content/uploads/2019/08/N16_f_.pdf
2 Available at: http://www.beltandroadforum.org/english/n100/2019/0427/c36-1312.html
3 何亚非：《中国与全球治理》，中国洲际出版社 2019 年版。
4 《锻造为应对全球基础设施挑战制定美国战略的快速路》，战略与国际问题研究中心（CSIS）全球基础设施工作组报告，该工作组是战略与国际问题研究中心（CSIS）重新连接亚洲项目的一部分，Charlene Barshefsky Stephen J. Hadley, Jonathan E. Hillman, Erol Yayboke (EDS), Washington, D.C., APRIL 2019, available at: https://csis-prod.s3.amazonaws.com/s3fs-public/publication/190423_Hadley%20et%20al_HigherRoads_report_WEB.pdf

尽管如此，贝拉博纳（Bellabona）和斯皮加雷利（Spigarelli）[1]认为，对于发达国家来说，中国的投资代表着一个机会，可以保护就业，并在停滞或衰退的行业中为对内部发展不再具有战略重要性的资产注入新的力量。对于发展中国家来说，中国提供了增长的可能性，为它们带来了资金、技术和技能资源。

在《中国的奇迹》一文中，研究中国的林毅夫回答了一个有趣的问题："其他发展中国家能否取得类似的经济表现？"

值得注意的是，林毅夫给出了一个持久的解决方案：

"……在改革过程中，发展中国家最好采取双轨制，为无法生存的企业提供一些暂时性的保护，以维持稳定，但允许进入该国具有相对优势的行业，以利用其后发优势。如果他们能做到这一点，其他发展中国家也可以在经济自由化进程中实现稳定和动态增长……"

在访问中国并对中国在法律全球化中的作用进行研究之后，我也准备回答同样的问题——其他发展中国家能否取得类似的经济表现？我可以向你保证答案是肯定的。

四 结论

联合国组织经济和社会事务部副秘书长刘振民先生曾宣布：

"为可持续发展促进和平与包容的社会，为所有人提供诉诸司法的机会，并在各级建立有效、负责和包容的机构"。[2]

本文考察了中国在法律全球化形成中的作用。中国积极参与全球治理改革和全球议程设置，共谋尊严、安全和互利共赢的未来。这篇文章揭示了世界其他地方需要更多关于中国的信息。中国有句谚语：博观而约取，厚积而薄发。因此，中国的经验证明，发展中国家应该把重点放在技术、人口和教育质量上。

1　Bellabona, P. and Spigarelli, F. (2007) 'Moving from Open Door to Go Global: China goes on the world stage', *Int. J. Chinese Culture and Management*, Vol. 1, No. 1, pp.93–107.

2　可持续发展目标16：关注公共机构。更多信息，请参见网址：http://workspace.unpan.org/sites/Internet/Documents/UNPAN99332.pdf

The Role of China in Formation of Legal Globalization: Setting Rules for a Common Prosperity

Ielyzaveta Lvova / Ukraine

Constitutional and International Law Department, Odessa State University of Internal Affairs / Professor

I. China's Actions in Legal Globalization and Governance

The phenomenon and impact of globalization on cultures and legal systems is colossal. Since the early 2000s national and supranational governments began to implement global rules for further integration and competitiveness, giving birth to legal globalization.[1]

In the era of globalization, the idea that openness and connectivity, mutual sharing and acceptance of the best achievements are to become key elements of foreign policy of modern state has been gradually developed.

China has actively participated in formation of legal globalization, since the

---

[1] Legal globalization (Globalization of law) may be defined as the worldwide progression of transnational legal structures and discourses along the dimensions of extensity, intensity, velocity, and impact (by Terrance C.Halliday and Pavel Osinsky) – For more see: Terence C. Halliday and Pavel Osinsky. Globalization of Law. *Annual Review of Sociology* Vol. 32 (2006), pp. 447-470.

Chinese Government first framed the Going Global Strategy for firms in China, making the outward expansion of business enterprises a major strategic initiative for the future economic development of the country[1].

Nowadays China gains its own role in globalizing legal norms and practices.

Firstly, China has developed new architectonic of a overall openness and cooperation with other countries in eco-environment protection alongside Belt and Road Initiative (BRI).

The Initiative has gained the features of a Global Project and covers the spirit and actions of two initiatives .

1.the new "Silk Road Economic Belt", which is primarily land-based and is projected to connect China with Central Asia, Eastern and Western Europe;

2. the "21st Century Maritime Silk Road" Initiative, which is a sea-based project aiming to bond China's southern coast to the Mediterranean, Africa, South-East Asia, and Central Asia.. By Xinmin Ma, this initiative "…calls for maritime cooperation among States based on the principles of consultation, contribution and shared benefits in order jointly cope with risks and challenges. China has advocated international cooperation and achieved fruitful outcomes in fields of international shipping, maritime scientific research, marine environmental protection, and maritime safety and security." [2]

It is obvious that China is a main driver of a world economic development, although China is a middle-income developing country, with a per capita GDP of 21,772 trillion International Dollars (2018). The most recent data from discussions on the 2019 Article IV Consultation of International Monetary Fund Mission to China (IMF 2019) give trend that"China's economic growth is expected to moderate

---

[1] Wang H., Miao L. (2016) "Going Global Strategy" and Global Talent. In: China Goes Global. Palgrave Macmillan Asian Business Series. Palgrave Macmillan, London, at p.144

[2] Xinmin Ma, "China and the UNCLOS: Practices and Policies" , in *The Chinese Journal of Global Governance,* Vol.5., I.1, 2019, P.9

to 6.2 percent and 6.0 percent in 2019 and 2020, respectively, as the planned policy stimulus partially offsets the negative impact from the recent US tariff hike on US$ 200 billion of Chinese exports. Growth is expected to gradually slow to 5.5 percent by 2024 as the economy moves towards a more sustainable growth path. Headline inflation is projected to rise to 2.3 percent in 2019, reflecting higher food prices. The near-term outlook remains particularly uncertain given the potential for further escalation of trade tensions."[1]

China's history of fast-growing wealth is based on foreign trade, foreign diplomacy closely linked with residence of foreigners. Prof. Branko Milanovic gives his own profs concerning reasons why China-foreign interactions experience is different than in the United States, Great Britain, France, Germany or Russia.

He explains that China was "…during most of that time either invaded by foreign troops, or had foreigners manage activities that are normally reserved for nationals (budget, trade policy, education); or because foreigners enjoyed exterritorial status (could not be judged by Chinese courts), or because they ruled parts of the county, or finally because China had foreigners heavily involved in its life be it as humanitarian workers, missionaries, technical experts or military advisers. Because of such intimate connection between major powers and China, Chinese internal political history is as much a history of dealing with foreigners as it is about inter-Chinese politics." [2]

Secondly, China actively participates in achieving of the 17 Sustainable Development Goals (SDGs) of the 2030 Agenda for Sustainable Development. To implement the SDGs the Chinese government released its National Plan on

---

1 IMF Press Release #19/196, available at: https://www.imf.org/en/News/Articles/2019/06/05/pr19196-china-imf-staff-completes-2019-article-iv-mission
2 BrankoMilanovic. History Without Ideology. A Review of Robert Bickers' "Out of China", Global Policy Journal, 01 August 2019, Available at :https://www.globalpolicyjournal.com/blog/01/08/2019/history-without-ideology-review-robert-bickers-out-china]

Implementation of the Agenda (2016).[1]

Thirdly, as a responsible major country, China is focused on importance of city planning as a main course of development strategy within the practice of "One Country, Two Systems". For example, in February 2019 the Central Government promulgated the Outline Development Plan for the Guangdong-Hong Kong-Macao Greater Bay Area.

II. Global City and the World: Shanghai in the Era of Openness and Reform

In order to understand the importance of Chinese central governmental actions for legal globalization, let us reveal the essence of Shanghai 2035 - a highly influential legal document that plays an exemplary role as the first master plan of a megacity to envision as far as 2035 and the first one approved by the State Council following the 19th National Congress of the CPC. "The document comprehensively implements the spirit of the 19th National Congress, takes Xi Jinping' s thought on socialism with Chinese characteristics for a new era for guiding ideas with a clear stand. It comprehensively implements the basic policy of upholding and developing socialism with Chinese characteristics for the new era."[2]

However, Shanghai is not situated in the center of China geographically, strategically speaking – Shanghai is a super international financial center, supreme region, a global city with an influence in economic, cultural and environmental protection.

According to Professor Pan Guang, from 1933 to 1941, Shanghai accepted almost 30,000 European Jews who escaped from Nazi Persecution and the Holocaust. Excluding those who left Shanghai for other countries, by the time of

---

1 Qin Tianbao, Hou Fang. China's National Plan on Implementation of the 2030 Sustainable Development Goals: from the Perspective of National Performance of Multilateral Environmental Agreements., in *Journal of Vasyl Stefanyk Precarpathian National University* http://jpnu.pu.if.ua vol. 5, no. 2 (2018), 55-66

2 Available at: http://www.shanghai.gov.cn/newshanghai/xxgkfj/2035004.pdf

the Japanese bombing of Pearl Harbor in December 1941, the city was sheltering 20,000 — 25,000 Jewish refugees. Prof. Pan Guang presents the data of the Simon Wiesenthal Centre on Holocaust Studies, according to which Shanghai took in more Jewish refugees than Canada, Australia, New Zealand, South Africa and India combined.[1]

Thanks to promotion of internationalization, since 1978 till spring of 1989 Shanghai faced huge economic changes and was a center of international finance.

In 1990, the government of Peoples Republic of China announced the launch of the project for development and further openness of the Pudong area, proposed by Deng Xiaoping. This program gave platform for Shanghai to participate in international economic dialogue together with other global cities - London, New-York, Tokyo and Paris. Since1992 up till now Shanghai has been known as the center of economic development.

Nowadays the Shanghai Master Plan 2016-2035 proposes a long time goal for a 15 years period for Shanghai to become an excellent global city. By 2020, Shanghai will gain global influence and will become a scientific and technological center. In addition, Shanghai will keep a strong position of cultural, ecological, maritime global influence city.

The Shanghai Master Plan 2016-2035 is organized and prepared by Shanghai Municipal People's Government and is approved by the State Council. It serves as the basis and official document for city planning, construction and management within the jurisdiction of Shanghai. It is also an important document to guide the future development of Shanghai, and a development blueprint to realize "Better City, Better Life".

It is interesting that the Moto "Better City, Better Life" first appeared as a motto

---

[1] Pan Guang. Shanghai: a Heaven for Holocaust Victims. In The Holocaust and the United Nations Outreach Programme, at P.65, available at: https://www.un.org/en/holocaustremembrance/docs/pdf/chapter6.pdf

for Expo 2010 and revealed idea of the exhibition in Shanghai.

China's first world's fair and the largest in history by size, attendance, and international participants, Expo 2010 saw the largest world's fair attendance in a single day: over one million of visitors on 16 October 2010.

Back to the history of the event, it is worth to mention that Shanghai Municipal People's Government has rated the World Expo Museum(WEM) project as a major cultural facility construction project in its "Twelfth Five-year Plan". The project started on November 23, 2010, when Shanghai Municipal People's Government and the Bureau of International Expositions (BIE) formally signed the Memorandum of Cooperation on the World Expo Museum in Paris, France, which defined the World Expo Museum as the only official museum and authorized documentation centre of BIE.

The WEM site is selected in Block 15-02, the 15th Neighborhood in the Culture Exposition Area of the original Expo Shanghai Site, north to East Longhua Road, south to Jumen Road, west to Block 15-01, and east to Mengzi Road. It takes a land area of 4 hectares, a total floor area of 46,550 square meters, and a total open management area of 90,580 square meters. The building height is 34.8 meters (6 floors are above ground and 1 floor underground). It was commenced at the end of December 2013, and the WEM is a new cultural landmark in Shanghai. [1]

Today the World Expo Museum helps to present how the World Cities are seen in China through expo pavilions and local exhibitions in general. Expos inspire cultural tourism and mass audiences visitors travel all over the world in one single city. [2]

Historically speaking, Chinese museums divulge strong economic, political and

---

1　Functional Positioning of World Expo Museum, available at: http://www.expo-museum.org/sbbwg/n137/n139/n216/n217/n221/u1ai20658.html
2　Upcoming Expos will take place in Dubai, United Arab Emirates, 2020 and in Buenos Aires, Argentina, 2023.

cultural ties with European and Post-Soviet Countries, including Ukraine. A great surge in Sino-Ukrainian cultural and economic cooperation is happening now.

During the 2nd Belt and Road Forum for International Cooperation (BRF) in Beijing on 25-27 April 2019, Ukrainian delegation offered a joint project portfolio: "development of port infrastructure, alternative energy facilities, construction of highways and bridges, development of railway and airport facilities, high technology, cooperation in aerospace, processing of agricultural products." Ukraine seeks to develop cooperation on the modernization of Ukrainian industry and to create joint production facilities. During the forum, the Ukrainian delegation agreed to sign an investment agreement between the governments of Ukraine and China totaling $ 340 million. USA to build a bridge across the Dnieper in Kremenchug. Advancing, Ukraine will participate in development of Ukraine-China BRI Road Map. [1]

According to the list of deliverables of the second BRF, Ukraine will participate in Multilateral Cooperation Mechanisms under the BRF Framework. The National Art Museum of China and 21 art museums or major fine arts institutions from 18 countries including Russia, the Republic of Korea, Greece, Belarus, Kazakhstan, Viet Nam, Sri Lanka, Ukraine, Lithuania, Bulgaria, Bangladesh, Hungary, Turkey, Moldova, Armenia and Poland, jointly founded the Silk Road International Alliance of Art Museums and Galleries.[2]

Ukraine will benefit from the best experience and effect of the museums and expos with the impact they made on the host cities and the result of achieving social goals, such as:

- support Peoples cultural confidence,

- improve historical basis for legal globalization,

---

[1] КовальО. Новий етап ініціативи "Поясу та шляху", «Україна-Китай» №2(16), 2019, с .17, available at: http://sinologist.com.ua/wp-content/uploads/2019/08/N16_f_.pdf
[2] Available at: http://www.beltandroadforum.org/english/n100/2019/0427/c36-1312.html

- promote patriotic campaign –e.g. WEM is the patriotic pride for a taining glory for China.

III. Chinese wisdom, mutual benefit and guides for developing countries

Waiting the above features of BRI's innovating China's verbal discourse, legal actions and ways of participation, it is worth to mention that the reform of the global governance system cannot be achieved without the injection of new forces. By He Yafei, China's success in domestic governance will bring oriental resources and Chinese wisdom to global governance. [1]

There is a strong vision among American researchers that initial political success of China's BRI is instructive. A long and still-growing list of countries has signed onto the BRI because it speaks to the hopes and aspirations of developing countries. As many countries have become wealthier, their interests have progressed from covering basic human needs to issues like energy, power, trade, and investment. China has tapped into these interests by offering large amounts of government financing, working bilaterally, and promising to deliver projects quickly. It has been successful largely because it is willing to assume risks that other investors have not, whether legal or illegal. In too many cases, China's offer is not the best choice but the only option for developing countries.[2]

Nevertheless, it is important to agree with Bellabona, P. and Spigarelli, F. that for developed countries, Chinese investments represent an opportunity to protect employment and to give new strength to assets no longer of strategic importance for internal development, in stagnant or declining sectors. For developing countries, China offers the possibility to grow, bringing them financial, technological and

---

1 He Yafei. China and Global Governance. China Intercontinental Press, 2019, XVII
2 The Higher Road Forging a U.S. Strategy for the Global Infrastructure Challenge. A Report of the CSIS Global Infrastructure Task Force as part of the CSIS Reconnecting Asia Project. Charlene Barshefsky Stephen J. Hadley, Jonathan E. Hillman, ErolYayboke (EDS), Washington, D.C., APRIL 2019, available at: https://csis-prod.s3.amazonaws.com/s3fs-public/publication/190423_Hadley%20 et%20al_HigherRoads_report_WEB.pdf

skills resources.[1]

In the article "The China Miracle Demystified" Chinese researcher Justin Yifu Lin gives his answers to an interesting question:

- "Can other developing countries achieve a similar economic performance?"

Remarkably, Justin Yifu Lin gives a durable solution:

"... In the reform process it is desirable for a developing country to adopt a dual-track approach, providing some transitory protections to nonviable firms to maintain stability but liberalizing entry into sectors in which the country has comparative advantages to tap the advantage of backwardness. If they can do this, other developing countries can also achieve stability and dynamic growth in their economic liberalization process..."

After visiting China and conducting my own research on China's role in legal globalization, I'm also ready to answer the same question - can other developing countries achieve a similar economic performance? I can reassure you: the answer is "YES!"

IV. Conclusion

Mr. Liu Zhenmin, Under-Secretary-General of the Department of Economic and Social Affairs at United Nations Organization once declared:

"Promote peaceful and inclusive societies for sustainable development, provide access to justice for all and build effective, accountable and inclusive institutions at all levels[2]".

This paper has surveyed the role of China in formation of legal globalization. China actively participates in global governance reform and global agenda setting

---

1 Bellabona, P. and Spigarelli, F. (2007) 'Moving from Open Door to Go Global: China goes on the world stage', *Int. J. Chinese Culture and Management,* Vol. 1, No. 1, pp.93–107.
2 For more see Sustainable Development Goal 16: Focus on public institutions , available at: http://workspace.unpan.org/sites/Internet/Documents/UNPAN99332.pdf

to chart the future of dignity, safety and mutual benefits. The article reveals that the rest of the world needs more information about China. Only by learning extensively and accumulating profound knowledge can one be ready to achieve something. Accordingly, Chinese experience is an evidence that developing countries should focus on technology, demographics and quality of education.